Back
to the
Lake

Back to the Lake

A READER

FOR WRITERS

Thomas Cooley

W • W • NORTON & COMPANY • NEW YORK • LONDON

W. W. Norton & Company has been independent since its founding in 1923, when William Warder Norton and Mary D. Herter Norton first published lectures delivered at the People's Institute, the adult education division of New York City's Cooper Union. The firm soon expanded its program beyond the Institute, publishing books by celebrated academics from America and abroad. By mid-century, the two major pillars of Norton's publishing program—trade books and college texts—were firmly established. In the 1950s, the Norton family transferred control of the company to its employees, and today—with a staff of four hundred and a comparable number of trade, college, and professional titles published each year—W. W. Norton & Company stands as the largest and oldest publishing house owned wholly by its employees.

Editor: Marilyn Moller
Associate editor: Erin Granville
Editorial assistant: Ana Cooke
Production editor: Rebecca A. Homiski
Production manager: Ben Reynolds
Copyeditor: Katharine Ings
Indexer: Sandi Schroeder
Design: Charlotte Staub / Antonina Krass / Carole Desnoes
Composition / Layout: PennSet / Carole Desnoes
Manufacturing: Courier—Westford, MA

Library of Congress Cataloging-in-Publication Data

Cooley, Thomas, 1942–
   Back to the lake : a reader for writers / Thomas Cooley. — 1st ed.
      p. cm.
   Includes bibliographical references and index.

ISBN: 978-0-393-92508-1 (pbk.)
ISBN: 978-0-393-93022-1 (Instructor's Edition; pbk.)

   1. College readers. 2. English language—Rhetoric—Problems, exercises, etc. 3. Report writing—Problems, exercises, etc. I. Title.
   PE1417.C6549 2009
   808'.0427—dc22

                              2008042962

W. W. Norton & Company, Inc., 500 Fifth Avenue, New York, NY 10110
www.wwnorton.com
W. W. Norton & Company Ltd., Castle House, 75/76 Wells Street, London W1T 3QT
1 2 3 4 5 6 7 8 9 0

Preface

*B*ack to the Lake takes its title from the classic essay "Once More to the Lake" by E. B. White, which I first read with awe and wonder as a freshman in a college writing course. Only years later did I realize that White worked his magic with common rhetorical techniques—narration, description, comparison, and the other modes of writing discussed in this book—that good writers use every day in all kinds of texts and contexts. Far from magic, as I discovered, the real wonder was that I could use these standard techniques in my own writing, whether to structure a paragraph or an entire essay, or, even more essentially, to generate ideas and organize my thoughts throughout the writing process.

We now take it for granted that the process of writing is one we can learn—and teach. This was not the case in White's day, however, as I discovered when, as a young assistant professor of English, I rashly fired off a letter asking him to explain how he composed "Once More to the Lake." To my astonishment, White not only responded to my letter, he said he didn't really know how he wrote anything. "The 'process,' " White confided, "is probably every bit as mysterious to me as it is to some of your students—if that will make them feel any better."

Fortunately for today's students and teachers, the scene has changed. After a generation of research in composition and rhetoric, we now know a lot more than we once did about how the writing process works and how to teach it. The goal of *Back to the Lake* is to apply this understanding of the writing process to show students how to make the basic moves—of narration, description, comparison, and the other fundamental modes of writing—that seasoned writers make all the time, whether consciously or otherwise, in their writing.

As its subtitle announces, *Back to the Lake* is a reader for writers. It includes more than 75 readings, some of them familiar, like the one by White, but many that have never been anthologized in a composition reader before now. The book is organized around the rhetorical modes as basic methods of discovery and development. Each method is covered in a chapter that includes 7 or 8 readings and practical guidelines that lead students through the process of composing a text by using that method, with tips (and even templates) for generating ideas, organizing and drafting, getting feedback, and revising and editing a final draft.

As a new rhetorically arranged reader and guide, *Back to the Lake* is both innovative and mindful of proven techniques for the successful teaching of writing. Among its innovations is the extensive use of everyday examples to help students recognize that they are already familiar with the methods taught in this book—and that they will have occasion to use them well beyond their writing classroom. A second innovation is templates that provide starting points for drafting in the various modes. Finally, recognizing that every kind of writing invites its own peculiar problems and errors, I've added to each chapter some tips on editing for errors that are common to the method under discussion.

An Overview of the Book

Chapter 1 introduces students to the principles of critical reading, taking them through the basic steps of reading with a critical eye.

Chapter 2 gives an overview of the writing process, preparing students to analyze assignments; to come up with topics on their own; to generate ideas; to draft and revise with a particular audience and purpose in mind; and to edit and proofread.

Chapters 3 through 11 each focus on one of the rhetorical modes as a basic method of discovery and development. Each method is amply demonstrated by 7 or 8 readings, including one written by a student. For teachers who want to show students how these standard methods of writing carry over into fiction and poetry, each chapter ends with a poem or short story. *Chapter 12* offers a number of readings that combine the methods, as much real-world writing does.

An Appendix on Using Sources completes the book, with guidance in finding and documenting sources. Up-to-date with the **2009 MLA guidelines**, it includes an annotated student research paper; we've also updated all the readings that use MLA style, providing additional models of the documentation style college students are often required to use.

Highlights

An engaging—and teachable—selection of readings, from the most classic ("Grant and Lee") to the most current (Barack Obama's speech on "A More Perfect Union"), to the best-selling (*Everything Bad Is Good for You*)—all demonstrating that the patterns taught in this book are ones that all good writers depend on. Each chapter includes one piece written by a student and one story or poem.

Tips and templates to help students get started drafting, providing language to help students make the moves needed to describe, compare, define, and so on.

Everyday examples, showing that the methods taught in this book are familiar ones—and that they are not used just in first-year writing; that a recipe, for example, relies on process analysis and that a Life Is Good T-shirt makes an argument.

Practical editing tips, to help students check for the kinds of errors that frequently occur with each of the rhetorical methods taught in this book—for instance, to check that verb tenses accurately reflect when actions occur in a narrative.

Help for multilingual students, with glosses for unfamiliar terms and cultural allusions, templates for getting started, and tips for dealing with predictable stumbling points—plus 15 readings that focus on issues across cultures.

Study questions follow each selection, helping students read the text closely and with an eye for how it was written. Each selection is also followed by at least two **suggestions for writing,** usually one for something short and one for a full essay.

Engaging visual texts, including photos, charts, cartoons, and other drawings, with instructions on how to use them responsibly and effectively in college writing.

Clusters of readings in the argument chapter debate three current issues: the legal drinking age, intellectual property rights, and ethics in a commercial culture. Each cluster includes at least three readings, showing students that there are always more than two sides to any debate.

A two-color design that makes the book easy to use, with all of the rhetoric, including the guidelines, printed on blue pages to make it easy to find. In addition, a **glossary / index** provides full definitions of all the key terms along with a list of the pages where they are covered in detail.

Beautifully written pedagogy, making the subject matter interesting, relevant, and easy to understand. This book practices what it preaches about good writing.

Acknowledgments

For help in the preparation and editing of this book, I wish to thank a number of people. As always, I am most grateful to Barbara Cooley, who deals equally well with issues of water quality and murky prose. Marilyn Moller, without your inspiration and experience at the editorial helm there would be no *Back to the Lake*; I thank you for keeping us all on course during a longer voyage than anyone expected. Thanks as well to Erin Granville, my hands-on editor at Norton, whose work ethic was inspiring; to Judy Voss, our expert from out of town; and, for assistance at an earlier stage of this project, to Nicole Netherton. I am also grateful to Mike Fleming for his good work on the headnotes and to Michal Brody for her work on the glosses and instructor's notes. In addition, I wish to thank Rebecca Homiski for her superb project editorial work; Katharine Ings for copyediting both this main text and the instructor's notes; Toni Krass and Carole Desnoes for the beautiful design; Nancy Rodwan and Margaret Gorenstein for clearing the many permissions; Kelly Mitchell for locating the photographs; Ben Reynolds for getting the book produced in good form despite the many deadlines some of us missed; Ana Cooke and Cat Spencer for helping to keep us all on track; and Marian Johnson and Julia Reidhead for their support of this ambitious project all along the way.

Thanks go as well to the following teachers who reviewed the manuscript: Mark Bernier, Blinn College at Brenham; Patricia Bostian, Central Piedmont Community College; Kathleen Dixon, University of North Dakota; Jean M. Evans, Norwalk, Connecticut, Public Schools; Lynn Ezzell, Cape Fear Community College; Adam Fischer, Bowie State University; Hannah Furrow, University of Michigan at Flint; Judy Gardner, University of Texas at San Antonio; Jim LaBate, Hudson Valley Community College; Mary Murray McDonald, Cleveland State University; Stephen Monroe, University of Mississippi; Daniel Olson, North Harris College; Joyce O'Shea, Wharton County Junior College; Jeffrey Powers-Beck, East Tennessee State University; Anita Tully, Nicholls State University; Mark Williams, California State University at Long Beach; Daniel Zimmerman, Middlesex County College; and Jamie L. Zorigian, Lehman College.

It is a great pleasure to name the teachers and experts in the field of composition and rhetoric who have given advice, or otherwise assisted me, at various stages in the evolution of this book. They include my colleagues at Ohio State, particularly Beverly Moss, Sara Garnes, and the late Edward P. J. Corbett; the late Dean McWilliams of Ohio University; Roy Rosenstein of the American University of Paris; and for his great generosity in allowing me to use the fruit of his research and experience in the research appendix, Richard Bullock of Wright State University.

Finally, I wish to thank Gerald Graff and Cathy Birkenstein, whose work inspired the writing templates in this book.

Contents

Chapter 3 Narration   49

" 'What? Do you support this lewd conduct? Are we living in an American movie? Since when have young people of mixed sexes been permitted to speak to each other *on the telephone?*' "

"Jarrah's objective was to crash his airliner into symbols of the American Republic, the Capitol or the White House. He was defeated by the alerted, unarmed passengers of United 93."

"If in that snowy backyard the driver of the black Buick had cut off our heads, Mikey's and mine, I would have died happy, for nothing has required so much of me since as being chased all over Pittsburgh . . . by this sainted, skinny furious red-headed man who wished to have a word with us."

"The fourth pitch is the mistake: the pitcher goes back to his change-up. Jeremy sees his arm coming through slowly again, and this time he knows to wait on it."

" 'Where did he get the bruises?' I ventured. . . . The mother looked at the scattered marks around the red-head's temples through her friendly librarian glasses, then up at me."

"Isn't that the kind of thing we fear strangers will do? Disturb. Betray. Prove they are not like us?"

"Her idea was to make the dog conditional. The conditions to be imposed would be numerous and severe, and I would be incapable of fulfilling them, so when I didn't get the dog it'd be my own fault. This was her logic, and the fact that she thought such a plan might work illustrates that some people should never be parents and that she was one of them."

Chapter 5 Example 166

DAVID BARBOZA, *Piling on the Cookies* 178
  "Finding old-fashioned Oreo sandwich cookies on supermarket shelves is no easy task these days."

THE ONION, *All Seven Deadly Sins Committed at Church Bake Sale* 183
  "In total, 347 individual acts of sin were committed at the bake sale, with nearly every attendee committing at least one of the seven deadly sins as outlined by Gregory the Great in the fifth century."

MICHAEL DIRDA, *Commencement Advice* 187
  "Literature offers various aesthetic pleasures, but it has also traditionally provided instruction and counsel on how to live, confront adversity, and find solace."

HORACE MINER, *Body Ritual among the Nacirema* 195
  "The fundamental belief underlying the whole system appears to be that the human body is ugly and that its natural tendency is to debility and disease. Incarcerated in such a body, man's only hope is to avert these characteristics through the use of the powerful influences of ritual and ceremony."

MONICA WUNDERLICH, *My Technologically Challenged Life* 202
  "In my house, technology does not exist, at least not for my parents. In fact it was 1995 when my father finally had to part with his beloved rotary phone."

ADRIENNE RICH, *Ritual Acts vi* 207
  "We would like to show but to not be obvious"

Chapter 8 Classification 306

"I once tried going a whole week without telling a lie, and it was paralyzing. I discovered that telling the truth all the time is nearly impossible."

"Women are often told they apologize too much. The reason they're told to stop doing it is that, to many men, apologizing seems synonymous with putting oneself down."

"Sociologists and linguists probably will tell you that a person's developing language skills are more influenced by peers. But I do think that the language spoken in the family, especially in immigrant families, . . . plays a large role."

"Many of us live in absurdly unlikely groupings because we have organized our lives that way."

"The next temperament is the fearful type. These are the more quiet and shy children."

"He argued that if wings were not the essential element in determining the difference between a hawk and an airplane, they were even less so in the recognition of angels."

Chapter 9 Definition 362

Chapter 10 Cause and Effect 429

"Married men make more money than single men. . . . The question is why."

"Yet it isn't a derogation of the black vernacular—a marvellously rich and inventive tongue—to point out that there's a language of the marketplace, too, and learning to speak that language has generally been a precondition for economic success, whoever you are."

"Most peasant farmers and herders, who constitute the great majority of the world's actual food producers, aren't necessarily better off than hunter-gatherers."

"Let us go back in time to what educational historians refer to as the later Paleolithic era in higher education, that is, the late 1960s, when I was in college. Here was how the used book market worked then."

"It is not uncommon for a dancer to walk into what she thinks will be her daily ballet class and find a scale set up in the center of the dance studio instead. . . . These weigh-ins are arranged ahead of time and kept secret from the dancers."

"When your name is Bob no one asks you, 'How do you spell that?' No so with Piscine Molitor Patel."

Chapter II Argument   487

"We hold these truths to be self-evident, that all men are created equal, that they are endowed by their Creator with certain unalienable Rights, that among these are Life, Liberty and the pursuit of Happiness."

"Let him be just and deal kindly with my people, for the dead are not powerless. Dead, did I say? There is no death, only a change of worlds."

"I have a dream that my four children will one day live in a nation where they will not be judged by the color of their skin but by the content of their character."

"But I have asserted a firm conviction—a conviction rooted in my faith in God and my faith in the American people—that working together we can move beyond some of our old racial wounds, and that in fact we have no choice if we are to continue on the path of a more perfect union."

"Had we but world enough, and time, / This coyness, lady, were no crime."

"Because the 21-year-old-drinking-age law is not working . . . it behooves us as a nation to change our current prohibition law and to teach responsible drinking techniques for those who choose to consume alcoholic beverages."

"My nephew knew two students who had died . . . and five others who had been paralyzed or seriously injured in car accidents because of binging."

Chapter 12 Combining the Methods 584

Appendix: Using Sources in Your Writing 638

Thematic Guide
to the Readings

Cultures and Ethnicities

Ethics and Religion

Fiction

Gender

History

Home and Family

Love and Marriage

Memories of Youth

Nature and the Environment

Poetry

Public Policy

Reading and Writers

Science and Technology

Sociology and Anthropology

Sports and Leisure

Student Writing

CHAPTER I

Good Writers
Are Good Readers

> The more that you read, the more things you will know. The more that you learn, the more places you'll go.　　　　　　　　　—Dr. Seuss

> Learning to write is similar to learning to play the piano. You have to practice daily to improve your skills. Studying good examples also helps.
> 　　　　　　　　　　　　　　　　　　　　—Juha Haataia

Let's start with the alphabet. If you can sing the alphabet song, it's because some-one—perhaps a teacher, parent, or sibling—sang it to you first and you learned from him or her. Learning to sing the alphabet, however, is much easier than learning to read or write it. Of the four basic human language skills, listening and speaking come naturally: we learn to speak as young children just by hearing other people talk and imitating them. Reading and writing require more instruction, especially to achieve real competence with the written word—but we start the same way. We learn even basic writing skills from others who have already acquired those skills themselves.

The writers you will encounter in this book have advanced well beyond their ABCs, but the lesson they offer is the same. To master the basic methods that accomplished writers have developed over the years to present their ideas effectively, you will need to study the work of other writers. You'll want to read closely, with a critical eye, the works of some skilled writers who have mastered the fundamentals of their craft.

This chapter focuses on how to engage in such close reading and provides some questions to help you read the essays in this book with an eye for what they can teach you about your own writing.

Reading Closely—and Critically

Like writing, reading is an active process. Even when you take a thriller to the beach and read for fun, your brain is at work translating words into mental images and ideas. When you read more purposefully, as with the essays in this book, your brain will get even more of a workout. In both instances, however, the words on the page form a text that can be analyzed and interpreted. The word *text*, like the word *textile*, derives from the Latin word for *weaving*. A text is a written fabric of words. When you read a text with a critical eye, you unravel that fabric, looking at how the words fit together to make meaning. You also question what you're reading and think more deeply about your own ideas on the subject.

Reading a text critically does not mean that you have to be judgmental. Instead, it means that you analyze the text as carefully and objectively as you can. This is why critical reading will be defined in this book as *close* reading: it sticks to the text as closely as possible and avoids reading too much (or too little) into the text.

The Reading Process

When you read any text, you engage in a number of activities. Among these are previewing, reading, and responding. Previewing a text means looking it over generally to get a rough sense of its subject, scope, and context. When you actually read the text, you comb through it systematically from beginning to end, trying to discern the author's main point, how it is supported, and whether any pertinent information is missing. As you respond to the text, you think about whether you agree or disagree (or both) with its ideas, and you may reread parts of the text that you have questions about. Let's take a closer look at each of these activities.

Previewing a Text

Before you plunge into a text, it's a good idea to take a few moments to survey the text as a whole. Get your pencil ready, because you may need it shortly, but resist the urge to underline until you have a better sense of where the text is going and what you want to focus on. Here are some tips for previewing the readings in this book:

- *Look at the headnote* to find out something about the author and the original context—the time, place, and circumstances in which the text was written and published. For example, a soldier's first-hand account of a battle has a far different context than a historian's account of the same battle written years later.

- *Think about the title.* What does it reveal about the topic and tone of the text? Are you expecting a serious argument, or an essay that pokes fun at its subject?

- *Skim the text for an overview*, noting any headings, boldfaced words, illustrations, charts, or footnotes.
- *Skim the introduction and conclusion*. What insight do they give you into the purpose and message of the text?
- *Think about your own expectations and purpose for reading*. Are you reading to obtain information, for entertainment, to fulfill an assignment? How will your purpose and prior knowledge affect what you focus on in the text?

Reading a Text

Reading a text closely is a little like investigating a crime scene. You look for certain clues; you ask certain questions. Your objective is to determine, as precisely and accurately as you can, both what the text has to say and how it says it. Your primary clues, therefore, are in the text itself—the actual words on the page.

If you've previewed the text carefully, you already have some idea of what it's about. Now is the time to examine it closely. So pull out your pencil, and perhaps a highlighter, and be ready to annotate the text as you go along—to jot down questions or comments in the margins, underline important points, circle key words, and otherwise mark places in the text that you may want to come back to.

The following paragraph, from an essay reprinted later in this chapter, was annotated by Judy Vassey, a student writer. See how she has identified and underlined the author's main point, circled a few words and phrases that she wants to investigate further, and raised a key question about the passage's many questions.

For some of us, reading begets rereading, and rereading begets writing. (Although there is no doubt which is first, and supreme; as Alberto Manguel writes in his wonderful *A History of Reading*, "I could perhaps live without writing. I don't think I could live without reading.") After a while the story is familiar, the settings known, the characters understood, and there is nothing left to discover but technique. Why that sentence structure and not something simpler, or more complex? Why that way of ordering events instead of something more straightforward, or more experimental? What grabs the reader by the throat? What sags and bags and fails? There are only two ways, really, to become a writer. One is to write. The other is to read.

—ANNA QUINDLEN, *How Reading Changed My Life*

Margin annotations: begets=Bible? main point — who's Manguel? — what story? — why all the questions?

Vassey is a good close reader, but on a first reading even she can't decipher all the important clues in a relatively complex passage like this. What does a good detective do to ensure that she hasn't missed any important clues? She returns to the scene of the crime—she rereads the text.

When Vassey reread the Quindlen text, she answered her own question about why Quindlen asks so many questions, noting that they show how a writer reads with an eye for methods and technique. Vassey noticed not only what Quindlen says but *how* she says it—what methods and techniques she uses. This should be your goal as a writer when you examine any text critically and closely.

QUESTIONS FOR READING

- *What is the writer's main point?* Is it clearly stated in a thesis? If so, where? If the main point is not stated directly, is it clearly implied?

- *What is the primary purpose of the text?* To provide information? Sell a product or service? Argue a point of view? Make us laugh? Tell a story?

- *Who is the intended audience?* Readers who are familiar with the topic? Those who know little about it? People who might be inclined to agree—or disagree?

- *What is the tone and style of the text?* Serious, informal, inspirational, strident?

- *How and where does the writer support the main point?* Can you point out specific details, facts, examples, visuals, expert testimony, personal experience, or other kinds of evidence?

- *Is the evidence sufficient?* Or does the supporting evidence fail to convince you? Are sources clearly identified so that you can tell where quotations, paraphrases, or summaries are coming from?

- *Has the writer fairly represented—and responded to—other points of view?* Has any crucial perspective been left out?

- *How is the text organized?* Do ideas flow logically from one to another? Where, if anywhere, is the text difficult to follow? Why?

- *What is the larger historical and cultural context of the text?* Who is the author? When was the text written and published? By whom? What other ideas or events does it reflect?

Responding to What You've Read

When you read a text, you can agree, disagree—or both—or withhold judgment. In fact, it is not unusual to disagree with or question some statements in a text even if you think the author has successfully presented and supported his or her thesis and done a good job overall.

After you have read and reread a text closely, think about and respond to it in writing. Here are a few tips for doing so:

- *Summarize what you've read in your own words.* If you can write a summary of the main point, you probably have a good grasp of what you've read.

- *Reread specific parts of the text to check your understanding and to answer any questions you might still have.* Further reading may also help if you're not yet sure whether you agree with the main point of the text.

- *Think about and record your own reactions.* Whether or not you agree with or like the text, did the writer accomplish what he or she set out to do?

- *Consider what you learned about writing.* Make note of any effective techniques used in the text that you might want to incorporate into your own writing. For example, does the piece have a catchy introduction, interesting and pertinent examples, striking visuals? If the text has elements you don't want to emulate—such as a weak conclusion—you might write those down as well.

Reading Visual Texts

Almost everywhere we look these days, we are surrounded by visuals—on blogs and websites, in magazines and textbooks, on billboards and subways. It is essential, then, to be able to read visuals closely, to look at them with a critical eye.

In many ways, reading a visual is similar to reading a written text in that you have to think critically about its purpose, its main point, and so on. Some visuals consist only of images—photographs, drawings, paintings—whereas other visuals—like graphs and diagrams—include words. Many kinds of advertising, for example, combine images and words to create an explicit message, urging us perhaps to buy a Honda, support the NRA, or quit smoking. Here are some tips for reading visuals:

- *What is the specific message—or main point—of the visual?* Does the message come across clearly, and does it do so with words as well as images?

- *How does the visual support its main point?* For example, does it use a poignant photograph, a quotation from an expert, or relevant statistics?

- *What is the source and purpose?* Was it developed by an individual, a corporation, a government agency? Is the source reputable? What does the nature of the source tell you about the purpose of the visual? Is the purpose to sell you something, to provide information, to persuade you to support a cause?

- *Who is the intended audience?* Is it aimed at a general audience or at a more specialized one: college students, parents, sports enthusiasts, experts in a particular field? How do you think the intended audience affects the argument the text makes?

- *What is the tone of the overall design—and what does that say about the message?* What word would you use to describe the design—bold, lively, tranquil, gloomy, cluttered, something else?

The book cover that appears below has been annotated by a student writer. A passage from this book begins on the next page. After you've read the passage, look back at this cover and think about how (and how well) the illustration supports the written text.

NATIONAL BESTSELLER

ANNA QUINDLEN

Author of *A Short Guide to a Happy Life*

HOW READING CHANGED MY LIFE

says lots of people bought this book

author must be well known if her name is larger than the title

ah, so she's also an expert on life!

woman seems to be floating, as if nothing matters but the book she is reading

pages of book are out-lined—implying their importance

what the book is about

Reading the Essays in This Book

Even if reading doesn't change your life, it will change your writing. Good writers are good readers because many of the basic skills of writing can only be learned by reading the work of other writers. In *Back to the Lake*, you will be reading and analyzing numerous essays by many different writers on a variety of topics. The essays are grouped into chapters according to the principal methods they use: NARRATION, DESCRIPTION, EXAMPLE, PROCESS, COMPARISON AND CONTRAST, CLASSIFICATION AND DIVISION, DEFINITION, CAUSE AND EFFECT, and ARGUMENT.

Experienced writers often employ more than one method in the same essay, and so there is also a final chapter called "Combining the Methods."

Your main goal in reading the essays in this book is to master the basic methods of development they demonstrate so you can use those methods in your own writing. As you study these model essays in detail, however, you will encounter many other useful strategies and techniques—ways of beginning, of using transitions to move a text along, of presenting certain kinds of information in lists or charts, and so on.

Each selection is introduced with a headnote that provides basic information about the author and the text's historical, social, or cultural context; and each selection is followed by study questions and writing prompts.

Look now at a very brief essay from Anna Quindlen's book *How Reading Changed My Life*. As you'll see, it's a fitting conclusion to a chapter claiming that "Good Writers Are Good Readers." Notice as well how the study questions that follow (shown here with answers) will help you read the selection *as a writer*.

ANNA QUINDLEN

How Reading Changed My Life

Anna Quindlen (b. 1952) grew up in the suburbs of Philadelphia in a neighborhood that was "the sort of place in which people dream of raising children—pretty, privileged but not rich, a small but satisfying spread of center-hall colonials, old roses, rhododendrons, and quiet roads." After graduating from Barnard College, Quindlen worked as a reporter, first for the New York Post *and then for the* New York Times, *where her regular column, "Public and Private," won a Pulitzer Prize in 1992.*

Though she still contributes a biweekly column to Newsweek, *Quindlen gave up full-time journalism in 1995 to concentrate on writing fiction. Her novels include* Rise *and* Shine *(2006),* Blessings *(2002), and* Black and Blue *(1998). She is also the author of* How Reading Changed My Life *(1998), from which this reading is taken. The personal story of her private life with books, Quindlen's narrative is also an account of how a writer learns the craft of writing by reading the work of other writers.*

In 1997 Katherine Paterson, whose novel *Bridge to Terabithia* has engaged several generations of young people with its story of friendship and loss—and also led to a policy in a school district in Kansas requiring a teacher to list each profanity in required reading and forward the list to parents—gave the Anne Carroll Moore Lecture at the New York Public Library.[1] It was a speech as fine as Ms. Paterson's books, which are fine indeed, and she spoke of the dedication of the children who are her readers: "I increasingly feel a sense of pity toward my fellow writers who spend their lives writing for the speeded-up audience of adults. They look at me, I realize, with a patronizing air, I who only write for the young. But I don't know any of them who have readers who will read their novels over and over again."

As someone who reads the same books over and over again, I think Ms. Paterson is wrong about that, although I know what she means. I have sat on the edge of several beds while *Green Eggs and Ham* was read, or recited more or less from memory; I read *A Wrinkle in Time* three times in a row once, when I was twelve, because I couldn't bear for it to end, wanted them all, Meg and Charles Murry and even the horribly pulsing brain called It, to be alive again as they could only live within my mind, so that I felt as if I killed them when I closed the cover and gave them the kiss of life when my eyes met the words that created their lives.[2] I still reread that way, always have, always will. I suspect there are more of us than Ms. Paterson knows. And I think I know who we are, and how we got that way. We are writers. We danced with the words, as children, in what became familiar patterns. The words became our friends and our companions, and without even saying it aloud, a thought danced with them: *I can do this. This is who I am.*

1. *Anne Carroll Moore (1871–1961):* an author of children's books and the first supervisor of Work with Children at the New York Public Library in Manhattan. *Bridge to Terabithia (1977):* in this novel, Katherine Paterson (b. 1932) tells the story of two children who create an imaginary kingdom in a forest. The book has twice, in 1985 and in 2007, been made into a movie.

2. *A Wrinkle in Time (1962):* a novel by Madeleine L'Engle (1918–2007) about three children, including Meg and Charles Murry, who are transported through the galaxy by transcendental beings. The book was not published at first because, according to L'Engle, many publishers considered it "too different." *Green Eggs and Ham (1960):* one of many popular children's books written and illustrated by Dr. Seuss (Theodor Seuss Geisel, 1902–1991), who believed that children learn to read through repetition and familiarity.

For some of us, reading begets rereading, and rereading begets writing. (Although 3
there is no doubt which is first, and supreme; as Alberto Manguel writes in his wonderful *A History of Reading*, "I could perhaps live without writing. I don't think I could
live without reading.")[3] After a while the story is familiar, the settings known, the
characters understood, and there is nothing left to discover but technique. Why
that sentence structure and not something simpler, or more complex? Why that
way of ordering events instead of something more straightforward, or more experimental? What grabs the reader by the throat? What sags and bags and fails? There
are only two ways, really, to become a writer. One is to write. The other is to read.

3. *Alberto Manguel* (b. 1948): a writer and editor now living in Buenos Aires, grew up in Israel,
where his father was the Argentinean ambassador. *A History of Reading* (1996) is his enthusiastic, the-
matic tour through the library imagined in a story by the Argentinean writer Jorge Luis Borges
(1899–1986).

READING CLOSELY

1. Quindlen thinks that "Ms. Paterson is wrong about that" (2). About what?
   What's at issue between these two writers—one who writes exclusively for children, the other who writes both for children and adults?

   *At issue is the nature of today's reading audience. Katherine Paterson claims that
   adult readers are too busy to reread anything. Thus, she feels "a sense of pity for my
   fellow writers" who do not write for children, because children read their favorite
   authors again and again (1).*

2. In her debate with Katherine Paterson, what position does Quindlen take?

   *Quindlen thinks there is at least one class of adult readers—those who are also writ-
   ers—who read and reread a favorite book over and over again. "I still reread that
   way," says Quindlen, "always have, always will" (2).*

3. In paragraph 3, Quindlen tells how her childhood reading inspired her to
   become a writer. What, according to Quindlen, do writers learn from reading
   and rereading a familiar text?

   They learn "familiar patterns" of writing (2).

STRATEGIES AND STRUCTURES

1. Quindlen begins by disagreeing with a fellow writer. How and how fairly does
   she represent the opposing point of view?

   *Before saying that Ms. Paterson is wrong, Quindlen praises her as a "fine" writer and
   speaker (1). She also says that she understands the opposing point of view and gives
   an example of herself as a repeat reader of children's books.*

2. What evidence does Quindlen give to support her contention that at least some adult readers are rereaders? How convincing do you find this evidence? Why?

   Most of Quindlen's evidence comes from her own experience, particularly of reading and rereading A Wrinkle in Time. *She might have given more of the experience of other writers to support her statement, "I suspect there are more of us than Ms Paterson knows" (2).*

3. The chair on the cover of Quindlen's book (p. 6) looks at first like it's upside down. Why do you think the designer chose this particular angle? What would happen to your view of the central figure (and what she's holding) if the chair were pictured from the side or front?

   It looks like the reader is floating—and could go anywhere as she reads. The angle of the visual also focuses our gaze on the book in the young woman's lap. If you look at it from a different angle, the book becomes less central to the picture.

4. *Other Methods.* Quindlen's personal NARRATIVE not only tells the story of how reading changed her life, it analyzes the EFFECTS of a life-changing experience. What are they?

   The main effect that reading had on her was to make her want to be a writer as well as a reader: "I can do this" (2). But Quindlen cites other effects as well: reading gave her an exciting mental life filled with imaginary companions—and rich memories to savor as an adult.

Thinking about Language

1. Ms. Paterson feels sorry for writers who must write for an audience that is "speeded-up" (1). Why do you think she chose this word instead of *sped up* or *hurried*?

   By emphasizing the word speed, *she draws the reader's attention to how fast-paced contemporary life has become, how we are accustomed to completing daily activities—including reading—as quickly as possible.*

2. Look up *begets* in a dictionary (3). What are the CONNOTATIONS of the term, and why do you think Quindlen chose it for describing how writing comes from reading?

   Beget *means "to father" or "to cause to exist." It connotes a close and natural relationship. Perhaps Quindlen is suggesting that learning to write from reading is a natural progression.*

3. What does Quindlen mean by "technique" (3)?

   From the examples she gives, it means practically every choice—of sentence structure, overall organization, audience appeal—that a writer makes to achieve the desired effect on the reader.

4. Quindlen is recalling her childhood from memory. Which particular phrases and sentences in her narrative do you find most memorylike in their flow and structure? Explain.

   Most of Quindlen's sentences are long, but when she recalls how reading enchanted her as a child—and still does—the words become almost dream-like in the way they mimic her thought processes. The best example is the sentence beginning, "I have sat on the edge of several beds" (2).

FOR WRITING

1. Write a paragraph or two explaining how you typically read a text.

2. Write a narrative about how you learned to read or write.

3. Choose a seemingly small moment from your childhood and write a narrative about the effect it has had on your life.

CHAPTER 2

The Writing Process

> Writing organizes and clarifies our thoughts. Writing is how we think our way into a subject and make it our own.   —WILLIAM ZINSSER

> I think I did pretty well, considering I started out with nothing but a bunch of blank paper.   —STEVE MARTIN

To learn to do anything well, from baking bread to programming a computer, we usually break it down into a series of operations. Writing is no exception. This chapter introduces all the steps of the writing process that will take you from a blank page to a final draft: planning; generating ideas; organizing and drafting; revising your draft as it progresses, both on your own and with the help of others; and editing and proofreading your work and putting it into final form.

Keep in mind, however, that writing is a recursive process—that is, it involves a certain amount of repetition. We plan, we draft, we revise; we plan, we draft, we revise again. Also, we tend to skip around as we write. For example, if we suddenly think of a great new idea, we may go back and rewrite what we have already written, perhaps revising it completely. Often, in fact, we engage in the various activities of writing more or less at the same time.

Planning

Most of the writing we do—and not just in school—starts with an assignment. An English teacher asks you to analyze a poem by Billy Collins. A prospective employer wants to know, on a job application form, why he or she should hire you. A college application includes an essay question, asking you to explain why you want to go to that school. Before you plunge headlong into any writing assignment, however, you need to think about where you're going. You need to plan.

To plan any piece of writing effectively, think about the nature of the assignment; the length and scope of the text you will need to write to respond to that assignment; your purpose in writing; and the audience you're writing for. You will also need to budget your time.

Managing Your Time

When is the assignment due? As soon as you get a writing assignment, make a note of the deadline. Some teachers deduct points for late papers; some don't accept them at all. Even if your instructor is lenient, learning to meet deadlines is part of surviving in college—and beyond. And remember that it's hard to plan well if you begin an assignment the night before it's due. With research papers and other long-range projects, especially, you should begin early so you have plenty of time to do everything the assignment requires.

What kind of research will you need to do? If you are writing a personal narrative or analyzing a process you know well (such as how to teach an Irish setter to catch a Frisbee), you may not need to do much research at all before you begin to write. On the other hand, if you are writing a full-scale research paper on global warming or the fiction of Henry James, the research may take longer than the actual writing. Most college writing assignments require at least some research. So as you plan any piece of writing, think about how much and what kind of research you will need to do, and allow plenty of time for that research.

Thinking about Purpose and Audience

We write for many reasons: to organize and clarify our thoughts, express our feelings, remember people and events, solve problems, persuade others to act or believe as we think they should.

For example, let's look at a paragraph from a 2007 *Time* magazine article on global warming:

> . . . If droughts and wildfires, floods and crop failures, collapsing climate-sensitive species and the images of drowning polar bears didn't quiet most of the remaining global warming doubters, the hurricane-driven destruction of New Orleans did. Dismissing a scientist's temperature chart is one thing. Dismissing the death of a major American city is something else entirely. What's more, the heat is only continuing to rise. This past year [2006] was the hottest on record in the U.S. The deceptively normal average temperature this winter masked record-breaking highs in December and record-breaking lows in February. That's the sign not of a planet keeping an even strain but of one thrashing through the alternating chills and night sweats of serious illness. —Jeffrey Kluger, "What Now?"

The main purpose of this passage is to persuade the reader that global warming can no longer be dismissed as an untested theory. The planet's temperature has been definitively taken, the author asserts, and by all accounts the patient is ailing.

Knowing what your main purpose is—whether to inform, entertain, persuade, show your knowledge of a subject, identify a problem, or something else—will help you determine what methods of development (such as narration, comparison, or definition) are best for fulfilling that purpose.

As you think about *why* you're writing, however, you also need to consider *who* your readers are. In his article on global warming, for example, Jeffrey Kluger speaks directly to his intended audience:

> Our feverish planet badly needs a cure. Climate change is caused by a lot of things, and it will take a lot of people to fix it. There's a role for big thinkers, power players, those with deep pockets—and the rest of us.

Kluger is speaking not to big thinkers or power players, but to "the rest of us"— ordinary folks who read *Time* magazine. Your intended audience can be yourself; someone you know, such as your roommate or your teacher; or someone you don't know. These different audiences have different needs, which you need to take into account. If *you* are the intended audience—as when you write in a diary or journal, or write a reminder for yourself—you can be as cryptic as you like:

> GW lecture tonight @ 8 in Denney.
> Joy @ Blue Dube, get notes, ask her to feed cat.

Once you plan to address someone else in writing, no matter what your purpose, you will need to fill in more blanks for the reader, even if you know that person well and are simply, as in the following example, leaving an informal message:

> Joy,
>
> I have to go to a global warming lecture tonight in Denney. Meet you at the Blue Danube at 6. May I borrow your ecology notes? Please feed Gen. Burnsides for me. Friskies in cabinet above fridge. Half a can.
> Thanks!
>
> Fred

Obviously, the writer of this message is familiar with his audience. He can assume, for example, that she knows Denney is the name of a building on campus and that General Burnsides is the name of a cat—but even Joy has to be told where the cat food is stashed and how much to serve. When you don't know your audience, or when you can't be sure they know what you're talking about, you need to supply them with even more information.

In each of the chapters that follow, you will find a section that will help you think about purpose and audience as you write. For now, here is a checklist of general guidelines to help you think about your intended audience and your purpose:

THINKING ABOUT PURPOSE AND AUDIENCE

- *What is the occasion for writing?* Are you taking a test? Writing a research paper? Applying for a job? Responding to an email? Commenting on a blog? Planning a toast for a wedding?

- *What is your purpose?* Do you want to tell your readers something they may not know? Entertain them? Convince them to do something? Change their minds?

- *Who is going to read (or hear) what you write?* Your classmates? Your teacher? Readers of a blog? Guests at a wedding?

- *What do you know about your audience's background?* For example, if you are writing an argument on how to stop global warming, you can expect readers who come from coal-mining regions to be more sympathetic if you look for ways of reducing the effects of carbon emissions than if you argue that all coal-burning power plants should be shut down.

- *How much does your audience already know about your subject?* If you are writing for a general audience, you may need to provide some background information and explain terminology that may be unfamiliar to them. For example, if you are writing about global warming for a newsmagazine, you might note that sequestration is a promising way to reduce carbon emissions—and then define sequestration, a process by which carbon emissions are stored underground. If you're writing for an audience of environmental scientists, on the other hand, you may be able to assume that they are familiar with sequestration.

- *What should you keep in mind about the demographics of your audience?* Does the gender of your audience matter? How about their age, level of education, economic status, or religion? Once you have sized up your audience, you're in a better position to generate ideas and evidence that will support what you have to say *and* appeal to that audience.

- *Who do you want your audience to be?* The language you use can let your readers know that you are writing to them—or not. In particular, be careful how you use the personal pronouns *we, us,* and *our.* For instance, if you write, "As Christians, we need to have compassion for others," be sure you want to limit your audience to Christians, for this language is likely to *exclude* anyone who is not.

Finding a Topic

Though we often use the words interchangeably, a *subject*, strictly speaking, is a broad field of study or inquiry, whereas a *topic* is a specific area within that field. If you are writing a paper for an ecology class, the subject of your paper is likely to be ecology. However, if your teacher asks what you're planning to write on and you reply simply, "on ecology," be prepared for a few more questions. You need to come up with a more specific topic.

Even if you said "climate change" or "global warming," your teacher would still want to know just what approach you planned to take. A good topic not only narrows down a general subject to a specific area within that field, it addresses a particular aspect of that more limited area, such as what global warming is, or what causes global warming, or what effects global warming has on the environment, or how to stop global warming.

With many writing assignments, you will be given a specific topic, or choice of specific topics, as part of the assignment. For example, an essay exam in Ecology 101 might ask: "Can global warming be stopped? How? Or why not?" Or it might say, more specifically: "Describe the key principles of the Kyoto Protocol." In a literature course, you might get a topic like this: "The narrator of Henry James's *The Turn of the Screw*: heroine or hysteric?" Or in a political science course, you may be asked to compare Marx's theory of revolution with Lenin's.

When you're given such a specific topic to write about, make sure you read the assignment carefully and know just what you are being asked to do. Pay close attention to how the assignment is worded. Look for key terms like *describe, define, analyze, compare and contrast, evaluate, argue*. Be aware that even short assignments may include more than one of these directives. For example, the same assignment may ask you not only to define global warming but to analyze its causes and effects, or to compare and contrast present-day climate conditions with those of an earlier time, or to construct an argument about what should be done to stop global warming.

Many teachers provide lists of possible topics when they make writing assignments. With longer assignments, however, you may have to work out a topic yourself, perhaps after meeting with your teacher. Start the conversation as soon as you get the assignment. Let your instructor know if there are any areas within your field of study you find particularly interesting or would like to learn more about. Ask your instructor for guidance and suggestions—and start looking on your own. If your school has a writing center, you might find it useful to discuss possible topics with someone there.

As you look for a specific topic to write about, refer to the following list, which suggests ways you can use the methods of development taught in this book to explore a topic.

USING THE METHODS TO EXPLORE A TOPIC

Use NARRATION to tell what happened—e.g., to tell what happened at the county fair. (Chapter 3)

Use DESCRIPTION to show how your subject looks, feels, smells, sounds, or tastes—e.g., to show what the Florida Keys are like. (Chapter 4)

Use EXAMPLE to give a "for instance"—e.g., to give an example of natural selection at work. (Chapter 5)

Use PROCESS to tell how something works or is made—e.g., to tell how a spellchecker works, or how to make cupcakes. (Chapter 6)

Use COMPARISON AND CONTRAST to trace similarities and differences—e.g., to tell how the religious beliefs of the Sunnis are different from those of the Shiites. (Chapter 7)

Use CLASSIFICATION to tell how something can be divided into categories, or what category it belongs to—e.g., to tell what kinds of dogs were at the American Kennel Club show. (Chapter 8)

Use DEFINITION to explain what something is—e.g., to explain what bipolar disorder is. (Chapter 9)

Use CAUSE AND EFFECT to explain what caused something or what its effects are—e.g., to explain how global warming will affect the California coastline. (Chapter 10)

Use ARGUMENT to make a case or justify a position—e.g., to make the case for buying a hybrid car instead of an SUV. (Chapter 11)

Generating Ideas

Once you have a topic to write about, it's time to start generating ideas. Where do you look for ideas? How do you go from nothing to something in a systematic way?

Over the years, writing teachers have developed a number of techniques to help writers find ideas. Freewriting, looping, listing, and brainstorming are ways to probe what you already know; clustering can help you connect ideas and begin organizing a written text around them; questioning can be particularly useful when you're trying to make a topic more specific; and keeping a journal can be helpful at any stage. All of these techniques, in fact, may come in handy at various points in the writing process, not just at the outset.

Freewriting

When you freewrite, you simply put pen to paper (or fingers to keyboard), and force yourself to jot down whatever pops into your head. Here are some tips for successful freewriting:

1. Write non-stop for a short period of time, say five or ten minutes. If nothing comes to mind at first, just write: "Nothing. I'm getting nothing. The words aren't coming." Eventually, the words *will* come—if you keep writing and don't stop until time runs out.

2. This is freewriting—so skip around freely and don't get bogged down.

3. Circle or underline words and ideas that you might want to come back to, but don't stop freewriting until your time is up. Then go back over what you have written and mark any passages that stand out as promising.

4. Freewrite again, using something you have marked in the previous session as your starting point. Do this over and over until you find an idea you want to explore further.

Here's an example of a ten-minute freewriting session by Zoe Shewer, a first-year writing student who was given the assignment "Write about an experience you've had that taught you something new about yourself."

> Write write write. Ten minutes. Okay, something I learned about myself. Yikes, what a question. I'm me. Blonde, not too tall—okay, looks really aren't the point here. I'm a pretty good athlete, love riding horses. I have a brother named Max and 2 dogs named Oz and Jazz. I tutor kids in Harlem—I like volunteering. I had a great time at Camp Robin Hood last summer. Working with all those different nonprofits was great. But did I learn anything about myself? I learned how to clean gutters, some American Sign Language, how to make spaghetti sauce. I learned that I'm not a good cook. Time.

Freewriting like this is more than a stretching exercise. It can lead to many new ideas if, each time you freewrite, you take something you have just said as the point of departure for more probing. Shewer's freewriting session led her to a possible source for an essay topic: her volunteer work.

Looping

To narrow down the subject you are exploring, try the more directed form of freewriting called *looping*. Looping not only helps you turn up a specific topic, it nudges you into writing sentences about it. Later on, you may want to use some of these sentences in your essay. Follow these steps for looping:

1. Freewrite for five or ten minutes, focusing on a single subject or idea and putting down everything about that subject that you can think of.

2. When you've finished the first loop, look over what you've written and summarize the most important part in a sentence: "I learned a lot volunteering last summer."

3. Use this summary sentence as the point of departure for your next loop. Write for another five or ten minutes without stopping. Then reflect on what you've just written, and compose another sentence summing it up: "Volunteering last summer taught me that I have a lot to learn."

4. Do as many loops as necessary until you have a direction in mind. If you already know the final destination of your essay, so much the better; but for now you're mainly looking for ways of refining your topic along the way.

Looping can be especially useful when you are trying to make an ABSTRACT subject more CONCRETE. Shewer summed up her freewriting exercise with the sentence "I learned a lot volunteering last summer" and used that sentence as the starting point for a new loop that helped her explore what she learned about herself.

Summary sentence from freewriting: I learned a lot volunteering last summer.

Loop 1: I learned a lot volunteering last summer. At Ready, Willing & Able, Seymour taught me to clean gutters. At ABC, I learned some American Sign Language, and I learned how strong those kids were. Every day, they came in determined to do everything. At the homeless shelter, I learned so much from Elsie about the city and how to survive in it. But did I learn anything about *myself?* At the end of the summer I had more admiration for Seymour, Elsie, and the kids at ABC. They all had so much more experience with life— even the kids. They had a lot of hard knocks and kept getting back up. Maybe I learned just how lucky I've been. But I think I already knew that. Maybe it was mostly that I learned that I really haven't experienced all that much.

Summary sentence: Volunteering taught me that I have a lot to learn.

Loop 2: Volunteering taught me that I have a lot to learn. Seymour told me a lot of stuff that I didn't know before, not just how to drain gutters but what his life was like. Elsie didn't talk much about her personal life, but she did tell me a lot about being homeless. And just being with the kids at ABC gave me insight into what it's like to be disadvantaged. They had to have so much determination. So did Seymour and Elsie. I don't have that kind of determination.

Summary sentence: Volunteering taught me to admire the determination that Seymour, Elsie, and the children I worked with had.

As these excerpts show, the purpose of looping is to bring ideas into sharper focus. By writing out her thoughts and looping back over them several times, Shewer was able to come up with concrete ideas about what she learned about herself by volunteering.

Keeping Lists

Most writing is better and clearer if it is detailed and specific instead of general and abstract. Keeping lists is a good way to generate ideas— and to illustrate those ideas with interesting examples and specific details. Here are some tips for keeping a list:

1. A list can be written anywhere: on paper, on a computer, in a notebook, on a napkin. Keep a pencil handy, so you can add to your lists at any time.

2. Don't worry about the form of your lists. But if the lists start to get long, group related items into piles, as you would if you were sorting your laundry.

3. Look for relationships not only *within* those piles but *between* them. Later, if you decide to construct a formal outline for your essay, you can build on the loosely arranged lists you already have.

Brainstorming

Brainstorming is a form of listing, but you write down words and ideas in one sitting rather than over time. Here are a few tips about brainstorming:

1. If you are brainstorming by yourself, first jot down a topic at the top of your page or screen. Then make a list of every idea or word that comes to mind.

2. Brainstorming is often more effective when you do it collaboratively, as part of a team, with everyone throwing out ideas and one person acting as scribe.

3. If you brainstorm with others, make sure everyone contributes. If one person monopolizes the session, the purpose of brainstorming is lost.

Clustering

Clustering helps you to make connections among ideas. Here is how to go about it:

1. Write down your topic in the center of the page, and circle it.

2. Outside this nucleus, jot down related topics and ideas, and circle each one. Draw a line from each of these satellite ideas to the central topic.

3. As you think of additional ideas, phrases, facts, or examples, group them in clusters and connect them to each other.

Zoe Shewer created the following cluster to group her ideas.

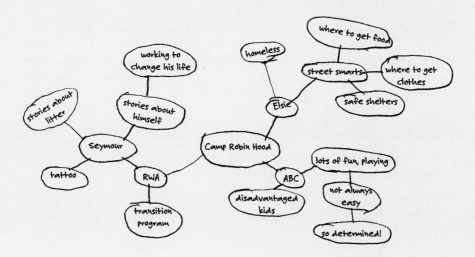

Asking Who, What, Where, When, Why, and How

Journalists ask *who, what, where, when, why,* and *how* to uncover the basic information that readers look for in a news story. These standard journalistic questions can be useful for all kinds of writing. Here is how you might use them in an essay about a car accident involving a member of your family:

1. *Who* was involved in the accident? What should I say about my sister (the driver)? About the passengers in the car (including the dog)? The police officer who investigated? The witnesses on the sidewalk?

2. *What* happened? What were the main events leading up to the crash? What did my sister do to avoid hitting the other car head-on? Should I mention that the dog got out of the car first?

3. *Where* did the accident occur? How much of the scene should I describe? The intersection itself? The hill leading up to it?

4. *When* did the accident take place? What time did my sister leave the party? Was it still raining?

5. *Why* did the accident happen? Did the other car swerve into her lane?

6. *How* could it have been avoided? Would my sister have reacted sooner if she hadn't been on her cell phone? Should I write about cell-phone usage as a contributing cause in traffic accidents?

Early in the writing process, asking key questions like these will help you turn up ideas and figure out which aspects of your subject you want to write about. Later on, the questions you choose to answer will determine, in part, the methods you use to organize your essay. For example, if you decided to explain in detail what happened on the day of your sister's accident, you would draw extensively on the techniques of NARRATION. Or if you decided to focus on the scene of the accident, you would write a largely DESCRIPTIVE essay.

Keeping a Journal

A personal journal can be a great source of raw materials for your writing. Here, for example, is part of a journal entry that Annie Dillard kept when she went on a camping trip in Virginia:

> Last night moths kept flying into the candle. They would hiss & spatter & recoil, lost upside down & flopping in the shadows among the pans on the table. Or—and this happened often, & again tonight—they'd burn their wings, & then their wings would <u>stick</u> to the next thing they'd touch—the edge of a pan, a lid. . . . These I could free with a quick flip with a spoon or something.

Two years after she made this journal entry, Dillard used some of those same details in an essay entitled "The Death of a Moth." In the published essay, the moth-drawn-to-the-flame becomes a vivid image of the dedicated writer who devotes all her energy to her work. Obviously, however, Dillard did not begin the writing process with a big idea like this in mind, and neither should you. She started with the homely details of pots and pans and ordinary moths as recorded in her journal. If you keep a journal regularly, as many writers do, you will have at your fingertips a world of concrete details to think and write about.

You can learn a lot about keeping a journal from an entry like Dillard's. Here are some pointers:

1. Write down your observations as close in time to the event as possible; don't wait until you get home from a camping trip to note what happened on the trip.

2. The observations in a journal do not have to deal with momentous events; record your everyday experiences.

3. Make each journal entry as detailed and specific as possible; don't just write "the bugs were bad" or "another beautiful day."

4. The entries in a journal do not have to be long or formally composed; they are for your eyes alone, so be as informal as you like.

5. You may not know the significance of a particular entry until months, even years, after you've written it.

Organizing and Drafting

Once you accumulate enough facts, details, and other raw material, your next job is to organize that material and develop it into a draft. The method (or methods) of development that you use will be determined by the main point you want your draft to make.

Stating Your Point

As you begin gathering materials for an essay, you probably won't know exactly what your thesis—your main point—is going to be (unless, of course, you've been given a specific main point as part of your assignment). Before you begin writing, however, try to state your thesis in one sentence. You may find as you write that you need to revise it, but you should start with a thesis in mind.

What makes a good thesis statement? First, let's consider what a thesis statement is not. A general announcement of your topic—"in this paper I plan to write about how you can fight global warming"—is *not* a thesis statement. A thesis statement tells the reader what your topic is, and it makes an interesting claim *about* your topic, one that is open to further discussion. This is why statements of fact are not thesis statements either: "The effects of global warming were first predicted in the 1890s by a little-known Swedish chemist." Historical and scientific facts may help support your thesis, but the thesis itself should say something about your subject that requires further discussion. For example:

The best way you can fight global warming is by reducing your personal carbon footprint.

The fight against global warming will be won or lost in developing nations such as India and China.

The United States is still the biggest energy hog on the planet.

When you draft an essay, make sure you state your thesis clearly, usually near the beginning. Like these examples, your thesis statement should be direct and specific, and let readers know what you'll be discussing in your essay.

Making an Outline

An informal outline is simply a list of your main points in the order they might appear in your draft. For example, after grouping her ideas into clusters, Zoe Shewer created this informal outline for her essay on an unexpected lesson:

Volunteering
 three nonprofits
 learned about myself
Ready, Willing & Able
 Seymour
 draining gutters
 telling stories
 his plans
Association to Benefit Children
 disadvantaged kids
 loved to play
 persevered
Homeless shelter
 Elsie
 street smarts
Learned that I have a lot to learn

For longer projects, such as a research paper, you may need a more detailed outline, indicating the order of both the main ideas and the less important ones. When you make a formal outline, you also show—by indenting and using letters and numbers—how all of your ideas fit together to support your THESIS:

Thesis statement: Working at Camp Robin Hood taught me that I have a lot to learn.
 I. Camp Robin Hood
  A. Crash course in volunteering
  B. Ready, Willing & Able
  C. Association to Benefit Children
  D. Homeless shelter
 II. Ready, Willing & Able
  A. Seymour

      B. Taught me to drain gutters
      C. Told me about his own life
  III. Association to Benefit Children
      A. Played with disadvantaged kids
      B. Read to them
      C. Admired their determination
  IV. Homeless shelter
      A. Elsie
      B. Depended on handouts and shelters
      C. Had figured out the system
   V. Conclusion
      A. Wanted to give something back
      B. Hope I helped others
      C. Sure I learned a lot myself

When you construct a formal outline like this, try to keep items that are at the same level in more or less the same grammatical form. Also, include at least two items for each level, otherwise you don't need to subdivide. Whatever kind of outline you make, however, change it as necessary as you write and revise.

Using the Basic Methods of Development

Once you've accumulated enough material to write about, have narrowed your subject down to a manageable topic, and have a workable thesis, you should choose one or more methods of development.

Zoe Shewer, for example, ultimately chose to write a narrative. This method of development is appropriate for her particular topic and thesis: an explanation of what she learned from doing volunteer work. Within a narrative framework, however, she also incorporated some DESCRIPTION and analyzed CAUSE AND EFFECT.

Often you will want to use several methods together. Let's look at brief example of each method.

Narration. Telling a story is one of the oldest ways of making a point. In this example, a journalist shows his mixed feelings toward his long-absent father by recalling the events of their last day together:

> He was living in a little house in Jacksonville, Alabama. . . . I knocked and a voice like an old woman's, punctuated with a cough that sounded like it came from deep in the guts, told me to come on in, it ain't locked. It was dark inside, but light enough to see what looked like a bundle of quilts on the corner of a sofa. Deep inside them was a ghost of a man, his hair and beard long

and going dirty gray, his face pale and cut with deep grooves. I knew I was in the right house because my daddy's only real possessions, a velvet-covered board pinned with medals, sat inside a glass cabinet on a table. But this couldn't be him. . . .

"It's all over but the shoutin' now, ain't it, boy," he said, and when he let the quilt slide from his shoulders I saw how he had wasted away, how the bones seemed to poke out of his clothes, and I could see how it killed his pride to look this way, unclean, and he looked away from me for a moment, ashamed.   —RICK BRAGG, *All Over But the Shoutin'*

Description. Description helps the reader to see, hear, feel, smell, or, taste whatever you're writing about. Descriptive writing uses specific details that appeal to the senses in order to create some DOMINANT IMPRESSION. In this example from a humor magazine, that impression is one of disgust and "horror" as a food critic describes how her subject looks and tastes:

Next on the menu was a can of Kal Kan Pedigree with Chunky Chicken. Chunky *chicken*? There were chunks in the can, certainly—big, purplish-brown chunks. I forked one chunk out (by now I was becoming more callous) and found that while it had no discernible chicken flavor, it wasn't bad except for the texture—like meat loaf with ground-up chicken bones.

In the world of canned dog food, a smooth consistency is a sign of low quality—lots of cereal. A lumpy, frightening, bloody, stringy horror is a sign of high quality—lots of meat. Nowhere in the world of wet dog foods was this demonstrated better than in the fanciest I tried—Kal Kan's Pedigree Select Dinners. . . .   —ANN HODGMAN, "No Wonder They Call Me a Bitch"

Example. Giving examples is one of the best ways to support a general statement or make a point, as in this observation about cultural differences in perception:

University of Michigan researchers reported that Asians and North Americans see the world differently. Shown a photograph, for example, North American students of European background paid more attention to the object in the foreground of a scene, while students from China spent more time studying the background and taking in the whole scene.
               —RANDOLPH E. SCHMID, "Dyslexia Differs by Language"

Process. Breaking an activity into steps is a good way to figure out and systematically explain how something works or is made. Often the purpose of a process analysis is to enable the reader to replicate the process, as in this set of instructions:

To start juggling, you begin by tossing a ball back and forth from left to right. This is the hardest part because you must learn where your hands must be positioned. Try to throw the ball to the same place each time.

Once you get this down, you are ready for the next step. . . .

Two balls is easy. Once you have one down, just throw the second ball up as the first ball starts to reach its peak (the highest point before descending). Don't worry if they occasionally collide. . . .

Once you have the pattern down for two balls, add a third ball. Throw the third ball when the second ball is at its peak height. At this point, the first ball should be passing your hand. Don't worry about catching it at first. Just get used to throwing all three balls at the right times.

After some practice at this, you will want to try to catch the first two balls. As you get the knack of throwing two balls and catching the first two, try to throw the first ball when the third is reaching its peak.

—CHRIS SEGUIN, "How to Juggle"

Comparison and contrast. Tracing similarities and differences tells readers how two or more subjects are alike, or different, or both. This example contrasts the experience of death in two cultures:

Once, a long time ago, living in Vietnam, we used to stare death in the face. The war, in many ways, had heightened our sensibilities toward living and dying. I saw dead bodies when I was five after a battle erupted near my house during the Tet Offensive. . . .

Though the fear of death and dying is a universal one, Vietnamese do not hide from it. We pray daily to the dead at our ancestral altar. We talk to ghosts. Death pervades our poems, novels, and sad-ending fairy tales. We dwell in its tragedy. We know that terrible things can and do happen to ordinary people.

But if agony and pain are part of Vietnamese culture, even to the point of being morbid, pleasure is at the center of American culture. While Vietnamese holidays are based on death anniversaries of famous kings and heroes, here we celebrate birth dates of presidents.

American popular culture treats death with humor. People laugh and scream at blood-and-guts movies. Zombie flicks are the rage. The wealthy sometimes freeze their dead relatives. Cemeteries are places of business, complete with colorful brochures. There are, I saw on TV the other day, drive-by funerals in some places in the Midwest where you don't have to get out of your car to pay your respects to the deceased.

—ANDREW LAM, "They Shut the Door on My Grandmother"

Classification. Dividing a subject into kinds helps explain a complex subject and can also suggest an outline for an entire essay. The following example divides conservation into three kinds:

> There are, as nearly as I can make out, three kinds of conservation currently operating. The first is the preservation of places that are grandly wild or "scenic" or in some other way spectacular. The second is what is called "conservation of natural resources"—that is, of the things of nature that we intend to use: soil, water, timber, and minerals. The third is what you might call industrial troubleshooting: the attempt to limit or stop or remedy the most flagrant abuses of the industrial system. All three kinds of conservation are inadequate, both separately and together.
>
> —WENDELL BERRY, "Conservation Is Good Work"

Definition. To explain what something is, identify its main characteristics. The following example identifies the main characteristics that many astronomers think are important for defining a planet in the solar system:

> The issue of a clear definition for *planet* came to a head in 2005 with the discovery of the trans-Neptunian object Eris, a body larger than the smallest then-accepted planet, Pluto. In its 2006 response, the International Astronomical Union (IAU), recognized by astronomers as the world body responsible for resolving issues of nomenclature, released its decision on the matter. This definition, which applies only to the Solar System, states that a planet is a body that orbits the Sun, is large enough for its own gravity to make it round, and has "cleared its neighborhood" of smaller objects. Pluto does not qualify as a planet under this definition, and the Solar System is thus considered to have eight planets: Mercury, Venus, Earth, Mars, Jupiter, Saturn, Uranus, and Neptune.
>
> —"Planet," Wikipedia (accessed January 3, 2008)

Cause and effect. Tracing causes and effects is a fundamental way of exploring relationships. The purpose of a cause-and-effect analysis is to demonstrate that one event (in the following example, a higher rate of behavioral disorders in young males) is actually the result of another event (hormones released in infant males before birth):

> Lest males of all ages feel unfairly picked upon, researchers point out that boys may be diagnosed with behavioral syndromes and disorders more often than girls for a very good reason: their brains may be more vulnerable. As a boy is developing in the womb, the male hormones released by his tiny testes accelerate the maturation of his brain, locking a lot of the wiring in place

early on; a girl's hormonal bath keeps her brain supple far longer. The result is that the infant male brain is a bit less flexible, less able to repair itself after slight injury that might come, for example, during the arduous trek down the birth canal. Hence, boys may well suffer disproportionately from behavioral disorders for reasons unrelated to cultural expectations.

—Natalie Angier, "Intolerance of Boyish Behavior"

Argument. When you argue a point, you make a claim and give evidence to support it, as in the following passage, which makes the case that we should all become vegetarians in order to save energy:

> Which is responsible for more global warming: your BMW or your Big Mac? Believe it or not, it's the burger. The international meat industry generates roughly 18 percent of the world's greenhouse-gas emissions—even more than transportation—according to a report last year from the U.N.'s Food and Agriculture Organization.
>
> Much of that comes from the nitrous oxide in manure and the methane that is, as the *New York Times* delicately put it, "the natural result of bovine digestion." Methane has a warning effect that is 23 times as great as that of carbon, while nitrous oxide is 296 times as great. . . .
>
> If you switch to vegetarianism, you can shrink your carbon footprint by up to 1.5 tons of carbon dioxide a year, according to research by the University of Chicago. Trading a standard car for a hybrid cuts only about one ton—and isn't as tasty.   —Bryan Walsh, "Skip the Steak"

The Parts of an Essay

No matter what methods of development you use, any essay you write should have a beginning, a middle, and an end. These three basic parts of an essay are usually referred to as the introduction, the body, and the conclusion.

In the introduction, you introduce the topic of your essay and state your thesis. That is, you tell the reader exactly what you're writing about and what your main point is. In the body of the essay—which may run anywhere from a few sentences or paragraphs to many pages—you offer evidence in support of your thesis. In the conclusion, you wrap up what you have to say, often by restating the thesis—but with some variation based on the evidence you have just cited.

For example, in the following short essay from *Time* magazine, the author states her thesis in the first paragraph. In the middle paragraph—the body of her essay—she cites facts and figures to support her thesis. And in the final paragraph, she concludes by restating that thesis—with a twist:

High-end hand-me-downs (the smart set calls them vintage) are more ecologically sound than new clothes. Why?

Introduction
States the thesis.

Buying a shirt the second time around means you avoid consuming all the energy used in producing and shipping a new one and, therefore, the carbon emissions associated with it. Every item of clothing you own has an impact on the environment. Some synthetic textiles are made with petroleum products. Cotton accounts for less than 3 percent of farmed land globally but consumes about a quarter of the pesticides.

Body
Supports the thesis with facts, figures, and other evidence.

One quick way to change your duds: invite friends over for a closet swap, to which everyone brings a few items they want to trade. It's easy on the environment—and your pocketbook.

Conclusion
Restates the thesis with a twist.

—COCO MASTERS, "Take Another Look at Vintage Clothes"

Any essay you write should have an introduction and a conclusion, as in this example. Usually, however, you will need more than a single paragraph in the body of your essay.

If you are writing about how individuals can combat global warming, for example, you may want to have a paragraph about recycling old clothes. But you will likely also include at least one additional body paragraph for each way of reducing carbon consumption that you discuss, such as making fewer left turns when we drive, eating less red meat, or planning a green wedding.

THE INTRODUCTION

Because it is the first thing the reader sees, the beginning of an essay requires special care. Here are a number of effective strategies for introducing an essay—all of which are intended to make the reader want to read more.

Start with a question. The following example opens with a serious question that grabs the reader's attention:

What's the difference between dementia and Alzheimer's? It's a common question, and doctors are some of the best at confusing us. Physicians seem to prefer the word "dementia," possibly because Alzheimer's has become such

a loaded word. "Dementia" somehow sounds less frightening to many people, and now even the experts have started using the words interchangeably.
—Molly Shomer, "What's the Difference Between Alzheimer's and Dementia?"

Start with a quotation or dialogue. In this example from *Outside* magazine, the author opens with an intriguing bit of dialogue, words that get the reader's interest and make a point about the beauty of nature:

"The thing is, there's this red dot," says Beau Turner, standing quietly in a longleaf-pine forest on his Avalon Plantation, 25,000 red-clay acres half an hour south of Tallahassee. It's 6:30 on a late-spring morning, and the humidity is rolling in like a fog; already I regret the hot coffee in my hand. One of our chores today is to band some new woodpecker chicks with Avalon identification, but then the red dot came up and I was anxious to see it. Not much bigger than the head of a pin, the red dot is a nearly Zen idea of nature's beauty. It sits behind the ear of the male red-cockaded woodpecker, an endangered species that Turner has spent the last four years trying to reintroduce to this land. —Jack Hitt, "One Nation, Under Ted"

Place your subject in a historical context. In the essay from which this introduction is taken, an economist makes the point that the rate of global warming may be higher than originally estimated; but first he puts the issue in historical perspective:

The 1995 consensus was convincing enough for Europe and Japan: the report's scientific findings were the basis for the Kyoto negotiations and the treaty they produced; those same findings also led most of the developed world to produce ambitious plans for reductions in carbon emissions. But the consensus didn't extend to Washington, and hence everyone else's efforts were deeply compromised by the American unwillingness to increase the price of energy. Our emissions continued to soar, and the plans of many of the Kyoto countries in Western Europe to reduce emissions sputtered.
—William McKibben, "Warning on Warming"

Open with an anecdote. Brief, illustrative anecdotes work especially well at the beginning of an essay. Here, the author is preparing to discuss how African American men are sometimes misperceived in public spaces:

My first victim was a woman—white, well dressed, probably in her early twenties. I came upon her late one evening on a deserted street in Hyde Park, a relatively affluent neighborhood in an otherwise mean, impoverished section of Chicago. As I swung onto the avenue behind her, there seemed to be a discreet, uninflammatory distance between us. Not so. She cast back a worried glance. To her, the youngish black man . . . seemed menacingly close. After a few more quick glimpses, she picked up her pace and was soon running in earnest. Within seconds she disappeared into a cross street . . . I was surprised, embarrassed, and dismayed all at once. Her flight made me feel like an accomplice in tyranny. It also made it clear that I was indistinguishable from the muggers who occasionally seeped into the area from the surrounding ghetto.   —Brent Staples, "Black Men and Public Space"

Shock or provoke the reader—mildly. You don't want to alarm your reader needlessly, but sometimes you may want to say "listen here" by being mildly provocative or controversial:

> Let's use the F word here. People say it's inappropriate, offensive, that it puts people off. But it seems to me it's the best way to begin, when it's simultaneously devalued and invaluable.
> Feminist. Feminist, feminist, feminist.
>   —Anna Quindlen, "Still Needing the F Word"

THE BODY PARAGRAPHS

The body of your essay supports and develops your thesis; it is where you give the evidence for the main point you're making. You can use many different kinds of evidence to develop paragraphs in the body of your essay:

Specific examples. Coco Masters uses an example to support her claim that buying vintage clothing is "ecologically sound." Buying a vintage shirt, she writes, "means you avoid consuming all the energy used in producing and shipping a new one."

Facts and figures. Masters provides specific figures to support her claim that reusing clothing is good for the environment: "Cotton accounts for less than 3 percent of farmed land globally but consumes about a quarter of the pesticides."

Expert testimony. To support the point that left turns waste fuel, editors of an online marketing magazine cite an executive at United Parcel Service (UPS): "According to UPS spokesman Steve Holmes, 'It seems small, but when you multiply it across 88,000 vehicles making nearly 15 million deliveries every day during the course of a year, it adds up.' "

Personal experience. To make the point that making left turns wastes time as well as fuel, you might cite your own personal experience: "First I made the trip through the Chicago Loop taking nothing but right turns. I travelled down Columbus Drive, took a right on Congress Parkway, and then took another right turn to my destination, the Dirksen Federal Building at Dearborn and Adams streets. Then I made the trip through the Loop to the Dirksen Building taking mostly left turns. The traffic was the same, but the left-turn trip took me three minutes and thirty seconds longer than the right-turn trip."

How much evidence is enough? In "Take Another Look at Vintage Clothes," for example, Coco Masters can adequately support her thesis in only a few sentences because it is so narrow in scope. A broader thesis on how we can combat global warming would require more evidence. Masters, however, limits her thesis to the claim that vintage clothes are better for the environment than new clothes. With such a narrow focus, a few examples of types of clothing and materials and figures on the energy required to produce and transport them will probably suffice to convince most readers.

Ultimately, however, it is the reader who determines whether or not your evidence is sufficient to support your thesis. The following questions can help you be sure your evidence will satisfy your readers.

- *Is your evidence concrete and specific?* Have you provided specific and concrete details that will make your point clear and interesting to the reader?

- *Is your evidence relevant to the case?* Will the reader understand immediately why you're citing particular facts, figures, personal experience, and other evidence? Do you need to explain further? Or choose other evidence?

- *Is your evidence sufficient to prove the case?* Have you cited enough evidence, or is the reader likely to require additional—or better—support before he or she will be convinced?

- *Are your sources fully and adequately documented?* Have you represented your sources fairly and accurately? Can readers locate them easily if they want to check your facts or interpretation? Have you scrupulously avoided representing the words or ideas of other writers as your own? (For more information on using and citing sources, see the appendix.)

THE CONCLUSION

The ending of an essay is your last chance to drive your point home with the reader—and to provide a sense of satisfaction and closure. Here are a few common approaches:

Restate your main point. But don't simply repeat it: remind the reader what you've said, *and*—as in this conclusion of an essay about *The Simpsons*—add a little "more than that":

At a time when it seems that society is being destroyed by its own designs, it is good to be able to hold up a mirror that shows us the extent of our problems. Neither escapist nor preachy, *The Simpsons* provides such a satiric mirror, a metaphoric reflection of our dissolving social foundation. More than that, *The Simpsons* is therapeutic: to be able to laugh in the face of such problems is the ultimate catharsis.

—BEN McCORKLE, "*The Simpsons*: A Mirror of Society"

End with a recommendation. This strategy is especially appropriate when you are completing an ARGUMENT, as in this study of the effect of handguns on the homicide rates in Seattle and Vancouver:

Our analysis of the rates of homicide in these two largely similar cities suggests that the modest restriction of citizens' access to firearms (especially handguns) is associated with lower rates of homicide. This association does not appear to be explained by differences between the communities in aggressiveness, criminal behavior, or response to crime. Although our findings should be corroborated in other settings, our results suggest that a more restrictive approach to handgun control may decrease national homicide rates.

—JOHN HENRY SLOAN et al., "Handgun Regulations, Crime, Assaults, and Homicide: A Tale of Two Cities"

Show the broader significance of your argument. See below the last paragraph of an essay on evolution. The essay opens by noting that the effects of the "great transition of animals from water to land" can be seen, for example, when modern humans shake hands. Now, many paragraphs later, the author concludes this explanation, and goes on to say something about how the study of evolutionary biology gives us a powerful tool for understanding the living world:

Let's return to our opening handshake. The structures we shook with—our shoulder, elbow, and wrist—were first seen in fish living in streams over 370 million years ago. Our firm clasp is made with a modified fish fin. Actually, we carry an entire branch of the tree of life inside of us, and it does not stop there. That broad smile we give when we shake hands? The jaws that form our grin arose during another ancient "great" transition. The pair of eyes we use to make eye contact? These were the product of an even more ancient "great" transition. The list goes on and on. . . . Perhaps that is what is so profound about evolution: Everyday biological processes can explain things that seem special or mysterious about the living world.

—NEIL SHUBIN, "The Great Transition"

Developing Paragraphs

Just as an essay is made up of a number of related paragraphs, a paragraph is made up of a number of related sentences. You can develop paragraphs by using the same methods—NARRATION, DESCRIPTION, EXAMPLE, CLASSIFICATION, and the others—that are also used to organize whole essays. Whatever method of development you use, however, you will need to tell the reader clearly and directly what your paragraph is about and where it's going. This is the purpose of the TOPIC SENTENCE.

WRITING TOPIC SENTENCES

Just as a thesis statement alerts readers to the main point of your essay, a topic sentence lets them know what to expect in a paragraph. A good topic sentence should not only tell the reader precisely what the topic of the paragraph is ("behavioral disorders in boys"), it should make a clear statement about that topic ("Doctors are now diagnosing behavioral disorders in boys more frequently than they used to"). Notice that each of the following topic sentences (from the passages on pp. 27–29) proposes something interesting—and arguable—about the topic:

> There are, as nearly as I can make out, three kinds of conservation currently operating. —WENDELL BERRY, "Conservation Is Good Work"

> But if agony and pain are part of Vietnamese culture, even to the point of being morbid, pleasure is at the center of America's culture.
> —ANDREW LAM, "They Shut the Door on My Grandmother"

> Lest males of all ages feel unfairly picked upon, researchers point out that boys may be diagnosed with behavioral syndromes and disorders more often than girls for a very good reason: their brains may be more vulnerable.
> —NATALIE ANGIER, "Intolerance of Boyish Behavior"

Each of these topic sentences appears at the beginning of a paragraph and tells the reader exactly where the paragraph is going. Sometimes, however, the topic sentence comes at the end and tells the reader where the paragraph has been, as in this example:

> There are 1.5 billion cattle and buffalo on the planet, along with 1.7 billion sheep and goats. Their populations are rising fast, especially in the developing world. Global meat production is expected to double between 2001 and 2050. Given the amount of energy consumed raising, shipping and selling livestock, a 16-oz. T-bone is like a Hummer on a plate.
> —BRYAN WALSH, "Skip the Steak"

No matter where it comes in the paragraph, your topic sentence should be supported by every other sentence in the paragraph. The supporting sentences can give examples, introduce facts and figures, or even tell an illustrative story; but they all need to connect logically with the topic sentence in ways that are apparent to the reader.

LINKING IDEAS TOGETHER

Each paragraph in your essay should lead logically to the next, with clear TRANSITIONS that indicate to the reader how the paragraphs are connected. Here are some transitional words and phrases that will help you tie your ideas together.

To give examples: for example, for instance, in fact, in particular, namely, specifically, that is

To compare: also, as, in a similar way, in comparison, like, likewise

To contrast: although, but, by contrast, however, on the contrary, on the other hand

To indicate cause and effect: as a result, because, because of, consequently, so, then

To indicate logical reasoning: accordingly, hence, it follows, therefore, thus, since, so

To indicate place or direction: across, across from, at, along, away, behind, close, down, distant, far, here, in between, in front of, inside, left, near, next to, north, outside, right, south, there, toward, up

To indicate time: at the same time, during, frequently, from time to time, in 1999, in the future, now, never, often, meanwhile, occasionally, soon, then, until, when

To indicate sequence or continuation: also, and, after, before, earlier, finally, first, furthermore, in addition, last, later, next

To summarize or conclude: in conclusion, in summary, in the end, consequently, so, therefore, thus, to conclude

Using Visuals

You may want to consider using visuals. Illustrations such as graphs and charts can be especially effective for presenting or comparing data, and photographs can help readers see things you describe in your written text.

Visuals should never be mere decoration or clip art, however. Any visuals should be directly relevant to your topic and must support your thesis in some way. For example, if you are writing about conserving energy by carrying a reusable cloth shopping bag, you might include an illustration showing the kind of bag you have in mind.

As with a written text, any visual material you include should be appropriate for your audience and purpose. A picture of a raven, for example, would not add much to an essay for a literature class on Edgar Allan Poe's famous poem—but it might be appropriate, if properly labeled, for a biology paper or a field guide to birds.

If you do decide that a visual illustration will genuinely enhance your argument, be sure to refer to it in your text and number it, if necessary, so that readers can find it ("see Fig. 1"). Position the visual as close as you can to the part of your text that it illustrates, and provide a caption that identifies and explains its point. If you found the visual in another source, identify the source and provide documentation in a Works Cited or References list.

This reusable bag lets you avoid using plastic shopping bags, thereby conserving energy and reducing landfill waste. © Doug Steley B/Alamy.

Revising

Revising is a process of re-vision, of looking again at your draft and making necessary changes in content, organization, or both. Occasionally when you revise, you discover only a few minor scrapes and bruises that need your attention. More often, however, revising requires some major surgery: adding new evidence, narrowing a thesis, cutting out paragraphs or entire sections, rewriting the beginning to appeal better to your audience, and so on.

Revising is not generally the time to focus on words or sentences, though you may change some words and smooth out awkward or unclear sentences as you revise. Nor is revising a matter of correcting errors, but rather of more general shaping and reshaping. Many writers try to revise far too soon. To avoid this pitfall, put aside your draft for a few hours—or better still, for a few days—before revising.

Reading a Draft with a Critical Eye

Start by reading your draft yourself, and then try to get someone else to look it over—a classmate, a writing tutor, your roommate, your grandmother. Whoever it is, be sure he or she is aware of your intended audience and purpose. Here's what you and the person with fresh eyes should look for as you read:

AN EFFECTIVE TITLE. Is the title more than a label? How does it pique the reader's interest? Does it indicate the subject of the essay—and if not, should it?

A CLEAR FOCUS. What is the main point? Is it clearly stated in a thesis statement—and if not, should it be? Is the thesis too broad? Sufficiently narrow?

SUFFICIENT INFORMATION FOR YOUR AUDIENCE. How familiar is the topic likely to be to your readers? Is there sufficient background information? Are there clear definitions for any terms and concepts readers might not know? Will readers find it interesting?

ADEQUATE SUPPORT FOR THE THESIS. What evidence supports the thesis? Is the evidence convincing and the reasoning logical? How could the draft be strengthened by adding more facts or specific details?

ORGANIZATION. Is the draft well organized? Does it have a clear beginning, middle, and ending? Are paragraphs related to each other by clear transitions? Does each paragraph contribute to the main point, or are some paragraphs off the topic? Does the ending give a sense of closure?

METHODS OF DEVELOPMENT. What is the main method of development? For example, is the draft primarily a NARRATIVE? A DESCRIPTION? An ARGUMENT? Is this method effective? If not, which other methods might be introduced? For instance, would more EXAMPLES, or DEFINITIONS, or a discussion of CAUSES be beneficial?

SOURCES. Is there material from other sources? If so, how are those sources incorporated—are they quoted? Paraphrased? Summarized? How are they acknowledged? In other words, is it clear to the reader whose words or ideas are being quoted, paraphrased, or summarized? How does the source material support the main point? Have all source materials been properly cited and documented?

PARAGRAPHS. Does each paragraph focus on one main idea and have a clear topic sentence? Does the structure of paragraphs vary, or are they too much alike? If they all begin with a topic sentence, should you consider rewriting some paragraphs to lead up to the topic sentence instead of down from it? Does every sentence in a paragraph support the point that the rest of the paragraph is making? Are there any long or complex paragraphs that should be broken into two? The more common problem, however, is that paragraphs are too short. Are there paragraphs that should be combined with other paragraphs, or developed more fully? How well does the draft flow from one paragraph to the next? If any paragraphs seem to break the flow, look to see if you need to add transitions or to use repetition to help the reader follow the text.

SENTENCE LENGTH AND VARIETY. Check the length of your sentences. If they are all approximately the same length, try varying them some. A short sentence in the middle of long sentences can provide emphasis. On the other hand, too many short sentences, one after the other, can sound choppy. Try combining some of them.

VISUALS. Does the draft include any visuals? If not, is there any material in the text that would be easier to understand in a chart or table? Any descriptive passages where a photo might help readers see what you're talking about? If there are visuals, are they relevant to the topic? How do they support the thesis?

A Sample Student Essay

Here is a first draft by Zoe Shewer, a student at Vanderbilt University who was assigned to write about an experience that taught her something new about herself.

FIRST DRAFT

How should I spend my summer vacation? Many college students have internships or summer jobs. Some travel. I spent last summer volunteering with three nonprofits through Camp Robin Hood.

Camp Robin Hood is a hands-on summer crash course in New York City nonprofit organizations. Every week, I worked at a different nonprofit: a day care center, a homeless shelter, and a transitional lifestyle program for ex-convicts and former addicts. At every organization, I learned something about working with the underprivileged, but at the end of the summer, I realized that I had also learned something about myself.

I began by working at Ready, Willing & Able, where ex-convicts and former addicts clean streets as part of a transitional lifestyle program. I'll never forget the street cleaning attendant I worked with there. Seymour was tall, tattooed, and a former addict. He was also calm and completely at ease in his RWA jumpsuit, sweeping the sidewalks and wheeling a huge blue trash can through the streets. Seymour taught me how to drain gutters by diverting the flow of water with a rolled up towel. He also taught me to "read" the back stories in the litter. It was like he saw a story in every piece of trash: a schoolgirl who discarded a bracelet in a temper tantrum, a closet eater who ate Twinkies in the street. He talked about his family, too, and his dreams and plans. I grew to respect him and admire his perseverance and determination, despite all the setbacks in his life.

That respect and admiration was something I would come to feel at each of the non-profits. At the Association to Benefit Children, an organization that provides services to underprivileged children, I played with and taught children who had many challenges. Like any kids, they loved singing, fingerpainting, and playing with toys. But there was no escaping the fact that these activities didn't always come easily to them. They worked hard for what they wanted. It was impossible not to admire their determination.

At a homeless shelter, where I handed out clean clothes and tickets for showers, I met people from every walk of life. Some had addiction problems or other illnesses, but many had simply fallen on hard times. The loss of a job or an unexpected medical problem ended up costing them their homes, and they had nowhere else to go. I spent many evenings talking to one woman in particular, Elsie. She had been homeless for several years and knew the streets of New York better than anyone I've ever met. She knew which restaurants would give out their leftover food and when you should appear at their back door for dinner. She knew which churches had the best soup kitchens, and which shelters were safest, and where to find the best cast-off clothing. I never found out how she'd become homeless, but she'd figured out the system and made it work for her. Although I grew up in New York City, her street smarts made me feel like I'd never really known the city.

I volunteered for Camp Robin Hood because I wanted to give something back. I know that my upbringing has been privileged, and I've been lucky to have never gone without. I wanted to do something for those who weren't so lucky. But I discovered that while I may have more tangible goods than those I was volunteering to help, they had a lot to teach me about the intangible: qualities like perseverance, determination, optimism and cheerfulness no matter what the circumstances. They taught me that I have a lot to learn.

Getting Response before Revising

After finishing her first draft, Shewer set it aside for a few hours and then reread it, using the guidelines for reading a draft with a critical eye (p. 37). She also asked a classmate to read it, and he offered her the following comments:

> I really like the topic of your essay, and I think it meets the assignment well. But maybe it would be more effective if you picked one of the three places you worked to focus on, so that you could talk about it more in-depth. I'd like to know more about them.
>
> You kind of state a thesis—"At every organization, I learned something about working with the underprivileged, but at the end of the summer, I realized that I had also learned something about myself"—but then you state it more directly at the end of the paper—"They taught me that I have a lot to learn." That works pretty well, and the body paragraphs do support this idea.
>
> You describe the people you meet, but it might be more interesting if there was more of a story.

Shewer agreed with her classmate's suggestions to focus on just one of the places she worked, and to incorporate more narration. She chose to write about her experience at Ready, Willing & Able, and to focus on her day working with Seymour. After some *brainstorming* about that day, she decided to add a *narrative* about one incident in particular. She then *revised her thesis* to reflect her narrower focus on that specific day. She also added a title, which she hadn't included in her first draft.

SECOND DRAFT

Ready, Willing, and Able

July is stifling in New York City, and I was not looking forward to wearing an oversized jumpsuit in the ninety-degree heat. I was suited up to clean streets as part of the Camp Robin Hood program. I was at the headquarters of Ready, Willing & Able. Most RWA employees are ex-convicts or former addicts for whom street cleaning is both a job and part of a transitional lifestyle program.

The program coordinator waved me towards a tall man who had apparently been waiting for me. His name was Seymour, and he was the street cleaning attendant I would be working with all day. As he reached out to shake my hand, I noticed that he had a tattoo on his forearm.

We headed out to the street, and while I fidgeted with the broom I carried, Seymour calmly wheeled a bright blue trash can behind him. As we began sweeping the sidewalks, Seymour not only showed me how to drain the gutters, he talked about who might have dropped certain kinds of trash and why and told me about his family and his desire to get his life back on track. Though I had lived in the city my entire life, I began to see things in a new light. I became so absorbed in Seymour's stories that I heard some girls laughing and almost didn't realize they were laughing at me. "I wonder what *she* did to deserve *that*!"

I looked up and saw a group of girls about my age laughing at me as they walked past. They obviously thought I was serving a juvenile court sentence. Ordinarily I may have laughed at the idea that I could be mistaken for a juvenile delinquent, but on this day I felt butterflies in my stomach.

What if Seymour thought I was just like those other girls? What if he thought I didn't want to be there and was counting down the minutes until the day would be over? I wanted to tell him that I had a lot of respect for his work and that I knew I couldn't possibly understand what he does just by shadowing him for a day. I wanted to tell him that I was not simply doing a day of community service so I could include it on a job résumé.

But Seymour broke the silence, saying, "Put some muscle in it, Goldilocks."

Revising a Second Draft

After setting her revision aside for a day, Shewer came back to her essay and reread it, following the questions for revision on pp. 38–39. She liked the story of her day working with Seymour, but she thought that now there was too much narration, and she needed to have *more descriptive details*. She also decided that she needed to explain more about the incident with the girls—how she felt and how that moment taught her something. Finally, she revised some of her sentences so they were not all the same length and tried to make some of her language more precise.

FINAL DRAFT

Ready, Willing, and Able

Wearing a canvas jumpsuit zipped up to my neck, I must have looked as though I was stepping onto the set of *ET: The Extra-Terrestrial,* but my actual destination was Madison Avenue, home to some of the fanciest boutiques in New York City. The bright blue jumpsuit I wore was far from high fashion: it was sized for a full-grown man, and it ballooned about my slender frame. My blonde hair was pulled back in a ponytail, and the only label I displayed was the bold-lettered logo on my back: Ready, Willing & Able. I was suited up to collect trash from the sidewalks of New York.

July is stifling in New York City, and I was not looking forward to wearing the oversized jumpsuit in the ninety-degree heat. As I made my way through the Ready, Willing & Able (RWA) head-quarters, I passed colorfully decorated bulletin boards bearing smiley-faced reminders: "Drug testing is on Monday!" "Curfew is midnight!" Most fulltime employees of RWA are ex-convicts or former addicts for whom street cleaning is the work-for-housing component of a transitional lifestyle program. For me, street cleaning was day one of Camp Robin Hood, a hands-on summer crash course in New York non-profit organizations. As I selected a broom from the supply closet, I reminded myself that I had volunteered to do this. Feeling like a new kid on the first day of school, I stood nervously next to the program supervisor who would be introducing me to the street cleaning attendant I would be helping.

If I was the awkward new kid, the street cleaning attendant to whom I was assigned, a tall man named Seymour, was undoubtedly the Big Man on Campus. Seymour wore his RWA cap slightly askew, and, as he reached out to shake my hand, I caught a glimpse of a tattoo under his sleeve. We headed out to the street together, and, while I nervously fidgeted with the broom I car-

Introduction

Beginning of narrative: the first day

Description of key character, with concrete details

ried, he calmly wheeled a bright blue trash can behind him. Seymour began sweeping the sidewalks, and I followed his lead. He not only showed me how to drain the gutters, he also taught me how to "read" the back stories in the litter. To Seymour, a torn hemp bracelet on the curb was a schoolgirl's temper tantrum; a Twinkie wrapper in the street was a closet eater's discarded evidence. Though I have lived in New York my entire life, I began to see my surroundings in a new light. The streets that had always felt so familiar seemed full of surprises. As our afternoon continued, Seymour also told me stories about his sister, his desire to get his life back on track after some time on the wrong side of the law, his love of Central Park, and his aspiration to travel across the country.

After several hours, I had more or less forgotten about my tent-sized, RWA jumpsuit when suddenly I heard someone laughing at me: "I wonder what *she* did to deserve *that*?!"

Dialogue and climax of narrative

I looked up and saw a group of girls my age looking in my direction and laughing as they walked past. My stomach tightened. They obviously thought I was being punished, perhaps serving a juvenile court sentence. Ordinarily I might have laughed at the idea that I could be mistaken for a juvenile delinquent, but on this day I felt a jumble of feelings—panic, shame, sadness, and admiration for a man whose history is suggested by his jumpsuit and the logo on his back. I will admit that a few hours earlier I was embarrassed about my ill-fitting uniform. Halfway through the work day, however, the girls' rude comments caused an entirely different kind of shame: What if Seymour thought *I* was anything like those girls? What if he thought that I was faking a smile and counting down the minutes until the day was over?

Effect of incident

Thesis indicated indirectly

I suddenly wanted to thank Seymour for this experience. I wanted to tell him that he was probably the best guide through these streets I had ever had, and that I knew I could not possibly

Significance of narrative

understand what he does by shadowing him for a day in a borrowed uniform. I wanted to explain to him that I volunteer regularly in New York: I am committed to working with at-risk children, and have done so for years at an after-school program in Harlem. I wanted to share how much I relate to his closeness with his family, his desire to travel, and his love of Strawberry Fields in Central Park. But the girls' mocking comments and laughter had left us in an uncomfortable silence, and I felt that anything I might say would make us feel even more awkward.

It was Seymour who broke this silence. As I stood next to the trash can and tried to avoid staring off in the direction of the latte-carrying girls, Seymour caught my eye, smiled and nodded towards my broom with one excellent piece of advice: "Put some muscle in it, Goldilocks."

Conclusion with dialogue

This final draft, Shewer felt, better blended the methods of narration and description, and it fulfilled the assignment to write about an experience that taught her something new about herself. She especially liked the concrete details she included and the dialogue that ended the essay.

Editing and Proofreading

When you finish revising your essay, you're still not quite done. You've put the icing on the cake, but you need to make sure all the candles are straight and to wipe the edge of the plate. That is, you need to edit and proofread your final draft before presenting it to the reader.

When you edit, you add finishing touches and correct errors in grammar, sentence structure, punctuation, and word choice that affect the sense and meaning of your text. When you proofread, you take care of misspellings, typos, problems with your margins and format, and other minor blemishes in the surface appearance of your document.

Certain types of errors are common to certain types of writing. Chapters 3–11 include sections on "Editing for Common Errors"—the kinds of errors that are likely with the method being discussed. Here are some tips that can help you check your drafts for some common errors.

Editing Sentences

Check to be sure that each sentence expresses a complete thought—that it has a subject (someone or something) and a verb performing an action or indicating a state of being.

Check capitalization and end punctuation. Be sure that each sentence begins with a capital letter and ends with a period, a question mark, or an exclamation point.

Look for sentences that begin with it or there. Often such sentences are vague or boring, and they are usually easy to edit. For example, if you've written "There is a doctor on call at every hospital," you could edit it to "A doctor is on call at every hospital."

Check for parallelism. All items in a list or series should have parallel forms—all nouns (Lincoln, Grant, Lee), all verbs (dedicate, consecrate, hallow), all phrases (of the people, by the people, for the people).

Editing Words

There, their. Use *there* to refer to place or direction, or to introduce a sentence (Who was there? There was no answer.). Use *their* as a possessive (Their intentions were good).

It's, its. Use *it's* to mean "it is" (It's difficult to say what causes dyslexia). Use *its* to mean "belonging to it" (Each car has its unique features).

Lie, lay. Use *lie* when you mean "recline" (She's lying down because she's tired). Use *lay* when you mean "put" or "place" (Lay the book on the table).

Editing Punctuation

Check for commas after introductory elements in a sentence.

> The day he disclosed his matrimonial ambitions for me, my uncle sat me at his right during lunch.　　　　　—SAIRA SHAH, "Longing to Belong"

Check for commas before and, but, or, nor, so, or yet in compound sentences.

> They divorced when I was in junior high school, and they agreed on little except that I was an impossible child.　　　　　—RICHARD RUSSO, "Dog"

Check for commas in a series.

> The hijackers had planned to take flights scheduled to depart at 7:45 (American 11), 8:00 (United 175 and United 93), and 8:10 (American 77).
> —THE 9/11 COMMISSION, "The Battle for United 93"

When you quote other people's words, be sure to put quotation marks at the beginning and end of the quotation.

> They quoted unnamed scouts from other teams saying things like, "He never met a pizza he didn't like." —MICHAEL LEWIS, "The Badger"

Check to be sure that you've put commas and periods inside quotation marks.

> "Put some muscle in it, Goldilocks."
> —ZOE SHEWER, "Ready, Willing, and Able"

> "He's not the most physically fit," Kubota had said.
> —MICHAEL LEWIS, "The Badger"

Check your use of apostrophes with possessives. Singular nouns should end in *'s,* whereas plural nouns should end in *s'.* The possessive pronouns *hers, his, its, ours, yours,* and *theirs* should not have apostrophes.

> Robert Bergman's radiant portraits of strangers provoked this meditation.
> —TONI MORRISON, "Strangers"

Morrison's meditation was provoked by the strangers' faces.

> Theirs was the life I dreamt about during my vacations in eastern North Carolina. —DAVID SEDARIS, "Remembering My Childhood
> on the Continent of Africa"

Proofreading and Final Formatting

Proofreading is the only stage in the writing process where you are *not* primarily concerned with meaning. Of course you should correct any substantive errors you discover, but your main concern when you proofread is the surface appearance of your text. Misspellings, margins that are too narrow or too wide, unindented paragraphs, missing page numbers—these are the kinds of imperfections you're looking for as you put the final touch on your document.

Such minor blemishes are especially hard to see when you're looking at your own work. So slow down as you proofread, and view your document more as a picture than as a written text. Use a ruler or piece of paper to guide your eye line by line as you scan the page; or read your entire text backward a sentence at a time; or read it out loud word by word. Use a spellchecker, too, but don't rely on it: a spellchecker doesn't know the difference, for example, between *spackling* and *spacing* or *Greek philosophy* and *Geek philosophy*.

After you've proofread your document word for word, check the overall format to make sure it follows any specific instructions that you may have been given. If your instructor does not have particular requirements for formatting, follow these standard guidelines:

Heading and title. Put your name, your instructor's name, the name and number of the course, and the date on separate lines in the upper-left-hand corner of your first page. Skip a line and center your title, but do not underline it or put it in quotation marks.

Typeface and size. Use ten- or twelve-point type in an easy-to-read typeface, such as Times New Roman, Courier, or Palatino.

Spacing. Double-space your document.

Margins. Leave at least an inch on each side and at the top and bottom of your text.

Paragraph indentation. Indent the first line of each paragraph five spaces.

Page numbers. Number your pages consecutively, and include your last name with each page number.

CHAPTER 3

Narration

Narrative is the oldest and most compelling method of holding someone's attention; everyone wants to be told a story.   —WILLIAM ZINSSER

Narration is the storytelling mode of writing. The minute you say to someone, "You won't believe what happened to me this morning," you have launched into a narrative.

To understand how narration works, let's have a look at the story of a young man's arrival, after an arduous journey, in the city of Philadelphia:

I walked up the street, gazing about till near the market-house I met a boy with bread. I had made many a meal on bread, and, inquiring where he got it, I went immediately to the baker's he directed me to, in Second-street, and ask'd for bisket, intending such as we had in Boston; but they, it seems, were not made in Philadelphia. Then I asked for a three-penny loaf, and was told they had none such. So not considering or knowing the difference of money, and the greater cheapness nor the names of his bread, I bade him give me three-penny worth of any sort. He gave me, accordingly, three great puffy rolls. I was surpriz'd at the quantity, but took it, and, having no room in my pockets, walk'd off with a roll under each arm, and eating the other. Thus I went up Market-street as far as Fourth-street, passing by the door of Mr. Read, my future wife's father; when she, standing at the door, saw me, and thought I made, as I certainly did, a most awkward, ridiculous appearance. Then I turned and went down Chestnut-street and part of Walnut-street, eating my roll all the way, and, coming round, found myself again at Market-street wharf, near the boat I came in, to which I went for a draught of the river water; and, being filled with one of my rolls, gave the other two to a woman and her child that came down the river in the boat with us, and were waiting to go farther. —BENJAMIN FRANKLIN, *Autobiography*

Defining Narrative:
Telling What Happened

What makes Franklin's text a narrative? Like all narratives, the story of his arrival in Philadelphia is an account of events. It answers the question "What happened?"—to a particular person in a particular place and time. Young Franklin arrived in the city, shopped for bread, ate, gazed and strolled about, saw a young woman, performed an act of charity.

Narratives focus on events, big and small. You do not have to live a life of high adventure or witness extraordinary acts in order to write a compelling narrative. The events in Franklin's story, you'll notice, are all perfectly ordinary; they could have happened to anybody. The interest, even the drama, that we all enjoy in a well-told story often comes not so much from the nature of the events themselves as from how they are presented.

In this chapter, we will examine how to come up with the raw materials for a story, how to select details from those raw materials to suit your purpose and audience, and how to organize those details as a narrative—by the use of chronology, transitions, verb tenses, and plot. But first, let's consider *why* we write narratives at all—and how they can help us to make a point.

Why Do We Write Narratives?

Everybody likes a good story. We tell stories for many reasons: to connect with other people, to entertain, to record what people said and did, to explain the significance of events, to persuade others to act in a certain way or to accept our point of view on an issue.

Ben Franklin tells his famous story at the beginning of his *Autobiography* in order to engage the reader's attention right off the bat. Franklin is not just entertaining the reader, however. He has a point to make, much as a graduation speaker opens with a humorous story or poignant tale before getting down to the serious business of talking about life after college.

Although a good story can be an end in itself, this chapter focuses on narratives that are written to make a point or support an argument. Such a narrative can be a brief part of a longer work, or it can be used to structure an entire essay. Very brief narratives, called ANECDOTES, appear in all kinds of writing. Writers often use them at the beginning of a text to get a reader's interest or to lead into their main point. Franklin's big point in his *Autobiography*, for example, is to show readers how he succeeded in life, and so he begins with an anecdote about his humble beginnings. That way, says Franklin, "you may in your mind compare such unlikely beginnings with the figure I have since made."

Suppose you are a geneticist, and you are writing about mitrochondrial DNA and how it can be used to study human evolution. (Mitrochondrial DNA is passed down, unaltered, from generation to generation on the mother's side.) Suppose, further, that you have isolated seven strains of mitrochondrial DNA and traced them back to the seven prehistoric female ancestors of all persons presently alive. How would you convey your exciting conclusions to a general audience?

Bryan Sykes, a professor of genetics at the Institute of Molecular Medicine at Oxford University, recently had to solve this problem because his research team had isolated seven separate lines of human descent. He decided to convey the findings by recreating the story of each of the "seven daughters of Eve," whose DNA can be identified by modern research methods. (You can find Sykes's "So, What Is DNA and What Does It Do?" on pp. 378–84.)

Here is how he concludes the narrative about one of them, a woman who lived forty-five thousand years ago:

> Ursula had no idea, of course, that both her daughters would give rise, through their children and grandchildren, to a continuous maternal line stretching to the present day. She had no idea she was to become the clan mother, the only woman of that time who could make that claim. Every single member of her clan can trace a direct and unbroken line back to Ursula. Her clan were the first modern humans successfully to colonize Europe. Within a comparatively short space of time they had spread across the whole continent, edging the Neanderthals into extinction. Today about 11 percent of modern Europeans are the direct maternal descendants of Ursula. They come from all parts of Europe, but the clan is particularly well represented in western Britain and Scandinavia . . .
>
> —BRYAN SYKES, *The Seven Daughters of Eve*

Sykes's story about Ursula efficiently explains a number of complicated points about genetic studies and human descent. By giving each of the maternal ancestors a story, Sykes makes his findings much easier to understand—and to remember. Sometimes there's no better way to make a point than by telling a good story—*if* it really fits the subject you are writing about and doesn't go off on a tangent.

Composing a Narrative

Let's go back to the adventures of Ben Franklin for a moment. How did Franklin know, on his first stroll around the city, that the young woman he saw standing at Mr. Read's door would one day be his wife? Obviously, he couldn't know this when he first saw her. Franklin's reference to his future wife shows us not that young Franklin was psychic but that his narrative has been carefully composed—after the fact, as all narratives are.

As the author of a narrative, you know everything that is going to happen, so you can present events in any order you please. However, if you want anyone else to understand the point you are trying to make, you need to compose your narrative carefully. Consider, first of all, your audience and your purpose for writing. Then think about which details to include and how to organize those details so that readers can follow your story and see your point in telling it. To make your story a compelling one, be sure to give it a plot and tell it from a consistent point of view.

Thinking about Purpose and Audience

The first thing to do as you compose a narrative is to think hard about the AUDIENCE you want to reach and the PURPOSE your narrative is intended to serve. Suppose you are telling about a visit to a computer store in an email to a friend, and your purpose is simply to say what you did yesterday. In this case, your narrative can ramble on about how you got to the store, discovered it was much larger than you expected, went into the monitor section and looked around, then wandered over to the printers and couldn't get a salesperson's attention, but eventually spoke to a very helpful manager, and so on. The story might end with your emerging triumphantly from the store with a good printer at a good price. It wouldn't matter much that your story goes on and on because you're writing to a friendly reader who is interested in everything you do and has time to listen.

Now suppose you are writing an advertisement, the purpose of which is to sell printers to the general public. You could still write about your visit to a computer store, but you would tell your story differently because you now have a different purpose and audience: "When I walked into ComputerDaze, I couldn't believe my eyes. Printers everywhere! And the cheap prices! Plus they give you a ream of paper absolutely free! I went home with a printer under each arm." Or suppose you are writing a column in a computer magazine, and your purpose is to show readers how to shop for a printer by telling them about the problems you dealt with as you shopped. You might write: "The first hurdle I encountered was the numbing variety of brands and models."

Whatever your purpose, you will want to think about how much your audience is likely to know about your subject—computers, for instance—so you can judge how much background information you need to give, how much technical language you can use, what terms you may need to define, and so on. If you are writing for an audience that knows nothing about computers and peripherals, for instance, you might even have to explain what an external hard drive is before you tell your readers how to buy or use one.

Generating Ideas:
Asking What Happened—and Who, Where, When, How, and Why

Before you can tell a good story, you have to have a story to tell. How do you come up with the raw materials for a narrative in the first place? Brainstorming, clustering, and other methods can help you GENERATE IDEAS. But a narrative is not just a kind of writing; it is also a way of thinking, one that can help you find ideas to write about. How do you get started? Let's look at an example.

Consider the following passage in which Annie Dillard tells about what happened one Saturday afternoon when her father was preparing to leave for a trip:

> Getting ready for the trip one Saturday, he roamed around our big brick house snapping his fingers. He had put a record on: Sharkey Bonano, "Li'l Liza Jane." I was reading Robert Louis Stevenson on the sunporch: *Kidnapped*. I looked up from my book and saw him outside; he had wandered out to the lawn and was standing in the wind between the buckeye trees and looking up at what must have been a small patch of wild sky. Old Low-Pockets. He was six feet four, all lanky and leggy; he had thick brown hair and shaggy brows, and a mild and dreamy expression in his blue eyes.
>
> —ANNIE DILLARD, *An American Childhood*

We can only imagine the exact process by which a superb writer like Dillard brought to light the vivid details of her past to form a passage like this. However, we do know that she wrote it many years after the fact, and so she must have probed her memory to find the details for her narrative.

As she prepared to write about her past experience, Dillard may well have asked herself the questions that journalists typically ask when developing a story: who, what, where, when, how, and why? Certainly her narrative answers most of those questions: who (she and her father), what (reading and listening to music), where (on the sunporch), when (one Saturday), why (to get ready for a trip).

If Dillard had stopped her questioning here, though, she would have turned up only the skeleton of a narrative, one that might read something like this:

Getting ready for his trip, Father roamed around the house listening to music while I read on the sunporch. He wandered outside and looked up at the sky. He was tall with thick hair and blue eyes.

This is the beginning of a narrative, but only the beginning, because it lacks the vivid details by which Dillard brings the past to life.

When you are planning a narrative, then, keep asking who, what, where, when, how, and why. Look for lots of particular details, both visual and auditory. "Just take a period," the writer John Steinbeck once advised a friend who was trying to write his life story. "Then try to remember it so clearly that you can see things: what colors and how warm or cold and how you got there. . . . It is important to tell what people looked like, how they walked, what they wore, what they ate." That way, instead of a generic girl with a nameless book and an anonymous man listening to unidentified music, your readers will see and hear Old Low-Pockets snapping his fingers as "Li'l Liza Jane" plays in the background and you pore over *Kidnapped*.

You will also want your readers to know *why* you're telling this particular story. In Dillard's case, the who, what, where, and when are vividly presented. We can see the scene clearly and everything that happens in it. But the *why*—Why is her father preparing for a trip? Why is she telling the story?—is not so immediately obvious.

As it happens, Dillard's father is about to leave his family in Pittsburgh and his job at the American Standard Company and take off down the Ohio River, heading, ultimately, to New Orleans, birthplace of jazz. Dillard could have simply told us that her father was an impractical man who suffered from wanderlust and a romantic notion of the cool life far away from the familiar world of manufacturing and plumbing fixtures. However, by constructing a narrative in which her father snaps his fingers to a jazz tune with a "dreamy expression" in his eyes, Dillard not only makes her point, she gives evidence in support of it at the same time. Every detail in her narrative is carefully selected to make that point.

Organizing and Drafting a Narrative

Once you have figured out what's going to happen in your narrative, it's time to get down to the business of organizing your material and writing a draft. As you draft a narrative, your task is to turn the *facts* of what happened into a *story* of what happened. To do this, you will need to put the events in chronological order, connect them with appropriate transitions and verb tenses, give your narrative a plot—and somehow indicate the point you are making. The tips on p. 56 can help you get started.

STATING YOUR POINT

Most of the narrative writing you do as a student will be for the purpose of making some kind of point, and sometimes you'll want to state that point explicitly. If you are writing about information technology for an economics class, for example, you might tell your story about going to a computer store; and you would probably want to explain why you were telling about the experience in a THESIS STATEMENT like this: "Go into any computer store today, and you will discover that information technology is the main product of American business."

FOLLOWING CHRONOLOGICAL ORDER

In his arrival narrative, Ben Franklin is looking back at his life through the perspective of time. Thus, as in most narratives, the events in his account are presented chronologically. First his arrival; then breakfast, followed by a stroll around the town; next comes the encounter with Miss Read; and, finally, the return to the wharf and the dispensing of the bread—all in the order in which they occurred *in time*. There is no law that says events in a narrative have to follow chronological order, and there are times when you will want to deviate from it. As a general rule, though, arrange events chronologically so your reader doesn't have to figure out what happened when.

ADDING TRANSITIONS

Notice the many direct references to time in Ben Franklin's narrative: *then, immediately, when, again.* No doubt, you can think of countless others: *first, last, not long after, next, while, thereafter, once upon a time.* Such direct references to the order of time can be boring in a narrative if they become too predictable, as in *first, second, third.* But used judiciously, such transitions provide smooth links from one event to another, as do other connecting words and phrases like *thus, therefore, consequently, what happened next, before I knew it, as he came back to the dock.*

USING APPROPRIATE VERB TENSES

In addition to clear transition words, your verb tenses, especially the sequence of tenses, can help you to connect events in time. To review for a moment: An action in the past perfect tense (he *had arrived*) occurs before an action in the past tense (he *arrived*), which occurs before an action in the present tense (he *arrives*), which occurs before an action in the future tense (he *will arrive*), which occurs before an action in the future perfect tense (he *will have arrived*). Actions in the present perfect (he *has arrived*) may start in the past and continue in the present.

Many of the verbs in Franklin's narrative are in the simple past tense: *walked, went, ask'd, thought, found, gave.* "I had made many a meal on bread," however, is in the past perfect tense because the action had already occurred many times *before* young Franklin asked for directions to the bakery.

Tense sequences mark the time of actions in relation to one another. Thus, all actions that happen more or less at the same time in your narrative should be in

TIPS AND TEMPLATES FOR DRAFTING

When you begin to draft a narrative, you need to say who or what the narrative is about, where it takes place, and what's happening as the story opens. These moves are fundamental to any narrative. See how Toni Morrison makes such moves in the beginning of her essay in this chapter:

> I am in this river place—newly mine—walking in the yard when I see a woman sitting on the seawall at the edge of a neighbor's garden.
> —TONI MORRISON, "Strangers"

Morrison says who her narrative is about ("I," "a woman"); where it takes place ("in this river place"); and what is happening as the story opens ("I see a woman"). Here are two more examples from this chapter:

> While traveling 35,000 feet above eastern Ohio, United 93 suddenly dropped 700 feet. —THE 9/11 COMMISSION, "The Battle for United 93"

> I closed the door to the sterile white examination room to face a thin, pale young boy, fourteen years old and sitting on the exam table with his knees pulled to his chest. —JEFF GREMMELS, "The Clinic"

The following templates can help you make some of these basic moves in your own writing. But don't take these as formulas where you just have to fill in the blanks. There are no easy formulas for good writing, but these templates can serve as starting points.

▶ This is a story about _____.

▶ The time and place of my story are _____ and _____.

▶ As the narrative opens, X is in the act of _____.

▶ What happened next was _____, followed by _____ and _____.

▶ At this point, _____.

▶ The climax of these events was _____.

▶ When X understood what had happened, he / she said "_____."

▶ The last thing that happened to X was _____.

▶ My point in telling this story is to show that _____.

the same tense: "The young man got off the boat, went to the bakery, and walked around the town." Don't shift tenses needlessly; but when you *do* need to indicate that one action happened before another in time, be sure to change tenses accordingly—and accurately. Sometimes you may need to shift out of chronological order altogether. (It's called a FLASHBACK if you shift back in time, a FLASH-FORWARD if you shift into the future.) Most of the time, however, stick to chronology.

Notice how often Franklin uses -*ing* forms of verbs: *gazing, inquiring, intending, considering, knowing, having, eating, passing, standing, eating* (again), *coming, being, waiting.* Putting -*ing* on the end of a verb makes the verb progressive. If Franklin's writing seems especially vivid, part of his secret lies in those progressive verb forms, which show past actions as if they are still going on as we read about them more than two centuries later.

DEVELOPING A PLOT

Connecting events in chronological order is always better than presenting them haphazardly. Chronology alone, however, no matter how faithfully followed, is insufficient for organizing a good narrative. A narrative, yes; a good narrative, no.

Suppose Ben Franklin returned for a visit to modern-day Philadelphia and filed the following account:

> I took 76 East (the Schuylkill Expressway) to 676 East, exited at Broad Street (the first exit) and continued straight on Vine Street to 12th Street. Then I turned right and proceeded two blocks to the Convention Center. There I paused for lunch (a Caesar salad with three great puffy rolls), afterward continuing my journey down 12th and back to Vine. Proceeding east for some distance, I then rounded Franklin Square, crossed the Franklin Bridge, and entered into New Jersey.

This account is, technically, a narrative, and it follows chronological order. By comparison with the original, however, it is pretty dull. If it went on like this for another paragraph or two, most readers would give up long before Franklin got back to Boston. Little more than an itinerary, this narrative moves steadfastly from place to place, but it doesn't really get anywhere because it has no PLOT.

Whether we read about pirates on the high seas or hobbits and rings of power, one of the most important elements that can make or break the story is how well it is plotted. It is no different when you write narratives of your own—events need to be related in such a way that one leads directly to, or causes, another. Taken together, the events in your narrative should have a beginning, a middle, and an end. Then your narrative will form a complete action: a plot.

One of the best ways to plot a narrative is to set up a situation; introduce a conflict; build up the dramatic tension until it reaches a high point, or CLIMAX; then release the tension and resolve the conflict. Consider the following little horror story, replete with a giant insect. First we set up the situation:

> Little Miss Muffet sat on a tuffet
> Eating her curds and whey.

Now comes the conflict:

> Along came a spider

Then the climax:

> Who sat down beside her

And finally the resolution:

> And frightened Miss Muffet away.

You knew all along how it was going to end; but it's still a satisfying story because it's tightly plotted with a keen sense of completion at the close.

Back to Ben Franklin's narrative. One reason this story of starting out in Philadelphia is among the most famous personal narratives in American literature, even though it's just one paragraph, is that it has a carefully organized plot—a *beginning* action (the hero's arrival); a *middle* (the stroll), in which a complication is introduced and the tension rises as the young hero sees his future wife and appears ridiculous; and an *ending* (the return to the wharf), in which the narrative tension is resolved as the hero comes back to his starting point and dispenses bounty in the form of the bread.

MAINTAINING A CONSISTENT POINT OF VIEW

Such is the difference between life and a *narrative* of life: life happens, often in disorderly fashion; a narrative, by contrast, must be carefully composed—from a particular POINT OF VIEW. Why do you think Annie Dillard wrote that her father looked up "at what must have been a small patch of wild sky"? Why didn't she just come out and say that the sky *was* wild? The reason is that, as the NARRATOR, or teller of her story, Dillard is speaking from the vantage point of herself as a child sitting on the sunporch. From that point of view, she could not logically have seen the sky as her father saw it.

As you construct a narrative, you need to maintain a logical and consistent point of view. Don't attribute perceptions to yourself or your narrator that are physically impossible ("I lay inside on the sofa while Old Low-Pockets wandered out to the lawn. His back to the house, he stared dreamily in the direction of his impending journey. A tear came into his eye"). If you do claim to see (or know) more than you reasonably can from where you sit, your credibility with the reader will soon be strained.

In a narrative written in the grammatical FIRST PERSON ("I" or "we"), like Dillard's, the speaker can be both an observer of the scene ("I looked up from my book and saw him outside") *and* a participant in the action ("I was reading Robert Louis Stevenson on the sunporch"). In a narrative written in the grammatical THIRD PERSON ("he," "she," "it," or "they"), as is the case in most articles and history books (and in Bryan Sykes's narrative about Ursula), however, the narrator is often merely an observer, though sometimes an all-knowing one.

ADDING DIALOGUE

In contrast to narratives told in the third person—which can have unlimited points of view—first-person narratives are *always* limited to telling us only what the narrator knows or imagines. There is a means, however, by which even first-person narrators can introduce the points of view of other people into a story. That is by the use of DIALOGUE, or quoting their direct speech. "Lie on your back," her mother tells young Dillard elsewhere in her narrative. "Look at the clouds and figure out what they look like."

As a first-person narrator, Dillard might have written, "My mother told me to look at the clouds and figure out what they look like." But these words would be filtered through Dillard's point of view. They would be a step removed from the person who said them and so would lack the immediacy of direct dialogue.

Suppose you are a witness to an accident in which a pedestrian was hit by a turning car, and you want to tell what happened—in a police report, say. Your narrative might begin with an account of how you noticed a car stopped at a red light and then saw another car approach suddenly from the right and pause. After the light changed, the first car went straight ahead; then the second car turned left. At the same time, a pedestrian, who had been trying to cross behind the first car, moved into the middle of the street and was hit by the turning car.

Why did the pedestrian cross the street against traffic? Your narrative can't say for sure because you don't know what was going on in the pedestrian's mind. If, however, you (or the police) approached the man and started asking him questions as he pulled himself to his feet, his point of view might be revealed in the ensuing dialogue.

Then, if you incorporated that dialogue into your narrative, you would not only capture another person's motives and point of view, but your narrative would be more interesting and lively:

"Why did you cross the street?"
"The stoplight was red and the little man on the pedestrian sign was on."
"Did you see the car turning in your direction as you crossed?"
"No, the stopped car was blocking my view."

"After it started up, did you see the other car?"

"Yes."

"Why did you cross anyway?"

"The little man told me to."

You can *tell* the reader of your narrative that someone is delusional or means well or would never hurt a fly. But if you let people in your narrative speak for themselves and *show* what they are thinking, the reader can draw his or her own conclusions. Then your story will seem more credible, your characters will come to life, and your whole narrative will have a greater dramatic impact.

USING OTHER METHODS

Narratives don't take place in a vacuum. As you tell what happens in your narrative, you'll likely need to draw on other methods of writing as well. For example, to show why your characters (the people in your narrative) do what they do, you may need to analyze the CAUSES AND EFFECTS of their actions. Or you may want to COMPARE AND CONTRAST one character with another. Almost certainly, you will want to DESCRIBE the characters and the physical setting of your narrative in some detail.

In Franklin's case, for instance, the description of his "awkward, ridiculous appearance" as he walks around the streets of Philadelphia "with a roll under each arm" is important to the story. The tattered young man may look foolish now—but not for long. This is an American success story, and already the new arrival is staking out his territory.

Reading a Narrative with a Critical Eye

Once you have drafted a narrative, it's always a good idea to ask someone else to read it. And, of course, you yourself will want to review what you have written from the standpoint of a critical reader. Here are some questions that you and any other reader might ask when checking a narrative:

PURPOSE AND AUDIENCE. Does the narrative serve the purpose it is intended to serve? Is it appropriate for its intended audience? Does it need any additional background information or definitions?

THE STORY. Does it consist mainly of actions and event? Do they constitute a plot, with a clear beginning, a middle, and an end? Is every action in the narrative necessary to the plot? Have any essential actions been left out?

THE POINT. Does the narrative have a clear point to make? What is it? Is it stated explicitly in a thesis? If not, should it be?

ORGANIZATION. Is the story line easy to follow? Are the events in chronological order? Are there any unintentional lapses in chronology or verb tense? Are intentional deviations from chronology, such as flashbacks, clearly indicated?

TRANSITIONS. Are there clear transitions to help readers follow the sequence of events? Check over each transition to see that it logically connects the adjoining parts of the narrative.

DIALOGUE AND POINT OF VIEW. If there is no dialogue in the narrative, would some direct speech help bring it to life? If there is dialogue, does it sound like real people talking? Is the narrative told from a consistent, plausible point of view?

DETAILS. Does the narrative have lots of concrete details, especially visual and auditory ones? Does it show as well as tell?

THE BEGINNING. Will the beginning of the narrative get the reader's attention? How? How well does it set up what follows? How else might the narrative begin?

THE ENDING. How satisfying is it? What does it leave the reader thinking or feeling? How else might the narrative end?

THE SUCCESS STORY

One common narrative pattern, which Ben Franklin practically invented in his famous *Autobiography*, is the success story. As in many fairy tales, the central event of such a narrative is the transformation of the hero or heroine. One reading in this chapter that demonstrates on this common narrative pattern is "The Badger," Michael Lewis's essay about an obscure college baseball player who turns into a star rookie for the Oakland A's.

To see how you can use the success-story pattern in your own writing— and how narratives differ from the actual events on which they are based— think of a successful person you might write about and make a list of key events in that person's life. Then identify a "turning point"—a particular event or series of events that changed the fortunes of your hero or heroine forever. Divide the rest of the events on your list into "before" and "after." Imagine the story you might construct around this outline.

Now take the same person and life events and consider how you would arrange them according to some other pattern, such as a journey or a fall from grace. This time, instead of dividing your narrative into before and after, imagine a different story line—a meandering path or a downward spiral. As you can see, you would end up telling a different story about the same person.

Editing for Common Errors in Narrative Writing

As with other kinds of writing, narration calls for distinctive patterns of language and punctuation—and thus invites certain kinds of errors. The following tips will help you check your writing for errors that often appear in narratives.

Check your verb tenses to make sure they accurately indicate when actions occur.

Because narrative writing focuses on actions or events—what happens or happened—it relies mightily on verbs. Some writers get confused about when to use the simple past tense (Ben *arrived*), the present perfect (Ben *has arrived*), and the past perfect (Ben *had arrived*).

Use the simple past to indicate actions completed at a specified time in the past.

> NOT He has completed the assignment this morning.
> BUT He completed the assignment this morning.

Use the present perfect to indicate actions begun and completed at some unspecified time in the past, or actions begun in the past and continuing into the present.

> NOT The war in the north goes on for five years now.
> BUT The war in the north has gone on for five years now.

> NOT For five years now, the insurgents fought in the north.
> BUT For five years now, the insurgents have fought in the north.

Use the past perfect to indicate actions completed *by* a specific time in the past or before another past action occurred.

> NOT The bobcats arrived next, but by then the muskrats moved out.
> BUT The bobcats arrived next, but by then the muskrats had moved out.

Check any dialogue to be sure it's punctuated correctly.

Narrative writing often includes dialogue, the direct quotation of what people say. Punctuating dialogue can be challenging because you have to deal with the punctuation in the dialogue itself and also with any punctuation necessary to integrate the dialogue into the text.

Commas and periods always go inside the quotation marks.

▶ "Perspective in painting is hard to define," my art history professor said.

▶ She then said that in Western painting, "perspective means one thing."

Semicolons and colons always go outside the quotation marks.

▶ But "in Asian painting, it means quite another"; or so she said.

▶ Asian painting presents the landscape "in layers": that was the main point she made in yesterday's lecture.

Question marks, exclamation points, and dashes go *inside* the quotation marks if they are part of the quoted text but *outside* if they are not part of the quoted text.

▶ The teacher asked, "Sam, how would you define perspective in art?"

▶ Did you say, "Divine perspective"?

A Vanity License Plate

In only two words, the license plate of this sports car tells a story. It may not tell the whole story—of the courtship and marriage *before* the divorce—but we know how the story ended: she got the Porsche. Narratives tell what happened (however briefly). To construct a compelling narrative, as this ad does, you need to set up a situation (such as a troubled marriage) in a particular time (the recent past) and place (a tree-shaded, urban neighborhood of elegant townhouses); then introduce a conflict (divorce proceedings would qualify); build up the tension (she wants his car); and resolve the conflict (she gets it). More than just a tale of conflict and revenge, however, this story has a point to make. The law firm of Sanders, Lyn & Ragonetti wants the readers' business, and it knows that narratives are a good way to attract the attention of potential clients—particularly women seeking a divorce who want to ride off into the sunset in style.

EVERYDAY NARRATION

SAIRA SHAH

Longing to Belong

Saira Shah (b. 1964) grew up in Britain, listening to stories about her family's "mytho-logical homeland" in Afghanistan. But when Shah first visited Afghanistan as a young journalist, the reality she encountered did not square with family myth. Afghanistan was at the time ruled by the fundamentalist Taliban and occupied by the Soviets. It was difficult for women to work or even to travel around the country, conditions Shah later captured dramatically in a documentary film, Beneath the Veil *(2001).*

The essay included here does not take place in Afghanistan, however, but in neigh-boring Pakistan, which Shah visited when she attended a family wedding at the age of seventeen. As the title suggests, it is a personal narrative about her "Longing to Belong"—in this case, to "experience the fairy tale" of her family's homeland. It was first published in 2003, in the New York Times Magazine.

THE DAY HE DISCLOSED his matrimonial ambitions for me, my uncle sat me at   1
his right during lunch. This was a sign of special favor, as it allowed him to feed me choice tidbits from his own plate. It was by no means an unadulterated pleasure. He would often generously withdraw a half-chewed delicacy from his mouth and lovingly cram it into mine—an Afghan habit with which I have since tried to come to terms. It was his way of telling me that I was valued, part of the family.

My brother and sister, Tahir and Safia, and my elderly aunt Amina and I were all   2
attending the wedding of my uncle's son. Although my uncle's home was closer than I'd ever been, I was not yet inside Afghanistan. This branch of my family lived in Peshawar, Pakistan. On seeing two unmarried daughters in the company of a female chaperone, my uncle obviously concluded that we had been sent to be married. I was taken aback by the visceral longing I felt to be part of this world. I had never realized that I had been starved of anything. Now, at 17, I discovered that like a princess in a fairy tale, I had been cut off from my origins. This was the point in the tale where, simply by walking through a magical door, I could recover my gardens and palaces. If I allowed my uncle to arrange a marriage for me, I would belong.

Over the next few days, the man my family wished me to marry was introduced   3
into the inner sanctum. He was a distant cousin. His luxuriant black mustache was generally considered to compensate for his lack of height. I was told breathlessly that he was a fighter pilot in the Pakistani Air Force. As an outsider, he wouldn't have been permitted to meet an unmarried girl. But as a relative, he had free run of the house. Whenever I appeared, a female cousin would fling a child into his arms. He'd pose with it, whiskers twitching, while the women cooed their admiration.

A huge cast of relatives had assembled to see my uncle's son marry. The wedding 4
lasted nearly 14 days and ended with a reception. The bride and groom sat on an
elevated stage to receive greetings. While the groom was permitted to laugh and
chat, the bride was required to sit perfectly still, her eyes demurely lowered. I
didn't see her move for four hours.

Watching this *tableau vivant*[1] of a submissive Afghan bride, I knew that marriage 5
would never be my easy route to the East. I could live in my father's mythological
homeland only through the eyes of the storyteller. In my desire to experience the
fairy tale, I had overlooked the staggeringly obvious: the storyteller was a man. If I
wanted freedom, I would have to cut my own path. I began to understand why my
uncle's wife had resorted to using religion to regain some control—at least in her
own home. Her piety gave her license to impose her will on others.

My putative fiancé returned to Quetta,[2] from where he sent a constant flow of 6
lavish gifts. I was busy examining my hoard when my uncle's wife announced that
he was on the phone. My intended was a favorite of hers; she had taken it upon
herself to promote the match. As she handed me the receiver, he delivered a line
culled straight from a Hindi movie: "We shall have a love-match, *ach-cha*?" Enough
was enough. I slammed down the phone and went to find Aunt Amina. When she
had heard me out, she said: "I'm glad that finally you've stopped this silly wild
goose chase for your roots. I'll have to extricate you from this mess. Wait here while
I put on something more impressive." As a piece of Islamic one-upmanship, she
returned wearing not one but three head scarves of different colors.

My uncle's wife was sitting on her prayer platform in the drawing room. Amina 7
stormed in, scattering servants before her like chaff. "Your relative . . . ," was
Amina's opening salvo, ". . . has been making obscene remarks to my niece." Her
mouth opened, but before she could find her voice, Amina fired her heaviest guns:
"Over the *telephone*!"

"How dare you!" her rival began. 8

It gave Amina exactly the opportunity she needed to move in for the kill. 9
"What? Do you support this lewd conduct? Are we living in an American movie?
Since when have young people of mixed sexes been permitted to speak to each
other *on the telephone*? Let alone to talk—as I regret to inform you your nephew
did—of love! Since when has love had anything to do with marriage? What a dangerous and absurd concept!"

My Peshawari aunt was not only outclassed; she was out-Islamed too. "My niece 10
is a rose that hasn't been plucked," Amina said. "It is my task as her chaperone to

---

1. *Tableau vivant*: French for "living picture." In a *tableau vivant*, costumed performers pose against
a scenic backdrop.
2. *Quetta*: city in west-central Pakistan.

ensure that this happy state of affairs continues. A match under such circumstances is quite out of the question. The engagement is off." My uncle's wife lost her battle for moral supremacy and, it seemed, her battle for sanity as well. In a gruff, slack-jawed way that I found unappealing, she made a sharp, inhuman sound that sounded almost like a bark.

READING CLOSELY

1. Why does Shah's Pakistani uncle assume that a marriage must be arranged for his visiting niece? Why does she go along with his plans at first?

2. What event causes young Shah to change her mind about an arranged marriage to her distant cousin? What does she come to realize?

3. Why does Aunt Amina help Shah instead of insisting that her niece follow tradition and go through with the marriage?

4. What does the title of the NARRATIVE tell us about Shah's main point? What do you think that point is?

5. According to Shah, what's wrong with the way the marriage story is told in her homeland? How would she (and Aunt Amina) change such narratives?

STRATEGIES AND STRUCTURES

1. In many fairy tales, the central event of the PLOT is a transformation—of a frog into a prince, for example. What transformation does Shah long for? In the last paragraph, who is transformed into what?

2. If the uncle's wife is the wicked stepmother in Shah's updated fairy tale, what role does Aunt Amina play? What other aspects of the traditional fairy-tale narrative does Shah retain? How is the traditional fairy-tale plot altered?

3. Shah doesn't introduce DIALOGUE into her narrative until paragraph 6. Why do you think she waits so long? How does the dialogue help to show her disillusionment?

4. *Other Methods.* In paragraph 2, Shah explicitly COMPARES the life she imagines for herself in her ancestral homeland to a fairy tale. How is her awareness of living in such a narrative similar to and different from the heroine's perspective in an actual fairy tale?

Thinking about Language

1. According to your dictionary, what are the DENOTATIONS of the following words: "visceral" (2), "luxuriant" (3), "*tableau vivant*" (5), "putative" (6)? What does language of this kind contribute to Shah's point?

2. An "inner sanctum" is the holiest of holy places in a shrine or temple (3). How is Shah's use of the phrase here IRONIC?

3. Babies are not literally "flung" into the arms of Shah's potential husband, nor are servants scattered "like chaff" (3, 7). What function does this HYPERBOLE serve in this essay?

4. Shah says that a "cast" of relatives assembles for her cousin's wedding (4). Where else in her narrative does Shah refer to life in her uncle's household as a show or spectacle? What does such imagery imply?

For Writing

1. Write a paragraph comparing real life in a place you have come to know to life in that place as you had imagined it.

2. Aunt Amina states that marrying for love is "a dangerous and absurd concept" (9). Write a narrative in which you test this concept, using it—or its opposite—as your THESIS.

The Battle for United 93

The 9/11 Commission was created by the U.S. Congress and President Bush in late 2002 as an independent, bipartisan commission with the mission of preparing a full account of the circumstances surrounding the terrorist attacks of September 11, 2001. The Commission was also charged with making recommendations for guarding against future attacks.

The 9/11 Commission Report, published in 2004, is like no other government report. Despite the fact that it was written by a ten-member committee and a staff of more than eighty people, the Report is a highly readable narrative that tells many gripping stories. How was this feat accomplished? The Commission and its staff included two historians, Philip Zelikow and Ernest R. May, and two professional editors, Alice Falk and Stephanie Kaplan. According to the Report, this team and the rest of the Commission "reasoned together over every page," carefully selecting from more than 2.5 million pages of documents. Included here is the story of the passengers of United Flight 93 who, at the cost of their lives, prevented their hijacked plane from reaching Washington. The notes that follow the selection are those that accompanied these parts of the Report and maintain its documentation style.

AT 8:42, UNITED AIRLINES FLIGHT 93 took off from Newark (New Jersey) 1
Liberty International Airport bound for San Francisco. The aircraft was piloted by Captain Jason Dahl and First Officer Leroy Homer, and there were five flight attendants. Thirty-seven passengers, including the hijackers, boarded the plane. Scheduled to depart the gate at 8:00, the Boeing 757's takeoff was delayed because of the airport's typically heavy morning traffic.[1]

The hijackers had planned to take flights scheduled to depart at 7:45 (Ameri- 2
can 11), 8:00 (United 175 and United 93), and 8:10 (American 77). Three of the flights had actually taken off within 10 to 15 minutes of their planned departure times. United 93 would ordinarily have taken off about 15 minutes after pulling away from the gate. When it left the ground at 8:42, the flight was running more than 25 minutes late.[2]

As United 93 left Newark, the flight's crew members were unaware of the 3
hijacking of American 11. Around 9:00, the FAA [Federal Aviation Administration], American, and United were facing the staggering realization of apparent multiple hijackings. At 9:03, they would see another aircraft strike the World Trade Center. Crisis managers at the FAA and the airlines did not yet act to warn other aircraft.[3] At the same time, Boston Center realized that a message transmitted just

before 8:25 by the hijacker pilot of American 11 included the phrase, "We have some planes."[4]

No one at the FAA or the airlines that day had ever dealt with multiple hijackings. Such a plot had not been carried out anywhere in the world in more than 30 years, and never in the United States. As news of the hijacking filtered through the FAA and the airlines, it does not seem to have occurred to their leadership that they needed to alert other aircraft in the air that they too might be at risk.[5]

United 175 was hijacked between 8:42 and 8:46, and awareness of that hijacking began to spread after 8:51. American 77 was hijacked between 8:51 and 8:54. By 9:00, FAA and airline officials began to comprehend that attackers were going after multiple aircraft. American Airlines' nationwide ground stop between 9:05 and 9:10 was followed by a United Airlines ground stop. FAA controllers at Boston Center, which had tracked the first two hijackings, requested at 9:07 that Herndon Command Center "get messages to airborne aircraft to increase security for the cockpit." There is no evidence that Herndon took such action. Boston Center immediately began speculating about other aircraft that might be in danger, leading them to worry about a transcontinental flight—Delta 1989—that in fact was not hijacked. At 9:19, the FAA's New England regional office called Herndon and asked that Cleveland Center advise Delta 1989 to use extra cockpit security.[6]

Several FAA air traffic control officials told us it was the air carriers' responsibility to notify their planes of security problems. One senior FAA air traffic control manager said that it was simply not the FAA's place to order the airlines what to tell their pilots.[7] We believe such statements do not reflect an adequate appreciation of the FAA's responsibility for the safety and security of civil aviation.

The airlines bore responsibility, too. They were facing an escalating number of conflicting and, for the most part, erroneous reports about other flights, as well as a continuing lack of vital information from the FAA about the hijacked flights. We found no evidence, however, that American Airlines sent any cockpit warnings to its aircraft on 9/11. United's first decisive action to notify its airborne aircraft to take defensive action did not come until 9:19, when a United flight dispatcher, Ed Ballinger, took the initiative to begin transmitting warnings to his 16 transcontinental flights: "Beware any cockpit intrusion—Two a/c [aircraft] hit World Trade Center." One of the flights that received the warning was United 93. Because Ballinger was still responsible for his other flights as well as Flight 175, his warning message was not transmitted to Flight 93 until 9:23.[8]

By all accounts, the first 46 minutes of Flight 93's cross-country trip proceeded routinely. Radio communications from the plane were normal. Heading, speed, and altitude ran according to plan. At 9:24, Ballinger's warning to United 93 was received in the cockpit. Within two minutes, at 9:26, the pilot, Jason Dahl, responded with a note of puzzlement: "Ed, confirm latest mssg plz—Jason."[9]

UNITED AIRLINES FLIGHT 93 (UA 93)
Newark to San Francisco

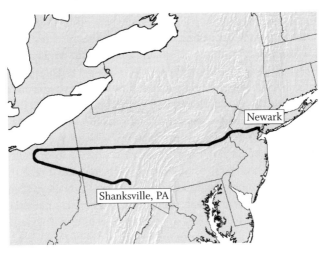

8:42	Takeoff
9:24	Flight 93 receives warning from UA about possible cockpit intrusion
9:27	Last routine radio communication
9:28	Likely takeover
9:34	Herndon Command Center advises FAA headquarters that UA 93 is hijacked
9:36	Flight attendant notifies UA of hijacking; UA attempts to contactthe cockpit
9:41	Transponder is turned off
9:57	Passenger revolt begins
10:03:11	Flight 93 crashes in field in Shanksville, PA

The hijackers attacked at 9:28. While traveling 35,000 feet above eastern Ohio, United 93 suddenly dropped 700 feet. Eleven seconds into the descent, the FAA's air traffic control center in Cleveland received the first of two radio transmissions from the aircraft. During the first broadcast, the captain or first officer could be heard declaring "Mayday" amid the sounds of a physical struggle in the cockpit. The second radio transmission, 35 seconds later, indicated that the fight was continuing. The captain or first officer could be heard shouting: "Hey get out of here— get out of here—get out of here."[10]

On the morning of 9/11, there were only 37 passengers on United 93—33 in addition to the 4 hijackers. This was below the norm for Tuesday mornings during the summer of 2001. But there is no evidence that the hijackers manipulated passenger levels or purchased additional seats to facilitate their operation.[11]

The terrorists who hijacked three other commercial flights on 9/11 operated in five-man teams. They initiated their cockpit takeover within 30 minutes of takeoff. On Flight 93, however, the takeover took place 46 minutes after takeoff and there were only four hijackers. The operative likely intended to round out the team for this flight, Mohamed al Kahtani, had been refused entry by a suspicious immigration inspector at Florida's Orlando International Airport in August.[12]

Because several passengers on United 93 described three hijackers on the plane, not four, some have wondered whether one of the hijackers had been able to use the cockpit jump seat from the outset of the flight. FAA rules allow use of this seat by documented and approved individuals, usually air carrier or FAA personnel. We have found no evidence indicating that one of the hijackers, or anyone else, sat there on this flight. All the hijackers had assigned seats in first class, and they seem to have used them. We believe it is more likely that Jarrah, the crucial pilot-trained member of their team, remained seated and inconspicuous until after the cockpit was seized; and once inside, he would not have been visible to the passengers.[13]

At 9:32, a hijacker, probably Jarrah, made or attempted to make the following announcement to the passengers of Flight 93: "Ladies and Gentlemen: Here the captain, please sit down keep remaining sitting. We have a bomb on board. So, sit." The flight data recorder (also recovered) indicates that Jarrah then instructed the plane's autopilot to turn the aircraft around and head east.[14]

The cockpit voice recorder data indicate that a woman, most likely a flight attendant, was being held captive in the cockpit. She struggled with one of the hijackers who killed or otherwise silenced her.[15]

Shortly thereafter, the passengers and flight crew began a series of calls from GTE airphones and cellular phones. These calls between family, friends, and colleagues took place until the end of the flight and provided those on the ground with firsthand accounts. They enabled the passengers to gain critical information, including the news that two aircraft had slammed into the World Trade Center.[16]

At 9:39, the FAA's Cleveland Air Route Traffic Control Center overheard a second announcement indicating that there was a bomb on board, that the plane was returning to the airport, and that they should remain seated.[17] While it apparently was not heard by the passengers, this announcement, like those on Flight 11 and Flight 77, was intended to deceive them. Jarrah, like Atta earlier, may have inadvertently broadcast the message because he did not know how to operate the radio and the intercom. To our knowledge none of them had ever flown an actual airliner before.

At least two callers from the flight reported that the hijackers knew that passengers were making calls but did not seem to care. It is quite possible Jarrah knew of the success of the assault on the World Trade Center. He could have learned of this from messages being sent by United Airlines to the cockpits of its transcontinental flights, including Flight 93, warning of cockpit intrusion and telling of the New York attacks. But even without them, he would certainly have understood that the attacks on the World Trade Center would already have unfolded, given Flight 93's tardy departure from Newark. If Jarrah did know that the passengers were making calls, it might not have occurred to him that they were certain to learn what had happened in New York, thereby defeating his attempts at deception.[18]

At least ten passengers and two crew members shared vital information with family, friends, colleagues, or others on the ground. All understood the plane had been hijacked. They said the hijackers wielded knives and claimed to have a bomb. The hijackers were wearing red bandanas, and they forced the passengers to the back of the aircraft.[19]

Callers reported that a passenger had been stabbed and that two people were lying on the floor of the cabin, injured or dead—possibly the captain and first officer. One caller reported that a flight attendant had been killed.[20]

One of the callers from United 93 also reported that he thought the hijackers might possess a gun. But none of the other callers reported the presence of a firearm. One recipient of a call from the aircraft recounted specifically asking her caller whether the hijackers had guns. The passenger replied that he did not see one. No evidence of firearms or of their identifiable remains was found at the aircraft's crash site, and the cockpit voice recorder gives no indication of a gun being fired or mentioned at any time. . . .[21]

Passengers on three flights reported the hijackers' claim of having a bomb. The FBI told us they found no trace of explosives at the crash sites. One of the passengers who mentioned a bomb expressed his belief that it was not real. Lacking any evidence that the hijackers attempted to smuggle such illegal items past the security screening checkpoints, we believe the bombs were probably fake.[22]

During at least five of the passengers' phone calls, information was shared about the attacks that had occurred earlier that morning at the World Trade Center. Five calls described the intent of passengers and surviving crew members to revolt against the hijackers. According to one call, they voted on whether to rush the terrorists in an attempt to retake the plane. They decided, and acted.[23]

At 9:57, the passenger assault began. Several passengers had terminated phone calls with loved ones in order to join the revolt. One of the callers ended her message as follows: "Everyone's running up to first class. I've got to go. Bye."[24]

The cockpit voice recorder captured the sounds of the passenger assault muffled by the intervening cockpit door. Some family members who listened to the recording report that they can hear the voice of a loved one among the din. We cannot identify whose voices can be heard. But the assault was sustained.[25]

In response, Jarrah immediately began to roll the airplane to the left and right, attempting to knock the passengers off balance. At 9:58:57, Jarrah told another hijacker in the cockpit to block the door. Jarrah continued to roll the airplane sharply left and right, but the assault continued. At 9:59:52, Jarrah changed tactics and pitched the nose of the airplane up and down to disrupt the assault. The recorder captured the sounds of loud thumps, crashes, shouts, and breaking glasses and plates. At 10:00:03, Jarrah stabilized the airplane.[26]

Five seconds later, Jarrah asked, "Is that it? Shall we finish it off?" A hijacker responded, "No. Not yet. When they all come, we finish it off." The sounds of fighting continued outside the cockpit. Again, Jarrah pitched the nose of the aircraft up and down. At 10:00:26, a passenger in the background said, "In the cockpit. If we don't we'll die!" Sixteen seconds later, a passenger yelled, "Roll it!" Jarrah stopped the violent maneuvers at about 10:01:00 and said, "Allah is the greatest! Allah is the greatest!" He then asked another hijacker in the cockpit, "Is that it? I mean, shall we put it down?" to which the other replied, "Yes, put it in it, and pull it down."[27]

The passengers continued their assault and at 10:02:23, a hijacker said, "Pull it down! Pull it down!" The hijackers remained at the controls but must have judged that the passengers were only seconds from overcoming them. The airplane headed down; the control wheel was turned hard to the right. The airplane rolled onto its back, and one of the hijackers began shouting "Allah is the greatest. Allah is the greatest." With the sounds of the passenger counterattack continuing, the aircraft plowed into an empty field in Shanksville, Pennsylvania, at 580 miles per hour, about 20 minutes' flying time from Washington, D.C.[28]

Jarrah's objective was to crash his airliner into symbols of the American Republic, the Capitol or the White House. He was defeated by the alerted, unarmed passengers of United 93.

Notes

1. The flight attendant assignments and seating included Chief Flight Attendant Deborah Welsh (first class, seat J1 at takeoff); Sandra Bradshaw (coach, seat J5); Wanda Green (first class, seat J4); Lorraine Bay (coach, seat J3); and CeeCee Lyles (coach, seat J6). See UAL response to Commission questions for the record, Apr. 5, 2004; FAA report, "Chronology of the September 11 Attacks and Subsequent Events Through October 24, 2001," undated; UAL records, copies of electronic boarding passes for Flight 93, Sept. 11, 2001; Bob Varcadipane interview (May 4, 2004); Newark Tower briefing (May 4, 2004).

2. Although the flight schedule indicates an 8:00 A.M. "departure," this was the time the plane left the gate area. Taxiing from the gate to the runway normally took about 15 minutes. Bob Varcadipane interview (May 4, 2004); Newark Tower briefing (May 4, 2004).

3. Commission analysis of FAA air traffic control data. On the FAA's awareness of multiple hijackings, see AAL transcript, telephone call from Nydia Gonzalez to Craig Marquis, Sept. 11, 2001; Craig Marquis interview (Nov. 19, 2003); AAL record, System Operations Command Center (SOCC) log,

Sept. 11, 2001; UAL System Operations Control briefing (Nov. 20, 2003); Rich Miles interview (Nov. 21, 2003); UAL report, "Timeline: Dispatch/SMFDO Activities—Terrorist Crisis," undated.

4. FAA audio file, Boston Center, position 46R, 8:24:38 and 8:24:56; Peter Zalewski interview (Sept. 23, 2003).

5. On September 6, 1970, members of the Popular Front for the Liberation of Palestine hijacked a Pan American Boeing 747, a TWA Boeing 707, and a Swissair DC-8. On September 9, a British airliner was hijacked as well. An attempt to hijack an Israeli airliner was thwarted. The Pan American plane landed in Cairo and was blown up after its passengers were released. The other three aircraft were flown to Dawson Field, near Amman, Jordan; the passengers were held captive, and the planes were destroyed. The international hijacking crisis turned into a civil war, as the Jordanian government used force to restore its control of the country. See FAA report, Civil Aviation Reference Handbook, May 1999, appendix D.

The FAA knew or strongly suspected that Flight 11 was a hijacking 11 minutes after it was taken over; Flight 175, 9 minutes after it was taken over. There is no evidence to indicate that the FAA recognized Flight 77 as a hijacking until it crashed into the Pentagon.

6. FAA audio file, Herndon Command Center, line 5114, 9:07:13; FAA audio file, Herndon Command Center, position 15, 9:19. At 9:07, Boston Air Traffic Control Center recommended to the FAA Command Center that a cockpit warning be sent to the pilots of all commercial aircraft to secure their cockpits. While Boston Center sent out such warnings to the commercial flights in its sector, we could find no evidence that a nationwide warning was issued by the ATC system.

7. Ellen King interview (Apr. 5, 2004). FAA air traffic control tapes indicate that at 9:19 the FAA Air Traffic Control System Command Center in Herndon ordered controllers to send a cockpit warning to Delta 1989 because, like American 11 and United 175, it was a transcontinental flight departing Boston's Logan Airport.

8. For American Airlines' response, see AAL briefing (Apr. 26, 2004). For Ballinger's warnings, see Ed Ballinger interview (Apr. 14, 2004). A companywide order for dispatchers to warn cockpits was not issued until 9:21. See UAL report, "Timeline: Dispatch/SMFDO Activities—Terrorist Crisis," undated. While one of Ballinger's colleagues assisted him, Ballinger remained responsible for multiple flights. See Ed Ballinger interview (Apr. 14, 2004). American Airlines' policy called for the flight dispatcher to manage only the hijacked flight, relieving him of responsibilities for all other flights. On American Airlines' policy, see Craig Marquis, Craig Parfitt, Joe Bertapelle, and Mike Mulcahy interview (Nov. 19, 2003). United Airlines had no such "isolation" policy. UAL System Operations Control briefing (Nov. 20, 2003).

9. On FDR, see NTSB report, "Specialist's Factual Report of Investigation—Digital Flight Data Recorder" for United Airlines Flight 93, Feb. 15, 2002; on CVR, see FBI report, "CVR from UA Flight #93," Dec. 4, 2003; Commission review of Aircraft Communication and Reporting System (ACARS) messages sent to and from Flight 93 (which indicate time of message transmission and receipt); see UAL record, Ed Ballinger ACARS log, Sept. 11, 2001. At 9:22, after learning of the events at the World Trade Center, Melody Homer, the wife of co-pilot Leroy Homer, had an ACARS message sent to her husband in the cockpit asking if he was okay. See UAL record, ACARS message, Sept. 11, 2001.

10. On FDR, see NTSB report, "Specialist's Factual Report of Investigation—Digital Flight Data Recorder" for United Airlines Flight 93, Feb. 15, 2002; on CVR, see FBI report, "CVR from UA Flight #93," Dec. 4, 2003; FAA report, "Summary of Air Traffic Hijack Events: September 11, 2001," Sept. 17, 2001; NTSB report, Air Traffic Control Recording—United Airlines Flight 93, Dec. 21, 2001.

11. The 37 passengers represented a load factor of 20.33 percent of the plane's seating capacity of 182, considerably below the 52.09 percent for Flight 93 on Tuesdays in the three-month period prior to September 11 (June 11–September 4, 2001). See UAL report, Flight 93 EWR-SFO load factors, undated.

Five passengers holding reservations for Flight 93 did not show for the flight. All five were interviewed and cleared by the FBI. FBI report, "Flight #93 'No Show' Passengers from 9/11/01," Sept. 18, 2001.

12. INS record, Withdrawal of Application for Admission for Mohamed al Kahtani, Aug. 4, 2001.

13. See FAA regulations, Admission to flight deck, 14 C.F.R. § 121.547 (2001); UAL records, copies of boarding passes for United 93, Sept. 11, 2001. One passenger reported that ten first-class passengers were aboard the flight. If that number is accurate, it would include the four hijackers. FBI report of investigation, interview of Lisa Jefferson, Sept. 11, 2001; UAL record, Flight 93 passenger manifest, Sept. 11, 2001. All but one of the six passengers seated in the first-class cabin communicated with the ground during the flight, and none mentioned anyone from their cabin having gone into the cockpit before the hijacking. Moreover, it is unlikely that the highly regarded and experienced pilot and co-pilot of Flight 93 would have allowed an observer into the cockpit before or after takeoff who had not obtained the proper permission. See UAL records, personnel files of Flight 93 pilots. For jumpseat information, see UAL record, Weight and Balance Information for Flight 93 and Flight 175, Sept. 11, 2001; AAL records, Dispatch Environmental Control/Weekly Flight Summary for Flight 11 and Flight 77, Sept. 11, 2001.

14. Like Atta on Flight 11, Jarrah apparently did not know how to operate the communication radios; thus his attempts to communicate with the passengers were broadcast on the ATC channel. See FBI report, "CVR from UA Flight #93," Dec. 4, 2003. Also, by 9:32 FAA notified United's headquarters that the flight was not responding to radio calls. According to United, the flight's nonresponse and its turn to the east led the airline to believe by 9:36 that the plane was hijacked. See Rich Miles interview (Nov. 21, 2003); UAL report, "United dispatch SMFDO activities—terrorist crisis," Sept. 11, 2001.

15. In accordance with FAA regulations, United 93's cockpit voice recorder recorded the last 31 minutes of sounds from the cockpit via microphones in the pilots' headsets, as well as in the over-head panel of the flight deck. This is the only recorder from the four hijacked airplanes to survive the impact and ensuing fire. The CVRs and FDRs from American 11 and United 175 were not found, and the CVR from American Flight 77 was badly burned and not recoverable. See FBI report, "CVR from UA Flight #93," Dec. 4, 2003; see also FAA regulations, 14 C.F.R. §§ 25.1457, 91.609, 91.1045, 121.359; Flight 93 CVR data. A transcript of the CVR recording was prepared by the NTSB and the FBI.

16. All calls placed on airphones were from the rear of the aircraft. There was one airphone installed in each row of seats on both sides of the aisle. The airphone system was capable of transmitting only eight calls at any one time. See FBI report of investigation, airphone records for flights UAL 93 and UAL 175 on Sept. 11, 2001, Sept. 18, 2001.

17. FAA audio file, Cleveland Center, position Lorain Radar; Flight 93 CVR data; FBI report, "CVR from UA Flight #93," Dec. 4, 2003.

18. FBI reports of investigation, interviews of recipients of calls from Todd Beamer, Sept. 11, 2001, through June 11, 2002; FBI reports of investigation, interviews of recipients of calls from Sandy Bradshaw, Sept. 11, 2001, through Oct. 4, 2001. Text messages warning the cockpit of Flight 93 were sent to the aircraft by Ed Ballinger at 9:24. See UAL record, Ed Ballinger's ACARS log, Sept. 11, 2001.

19. We have relied mainly on the record of FBI interviews with the people who received calls. The FBI interviews were conducted while memories were still fresh and were less likely to have been affected by reading the accounts of others or hearing stories in the media. In some cases we have conducted our own interviews to supplement or verify the record. See FBI reports of investigation, interviews of recipients of calls from Todd Beamer, Mark Bingham, Sandy Bradshaw, Marion Britton, Thomas Burnett, Joseph DeLuca, Edward Felt, Jeremy Glick, Lauren Grandcolas, Linda Gronlund, CeeCee Lyles, Honor Wainio.

20. FBI reports of investigation, interviews of recipients of calls from Thomas Burnett, Sept. 11, 2001; FBI reports of investigation, interviews of recipients of calls from Marion Britton, Sept. 14,

2001, through Nov. 8, 2001; Lisa Jefferson interview (May 11, 2004); FBI report of investigation, interview of Lisa Jefferson, Sept. 11, 2001; Richard Belme interview (Nov. 21, 2003).

21. See Jere Longman, *Among the Heroes—United Flight 93 and the Passengers and Crew Who Fought Back* (Harper-Collins, 2002), p. 107; Deena Burnett interview (Apr. 26, 2004); FBI reports of investigation, interviews of recipients of calls from Jeremy Glick, Sept. 11, 2001, through Sept. 12, 2001; Lyzbeth Glick interview (Apr. 22, 2004). Experts told us that a gunshot would definitely be audible on the CVR. The FBI found no evidence of a firearm at the crash site of Flight 93. See FBI response to Commission briefing request no. 6, undated (topic 11). The FBI collected 14 knives or portions of knives at the Flight 93 crash site. FBI report, "Knives Found at the UA Flight 93 Crash Site," undated.

22. FBI response to Commission briefing request no. 6, undated (topic 11); FBI reports of investigation, interviews of recipients of calls from Jeremy Glick, Sept. 11, 2001, through Sept. 12, 2001.

23. See FBI reports of investigation, interviews of recipients of calls from United 93.

24. FBI reports of investigation, interviews of recipients of calls from United 93. For quote, see FBI report of investigation, interview of Philip Bradshaw, Sept. 11, 2001; Philip Bradshaw interview (June 15, 2004); Flight 93 FDR and CVR data. At 9:55:11 Jarrah dialed in the VHF Omni-directional Range (VOR) frequency for the VOR navigational aid at Washington Reagan National Airport, further indicating that the attack was planned for the nation's capital.

25. Flight 93 FDR and CVR data.

26. Ibid.

27. Ibid.

28. Ibid. The CVR clearly captured the words of the hijackers, including words in Arabic from the microphone in the pilot headset up to the end of the flight. The hijackers' statements, the clarity of the recording, the position of the microphone in the pilot headset, and the corresponding manipulations of flight controls provide the evidence. The quotes are taken from our listening to the CVR, aided by an Arabic speaker.

Reading Closely

1. How did the passengers on United Airlines Flight 93 first learn that they were being hijacked? Approximately how long did the ensuing battle last?

2. The terrorist attack on United Flight 93 differed in several particulars from the other three hijackings of airliners that took place on 9/11. What were some of those differences and why, according to the Commission, did they occur?

3. According to the 9/11 Commission, what would have happened if the passengers had not forced the terrorists to down the plane?

4. Why do you think the Commission makes a point of saying that the passenger assault was "sustained" and that it was "continuing" when the plane hit the ground (24, 27)?

STRATEGIES AND STRUCTURES

1. For what PURPOSE(S) does the 9/11 Commission tell the story of the passengers on United Airlines Flight 93 and their final efforts?

2. The first part of this selection is told almost exclusively in the THIRD PERSON. Why? Point out the few places where the Commission intrudes with the FIRST PERSON ("we" or "our"). Why the switch in grammatical POINT OF VIEW in these particular instances?

3. *The 9/11 Commission Report* includes direct quotations from the passengers and hijackers. How would the NARRATIVE be different without such DIALOGUE? What examples of dialogue do you find particularly effective? Why?

4. *Other Methods*. Compare the chronology of Flight 93 on p. 72 with that narrated in the *Report*. Both the list and the narrative cover the same events, but in a different manner. How does the narrative use CAUSE-AND-EFFECT ANALYSIS to tie events together into a plot instead of simply listing one event after the other? What is the effect of reading the list after reading the narrative?

THINKING ABOUT LANGUAGE

1. In paragraph 6, the Commission notes that the statements of some FAA officials did not "reflect an adequate appreciation of the FAA's responsibility for the safety and security of civil aviation." What are the implications of the phrase "adequate appreciation"? What other terms might the Commission have used to describe the responsibilities of the FAA?

2. The Commission often speculates (or questions the speculations of others) about what happened aboard United 93. What are some of the words and phrases that the writers use to distinguish speculation from fact?

FOR WRITING

1. Write a brief chronological narrative telling where you were and what you thought and did when you first heard about the crash of United Flight 93 (or some other event on 9/11).

2. Write a narrative essay reporting about an event that you have not experienced first-hand. Assume that your audience is your classmates and that your purpose is to tell them what happened and why it matters. Within your narrative, be careful to answer the questions *who, what, where, when, how,* and *why.*

ANNIE DILLARD

An American Childhood

Annie Dillard (b. 1945) grew up in Pittsburgh with a book in her hand. Her master's thesis at Hollins College was on Thoreau's Walden, *to which her work has been compared. Dillard is known for her meditative essays on nature, collected in* A Pilgrim at Tinker Creek (1974), *which won the Pulitzer Prize for nonfiction, and* Teaching a Stone to Talk (1982). *She's published two memoirs,* A Writing Life (1989), *and* An American Childhood (1987), *from which the following selection was taken.*

This selection is a narrative of childhood, an adventure through Dillard's old neighborhood—and her imagination. Her inspiration? Classic narratives of adventure, such as Robert Louis Stevenson's Kidnapped. *According to Dillard, "you have enough experience by the time you're five years old" to create your own adventure narrative. "What you need is the library. . . . What you have to learn is the best of what is being thought and said. If you [have] a choice between spending a summer in Nepal and spending a summer in the library, go to the library."*

SOME BOYS TAUGHT ME TO PLAY FOOTBALL. This was fine sport. You thought up a new strategy for every play and whispered it to the others. You went out for a pass, fooling everyone. Best, you got to throw yourself mightily at someone's running legs. Either you brought him down or you hit the ground flat on your chin, with your arms empty before you. It was all or nothing. If you hesitated in fear, you would miss and get hurt: you would take a hard fall while the kid got away, or you would get kicked in the face while the kid got away. But if you flung yourself wholeheartedly at the back of his knees—if you gathered and joined body and soul and pointed them diving fearlessly—then you likely wouldn't get hurt, and you'd stop the ball. Your fate, and your team's score, depended on your concentration and courage. Nothing girls did could compare with it. 1

Boys welcomed me at baseball, too, for I had, through enthusiastic practice, what was weirdly known as a boy's arm. In winter, in the snow, there was neither baseball nor football, so the boys and I threw snowballs at passing cars. I got in trouble throwing snowballs, and have seldom been happier since. 2

On one weekday morning after Christmas, six inches of new snow had just fallen. We were standing up to our boot tops in snow on a front yard on trafficked Reynolds Street, waiting for cars. The cars traveled Reynolds Street slowly 3 and evenly; they were targets all but wrapped in red ribbons, cream puffs.[1] We couldn't miss.

I was seven; the boys were eight, nine, and ten. The oldest two Fahey boys were there—Mikey and Peter—polite blond boys who lived near me on Lloyd Street, and who already had four brothers and sisters. My parents approved Mikey and Peter Fahey. Chickie McBride was there, a tough kid, and Billy Paul and Mackie Kean too, from across Reynolds, where the boys grew up dark and furious, grew up skinny, knowing, and skilled. We had all drifted from our houses that morning looking for action, and had found it here on Reynolds Street.

It was cloudy but cold. The cars' tires laid behind them on the snowy street a complex trail of beige chunks like crenellated castle walls. I had stepped on some earlier; they squeaked. We could have wished for more traffic. When a car came, we all popped it one. In the intervals between cars we reverted to the natural solitude of children.

I started making an iceball—a perfect iceball, from perfectly white snow, perfectly spherical, and squeezed perfectly translucent so no snow remained all the way through. (The Fahey boys and I considered it unfair actually to throw an iceball at somebody, but it had been known to happen.)

I had just embarked on the iceball project when we heard tire chains come clanking from afar. A black Buick was moving toward us down the street. We all spread out, banged together some regular snowballs, took aim, and, when the Buick drew nigh, fired.

A soft snowball hit the driver's windshield right before the driver's face. It made a smashed star with a hump in the middle.

Often, of course, we hit our target, but this time, the only time in all of life, the car pulled over and stopped. Its wide black door opened; a man got out of it, running. He didn't even close the car door.

He ran after us, and we ran away from him, up the snowy Reynolds sidewalk. At the corner, I looked back; incredibly, he was still after us. He was in city clothes: a suit and tie, street shoes. Any normal adult would have quit, having sprung us into flight and made his point. This man was gaining on us. He was a thin man, all action. All of a sudden, we were running for our lives.

Wordless, we split up. We were on our turf; we could lose ourselves in the neighborhood backyards, everyone for himself. I paused and considered. Everyone had vanished except Mikey Fahey, who was just rounding the corner of a yellow brick house. Poor Mikey, I trailed him. The driver of the Buick sensibly picked the two of us to follow. The man apparently had all day.

---

1. *Cream puffs:* pastries filled with whipped cream. Metaphorically, a cream puff is a timid person or a task that is easily accomplished.

He chased Mikey and me around the yellow house and up a backyard path we 12
knew by heart: under a low tree, up a bank, through a hedge, down some snowy
steps, and across the grocery store's delivery driveway. We smashed through a gap
in another hedge, entered a scruffy backyard and ran around its back porch and
tight between houses to Edgerton Avenue; we ran across Edgerton to an alley and
up our own sliding woodpile to the Halls' front yard; he kept coming. We ran up
Lloyd Street and wound through mazy backyards toward the steep hilltop at
Willard and Lang.

He chased us silently, block after block. He chased us silently over picket fences, 13
through thorny hedges, between houses, around garbage cans, and across streets.
Every time I glanced back, choking for breath, I expected he would have quit. He
must have been as breathless as we were. His jacket strained over his body. It was
an immense discovery, pounding into my hot head with every sliding, joyous step,
that this ordinary adult evidently knew what I thought only children who trained
at football knew: that you have to fling yourself at what you're doing, you have to
point yourself, forget yourself, aim, dive.

Mikey and I had nowhere to go, in our own neighborhood or out of it, but away 14
from this man who was chasing us. He impelled us forward; we compelled him to follow our route. The air was cold; every breath tore my throat. We kept running, block
after block; we kept improvising, backyard after backyard, running a frantic course
and choosing it simultaneously, failing always to find small places or hard places to
slow him down, and discovering always, exhilarated, dismayed, that only bare speed
could save us—for he would never give up, this man—and we were losing speed.

He chased us through the backyard labyrinths of ten blocks before he caught us 15
by our jackets. He caught us and we all stopped.

We three stood staggering, half blinded, coughing, in an obscure hilltop back- 16
yard: a man in his twenties, a boy, a girl. He had released our jackets, our pursuer,
our captor, our hero: He knew we weren't going anywhere. We all played by the
rules. Mikey and I unzipped our jackets. I pulled off my sopping mittens. Our
tracks multiplied in the backyard's new snow. We had been breaking new snow all
morning. We didn't look at each other. I was cherishing my excitement. The man's
lower pants legs were wet; his cuffs were full of snow, and there was a prow of
snow beneath them on his shoes and socks. Some trees bordered the little flat
backyard, some messy winter trees. There was no one around: a clearing in a grove,
and we the only players.

It was a long time before he could speak. I had some difficulty at first recalling 17
why we were there. My lips felt swollen; I couldn't see out of the sides of my eyes;
I kept coughing.

"You stupid kids," he began perfunctorily. 18

We listened perfunctorily indeed, if we listened at all, for the chewing out was 19 redundant, a mere formality, and beside the point. The point was that he had chased us passionately without giving up, and so he had caught us. Now he came down to earth. I wanted the glory to last forever.

But how could the glory have lasted forever? We could have run through every 20 backyard in North America until we got to Panama. But when he trapped us at the lip of the Panama Canal, what precisely could he have done to prolong the drama of the chase and cap its glory? I brooded about this for the next few years. He could only have fried Mikey Fahey and me in boiling oil, say, or dismembered us piece-meal, or staked us to anthills. None of which I really wanted, and none of which any adult was likely to do, even in the spirit of fun. He could only chew us out there in the Panamanian jungle, after months or years of exalting pursuit. He could only begin, "You stupid kids," and continue in his ordinary Pittsburgh accent with his normal righteous anger and the usual common sense.

If in that snowy backyard the driver of the black Buick had cut off our heads, 21 Mikey's and mine, I would have died happy, for nothing has required so much of me since as being chased all over Pittsburgh in the middle of winter—running ter-rified, exhausted—by this sainted, skinny, furious red-headed man who wished to have a word with us. I don't know how he found his way back to his car.

READING CLOSELY

1. When she was growing up in Pittsburgh, says Dillard, nothing that girls nor-mally did "could compare with" playing football (1). What was so special to her about this "boys" sport?

2. How old is Dillard at the time of the big chase? Does it matter that she is the youngest in the game—and the only girl? Why or why not?

3. As the chase goes on, Dillard's pursuer becomes her "hero" (16). Why? How, according to Dillard, is true "glory" to be achieved in any pursuit (19)?

4. What do the man's appearance and behavior tell us about the America of Dil-lard's childhood?

STRATEGIES AND STRUCTURES

1. Dillard begins her NARRATIVE with an account of learning to play football and other boys games. Why is this introduction necessary to the PLOT of the story?

2. As the chase unfolds, Dillard steadily increases the tension between the adver-saries. How? Give examples from the text.

3. Dillard gives only the beginning of the victor's lecture, "You stupid kids" (18). Why doesn't she quote his whole speech?

4. What does the young Dillard learn by imagining different outcomes to the chase? What does this lesson reveal about her PURPOSE for writing?

5. *Other Methods.* Dillard's narrative includes vivid DESCRIPTION. Imagine the chase scene without the descriptive detail—of a perfect iceball, for instance, or of what the man was wearing. How does such description contribute to the point Dillard is making in this essay? What do you think that point is?

THINKING ABOUT LANGUAGE

1. What is "righteous anger" (20)? How does it differ from other kinds? Why is such anger "normal" in the time and place that Dillard is describing (20)?

2. What is the meaning of "perfunctorily" (18, 19)? Why is the word appropriate here?

3. They were "the only players," says Dillard, when the chase comes to an end (16). In what sense(s) is she using the word *players* here? How is she using "grove" (16)?

FOR WRITING

1. Did you ever get in trouble while playing a childhood sport or game? Write a paragraph about what happened.

2. Write a narrative essay about an early childhood encounter in which adults did not behave as you expected them to. Be careful to establish a consistent POINT OF VIEW—whether that of a child or of an adult looking back.

3. Write a narrative essay in which the setting is one of your old neighborhoods. Show and tell the reader about something that you and your friends typically did there. Write as an adult looking back, but try to capture your POINT OF VIEW as a child as well.

MICHAEL LEWIS

The Badger

Michael Lewis (b. 1960) is a native of New Orleans, and was educated at Princeton University and the London School of Economics. Before becoming a professional writer, he spent four years as a bond salesman on Wall Street, the subject of his best-selling book Liar's Poker *(1989). This selection is a chapter from* Moneyball *(2003), Lewis's investigation of the new economics of baseball, as exemplified by the Oakland Athletics and their enterprising general manager, Billy Beane.*

"The Badger" tells what happened to rookie catcher Jeremy Brown soon after he was drafted from the University of Alabama to play for the Oakland A's. At "five foot eight and 215 pounds," Brown did not look like a star athlete, but his performance on the field changed everyone's perception of him, including his own. Try reading Brown's story as a Cinderella story, and think about how it illustrates Lewis's general point in Moneyball *that baseball is a financial market, and that baseball players, like stocks or bonds, can be misvalued even when professionals are analyzing them closely.*

THE JEREMY BROWN who steps into the batter's box in early October is, and is not, the fat catcher from Hueytown, Alabama, that the Oakland A's had made the least likely first-round draft choice in recent memory. He was still about five foot eight and 215 pounds. He still wasn't much use to anyone hoping to sell jeans. But in other ways, the important ways, experience had reshaped him.

Three months earlier, just after the June draft, he'd arrived in Vancouver, Canada, to play for the A's rookie ball team.[1] Waiting for him there was a seemingly endless number of jokes to be had at his expense. The most widely read magazine in the locker room, *Baseball America*, kept writing all these rude things about his appearance. They quoted unnamed scouts from other teams saying things like, "He never met a pizza he didn't like." They pressed the A's own scouting director, Erik Kubota, to acknowledge the perversity of selecting a young man who looked like Jeremy Brown with a first-round draft choice. "He's not the most physically fit," Kubota had said, sounding distinctly apologetic. "It's not a pretty body. . . . This guy's a great baseball player trapped in a bad body." The magazine ran Jeremy's college yearbook picture over the caption: "Bad Boy Rap." His mother back in Huey-

---

1. *Rookie ball team:* major league baseball in the United States draws its players from minor league teams. Each major league team has its own group of minor league teams, arranged by skill in seven levels. The rookie league is the lowest of the seven levels; it is where many of the youngest players start out.

town read all of it, and every time someone made fun of the shape of her son, she got upset all over again. His dad just laughed.

The other guys on the rookie ball team thought it was a riot. They couldn't wait 3 for the next issue of *Baseball America* to see what they'd write about Jeremy this time. Jeremy's new friend, Nick Swisher, was always the first to find whatever they'd written, but Swish approached the thing with defiance. Nick Swisher, son of former major league player Steve Swisher, and consensus first-round draft pick, took shit from no one. Swish didn't wait for other people to tell him what he was worth; he told them. He was trying to instill the same attitude, without much luck, in Jeremy Brown. One night over dinner with a few of the guys, Swish had said to him, "All that stuff they write in *Baseball America*—that's bull. . . . You can play. That's all that matters. You can play. You think Babe Ruth was a stud? Hell no. . . ." Jeremy was slow to take offense and it took him a second or two to register the double-edged nature of Swish's pep talk. "Babe Ruth was a fat piece of shit," he said. "Just like Brown." And everyone at the table laughed.

A few weeks after he'd arrived in Vancouver, Jeremy Brown and Nick Swisher 4 were told by the team's trainer that the coaches wanted to see them in their office. Jeremy's first thought was "Oh man, I know I musta done something dumb." That was Jeremy's instinctive reaction when the authorities paid special attention to him: he'd done something wrong. What he'd done, in this case, was get on base an astonishing half the time he came to the plate. Jeremy Brown was making rookie ball look too easy. Billy Beane wanted to test him against stiffer competition; Billy wanted to see what he had. The coach handed Jeremy and Nick Swisher plane tickets and told them that they were the first guys from Oakland's 2002 draft to get promoted to Single-A ball.[2]

It took them forever to get from Vancouver, Canada, to Visalia, California. They 5 arrived just before a game, having not slept in thirty-one hours. No one said anything to them; no one wanted to have anything to do with them. That's the way it was as you climbed in the minors: your new teammates were never happy to see you. "Everybody just kind of looks at you and doesn't say anything," said Jeremy. "You just try to be nice. You don't want to get off on the wrong foot."

That first night in Visalia, he and Swish dressed and sat on the end of the bench. 6 They might as well have been on the visiting team. No one even came down to say hello; if Swish hadn't been on hand to confirm the fact Jeremy might have wondered if he still existed. In the third inning the team's regular catcher, a hulk named Jorge Soto, came to the plate. Jeremy had never heard of Soto but he assumed, rightly, that he was competing with Soto for the catching job. On the first pitch Soto hit a shot the likes of which neither Jeremy nor Swish had ever seen. It

---

2. *Single-A ball*: a level of minor league baseball three steps down from the major leagues.

was still rising as it flew over the light tower in left center field. It cleared the parking lot and also the skate park on the other side of the parking lot. It was the farthest ball Jeremy had ever seen hit live. Five hundred and fifty feet, maybe more. As Soto trotted around the bases, Jeremy turned to Swish and said, "I don't think I'm ever going to catch here."

If it was up to his new teammates, he wouldn't have. They locked the door; if Jeremy Brown and Nick Swisher wanted in, they'd have to break it down. One day he was walking through the Visalia clubhouse when someone shouted in a mocking tone, "Hey, Badger." Jeremy had no clue what the guy was talking about. He soon learned. His teammates, who still weren't saying much to him, had nicknamed him "The Badger." "It was 'cause when I get into the shower I kind of got a lot of hair on my body," Jeremy explained. Behind his back, they were all still having fun at his expense. Jeremy just did what he always did, smiled and got along.

Along with most of the other players drafted by the Oakland A's in 2002, Jeremy Brown had been invited to the Instructional League in Arizona at the end of the season. By then, three months after he'd been promoted to Visalia, no one was laughing at him. In Visalia, he'd quickly seized the starting catching job from Jorge Soto, and led the team in batting average (.310), on-base percentage (.444) and slugging percentage (.545). In fifty-five games, he'd knocked in forty runs. So artfully had he ripped through the pitching in high Single-A ball that Billy Beane had invited him to the 2003 big league spring training camp—the only player from the 2002 draft so honored. Every other player in the Oakland A's 2002 draft—even Nick Swisher—had experienced what the A's minor league director Keith Lieppman called "reality." Reality, Lieppman said, "is when you learn that you are going to have to change the way you play baseball if you are going to survive." Jeremy alone didn't need to change a thing about himself; it was the world around him that needed to change. And it did. The running commentary about him in *Baseball America* hung a U-turn. When the magazine named him one of the top three hitters from the entire 2002 draft, and one of the four top prospects in the Oakland A's minor league system, his mom called to tell him: someone had finally written something nice about him. His teammates in Visalia no longer called him "The Badger." Everyone now just called him "Badge."

When Jeremy Brown comes to the plate on this mid-October afternoon in Scottsdale, Arizona, it's the bottom of the second inning. There's no score, and there's no one on base. The big left-hander on the other team has made short work of the A's first three hitters. He throws Jeremy a fastball off the plate. Jeremy just looks at it. Ball one. Pitch number two is a change-up on the outside corner, where Jeremy can't do much with it anyway, so he just lets it be. Strike one. Jeremy Brown knows something about pitchers: "They almost always make a mistake," he says. "All you have to do is wait for it." Give the game a chance to come to you and often

enough it will. When he takes the change-up for a called strike, he notices the possibility of a future mistake. The pitcher's arm motion, when he throws his change-
up, is noticeably slower than it is when he throws his fastball.

The pitcher's next pitch is a fastball off the plate. Ball two. It's 2–1: a hitter's 10
count.

The fourth pitch is the mistake: the pitcher goes back to his change-up. Jeremy 11
sees his arm coming through slowly again, and this time he knows to wait on it.
The change-up arrives waist-high over the middle of the plate. The line drive
Jeremy hits screams over the pitcher's right ear and into the gap in left center field.

As he leaves the batter's box, Jeremy sees the left and center fielders converging 12
fast. The left fielder, thinking he might make the catch, is already running himself
out of position to play the ball off the wall. Jeremy knows he hit it hard, and so he
knows what's going to happen next—or imagines he does. The ball is going to hit
the wall and ricochet back into the field. The left fielder, having overrun it, will
have to turn around and chase after it. Halfway down the first-base line, Jeremy
Brown has one thought in his mind: *I'm gonna get a triple.*

It's a new thought for him. He isn't built for triples. He hasn't hit a triple in 13
years. He thrills to the new idea: Jeremy Brown, hitter of triples. A funny thing has
happened since he became, by some miracle, the most upwardly mobile hitter in
the Oakland A's minor league system. Surrounded by people who keep telling him
he's capable of almost anything, he's coming to believe it himself.

He races around first ("I'm haulin' ass now") and picks up the left fielder, run- 14
ning with his back to him, but not the ball. He's running as hard as he's ever run—
and then he's not. Between first and second base his feet go out from under him
and he backflops into the dirt, like Charlie Brown. He notices, first, a shooting pain
in his hand: he's jammed his finger. He picks himself up, to scramble back to the
safety of first base, when he sees his teammates in the dugout. The guys are falling
all over each other, laughing. Swish. Stanley. Teahen. Kiger. Everybody's laughing
at him again. But their laughter has a different tone; it's not the sniggering laughter of the people who made fun of his body. It's something else. He looks out into
the gap in left center field. The outfielders are just standing there: they've stopped
chasing the ball. The ball's gone. The triple of Jeremy Brown's imagination, in reality, is a home run.

Reading Closely

1. Why and how does Jeremy Brown get the nickname "The Badger" (7)?

2. In the months after he is drafted from college baseball to play for the Oakland A's, Brown does not change much physically. He does, however, change "in other ways, the important ways" (1). What are some of them?

3. What is the significance of the change in Brown's nickname from "The Badger" to just "Badge" (8)? What brings about this change?

4. If "The Badger" is an essay about success, what is Lewis's main point?

Strategies and Structures

1. Why do you think Lewis pays so much attention throughout his NARRATIVE to the physical characteristics of "the fat catcher from Hueytown, Alabama" (1)? With whom does he CONTRAST Brown's physical appearance? Why?

2. When sports writers and announcers speak of a Cinderella story, what are they referring to? How does Jeremy Brown's story fit the fairy-tale pattern?

3. Paragraphs 2–8 of "The Badger" take the reader back three months in time to when Brown was first drafted into professional baseball. What is the purpose of this FLASHBACK? How and where does a change in verb tense alert you that the flashback has ended?

4. In paragraph 12, Brown "imagines," incorrectly, that he has hit a triple. Why do you think Lewis leaves the reader in the dark as to the "reality" of what has happened until the last sentence of the narrative (14)?

5. *Other Methods.* What are the main CAUSES of the changes in Brown? What EFFECTS do those causes have?

Thinking about Language

1. "By some miracle," says Lewis, the A's rookie catcher has become an "upwardly mobile hitter" (13). Fairy tales deal with the miraculous, but *upward mobility* sounds like social science. Why do you think Lewis combines such terms here?

2. How does Keith Lieppman, the director of the A's minor-league teams, DEFINE "reality" (8)? Why do you think Lewis repeats the word again at the end of his narrative?

3. What if Lewis's hero had been nicknamed "The Fox" or "The Babe"? In what ways does "The Badger" serve Lewis's narrative purposes?

4. What are the implications of the term "reshaped" (1)?

5. What new EPITHET does Brown imagine for himself in paragraph 13, and what does it contribute to Lewis's point?

FOR WRITING

1. Have you ever "hit a triple" when you were not expecting to? Write a letter to a close friend or relative about some unexpected success you've had, telling what happened and how it affected who you are.

2. Paragraphs 9–14 focus on one baseball game. Rewrite them as a news article reporting on the game. State the most important *who, what, where, when, how,* and *why* in your opening paragraph and then develop the answers to those questions in the following paragraphs.

JEFF GREMMELS

The Clinic

Jeff Gremmels (b. 1972) was a medical student at the University of Illinois College of Medicine at Rockford when he wrote "The Clinic." As part of his training, Gremmels saw patients weekly at one of the university's primary care centers. This selection centers on a particularly difficult case—one in which the novice doctor needs to look beyond physical explanations. An experienced physician comes to his aid, and the doctor-in-training discovers how much more he has to learn.

"The Clinic" won first prize in an essay competition sponsored by the University of Illinois College of Medicine. Why would a college of medicine promote a writing contest? "Because writing is a good way to clarify our thoughts and feelings," said Margaret Maynard, the microbiologist in charge of the contest. Also, she notes, the college "wanted to foster a compassionate, humanitarian approach to the practice of medicine. . . . to graduate caring, concerned doctors, not just technically gifted ones." "The Clinic" suggests that the author, now a practicing radiologist in Boston, was well on his way to becoming just such a physician. First published in the Rockford Register Star *in 1998, this essay has also appeared in* Becoming Doctors, *an anthology of essays by medical students.*

EVERY WEDNESDAY, as part of my second-year medical student experience in   1
Rockford, I travel north to see patients at the UIC University Primary Care Clinic at Rockton. Early this past winter, I was handed the chart of a new patient and I was told I was seeing him for "stomachaches." I closed the door to the sterile white examination room to face a thin, pale young boy, fourteen years old and sitting on the exam table with his knees pulled to his chest. His head jumped as the exam door snapped briskly shut. I introduced myself and crouched at eye-level next to him. He tightened the grip on his knees. "What's wrong?" Silence filled the bleach-tinged air, and his eyes stared at me, unblinking.

"He's not eating anything, says his stomach hurts." The voice came from the   2
mother in the corner of the room. I hadn't even noticed her as I entered, all my attention focused immediately on the tensed figure on the bed. "For the past two weeks, it's been nothing but cereal, and only a handful of that." I listened to the mother sketch a history of nausea, stomachaches, and absent stares. It gave the impression of more than the typical stomachache, and I plied ahead, waiting to finally ask the key question that slipped the knot on this mystery and sent the bacteria or virus or swallowed garden flower culprit plummeting into my lap. The knot refused to give.

"Where did he get the bruises?" I ventured, hoping to unearth some bleeding 3 disorder with a forgotten manifestation of gastrointestinal symptoms. The mother looked at the scattered marks around the red-head's temples through her friendly librarian glasses, then up at me.

"He's very active, normally, and gets into all sorts of spots. He comes in from the 4 woods with new cuts and scrapes every night. You should have seen him after the big rains, all mud and torn jeans." With this she looked back at the alabaster boy huddling on the bed and smiled with the memory of his past spirit.

A professor teaching our physical diagnosis class told us we should know 80 per- 5 cent of the cases coming before us by hearing the history alone. This case was quickly proving itself the undesired 20 percent. I moved to the physical exam. The boy was not keen on the concept of my examining him, and made his desires very clear as he refused every request to look up at me or to open his clamped mouth. I wanted to solve this puzzle and began to insist more forcefully until finally, with his surprisingly strong mother, I managed to pull his loose shirt over his head. Beneath that shirt lay pale doughy skin, its spongy texture belying the taut muscu- lature beneath. On the surface of the skin was a continuation of the light bruising around his temples. As the mother sat down and the boy resumed his curled-ball posture, my eyes picked out almost one-dozen small, red "U"s, with two small bars between the uprights like a German umlaut.[1] Raised and bright, more like a rash or burn than a bruise, I hoped these would be the clues I needed to solve my mystery of the afternoon. Further examination revealed nothing more than a continuation of the pattern down to his ankles.

I combed my cloudy memories of past lectures for anything reminiscent of this 6 strange mark as I walked up the hall to find a doctor. The search failed to exhume any diseases with ties to Germanic vowels.

As I explained my cryptic findings to the attending physician, I saw her eyes 7 quickly open, contradicting my belief that she was actually asleep. Pushing insur- ance papers towards me, she quickly stated, "I'm going to look at him. I want you to have the mother fill these out in the waiting room." I followed her white lab coat to the exam room and completed my assigned mission. I returned from the waiting room—despite the mother's distant protests of having already completed the same forms—to find the attending physician on the phone and admitting my patient directly to hospital care.

Twenty-five minutes later, I again sat in her office, listening to the diagnosis. 8 "The wheels of a lighter, a disposable lighter, leave those two umlaut marks—noth- ing else looks like it. It's almost always abuse in his age group." I couldn't think of

---

1. *Umlaut*: the German name for the marking on certain vowel letters to indicate specific sounds. The umlaut appears as two dots above a letter, for example, ü or ä.

any reply, and we spent several minutes gazing into the carpet, silent and introspective. I left the clinic alone and went directly to my apartment, missing the evening lecture on "Insulin and Diabetic Control."

Four days later, I went to the hospital to see the boy who was once my patient. I 9 read the psychiatrist's chart notes slowly, rereading the passages describing the boy's abuse by his stepfather and his three-year history of self-mutilation and depression. It never entered my mind, so avid for a solution, to ask for a history of hospitalizations or illness, and I felt the cavernous shadows of my own missing knowledge hinting at their depth. My focus had always been on the disease, the physiologic atrocity accosting the patient's unsuspecting organs and cells. This was my first glimpse into an arena I had utterly neglected—the patient's psyche—quietly present in everyone and in every disease.

Entering the boy's room, I found him asleep, an IV pole standing sentry over his 10 frail visage. I picked up a crumpled note from the floor, smoothing it to reveal the young patient's shaky handwriting:

> I wish I were a paper airplane,
> Soaked in gas, shooting red flames,
> burning with an orange glow, over
> all the people below.
> I could fall through the sky
> like a comet or a meteorite.
> I could become a UFO,
> become someone I did not know.

Years of lectures, labs, and research could not match the education I received in 11 five days with this single boy.

Reading Closely

1. Why is Gremmels unable, on his own, to determine what is wrong with his patient? How does the attending physician figure it out?

2. When the attending physician explains the strange marks on the patient's body, Gremmels says he "couldn't think of any reply" (8). Why is the student doctor left speechless?

3. A key question to ask about any NARRATIVE is "Whose story is it?" Would you say "The Clinic" is the boy's story or the medical student's? Or both? Why?

Strategies and Structures

1. What is Gremmels's PURPOSE in writing about this particular experience? How do you know?

2. "The Clinic" is told as a medical detective story. Why do you think Gremmels chose that genre?

3. Make a list of the main clues in this case. How does Gremmels reveal them to the reader, and how do these clues advance the NARRATIVE?

4. The last sentence of his essay, Gremmels says, "was put there because I suspected the medical school judges would like it. I, personally, think the story should end with the poem." What do you think? Why?

5. *Other Methods.* As a rule, mystery stories present EFFECTS, and the detective has to figure out CAUSES. Is this true of "The Clinic"? Explain.

Thinking about Language

1. Why does Gremmels introduce the METAPHOR of the knot in paragraph 2?

2. The DENOTATION of "exhume" is "to find or uncover" (6). What are the CONNOTATIONS of the word here, and what does the word contribute to the narrative?

3. In paragraph 9, the second-year medical student mentions the "cavernous shadows of my own missing knowledge." Is this phrase appropriate, in your opinion? Why or why not? How does it affect the TONE of the essay? Explain.

For Writing

1. Write a paragraph or two narrating from your perspective a visit to a doctor—or a teacher, counselor, or someone else you've gone to for help. Put the events of the visit in chronological order, and use transitions as needed to lead your reader through the story. Pay particular attention to the first sentence; see if you can make it introduce your main point. Then, switch perspectives, and rewrite your narrative from the POINT OF VIEW of the other person. Keep in mind how he or she might see both you—and the visit—differently than you do.

2. Write a narrative essay about some problem you had to diagnose and solve. The problem can be about anything—a car or computer, for example, or a friend or family member. Try to develop a PLOT that will get and hold readers' interest.

TONI MORRISON

Strangers

Toni Morrison (b. 1931) is a native of Lorain, Ohio. A graduate of Howard University and Cornell, she is now a professor of humanities at Princeton. She is the author of such well-known works as The Bluest Eye *(1970),* Song of Solomon *(1977),* Tar Baby *(1981),* Beloved *(1987), and other portrayals of African American experience. In 1993, she was awarded the Nobel Prize for literature. Her acceptance speech took the form of a narrative about an old blind woman, a storyteller, who demonstrates to a skeptical audience the power of narrative.*

"Strangers" begins with an account of another old woman who tells Morrison a story. The encounter leads Morrison to meditate on how strangers help us to understand ourselves and our humanity. "Strangers" originally appeared as the introduction to A Kind of Rapture *(1998), a book of photographs by Robert Bergman.*

I AM IN THIS RIVER PLACE—newly mine—walking in the yard when I see a woman sitting on the seawall at the edge of a neighbor's garden. A homemade fishing pole arcs into the water some twenty feet from her hand. A feeling of welcome washes over me. I walk toward her, right up to the fence that separates my place from the neighbor's, and notice with pleasure the clothes she wears: men's shoes, a man's hat, a well-worn colorless sweater over a long black dress. The woman turns her head and greets me with an easy smile and a "How you doing?" She tells me her name (Mother Something) and we talk for some time—fifteen minutes or so—about fish recipes and weather and children. When I ask her if she lives there, she answers no. She lives in a nearby village, but the owner of the house lets her come to this spot any time she wants to fish, and she comes every week, sometimes several days in a row when the perch or catfish are running and even if they aren't because she likes eel, too, and they are always there. She is witty and full of the wisdom that older women always seem to have a lock on. When we part, it is with an understanding that she will be there the next day or very soon after and we will visit again. I imagine more conversations with her. I will invite her into my house for coffee, for tales, for laughter. She reminds me of someone, something. I imagine a friendship, casual, effortless, delightful.

She is not there the next day. She is not there the following days, either. And I look for her every morning. The summer passes, and I have not seen her at all. Finally, I approach the neighbor to ask about her and am bewildered to learn that the neighbor does not know who or what I am talking about. No old woman fished from her wall—ever—and none had permission to do so. I decide that the fisher-

95

woman fibbed about the permission and took advantage of the neighbor's frequent absences to poach. The fact of the neighbor's presence is proof that the fisher-woman would not be there. During the months following, I ask lots of people if they know Mother Something. No one, not even people who have lived in nearby villages for seventy years, has ever heard of her.

I feel cheated, puzzled, but also amused, and wonder off and on if I have ³ dreamed her. In any case, I tell myself, it was an encounter of no value other than anecdotal. Still. Little by little, annoyance then bitterness takes the place of my original bewilderment. A certain view from my windows is now devoid of her, reminding me every morning of her deceit and my disappointment. What was she doing in that neighborhood, anyway? She didn't drive, had to walk four miles if indeed she lived where she said she did. How could she be missed on the road in that hat, those awful shoes? I try to understand the intensity of my chagrin, and why I am missing a woman I spoke to for fifteen minutes. I get nowhere except for the stingy explanation that she had come into my space (next to it, anyway—at the property line, at the edge, just at the fence, where the most interesting things always happen), and had implied promises of female camaraderie, of opportunities for me to be generous, of protection and protecting. Now she is gone, taking with her my good opinion of myself, which, of course, is unforgivable.

Isn't that the kind of thing that we fear strangers will do? Disturb. Betray. Prove ⁴ they are not like us. That is why it is so hard to know what to do with them. The love that prophets have urged us to offer the stranger is the same love that Jean-Paul Sartre¹ could reveal as the very mendacity of Hell. The signal line of "No Exit," "L'enfer, c'est les autres," raises the possibility that "other people" are responsible for turning a personal world into a public hell. In the admonition of a prophet and the sly warning of an artist, strangers as well as the beloved are understood to tempt our gaze, to slide away or to stake claims. Religious prophets caution against the slide, the looking away; Sartre warns against love as possession.

The resources available to us for benign access to each other, for vaulting the ⁵ mere blue air that separates us, are few but powerful: language, image, and experience, which may involve both, one, or neither of the first two. Language (saying, listening, reading) can encourage, even mandate, surrender, the breach of distances among us, whether they are continental or on the same pillow, whether they are distances of culture or the distinctions and indistinctions of age or gender, whether they are the consequences of social invention or biology. Image increasingly rules the realm of shaping, sometimes becoming, often contaminating, knowledge. Provoking language or eclipsing it, an image can determine not only what we know and

---

1. *Jean-Paul Sartre* (1905–1980): French existentialist philosopher; this line from his play *No Exit* (1944) is usually translated as "Hell is other people."

feel but also what we believe is worth knowing about what we feel.

These two godlings, language and image, feed and form experience. My instant embrace of an outrageously dressed fisherwoman was due in part to an image on 6 which my representation of her was based. I immediately sentimentalized and appropriated her. I owned her or wanted to (and I suspect she glimpsed it). I had forgotten the power of embedded images and stylish language to seduce, reveal, control. Forgot, too, their capacity to help us pursue the human project—which is to remain human and to block the dehumanization of others.

But something unforeseen has entered into this admittedly oversimplified menu of our resources. Far from our original expectations of increased intimacy 7 and broader knowledge, routine media presentations deploy images and language that narrow our view of what humans look like (or ought to look like) and what in fact we are like. Succumbing to the perversions of media can blur vision, resisting them can do the same. I was clearly and aggressively resisting such influences in my encounter with the fisherwoman. Art as well as the market can be complicit in the sequestering of form from formula, of nature from artifice, of humanity from commodity. Art gesturing toward representation has, in some exalted quarters, become literally beneath contempt. The concept of what it is to be human has altered, and the word *truth* needs quotation marks around it so that its absence (its elusiveness) is stronger than its presence.

Why would we want to know a stranger when it is easier to estrange another? Why would we want to close the distance when we can close the gate? Appeals in 8 arts and religion for comity in the Common Wealth are faint.

It took some time for me to understand my unreasonable claims on that fisher-woman. To understand that I was longing for and missing some aspect of myself, 9 and that there are no strangers. There are only versions of ourselves, many of which we have not embraced, most of which we wish to protect ourselves from. For the stranger is not foreign, she is random, not alien but remembered; and it is the randomness of the encounter with our already known—although unacknowl-edged—selves that summons a ripple of alarm. That makes us reject the figure and the emotions it provokes—especially when these emotions are profound. It is also what makes us want to own, govern, administrate the Other. To romance her, if we can, back into our own mirrors. In either instance (of alarm or false reverence), we deny her personhood, the specific individuality we insist upon for ourselves.

READING CLOSELY

1. At first, Morrison is merely puzzled and annoyed by the behavior of the old woman she finds fishing on the seawall of the property next door. Then "bitterness" sets in (3). What makes Morrison bitter about the encounter?

2. Why, according to Morrison, is it "so hard to know what to do with" strangers (4)?

3. In Morrison's view, what are the three main "resources" that human beings have for getting in touch with one another (5)? How are they related to each other?

4. Whose story is Morrison telling here, the fisherwoman's or her own? Why do you think so, and why does it matter whose story this is?

STRATEGIES AND STRUCTURES

1. "Strangers" begins as a series of interlocking NARRATIVES, the first of which is the story of Morrison's encounter with the fisherwoman, "Mother Something" (1). What happens in this brief narrative, and how effectively does it capture the reader's attention?

2. What is Morrison's main point about "the human project" in this essay (6)? Why do you think she uses stories to make her point? How effective do you find this strategy?

3. How does Morrison use her encounter with the fisherwoman to EXEMPLIFY what she has to say about strangers and our relation to them?

4. In Morrison's analysis, what EFFECT do the media have on our perceptions of how people, including ourselves, ought to look and be? What CAUSES does she cite for this effect?

5. *Other Methods.* Morrison wrote this essay as the introduction to a collection of photographs. How—and how effectively—does her DESCRIPTION of "Mother Something" help to lead the reader from one form of communication (language) to the other (images)?

THINKING ABOUT LANGUAGE

1. Morrison meets her stranger "at the edge, just at the fence," of the neighboring property (3). What space is she talking about when she says this is "where the most interesting things always happen" (3)?

2. Morrison does not use the term, but in what sense(s) might the old woman she meets be called a *marginal* figure? How does the concept of a "margin" relate to photographs and other images? To narratives?

3. Why do you think Morrison refers to "language and image" as "godlings" (6)? Why doesn't she just call them "gods," or even "Gods"?

For Writing

1. Morrison's essay is the introduction to *A Kind of Rapture*, Robert Bergman's book of color photographs of ordinary people. Find a photograph that captures your interest and write a paragraph or two responding to it. You could look at pictures in *A Kind of Rapture*, or search the Web for images by other photographers such as Annie Leibovitz, Dorothea Lange, or Joel Sternfeld, or you could find a photo in a magazine or newspaper. You might imagine meeting the person in the photo, or imagining what he or she is thinking, or you may just want to write down your thoughts as inspired by the photo.

2. Write a narrative essay about an encounter with someone—a stranger, or even a friend or relative—that left you wanting to know that person better. Tell the story in such a way that the reader understands what attracted you to this person and why you wanted to strike up a friendship with him or her.

RICHARD RUSSO

Dog

Richard Russo (b. 1949) is a novelist. He is the author of, among other works,
Nobody's Fool *(1991) and* Empire Falls *(2002), which received the Pulitzer Prize in
fiction. Before he turned exclusively to writing, Russo taught fiction writing at Southern Illinois University and Colby College. Out of this experience came his academic
novel,* Straight Man *(1997), about William Henry Devereaux Jr., the son of two English professors and himself the chair of the English department at the mythical West
Central Pennsylvania University. "Dog," which first appeared as a short story in the*
New Yorker *in 1996, is the prologue to that novel.*

*In "Dog" we return to the narrator's childhood. His parents are in the process of
splitting up, though their son doesn't know it yet. All he wants is a dog, and he sets out
relentlessly to get one. As you'll see, though, this is far more than a boy-meets-dog
narrative.*

They're nice to have. A dog.   —F. Scott Fitzgerald, *The Great Gatsby*

Truth be told, I'm not an easy man. I can be an entertaining one, though it's   1
been my experience that most people don't want to be entertained. They want to
be comforted. And, of course, my idea of entertaining might not be yours. I'm in
complete agreement with all those people who say, regarding movies, "I just want
to be entertained." This populist position is much derided by my academic colleagues as simpleminded and unsophisticated, evidence of questionable analytical
and critical acuity. But I agree with the premise, and I too just want to be entertained. That I am almost never entertained by what entertains *other* people who
just want to be entertained doesn't make us philosophically incompatible. It just
means we shouldn't go to movies together.

The kind of man I am, according to those who know me best, is exasperating.   2
According to my parents, I was an exasperating child as well. They divorced when
I was in junior high school, and they agree on little except that I was an impossible
child. The story they tell of young William Henry Devereaux, Jr., and his first dog is
eerily similar in its facts, its conclusions, even the style of its telling, no matter
which of them is telling it. Here's the story they tell.

I was nine, and the house we were living in, which belonged to the univer-   3
sity, was my fourth. My parents were academic nomads, my father, then and
now, an academic opportunist, always in the vanguard of whatever was trendy
and chic in literary criticism. This was the fifties, and for him, New Criticism[1]

was already old. In early middle age he was already a full professor with several published books, all of them "hot," the subject of intense debate at English department cocktail parties. The academic position he favored was the "distinguished visiting professor" variety, usually created for him, duration of visit a year or two at most, perhaps because it's hard to remain distinguished among people who know you. Usually his teaching responsibilities were light, a course or two a year. Otherwise, he was expected to read and think and write and publish and acknowledge in the preface of his next book the generosity of the institution that provided him the academic good life. My mother, also an English professor, was hired as part of the package deal, to teach a full load and thereby help balance the books.

The houses we lived in were elegant, old, high-ceilinged, drafty, either on or close to campus. They had hardwood floors and smoky fireplaces with fires in them only when my father held court, which he did either on Friday afternoons, our large rooms filling up with obsequious junior faculty and nervous grad students, or Saturday evenings, when my mother gave dinner parties for the chair of the department, or the dean, or a visiting poet. In all situations I was the only child, and I must have been a lonely one, because what I wanted more than anything in the world was a dog. 4

Predictably, my parents did not. Probably the terms of living in these university houses were specific regarding pets. By the time I was nine I'd been lobbying hard for a dog for a year or two. My father and mother were hoping I would outgrow this longing, given enough time. I could see this hope in their eyes and it steeled my resolve, intensified my desire. What did I want for Christmas? A dog. What did I want for my birthday? A dog. What did I want on my ham sandwich? A dog. It was a deeply satisfying look of pure exasperation they shared at such moments, and if I couldn't have a dog, this was the next best thing. 5

Life continued in this fashion until finally my mother made a mistake, a doozy of a blunder born of emotional exhaustion and despair. She, far more than my father, would have preferred a happy child. One spring day after I'd been badgering her pretty relentlessly she sat me down and said, "You know, a dog is something you earn." My father heard this, got up, and left the room, grim acknowledgment that my mother had just conceded the war. Her idea was to make the dog conditional. The conditions to be imposed would be numerous and severe, and I would be incapable of fulfilling them, so when I didn't get the dog it'd be my own fault. This was her logic, and the fact that she thought such a plan might work illustrates that some people should never be parents and that she was one of them. 6

---

1. *New Criticism*: a literary theory of the twentieth century in America and Britain that stressed the close reading of texts.

I immediately put into practice a plan of my own to wear my mother down.   7
Unlike hers, my plan was simple and flawless. Mornings I woke up talking about
dogs and nights I fell asleep talking about them. When my mother and father
changed the subject, I changed it back. "Speaking of dogs," I would say, a forkful of
my mother's roast poised at my lips, and I'd be off again. Maybe no one *had* been
speaking of dogs, but never mind, we were speaking of them now. At the library I
checked out a half dozen books on dogs every two weeks and left them lying open
around the house. I pointed out dogs we passed on the street, dogs on television,
dogs in the magazines my mother subscribed to. I discussed the relative merits of
various breeds at every meal. My father seldom listened to anything I said, but I
began to see signs that the underpinnings of my mother's personality were beginning to corrode in the salt water of my tidal persistence, and when I judged that
she was nigh to complete collapse, I took every penny of the allowance money I'd
been saving and spent it on a dazzling, bejeweled dog collar and leash set at the
overpriced pet store around the corner.

During this period when we were constantly "speaking of dogs," I was not a   8
model boy. I was supposed to be "earning a dog," and I was constantly checking
with my mother to see how I was doing, just how much of a dog I'd earned, but I
doubt my behavior had changed a jot. I wasn't really a bad boy. Just a noisy, busy,
constantly needy boy. Mr. In and Out, my mother called me, because I was in and
out of rooms, in and out of doors, in and out of the refrigerator. "Henry," my
mother would plead with me. "Light somewhere." One of the things I often needed
was information, and I constantly interrupted my mother's reading and paper grad-
ing to get it. My father, partly to avoid having to answer my questions, spent most
of his time in his book-lined office on campus, joining my mother and me only at
mealtimes, so that we could speak of dogs as a family. Then he was gone again,
blissfully unaware, I thought at the time, that my mother continued to glare homi-
cidally, for long minutes after his departure, at the chair he'd so recently occupied.
But he claimed to be close to finishing the book he was working on, and this was a
powerful excuse to offer a woman with as much abstract respect for books and
learning as my mother possessed.

Gradually, she came to understand that she was fighting a battle she couldn't   9
win and that she was fighting it alone. I now know that this was part of a larger
cluster of bitter marital realizations, but at the time I sniffed nothing in the air but
victory. In late August, during what people refer to as "the dog days," when she
made one last, weak condition, final evidence that I had earned a dog, I relented
and truly tried to reform my behavior. It was literally the least I could do.

What my mother wanted of me was to stop slamming the screen door. The   10
house we were living in, it must be said, was an acoustic marvel akin to the Whispering Gallery in St. Paul's, where muted voices travel across a great open space

and arrive, clear and intact, at the other side of the great dome. In our house the screen door swung shut on a tight spring, the straight wooden edge of the door encountering the doorframe like a gunshot played through a guitar amplifier set on stun, the crack transmitting perfectly, with equal force and clarity, to every room in the house, upstairs and down. That summer I was in and out that door dozens of times a day, and my mother said it was like living in a shooting gallery. It made her wish the door wasn't shooting blanks. If I could just remember not to slam the door, then she'd see about a dog. Soon.

I did better, remembering about half the time not to let the door slam. When I forgot, I came back in to apologize, sometimes forgetting then too. Still, that I was trying, together with the fact that I carried the expensive dog collar and leash with me everywhere I went, apparently moved my mother, because at the end of that first week of diminished door slamming, my father went somewhere on Saturday morning, refusing to reveal where, and so of course I knew. "What *kind*?" I pleaded with my mother when he was gone. But she claimed not to know. "Your father's doing this," she said, and I thought I saw a trace of misgiving in her expression. 11

When he returned, I saw why. He'd put it in the backseat, and when my father pulled the car in and parked along the side of the house, I saw from the kitchen window its chin resting on the back of the rear seat. I think it saw me too, but if so it did not react. Neither did it seem to notice that the car had stopped, that my father had gotten out and was holding the front seat forward. He had to reach in, take the dog by the collar, and pull. 12

As the animal unfolded its long legs and stepped tentatively, arthritically, out of the car, I saw that I had been both betrayed and outsmarted. In all the time we had been "speaking of dogs," what I'd been seeing in my mind's eye was puppies. Collie puppies, beagle puppies, Lab puppies, shepherd puppies, but none of that had been inked anywhere, I now realized. If not a puppy, a young dog. A rascal, full of spirit and possibility, a dog with new tricks to learn. *This* dog was barely ambulatory. It stood, head down, as if ashamed at something done long ago in its puppydom, and I thought I detected a shiver run through its frame when my father closed the car door behind it. 13

The animal was, I suppose, what might have been called a handsome dog. A purebred, rust-colored Irish setter, meticulously groomed, wonderfully mannered, the kind of dog you could safely bring into a house owned by the university, the sort of dog that wouldn't really violate the no pets clause, the kind of dog, I saw clearly, you'd get if you really didn't want a dog or to be bothered with a dog. It'd belonged, I later learned, to a professor emeritus of the university who'd been put into a nursing home earlier in the week, leaving the animal an orphan. It was like a painting of a dog, or a dog you'd hire to pose for a portrait, a dog you could be sure wouldn't move. 14

Both my father and the animal came into the kitchen reluctantly, my father   15
closing the screen door behind them with great care. I like to think that on the way
home he'd suffered a misgiving, though I could tell that it was his intention to play
the hand out boldly. My mother, who'd taken in my devastation at a glance, studied
me for a moment and then my father.

"What?" he said.   16

My mother just shook her head.   17

My father looked at me, then back at her. A violent shiver palsied the dog's   18
limbs. The animal seemed to want to lie down on the cool linoleum, but to have
forgotten how. It offered a deep sigh that seemed to speak for all of us.

"He's a good dog," my father said, rather pointedly, to my mother. "A little high-   19
strung, but that's the way with purebred setters. They're all nervous."

This was not the sort of thing my father knew. Clearly he was repeating the   20
explanation he'd just been given when he picked up the dog.

"What's his name?" my mother said, apparently for something to say.   21

My father had neglected to ask. He checked the dog's collar for clues.   22

"Lord," my mother said. "Lord, lord."   23

"It's not like we can't name him ourselves," my father said, irritated now. "I   24
think it's something we can manage, don't you?"

"You could name him after a passé school of literary criticism," my mother sug-   25
gested.

"It's a she," I said, because it was.   26

It seemed to cheer my father, at least a little, that I'd allowed myself to be drawn   27
into the conversation. "What do you say, Henry?" he wanted to know. "What'll we
name him?"

This second faulty pronoun reference was too much for me. "I want to go out   28
and play now," I said, and I bolted for the screen door before an objection could be
registered. It slammed behind me, hard, its gunshot report even louder than usual.
As I cleared the steps in a single leap, I thought I heard a thud back in the kitchen,
a dull, muffled echo of the door, and then I heard my father say, "What the hell?"
I went back up the steps, cautiously now, meaning to apologize for the door.
Through the screen I could see my mother and father standing together in the middle of the kitchen, looking down at the dog, which seemed to be napping. My
father nudged a haunch with the toe of his cordovan loafer.[2]

He dug the grave in the backyard with a shovel borrowed from a neighbor. My   29
father had soft hands and they blistered easily. I offered to help, but he just looked
at me. When he was standing, midthigh, in the hole he'd dug, he shook his head
one last time in disbelief. "Dead," he said. "Before we could even name him."

---

2. *Cordovan loafer*: a style of casual but expensive men's shoes made from fine horse leather.

I knew better than to correct the pronoun again, so I just stood there thinking 30 about what he'd said while he climbed out of the hole and went over to the back porch to collect the dog where it lay under an old sheet. I could tell by the careful way he tucked that sheet under the animal that he didn't want to touch anything dead, even newly dead. He lowered the dog into the hole by means of the sheet, but he had to drop it the last foot or so. When the animal thudded on the earth and lay still, my father looked over at me and shook his head. Then he picked up the shovel and leaned on it before he started filling in the hole. He seemed to be waiting for me to say something, so I said, "Red."

My father's eyes narrowed, as if I'd spoken in a foreign tongue. "What?" he said. 31

"We'll name her Red," I explained. 32

In the years after he left us, my father became even more famous. He is some- 33 times credited, if credit is the word, with being the Father of American Literary Theory. In addition to his many books of scholarship, he's also written a literary memoir that was short-listed for a major award and that offers insight into the personalities of several major literary figures of the twentieth century, now deceased. His photograph often graces the pages of the literary reviews. He went through a phase where he wore crewneck sweaters and gold chains beneath his tweed coat,[3] but now he's mostly photographed in an oxford button-down shirt, tie, and jacket, in his book-lined office at the university. But to me, his son, William Henry Devereaux, Sr., is most real standing in his ruined cordovan loafers, leaning on the handle of a borrowed shovel, examining his dirty, blistered hands, and receiving my suggestion of what to name a dead dog. I suspect that digging our dog's grave was one of relatively few experiences of his life (excepting carnal ones) that did not originate on the printed page. And when I suggested we name the dead dog Red, he looked at me as if I myself had just stepped from the pages of a book he'd started to read years ago and then put down when something else caught his interest. "What?" he said, letting go of the shovel, so that its handle hit the earth between my feet. "What?"

It's not an easy time for any parent, this moment when the realization dawns 34 that you've given birth to something that will never see things the way you do, despite the fact that it is your living legacy, that it bears your name.

---

3. *Crewneck sweaters and gold chains beneath his tweed coat*: tweed coats are stereotypical clothing for professors and other academics. Crewneck sweaters worn with heavy gold chains were a macho style of the 1970s.

Reading Closely

1. Why does Henry want a dog?

2. How and why does young Henry earn the nickname "Mr. In and Out" (8)? How appropriate is the name?

3. What plan does Henry set into motion in paragraph 7? How well does it work?

4. Henry relents from his plan and tries hard not to slam the screen door. What does this change of heart show the reader about his character and personality? What can we make of his final screen-door slam (28)?

Strategies and Structures

1. Russo's story of a boy and his dog doesn't actually begin until paragraph 4. What is the PURPOSE of the first two paragraphs of the NARRATIVE?

2. Where and why does Russo's story engage in a FLASH FORWARD to a time in the future? How does he bring the story back to the past?

3. Besides telling a boy-meets-dog story, Russo's narrator is also telling the story of how he became "the kind of man I am" (2). What kind of man is he, and what are some of the CAUSES?

4. Russo does not introduce DIALOGUE into his story until paragraph 11. Why do you think he waits until this particular point before letting his characters speak?

5. *Other Methods.* Russo DESCRIBES in detail the "acoustic marvel" of a house in which the Devereaux family is living (10). Why does he pay so much attention to the screen door in particular? Point out other places where Russo's descriptions support the actions of the story.

Thinking about Language

1. Russo uses the following academic language in paragraph 1: "populist position," "much derided," "questionable analytical and critical acuity," "premise," "philosophically incompatible." Why does he use such language so early in his story?

2. Why does Henry's father refer to the new dog as "he"? What does the boy's reaction to this "faulty pronoun reference" tell you about his upbringing and future (28)? Give examples of other times when Henry challenges his father.

3. When his parents tell the story of him and his first dog, says Henry, the story is "eerily similar in . . . its telling" (2). Why does he consider their mutual agreement about the story to be "eerie"?

FOR WRITING

1. Write a paragraph or two narrating your efforts to convince your family to acquire a pet or something else you've wanted.

2. Write a narrative essay about something that mattered a lot to you when you were a child—a dog, a doll, a game, etc. Your essay should tell about some memorable incident. Make sure the essay has a beginning, middle, and ending, and choose details that will bring the incident alive for the reader. Be sure to indicate why the incident was significant to you.

3. The writer Annie Proulx has praised Russo for creating characters "as real as we are," ones readers can see "coming out of doorways, lurching through life." Write a narrative essay about some real person you know. Focus on an incident (to be sure you write a narrative, not just a DESCRIPTION). Choose details that will give readers a sense of who the person is, and arrange actions carefully to lead readers through the story.

CHAPTER 4

Description

In his classic essay "Once More to the Lake," E. B. White describes what he sees, hears, and feels early one morning as he goes out in a rowboat with his young son:

> We went fishing the first morning. I felt the same damp moss covering the worms in the bait can, and saw the dragonfly alight on the tip of my rod as it hovered a few inches from the surface of the water. . . . The small waves were the same, chucking the rowboat under the chin as we fished at anchor, and the boat was the same boat, the same color green and the ribs broken in the same places, and under the floorboards the same freshwater leavings and debris—the dead helgramite, the wisps of moss, the rusty discarded fishhook, the dried blood from yesterday's catch. We stared silently at the tips of our rods, at the dragonflies that came and went. I lowered the tip of mine into the water, tentatively, pensively dislodging the fly, which darted two feet away, poised, darted two feet back, and came to rest again a little farther up the rod.

You can picture the tranquil scene—the lake, father and son in the boat, waves lapping the bow, the dragonfly at the end of the rod—because this passage is a little masterpiece of descriptive writing.

Defining Description:
Telling How Something Looks, Sounds, Feels, Smells, or Tastes

Description appeals to the senses: it gives the reader something to look at (the green boat, the rusty fishhook, the hovering dragonfly); to feel (the damp moss); to hear (the small waves); and to smell (the drying fish blood). As for taste, White appeals more directly to that sense later in his essay, when he and his young son go to a nearby farmhouse for dinner (fried chicken, apple pie). What does a subject look, feel, smell, sound, or taste like? These are the fundamental questions that descriptive writing addresses.

In this chapter we will see where to look for the specific physical details you need for building a good description. We will examine ways to give your description a sharp focus by selecting from those details to suit your purpose and audience. And we will look at a number of strategies for organizing those details as you compose and revise your description.

Why Do We Describe?

Description is a means of showing rather than telling. We describe something—a person, a lake, a memory, a chemical reaction—so that the reader can experience it directly as we do. Description makes anything we write less ABSTRACT, or general, and more CONCRETE, referring to specific things we can see, feel, smell, hear, or taste. White, for example, could tell us that time seemed to stand still on the lake, but he makes that abstract idea much easier to grasp by showing us specific details—the green boat, the waves, and the dragonfly hovering (like time) at the end of his fishing rod.

Composing a Description

Your reader will find almost anything you write easier to comprehend if you describe your subject in vivid detail. However, in a personal essay about your grandmother's cooking, you will probably describe things differently than in a lab report on dissecting a shark.

There are basically two ways of describing something—objectively or subjectively. An OBJECTIVE description presents its subject impartially. Its purpose is to provide the reader with information, as in this description of a watershed in southern Alaska:

Duck Creek is a small anadromous [running upriver from the sea] fish stream located in an old outwash channel of the Mendenhall Glacier in the center of the most populated residential area of Alaska's capital, Juneau. Duck Creek supports a large over-wintering population of coho salmon juveniles that migrate into the stream each fall from the estuarine wetlands.

—Environmental Protection Agency,
"Make Way for Salmon in Duck Creek"

The EPA's description is objective not only because it uses precise scientific terms ("anadromous," "estuarine") but because it is made up entirely of factual information about its subject—the size and age of the creek, where it is located, the type of fish that inhabit it, and so on.

A SUBJECTIVE description provides information, too. But it also conveys the writer's personal response to the subject being described, as in this description from an article about a visit to the 2008 Iowa State Fair:

And then I wound up at an open-air brick pavilion for the llama judging. Llamas are gentle, dignified beasts, and here were four of them being shown by teenagers. The animal's military bearing, heads high, their stately gait, their dark soulful eyes—they looked as if they'd walked straight out of *Dr. Doolittle*. . . . According to a poster, they are raised for "fiber, showing, carting, gaurdians and companionship." One girl stood by her llama and blew gently on its nose, and he looked lovingly into her eyes. A sort of conversation. If every teenager had his or her own llama, this would be a very different country.   —Garrison Keillor, "A Sunday at the State Fair"

This is a subjective description: the author feels or imagines that the llamas are dignified and loving—and that one of them is having a "conversation" with his keeper.

However, many of the other details in Keillor's description—including the physical location, the number of llamas on display, who the exhibitors are, and the exact words of the poster explaining what llamas are raised for—are rendered objectively. Most descriptions include a combination of subjective and objective elements as here. And even the most subjective description should be grounded in the concrete physical features of the person, place, or thing it describes—which is why White's description of the lake is so effective.

Not all subjective descriptions are so successful, however. Consider the following passage, which refers to the same lake described by E. B. White. According to the region's official website, the area around that lake is "famous for its sparkling scenic streams and chain of seven lakes, its panoramic views of fields, hills and woodlands, its inviting towns and villages."

Sparkling streams, panoramic views. Sounds like a nice place. The same could be said, however, of a large car wash with a picture window in the waiting room. This subjective description offers no definite impression of the lakes because it merely names abstract qualities. So does the rest of the site, which says that the region is "picturesque and welcoming," providing "a retreat for peace and tranquility."

Picturesqueness and tranquility are difficult to smell or taste. The problem with this tourist-brochure prose is that it tells the reader what to think *about* the place; it doesn't capture the place itself. The fundamental purpose of descriptive writing, whether subjective or objective, is to recreate the characteristics of its subject so vividly that readers perceive it with their own eyes and ears—and mind.

Good descriptive writing is built on concrete particulars rather than abstract qualities. So don't just write, "It was a dark and stormy night"; try to make your reader see, hear, and feel the wind and rain.

Thinking about Purpose and Audience

Your purpose in describing something—whether to picture your subject as objectively as possible, capture it in a certain light or mood, express your feelings about it, persuade the reader to visit (or avoid) it, or merely to amuse the reader—will determine the details you'll want to include in your description. For example, the official Belgrade Lakes website describes family vacations; and like E. B. White, it dwells on the beauty, peace, and tranquility of the place, as well as the fishing and boating. Its slogan—"Where Memories Last a Lifetime"—might almost have been drawn from White's essay. The website, however, aims to persuade the general public to visit the area and thus emphasizes "wholesome family fun" and "activities for all ages"—and leaves out the storm clouds that gather in White's essay.

Suppose you were describing Belgrade Lakes to friends who were thinking of going there and wanted information about the area. You might express your feelings toward the region, but your main purpose would be to inform your friends about it—as objectively as possible—so they could decide for themselves whether or not to go. You would talk about the peace and quiet, of course; but you would also include other aspects of the scene, such as the pebble beaches, touristy shops, and local restaurants—not to mention the night crawlers at the Pickled Trout Saloon. Instead of selecting details that presented only one aspect of the place, you would choose representative details that painted a fair and accurate picture of what it was like.

Whatever your purpose, you need to take into account how much your audience already knows (or does not know) about the subject you are describing. For example, if you want to describe to someone who has never been on your campus the mad rush that takes place there when classes change, you're going to have to fill in the background for them: the main quadrangle with its sun worshipers in bathing suits, the brick-and-stone classroom buildings on either side, the library looming at one end. On the other hand, if you were to describe this same scene to fellow students who already know the territory well, you could skip the background description and go directly to the mob scene.

Generating Ideas:
Asking How Something Looks, Sounds, Feels, Smells, and Tastes

Good descriptive writing begins and ends with the concrete physical characteristics of whatever you are describing. To gather those details, you need to ask what your subject looks, sounds, feels, smells, or tastes like. Methods like BRAINSTORMING and LISTING can help you probe for ideas as you run through each of the five senses.

One resource for answering these questions is direct experience and observation. Even if you are describing a familiar subject—a lake you've often visited, your old neighborhood, a person from your hometown—go back to the source. Try to see your subject objectively as well as subjectively; take notes—much like a reporter on assignment, or a traveler in a strange land.

One of your richest sources of ideas for a description, especially if you are describing something from the past, is memory. Ask others—friends, parents—to help you remember things accurately and truthfully. Tap your senses. Let's assume you're describing your hometown. Pick a spot, maybe the main shopping street or town square. Ask yourself what it looked like, and in your mind's eye, try to see specific details—colors, landmarks, signs on the buildings. Then try to recall sounds, smells, textures—and what you did there. As sensations stand out in your memory, let them dominate your description. This example recalls a town in Kentucky:

> Food was better in town, we thought. It wasn't plain and everyday. The centers of pleasure were there—the hamburger and barbecue places, the movie shows, all the places to buy things. Woolworth's, with the pneumatic tubes overhead rushing money along a metallic mole tunnel up to a balcony; Lochridge & Ridgway, with an engraved sign on the third-story cornice: STOVES, APPLIANCES, PLOWS . . . A circuit of the courthouse took you past the grand furniture stores, the two dime stores, the shoe stores, the men's stores, the ladies' stores, the banks, the drugstores. You'd walk past the poolroom and an exhaust fan would blow the intoxicating smell of hamburgers in your face.   —Bobbie Ann Mason, "Being Country"

What makes this description so vivid is the specific details—the pneumatic tubes in Woolworth's, the engraved words on the appliance store.

How did the writer generate such details? As she searched her memory, we can imagine Mason asking herself, "What *did* the place look like exactly? What did it sound like? What did it smell and taste like?" Many writers find that tastes and smells are particularly evocative. In fact, it is the "intoxicating" smell of hamburgers from the poolroom that provides the highpoint of Mason's description—and that may have brought the place to life for her as she searched her memory for ideas.

The pond of memory is a rich reservoir of sensations for the writer of description. The process of recovering its treasures is a little like fishing: think back to the spots you knew well; bait the hook by asking the key questions; weigh and measure everything you pull up. As you revise, you can always throw back the ones you can't use. Just the right details for capturing your subject on paper *are* lurking there, often in plain sight—or just below the surface. Your job as a writer is to bring those details to light, with the life still in them.

Organizing and Drafting a Description

Once you've gathered the specific details that capture your subject, you're ready to begin organizing and drafting. As you write, let those details speak for themselves—give enough of them so that readers can picture your subject clearly. Be careful to arrange the details so that they make a dominant impression on your readers, and to maintain a consistent vantage point. Finally, make sure readers know the point of your description. The tips on p. 115 can help you get started with your draft.

STATING YOUR POINT

Description is seldom an end in itself. Ordinarily, we describe something to someone for a reason. Why are you describing a particular fishing trip, or a woman hanging out laundry, or bloody footprints in the snow? You need to let the reader know. It can be by way of an explicit THESIS STATEMENT: "This description of Washington's ragged army at Yorktown shows that the American general faced many of the same challenges as Napoleon in the winter battle for Moscow, but Washington turned them to advantage."

Or your reasons can be stated more informally. Consider the following description of the streets of Havana, Cuba:

> Everywhere I went, there were men and women waiting in lines. There were lines to get water, lines to have cheap cigarette lighters repaired, lines to get into the city's lone merchandise store in Miramar where a simple sledgehammer cost fifty-six dollars. At the nationalized health care clinics, the lines wrapped away for blocks; the somber aged, the ill, the expectant young mothers, all waiting, patiently enduring.
>
> —RANDY WAYNE WHITE, *Last Flight Out*

The point of this description is to show that everyday life is difficult in a Communist system where everything is centrally controlled, including simple consumer goods and services. Randy Wayne White is writing a descriptive travel essay, however, not a political treatise. So he states his point informally, as a personal observation: "A few weeks of living like that, and I myself—not the bravest of men—would consider worming into an inner tube and paddling north."

You don't always have to make a formal statement of your thesis—"Communism failed as a social system because it failed as an economic system"—when you write a description. But you *should* include a clear statement, however informal, of why you're writing the description.

BEGINNING WITH DETAILS

One way *not* to begin a description is to leap immediately into a general statement of the impression your subject is supposed to make. Instead, you should begin with descriptive details, and let your readers form that impression for themselves. The following statement, for example, would not be the best way to begin a description of the Grand Canyon: "As the abyss yawned at my feet, I was swept away by the beauty and majesty of the scene."

Few writers have taught us this lesson better than Ernest Hemingway, whose stories and newspaper correspondence are full of powerful descriptions that show us a place or object long before telling us what to think of it. Here's Hemingway's rendition of a father and son fishing on a lake early in the morning:

> They were seated in the boat, Nick in the stern, his father rowing. The sun was coming up over the hills. A bass jumped, making a circle in the water. Nick trailed his hand in the water. It felt warm in the sharp chill of the morning.   —ERNEST HEMINGWAY, "Indian Camp"

The boy in the story, Nick Adams, has just witnessed a grisly suicide. As Nick and his father row home, the boy is soothed by the morning sun, the leaping bass, and the warm water. Nature seems kind, and the story ends with a direct statement of what the boy thinks about the scene: "In the early morning on the lake sitting in the stern of the boat with his father rowing, he felt quite sure that he would never die."

The purpose of Hemingway's description is to show us the boy's naïveté. However, Hemingway does not deliver the punch line—the boy's stated feeling about the scene—until he has given us the physical details on which that feeling is based. You could organize an entire descriptive essay on this model: detail (early morning), detail (lake), detail (boat), detail (boy sitting in the stern), detail (father rowing)—DOMINANT IMPRESSION (boy feeling "quite sure he would never die").

TIPS AND TEMPLATES FOR DRAFTING

When you begin to draft a description, you need to identify who or what you're describing, say what your subject looks or feels like, and indicate the traits you plan to focus on. These moves are fundamental to any description. See how Judith Ortiz Cofer makes such moves in the beginning of her essay in this chapter:

> My grandmother's house is like a chambered nautilus; it has many rooms, yet is not a mansion. Its proportions are small and its design simple.   —JUDITH ORTIZ COFER, "More Room"

Ortiz Cofer identifies what she's describing ("my grandmother's house"); says something about what her subject looks like ("a chambered nautilus"); and indicates some of the physical characteristics (the proportions and design of the house) that she plans to discuss. Here is one more example from this chapter:

> Dead Man's Hole is a large green mineral pool gouged out of a circular limestone cliff, so deep into the hill country of Texas that it's hardly got an address.   —LANCE ARMSTRONG and SALLY JENKINS, "Pitched Back"

The following templates can help you make some of these basic moves in your own writing. But don't take these as formulas where you just have to fill in the blanks. There are no easy formulas for good writing, but these templates can serve as starting points.

▶ *X* is like a _____; it has _____, _____, and _____.

▶ He / she looked a lot like _____, except for _____, which _____.

▶ From the perspective of _____, however, *X* could be described as _____.

▶ In some ways, namely _____, *X* resembles _____; but in other ways, *X* is more like _____.

▶ *X* is not at all like _____ because _____.

▶ Mainly because of _____ and _____, *X* gives the impression of being _____.

▶ From this description of *X*, you can see that _____.

CREATING A DOMINANT IMPRESSION

Some descriptions, such as Hemingway's, appeal to several different senses—the sight of the rising sun, the sound of the jumping bass, the touch of the warm water in the chilled air. Don't feel that you have to give equal attention to all five senses when you write a description; but whether you appeal to a single sense or several, make sure they all contribute to the dominant impression you want your description to make upon the reader.

The dominant impression conveyed by Hemingway's description of fishing on the lake, for example, is that of peace and calm—the soothing tranquility of nature. Now, suppose you were to describe a similar morning scene on a freshwater lake in a rowboat. But instead of bass and sunrise, you call the reader's attention to an ominous dark cloud in the distance, drawing nearer. The wind rises. The reader hears a nasty grating sound as the little boat scrapes over a sunken log in the fast-flowing current. Instead of gently chucking the boat under the chin, the waves, now grown to white caps, flip it over with a crash, throwing you into the icy water. Nature, the reader concludes as you disappear beneath the surface, is not kind. The reader is left with the dominant impression of danger because you have chosen to build your description on particular details (mostly sounds) that contribute to a sense of danger and foreboding.

ARRANGING THE DETAILS

While the events in a NARRATIVE are usually organized chronologically, the physical elements of a description are often organized according to their location.

So as you begin to get your description down on paper, the physical configuration of whatever you're describing will often suggest a pattern of organization to you. Bobbie Ann Mason's description on p. 112 of the sights and smells of her hometown in Kentucky, for example, follows the "circuit" of the courthouse square. In Mason's description, we get the furniture stores, then the dime stores, then the men's and ladies' stores and the banks, and, finally, the poolroom, because that is the order in which young Mason would have seen them all, starting where she did and walking around the main square of the town.

Descriptions of places are often organized, like Mason's, by physical direction— around the block, north to south, front to back, left to right, inside to outside, near to far, top to bottom. If you were describing a room, for example, you might use an outside-to-inside order, starting with the door (don't forget the knob and other details). Next you could present the main physical features of the room as they might appear to someone just crossing the threshold (oak floors, high ceilings, ancient fireplace). Then would come the grand piano, the candle on a stand, the old lady mending a tapestry—just as these objects might appear to a person entering the room and adjusting his or her eyes to the light.

An object can suggest an order of arrangement as well as a place can. If you were describing a large fish, for instance, you might let the anatomy of the fish guide your description. Notice how the details are ordered in the following description of a tarpon, which was written to describe the fish to a blind boy who has just caught it.

> He's mostly silver, but the silver is somehow made up of *all* the colors. . . . He has all these big scales, like armor all over his body. They're silver, too, and when he moves they sparkle. He has a strong body and a large powerful tail. He has big round eyes, bigger than a quarter, and a lower jaw that sticks out past the upper one and is very tough. His belly is almost white and his back is a gunmetal gray. When he jumped he came out of the water about six feet, and his scales caught the sun and flashed it all over the place.
> —CHEROKEE PAUL MCDONALD, "A View from the Bridge"

McDonald's description begins and ends with the colors of the fish, its most noticeable feature (to a sighted person) in the glinting sun. Most of his description, however, is organized according to the parts of the subject itself, moving from the body of the tarpon as a whole to the tail, eyes, belly, and back. From whole to parts, or parts to whole: you can go either way when constructing a description. Or you can describe the most important or unusual features of your subject first, then the least important or most familiar ones (or vice versa). Or you can go from the largest to smallest, or from specific to general, or from concrete to abstract—or vice versa—so long as you maintain a consistent vantage point.

MAINTAINING A VANTAGE POINT

In McDonald's essay, as the title suggests, the vantage point is from the bridge. Here's the beginning of the essay, before the boy catches the tarpon:

> I was coming up on the little bridge in the Rio Vista neighborhood of Fort Lauderdale, deeping my stride and breathing to negotiate the slight incline without altering my pace. And then, as I neared the crest, I saw the kid.
>
> He was a lumpy little guy with baggy shorts, a faded T-shirt and heavy sweat socks falling down over old sneakers.
>
> Partially covering his shaggy blond hair was one of those blue baseball caps with gold braid on the bill and a sailfish patch sewn onto the peak. Covering his eyes and part of his face was a pair of those stupid-looking '50's-style wrap-around sunglasses.

Like his description of the tarpon, McDonald's description of the boy moves from the whole (lumpy little guy in shorts and T-shirt) to the parts (hair, cap, patch, eyes, face, glasses). It also presents those details in the order in which the observer perceives them from his vantage point. That is, the reader of McDonald's essay sees only what the writer sees as he comes over the bridge. For example, at this point in his description, the writer does not yet know why the boy is wearing "stupid-looking" sunglasses. As you compose a description, be careful to maintain a consistent vantage point, as McDonald does.

USING FIGURATIVE LANGUAGE

Because descriptive writing presents the reader with images of the physical world, it lends itself to the use of figurative language. The three figures of speech you are most likely to use in composing a description are similes, metaphors, and personification.

Similes tell the reader what something looks, sounds, or feels like, using *like* or *as*:

> She was like a pretty kite that floated above my head.   —Maya Angelou

> Suspicion climbed all over her face like a kitten, but not so playfully.
> —Raymond Chandler

> Two policemen . . . were leaning into a third woman as if she were a stalled car.
> —T. C. Boyle, *Talk, Talk*

Metaphors make implicit comparisons, without *like* or *as*:

> All the world's a stage.

> You are my sunshine.

> Papa was a rolling stone.

Metaphors have two parts: the subject of the description (world, you, Papa); and the thing (stage, sunshine, rolling stone) to which that subject is being implicitly compared.

Personification assigns human qualities to inanimate objects, as in this poetic description of a mirror:

> *I am silver and exact.*
> *I have no preconceptions.*
> *Whatever I see I swallow immediately*
> *Just as it is, unmisted by love or dislike.*
> —Sylvia Plath, "Mirror"

USING OTHER METHODS

When you describe something, you will often have reason to use other methods as well—to DEFINE it, ANALYZE what CAUSED it, and so on. Especially if you are describing something that is unfamiliar to the reader—such as this description of a cemetery in rural El Salvador—consider COMPARING it with something the reader already knows about:

> Plunged like daggers to the ground are the crosses, mainly a fabulous aqua color, though some are bleached white and some are unpainted. . . . It looks like the aftermath of a piñata party, with crepe-paper chains strewn like leis about the necks of the gravestone markers, plastic red roses wreathed at the feet, errant scraps of yellow paper and transparent cellophane trapped between the blades of grass. —BETH KEPHART, *Still Love in Strange Places*

"Daggers" imply violence, of course; but the cemetery in this colorful description is far from somber. The dominant impression is a sense of festive disorder, as Kephart compares this strange scene to a more familiar one in which children have just left after hammering a piñata to release the candy and toys inside.

Reading a Description with a Critical Eye

Once you have drafted a description, try it out on someone else to get a sense of what's working and what needs revision. Then read it over yourself with a critical eye. The following questions will help you and any reader think about the key elements of descriptive writing.

PURPOSE AND AUDIENCE. Who is the intended audience, and why will they be reading this description? Does it tell them everything they will need to know, or will they need more background information?

SPECIFIC DETAILS. Are there enough details to give the reader a vivid impression of the subject? To which senses in particular does the description appeal—Sight? Sound? Smell? Touch? Taste?

DOMINANT IMPRESSION. What dominant impression does the description give? Does every detail contribute directly to that impression? What additional details would make the dominant impression clearer or stronger? Do any details detract from that impression?

THE POINT. Does the description have a clear point? Is the point stated in a thesis statement? If not, should it be?

ORGANIZATION. How are the details of the description presented—by moving from part to whole? Whole to part? North to south? Most important to least important? Some other way?

OBJECTIVE OR SUBJECTIVE? Are the details of the description presented objectively, subjectively, or both? Is the degree of objectivity appropriate for the overall purpose and audience of the description? If not, how can it be made more inform-ative and less emotional (or vice versa)?

VANTAGE POINT. From what perspective are the various aspects of the subject described? Near and intimate? Far and detached? Somewhere in between? Is that perspective maintained consistently throughout the description?

FIGURATIVE LANGUAGE. What figures of speech, such as metaphors, similes, or personification, does the description use? Are they appropriate for this purpose and audience?

OTHER METHODS. Has the description been expanded to include other methods of development—for example, by analyzing what caused something, or by comparing its attributes to those of other things with which the reader may already be familiar?

Editing for Common Errors in Descriptive Writing

Certain kinds of errors are typical of descriptive writing. The following guidelines will help you check over your description for these common problems—and make the necessary corrections.

Check your details to see if you can make them more concrete.

ABSTRACT Great Pond is so amazing and incredible that floating on it in a boat seems like floating on air.

CONCRETE Great Pond is so clear and deep that floating on it in a boat seems like floating on air.

Amazing and *incredible* are abstract terms; *clear* and *deep* describe the water in more concrete terms.

ABSTRACT The Belgrade region is famous for its charming views.

CONCRETE The Belgrade region is famous for its panoramic views of fields, hills, and woodlands.

The second sentence says more precisely what makes the views charming.

Check for filler words like *very, quite, really,* and *truly.*

VAGUE The lake was very secluded.

SPECIFIC The lake was fifteen miles from the nearest village.

If you've used several adjectives together, be sure they are in the right order.

Subjective adjectives (those that reflect the writer's own opinion) go before objective adjectives (those that are strictly factual): write "fabulous four-door Chevrolet" rather than "four-door fabulous Chevrolet." Beyond that, adjectives usually go in the following order: number, size, shape, age, color, nationality.

NOT The streets of Havana were lined with many old big American cars.

BUT The streets of Havana were lined with many big old American cars.

Check for common usage errors.

UNIQUE, PERFECT

Don't use *more* or *most*, *less* or *least*, or *very* before words like *unique*, *equal*, *perfect*, or *infinite*. Either something is unique or it isn't. Write that your holiday was "perfect," not that it was "very perfect."

AWESOME, COOL

Not only are these modifiers too abstract, they're overused. You probably should delete them or replace them with fresher words no matter how grand the scene you're describing. Instead of writing that the river was "awesome," call it "majestic"—or be more specific: "The Mississippi is the second longest river in the United States."

A Nike Sneaker

When you describe something, such as a pair of classic Nike sneakers, you tell what qualities distinguish it from other, similar objects. First released in 1984, the original Nike "Vandals," for example, had uppers "made of thick canvas" rather than leather, the material of more mundane sneakers of the day. All editions were designed as basketball shoes. The more expensive Vandal "Supremes," however, could be further distinguished from the basic model by uppers composed of nylon. They also "came with two different colored sets of laces and a Velcro ankle support strap (with a three-way color scheme)." These last physical details, in particular, contribute to the DOMINANT IMPRESSION that the writer of this description wanted to leave with the audience, those who collect sneakers: that the classic Vandal was "one of the first fashionable basketball shoes" and has never been surpassed for style and quality.

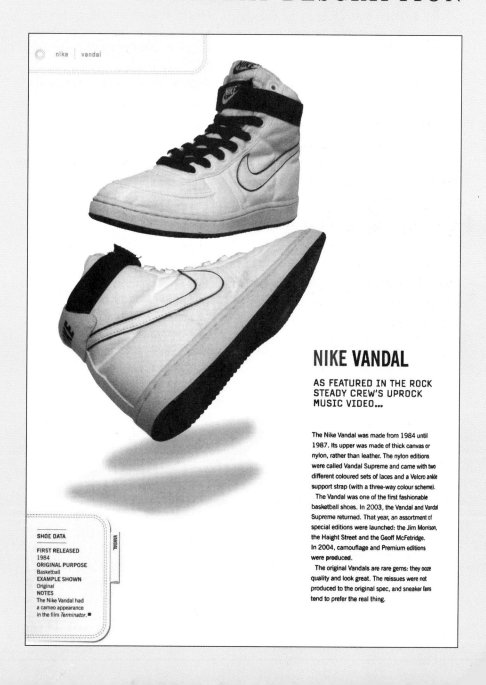

nike | vandal

NIKE **VANDAL**

AS FEATURED IN THE ROCK STEADY CREW'S UPROCK MUSIC VIDEO...

The Nike Vandal was made from 1984 until 1987. Its upper was made of thick canvas or nylon, rather than leather. The nylon editions were called Vandal Supreme and came with two different coloured sets of laces and a Velcro ankle support strap (with a three-way colour scheme).

The Vandal was one of the first fashionable basketball shoes. In 2003, the Vandal and Vandal Supreme returned. That year, an assortment of special editions were launched: the Jim Morrison, the Haight Street and the Geoff McFetridge. In 2004, camouflage and Premium editions were produced.

The original Vandals are rare gems: they ooze quality and look great. The reissues were not produced to the original spec, and sneaker fans tend to prefer the real thing.

SHOE DATA

FIRST RELEASED
1984
ORIGINAL PURPOSE
Basketball
EXAMPLE SHOWN
Original
NOTES
The Nike Vandal had a cameo appearance in the film *Terminator*. ■

VANDAL

More Room

Judith Ortiz Cofer (b. 1952) is a native of Puerto Rico but moved to Paterson, New Jersey, as a small child. Though Ortiz Cofer grew up and went to school on the "mainland," she often returned for extended visits to her grandmother's home in Puerto Rico, the "casa de Mamá" described in "More Room." This bicultural experience is the basis of much of Ortiz Cofer's writing, including her novel The Meaning of Consuelo *(2003), which won the Americas Award, and* The Latin Deli *(1993). A poet as well as a novelist, Ortiz Cofer teaches creative writing at the University of Georgia, where she is Franklin Professor of English.*

"More Room" is from Silent Dancing *(1990), a memoir of Ortiz Cofer's childhood in Puerto Rico and New Jersey. In this description, Ortiz Cofer shows how a few remembered details can bring back an entire scene and the people in it.*

M Y GRANDMOTHER'S HOUSE is like a chambered nautilus; it has many rooms, yet it is not a mansion. Its proportions are small and its design simple. It is a house that has grown organically, according to the needs of its inhabitants. To all of us in the family it is known as *la casa de Mamá*. It is the place of our origin; the stage for our memories and dreams of Island life.

I remember how in my childhood it sat on stilts; this was before it had a downstairs. It rested on its perch like a great blue bird, not a flying sort of bird, more like a nesting hen, but with spread wings. Grandfather had built it soon after their marriage. He was a painter and housebuilder by trade, a poet and meditative man by nature. As each of their eight children were born, new rooms were added. After a few years, the paint did not exactly match, nor the materials, so that there was a chronology to it, like the rings of a tree, and Mamá could tell you the history of each room in her *casa*, and thus the genealogy of the family along with it.

Her room is the heart of the house. Though I have seen it recently, and both woman and room have diminished in size, changed by the new perspective of my eyes, now capable of looking over countertops and tall beds, it is not this picture I carry in my memory of Mamá's *casa*. Instead, I see her room as a queen's chamber where a small woman loomed large, a throne-room with a massive four-poster bed in its center which stood taller than a child's head. It was on this bed where her own children had been born that the smallest grandchildren were allowed to take naps in the afternoons; here too was where Mamá secluded herself to dispense private advice to her daughters, sitting on the edge of the bed, looking down at whoever sat on the rocker where generations of babies had been sung to sleep. To me she looked like a wise empress right out of the fairy tales I was addicted to reading.

Though the room was dominated by the mahogany four-poster, it also contained   4 all of Mamá's symbols of power. On her dresser instead of cosmetics there were jars filled with herbs: *yerba buena, yerba mala*,[1] the making of purgatives and teas to which we were all subjected during childhood crises. She had a steaming cup for anyone who could not, or would not, get up to face life on any given day. If the acrid aftertaste of her cures for malingering did not get you out of bed, then it was time to call *el doctor*.

And there was the monstrous chifforobe she kept locked with a little golden key   5 she did not hide. This was a test of her dominion over us; though my cousins and I wanted a look inside that massive wardrobe more than anything, we never reached for that little key lying on top of her Bible on the dresser. This was also where she placed her earrings and rosary at night. God's word was her security system. This chifforobe was the place where I imagined she kept jewels, satin slippers, and elegant sequined, silk gowns of heartbreaking fineness. I lusted after those imaginary costumes. I had heard that Mamá had been a great beauty in her youth, and the belle of many balls. My cousins had other ideas as to what she kept in that wooden vault: its secret could be money (Mamá did not hand cash to strangers, banks were out of the question, so there were stories that her mattress was stuffed with dollar bills, and that she buried coins in jars in her garden under rosebushes, or kept them in her inviolate chifforobe); there might be that legendary gun salvaged from the Spanish-American conflict over the Island. We went wild over suspected treasures that we made up simply because children have to fill locked trunks with something wonderful.

On the wall above the bed hung a heavy silver crucifix. Christ's agonized head   6 hung directly over Mamá's pillow. I avoided looking at this weapon suspended over where her head would lay; and on the rare occasions when I was allowed to sleep on that bed, I scooted down to the safe middle of the mattress, where her body's impression took me in like a mother's lap. Having taken care of the obligatory religious decoration with a crucifix, Mamá covered the other walls with objects sent to her over the years by her children in the States. *Los Nueva Yores*[2] were represented by, among other things, a postcard of Niagara Falls from her son Hernán, postmarked, Buffalo, N.Y. In a conspicuous gold frame hung a large color photograph of her daughter Nena, her husband and their five children at the entrance to Disneyland in California. From us she had gotten a black lace fan. Father had brought it to her from a tour of duty with the Navy in Europe (on Sundays she would remove it

---

1. *Yerba buena, yerba mala*: good herb, bad herb.
2. *Los Nuevas Yores*: the New Yorkers.

from its hook on the wall to fan herself at mass). Each year more items were added as the family grew and dispersed, and every object in the room had a story attached to it, a *cuento* which Mamá would bestow on anyone who received the privilege of a day alone with her. It was almost worth pretending to be sick, though the bitter herb purgatives of the body were a big price to pay for the spirit revivals of her story-telling.

Mamá slept alone on her large bed, except for the times when a sick grandchild   7 warranted the privilege, or when a heartbroken daughter came home in need of more than herbal teas. In the family there is a story about how this came to be.

When one of the daughters, my mother or one of her sisters, tells the *cuento* of   8 how Mamá came to own her nights, it is usually preceded by the qualifications that Papá's exile from his wife's room was not a result of animosity between the couple, but that the act had been Mamá's famous bloodless coup for her personal freedom. Papá was the benevolent dictator of her body and her life who had had to be banished from her bed so that Mamá could better serve her family. Before the telling, we had to agree that the old man was not to blame. We all recognized that in the family Papá was as an *alma de Dios*, a saintly, soft-spoken presence whose main pleasures in life, such as writing poetry and reading the Spanish large-type editions of *Reader's Digest*, always took place outside the vortex of Mamá's crowded realm. It was not his fault, after all, that every year or so he planted a baby-seed in Mamá's fertile body, keeping her from leading the active life she needed and desired. He loved her and the babies. Papá composed odes and lyrics to celebrate births and anniversaries and hired musicians to accompany him in singing them to his family and friends at extravagant pig-roasts he threw yearly. Mamá and the oldest girls worked for days preparing the food. Papá sat for hours in his painter's shed, also his study and library, composing the songs. At these celebrations he was also known to give long speeches in praise of God, his fecund wife, and his beloved island. As a middle child, my mother remembers these occasions as a time when the women sat in the kitchen and lamented their burdens, while the men feasted out in the patio, their rum-thickened voices rising in song and praise for each other, *compañeros* all.

It was after the birth of her eighth child, after she had lost three at birth or in   9 infancy, that Mamá made her decision. They say that Mamá had had a special way of letting her husband know that they were expecting, one that had begun when, at the beginning of their marriage, he had built her a house too confining for her taste. So, when she discovered her first pregnancy, she supposedly drew plans for another room, which he dutifully executed. Every time a child was due, she would demand, *more space, more space*. Papá acceded to her wishes, child after child, since he had learned early that Mamá's renowned temper was a thing that grew like a monster along with a new belly. In this way Mamá got the house that she wanted, but with each child she lost in heart and energy. She had knowledge of her body and perceived that if she had any more children, her dreams and her plans would have to be permanently forgotten, because she would be a chronically ill woman, like Flora with her twelve children: asthma, no teeth, in bed more than on her feet.

And so, after my youngest uncle was born, she asked Papá to build a large room 10 at the back of the house. He did so in joyful anticipation. Mamá had asked him special things this time: shelves on the walls, a private entrance. He thought that she meant this room to be a nursery where several children could sleep. He thought it was a wonderful idea. He painted it his favorite color, sky blue, and made large windows looking out over a green hill and the church spires beyond. But nothing happened. Mamá's belly did not grow, yet she seemed in a frenzy of activity over the house. Finally, an anxious Papá approached his wife to tell her that the new room was finished and ready to be occupied. And Mamá, they say, replied: "Good, it's for you."

And so it was that Mamá discovered the only means of birth control available to 11 a Catholic woman of her time: sacrifice. She gave up the comfort of Papá's sexual love for something she deemed greater: the right to own and control her body, so that she might live to meet her grandchildren—me among them—so that she could give more of herself to the ones already there, so that she could be more than a channel for other lives, so that even now that time has robbed her of the elasticity of her body and of her amazing reservoir of energy, she still emanates the kind of joy that can only be achieved by living according to the dictates of one's own heart.

READING CLOSELY

1. Mamá's house in Puerto Rico was originally built on stilts to avoid high water, but the lower level got filled in when the family needed more room. How are these old additions different from the new room with shelves and a private entrance?

2. Mamá exercises "dominion" over all her house and family (5). Her grandchildren ascribe her power to the exotic items in her room, but what is the true source of her power?

3. If Mamá is the "queen" of the house and household that Ortiz Cofer DESCRIBES, what are some of Papá's other roles (besides that of prince consort) (3)?

4. When Papá is preparing birthday odes and patriotic hymns to be sung at annual feasts, what are the women in the family doing? Why? What is Ortiz Cofer suggesting about the culture she is describing?

5. Why does Mamá need more room? What point is Ortiz Cofer making about women and families by describing her grandmother's home?

Strategies and Structures

1. Ortiz Cofer describes the outside of her grandmother's house before moving to the inside. What specific details does she focus upon?

2. Once she moves inside the house, which room does Ortiz Cofer single out? Why? What does it contribute to her description of Mamá?

3. Ortiz Cofer is not so much describing her grandmother's house as it is today as the house as it exists in her memory. How is this "picture" different from present-day reality (3)? How does she capture the place from the viewpoint of a child?

4. Mamá's house is full of her "symbols of power" (4). What DOMINANT IMPRESSION of the place and of her do they help convey to the reader?

5. *Other Methods.* In addition to describing her grandmother's house and its contents, "More Room" tells the story of a "bloodless coup" (8). What coup? How does this NARRATIVE relate to Ortiz Cofer's description of the house?

Thinking about Language

1. "Build three more stately mansions, O my soul. / As the swift seasons roll!" So begins the final stanza of "The Chambered Nautilus" (1858) by Oliver Wendell Holmes. How does Ortiz Cofer make use of this ALLUSION?

2. *Cuento* (6, 8) is the Spanish word for story. Why does Ortiz Cofer mention the telling of stories in her description?

3. Mamá's room, says Ortiz Cofer, is the "heart" of the house (3). What are the implications of this METAPHOR?

For Writing

1. Write a paragraph or two in which you COMPARE the present-day aspects of a house, room, or other place with those of the place as you picture it in memory.

2. Write a description of a house or other place that captures the tension (or harmony) among its inhabitants by describing the physical features of the place.

ZORA NEALE HURSTON

How It Feels to Be Colored Me

Zora Neale Hurston (1891–1960) was a novelist and folklorist who was born in Alabama but lived most of her life in Florida. After studying anthropology at Barnard College and Columbia University, she collected folklore in the South, particularly Florida, and in Jamaica, Haiti, Bermuda, and Honduras. In the 1950s, she worked as a maid, freelance writer, librarian, newspaper writer, and teacher. Late in life, she was a librarian for the Library of Congress and a professor of drama at North Carolina College. She is best known for her novel Their Eyes Were Watching God *(1937).*

"How It Feels to Be Colored Me" was first published in The World Tomorrow, *a Christian socialist magazine, in 1928, the year Hurston graduated from Barnard. It opens with a description of Hurston's childhood experience in the all-black community of Eatonville, Florida. When Hurston was thirteen, her mother died, and she was obliged to leave Eatonville for Jacksonville, Florida. "How It Feels to Be Colored Me" describes the difference Hurston feels between being black in an all-black community and being black "against a sharp white background."*

I AM COLORED but I offer nothing in the way of extenuating circumstances except the fact that I am the only Negro in the United States whose grandfather on the mother's side was *not* an Indian chief.

I remember the very day that I became colored. Up to my thirteenth year I lived in the little Negro town of Eatonville, Florida. It is exclusively a colored town. The only white people I knew passed through the town going to or coming from Orlando. The native whites rode dusty horses, the Northern tourists chugged down the sandy village road in automobiles. The town knew the Southerners and never stopped cane chewing when they passed.[1] But the Northerners were something else again. They were peered at cautiously from behind curtains by the timid. The more venturesome would come out on the porch to watch them go past and got just as much pleasure out of the tourists as the tourists got out of the village.

The front porch might seem a daring place for the rest of the town, but it was a gallery seat for me. My favorite place was atop the gate-post. Proscenium box[2] for a born first-nighter. Not only did I enjoy the show, but I didn't mind the actors knowing that I liked it. I usually spoke to them in passing. I'd wave at them and when they returned my salute, I would say something like this: "Howdy-do-well-I-thank-

---

1. *Cane:* sugar cane.
2. *Proscenium box:* theater seats that are next to and above the stage.

you-where-you-goin' ?" Usually automobile or the horse paused at this, and after a queer exchange of compliments, I would probably "go a piece of the way" with them, as we say in farthest Florida. If one of my family happened to come to the front in time to see me, of course negotiations would be rudely broken off. But even so, it is clear that I was the first "welcome-to-our-state" Floridian, and I hope the Miami Chamber of Commerce will please take notice.

During this period, white people differed from colored to me only in that they 4 rode through town and never lived there. They liked to hear me "speak pieces" and sing and wanted to see me dance the parse-me-la,[3] and gave me generously of their small silver for doing these things, which seemed strange to me for I wanted to do them so much that I needed bribing to stop. Only they didn't know it. The colored people gave no dimes. They deplored any joyful tendencies in me, but I was their Zora nevertheless. I belonged to them, to the nearby hotels, to the county—everybody's Zora.

But changes came in the family when I was thirteen, and I was sent to school in 5 Jacksonville. I left Eatonville, the town of the oleanders, as Zora. When I disembarked from the river-boat at Jacksonville, she was no more. It seemed that I had suffered a sea change. I was not Zora of Orange County any more, I was now a little colored girl. I found it out in certain ways. In my heart as well as in the mirror, I became a fast brown—warranted not to rub nor run.

But I am not tragically colored. There is no great sorrow dammed up in my soul, 6 nor lurking behind my eyes. I do not mind at all. I do not belong to the sobbing school of Negrohood who hold that nature somehow has given them a lowdown dirty deal and whose feelings are all hurt about it. Even in the helter-skelter skirmish that is my life, I have seen that the world is to the strong regardless of a little pigmentation more or less. No, I do not weep at the world—I am too busy sharpening my oyster knife.

Someone is always at my elbow reminding me that I am the granddaughter of 7 slaves. It fails to register depression with me. Slavery is sixty years in the past. The operation was successful and the patient is doing well, thank you. The terrible struggle that made me an American out of a potential slave said "On the line!" The Reconstruction said "Get set!"; and the generation before said "Go!"[4] I am off to a flying start and I must not halt in the stretch to look behind and weep. Slavery is the price I paid for civilization, and the choice was not with me. It is a bully adventure and worth all that I have paid through my ancestors for it. No one on earth

3. *Parse-me-la*: a dance popular in the southern United States in the 1890s.
4. *The terrible struggle . . . "Go!"*: Hurston is comparing the U.S. Civil War (1861–1865) and the period immediately following to the beginning of a race.

ever had a greater chance for glory. The world to be won and nothing to be lost. It is thrilling to think—to know that for any act of mine, I shall get twice as much praise or twice as much blame. It is quite exciting to hold the center of the national stage, with the spectators not knowing whether to laugh or to weep.

The position of my white neighbor is much more difficult. No brown specter 8 pulls up a chair beside me when I sit down to eat. No dark ghost thrusts its leg against mine in bed. The game of keeping what one has is never so exciting as the game of getting.

I do not always feel colored. Even now I often achieve the unconscious Zora of 9 Eatonville before the Hegira.[5] I feel most colored when I am thrown against a sharp white background.

For instance at Barnard. "Beside the waters of the Hudson" I feel my race.[6] 10 Among the thousand white persons, I am a dark rock surged upon, and overswept, but through it all, I remain myself. When covered by the waters, I am; and the ebb but reveals me again.

Sometimes it is the other way around. A white person is set down in our midst, but 11 the contrast is just as sharp for me. For instance, when I sit in the drafty basement that is The New World Cabaret with a white person, my color comes. We enter chatting about any little nothing that we have in common and are seated by the jazz waiters. In the abrupt way that jazz orchestras have, this one plunges into a number. It loses no time in circumlocutions, but gets right down to business. It constricts the thorax and splits the heart with its tempo and narcotic harmonies. This orchestra grows rambunctious, rears on its hind legs and attacks the tonal veil with primitive fury, rending it, clawing it until it breaks through to the jungle beyond. I follow those heathen—follow them exultingly. I dance wildly inside myself; I yell within, I whoop; I shake my assegai above my head, I hurl it true to the mark *yeeeeooww!*[7] I am in the jungle and living in the jungle way. My face is painted red and yellow and my body is painted blue. My pulse is throbbing like a war drum. I want to slaughter something—give pain, give death to what, I do not know. But the piece ends. The men of the orchestra wipe their lips and rest their fingers. I creep back slowly to the veneer we call civilization with the last tone and find the white friend sitting motionless in his seat, smoking calmly.

"Good music they have here," he remarks, drumming the table with his fingertips. 12

5. *Hegira*: great escape; literally, Muhammad's flight from Mecca in A.D. 622.

6. *"Beside the waters of the Hudson"*: in Psalm 137, the Jewish people, exiled from Jerusalem, long for their homeland as they mourn "by the rivers of Babylon." *Barnard College*: a women's college in New York City, located near the Hudson River.

7. *Assegai:* African hunting spear.

Music. The great blobs of purple and red emotion have not touched him. He has   13
only heard what I felt. He is far away and I see him but dimly across the ocean and
the continent that have fallen between us. He is so pale with his whiteness then
and I am so colored.

At certain times I have no race, I am *me*. When I set my hat at a certain angle and   14
saunter down Seventh Avenue, Harlem City, feeling as snooty as the lions in front
of the Forty-Second Street Library, for instance. So far as my feelings are concerned, Peggy Hopkins Joyce on the Boule Mich[8] with her gorgeous raiment,
stately carriage, knees knocking together in a most aristocratic manner, has nothing on me. The cosmic Zora emerges. I belong to no race nor time. I am the eternal
feminine with its string of beads.

I have no separate feeling about being an American citizen and colored. I am   15
merely a fragment of the Great Soul that surges within the boundaries. My country,
right or wrong.

Sometimes, I feel discriminated against, but it does not make me angry. It   16
merely astonishes me. How *can* any deny themselves the pleasure of my company?
It's beyond me.

But in the main, I feel like a brown bag of miscellany propped against a wall.   17
Against a wall in company with other bags, white, red and yellow. Pour out the contents, and there is discovered a jumble of small things priceless and worthless. A
first-water diamond, an empty spool, bits of broken glass, lengths of string, a key to
a door long since crumbled away, a rusty knife-blade, old shoes saved for a road
that never was and never will be, a nail bent under the weight of things too heavy
for any nail, a dried flower or two still a little fragrant. In your hand is the brown
bag. On the ground before you is the jumble it held—so much like the jumble in
the bags, could they be emptied, that all might be dumped in a single heap and the
bags refilled without altering the content of any greatly. A bit of colored glass more
or less would not matter. Perhaps that is how the Great Stuffer of Bags filled them
in the first place—who knows?

8. *Boule Mich:* Boulevard Saint-Michel, a street in Paris once famous for the intellectuals and
artists who dominated its shops and cafes. *Peggy Hopkins Joyce:* an American actress and celebrity in
the 1920s known for her extravagant style.

READING CLOSELY

1. Which is more important in Zora Neale Hurston's view: race or personal identity? Explain.

2. Before young Zora "became colored" (2), what was the only difference between
   white folks and colored folks?

3. What happened to change Hurston's sense of race and color? What effects did this experience have upon her life?

4. When and why does Hurston "feel" her race most sharply?

5. Why does Hurston say that the position of her white neighbor is "much more difficult" (8)?

STRATEGIES AND STRUCTURES

1. Hurston begins her DESCRIPTION of how she feels by denying that she is the granddaughter of an Indian chief. What point is she making about her identity?

2. In the next three paragraphs, Hurston describes her childhood self. What are some of the main characteristics and qualities of "Zora of Orange County" (5)? What DOMINANT IMPRESSION of her childhood does Hurston convey here?

3. What qualities does Hurston assign to her adult self when she feels surrounded by a sea of whiteness—as, for example, when she is in college?

4. Hurston's essay originally appeared in a magazine intended for a liberal Christian readership. In what ways is her message addressed to such an audience?

5. *Other Methods.* Hurston ends by COMPARING the contents of various mixed bags of odds and ends (17). What is the point of this comparison?

THINKING ABOUT LANGUAGE

1. Notice the PUN in Hurston's title. How would the meaning change if she had said "colored *like* me"?

2. Hurston refers to her front porch in Eatonville as a "gallery" (3) and to the passers-by as "actors" (3). Where else does she use METAPHORS from the theater to describe her experience of race in America?

3. "The operation was successful," says Hurston (7). What operation is she talking about? Why the surgical metaphor?

4. A trained anthropologist, Hurston claims to return to the jungle in paragraph 11. How does her language in this paragraph—"circumlocutions," "tonal veil," "primitive fury," "the veneer we call civilization"—bear upon that claim?

FOR WRITING

1. You have just entered a favorite nightspot, real or imagined. The music is playing. You are not alone. Describe the scene in a paragraph or two.

2. Write an essay describing your own first experience with racial, economic, or gender differences.

LANCE ARMSTRONG AND SALLY JENKINS

Pitched Back

Lance Armstrong (b. 1971), a native of Plano, Texas, is the only cyclist in history to win the Tour de France seven times. In 1996, he was diagnosed with testicular cancer that had already spread to his brain and lungs. His chances for recovery slim, Armstrong began aggressive chemotherapy anyway—and went on to win his first Tour in 1999. Armstrong tells the story of his experience with cancer and his stunning recovery in It's Not About the Bike *(2001). "Pitched Back" is from the introduction to* Every Second Counts *(2003), in which Armstrong continues that story. Both books were co-written with Sally Jenkins, a sports columnist for the* Washington Post.*

"Pitched Back" describes the hardships of the Tour de France, the world's most grueling bicycle race—but only briefly. Taking its title from a remark about his illness by one of Armstrong's Texas friends, "Pitched Back" is more about daily life in the Armstrong family household in Austin, describing places closer to Armstrong's roots, including a mineral pond called "Dead Man's Hole" into whose chilly waters Armstrong sometimes dives.

So, it looks as though I'm going to live—at least for another 50 years or more. But whenever I need to reassure myself of this, as I sometimes do, I go out to a place called Dead Man's Hole, and I stare down into it, and then, with firm intent, I strip off my shirt and I leap straight out into what you might call the great sublime.

Let's say it's my own personal way of checking for vital signs. Dead Man's Hole is a large green mineral pool gouged out of a circular limestone cliff, so deep into the hill country of Texas that it's hardly got an address. According to conflicting legends, it's either where Confederates tossed Union[1] sympathizers to drown, or where Apaches lured unsuspecting cowboys who didn't see the fall coming. In any event, I'm drawn to it, so much so that I bought 200 acres of brush and pasture surrounding it, and I've worn a road into the dirt by driving out there. It seems only right that a place called Dead Man's Hole should belong to a guy who nearly died—and who, by the way, has no intention of just barely living.

I stand there next to a 45-foot waterfall and examine the drop—and myself, while I'm at it. It's a long drop, so long that it makes the roof of my mouth go dry just looking at it. It's long enough for a guy to actually think on the way down, and to think more than one thought, too. Long enough to think first one thing, *A little*

---

1. *Confederate* and *Union*: the two sides in the U.S. Civil War, 1861–1865.

fear is good for you, and then another, *It's good for you if you can swim,* and then one more thing as I hit the water: *Oh fuck, it's cold.* As I jump, there are certain unmistakable signs that I'm alive: the press of my pulse, the insistent sound of my own breathing, and the whanging in my chest that's my heart, which by then sounds like an insubordinate prisoner beating on the bars of my ribcage.

I come up whooping through the foam and swim for the rocks. Then I climb   4
back up and towel off, and I drive home to my three kids. I burst through the door, and I shout at my son, Luke, and my twin daughters, Grace and Isabelle, and I kiss them on the necks, and I grab a Shiner Bock beer with one hand and an armful of babies with the other.

The first time I ever did it, my wife, Kik, just looked at me and rolled her eyes.   5
She knew where I'd been.

"Was that clarifying for you?" she said.   6

At what point do you let go of not dying? Maybe I haven't entirely and maybe I   7
don't want to.

I know they're out there, lying in their hospital beds, with those damn drip   8
poles, watching the damn chemo slide into their veins, and thinking, *This guy had the same thing I do. If he can do it, I can, too.* I think of them all the time.

My friend Lee Walker says I got "pitched back." What he means is, I almost died,   9
and possibly even did die a little, but then I got pitched back into the world of the living. It's as good a description as any of what happened. I was 25 when cancer nearly killed me: advanced choriocarcinoma spread to my abdomen, lungs, and brain and required two surgeries and four cycles of chemotherapy to get rid of. I wrote an entire book about death, called *It's Not About the Bike,* about confronting the possibility of it, and narrowly escaping it.

"Are you sure?" I asked the doctor.   10

"I'm sure."   11

"How sure?"   12

"I'm very sure."   13

"How can you be so sure?"   14

"I'm so sure that I've scheduled you for surgery at 7 A.M. tomorrow."   15

Mounted on a light table, the X-ray showed my chest. Black meant clear; white meant   16
cancer. My chest looked like a snowstorm.

What I didn't and couldn't address at the time was the prospect of life. Once you   17
figure out you're going to live, you have to decide how to, and that's not an uncomplicated matter. You ask yourself: *now that I know I'm not going to die, what will I do? What's the highest and best use of my self?* These things aren't linear, they're a mysterious calculus. For me, the best use of myself has been to race in the Tour de France, the most grueling sporting event in the world.

Every time I win another Tour, I prove that I'm alive—and therefore that others   18
can survive, too. I've survived cancer again, and again, and again, and again. I've
won four Tour titles, and I wouldn't mind a record-tying five. That would be some
good living.

But the fact is that I wouldn't have won even a single Tour de France without   19
the lesson of illness. What it teaches is this: pain is temporary. Quitting lasts forever.

To me, just finishing the Tour de France is a demonstration of survival. The   20
arduousness of the race, the sheer unreasonableness of the job, the circumnaviga-
tion of an entire country on a bicycle, village to village, along its shores, across its
bridges, up and over the mountain peaks they call cols, requires a matchless stamina. The Tour is so taxing that Dutch rider Hennie Kuiper once said, after a long
climb up an alp, "The snow had turned black in my eyes." It's not unlike the stamina of people who are ill every day. The Tour is a daily festival of human suffering,
of minor tragedies and comedies, all conducted in the elements, sometimes terrible weather and sometimes fine, over flats, and into headwinds, with plenty of
crashes. And it's three weeks long. Think about what you were doing three weeks
ago. It feels like last year.

The race is very much like living—except that its consequences are less dire and   21
there's a prize at the end. Life is not so neat.

There was no pat storybook ending for me. I survived cancer and made a suc-   22
cessful comeback as a cyclist by winning the 1999 Tour, but that was more of a
beginning than an end. Life actually went on, sometimes in the most messy, inconvenient, and untriumphant ways. In the next five years I'd have three children, take
hundreds of drug tests (literally), break my neck (literally), win some more races,
lose some, too, and experience a breakdown in my marriage. Among other adventures.

When you walk into the Armstrong household, what you see is infants crawling   23
everywhere. Luke was born in the fall of 1999 to Kristin (Kik) Armstrong and me
shortly after that first Tour, and the twins came in the fall of 2001. Grace and
Isabelle have blue saucer eyes, and they toddle across the floor at scarcely believable speeds. They like to pull themselves upright on the available furniture and
stand there, wobbling, while they plan how to make trouble. One of Isabelle's
amusements is to stand up on the water dispenser and press the tap until the
kitchen floods, while she laughs hysterically. I tell her, "No, no, no," and she just
shakes her head back and forth and keeps laughing, while the water runs all over
the floor. I can't wait for their teen years.

Luke adds to the bedlam by riding his bike in the living room, or doing laps in a   24
plastic car, or tugging the girls around in separate red wagons. He is sturdy and
hardheaded. He wears his bike helmet inside the house and refuses to take it off,

even when we go out to dinner. We get some interesting stares—but anything is better than the fight that ensues if you try to remove the helmet. He insists on wearing it just in case he might get to go cycling with me. To him, a road is what his father does for a living. I'm on the road so much that when the phone rings, he says, "Daddy."

One afternoon I went to pick my family up at an airport. Luke gave me a long 25 stare and said, "Daddy, you look like me."

"Uh, I look like *you*?" I said. 26

"Yeah." 27

"Are you sure it's not the other way around?" 28

"Yeah, I'm sure. It's definitely you that looks like me." 29

Also milling around our house are a cat named Chemo and a small white dog 30 named Boone. I trip around all of them, watching my feet, careful not to step on a critter or a kid. It's been a chaotic few years, and not without its casualties. There have been so many children and adults and animals to feed that sometimes things get confused and the dog winds up with the baby food. One day Kik handed me what was supposed to be a glass of water.

"This tastes like Sprite," I said. 31

"Just drink it," she said. 32

I could never seem to find the right keys to anything. One time I pulled the ring 33 of keys from my pocket and stared at them in their seeming hundreds, and said to Kik, wonderingly, "I have the keys to the whole world." She just said, "Perfect."

The reason I have so many keys is because I need so many homes and vehicles, 34 in various countries and counties. I spend most of the spring and summer in my European home in Girona, Spain, while I prepare for the Tour. When the racing season is over, I come back to Austin. Our family lives in a house in central Austin, and we also have the ranch in the hill country. But my favorite home is a small hideaway, a one-room cabin just outside Austin, in the hills overlooking the Colorado River. Across the river there's a rope swing dangling from an old bent oak, and on hot days I like to swing on the rope and hurl myself into the current.

I love the tumult of my large family, and I've even been accused of fostering a 35 certain amount of commotion, because I have no tolerance for peace and quiet. I'm congenitally unable to sit still; I crave action, and if I can't find any, I invent it.

My friends call me Mellow Johnny. It's a play on the French term for the leader 36 of the Tour de France, who wears a yellow jersey: the *maillot jaune*. We like to joke that Mellow Johnny is the Texan pronunciation. The name is also a play on my not-so-mellow personality. I'm Mellow Johnny, or Johnny Mellow, or, if you're feeling formal, Jonathan Mellow.

Sometimes I'm just Bike Boy. I ride my bike almost every day, even in the off- 37 season, no matter the weather. It could be hailing, and my friends and riding partners dread the call that they know is going to come: they pick up the phone, and they hear Bike Boy on the other end, demanding, "You ridin', or you *hidin'*?"

One famous November day during the off-season, I rode four and a half hours 38 through one of the strongest rainstorms on record. Seven inches of precipitation, with flash floods and road closures everywhere. I loved it. People thought I was crazy, of course. But when I'm on the bike, I feel like I'm 13 years old. I run fewer red lights now, but otherwise it's the same.

Some days, though, I feel much older than a man in his thirties; it's as if I've 39 lived a lot longer. That's the cancer, I guess. I've spent a lot of time examining what it did to me—how it aged me, altered me—and the conclusion I've come to is, it didn't just change my body; it changed my mind.

I've often said cancer was the best thing that ever happened to me. But every- 40 body wants to know what I mean by that: how could a life-threatening disease be a good thing? I say it because my illness was also my antidote: it cured me of lazi-ness.

Before I was diagnosed, I was a slacker. I was getting paid a lot of money for a 41 job I didn't do 100 percent, and that was more than just a shame—it was wrong. When I got sick, I told myself: if I get another chance, I'll do this right—and I'll work for something more than just myself.

I have a friend, a fellow cancer survivor named Sally Reed, who sums up the 42 experience better than anyone I know. "My house is burned down," she says, "but I can see the sky."

Sally was diagnosed with rampant breast cancer in the spring of 1999. The dis- 43 ease had reached Stage Three and spread to her lymphatic system. She was facing both radiation and chemotherapy. Right away, all of her smaller fears disappeared, replaced by this new one. She had been so afraid of flying that she hadn't flown in more than 15 years. But after she got the diagnosis, she called an airline and booked a flight to Niagara Falls. She went there by herself and stood overlooking the roar-ing falls.

"I wanted to see something bigger than me," she says. 44

Mortal illness, like most personal catastrophes, comes on suddenly. There's no 45 great sense of foreboding, no premonition, you just wake up one morning and something's wrong in your lungs, or your liver, or your bones. But near-death cleared the decks, and what came after was a bright, sparkling awareness: time is limited, so I better wake up every morning fresh and know that I have just one chance to live this particular day right, and to string my days together into a life of action, and purpose.

If you want to know what keeps me on my bike, riding up an alp for six hours in 46 the rain, that's your answer.

Reading Closely

1. Lance Armstrong and Sally Jenkins DESCRIBE the Tour de France as "very much like living" (21). How so? What characteristics do they have in common, according to Armstrong? How are they different?

2. Where and how did Armstrong get the nickname "Mellow Johnny" (36)? How and how well does it capture his personality?

3. Armstrong says he got "pitched back" (9). Pitched back from what? How?

4. What is Armstrong's main point about how to live? Where is this point most clearly expressed?

Strategies and Structures

1. Armstrong and Jenkins describe Dead Man's Hole as a "large green mineral pool gouged out of a circular limestone cliff" (2). What other characteristics, physical and mental, do they assign to this special place? Why is Armstrong so drawn to it—and why do you think he describes it in such detail?

2. In paragraph 4, Armstrong and Jenkins start to describe life in the Armstrong family home in Austin, but then they switch to the subject of Armstrong's cancer. Where do they come back to describe the Armstrong family? How do they tie the two subjects together?

3. Where do Armstrong and Jenkins use DIALOGUE? What does it contribute to their descriptions?

4. Point out specific details and EXAMPLES in Armstrong's and Jenkins's descriptions that you find particularly effective. Why do they work so well?

5. *Other Methods.* Where and how does Armstrong COMPARE AND CONTRAST his old self with his new, post-cancer self?

Thinking about Language

1. Armstrong describes the entire experience of surviving mortal illness as being "pitched back." How and how well do you think this phrase does the job?

2. His chest X-ray, says Armstrong, "looked like a snowstorm" (16). Point out other places where he and Jenkins use SIMILES to describe things. Do you find them effective? Why or why not?

3. Why does Armstrong's wife introduce the term "clarifying" (6) to describe his plunge into the mineral pool?

4. How does the name of the pool, Dead Man's Hole, resonate throughout this text?

FOR WRITING

1. In a paragraph or two, describe the chaos (or calm and order) in a household with which you are familiar. Think about the DOMINANT IMPRESSION you want to give, and choose details accordingly.

2. Write an essay describing a special place that you find "clarifying" to visit.

3. Have you (or someone you know) ever been "pitched back" from a difficult situation? Describe the experience.

THOMAS BELLER

The Ashen Guy: Lower Broadway, September 11, 2001

Thomas Beller (b. 1965) is the webmaster of mrbellersneighborhood.com, a website where New Yorkers publish true stories of life in the big city. Following the events of September 11, 2001, Beller received many eyewitness accounts of the attacks, which he collected in Before & After: Stories from New York *(2002). Beller is also the author of a collection of short stories,* Seduction Theory *(1995), and a novel,* The Sleep-Over Artist *(2000).*

"The Ashen Guy," written by Beller himself, takes place just after the first World Trade Center tower has fallen and just before the collapse of the second tower. An eye-witness description of the scene from a few blocks north of Ground Zero, it focuses on a single man in the retreating crowd, a survivor from the eighty-first floor of the collapsed building who is not about to look back even when the second tower falls.

AT BROADWAY AND UNION SQUARE a woman moved with the crowd talking   1
on her cell phone. "It's a good thing," she began. I biked south. At Tenth Street the bells of Grace Church pealed ten times.[1] Everyone was moving in the same direction, orderly, but with an element of panic and, beneath that, a nervous energy. Their clothes were crisp and unrumpled, their hair freshly combed. Below Houston Street, a fleet of black shiny SUVs with sirens sped south, toward the smoky horizon somewhere south of Canal Street. A messenger biked beside me. I almost asked him if he was making a delivery.

At Thomas Street, about six blocks north of the World Trade Center, the nature   2
of the crowd on the street changed. There was more urgency and less mirth. Cop cars parked at odd angles, their red sirens spinning. The policemen were waving their arms, shouting, and amidst the crowd was a guy who had been on the eighty-first floor of Two World Trade Center when the plane hit. It was just after 10 A.M. Two World Trade had just collapsed, and One World Trade stood smoldering behind him.

At first glance he looked like a snowman, except instead of snow he was covered   3
in gray, asbestos-colored ash. He was moving along with the crowd, streaming north, up Broadway. His head and neck and shoulders and about halfway down his chest were covered in gray ash. You could make out a pair of bloodshot eyes, and he was running his hand over his head. A small plume of dust drifted off the top of his

---

1. *Pealed ten times:* ten chimes indicates that the time was 10 A.M. At that hour, the two planes had hit the two towers and the attack had already been reported on the news media.

head as he walked, echoing the larger plume of smoke drifting off of One World Trade behind him.

"There were about 230 people on the eighty-first floor and I was one of the last ones out. We took the stairs. There was smoke, but it wasn't fire smoke, it was dry wall smoke and dust. The fire was above us."   4

He was shaking. His eyes were red from dust and maybe tears. He didn't seem like the sort of man who cried. He had fair skin and a sandy-colored crew cut. He was wearing chinos and Docksiders and his shirt was a checked button-down.   5

He was walking with the crowd, but his body language was a little different. Everyone, even those who weren't looking back, had about them a certain nervous desire to look behind them, to see, to communicate to their neighbor, but this guy had no interest in anything but in getting away from where he had just been. It radiated from every muscle in his body. To get away.   6

"I was almost out. I got down to the lobby, right near the Borders book store. And then there was this explosion. I don't know, I just got thrown to the ground and all this stuff fell on top of me."   7

By now he had dusted his head off and you could see his skin. It was pale and ashen, one of his eyes was very red. At first I thought maybe it was the dust and perhaps tears that had made his eyes bloodshot; looking closer I saw that one eye was badly inflamed.   8

He was joined by another man, a blue oxford shirt with a tie, mid-forties, lawyerly, who worked in the building across the street.   9

"I watched the whole thing. I saw the second plane hit, the explosion. No one told us to evacuate, and then the building just collapsed and I thought I better get out of here because my building could go too."   10

On Franklin Street the police were screaming: "There's a package! There's a package! Keep moving!"   11

They were herding everyone to the left, towards West Broadway. "People! Trust me! Let's go! People let's go! There's an unidentified package across the street!"   12

The view on West Broadway and Franklin was very good. One tower, gray sky billowing, the sky darkening.   13

"Do you know which way the tower fell?" a woman asked. A tall man stood behind her, scruffy beard and longish hair, his hand on her shoulder.   14

"It fell straight down!" someone said.   15

"Because we live one block away and . . . does anyone know which way the building fell?"   16

The man behind her, her husband, I assumed, had this very sad look on his face, as though he understood something she didn't. It was as if that consoling hand on her shoulder was there to make sure she didn't try and make a run for it.   17

"I don't know what happened," said the ashen guy. "I just hit the ground, don't 18 know if something hit me or . . ."

"It was the force of the building collapsing," said the lawyer. 19

"I got up and just started walking," said the ashen guy. 20

There was a huge rumbling sound accompanied by the sound of people shriek- 21 ing. Everyone who wasn't already looking turned to see the remaining building start to crumble in on itself, a huge ball of smoke rising out from beneath it, a mushroom cloud in reverse. The whole street paused, froze, screamed, some people broke into tears, many people brought their hands up to their mouths, everyone was momentarily frozen, except for the ashen guy, who just kept walking.

Reading Closely

1. Though he DESCRIBES him in detail, Beller never identifies the Ashen Guy by name. Why not? Who might he be or stand for?

2. The people in Beller's description walk as if they were in a dream. How and how well does this dreamlike atmosphere fit the events of September 11, 2001, as Beller describes them?

3. Why doesn't the Ashen Guy look back when the second tower falls?

4. Beller is describing a survivor. Why? What point is he making in the immediate aftermath of the attacks?

Strategies and Structures

1. How is Beller traveling when he comes upon the Ashen Guy? What advantages does this mode of transportation give him as a narrator?

2. "At first glance he looked like a snowman," says Beller of the man who is the focal point of his description (3). Why is he mistaken at first? Why does he report this mistake in perception?

3. How does Beller give the impression in paragraph 8 that he is getting closer to his mysterious man?

4. What specific details does Beller supply to the reader through the use of DIA-LOGUE? Why doesn't he just tell the reader what happened?

5. *Other Methods.* Beller's essay includes many elements of NARRATION. What are some of them, and how do they contribute to his description?

THINKING ABOUT LANGUAGE

1. How appropriate do you find Beller's use of the word "ashen" in this description of a national nightmare? Explain.

2. Why do you think Beller calls his lone survivor a "guy" rather than a man, or person, or figure?

3. In paragraph 3, Beller writes, "A small plume of dust drifted off the top of his head as he walked, echoing the larger plume of smoke drifting off of One World Trade behind him." What do you think of Beller's use of the word "echoing" in this sentence? How about "plume"?

4. Give several other examples of Beller's figurative linking of the man and the tower. At the end of his description, the tower falls. How about the man?

FOR WRITING

1. Where were you on September 11, 2001? Write a paragraph or two describing who and what you saw and heard on that day.

2. Recall a person you know or have read about who has survived a catastrophic event—such as 9/11, Hurricane Katrina, or some personal crisis. Write an essay describing that person and his or her behavior in response to the event.

E. B. WHITE

Once More to the Lake

*Elwyn Brooks White (1899–1985) was born in Mount Vernon, New York. He gradu-
ated from Cornell University in 1921 and worked as a journalist and advertising copy-
writer before joining the staff of the* New Yorker *in 1926. From 1938 to 1943, he also
wrote a regular column for* Harper's *magazine. White's numerous books include the
children's classic* Charlotte's Web *(1952) and his updating of William Strunk's 1918*
Elements of Style *(1959), a guide to writing.*

*Written in August 1941 on the eve of World War II, "Once More to the Lake" origi-
nally appeared in* Harper's *and helped to establish White's reputation as a leading
essayist of his day. The lake described here is Great Pond in south-central Maine. As
White returns to this familiar scene, it seems unchanged—at first.*

O NE SUMMER, along about 1904, my father rented a camp on a lake in Maine 1
and took us all there for the month of August. We all got ringworm from some kit-
tens and had to rub Pond's Extract on our arms and legs night and morning, and
my father rolled over in a canoe with all his clothes on; but outside of that the vacation was a success and from then on none of us ever thought there was any place in
the world like that lake in Maine. We returned summer after summer—always on
August 1 for one month. I have since become a salt-water man, but sometimes in
summer there are days when the restlessness of the tides and the fearful cold of the
sea water and the incessant wind that blows across the afternoon and into the
evening make me wish for the placidity of a lake in the woods. A few weeks ago this
feeling got so strong I bought myself a couple of bass hooks and a spinner and
returned to the lake where we used to go, for a week's fishing and to revisit old
haunts.

I took along my son, who had never had any fresh water up his nose and who 2
had seen lily pads only from train windows. On the journey over to the lake I began
to wonder what it would be like. I wondered how the time would have marred this
unique, this holy spot—the coves and streams, the hills that the sun set behind, the
camps and the paths behind the camps. I was sure that the tarred road would have
found it out, and I wondered in what other ways it would be desolated. It is strange
how much you can remember about places like that once you allow your mind to
return into the grooves that lead back. You remember one thing, and that suddenly
reminds you of another thing. I guess I remembered clearest of all the early mornings, when the lake was cool and motionless, remembered how the bedroom
smelled of the lumber it was made of and of the wet woods whose scent entered

through the screen. The partitions in the camp were thin and did not extend clear to the top of the rooms, and as I was always the first up I would dress softly so as not to wake the others, and sneak out into the sweet outdoors and start out in the canoe, keeping close along the shore in the long shadows of the pines. I remembered being very careful never to rub my paddle against the gunwale for fear of disturbing the stillness of the cathedral.

The lake had never been what you would call a wild lake. There were cottages 3 sprinkled around the shores, and it was in farming country although the shores of the lake were quite heavily wooded. Some of the cottages were owned by nearby farmers, and you would live at the shore and eat your meals at the farmhouse. That's what our family did. But although it wasn't wild, it was a fairly large and undisturbed lake and there were places in it that, to a child at least, seemed infinitely remote and primeval.

I was right about the tar: it led to within half a mile of the shore. But when I got 4 back there, with my boy, and we settled into a camp near a farmhouse and into the kind of summertime I had known, I could tell that it was going to be pretty much the same as it had been before—I knew it, lying in bed the first morning, smelling the bedroom and hearing the boy sneak quietly out and go off along the shore in a boat. I began to sustain the illusion that he was I, and therefore, by simple transposition, that I was my father. This sensation persisted, kept cropping up all the time we were there. It was not an entirely new feeling, but in this setting, it grew much stronger. I seemed to be living a dual existence. I would be in the middle of some simple act, I would be picking up a bait box or laying down a table fork, or I would be saying something, and suddenly it would be not I but my father who was saying the words or making the gesture. It gave me a creepy sensation.

We went fishing the first morning. I felt the same damp moss covering the 5 worms in the bait can, and saw the dragonfly alight on the tip of my rod as it hovered a few inches from the surface of the water. It was the arrival of this fly that convinced me beyond any doubt that everything was as it always had been, that the years were a mirage and that there had been no years. The small waves were the same, chucking the rowboat under the chin as we fished at anchor, and the boat was the same boat, the same color green and the ribs broken in the same places, and under the floorboards the same freshwater leavings and débris—the dead helgramite, the wisps of moss, the rusty discarded fishhook, the dried blood from yesterday's catch. We stared silently at the tips of our rods, at the dragonflies that came and went. I lowered the tip of mine into the water, tentatively, pensively dislodging the fly, which darted two feet away, poised, darted two feet back, and came to rest again a little farther up the rod. There had been no years between the ducking of this dragonfly and the other one—the one that was part of memory. I looked at the boy, who was silently watching his fly, and it was my hands that held his rod, my eyes watching. I felt dizzy and didn't know which rod I was at the end of.

We caught two bass, hauling them in briskly as though they were mackerel, 6 pulling them over the side of the boat in a businesslike manner without any landing net, and stunning them with a blow on the back of the head. When we got back for a swim before lunch, the lake was exactly where we had left it, the same number of inches from the dock, and there was only the merest suggestion of a breeze. This seemed an utterly enchanted sea, this lake you could leave to its own devices for a few hours and come back to, and find that it had not stirred, this constant and trustworthy body of water. In the shallows, the dark, water-soaked sticks and twigs, smooth and old, were undulating in clusters on the bottom against the clean ribbed sand, and the track of the mussel was plain. A school of minnows swam by, each minnow with its small individual shadow, doubling the attendance, so clear and sharp in the sunlight. Some of the other campers were in swimming, along the shore, one of them with a cake of soap, and the water felt thin and clear and unsubstantial. Over the years there had been this person with the cake of soap, this cultist, and here he was. There had been no years.

Up to the farmhouse to dinner through the teeming, dusty field, the road under 7 our sneakers was only a two-track road. The middle track was missing, the one with the marks of the hooves and the splotches of dried, flaky manure. There had always been three tracks to choose from in choosing which track to walk in; now the choice was narrowed down to two. For a moment I missed terribly the middle alternative. But the way led past the tennis court, and something about the way it lay there in the sun reassured me; the tape had loosened along the backline, the alleys were green with plantains and other weeds, and the net (installed in June and removed in September) sagged in the dry noon, and the whole place steamed with midday heat and hunger and emptiness. There was a choice of pie for dessert, and one was blueberry and one was apple, and the waitresses were the same country girls, there having been no passage of time, only the illusion of it as in a dropped curtain—the waitresses were still fifteen; their hair had been washed, that was the only difference—they had been to the movies and seen the pretty girls with the clean hair.

Summertime, oh, summertime, pattern of life indelible, the fade-proof lake, the 8 woods unshatterable, the pasture with the sweetfern and the juniper forever and ever, summer without end; this was the background, and the life along the shore was the design, the cottages with their innocent and tranquil design, their tiny docks with the flagpole and the American flag floating against the white clouds in the blue sky, the little paths over the roots of the trees leading from camp to camp and the paths leading back to the outhouses and the can of lime for sprinkling, and at the souvenir counters at the store the miniature birch-bark canoes and the postcards that showed things looking a little better than they looked. This was the American family at play, escaping the city heat, wondering whether the newcomers in the camp at the head of the cove were "common" or "nice," wondering whether it was true that the people who drove up for Sunday dinner at the farmhouse were turned away because there wasn't enough chicken.

It seemed to me, as I kept remembering all this, that those times and those summers had been infinitely precious and worth saving. There had been jollity and peace and goodness. The arriving (at the beginning of August) had been so big a business in itself, at the railway station the farm wagon drawn up, the first smell of the pine-laden air, the first glimpse of the smiling farmer, and the great importance of the trunks and your father's enormous authority in such matters, and the feel of the wagon under you for the long ten-mile haul, and at the top of the last long hill catching the first view of the lake after eleven months of not seeing this cherished body of water. The shouts and cries of the other campers when they saw you, and the trunks to be unpacked, to give up their rich burden. (Arriving was less exciting nowadays, when you sneaked up in your car and parked it under a tree near the camp and took out the bags and in five minutes it was all over, no fuss, no loud wonderful fuss about trunks.)

Peace and goodness and jollity. The only thing that was wrong now, really, was the sound of the place, an unfamiliar nervous sound of the outboard motors. This was the note that jarred, the one thing that would sometimes break the illusion and set the years moving. In those other summertimes all motors were inboard; and when they were at a little distance, the noise they made was a sedative, an ingredient of summer sleep. They were one-cylinder and two-cylinder engines, and some were make-and-break and some were jump-spark,[1] but they all made a sleepy sound across the lake. The one-lungers throbbed and fluttered, and the twin-cylinder ones purred, and purred, and that was a quiet sound, too. But now the campers all had outboards. In the daytime, in the hot mornings, these motors made a petulant, irritable sound; at night, in the still evening when the afterglow lit the water, they whined about one's ears like mosquitoes. My boy loved our rented outboard, and his great desire was to achieve single-handed mastery over it, and authority, and he soon learned the trick of choking it a little (but not too much), and the adjustment of the needle valve. Watching him I would remember the things you could do with the old one-cylinder engine with the heavy flywheel, how you could have it eating out of your hand if you got really close to it spiritually. Motorboats in those days didn't have clutches, and you would make a landing by shutting off the motor at the proper time and coasting in with a dead rudder. But there was a way of reversing them, if you learned the trick, by cutting the switch

9

10

1. *Make-and-break* and *jump-spark*: two common types of ignition systems in old marine engines.

and putting it on again exactly on the final dying revolution of the flywheel, so that it would kick back against compression and begin reversing. Approaching a dock in a strong following breeze, it was difficult to slow up sufficiently by the ordinary coasting method, and if a boy felt he had complete mastery over his motor, he was tempted to keep it running beyond its time and then reverse it a few feet from the dock. It took a cool nerve, because if you threw the switch a twentieth of a second too soon you would catch the flywheel when it still had speed enough to go up past center, and the boat would leap ahead, charging bull-fashion at the dock.

We had a good week at the camp. The bass were biting well and the sun shone 11 endlessly, day after day. We would be tired at night and lie down in the accumulated heat of the little bedrooms after the long hot day and the breeze would stir almost imperceptibly outside and the smell of the swamp drift in through the rusty screens. Sleep would come easily and in the morning the red squirrel would be on the roof, tapping out his gay routine. I kept remembering everything, lying in bed in the mornings—the small steamboat that had a long rounded stern like the lip of a Ubangi, and how quietly she ran on the moonlight sails, when the older boys played their mandolins and the girls sang and we ate doughnuts dipped in sugar, and how sweet the music was on the water in the shining night, and what it had felt like to think about girls then. After breakfast, we would go up to the store and the things were in the same place—the minnows in a bottle, the plugs and spinners[2] disarranged and pawed over by the youngsters from the boys' camp, the Fig Newtons and the Beeman's gum. Outside, the road was tarred and cars stood in front of the store. Inside, all was just as it had always been, except there was more Coca-Cola and not so much Moxie[3] and root beer and birch beer and sarsaparilla. We would walk out with the bottle of pop apiece and sometimes the pop would backfire up our noses and hurt. We explored the streams, quietly, where the turtles slid off logs and dug their way into the soft bottom; and we lay on the town wharf and fed worms to the tame bass. Everywhere we went I had trouble making out which was I, the one walking at my side, the one walking in my pants.

One afternoon while we were there at that lake a thunderstorm came up. It was 12 like the revival of an old melodrama that I had seen long ago with childish awe. The second-act climax of the drama of the electrical disturbance over a lake in America has not changed in any important respect. This was the big scene, still the big scene. The whole thing was so familiar, the first feeling of oppression and heat and a general air around camp of not wanting to go very far away. In midafternoon (it was all the same) a curious darkening of the sky, and a lull in everything that had made life tick; and then the way the boats suddenly swung the other way at

---

2. *Plugs and spinners*: types of fishing lures.
3. *Moxie*: the brand name of an old-fashioned soft drink.

their moorings with the coming of a breeze out of the new quarter, and the premonitory rumble. Then the kettle drum, then the snare, then the bass drum and cymbals, then crackling light against the dark, and the gods grinning and licking their chops in the hills. Afterward the calm, the rain steadily rustling in the calm lake, the return of light and hope and spirits, and the campers running out in joy and relief to go swimming in the rain, their bright cries perpetuating the deathless joke about how they were getting simply drenched, and the children screaming with delight at the new sensation of bathing in the rain, and the joke about getting drenched linking the generations in a strong indestructible chain. And the comedian who waded in carrying an umbrella.

When the others went swimming, my son said he was going in, too. He pulled 13
his dripping trunks from the line where they had hung all through the shower and wrung them out. Languidly, and with no thought of going in, I watched him, his hard little body, skinny and bare, saw him wince slightly as he pulled up around his vitals the small, soggy, icy garment. As he buckled the swollen belt, suddenly my groin felt the chill of death.

READING CLOSELY

1. When and with whom did E. B. White first visit the lake he DESCRIBES so palpably in "Once More to the Lake"? With whom—and in approximately what time period—does he return to the lake, as described in his essay?

2. What DOMINANT IMPRESSION of the lake and its surrounding do you take away from White's description? Explain.

3. In paragraph 2, is White describing the lake as it was in the past, or as it is in the present time of his essay? How about in paragraphs 4–6? And in paragraph 11? Explain.

4. In addition to his own adventures on the lake, White is also describing those of "the American family at play" (8). What sentiments and behaviors does he identify as particularly "American"?

5. Do American families still take summer vacations "at the lake"? How has the pattern of family play—on a lake or elsewhere—changed since White wrote his essay? How has it remained the same?

STRATEGIES AND STRUCTURES

1. In his description of the "primeval" (3) lake, White stresses its qualities of calm and timelessness. What particular details contribute most effectively to this impression? What is his point in making it?

2. When he returned to the lake with his young son, the two of them, says White, went fishing "the first morning" (5). Point out other direct references to time in White's essay. How does he use CHRONOLOGY and the passing of time to organize his entire description?

3. One way in which the lake of his childhood has definitely changed, says White, is in its sounds. What new sounds does he describe? How does he incorporate this change into his description of the lake as a timeless place?

4. How would White's essay have been different without the last paragraph, in which he watches his young son get ready to go swimming?

5. *Other Methods.* As White describes the lake, he also tells a story about it. What's the PLOT of that story? How does White's NARRATIVE fit in with and support his description?

THINKING ABOUT LANGUAGE

1. What is the difference between an illusion and a "mirage" (5)? How and where do White's physical descriptions of the lake lead him to willful misinterpretations of the scene?

2. When he describes the lake as not only "constant" but "trustworthy" (6), White has PERSONIFIED the natural scene. When and where does it seem to take on a mind of its own in sharp contrast to his desires?

3. Why does White repeat the word *same* in paragraph 5?

4. When out in the boat alone as a boy, White did not want to disturb the "stillness of the cathedral" (2). What are the implications of this phrase? In what ways is White's son depicted as a chip off the old block?

5. The lake that White describes might be said to reside as much in memory as in the state of Maine. Why might fishing in a pond or lake provide an especially apt METAPHOR for probing memory—and writing about it?

FOR WRITING

1. Briefly describe a memorable family vacation or other outing. What do you remember most about it, and why? Try to recall the details that led you to this memory.

2. Recall a place that seemed "unique" or "holy" to you when you first visited it. Write an essay describing how it has changed since then, and how it has remained the same. In choosing details to include, think about what DOMINANT IMPRESSION you want to give.

3. Write an essay describing how a familiar sight, taste, or sound triggers your remembrance of things past. Try to tie what you find back in with the present.

ERNESTO MESTRE-REED

There Is a Spitting Tree in Spanish Brooklyn

Ernesto Mestre-Reed (b. 1964) is a native of Cuba but grew up in Miami, Florida. He attended Tulane University and now teaches creative writing at Sarah Lawrence College. He is the author of two novels, The Lazarus Rumba *(1999) and* The Second Death of Unica Aveyano *(2004).*

"The Spitting Tree" was first published in 2004 in the New York Times. *It describes a ginkgo tree in Brooklyn, where Mestre-Reed now lives; the mangoes, nisperos, and mammees that he came upon one day in Mexico; and a tall guava tree that grew in his grandfather's yard in Cuba. Encountering the fruits of his childhood even in Brooklyn, Mestre-Reed takes them back to his apartment to ripen in a dark closet. Here, miraculously, among old paint cans and cleaning supplies, they "flourish and sweeten" as naturally as they would "under the bright tropical sun."*

A MONG THE MANY FRUIT TREES in my grandparents' yard in Cuba was a tall guava tree. It stood over the patio and in the summers it produced so much fruit that my brothers and I could not eat enough to keep up with it, though we tried, scurrying up its narrow trunk and picking as many as we thought we could handle. [1]

Eventually the tree would drop its ripe fruit, leaving dark black stains on the bricked-up ground. Our grandfather told us that that's how the guava tree spat. So we would sidestep the splotches of rotted fruit. [2]

Our grandfather was an expert at spitting—because of either the endless number of cigars he was always smoking, or chomping on from end to tip when they were not lighted, or because of some hormone that made his saliva glands overcompensate. [3]

He would spit anywhere and anytime—while sitting down reading the newspaper in the morning, in the kitchen before drinking his cafecito after his siesta, at the dining room table during meals. With the precision of a veteran bombardier he never missed his mark by more than a few millimeters. [4]

Despite constant practice, my brothers and I could not surpass him. Unfortunately for our grandmother, our games left her beautiful tile floors with wine-dark stains that rivaled those of the spitting guava tree. [5]

But lest you get the wrong impression of my family, please know this: Our grandfather was more than just a great spitter—he was our town's haberdasher. In [6] his pressed guayaberas and perfectly tilted Panamas,[1] with his full head of hair the color of orange blossoms, he was as elegant as any man around. That's why we thought the secret spitting was so hilarious.

My grandfather died some years ago and, as is natural, my memories of our childhood spitting games receded from memory until this May, when I visited a friend's house in Merida, in the Yucatan peninsula of Mexico. [7]

I walked onto a patio speckled with dark stains, as if the heavens had been spitting down on it. I looked up; there were the two trees responsible. One was a lollipop mango tree. Lollipop mangos are little heart-shaped mangos that you eat not by peeling and slicing the flesh, but by biting off their heads and sucking out the juices. The other was a nispero tree. A nispero (called a loquat in English) is a golf-ball-sized tropical fruit, with a thin rind the color of a deer's coat and sweet golden flesh. [8]

Beyond the patio, I saw a mammee tree, which bears large, football-shaped fruit. The fruit's flesh is just as sweet as the nispero's, but it's much more suggestive— with its carmine hues and its ominous single black seed. [9]

In the Cuba of my childhood, nisperos and mammees were so abundant we ate them in every way: on the side at breakfast, lunch and dinner, pulped and made into shakes with coconut milk as an afternoon snack. In a country where milk, cigarettes, coffee and pork chops were marked off on a ration card the fruit trees offered rare abundance. [10]

In America, where we are surrounded by abundance, it's easy to lose awareness of it, even to forget about it. For a few months every summer, I can even buy nisperos and mammees at the delis in the Latino enclaves in Brooklyn. [11]

But these fruits are not soft and ripe like the ones sold in the open air markets in Merida—the mammees with a thin slice cut out to entice customers. The trees that spit them down belong to another place and time. My Brooklyn fruits, though, become a reminder of abundance amid abundance, for it takes work to coax the fruits to the ripened state I remember from my youth. [12]

Although I often pay as much as $10 for a single mammee, the excitement is worth it: I feel as if I'm carrying my childhood in a paper bag as I climb the stairs to my apartment. Once I'm home, I wrap them in clear plastic bags and stick them in a dark closet. Somehow, the darkness of a New York City closet lets these fruits flourish and sweeten as naturally as they do under the bright tropical skies. [13]

---

1. *Panama*: a traditional straw hat from Ecuador. Its name comes from the fact that it was widely exported from Panama. *Guayabera*: a style of men's shirt that is considered dressy and elegant in Cuba and other parts of Latin America. The shirt has pleats down the front and back and is worn loose outside the pants.

On special occasions, I pull them one by one from the plastic bags in the dark   14
closet, where they are tucked between the old paint cans and the tool box and the
cleaning supplies. They are eaten for dessert after a particularly good dinner, or
with a glass of Champagne.

New Yorkers are fond of thinking that we can get anything here. If you experi-   15
enced something anywhere else (a great love affair, an unforgettable summer, a
piece of fruit), we believe that we can not only duplicate it here, but also improve
upon it.

There is no denying this. After their sojourn in the closet, the nisperos and   16
mammees that I buy in Brooklyn are as sweet as the ones I had in my childhood. I
have also begun to notice a ginkgo tree on Seventh Avenue in Brooklyn. It spits its
fruit onto the sidewalk with perfect, gross consistency. I know it would have made
my grandfather proud.

READING CLOSELY

1. What is Ernesto Mestre-Reed's secret for getting tropical fruit to ripen properly
   in New York City? Where and how does he reveal and DESCRIBE his method?

2. When his grandfather died, Mestre-Reed's memories of the old man's spitting
   habits naturally receded. What brought them back to him?

3. Why does Mestre-Reed feel that he is "carrying my childhood in a paper bag"
   when he buys a piece of tropical fruit from a vendor in Brooklyn (13)?

4. According to Mestre-Reed, why is it easy to "lose awareness" of the succulence
   offered by the mangos, mammees, and other tropical fruits that can be purchased in the city (11)?

STRATEGIES AND STRUCTURES

1. How does memory serve Mestre-Reed as a source of raw material for his
   descriptions in this essay?

2. In paragraphs 13 and 14, Mestre-Reed describes the PROCESS of storing the fruit,
   letting it ripen, and retrieving it on special occasions. How might this process
   be said to resemble that of retrieving items from memory, as described throughout his essay? Explain.

3. Mestre-Reed addresses his fellow New Yorkers several times. What particular
   message does he direct to them? Who else is he speaking to, and what is his
   main purpose in recalling the fruits of his childhood?

4. Why do you think Mestre-Reed ends his essay with a description of the ginkgo
   tree he finds on Seventh Avenue in Brooklyn?

5. *Other Methods.* The fruit of the nispero tree, says Mestre-Reed, has a rind "the color of a deer's coat" (8). Where else does Mestre-Reed describe unfamiliar objects by COMPARING them to ones his audience is likely to be more familiar with? Is this an effective strategy? Why or why not?

THINKING ABOUT LANGUAGE

1. Back in Cuba, Mestre-Reed's grandfather was a haberdasher (6). What is a haberdasher, and why do they know about Panamas and guayaberas?

2. What color is *carmine* (9)?

3. How does Mestre-Reed use tropical fruit trees as METAPHORS for his Cuban childhood?

4. How does Mestre-Reed's description of exotic fruit balance or counteract the "perfect, gross consistency" of the spitting trees—and man (16)?

FOR WRITING

1. Write a paragraph or two describing a relative, family friend, or other person whom you found fascinating as a child. What qualities, physical or otherwise, do you particularly remember?

2. Write an essay describing someone or something—for example, a vegetable, regional dish, or animal—that a queasy reader might at first find less than appetizing but will come to appreciate because of your sensitivity in describing it.

THOMAS HITCHNER

The Places Reading Has Taken Me

Thomas Hitchner grew up in Berkeley, California, and wrote this essay for an English class at the University of California at Irvine. The essay won the 2004 Nellie Ansley Reeves Essay Contest, which is sponsored by the U.C. Irvine libraries.

"The Places Reading Has Taken Me" is a reading of Robert Browning's poem "My Last Duchess." As Hitchner interprets the poem, he not only describes in detail the locations this particular act of reading has taken him—some real, some imagined—he describes reading itself as a creative act. (Although you can enjoy the essay without reading the poem, if you'd like to read it, see p. 162.)

> *That's my last Duchess painted on the wall,*
> *Looking as if she were alive.*
>
> —ROBERT BROWNING, "My Last Duchess"

WHEN WE ARE YOUNG, adults try to instill a love of literacy in us by suggesting that books somehow have the power to transport us to strange and wonderful places. We hear this from our parents, or our teachers and librarians; often, ironically, we hear it from our children's TV programs. We are told that by reading about new worlds and new people, we can actually visit those worlds and meet those people. Books, say the grownups, can take us anywhere.

The drive to make literary pilgrimages begins in us, I think, when we first realize this is not actually so. We begin to recognize how much agency is required from us when we read, how much we are training our minds to create the details tantalizingly omitted from the text. The metaphor of a book as a transporter, or a time machine, assigns a depressingly passive role to the reader; when we read, too much is required of us to claim that we are being taken on a ride. Books and poems cannot, of their own power, transport us anywhere, any more than a map or travel guide can. They can point the way, but we have to make the trip ourselves. And for those of us of a certain literal bent, that means just what it sounds like.

And so, in the early spring of 2002, I found myself in Ferrara, in northern Italy, standing in front of the Castello d'Este. I was there because of a fifty-six line poem by Robert Browning, written 160 years before, which takes place at that castle. Even after having planned my trip weeks earlier, and having spent some hours traveling here, I still found what I had done somewhat startling: I had stepped off a train into fiction. No longer a mere reader, I was making myself an eyewitness, visiting the scene of "My Last Duchess."

At that time, I had only recently begun making literary pilgrimages, and I had found them disappointing, to put it mildly. I was studying in England that year, and as soon as I arrived I found myself exhilaratingly close to so many landmarks of great literature. Two weeks after arriving, I visited Shakespeare's birthplace at Stratford-upon-Avon; that winter, I crossed the Channel to Paris and visited the graves of Oscar Wilde and Gertrude Stein. Yet these places left me feeling cheated, as I found no trace of the great writers' spirits at these sites. Shakespeare, whose continual relevance never ceases to startle, is represented in Stratford by an artificially preserved cottage surrounded by similarly artificial restaurants and tourist shops, as if the pleasure of his plays and sonnets is equivalent to that of a Renaissance Faire.[1] Wilde, whose skewering of conventions was the only thing he ever took seriously, is buried in Paris under a tombstone earnest enough to make one ill.

I realize now what made these sites so unsatisfying: they were not about the writing, but the writer, and a bowdlerized, diluted version of the writer at that. The writers had been trapped by conventionality at birth and at death, the only times in their lives when they did not have the power to speak for themselves. Rather than visiting the brackets of the writers' careers, I should have been visiting the words themselves, the fields and towns and buildings that they had made mythical. So I went to Ferrara, to see if I could recreate the excitement and fearful recognition I had felt when I first read "My Last Duchess."

I never visit a castle without feeling, with a childish thrill, that I am walking into a storybook. (Far from fiction taking me places, then, places have often taken me to fiction.) My first sighting of the Castello d'Este evoked those feelings again, but with a dark inversion. In Browning's poem, this was not a place of heroism, but of cruelty. The castle did not protect, so much as conceal. The poem is a wandering soliloquy spoken by the Duke of Ferrara, discussing the late Duchess of the title. The Duke's "Last Duchess" is not his last for all time, but merely the last in a series—a series he is hoping to extend, as he is speaking the poem to a wedding agent sent by the Count of Tyrol. As he flaunts the different *objets d'art* that decorate his palace, he comes to a portrait of his late wife. With a casualness that is slowly chilling, yet also suggests a certain forced composure, the Duke describes how he grew dissatisfied with his wife and so gave orders that she be murdered. The Duke's story is so offhand that the many first-time readers do not realize the crime he is describing, as I did not when I first read it, but even when this essential fact is missed the reader senses that something is terribly wrong with this man. He explains, unprompted, that even if he had the verbal talents to describe his wife's

1. *Renaissance Faire*: an outdoor festival loosely based on those of sixteenth-century England. Musicians, actors, and jugglers dress in Elizabethan costume, and booths sell Elizabethan food, crafts, and clothing.

failings to her in the hopes of correcting them, he would not: "E'en then would be some stooping; and I choose / Never to stoop" (lines 42–43). At every line, the Duke's easy conversation betrays his horrifying pride and cruelty.

My photographs from that day are pleasant, but unenlightening. They are pretty pictures of a red brick castle on a cloudy day. They do a decent job of showing the mixture of architectural styles—Arabic, Roman, northern European—that are combined in the squat structure. They convey enjoyable surprise that derives from the incongruity, never old to Americans in Europe, of seeing a castle and moat in the middle of a city, like a cut jewel sitting in a pile of pebbles. But the pictures do nothing to suggest what the castle meant to me, thanks to Browning's poem; they do not evoke the excitement, nor the apprehensive chill I felt when I looked at the castle where the Duke had dispassionately negotiated a replacement for his wife. My photographs show none of this, and so they give lie to another commonplace about the power of art: that it can preserve or even recreate memories, and that those memories can then be easily transmitted to others. In the pictures, the castle is only a castle.

Of course, Browning himself spends almost no time in his poem discussing the Castello d'Este; in regards to the castle, as with humanity, he is concerned with what lurks inside. To be sure, Browning is interested in the aesthetic facades of wealth and refinement, but unlike the Duke who narrates the poem Browning never lets himself forget the darkness and cruelty that is hidden—even caused—by the obsession with ornamental beauty. The Duchess dies, in fact, because her husband cannot tell the difference between a woman with a pleasant demeanor and a work of art that should belong to him alone. "She liked whate'er / She looked on," he tells the agent from Tyrol, "and her looks went everywhere" (lines 23–24). While alive, she had control of her gaze, and her beauty. Now she is nothing more than a painting on a wall, and the Duke has full control of who can view her. "None puts by / The curtain I have drawn for you, but I" (lines 9–10), he boasts, fully unaware that at that moment Browning is parting the curtain that covers up his murderous jealousy.

The painting, of course, does not appear in the interior of the castle. "Frà Pandolf," the supposed painter of the portrait, is fictional, just as the accusation the poem tacitly levies against the Duke is based on evidence that is questionable at best. The castle, as I was subjectively viewing it, was therefore a fictional creation. But of course, this served my purposes all the more. If I had been visiting the site of an actual historical event, like a Civil War battlefield, it would be interesting, and no doubt at least as moving as this castle, but the mystery of artistic creation would not be present. Generals and lords and statesmen create battlefields, and castles for that matter, but only artists can do what Browning had done: augment the stones of those castles with stories that we feel to be true, whether they happened or no. Visiting the castle did not make the poem more concrete in my eyes; on the contrary, it fictionalized the castle. I was amazed at the degree to which I felt I had been there before.

And so, though the view of Ferrara from the tower was beautiful it was the dungeon I wanted to see: the place where, it seemed reasonable to assume, the Duchess would have been murdered at her husband's fiat. The Duke does not say so, of course—"I gave commands" (line 45) is all he will tell us, perhaps not so much secretive as uninterested—but to me it is the logical place. The Duke would want to keep the sordid act out of sight, much as he now hides her painted image behind a curtain so that only he may view it. This is how I know Browning was a great poet: who else could, in a beautiful Italian castle like this one, make me care most about an unremarkable basement? For it was unremarkable, as dungeons go, with the standard cells, barred windows, and oppressive damp. Yet how was it that I had never before realized what a horrible place a dungeon is? I had visited perhaps a half-dozen castles in my year abroad, and all of them had been tourist attractions to me. Now, though, I saw it for what it was: the place where "all smiles stopped together" (line 46). The first thing we know about the poem is that it is set in Ferrara (it says so, right under the title), and yet Browning universalizes the poem's tragedy. What happened here could happen in Tyrol, or at any of the noble houses in Europe where a love of beauty warps into a never-ending craving for possession.

"There she stands / As if alive" (lines 46–47), the Duke says before turning away from the portrait. One can read almost anything into that distracted statement: guilt at his act, triumph that he has confined his last Duchess into a form that he can control. To me, though, the Duke is not so self-reflective as to think either of these things. I see him as expressing, with an almost heartbreaking innocence and simplicity, what we love about art when we are young, what the Duke himself must have loved about it before he was transformed into a man driven only by his bizarre aesthetic greed: the feeling that the artist is creating worlds, and people. This is what makes us think we would like to meet the people we read about, even if they scare us, even if we find ourselves hating them. I had brought myself as close as I would ever come to meeting those characters. There, in Ferrara, the Duke stood, as if alive. And the Duchess, as well, with "depth and passion" in her "earnest glance" (line 8). Thanks to Browning, there was no curtain to cover her.

Reading Closely

1. Thomas Hitchner is simultaneously describing a poem by Robert Browning; a castle in Italy; that same castle as it exists in his imagination; and what else?

2. According to Hitchner, what's wrong with the idea of a book or other written text as a "transporter" or "time machine" (2)?

3. What other "commonplace about the power of art" does Hitchner call into question here (7)?

4. When Hitchner first embarked on literary pilgrimages in Europe, what made the sites of his early visits so "unsatisfying" (5)?

5. Why does Hitchner find the Duke's castle so enticing? Why is he particularly fascinated by the dungeon? What insight does he gain from observing it?

Strategies and Structures

1. Hitchner uses the photographs he took on the day he first saw the Castello d'Este as a means of describing the place objectively. Why do you think he does so before telling "what the castle meant to me" (7)? Why doesn't he simply leap into the subjective description?

2. What dominant impression of the castle does Hitchner convey? Does he do so by describing the actual castle or the castle of his imagination? Explain.

3. Hitchner does not begin to describe Browning's poem in any detail until paragraph 6, about a third of the way through the essay. Why do you think he waits until this point instead of summarizing the poem at the beginning?

4. Hitchner organizes his essay into three distinct parts. What is the function of each part?

5. Hitchner quotes little more than half a dozen lines from the Browning poem. How well-chosen do you find the lines he cites? Should he have quoted more? Why or why not?

6. What role does memory play in Hitchner's description of the Castello d'Este? Since he has never been there before, how is it that he "remembers" it?

7. *Other Methods.* How does Hitchner's reading of "My Last Duchess" exemplify the reading process as he thinks it should be?

Thinking about Language

1. What does Hitchner mean by "agency" (2)?

2. Browning's poet, says Hitchner, "augments" the stones of the castle (9). What do you think of his use of this word?

3. To what curtain is Hitchner referring at the end of his essay? How does the curtain function as a METAPHOR—that is, in what sense has he been lifting a curtain throughout?

4. Why does Hitchner COMPARE a book to a "map" instead of a landscape (2)?

For Writing

1. Where has reading taken you? Write a paragraph or two describing a literary or historical site you have visited. Try to picture the site both as it was and as you had expected it to be.

2. Write an essay describing one of your own adventures in reading and what it taught you about the act of reading itself. You might base your essay on a reading of a favorite text, as Hitchner does.

ROBERT BROWNING

My Last Duchess

Robert Browning (1812–1889) grew up in England, where his father was a bank clerk and collector of antiquities and his mother was a pianist. By age fourteen, Browning had learned French, Greek, and Latin. His first major work, Pauline, was published in 1840. In 1846, Browning married the poet Elizabeth Barrett, and they moved to Italy. In 1849, his Collected Poems was published. Browning's intensely psychological poems are known for showing human motives at work—instead of merely telling about them—through such devices as the dramatic monologue. After his wife's death in 1861, Browning returned to London and continued to write poems until his death in 1899. He is buried in Westminster Abbey in the "Poet's Corner."

"My Last Duchess" (1842) is loosely based on the life of Alfonso II, the Duke of Ferrara, in northern Italy, who lived in the sixteenth century. In Browning's poem, the Duke stands in front of a life-like portrait of his last wife and describes her, both as she was in life and as she is pictured in the portrait, to a marriage broker (a representative of a count whose daughter the Duke wishes to marry).

Ferrara

That's my last Duchess painted on the wall,   1
Looking as if she were alive. I call
That piece a wonder, now: Frà Pandolf's hands
Worked busily a day, and there she stands.
Will't please you sit and look at her? I said   5
"Frà Pandolf" by design, for never read
Strangers like you that pictured countenance,
The depth and passion of its earnest glance,
But to myself they turned (since none puts by
The curtain I have drawn for you, but I)   10
And seemed as they would ask me, if they durst,
How such a glance came there; so, not the first
Are you to turn and ask thus. Sir, 'twas not
Her husband's presence only, called that spot
Of joy into the Duchess' cheek: perhaps   15
Frà Pandolf chanced to say "Her mantle laps
Over my lady's wrist too much," or "Paint
Must never hope to reproduce the faint
Half-flush that dies along her throat": such stuff

Was courtesy, she thought, and cause enough   20
For calling up that spot of joy. She had
A heart—how shall I say?—too soon made glad,
Too easily impressed; she liked whate'er
She looked on, and her looks went everywhere.
Sir, 'twas all one! My favor at her breast,   25
The dropping of the daylight in the West,
The bough of cherries some officious fool
Broke in the orchard for her, the white mule
She rode with round the terrace—all and each
Would draw from her alike the approving speech,   30
Or blush, at least. She thanked men,—good! but thanked
Somehow—I know not how—as if she ranked
My gift of a nine-hundred-years-old name
With anybody's gift. Who'd stoop to blame
This sort of trifling? Even had you skill   35
In speech—which I have not—to make your will
Quite clear to such an one, and say, "Just this
Or that in you disgusts me; here you miss,
Or there exceed the mark"—and if she let
Herself be lessoned so, nor plainly set   40
Her wits to yours, forsooth, and made excuse,
—E'en then would be some stooping; and I choose
Never to stoop. Oh sir, she smiled, no doubt,
Whene'er I passed her; but who passed without
Much the same smile? This grew; I gave commands;   45
Then all smiles stopped together. There she stands
As if alive. Will't please you rise? We'll meet
The company below, then. I repeat,
The Count your master's known munificence
Is ample warrant that no just pretense   50
Of mine for dowry will be disallowed;
Though his fair daughter's self, as I avowed
At starting, is my object. Nay, we'll go
Together down, sir. Notice Neptune, though,
Taming a sea-horse, thought a rarity,   55
Which Claus of Innsbruck cast in bronze for me!

READING CLOSELY

1. The Duke in Browning's poem has ordered the death of his last duchess, whose portrait now hangs behind a curtain on the wall. How do we know this?

2. "I call / That piece a wonder, now" (2–3). In the opening lines of Browning's poem, the Duke is describing his dead lady's portrait. To whom (besides the reader)? Why is this visitor present?

3. It is the lady's painted "glance" (8, 12), in particular, that the Duke and the visiting stranger "read" (6) as they first look at the portrait. What specific qualities does the Duke ascribe to that glance?

4. The Duke points out a "spot / Of joy" in the painting (14–15). What is he referring to? How did it get there?

5. Why does the Duke ask his visitor to "rise" in line 47? What has he been doing? Where are the Duke and his visitor going at the end of the poem, as the Duke calls the stranger's attention to a rare bronze sculpture of Neptune?

STRATEGIES AND STRUCTURES

1. Having described the wonderful portrait at the beginning of Browning's poem, the Duke directs his guest to "notice," at the end, another work of art in his collection (54). What does the Duke's preoccupation with these fine possessions reveal about his character?

2. What particular qualities of mind and heart does the Duke focus on as he describes the lady's character? Why do these traits "disgust" him (38)?

3. How do the "dropping of the daylight in the West," the "bough of cherries," and "the white mule" (26–28) contribute to the Duke's description of the lady? Cite other details in his description that help complete the picture.

4. What DOMINANT IMPRESSION of his (former) lady does the Duke's description leave you with?

5. *Other Methods.* Browning's poem has a PLOT worthy of a murder mystery. The Duke tells the story of the murder in a single sentence, however. Which one? Why do you think Browning reduces the NARRATIVE of the actual murder (or of the confession) to such a minimum in his description? What happens next, after the Duke lets the secret out?

THINKING ABOUT LANGUAGE

1. The Duke says he did not have enough "skill / In speech" (35–36) to explain his objections to the lady even if he wanted to. Explain the IRONY of this claim.

2. The Duke thinks the lady should be "lessoned" (40). What are the CONNOTATIONS of this term, and why might the arrogant Duke use it?

3. What does the Duke mean by "stooping" (42)? What does his choice of this word reveal about his character?

FOR WRITING

1. Write a brief portrait in words that captures the spirit and conduct of a person you have observed.

2. Write a DESCRIPTION of a painting that has captured your imagination. Describe the painting in detail, and also describe your reaction to the image in such a way that the reader understands why it affects you as it does.

CHAPTER 5

Example

<hr>

Few things are harder to put up with than the annoyance of a good
example.   —MARK TWAIN, *Pudd'nhead Wilson*

An art dealer knows at a glance that a supposedly ancient statue is a fake. After
five minutes in a new course, a student accurately predicts that the professor is
going to be a brilliant teacher—or a bore. Listening to a husband and wife bicker in
his office, a trained psychologist can tell, with ninety percent accuracy, whether the
couple will still be together in fifteen years. These are all EXAMPLES that journalist
Malcolm Gladwell uses to illustrate "thin-slicing," the idea that human beings can
make accurate judgments based on "the very thinnest slice" of information.

Examples help us to understand such concepts by making them more concrete
and specific. Because a single good example is often worth a dozen lengthy explanations, we use examples all the time to support or explain what we have to say.
The use of examples—exemplification—is so basic to human communication, in
fact, that it is hard to imagine writing without them.

Defining Exemplification:
Giving a "For Instance"

When you define something, such as thin-slicing or the law of supply and demand,
you say what it is. When you exemplify something, you give an instance or illustration. To show us what he means by thin-slicing, Gladwell cites the example of an
experienced policeman who knows from the look of fear on a gang member's face
that he doesn't have to shoot, even though the youth is in the act of pulling a gun:

"He was fourteen, looked like he was nine. If he was an adult I think I probably would have shot him. I sure perceived the threat of that gun. . . . I think
the fact that I was an experienced officer had a lot to do with my decision. I
could see a lot of fear in his face, which I also perceived in other situations,
and that led me to believe that if I would just give him just a little bit more
time that he might give me an option to not shoot him."

—MALCOLM GLADWELL, Blink

This is, as Gladwell goes on to say, "a beautiful example" of the complicated psychological process he is explaining.

Examples are specific items or instances—a crispy taco with guacamole, "The
Raven," a fast-thinking cop who decides not to shoot a teenager—that can be taken
to represent a whole group—Tex-Mex food, the poems of Edgar Allan Poe, psychological thin-slicing.

In this chapter, we will see how to choose examples that truly represent—or
exemplify—your subject. We will consider how many and what kinds of examples
are sufficient to make your point about that subject, and we will discuss how to
organize an entire essay around those examples.

Why Do We Cite Examples?

For most of us, it is easier to digest a piece of pie than the whole pie at once. The
same goes for examples: They make general concepts easier to grasp (and swal-
low), and they give the flavor of the whole in a single bite. As writers, we cite
examples to explain an ABSTRACT idea, to provide support for an ARGUMENT, or just
to make something interesting.

Suppose we were writing about a street bazaar and wanted to make the point
that "everything was for sale." This seems like a straightforward statement, but
"everything" could refer to almost anything—from livestock to homemade bread. To
clarify what we mean, we would need to give specific examples, as in the following:

Everything was for sale—flowers, bolts of cloth, candles, fruits and vegetables, shoes, coffee beans, toys, cheap jewelry, canned goods, religious articles,
books, kerosene, candy, nylons, towels—all of it spilling onto the street in
colorful profusion. —FRANK CONROY, Stop-Time

Using examples like this helps us (and our readers) to narrow down the universe
from "everything" to something a little more specific. It shows just what corner of
the great bazaar we're talking about, and it gives the reader a CONCRETE sense of
the bazaar's "colorful profusion." Even more important, by using concrete examples

like bolts of cloth and kerosene, Conroy explains exactly what was for sale, making his statement clearer and more interesting.

Composing an Exemplification Essay

An exemplification essay consists of basically two parts: a generalization ("everything was for sale") and the examples that demonstrate and support the generalization ("bolts of cloth, candles, fruits and vegetables, shoes, coffee beans, toys, cheap jewelry" etc.). As you compose such an essay, then, think first about your main point and let that point guide you in choosing which qualities of your subject to emphasize.

For example, if you are making a point about the abundance of goods at a street market, you would focus, as Frank Conroy does, on the number and variety of the items for sale at the market. Once you have decided which qualities (abundance and low prices) are essential characteristics of your subject, your next task is to look for concrete and specific examples—all those bolts of cloth and canned goods—that exemplify these characteristics.

As you come up with representative examples of your subject, you will need to decide not only which particular examples to cite, but also how to organize and present them. The exact number and kinds of examples you give, however, will depend as much upon your audience and purpose as upon your subject.

Thinking about Purpose and Audience

Before you begin writing, think about your purpose. Is it to entertain? Inform? Persuade? Each purpose requires a different kind of example. For instance, consider the satirical bake sale piece from *The Onion* on p. 183, "All Seven Deadly Sins Committed at Church Bake Sale." The purpose of this piece is to entertain, so it offers humorous examples of incidents at the bake sale.

But suppose you wanted to write a straightforward, informative report about the bake sale for the church bulletin. In that case, you would focus on examples not of the deadly sins, but of the people staffing the booths and the kinds of baked goods sold. On the other hand, if you were writing about the bake sale in order to persuade others to participate next time, you might offer examples of the money earned at various booths, how much fun participants had, and what good causes the money will be used for. In every case, your purpose determines the kinds of examples you use.

Before you can select examples that are particularly effective, you will have to take into account how much your AUDIENCE already knows about your subject and how sympathetic they are likely to be to your position. Suppose you are writing a paper for a course in health and nutrition, and your PURPOSE is to demonstrate that the health of Americans in general has declined over the last decade. If you were writing for your teacher alone—or for an audience of doctors and nutritionists—a few key examples would probably suffice to make your point.

Your paper, however, is intended for a more general audience, such as your classmates. So you will need to give more background information and cite more (and more basic) examples than you would if you were addressing an audience of specialists. If your readers are unfamiliar with your subject or not likely to see it as you do, you are going to have to work even harder to come up with sufficient examples. For instance, you may have to give extra examples to remind the athletes in your audience that their physical condition is not necessarily representative of the general state of health among all Americans.

Generating Ideas: Finding Good Examples

Techniques like LISTING, BRAINSTORMING, and CLUSTERING can help you come up with examples on almost any subject. As you look for examples, look for ones that display as many of the typical characteristics of your subject as possible.

Suppose you were writing an essay about the seven deadly sins, and you decided to focus on the sin of gluttony. One characteristic of gluttony is overeating. As you looked around for good examples of this characteristic, you might be tempted to choose someone like the international speed-eating champion, Sonya Thomas, who holds world records for devouring chicken wings (157 in thirty-two minutes), tacos (43 in eleven minutes), and eggs (65 in seven minutes). She would seem to be a prime example of gluttony. Thomas, however, weighs only about a hundred pounds; and though she eats a lot, she has many other characteristics, such as discipline and endurance, that we typically associate with great athletes. Perhaps she isn't such a good example of a glutton after all.

So as you look for examples, search for ones that exemplify *all* the essential traits of the subject you're exemplifying. Gluttons, for instance, not only eat a lot; they are often lazy. To exemplify the concept of gluttony more accurately and completely, therefore, we need to look for something or someone who exhibits both of these essential traits. How about Jabba the Hutt, the obese alien of *Star Wars* fame? Would he, perhaps, make a better example of gluttony than Sonya Thomas?

Jabba eats a lot—that's why he is so grossly overweight. Also, when not eating, he is forever tugging at his water pipe, another sign of overindulgence. What about lethargy, a prime characteristic of the glutton? Jabba can hardly rise from his cushions, much less dart around the galaxy participating in eating contests. And when he does attempt to walk, he waddles heavily from side to side. Since Jabba embodies most of the chief characteristics of a glutton—he is both fat *and* lazy—he would make a better example of gluttony than the trim and energetic Thomas.

Organizing and Drafting an Exemplification Essay

Once you have a number of examples that exhibit the chief characteristics of your subject, you're ready to organize them and put them in a draft. The simplest way to organize an exemplification essay is to state your THESIS at the beginning and then give your best examples to support it. You could also present your examples in order of increasing importance or interest, perhaps saving the best for last. Or, if you plan to use a large number of examples, you might organize them into categories.

However you organize your essay, you'll need to clearly state your point, provide sufficient and representative examples, and use transitions to help readers follow your text. The tips on p. 171 can help you with your draft.

STATING YOUR POINT

Usually, in an exemplification essay, you will state your point directly in a THESIS STATEMENT in your introduction. For example:

> College teams depend upon teamwork more than star athletes for success.

> In general, the health of Americans has declined in the last ten years.

> Hillary Clinton's 2008 campaign for the U.S. presidency made a number of tactical errors.

> From a close reading of almost any major scene in *The Great Gatsby*, we can conclude that Fitzgerald's narrator, Nick Carraway, is not to be trusted.

> As indicated by the increasing popularity of websites devoted to harmful campus gossip, online anonymity poses serious ethical problems.

Each of these thesis statements cries out for specific examples to support it. How many specific examples would you need to do the job sufficiently—and what kinds?

PROVIDING SUFFICIENT EXAMPLES

As you select examples to support a thesis, you have basically two choices: you can use multiple brief examples or one or two extended examples. Which method you choose will depend, in part, on the kind of generalization you're making.

Multiple examples work well when you are dealing with different aspects of a large subject (the Clinton presidential campaign strategy) or exemplifying trends involving large numbers of people (Americans whose health has declined, college athletes). Extended examples, on the other hand, work better when you are talking about the implications of a particular case (a single scene in a novel; a particular website).

TIPS AND TEMPLATES FOR DRAFTING

When you begin to draft an essay based on examples, you need to identify the subject, say what its main characteristics are, and indicate specific examples that exhibit those characteristics. These moves are fundamental to exemplification. See how David Barboza makes such moves in the beginning of his essay in this chapter:

> Marketing experts call it extending the heritage brand . . . stocking the shelves with new twists on old, familiar names. Snickers, for instance, flavor Edy's ice cream. Nestlé candies are sprinkled on Chips Ahoy cookies. —DAVID BARBOZA, "Piling on the Cookies"

Barboza identifies his subject (the marketing practice of "extending the heritage brand"), says what the main characteristic of that practice is ("stocking the shelves with new twists on old, familiar names"), and indicates specific examples that exhibit that characteristic (Snickers on Edy's ice cream; Nestlé candies on Chips Ahoy cookies). Here is one more example from this chapter:

> Since commencement speakers traditionally offer advice to the young in June, here, in no particular order, are a dozen of the quotations that one reader calls to mind in moments of confusion, stress, and sorrow. —MICHAEL DIRDA, "Commencement Advice"

The following templates can help you make some of these basic moves in your own writing. But don't take these as formulas where you just have to fill in the blanks. There are no easy formulas for good writing, but these templates can serve as starting points.

▶ About X, it can generally be said that _____; a good example would be _____.

▶ The main characteristics of X are _____ and _____, as exemplified by _____, _____ and _____.

▶ For the best example(s) of X, we can turn to _____.

▶ _____ is a particularly representative example of X because _____.

▶ Additional examples of X include _____, _____, and _____.

▶ From these examples of X, we can conclude that _____.

Take the proposition that the health of Americans, on average, has declined in the last ten years. To support a sweeping general statement like this, which applies to millions of people, you would probably need to use multiple examples rather than one or two extended ones.

On its website, the American Public Health Association lists eighteen indicators of the nation's health. If you were drawing on this data to make your point about the decline in health among Americans in recent years, you would not likely focus on only one or two of these indicators, since health is a broad topic that encompasses many factors. Instead, you would want to cite multiple examples—increased rates of infant mortality, greater obesity and addiction to smoking, shorter average life expectancies, and a decrease in spending for health care—of the many different factors that contribute to the general decline you are illustrating.

Now let's consider how a newspaper columnist uses a single, brief example to support his thesis about the problem of anonymity on the Internet:

> One site, called JuicyCampus.com, which maintains message boards on 59 university campuses, has been attracting special attention. As a recent article in *Radar Magazine* put it, JuicyCampus.com is "a virtual bathroom wall upon which college students across the country scrawl slurs, smears, and secrets, true or otherwise, about their classmates." In one feature, to take one modest example, . . . there were 47 postings in response, several of which gave names, apparently real ones.
>
> —RICHARD BERNSTEIN, "The Growing Cowardice of Online Anonymity"

Bernstein's thesis—that Internet anonymity raises serious ethical problems—addresses a large issue; but here is a case where a single example might be sufficient to make the point because most readers can easily imagine themselves as victims of the practice that Bernstein describes. However, if your audience is likely to be divided on an issue, such as the coverage of a political candidate by the national media, you would need to give more examples.

Sufficiency isn't strictly a matter of numbers. Often a few good examples will suffice, which is what sufficiency implies: enough to do the job, and no more. Ultimately, whether or not your examples are sufficient to prove your point depends on your audience. If your readers are inclined to agree with you, sometimes a single extended example may be enough. On the other hand, if your readers bring a wide range of opinions to your subject, you will probably need more examples, no matter what your point is.

In other words, whether or not your examples are sufficient to support your thesis is not determined by the number of examples you give so much as by how persuasive those examples will seem to your readers. So consider your intended readers, and choose examples you think they will find interesting and convincing.

USING A RANGE OF REPRESENTATIVE EXAMPLES

Be sure that your examples fairly and accurately support the point you're making. In an essay on how college athletic teams depend on teamwork for success, for instance, you would want to choose examples from several different teams. Similarly, if you are trying to convince readers that Hillary Clinton made many tactical errors in her campaign for the presidency, you would need to show a number of those errors, from several different points in the campaign.

And make sure that any examples you give are representatives. For this reason, you'll want to steer clear of highly unusual examples. If you are writing about the benefits of swimming every day, for instance, Michael Phelps is not a typical swimmer and should not be your only example. Better to cite several swimmers, ones who can demonstrate several different benefits.

USING TRANSITIONS BETWEEN EXAMPLES

To make a point with examples, you need to do more than state your claim and then give examples, no matter how effective they may be. You need to relate those examples to each other and to the point you're making by using clear TRANSITIONS and other connecting words and phrases.

You can always use the phrases "for example" and "for instance": "The sloth, for example, is one of many animals that survive because of their protective coloration. Other animals—for instance, wolves and wild dogs—do so by going around in packs." But consider using other transitions and connecting phrases as well, such as: *more specifically, exactly, precisely, thus, namely, indeed, that is, in other words, in fact, in particular.* ("The sloth, in particular, survives by blending in with its surroundings.") Or try using a rhetorical question, which you then go on to answer: "So what strategy of survival does the sloth exemplify?"

USING OTHER METHODS

Other methods of writing are often useful in an exemplification essay. Because the purpose of examples is to make your topic concrete and specific, you might want to DESCRIBE them in some detail. Or you might NARRATE what happens when your subject behaves in its typical fashion. Or you might ANALYZE THE CAUSES by which your subject came to have its distinctive attributes.

Reading an Exemplification Essay with a Critical Eye

When you write an essay based on examples, those examples should not only be clear and interesting, they should clearly illustrate what you say they do. Do your examples meet these requirements? Once you've drafted your essay, ask someone else to read it and tell you which examples they find especially effective and which ones, if any, they think should be replaced or developed more sharply. Here are some questions that you or other readers might ask when checking over an exemplification essay.

PURPOSE AND AUDIENCE. What is the overall purpose of the essay—to inform? Entertain? Persuade? How well does the text achieve that purpose? How familiar is the intended audience likely to be with the subject of the essay? What additional information might they find useful? What terms might they need to have defined or further explained?

THE POINT. What is the main point of the essay? Is it stated in a thesis? If not, should it be? How and how well do the examples support the thesis?

ORGANIZATION. Does the essay use multiple shorter examples, a few extended examples, or a combination of the two? Is this arrangement appropriate to the kind of generalization the essay makes—using multiple examples, for instance, to support a generalization that applies in many instances and extended examples to illustrate particular cases?

SUFFICIENT EXAMPLES. Are the examples presented in the essay sufficient to illustrate its key point or points? If not, how could the examples be made more persuasive? Would more examples be more convincing?

CONCRETE AND SPECIFIC EXAMPLES. Do the examples explain the topic in ways that are concrete (perceptible to the senses) and specific (narrowed down)? If not, how might they be sharpened?

REPRESENTATIVE EXAMPLES. Do the examples fairly and accurately represent the group they claim to represent? If the essay is based on one or two extended examples, do they represent *all* the important characteristics of the subject?

TRANSITIONS. Check all the transition words and phrases in the essay. How effectively do they introduce and link the examples? Do they explicitly connect the examples to the ideas they are illustrating? Where might transitions be added or strengthened?

OTHER METHODS. Does the essay incorporate any other methods of development? Would it be improved by including some description or narration, for example?

Editing for Common Errors in Examples

Exemplification invites certain kinds of errors. The following tips will help you check your writing for some of them.

If you list a series of examples, check to be sure they are parallel in structure.

NOT   Animals avoid predators in many ways. They travel in groups, move fast, blending in with their surroundings, and looking threatening.

BUT   Animals avoid predators in many ways. They travel in groups, move fast, blend in with their surroundings, and look threatening.

Edit out *etc.*, *and so forth*, or *and so on* when they add nothing of substance to a sentence.

NOT   Animals typically avoid predators by traveling in groups, moving fast, blending in with their surroundings, etc.

BUT   Animals typically avoid predators by traveling in groups, moving fast, and blending in with their surroundings.

Check your use of *i.e.* and *e.g.*

These abbreviations of Latin phrases are often used interchangeably to introduce examples, but they do not mean the same thing: *i.e.* means "that is" and *e.g.* means "for example." Since most of your readers do not likely speak Latin, it is a good idea to use the English equivalents.

▶ The chameleon is an animal that uses protective coloration—that is, it changes color to blend in with its surroundings.

▶ Some animals change colors to blend in with their surroundings—for example, the chameleon.

An eBay Ad

Whatever you're looking for, you can get it on eBay. Such is the claim of this topiary advertisement for the world's largest Internet auction service. When you make such a claim in writing you need to support it with concrete, specific examples—like hula skirts, lawnmowers, and artificial turf. The bigger the claim, the more examples you are likely to need. The exact number and kind of examples you give, however, will depend on your audience, and on how well your examples represent your subject. Good examples can represent an entire domain of possibilities. That's why advertisers like eBay can hope to attract buyers to a vast inventory of goods and services by giving just twenty-one specific examples—in this case all carefully chosen to evoke a green world of recreation and the outdoors.

EVERYDAY EXAMPLE

search.ebay.com/hula skirts
   /portable video games
   /mystery novels
   /baseball tickets
   /all-terrain tires
   /dome tents
   /stain removers

/ranch land
/hedge trimmers
/golf shoes
/video cellphones
/flip-flops
/digital sports watches
/horseshoe sets

/laptops
/swimming trunks
/digital cameras
/sprinklers
/sun hats
/lawnmowers
/artificial turf

you can get **it** on

DAVID BARBOZA

Piling on the Cookies

David Barboza was still an undergraduate at Boston University when he became a part-time correspondent for the New York Times. *Seven years after graduation, in 1997, the newspaper hired him as a staff writer for the business section. Over the course of his career, Barboza has made a specialty of spotting trends—as in "Piling on the Cookies."*

This article makes clear that sometimes the best way to tell a story is by detailing a well-chosen example. Here, Barboza uses the Oreo cookie as an extended example of a significant trend in modern marketing: what industry insiders call "line extension." Barboza's article first appeared in the New York Times *in October 2003.*

FINDING OLD-FASHIONED Oreo sandwich cookies on supermarket shelves is no 1
easy task these days.

The toothsome snack's progeny, like the flashier Fudge Mint Covered Oreo, the 2
heftier Oreo Double Stuf and the bite-sized Mini Oreo, now crowd the cookie aisle,
leaving the 91-year-old original wedged into the tiniest of corners.

Marketing experts call it extending the heritage brand. Rather than spending 3
millions to develop and market new brands, food marketers are stocking the
shelves with new twists on old, familiar names. Snickers, for instance, flavor Edy's
ice cream. Nestlé candies are sprinkled on Chips Ahoy cookies. Trix cereal has
migrated into Yoplait yogurt. And Reese's Pieces have become a cereal called
Reese's Puffs.

But few foods are as ubiquitous as the humble charcoal-colored Oreo, which has a 4
basketful of spinoffs, from candy bars to ice cream to pie crusts. Such versatility has
helped to more than double the sale of all things Oreo over the last decade—close to
$1 billion. Not bad for a brand that is older than the automobile assembly line.

There are, for instance, Oreo O's breakfast cereal, Oreo ice cream, Oreo Jell-O, 5
Oreo pudding crust, cake mix, frosting, brownies, granola bars, and, just in time for
Halloween, Oreos with pumpkin-colored cream fillings.

Marketing experts say Oreo is not just a cookie anymore, it's practically a flavor. 6
But, they warn, there are dangers in tinkering with valuable brands. Chiefly, they
worry about saturating the market, and there are some signs from Kraft Foods Inc.
that cookie sales are slowing.

Still, they marvel at how Kraft and Nabisco have found so many new ways to use 7
Oreos and to get people to buy them. Nabisco, the creator of Oreos, merged with
Kraft in 2000 and Kraft was spun off from Philip Morris a year later.

"The industry term for this phenomena is line extension," says Alan Brew, a 8

**DOUBLE DELIGHT
MINT 'N CREME**
Introduced in 2003

**DOUBLE DELIGHT
PEANUT BUTTER &
CHOCOLATE**
2003

**DOUBLE DELIGHT
COFFEE 'N CREME**
2003

UH OH OREO
(Vanilla cookie, chocolate filling)
2003

CHOCOLATE CREME OREO
2001

FOOTBALL OREO
(Football design on biscuit)
Seasonal

DOUBLE STUFF
1974

ORIGINAL
1912

Piling on the Cookies
In the Oreo's first eight decades,
Nabisco tried only a handful of
variations on the original. But
in recent years, it has stretched
the line to more than two dozen
by varying the size, the filling,
the biscuit recipe—nearly
everything but the brand name.
Here are some examples now
on store shelves.

marketing expert at Addison, a corporate branding consultant in San Francisco. "This widens the franchise. And it's defensive. To stop a micro-product from coming in, you attack yourself, all the time, before someone else attacks you."

Yet close comparisons are hard to come by. Coke evolved into Diet Coke, Cherry 9 Coke, Diet Cherry Coke, and even Vanilla Coke. But that was nothing like the hyper-evolving, perpetually repackaged, category-migrating Oreo.

There is the Double Delight Oreo, the Uh-Oh Oreo (vanilla cookie with choco- 10 late filling), Oreo Cookie Barz, Football Oreos, Oreos Cookies & Creme Pie, Oreos in Kraft Lunchables, for kids, and Oreo cookies with a variety of cream fillings (mint, chocolate, coffee) and sizes (6-pack, 12-pack, snack pack and more).

According to the latest Oreo promotions, there is even an Oreo cookie that, 11 when liberally dunked in a glass of milk, will turn the milk blue and win some lucky Oreo dunker a $1 million prize.

"Every year we talk to consumers and Oreo lovers," says Daryl Brewster, Kraft's 12 president of the biscuits, snacks and confections. "And what we found is tremendous amounts of desire for the next Oreo experience."

These days, food companies like to talk of eating "experiences." Ketchup isn't 13 just ketchup, it's jazzed up with green food coloring and made into a kind of finger paint for finger food—for children to play with and squirt on mashed potatoes.

Kraft approaches the Oreo in the same way. Eating an Oreo isn't just eating an 14 Oreo, they say, it's the experience of dunking it in milk, twisting it apart and licking it clean.

Believing as they do in the Oreo experience, the issue for Kraft executives boils 15 down to this: Why introduce a new cookie brand when you can just keep reinventing the Oreo?

"It's much more economical to extend a brand rather than create a new one," 16 says Judy Hopelain, a brand strategist at Prophet, a consulting firm in San Francisco. "It's also probably a lot easier to get shelf space for a well-known brand."

The strategy seems to have worked, analysts said. 17

"Between 1998 and 2001, the Oreo had annual compound growth of 13 per- 18 cent," says John McMillin, a longtime food analyst at Prudential Securities. "These days, few things in the food industry even grow 3 percent."

But Kraft's most recent profit report suggests the Oreo gravy train may be slow- 19 ing. The company said that cookie sales overall have weakened, but some of that weakness was offset by a strong introduction this year [2003] of the Uh-Oh Oreo.

Some Wall Street analysts are now warning of trouble ahead because cookie 20 sales generally are forecast to continue to fall. Kraft officials declined to say whether Oreo sales were declining, or whether the drop was in other brands, like Chips Ahoy or Ritz crackers.

"The Oreo line extensions have been successful," said William Leach, a consumer analyst at Neuberger Berman, an investment firm based in New York, "but the whole line is getting soft." 21

There are other problems, as well. The Oreo, like most mass-produced cookies, gets some of its texture from trans fatty acids, which raise the level of fat and cholesterol in the blood, and may lower the level of high density lipoproteins, often called good cholesterol. Last year the National Academy of Sciences said the level of trans fats in the diet should be as low as possible. 22

Kraft and Nabisco have responded to the controversy in a familiar way, by introducing yet another kind of Oreo, a reduced-fat variety to join the double-filled and the fudge-covered. 23

Kraft executives say that for the last few years, focus groups and market research shows that consumers want more and more varieties of the Oreo, which was created in 1912 by the National Biscuit Company, later known as Nabisco. 24

But there is a concern that too much tinkering could tarnish the brand. The lesson of New Coke—introduced and then withdrawn by the Coca-Cola Company after complaints from faithful customers—has not been lost on Kraft. 25

That is not to say that Oreo fans will not test the limits on their own. Just ask those people who delight in making deep-fried Oreos by soaking them in pancake batter before frying them in cooking oil. 26

Is Kraft, which has already blanketed the world with its billion-dollar cookie, running out of ideas? 27

Nope. 28

"There are some places we won't go," Mr. Brewster, at Kraft, says. "But there are still a lot of places. As long as we continue to listen to consumers, we'll be O.K." 29

READING CLOSELY

1. According to David Barboza, why are "old-fashioned" Oreos hard to find on grocery shelves these days (1)?

2. What is Barboza's main point, and how does his example of the hard-to-find "original" cookie illustrate that point (2)?

3. Why, according to marketing experts, do companies extend old brands instead of introducing entirely new product lines?

4. Although Kraft Foods has been successful in extending the Oreo brand, what are some problems in the food industry in general?

STRATEGIES AND STRUCTURES

1. Barboza begins his article by explaining the concept of "line extension." What CONCRETE and specific examples does he use to illustrate that general concept?

2. What is Barboza's PURPOSE in writing about marketing strategies? Who is his intended AUDIENCE? How can you tell?

3. Barboza explains how the executives at Kraft Foods have extended the Oreo line in particular. What specific examples does he give? Are they sufficient to make his point? Why or why not?

4. Barboza often makes a general statement and then immediately gives a concrete example to back it up. Point out several instances, and explain how (and how well) this author's examples actually represent his ideas.

5. Throughout his article, Barboza uses transitions and connectors like *for instance*. What other transitions does Barboza use, and how do they help him remind readers of his main point?

6. *Other Methods.* Oreo, says Barboza, is no longer just a cookie but "practically a flavor" (6), and consuming an Oreo is not just an act of eating but "an experience" (13–14). How does he use examples to illustrate these new DEFINITIONS?

THINKING ABOUT LANGUAGE

1. In paragraph 2, why do you think Barboza uses the word "progeny" instead of *descendants* or *offspring* (2)?

2. What is a "spinoff," and how does Barboza apply the word to companies as well as products (4, 7)?

3. How do the hyphenated words in paragraph 9 help to illustrate what Barboza is saying about the evolution of the humble Oreo?

4. What makes a vanilla cookie filled with chocolate an "Uh-Oh Oreo" (10)?

5. Explain the PUN on "gravy train" in paragraph 19.

FOR WRITING

1. Write a paragraph exemplifying an eating "experience" you have had (13–14).

2. Many companies extend their products and brands, as, for example, Nike and Adidas have done with their athletic shoes, or auto manufacturers do with frequent changes in models and styling and with add-ons, such as mud-flaps and magnesium wheels. Using a product, brand, or service you are familiar with, write an exemplification essay illustrating line extension.

All Seven Deadly Sins Committed
at Church Bake Sale

The Onion is a satirical weekly newspaper that was founded in 1988 by two juniors at the University of Wisconsin, Tim Keck and Christopher Johnson, who distributed a handful of copies to their friends around the Madison area. Today The Onion *boasts more than three million regular readers nationwide and attributes its success to "fearless reporting and scathing commentary." Consider, for instance, these* Onion *headlines: "Cases of Glitter Lung on the Rise among Elementary-School Art Teachers," "Study Reveals Pittsburgh Unprepared for Full-Scale Zombie Attack," "Bush Vows to Eliminate U.S. Dependence on Oil By 4920." Such satire has won* The Onion *a Thurber Prize for American Humor and a handful of Webby Awards for theonion.com. Two collections of its articles have made the* New York Times *bestseller list:* Ad Nauseam *(2003) and* Our Dumb Century *(2004).*

The Onion's brand of satire is marked by its pitch-perfect mimicry of the reporting styles that many papers routinely use to inflate the banal into the newsworthy. In the following article, an Onion *investigative reporter sniffs out numerous concrete and specific examples of the "deadly sins" committed at a church bake sale.*

Gᴀᴅꜱᴅᴇɴ, AL—The seven deadly sins—avarice, sloth, envy, lust, gluttony, pride, and wrath—were all committed Sunday during the twice-annual bake sale at St. Mary's of the Immaculate Conception Church.

In total, 347 individual acts of sin were committed at the bake sale, with nearly every attendee committing at least one of the seven deadly sins as outlined by Gregory the Great in the fifth century.

"My cookies, cakes, and brownies are always the highlight of our church bake sales, and everyone says so," said parishioner Connie Barrett, 49, openly committing the sin of pride. "Sometimes, even I'm amazed by how well my goodies turn out."

Fellow parishioner Betty Wicks agreed.

"Every time I go past Connie's table, I just have to buy something," said the 245-pound Wicks, who commits the sin of gluttony at every St. Mary's bake sale, as well as most Friday nights at Old Country Buffet. "I simply can't help myself—it's all so delicious."

The popularity of Barrett's mouth-watering wares elicited the sin of envy in many of her fellow vendors.

"Connie has this fantastic book of recipes her grandmother gave her, and she won't share them with anyone," church organist Georgia Brandt said. "This year, I made white-chocolate blondies and thought they'd be a big hit. But most people just went straight to Connie's table, got what they wanted, and left. All the while, Connie just stood there with this look of smug satisfaction on her face. It took every ounce of strength in my body to keep from going over there and really telling her off."

While the sins of wrath and avarice were each committed dozens of times at the event, Barrett and longtime bake-sale rival Penny Cox brought them together in full force.   8

"Penny said she wanted to make a bet over whose table would make the most money," said Barrett, exhibiting avarice. "Whoever lost would have to sit in the dunk tank at the St. Mary's Summer Fun Festival. I figured it's for such a good cause, a little wager couldn't hurt. Besides, I always bring the church more money anyway, so I couldn't possibly lose."   9

Moments after agreeing to the wager, Cox became wrathful when Barrett, the bake sale's co-chair, grabbed the best table location under the pretense of having to keep the coffee machine full. Cox attempted to exact revenge by reporting an alleged Barrett misdeed to the church's priest.   10

"I mentioned to Father Mark [O'Connor] that I've seen candles at Connie's house that I wouldn't be surprised one bit if she stole from the church's storage closet," said Cox, who also committed the sin of sloth by forcing her daughter to set up and man her booth while she gossiped with friends. "Perhaps if he investigates this, by this time next year, Connie won't be co-chair of the bake sale and in her place we'll have someone who's willing to rotate the choice table spots."   11

The sin of lust also reared its ugly head at the bake sale, largely due to the presence of Melissa Wyckoff, a shapely 20-year-old redhead whose family recently joined the church. While male attendees ogled Wyckoff, the primary object of lust for females was the personable, boyish Father Mark.   12

Though attendees' feelings of lust for Wyckoff and O'Connor were never acted on, they did not go unnoticed.   13

"There's something not right about that Melissa Wyckoff," said envious and wrathful bake-sale participant Jilly Brandon, after her husband Craig offered Wyckoff one of her Rice Krispie treats to "welcome her to the parish." "She might have just moved here from California, but that red dress of hers should get her kicked out of the church."   14

According to St. Mary's treasurer Beth Ellen Coyle, informal church-sponsored events are a notorious breeding ground for the seven deadly sins.   15

"Bake sales, haunted houses, pancake breakfasts . . . such church events are rife with potential for sin," Coyle said. "This year, we had to eliminate the 'Guess Your Weight' booth from the annual church carnival because the envy and pride had got-   16 ten so out of hand. Church events are about glorifying God, not violating His word. If you want to do that, you're no better than that cheap strumpet Melissa Wyckoff."

READING CLOSELY

1. Who established the names and number of the seven deadly sins as we know them today?

2. How "deadly" do you find the sins reported here? That is, how well do the reporter's examples represent the general concept he says he is exemplifying?

3. The *Onion* reporter records "347 individual acts of sin" at the church bake sale (2). Is anything suspicious about these statistics? How do you suppose the reporter came up with this number?

4. Which sins does parishioner Connie Barrett commit? How does her bake-sale success encourage the sins of others?

5. Which single sin among the seven do the patrons of the bake sale only contemplate, rather than act upon? Who inspires it?

STRATEGIES AND STRUCTURES

1. A spoof is a gentle PARODY or mildly satirical imitation. What general PURPOSE does a spoof or parody usually serve? What is the writer's specific purpose here, and who do you think is the intended AUDIENCE?

2. Pride, avarice, and the other "deadly sins" are ABSTRACT concepts. How do the reporter's examples make them more CONCRETE and specific? Are the examples sufficient, or should there be more? Explain.

3. The reporter gives numerous examples of what people say at the church bake sale. Why? What purpose do these verbal examples serve?

4. *Other Methods.* To bolster the examples, the reporter uses elements of NARRATIVE. What are some of them, specifically?

THINKING ABOUT LANGUAGE

1. What, exactly, is a "strumpet," and why do you think the reporter uses this rather than a stronger word to describe Melissa Wyckoff (16)?

2. Deadly (or mortal) sins can be distinguished from venial sins. According to your dictionary, what is the difference between the two kinds? Give examples.

3. Give a SYNONYM for each of the following words: "avarice," "sloth," "gluttony," and "wrath" (1).

4. Another word for *pride* is *hubris*. What is the difference between the two, according to your dictionary?

For Writing

1. Write a paragraph about one sin you would add to the traditional list.
2. Write an exemplification essay illustrating how the seven deadly sins are routinely committed in the library, in your classes, or in some other place at your school.

MICHAEL DIRDA

Commencement Advice

Michael Dirda (b. 1948) is an author, critic, and English professor, but at heart he's still the bookworm whose father once complained, "All that kid wants to do is stick his nose in a book." For the past twenty-five years Dirda has been senior editor of the Washington Post Book World, *and in 1993 he won the Pulitzer Prize for distinguished criticism.*

It should come as no surprise that such a passionate reader is a passionate educator as well. Author of Bound to Please: An Extraordinary One-Volume Literary Education (2004), *Dirda teaches literature at McDaniel College in Westminster, Maryland. "Commencement Advice," first published in the* Washington Post Book World *in 1999, illustrates its teachings with copious examples from the author's reading and personal experience.*

ANYONE WHO'S EVER GONE TO SCHOOL is likely to feel a certain jauntiness   1
come the end of June. Summer is here. No more classes, no more books, no more teacher's dirty looks.[1] Swimming pools and parks beckon; trips to the mountains, beaches, or grandparents loom. The world, once more, seems, as Matthew Arnold said, "a land of dreams, so various, so beautiful, so new."[2]

For a 17- or 18-year-old graduate, that elation is multiplied a hundredfold. School is   2
not only out for the summer; it's over with for good. Oh, for many there's college in the offing, but that's somehow different: an Eden of parties and romance, broken hearts that rapidly heal, kegs of foaming beer, lazy Saturday afternoons at the stadium watching football, and—after four years of mind-numbing, dizzying bliss—a degree, rapidly followed by a high-paying job, a Porsche 911, and that first million. So goes the pastoral daydream. Alas, our barefoot boy or girl will discover soon enough that the world is actually, as Arnold also reminded us, a "darkling plain / Swept with confused alarms of struggle and flight, / Where ignorant armies clash by night."

Literature offers various aesthetic pleasures, but it has also traditionally provided   3
instruction and counsel on how to live, confront adversity, and find solace. The moral

---

1. *No more [pencils], no more books, no more teacher's dirty looks*: a chant sung gleefully by U.S. children on the last day of school.

2. *Matthew Arnold* (1822–1888): a major poet and literary critic of Victorian Britain. This quotation and the one in the next paragraph are from his poetic meditation on the uncertainty of love and life, "Dover Beach" (1867).

essay—from Marcus Aurelius to Montaigne[3] to Matthew Arnold—has a long tradition, and one that still lingers on in bestselling manuals about the lessons we learn from kindergarten and the soul's need for chicken soup.[4] Over the years I have been an occasional skimmer of such guides but have found that most of my own ground rules for better living—or at least for getting through life—derive from some of the less obvious byways of my reading. Since commencement speakers traditionally offer advice to the young in June, here, in no particular order, are a dozen of the quotations that one reader calls to mind in moments of confusion, stress, and sorrow.

1. "Life is trouble." So proclaims the hero of Nikos Kazantzakis's novel *Zorba the Greek.*[5] Struggle, conflict, tension, disappointment, failure—these are all signs that one is alive. If you try new things, some of them simply aren't going to work out. But one ought to shine in use, and the all too common desire for a Lotos-land existence of endless summer is really an unacknowledged death wish.[6] Expect the worst, says Carl Sandburg in his forgotten poem. "The People, Yes,"[7] and you won't be disappointed. Life is trouble. Only death is no trouble at all.

2. Keep an "interior citadel." The philosopher-emperor Marcus Aurelius passed much of his reign on battlefields. But even on the fraying edges of the Roman Empire he always strove to maintain a stoic's inner tranquility, amounting almost to indifference to the world outside. He accomplished this by retreating regularly to an "interior citadel," a place in the mind where he could fortify himself against what Hamlet, that failed Danish stoic, called the "slings and arrows of outrageous fortune."[8] From there, atop the crenelated ramparts, one can metaphorically look down

3. *Michel Eyquem de Montaigne* (1533–1592): French moralist who published his *Essays* in 1580. *Marcus Aurelius* (121–180 C.E.): Roman emperor who wrote his *Meditations* while on a military campaign during the last decade of his life.

4. *Lessons . . . chicken soup*: references to Robert Fulghum's *All I Really Need to Know I Learned in Kindergarten* (1986) and the *Chicken Soup for the Soul* series (first book published in 1993). Both offer inspirational stories and folk wisdom.

5. *Zorba the Greek*: best-known work by the Greek novelist, poet, and philosopher. Kazantzakis (1883–1957) published *Zorba* in English translation in 1946.

6. *Lotos-land*: a dual literary reference. In Homer's *Odyssey*, Odysseus and his crew are shipwrecked on an island where the men eat a flower that causes forgetfulness and lassitude. Alfred, Lord Tennyson's 1843 poem "The Lotos-Eaters" describes the same land as a place where it is always afternoon. The flowers they wrote about were the Egyptian blue lotus, also known as the blue waterlily, which is reputed to produce narcotic effects in those who eat it.

7. *"The People, Yes"*: Sandburg (1878–1967) published this epic poem of the American language and people in 1936. He is best remembered for his *Chicago Poems* (1916) and for his biography of Lincoln.

8. *"Slings . . . fortune"*: The line is from Hamlet's "to be, or not to be" soliloquy in Act III of Shakespeare's play.

on troubles from a great height, serene and detached. As Satan once observed, the mind is its own place, and in itself can make a Heaven of Hell, a Hell of Heaven.[9]

3. "Constant work is the law of art as it is of life." Balzac followed every word [6] of this sentence to the letter, burning many candles at both ends so that he could write all night the magnificent, melodramatic novels of *La Comédie humaine*.[10] If you hope to accomplish something worthwhile during your time on earth, you will have to work. As a young man or woman, your goal should be to find the kind of job, craft, profession, or useful activity that you are willing to marry, till death do you part. After all, to miss out on one's proper work may be the greatest mistake of a lifetime. If you are born to be an artist, don't settle for being a mere lawyer or stockbroker. Compared to satisfying work, even pleasure pales to insignificance.

4. "Do what you are doing." This, I believe, is both a Jesuit motto and a Zen [7] imperative. That is, if you are making dinner or playing soccer or writing a memo, really focus your whole being on just that. Do it well. Thereby, you invest even the most trivial activities with significance, turning the mundane into the spiritual, perhaps even the ecstatic. A monk tending a garden at dawn is praying. By concerted acts of attention, you can make everything you do a kind of poetry.

5. "The most effective weapon of any man is to have reduced his share of [8] **histrionics to a minimum."** This was the watchword of André Malraux,[11] the larger-than-life novelist, adventurer, art historian, politician. Malraux believed in maturity, in being a grown-up. Our natural tendency is to exaggerate our sorrows, anger, and desires. But deep within we know that we are overreacting, indeed overacting. We get caught up in the situation, carried away by our own pleasure in personal melodrama. So we perform for the audience, sometimes an audience of only one. Instead of such staginess, we should remind ourselves that clarity is as much a mental and emotional virtue as it is a stylistic one. Do we really feel this riot of emotion? Is there any point to all this brouhaha? Should a grown-up behave like this?

6. "Cover your tracks."[12] Bertolt Brecht made this the refrain to one of his [9] political poems. When you go into the big city, he says, know that you are never

---

9. *The mind . . . Heaven:* allusion to the words of Satan in *Paradise Lost* (1667; Book 1, line 255) by the British poet John Milton (1608–1674).

10. *La Comédie humaine: The Human Comedy* is the collective name of the works of the French novelist Honoré de Balzac (1799–1850). The quotation is from *Cousin Bette* (1848).

11. *André Malraux* (1901–1976): French writer and statesman who spoke of the need to act like a grown-up in his autobiography, *Anti-Memoirs* (1968).

12. *"Cover your tracks":* German dramatist and poet Bertolt Brecht (1898–1956) gives this advice in "Handbook for City Dwellers" (1926).

safe; people will be watching every move you make. Your only hope of getting out alive is to "cover your tracks." "Whatever you say, don't say it twice. / If you find your ideas in anyone else, disown them. / The man who hasn't signed anything, who has left no picture / Who was not there, who said nothing: / How can they catch him? / Cover your tracks." For me, this phrase stands as the rough equivalent to the more famous "Trust no one" formula of *The X-Files*.[13] In fact, one should trust everyone but give away nothing that really matters—except to those who love you. "Cover your tracks" means to be careful, destroy your rough drafts, and never let them see you sweat.

7. "A thing is only worth so much time." Parents tend to specialize in certain slogans, and this was my father's favorite. It is a doctrine that needs to be applied with caution, because some things—painting a picture, writing a poem—require that we spend whatever time is needed to do them right. But many activities can needlessly absorb immense chunks of our lives. You can spend every Saturday afternoon for a year test-driving new cars before you pick the wrong one anyway. You can agonize for weeks whether to go for a physical or not. You can work fourteen-hour days downtown. But should you? Aren't there more important matters to attend to? "The cost of a thing," wrote Thoreau, "is the amount of what I will call life which is required to be exchanged for it immediately or in the long run."[14] This leads on to the following, associated motto:

8. "Get on with your work." At moments of emotional crisis, people sometimes just want to plop down and cry. You can do this for a minute or two, and probably should, but also remember that, as Disraeli[15] said, "Grief is the agony of an instant: the indulgence of grief the blunder of a life." When I grow melancholy—the occupational disease of writers—I start doing household chores: I wash dishes and clothes, dust and vacuum, reorganize my bureau, box up books. While performing such activities, I'm allowed to be as depressed as I want, provided I keep on working. That's the key. Usually, within a few hours I feel better. At the very least I end up with a clean house.

9. "We must laugh before we are happy, for fear of dying without having laughed at all." A corollary to this insightful observation from La Bruyere is

13. *The X-Files*: TV show that ran from 1993 to 2002, in which FBI agents Dana Scully and Fox Mulder investigated paranormal phenomena and ran afoul of government conspiracies—hence the advice to "trust no one."

14. *"The cost . . . long run"*: Henry David Thoreau (1817–1862) offers this definition in the "Economy" chapter of *Walden* (1854).

15. *Benjamin Disraeli* (1804–1881) was twice prime minister of Britain.

William James's dictum that if you act as though you were happy, even when you're not, your mind will eventually trick itself into a cheerier mood.[16] What better gift, though, could the gods bestow than a sense of humor? "One can pretend to be serious," said the French playwright Sacha Guitry,[17] "but one can't pretend to be witty." If you don't naturally possess a lighthearted spirit, at least try to acquire a sense of irony and compassion, and learn to smile at your own foolishness—and the world's. As a dear friend used to remind me, self-pity is most unattractive.

10. **"Live all you can. It's a mistake not to,"** announces Lambert Strether in a climactic moment of Henry James's late masterpiece *The Ambassadors*. As the years roll by, it is tempting to settle for a half-life of routine, order, and accommodation. But all of us ought to strive to be overreachers, ever restless, ever adventurous. T. S. Eliot said, "Old men should be explorers,"[18] but so should young men and women and 50-year-olds. Henry James also provides excellent advice for cultivating one's spirit: "Be one on whom nothing is lost." That is, pay attention, observe, learn, be as sensitive and responsive as your nature permits.   13

11. **Choose some heroes and imitate them.** To me, Montaigne, Samuel Johnson, Stendhal, Jane Austen, Chekhov, and Colette[19] are not merely great writers; they are also wonderfully humane and sympathetic human beings. Shrewd, self-aware, free of cant, urbane, kindly—they are my secular saints. Once you have imbibed the personalities of such master spirits, you can turn to them as guides through life's moral thickets and ethical swamps. What would Samuel Johnson say in this situation? What counsel would Colette give? How would Stendhal react?   14

12. **"Memento mori."** We must all die, and doubtless it will be on a sunny day when the whole world seems young and fresh. No one likes to think about that last bad quarter-hour, but it will come round eventually. Theologians in earlier centuries insisted that we meditate on death, so that we might review our lives,   15

16. *"If you act . . . cheerier mood":* Dirda is paraphrasing the pragmatic philosophy of the American psychologist William James (1843–1916). *Jean de La Bruyere (1645–1696):* French moralist and essayist; his *Characters* appeared in 1688.

17. *Sacha Guitry:* born in Russia in 1885 and died in Paris in 1957; he was the son of a French actor.

18. *"Old man . . . explorers":* a line from *Four Quartets*, which Eliot (1888–1965) published in book form in 1943.

19. *Colette (1873–1954):* pen-name of the French novelist Sidonie-Gabrielle Colette. *Anton Pavlovich Chekhov (1860–1904):* Russian master of the short story who was also a playwright. *Jane Austen (1775–1817):* known for her novels of polite British society. *Stendhal (1783–1842):* pen-name of the French novelist Marie-Henri Beyle. *Dr. Samuel Johnson (1709–1784):* British lexicographer, essayist, and literary critic.

amending them where needed. That same practice can help even the most profane among us. If I were to die now, would I be wracked with regrets? Are there matters I should have attended to? Be prepared. In one of Tolstoy's[20] parables, a peasant is plowing a field. The narrator asks the old man what he would do if he knew that Death was coming to take him away within the hour. The peasant answers, "Keep plowing." How many of us could offer a comparably serene reply?

So there's my advice to this year's graduates. Easy enough to give, I realize, and hard to follow—as I know, too. But let me conclude with one strongly personal plea, making a baker's dozen: Read the classics. The world is awash in bestsellers and frivolous nonfiction, but just as our bodies need physical exercise, so our brains need demanding books. Set aside some part of the day for real reading. Work your way through Plato; be touched by Cather's *A Lost Lady* and shocked by Rousseau's *Confessions*; feel the burning fever of *Death in Venice*; listen in on Samuel Johnson's repartee, and marvel before *One Hundred Years of Solitude*.[21] Books, like great art and music and love, make us feel passionately alive. And isn't that what we all want? 16

20. *Lev Nikolayevich Tolstoy (1828–1910)*: Russian novelist and philosopher; his parables are collected in *Master and Man and Other Parables and Tales* (1895).

21. *One Hundred Years of Solitude (1967)*: a book by Colombian novelist Gabriel García Márquez (b. 1928), who is known for his use of magical realism. *Death in Venice (1912)*: the work of German novelist Thomas Mann (1875–1955). *Jean-Jacques Rousseau (1712–1778)*: French writer and political theorist whose *Confessions* appeared in 1782. *Willa Cather (1873–1947)*: American novelist who published *A Lost Lady* in 1923. *Plato (427–347 B.C.E.)*: Greek philosopher who was a student of Socrates and the teacher of Aristotle.

READING CLOSELY

1. Michael Dirda's essay consists of three paragraphs of introduction followed by a list of EXAMPLES. What, exactly, is he exemplifying? What is Dirda's main point?

2. What mistaken idea is Dirda exemplifying in paragraph 2 by referring, among other delights, to "lazy Saturday afternoons at the stadium watching football . . . followed by a high-paying job, a Porsche 911, and that first million"? Why do you think he introduces this false notion?

3. According to Dirda, why should we maintain an "interior citadel" (5)?

4. In Dirda's view, how important is a person's job or profession? Do you agree with Dirda about "satisfying work" (6)? Explain.

5. Dirda bases his essay (and the advice it gives) on a particular view of the role of

literature and reading. What is that view, and where does he state it most directly? Do you agree? Why or why not?

STRATEGIES AND STRUCTURES

1. How and where does Dirda identify his AUDIENCE and state his PURPOSE? Why do you think Dirda immediately qualifies his purpose?

2. Given his purpose and audience, why do you think Dirda builds his essay around many multiple examples rather one or two extended examples?

3. In addition to using numerous examples from literature, Dirda incorporates CONCRETE, specific examples from his own experience and from everyday life. Which of Dirda's examples do you find especially interesting or appropriate? How and how well do they illustrate his point, in your opinion?

4. Dirda presents his articles of advice "in no particular order" (3). Why doesn't he arrange them in order of importance?

5. Each of Dirda's paragraphs is a mini-essay that states its point with a quotation, gives a number of specific examples, and then states its point again with some variation. Is this an effective strategy? Why or why not?

6. Within paragraphs, Dirda's ideas are clearly connected to one another. Should he have included more transitions and other connecting words *between* paragraphs to link the parts of his essay together as a whole? Why or why not?

7. *Other Methods.* Besides exemplifying his topic, Dirda is also analyzing a PROCESS. What is he explaining how to do, and what is the intended result of the process?

THINKING ABOUT LANGUAGE

1. Since graduation occurs at the *end* of high school or college, why is Dirda giving *commencement* advice?

2. One meaning of *moral* is "pertaining to right and wrong"; another is "teaching a lesson." In which sense is Dirda using the word when he refers to the tradition of "the moral essay" (3)?

3. Usually, a "pastoral" poem or tale is set in the country and deals with the simple life (2). Explain the IRONY in Dirda's allusion to this tradition.

4. What is a "baker's dozen," and where does the term come from (16)? Why does Dirda give us just that many articles of advice?

5. What does Dirda mean by "destroy your rough drafts" (9)? Explain the ANALOGY he is using here.

6. What is a maxim and how might the word be applied to Dirda's essay?

For Writing

1. Choose one of Dirda's sayings and write a paragraph illustrating it with specific EXAMPLES of your own.

2. Write an exemplification essay giving commencement advice to the new graduates of your high school or college.

3. Write an essay exemplifying how reading good literature provides (or does not provide) instruction on how to live.

HORACE MINER

Body Ritual among the Nacirema

Horace Miner (1912–1993) grew up in Lexington, Kentucky, where his father was a professor at the University of Kentucky. As an undergraduate, Miner developed an interest in archeology and anthropology; he later became the curator of the University of Kentucky's Museum of Anthropology. After receiving a doctorate in anthropology from the University of Chicago in 1937, Miner began a long teaching career, culminating in twenty-eight years at the University of Michigan. He is the author of a number of books, including Culture and Agriculture *(1949),* The Primitive City of Timbuctoo *(1953),* Oasis and Casbah *(1960), and* City in Modern Africa *(1967).*

Miner's academic specialty was the study of traditional cultures closely tied to the land they inhabit. Although his expertise chiefly centered on Africa, his best-known work, "Body Ritual among the Nacirema" (first published in the American Anthropologist *in 1956), examines a curious North American tribe. Many examples of Nacirema customs and folkways are recorded here, using the rigorous methodology and language of the observational sciences. From these peculiar behaviors, a general picture emerges of a culture at once remote and strangely familiar.*

THE ANTHROPOLOGIST has become so familiar with the diversity of ways in which   1
different peoples behave in similar situations that he is not apt to be surprised by even
the most exotic customs. In fact, if all of the logically possible combinations of behavior have not been found somewhere in the world, he is apt to suspect that they must be present in some yet undescribed tribe. This point has, in fact, been expressed with respect to clan organization by Murdock.[1] In this light, the magical beliefs and practices of the Nacirema present such unusual aspects that it seems desirable to describe them as an example of the extremes to which human behavior can go.

Professor Linton first brought the ritual of the Nacirema to the attention of   2
anthropologists twenty years ago, but the culture of this people is still very poorly understood. They are a North American group living in the territory between the Canadian Cree, the Yaqui and Tarahumare of Mexico, and the Carib and Arawak of the Antilles.[2] Little is known of their origin, although tradition states that they came from the east . . . .

1. *George Peter Murdock* (1897–1985): American anthropologist who was an authority on primitive cultures.

2. *Cree, Yaqui, Tarahumare, Carib, and Arawak:* Native American tribes that once inhabited the Saskatchewan region of Canada, western Mexico, and the West Indies.

Nacirema culture is characterized by a highly developed market economy which   3
has evolved in a rich natural habitat. While much of the people's time is devoted to
economic pursuits, a large part of the fruits of these labors and a considerable portion of the day are spent in ritual activity. The focus of this activity is the human
body, the appearance and health of which loom as a dominant concern in the ethos
of the people. While such a concern is certainly not unusual, its ceremonial aspects
and associated philosophy are unique.

The fundamental belief underlying the whole system appears to be that the   4
human body is ugly and that its natural tendency is to debility and disease. Incarcerated in such a body, man's only hope is to avert these characteristics through the
use of the powerful influences of ritual and ceremony. Every household has one or
more shrines devoted to this purpose. The more powerful individuals in the society
have several shrines in their houses and, in fact, the opulence of a house is often
referred to in terms of the number of such ritual centers it possesses. Most houses
are of wattle and daub[3] construction, but the shrine rooms of the more wealthy are
walled with stone. Poorer families imitate the rich by applying pottery plaques to
their shrine walls.

While each family has at least one such shrine, the rituals associated with it are   5
not family ceremonies but are private and secret. The rites are normally only discussed with children, and then only during the period when they are being initiated into these mysteries. I was able, however, to establish sufficient rapport with
the natives to examine these shrines and to have the rituals described to me.

The focal point of the shrine is a box or chest which is built into the wall. In this   6
chest are kept the many charms and magical potions without which no native
believes he could live. These preparations are secured from a variety of specialized
practitioners. The most powerful of these are the medicine men, whose assistance
must be rewarded with substantial gifts. However, the medicine men do not provide the curative potions for their clients, but decide what the ingredients should
be and then write them down in an ancient and secret language. This writing is
understood only by the medicine men and by the herbalists who, for another gift,
provide the required charm.

The charm is not disposed of after it has served its purpose, but is placed in the   7
charm-box of the household shrine. As these magical materials are specific for certain ills, and the real or imagined maladies of the people are many, the charm-box
is usually full to overflowing. The magical packets are so numerous that people forget what their purposes were and fear to use them again. While the natives are very
vague on this point, we can only assume that the idea in retaining all the old magi-

---

3. *Wattle and daub*: a type of building construction that covers a lattice work of wooden stakes
(wattles) with an adhesive mixture (daub) made from clay and sand or other available substances.

cal materials is that their presence in the charm-box, before which the body rituals are conducted, will in some way protect the worshipper.

Beneath the charm-box is a small font. Each day every member of the family, in 8 succession, enters the shrine room, bows his head before the charm-box, mingles different sorts of holy water in the font, and proceeds with a brief rite of ablution. The holy waters are secured from the Water Temple of the community, where the priests conduct elaborate ceremonies to make the liquid ritually pure.

In the hierarchy of magical practitioners, and below the medicine men in pres- 9 tige, are specialists whose designation is best translated "holy-mouth-men." The Nacirema have an almost pathological horror of and fascination with the mouth, the condition of which is believed to have a supernatural influence on all social relationships. Were it not for the rituals of the mouth, they believe that their teeth would fall out, their gums bleed, their jaws shrink, their friends desert them, and their lovers reject them. They also believe that a strong relationship exists between oral and moral characteristics. For example, there is a ritual ablution of the mouth for children which is supposed to improve their moral fiber.

The daily body ritual performed by everyone includes a mouth-rite. Despite the 10 fact that these people are so punctilious about care of the mouth, this rite involves a practice which strikes the uninitiated stranger as revolting. It was reported to me that the ritual consists of inserting a small bundle of hog hairs into the mouth, along with certain magical powders, and then moving the bundle in a highly for-malized series of gestures.

In addition to the private mouth-rite, the people seek out a holy-mouth-man 11 once or twice a year. These practitioners have an impressive set of paraphernalia, consisting of a variety of augers, awls, probes, and prods. The use of these objects in the exorcism of the evils of the mouth involves almost unbelievable ritual torture of the client. The holy-mouth-man opens the client's mouth and, using the above mentioned tools, enlarges any holes which decay may have created in the teeth. Magical materials are put into these holes. If there are not naturally occurring holes in the teeth, large sections of one or more teeth are gouged out so that the supernatural substance can be applied. In the client's view, the purpose of these ministrations is to arrest decay and to draw friends. The extremely sacred and tra-ditional character of the rite is evident in the fact that the natives return to the holy-mouth-men year after year, despite the fact that their teeth continue to decay.

It is to be hoped that, when a thorough study of the Nacirema is made, there 12 will be careful inquiry into the personality structure of these people. One has but to watch the gleam in the eye of a holy-mouth-man, as he jabs an awl into an exposed nerve, to suspect that a certain amount of sadism is involved. If this can be established, a very interesting pattern emerges, for most of the population shows definite masochistic tendencies. It was to these that Professor Linton referred in discussing a distinctive part of the daily body ritual which is performed only by men. This part of the rite involves scraping and lacerating the surface of the face with a sharp instrument. Special women's rites are performed only four times during each lunar month, but what they lack in frequency is made up in barbarity. As part of this ceremony, women bake their heads in small ovens for about an hour. The theoretically interesting point is that what seems to be a preponderantly masochistic people have developed sadistic specialists.

The medicine men have an imposing temple, or *latipso*, in every community of any size. The more elaborate ceremonies required to treat very sick patients can only be performed at this temple. These ceremonies involve not only the thaumaturge but a permanent group of vestal maidens who move sedately about the temple chambers in distinctive costume and headdress. 13

The *latipso* ceremonies are so harsh that it is phenomenal that a fair proportion of the really sick natives who enter the temple ever recover. Small children whose indoctrination is still incomplete have been known to resist attempts to take them to the temple because "that is where you go to die." Despite this fact, sick adults are not only willing but eager to undergo the protracted ritual purification, if they can afford to do so. No matter how ill the supplicant or how grave the emergency, the guardians of many temples will not admit a client if he cannot give a rich gift to the custodian. Even after one has gained admission and survived the ceremonies, the guardians will not permit the neophyte to leave until he makes still another gift. 14

The supplicant entering the temple is first stripped of all his or her clothes. In everyday life the Nacirema avoids exposure of his body and its natural functions. Bathing and excretory acts are performed only in the secrecy of the household shrine, where they are ritualized as part of the body-rites. Psychological shock results from the fact that body secrecy is suddenly lost upon entry into the *latipso*. A man, whose own wife has never seen him in an excretory act, suddenly finds himself naked and assisted by a vestal maiden while he performs his natural functions into a sacred vessel. This sort of ceremonial treatment is necessitated by the fact that the excreta are used by a diviner to ascertain the course and nature of the client's sickness. Female clients, on the other hand, find their naked bodies are subjected to the scrutiny, manipulation and prodding of the medicine men. 15

Few supplicants in the temple are well enough to do anything but lie on their hard beds. The daily ceremonies, like the rites of the holy-mouth-men, involve discomfort and torture. With ritual precision, the vestals awaken their miserable charges each dawn and roll them about on their beds of pain while performing ablutions, in the formal movements of which the maidens are highly trained. At other times they insert magic wands in the supplicant's mouth or force him to eat substances which are supposed to be healing. From time to time the medicine men come to their clients and jab magically treated needles into their flesh. The fact 16 that these temple ceremonies may not cure, and may even kill the neophyte, in no way decreases the people's faith in the medicine men.

There remains one other kind of practitioner, known as a "listener." This witch- 17 doctor has the power to exorcise the devils that lodge in the heads of people who have been bewitched. The Nacirema believe that parents bewitch their own children. Mothers are particularly suspected of putting a curse on children while teaching them the secret body rituals. The counter-magic of the witchdoctor is unusual in its lack of ritual. The patient simply tells the "listener" all his troubles and fears, beginning with the earliest difficulties he can remember. The memory displayed by the Nacirema in these exorcism sessions is truly remarkable. It is not uncommon for the patient to bemoan the rejection he felt upon being weaned as a babe, and a few individuals even see their troubles going back to the traumatic effects of their own birth.

In conclusion, mention must be made of certain practices which have their base 18 in native esthetics but which depend upon the pervasive aversion to the natural body and its functions. There are ritual fasts to make fat people thin and ceremonial feasts to make thin people fat. Still other rites are used to make women's breasts larger if they are small, and smaller if they are large. General dissatisfaction with breast shape is symbolized in the fact that the ideal form is virtually outside the range of human variation. A few women afflicted with almost inhuman hyper-mammary development are so idolized that they make a handsome living by simply going from village to village and permitting the natives to stare at them for a fee.

Reference has already been made to the fact that excretory functions are ritual- 19 ized, routinized, and relegated to secrecy. Natural reproductive functions are similarly distorted. Intercourse is taboo as a topic and scheduled as an act. Efforts are made to avoid pregnancy by the use of magical materials or by limiting intercourse to certain phases of the moon. Conception is actually very infrequent. When pregnant, women dress so as to hide their condition. Parturition takes place in secret, without friends or relatives to assist, and the majority of women do not nurse their infants.

Our review of the ritual life of the Nacirema has certainly shown them to be a 20 magic-ridden people. It is hard to understand how they have managed to exist so long under the burdens which they have imposed upon themselves. But even such exotic customs as these take on real meaning when they are viewed with the insight provided by Malinowski[4] when he wrote:

"Looking from far and above, from our high places of safety in the developed 21 civilization, it is easy to see all the crudity and irrelevance of magic. But without its power and guidance early man could not have mastered his practical difficulties as he has done, nor could man have advanced to the higher stages of civilization."

---

4. *Bronislaw Kasper Malinowski* (1884–1942): Polish-born anthropologist.

READING CLOSELY

1. Who are these strange people, the Nacirema? How did they get their name?

2. What are the "shrine rooms" and "charm-boxes" that are used in the morning rituals of the Nacirema (4, 7)?

3. Why do the Nacirema put "hog hairs" in their mouths (10)? What is the "ritual ablution of the mouth," and why is it believed to improve children's moral fiber?

4. Who is the "listener," and why do the Nacirema think that "parents bewitch their own children" (17)?

5. What is the real meaning of the Nacirema's exotic customs when viewed in the light of Malinowski's statement at the end of the essay (20–21)? What point is Miner making about the field of modern anthropology?

STRATEGIES AND STRUCTURES

1. Miner begins with general observations about the Nacirema, in paragraphs 1–4, and then gives EXAMPLES of specific behaviors. How effective is this strategy? How else might he have organized the essay?

2. What is Miner's PURPOSE in writing about the behavior of this strange tribe? Who is his intended AUDIENCE? Do you think a mock-scientific paper is an effective means of accomplishing this purpose? Why or why not?

3. Are Miner's examples representative of the Nacirema? Why or why not? What other rituals and customs might he have used as representative examples?

4. Most of the time when we exemplify something strange, we try to make it more familiar to the reader. Miner, however, makes the familiar seem strange. Give examples of how he accomplishes this.

5. As a social anthropologist, Miner follows certain professional conventions in this journal article. What are some of them? How, specifically, does Miner give his essay the flavor of a scientific article or report? Pay special attention to paragraphs 1–3 and 18–21.

6. *Other Methods.* Miner combines detailed DESCRIPTIONS with his examples. Which details first made you suspect that Miner was writing tongue-in-cheek?

THINKING ABOUT LANGUAGE

1. Where do the Nacirema get the word *latipso* for their temples of the sick (13)?

2. What is a "thaumaturge" (13)? What are the Nacirema's usual names for the following persons: "herbalist" (6), "medicine men" (6), "holy-mouth-men" (9), "diviner" (15)?

3. Why do you think Miner uses such clinical terms as "excreta" (15), "hyper-mammary" (18), and "parturition" (19)? Give other examples.

4. Consult your dictionary for any of the following words you do not already know: "ethos" (3), "incarcerated" (4), "opulence" (4), "ablution" (8), "patholog-ical" (9), "punctilious" (10), "paraphernalia" (11), "sadism" (12), "masochistic" (12), "supplicant" (14), "neophyte" (14), "scrutiny" (15), "aversion" (18), "taboo" (19), "parturition" (19).

For Writing

1. Make a list of other examples of Nacirema customs—for example, those associ-ated with wearing clothes or purchasing goods—that bear out Miner's findings about the tribe.

2. Although Miner says in paragraph 3 that the Nacirema have a "highly developed market economy," he does not explain their "economic pursuits." Write an essay exemplifying their economic activities to show that these people who find the body ugly nevertheless find treasure to be beautiful.

3. Pretend that you are seeing a place, such as a barbershop or beauty salon, gym, swimming pool, or a doctor's office, for the first time and do not know the names or purposes of anything. Then write an essay exemplifying what typically goes on at that familiar location. Make up descriptive names for people and objects, and use the method of CAUSE AND EFFECT to explain the surface appear-ance of events.

MONICA WUNDERLICH

My Technologically Challenged Life

Monica Wunderlich had no computer at home while she was growing up and, until 1995, no touch-tone phone. Her family is still not connected to the Internet. Her "technologically crippled" condition plagued Wunderlich as a student and when she went to work at a health-care facility for elderly patients. She has finally purchased a computer, but Wunderlich wonders if she will ever catch up.

"My Technologically Challenged Life" appeared in 2004 in Delta Winds, *an anthology of student writing published each year by the English department of San Joaquin Delta College in Stockton, California. Wunderlich first wrote the essay as an assignment for an English course. It gives many humorous examples of the difficulties she has encountered with ordinary technology (or the lack of it) in her everyday life. At the nursing facility where the author worked while attending college, however, the lack of up-to-date equipment was no laughing matter—as Wunderlich's more disturbing examples make clear.*

I**T PROBABLY SEEMS EASY** for someone to use a computer to solve a task or call a 1 friend on a cellular phone for the solution. I, however, do not have access to such luxuries. My home, workplace, and automobile are almost barren of anything electronic. It's not as if I don't want technology in my life, but I feel as if technology has taken on the role of a rabbit, and I am the fox with three legs that just can't seem to get it. And after many useless attempts at trying to figure it out, I have almost given up.

In my house, technology does not exist, at least not for my parents. In fact it was 2 1995 when my father finally had to part with his beloved rotary phone,[1] not because it was worn out, but because it would not work with the new automated menus that companies were using. Reaching an actual person was difficult the old way because of the physical impossibility of being able to *push* 1, 2, or 3 when a phone possesses no buttons. It was quite embarrassing, especially since I was fifteen and all of my friends had "normal" phones. My dad's biggest argument was that "It's a privacy issue. No one can tap into our phone calls and listen to our conversations." Well, the last time I had checked, none of us were trafficking dope.

I also had the privilege of not using a computer. It was hard going through high 3 school without one, for I had many teachers who demanded many essays from me.

---

1. *Rotary phone*: the type of telephone in widespread use throughout much of the twentieth century until it was replaced by the now-familiar touch-tone phone. While a touch-tone phone has a keypad, a rotary phone has a dial.

Yet I had no way to type them. My sister was in the same boat, so we tried tag-teaming[2] my parents into getting us a computer. But to no avail. We kept getting things like "They're too expensive," or "We have no room for one," or "We'll get one later." Later! My parents should have just said NEVER! So my sister and I resorted to spending hours at our friends' houses, because their parents were nice to them and bought computers. The only problem was that our friends had lives and weren't always around at our disposal. So Plan B for essay completion was using a cheesy electronic word processor that my dad had borrowed from my *grandparents* to supposedly "help us out." This beast of a machine wasn't much help, though, because it was a pain in the neck to use. It had a teeny tiny little screen that wouldn't show the entire typed line, so by the time the line was printed, I'd find about ten uncorrected mistakes, and I'd have to start over. However, nothing is permanent and walls do come down, and so be it—the Wunderlichs buy their first computer! Two years after I graduate high school. As of yet, we still do not have the Internet.

My job is another place where technology is lacking. I work in a home for the elderly, and I take care of about eight to ten patients a night. I have to take some of these patients' vital signs, and I speak on behalf of anyone who has ever worked in the medical profession when I say that the most efficient way to take vital signs is electronically. However, my employers do not grant us the equipment for electronic vitals. We are still using glass thermometers, which are not only a waste of time (3 seconds vs. 3 minutes for an oral temp), but they are extremely dangerous. Residents are known to bite down on the thermometers, exposing themselves to harmful mercury. I can't even begin to count how many thermometers I have dropped and broken since I've worked there. One time I dropped a thermometer and didn't realize I had broken it. So I picked it up to shake it down, but instead I flung mercury everywhere. An electronic thermometer just makes more sense when trying to make the residents' environment as safe as possible.

We also have to use manual blood pressure cuffs. They're just the normal cuffs that are wrapped around the arm, pumped up, and read using the bouncing needle. The problem is that none of our blood pressure cuffs are calibrated correctly, and the needles are way out of kilter. This makes it impossible to get an accurate reading. An ingenious solution would be digital cuffs, but that is highly unlikely. Actually, the home did try to supply some digital cuffs, but they were stolen. One man's sticky fingers equals inconvenience for the rest of us, and the home no longer supplied us with such time-saving technology. Using manual equipment is hard not only for us but also for the nurses. The care home does not allow feeding machines

---

2. *Tag-teaming*: a wrestling term, now in common usage, referring to two people working as a team in alternate turns.

in the facility, yet people who need to be fed by a stomach tube are still admitted. This means that the nurses have to allot a special time from their med pass to hook up a syringe to the patient's stomach tube and pour their "steak dinner in a can" down the tube little by little. This tedious process takes about twenty minutes, and nurses don't really have twenty minutes to throw around, so it really crowds their schedules. If we had feeding machines, the nurses would only have to change a bag when a machine beeps. Problem solved if things went my way.

Another part of my life that is technologically crippled is my car. As much as I like my car, I still think it could use a few more bells and whistles. I drive a 2002 Volkswagen Jetta, which would probably make the reader think "Oh, a new car. There must be plenty of technology in that new car." My answer to that is "No, there isn't." The only technology is the 5 billion standard airbags for when I do something really stupid. Other than that I have to shift it manually. If I want to roll down my window, I have to turn a crank. My car did not come with a CD player, so I shelled out $500 for one. I've had this stereo since last May, and I still can't figure out how to set the clock or preset stations. Volkswagen technology could not stop my car from exercising its "check engine light" once every three weeks. Even though the design techs included a cute warning light, my blood still boiled every time the light would come on proudly, and I made yet another pilgrimage to the dealership . . . on my day off. It would be nice if my car came equipped with one of those Global Positioning System things as well. I am really good at getting lost, and if I had one of these systems a year ago, I would not have found myself driving over both the Bay Bridge and the Golden Gate Bridge when I was supposed to be on the Richmond Bridge. (Ironically enough, I did this during the weekend that terrorists were supposed to be blowing up the Bay and Golden Gate Bridges.) And if I had had any passengers while tempting fate that day, I could have kept them distracted from the fact that we were lost (and possibly going to die) by letting them watch a movie on one of those in-car DVD players. But of course I don't have an in-car DVD player, so my hypothetical passengers would probably have been frantic. 6

No matter how much technology is out there, I seem to be getting through the day without most of it. It would seem hard to imagine someone else living without such modern conveniences, and, yes, at times I feel very primitive. However, I am slowly catching on to what's new out there even though incorporating every modern convenience into my day is out of the question. I am learning even though it is at a snail's pace. Hopefully I'll have it all figured out by the time cars fly, or else I will be walking. 7

READING CLOSELY

1. What role do Wunderlich's parents play in limiting her access to technology? How do they explain their behavior to her and her sister? Does their reasoning sound familiar to you? How so?

2. At times, Wunderlich blames herself for her technological difficulties. Who or what else is at fault, especially at the health-care facility? What three examples does she give about serious technological problems at work?

3. Why does Wunderlich refer to the weekend when terrorists were "supposed to be blowing up" two of San Francisco's main bridges (6)? What does this observation have to do with technology?

STRATEGIES AND STRUCTURES

1. Since Wunderlich's essay was written as an assignment for an English class, her main PURPOSE was to amuse her teacher and classmates and to inform them about the technological "challenges" she faces every day. How well do you think she achieves this purpose? Explain.

2. Wunderlich's title tells the reader that her life is "technologically challenged," a point she supports with EXAMPLES throughout her essay. Should she have made this main point more explicitly in a THESIS STATEMENT? Why or why not?

3. Wunderlich organizes her examples by grouping them according to each "part of my life" (6). What are those parts? How and how well do you think they help her to structure her essay?

4. What is IRONIC about the example of Wunderlich's car?

5. *Other Methods.* When she writes about the lack of technology in the facility where she works, Wunderlich is also presenting an ARGUMENT about working conditions and the quality of patient care. To whom is this argument addressed? Are her examples sufficient to support it? Why or why not?

THINKING ABOUT LANGUAGE

1. Look up the term *Luddite*. What does the name mean, and where does it come from? Who might Wunderlich consider a Luddite?

2. Wunderlich compares herself to a three-legged fox chasing a rabbit (1). How effective do you find this ANALOGY?

3. What does Wunderlich's METAPHOR of "tag-teaming" (3) imply about the extent of her and her sister's persistence?

4. "Hopefully," says Wunderlich about her attempt to catch up with technology, "I'll have it all figured out by the time cars fly" (7). Where else in her essay, and for what purposes, does Wunderlich use HYPERBOLE like this?

FOR WRITING

1. Is your personal life or work "challenged" in some way, technologically or otherwise? Using examples, write a paragraph or two about a particular challenge and how you deal with it (or fail to do so).

2. If you could have the latest technology in every field, what specific devices, gadgets, and gear would you go for? Write an essay giving examples of the choices you would make and why.

3. What is a Global Positioning System and what does it do? Write an essay giving copious examples of the functions and uses of GPS technology.

ADRIENNE RICH

Ritual Acts vi

Adrienne Rich (b. 1929) has been a major voice in American poetry for more than half a century. A 1951 graduate of Radcliffe College, she won the Yale Series of Younger Poets Competition that year for her first book, A Change of World. *Rich's early work revealed her quiet mastery of traditional poetic themes and approaches, but she moved decisively away from such formalism with her third book,* Snapshots of a Daughter-in-Law *(1963). During this period, she also became an increasingly outspoken political activist, advocating racial and sexual equality and opposing the Vietnam War. In 1973 she won the National Book Award for her collection* Diving into the Wreck. *She has published more than twenty-five books of poetry and prose.*

The following excerpt is the concluding section of the poem "Ritual Acts," from The School among the Ruins, *Rich's 2004 collection. Here, as earlier in the poem, Rich is describing a "ruined" world in which poetry is "a kind of teaching."*

A goat devouring a flowering plant 1
A child squeezing through a fence to school
A woman slicing an onion
A bare foot sticking out
A wash line tied to a torn-up tree 5
A dog's leg lifted at a standpipe[1]
An old man kneeling to drink there
A hand on the remote

We would like to show but to not be obvious
except to the oblivious 10
We want to show ordinary life
We are dying to show it

---

1. *Standpipe:* a vertical pipe connected to a central water supply. Refers here to the only source of water in poor third-world villages.

READING CLOSELY

1. What is Adrienne Rich EXEMPLIFYING in this poem? How do you know?

2. Assuming that "we" refers to the poet, or to poets in general, what main point is Rich making about the writing of poetry?

STRATEGIES AND STRUCTURES

1. Rich begins with specific EXAMPLES and then tells us explicitly what she is illustrating. Why do you think she follows this order, instead of stating her thesis first and *then* giving her examples?

2. What is Rich's PURPOSE in writing this poem? Who are "the oblivious," and why might the poet make an exception of them (9)?

3. Rich's EXAMPLES consist mainly of CONCRETE, specific "acts." Why does she represent her particular subject with people (and animals) doing things?

4. *Other Methods.* Actions are the soul of NARRATIVE writing. Do Rich's examples present us with a coherent story? Why or why not?

THINKING ABOUT LANGUAGE

1. "Ritual" acts are repeated actions that form part of a rite or ceremony. Why might Rich refer to the events of everyday life as a ceremony?

2. How does Rich use parallel grammatical structures in this poem?

3. Why do you think a poet would use the word "show," rather than *tell* or *explain*, to describe her craft (9, 11–12)?

4. Is Rich using the word "dying" in a strictly literal sense (11)? Or is she speaking figuratively, too? Explain.

FOR WRITING

1. Make a list of the acts you would choose to exemplify the rituals of ordinary life.

2. Write an ANALYSIS of Rich's use of CONCRETE examples in this or another poem.

CHAPTER 6

Process Analysis

Writing is a multistage process. . . . The stages are interactive and frequently occur simultaneously. The writing process consists of prewriting, drafting, revising, editing, and publishing.
—Nora M. Kneebone, West Iron County Middle School

How to undecorate the tree is my business. There's no one around to give advice, so I do it my way. I take the end of a rope of gold tinsel and give it a jerk. The tree spins around, and I clean the whole thing off in eight seconds.
—Erma Bombeck

What does taking down a Christmas tree have in common with replacing an empty roll of toilet tissue, painting baseboards, or removing a splinter with a needle? According to the household humorist Erma Bombeck, these are all lonely jobs; when it comes time to do them, the rest of the family has disappeared, so no one is around to help. These activities have something else in common, too. Like the business of writing about them, each one constitutes a process that can be understood and explained through PROCESS ANALYSIS.

Defining Process Analysis:
Telling How or How To

A process is a series of actions that produces an end result, such as getting rid of last year's Christmas tree. When you analyze a process, you separate those actions into a number of steps: unplug the lights on the tree, remove the ornaments and store them away till next year, unwind the lights and tinsel, gently lower the tree onto an old sheet, and so on.

There are two basic kinds of process analysis, directive and explanatory. A directive process analysis tells the reader how to do something, such as take down a

Christmas tree, throw a boomerang, treat attention deficit disorder, or avoid being eaten by an alligator. An explanatory process analysis tells the reader how something works—a DVD player, cloning, the United States Senate.

In this chapter, we will explore how to analyze a process—how to break it into a sequence of steps; how to select the specific details that best suit your purpose and audience; and how to organize and present those details effectively. We will also review the critical points to watch for as you read over a process analysis, as well as common errors to avoid when you edit.

Why Do We Analyze Processes?

The human mind is naturally analytical, inclined to take things apart to see how the pieces fit together. There are basically two reasons for analyzing a process. Sometimes we want to understand how something works, as when we analyze how wind flowing over a curved wing creates a difference in pressure that lifts an airplane. Other times we want to know how to do something, such as how to fly a plane. If the process produces an undesirable result, as with the spread of a disease, our purpose in analyzing it may be to prevent it from occurring again.

Composing a Process Analysis

When you compose a process analysis, your first task is to break down the process into its main steps. If you are analyzing how to take down a Christmas tree using the Bombeck method, the process is simple and the steps are few: grab a rope of tinsel by one end, give it a jerk, and catch the ornaments as they spin off. Even in this simple case, you'll notice, the steps of the process must be presented to the reader in a particular order, usually CHRONOLOGICAL. With a multistage process—such as writing an essay or playing a video game—figuring out that order can be challenging, especially if the process has more than one possible outcome.

Removing the decorations from a Christmas tree is a process that *could* be accomplished in a single step. (All you really have to do is shake the tree.) Let's take a more challenging example, such as that of a complicated natural process, one we can analyze but not necessarily control—the spread of the bubonic plague.

The spread of the plague is an excellent example of a natural process we'd like to eradicate. A carrier, usually a flea, bites an infected animal, usually a rat. The flea picks up infected blood and transfers the bacilli that cause the plague to the human victim, again by biting. Having entered the bloodstream, the bacilli travel to the lymph nodes, where they begin to replicate. Eventually the lymph nodes swell, creating what Wendy Orent describes in *Plague* as "the huge, boggy, exquisitely painful mass we know as a bubo." The order is always the same—up to a point. The buboes never appear before the victim is infected. And the victim is never infected before the flea bites. What happens after the buboes appear, however—whether the victim lives or dies—is not fixed.

The order of events in most natural disasters, in fact, can be difficult to determine with certainty. In an earthquake or hurricane, for example, it is true that the ground trembles or the wind blows first; but then many things start to happen all at once. In other words, the actions and events of many processes are, as Nora Kneebone observed, "interactive and frequently occur simultaneously." When you write about a process, however, you must present events in an orderly sequence. Whatever it turns out to be, the sequence in which you choose to relate those events will provide the main principle for organizing your written analysis.

Thinking about Purpose and Audience

One purpose for writing a process anlaysis is to tell your readers how to do something. For this purpose, a basic set of instructions or directions will usually do the job, as when you give someone the recipe for your Aunt Mary's famous pound cake.

When, however, you want your audience to understand, not duplicate, a complicated process—such as the spread of a disease, the cloning of a sheep, or the chemistry that makes a cake rise—your analysis should be more explanatory than directive. So instead of giving instructions ("add the sugar to the butter"), you would go over the inner workings of the process in some detail, telling readers, for example, *what happens* when they add baking powder to the cake mixture.

Here's a chef's analysis of the baking process:

> The first step in making a pound cake is to take a fat, such as butter or shortening, or a combination of the two, and beat it with an electric mixer. This incorporates air bubbles. Then, sugar is sprinkled slowly into the butter. As the sharp sugar crystals cut into the butter, tiny pockets are formed and fill with air as the mixer blades pull more butter over the top of the hole to close it. This makes the butter double in volume and become creamy in texture, which is why this procedure is called "creaming." . . . Then, the eggs are usually added, which adds more volume and allows the mixture to hold even more air. The dry ingredients, including the baking soda or powder, are then added, usually alternating with liquid. When the baking soda or powder comes into contact with liquid, carbon dioxide is released. As the batter heats up, bubbles form and the batter rises.
>
> —RICK MCDANIEL, "Chemistry 101 for Pound Cakes"

This is much more information than your readers will need if you are just giving them a recipe for pound cake. However, if you are writing for a food magazine and you want readers to understand why their cakes may fall if they open the oven door during the baking process—it's because the bubbles collapse before the batter sets up—then such explanatory details are appropriate.

The nature of your audience, too, will affect the information you include in your analysis. How much does your intended reader already know about the process you're analyzing? Why might he or she want to know more, or less? If you are giving a set of instructions, will the reader require any special tools or equipment? What problems or glitches is the reader likely to encounter? Will you need to indicate where he or she can look for more information on your topic? Ask questions like these, and select the steps and details you present accordingly.

Generating Ideas: Asking How Something Works

BRAINSTORMING, LISTING, and other methods can help you generate ideas for your process analysis. When you analyze a process, the essential question to ask yourself is *how*. How does a cake rise? How do I bake a German chocolate cake? How does an engine work? How do I back out of the garage?

When you're thinking about writing a process analysis, ask yourself a "how" question about your topic, research the answer, and write down all of the steps involved. These will form the foundation of your process analysis. For instance, "How do I back out of the garage?" might result in a list like this:

step on the gas
turn the key in the ignition
put the car in reverse
cut the steering wheel to the right
back out of the garage

This list includes all the essential steps for backing a car out of a garage, but you wouldn't want your reader to try to follow them in this order. Once you have a list of all the steps in your process, you need to begin thinking about the best order in which to present them to your reader.

Organizing and Drafting a Process Analysis

Once you've identified the steps in a process, you need to organize and begin drafting. First you'll need to put the steps in a certain order; then you'll need to state your point and think about whether you should demonstrate the process visually. Finally, you'll want to choose appropriate transitions and think about your pronouns and verbs. The tips on p. 214 can help you get started.

PUTTING THE STEPS IN ORDER

Many processes, especially those linked by CAUSE AND EFFECT, follow a prescribed order. For example, before the bacillus that causes bubonic plague can enter a victim's bloodstream, a flea must first bite an infected rat, then bite the human. The process of infection won't work if the steps that make up the process unfold in any other order.

But sometimes the steps that make up a process can take place in almost any order. Consider the following tongue-in-cheek analysis of the men's movement:

> The Wild Man process involves five basic phases: Sweating, Yelling, Crying, Drum-Beating, and Ripping Your Shirt Off Even If It's Expensive.
> —JOE BOB BRIGGS, "Get in Touch with Your Ancient Spear"

A man in the process of reverting to his "wild" self would not necessarily go through the phases of the process in the exact order indicated here. For example, he might tear his shirt off first, before sweating or yelling. (Yelling first might even help to induce the sweating phase.)

When you write about the wild man (or any other) process, however, you must organize and present the main steps of the process in *some* order. If the process is a linear one, such as driving to a particular address in Dallas, you simply start at the earliest point in time and move forward, step by step, to the end result. If the process is cyclical, such as what's happening in your car engine as you drive, you will have to pick a logical point in the process and then proceed through the rest of the cycle. If, however, the process you are analyzing does not naturally follow chronology, try arranging the steps of your analysis from most important to least important, or the other way around.

STATING YOUR POINT

A good process analysis should have a point to make—a thesis. That point should be clearly expressed in a thesis statement so the reader will know why you're analyzing the process and what to expect. In addition, your thesis statement should in some way identify the process and indicate its end result. For example:

> You cannot understand how the Florida citrus industry works without understanding how fresh orange juice gets processed into "concentrate."
> —JOHN MCPHEE, *Oranges*

TIPS AND TEMPLATES FOR DRAFTING

When you begin to draft a process analysis, you need to say what process you're analyzing and to identify some of the most important steps in the process. These moves are fundamental to any process analysis. See how Diane Ackerman makes such moves in her essay in this chapter:

> But how do the colored leaves fall? As a leaf ages, the growth hormone, auxin, fades, and cells at the base of the petiole divide. Two or three rows of small cells, lying at right angles to the axis of the petiole, react with water, then come apart, leaving the petioles hanging on by only a few threads of xylem. A light breeze, and the leaves are airborne.
>
> —DIANE ACKERMAN, "Why Leaves Turn Color in the Fall"

Ackerman identifies the process she's analyzing (the falling of leaves) and indicates some important steps in the process (leaf ages; growth hormone fades; stem cells divide, react with water, and come apart; leaf drops). Here is one more example from this chapter:

> The most sensible way to avoid these threats, according to the instructor, is to remain alert, use common sense, be inconspicuous, and avoid dangerous areas, such as the planet Earth.
>
> —DAVE BARRY, "I Will Survive . . . Or at Least I'll Be Delayed"

The following templates can help you make some of these basic moves in your own writing. But don't take these as formulas where you just have to fill in the blanks. There are no easy formulas for good writing, but these templates can serve as starting points.

▶ In order to understand how process X works, we can divide it into the following steps: _____, _____, _____, and _____.

▶ The various steps that make up X can be grouped into the following stages: _____, _____, and _____.

▶ The end result of X is _____.

▶ In order to repeat X, you must first _____; then _____ and _____; and finally _____.

▶ The tools and materials you will need to replicate X include _____, _____, and _____.

▶ The most important reasons for understanding / repeating X are _____, _____, and _____.

This thesis statement clearly tells the reader what process you're analyzing (making "concentrate" from fresh orange juice), why you're analyzing it, (as a foundation for understanding the Florida citrus industry), and what the end result of the process is (orange juice concentrate). As you begin to draft a process analysis, make sure your thesis statement includes all of this information, so that your reader knows just what to expect from your analysis.

USING TRANSITIONS

As you recount the main steps in the process one by one, let the reader know when you are moving from one step to another by including clear TRANSITIONS, such as *next, from there, after five minutes, then*. The actions and events that make up a process are repeatable—unlike those in a narrative, which happen only *once* upon a time. So you will frequently use such expressions as *usually, normally, in most cases, whenever*. But also note any deviations from the normal order that might occur by using transitions like *sometimes, rarely, in one instance*.

USING APPROPRIATE PRONOUNS

In an explanatory process analysis, you need to focus on the things (fleas, rats, engines, oranges) and activities (infection, compression and combustion, culling and scrubbing) that make up the process. Thus you will write about the process most of the time in the third person (*he, she, it,* and *they*):

> Moving up a conveyer belt, oranges are scrubbed with detergent before they roll on into the juicing machines. —JOHN MCPHEE, *Oranges*

In a directive process analysis, by contrast, you are telling the reader directly how to do something. So you should typically use the second person (*you*): "When making orange juice, first you need to cut the oranges in half."

USING APPROPRIATE VERB FORMS

In an explanatory process analysis, you indicate how something works or is made, so your verbs should be in the indicative mood:

> As the rotor <u>moves</u> around the chamber, each of the three volumes of gas alternately <u>expands</u> and <u>contracts</u>. It is this expansion and contraction that <u>draws</u> air and fuel into the engine, <u>compresses</u> it, and <u>makes</u> useful power. —KARIM NICE, "How Rotary Engines Work"

In a directive process analysis, on the other hand, you are telling the reader how to do something, so your verbs should be in the imperative mood, as in these instructions for reviewing for exams:

<u>Start</u> preparing for your exams the first day of class. . . . <u>Plan</u> reviews as part of your regularly weekly study schedule. . . . <u>Read</u> over your lecture notes and <u>ask</u> yourself questions on the material you don't know well. . . . <u>Review</u> for several short periods rather than one long period.
— *Student Handbook*, University of Minnesota at Duluth

Notice that the verbs in these two examples are both in the present tense. That is because they express habitual actions. Instructions are always written in the present tense because they tell how something is (or should be) habitually done: "As you place the oranges on the conveyor belt, keep hair and fingers clear of the rollers."

Explanations, on the other hand, are written in the present tense when they tell how a process is habitually performed:

At low tide, researchers collect the algae by the handful and place it in plastic baggies. Back at the lab, they separate out the different strains and examine each type under a microscope.

But explanations are written in the *past* tense when they explain how a process was performed on a particular occasion, even though the process itself is repeatable:

At low tide, researchers collected the algae by the handful and placed it in plastic baggies. Back at the lab, they separated out the different strains and examined each type under a microscope.

Be careful not to switch between past tense and present tense in your analysis, unless you're intentionally switching from explaining how a process is usually performed (present tense) to how it was performed on a particular occasion (past tense).

EXPLAINING A PROCESS VISUALLY

Sometimes a process is best explained by *showing* how it works. (Just try writing a paragraph telling readers how to tie their shoes, for example.) If that's the case with some part of the process you're analyzing, you may want to include a diagram or drawing, such as the one on p. 217.

Notice that there are words to accompany each visual step. You'll want to make sure that the visual is clearly labeled for the reader, whether that means describing what the visual shows and indicating the sequence of events, as here, or labeling parts of a diagram (for instance, the parts of an engine).

How to Tie a Half Windsor

 1. Place the necktie around your collar and arrange the tie so that the wider end (A) is longer than the narrow end (B), then cross A over B.

 2. Twist A around and behind B.

 3. Bring A up.

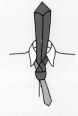 4. Pull A down through the loop.

 5. Bring A around front, crossing over B from left to right.

 6. Again thread A up and through the loop.

 7. Pull A down through the front of the knot.

 8. Tighten the knot: hold B with one hand and pull the knot up toward the collar with the other hand.

CONCLUDING A PROCESS ANALYSIS

A process is not complete until it produces an end product or final result. Likewise, a process analysis is not complete until it explains how the process ends—and what this result means for the reader.

The process of turning orange juice into concentrate, for example, does not end when the juice is extracted from the fruit. The extracted juice must be further processed and then shipped to the consumer, as John McPhee explains in the conclusion of his analysis: "From the extractor the orange concentrate flows into holding tanks from which it is later tapped, packaged, frozen, and shipped to grocery stories all over the country." And that, he might have added, is how you get your "fresh" o.j. in the morning.

Even this is not the end of the story, however. If you were writing a directive analysis of the process of making orange juice from concentrate, you would need, in conclusion, to remind readers to add cold water to the concentrate before serving.

USING OTHER METHODS

Analyzing the likely outcomes of a process and the steps leading to it may not always tell your readers everything they want or need to know. To explain a complicated process fully and completely, you may need to draw on other methods besides process analysis. Take, for instance, the process by which teenagers become addicted to tobacco. A teenager, let's call her Courtney, crosses the threshold from casual smoking to addiction. (Already we are expanding our analysis by giving an EXAMPLE.) Courtney now smokes half a dozen cigarettes every day. The process goes on—and on.

Over the next five years, Courtney gradually increases her intake of nicotine, a few cigarettes at a time, until one day she is a confirmed pack-a-day-plus smoker. Why? Why does Courtney become addicted while her sister, Brittany, never goes beyond a few cigarettes a day? Merely knowing *how* the process of addiction occurs—that it takes place in phases, from non-smoking to experimentation to addiction—isn't necessarily going to tell us *why* it occurs, though that's an important question to consider.

For the answer—and to make our analysis more meaningful—we could draw on the other methods discussed in this book. For example, we could CLASSIFY and DIVIDE teenage smokers into types: quitters (those who experiment with smoking but soon give it up); chippers (those who continue to smoke but never get addicted to tobacco); and addicts (those who regularly smoke six or more cigarettes a day).

Analyzing what categories teenage smokers fall into still doesn't tell us why some chippers become addicts while others never do. To learn why individual smokers cross the line, we also need to ANALYZE THE CAUSES of nicotine addiction.

It turns out that as long as Courtney smokes about five cigarettes a day and no more, she can go on for years without becoming addicted. Once she starts smoking more than that, however, the balance tips, and she slowly slides into addiction.

When we analyze a noxious process, such as a disease or addiction, our ultimate purpose is usually to combat it. For this purpose, we find ourselves ARGUING for a solution to the problem.

Reading a Process Analysis with a Critical Eye

One complex process that doesn't proceed in linear fashion is the writing process. Although the phases of the writing process are sequential—that is, you have to organize and draft an essay before you can revise and edit it—they are also repeatable, unlike the steps in most strictly linear processes. (You wouldn't want to bake a cake, for example, and then take it out of the oven and stir it again.) So once you've "completed" your draft, go back, check it over thoroughly, and revise what you've written. Repeat as necessary.

Since the heart of your analysis is the process itself, you need to make sure, first of all, that your reader will be able to follow every step. So ask a friend or classmate to review your draft and tell you whether he or she has any questions about how the process works—or any suggestions for making it clearer. The following questions focus on the main points to check over in a process analysis.

PURPOSE AND AUDIENCE. Is the purpose of the analysis to tell the audience how to do something, or is it to explain how something works or is made? How likely is the intended audience to want or need this information? What additional information, if any, should the analysis provide? For example, is there any special equipment that readers might need to know about? Any terms that need to be defined?

ORGANIZATION. Are all of the important steps of the process included? Are they arranged chronologically, or in some other order that makes sense—such as from most important to least important? Are there clear TRANSITIONS between each step?

THE POINT. What is the point of the analysis? Is there a THESIS STATEMENT at the beginning that tells the reader why this particular process is being analyzed and what to look for in the rest of the essay? Is the significance or end result of the process clearly indicated?

PRONOUNS. Is the analysis primarily directive or explanatory? If it's directing the reader to do something, is it written mostly in the second person, referring to the reader as *you*? If the analysis is primarily explanatory, is it written mostly in the third person (*he, she, it,* and *they*)?

VERBS. If the analysis is directive, are the verbs in the imperative (or commanding) mood? If it's explanatory, are they in the indicative mood? Is there any needless switching between the two moods? With verbs in the imperative mood, remember, the pronoun *you* is often understood rather than explicitly stated: (You) "Check over every aspect of your draft carefully."

VISUALS. Are any charts, drawings, or other illustrations included to help explain the process? If not, should there be? Are the visuals appropriately labeled?

CONCLUSION. Does the analysis end with a clear indication of the outcome of the process? If there are several possible outcomes, does it indicate what they are and which results are most likely?

OTHER METHODS. Does the analysis include other methods of development? For instance, does it give EXAMPLES of the process? Does it ANALYZE WHAT CAUSED key actions or events in the process and what EFFECTS they might have? Does it CLASSIFY or DIVIDE part of the process? Does it offer an ARGUMENT about the process?

Editing for Common Errors in a Process Analysis

Process analysis invites certain kinds of errors. Following are some tips that can help you check for two common problems.

Check your pronouns.

Remember to use third-person pronouns (*he, she, it, they*) when you're explaining how something works or is done—and to use the second-person pronoun (*you*) when you're telling someone how to do something.

NOT When trees are harvested, you have to cut down each one by hand.

BUT When trees are harvested, they are cut down by hand.

The reader is not actually harvesting the trees.

NOT To harvest trees properly, they must be cut by hand.

BUT To harvest trees properly, you must cut them down by hand.

Here the reader is the one harvesting the trees.

Check your verbs to make sure you haven't switched needlessly between the indicative and the imperative.

NOT According to the recipe, we should stir in the nuts last. Then sprinkle cinnamon on top.

BUT According to the recipe, we should stir in the nuts last and then sprinkle cinnamon on top.

OR Stir in the nuts last and then sprinkle cinnamon on top.

Making Guacamole

A process analysis tells how something works or is made. Recipes, such as the directions for cutting an avocado to make guacamole, are typical examples of the kinds of process analysis that we do every day. When you analyze a process, you break it down into the steps and stages that compose the process. The first stage in making guacamole, for example, is to get the avocado ready to mash and mix with the other ingredients. This preparation stage, in turn, can be broken down into the three steps pictured here—cutting, removing the pit, and scraping. When you write about a process, you present the various steps to the reader in the order in which they usually occur. You wouldn't want to write a recipe for guacamole that told the reader to scrape out the avocado, cut it in two, and then remove the pit. The reader would have trouble following these directions; and one reason you analyze a process in the first place, particularly in a recipe, is often so your reader can repeat the process.

EVERYDAY PROCESS

Cutting an avocado in half,

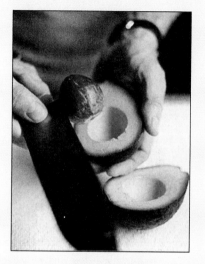

. . . removing the pit,

. . . and scraping flesh from skin for guacamole.

JOSHUA PIVEN, DAVID BORGENICHT, AND JENNIFER WORICK

How to Pull an All-Nighter

Joshua Piven, David Borgenicht, and Jennifer Worick have made a small industry out of teaching people how to deal with situations they are unlikely to get into. In 1998, while watching a movie in which a man without piloting experience was forced to land a plane, Borgenicht concluded that life is filled with "worst-case scenarios" for which the average person is utterly unprepared. He recruited Piven, a fellow University of Pennsylvania graduate, to help him research and write a manual for such situations—The Worst-Case Scenario Survival Handbook (1999). Addressing situations that range from the merely improbable (How to Deliver a Baby in a Taxicab) to the barely imaginable (How to Win a Sword Fight), the book was so popular that there are now Worst-Case Scenario handbooks for everything from holidays and golfing to weddings and dating.

The Worst-Case Scenario Survival Handbook: College (2004), co-authored by Jennifer Worick, brings the Worst-Case outlook to college life. "How to Pull an All-Nighter" is from that collection and deals with a process that some students might actually engage in—staying up all night to study. As with the authors' instructions for surviving a stadium riot or shark attack, however, readers of this point-by-point analysis might be better advised to avoid the situation in the first place.

Eat a light dinner. Do not skip a meal, but do not eat to the point of drowsiness or sluggishness. Select foods with protein, like chicken breast, and complex carbohydrates, such as whole-wheat bread, brown rice, or beans, to provide you with energy and stamina for a long night. Later, when you feel your energy ebb, eat an energy bar.   1

Consume peppermint. Peppermint is a stimulant; even a whiff of it will make you more alert and awake. Eat peppermint candy, chew peppermint gum, or drink peppermint-flavored herbal tea. Rub peppermint oil on your temples or wrists.   2

Turn on the radio or television. A bit of white noise in the background will engage your senses. Select a classical or jazz station on the radio. If you turn on the television, turn to an infomercial or shopping channel. Keep the volume low. Do not select a rerun of your favorite situation comedy or anything you might otherwise be interested in.   3

Turn on a strong overhead light. A bright light will help you see what you are reading as well as prevent you from falling into a deep sleep. Close the curtains   4 and put clocks out of sight; your body will become confused as to what time of night it is.

Turn down the thermostat. The cold temperature will help keep you awake. 5 Make sure the temperature does not dip below 50°F, at which you are susceptible to hypothermia, especially if you have wet hair or skin. A high temperature slows your pulse and makes you drowsy.

Do not lie down. Pinch yourself or wear tight shoes and constricting underwear. 6 Physical discomfort will keep you distracted and awake.

Consume caffeine. Drink caffeinated beverages or eat a few caffeinated mints, 7 but proceed with caution: Too much caffeine can leave you distracted and wired. Three hundred milligrams is considered a safe daily amount of caffeine for adults, which translates into a six-pack of soda or three to four cups of brewed coffee.

Breathe deeply. Go to an open window or step outside for a few minutes. Stand 8 up straight, close your eyes, and inhale deeply through your nose. Hold the breath for as long as you can. Exhale slowly through your nose or mouth. Repeat several times. Deep breathing will clear your mind and give you a shot of energy.

Stretch. Stretch your limbs by taking a walk or doing a few yoga poses. This will 9 work out any tension you are holding in your muscles.

- Lift your arms over your head and reach for the sky, alternating arms.
- Lean over to each side and then lean forward from the waist, bringing your arms out in front of you and down to the ground.
- Let your arms dangle; swing them from side to side.

Do a headstand. Increase your circulation by standing on your head. 10

- Find an area of clear floor space next to a wall.
- Kneel on the floor, facing the wall.
- Place your head on the floor a few inches from the wall.
- Place your forearms on the floor on either side of your head.
- Raise your body and legs slowly up the wall. Keep your body weight on your arms, not your head. Lean against the wall as needed.

Raise your heart rate. If you find yourself nodding off, do a few calisthenics to 11 raise your heart rate. Do 25 jumping jacks, or skip rope or jog in place for 5 minutes.

Standing on your head will increase circulation.

Get a study partner. Even if he is not cramming for the same exam, you and your   12
partner can quiz each other and talk as you start to get drowsy. Do not stay up with
someone you know will distract you with either idle chatter or sexual tension.

Be Aware

Even if you don't plan on going to sleep, set your alarm clock. To make sure that   13
you are awake when you need to be, set every alarm you can find—watches, computers, cell phones, and hand-held electronic devices often have built-in alarms.
Arrange for a friend or your roommate to back up the alarms with a wake-up call.

READING CLOSELY

1. What are the main steps into which the authors of this selection divide the
   process of pulling an all-nighter?

2. Which steps do you think would be most effective? Least effective? Why?

3. What steps would you add to (or remove from) this process analysis?

STRATEGIES AND STRUCTURES

1. Who might be interested in the process that Piven, Borgenicht, and Worick are explaining? What audience in particular do they have in mind? How can you tell?

2. The authors of this selection do not say why they are explaining how to pull an all-nighter. What might their purpose be, and should they state it more directly? Why or why not?

3. The instructions in this selection could be followed in almost any order. Why? On the other hand, why do individual directives—such as those for breathing deeply, stretching, and doing a headstand—actually require the reader to follow a particular sequence?

4. An essay has an introduction, a body, and a conclusion. What parts of the essay form are missing from "How to Pull an All-Nighter"? If this selection is not really an essay, what it is? Explain.

5. How and how well does the illustration in this selection take the place of verbal explanations?

6. *Other Methods.* As Piven et al. analyze the process of staying awake all night, they give a number of specific EXAMPLES. Which ones do you think contribute most to the analysis? Why?

THINKING ABOUT LANGUAGE

1. The verbs in the headings that introduce each section of this text are all in the imperative mood. Why?

2. What pronoun is understood in each heading? What grammatical "person" is it in? Why?

3. In what sense are the authors of the selection using the word "translates" (7)?

FOR WRITING

1. Write a paragraph or two telling someone how to pull an all-nighter.

2. Write an essay explaining how to study so as to avoid all-nighters and other educational pitfalls.

DAVE BARRY

I Will Survive . . . Or at Least I'll Be Delayed

Dave Barry (b. 1947) is the author of more than thirty books of humor. A graduate of Haverford College, Barry taught writing for a consulting firm before joining The Miami Herald *as a humor columnist in 1983. (When you write a business letter, Barry advised his students, do not say things like, "Enclosed, please find the enclosed enclosures.") Barry's columns—collected in such volumes as* Dave Barry Is Not Making This Up *(1995) and* Dave Barry: Boogers Are My Beat *(2003)—earned him a Pulitzer Prize for Commentary in 1988 and appeared weekly until 2005. In addition to the occasional column and a blog, Barry is now working on a children's book and a film based on his* Complete Guide to Guys *(1991). The most recent of his satirical "guides"—which bring a "guy's" perspective to everything from "marriage and/or sex" to parenting, politics, and personal finances—is* Dave Barry's Money Secrets *(2006).*

"I Will Survive . . . Or at Least I'll Be Delayed" is a garbled review of the lessons that Barry learned in Hostile Environment Training—and a parody of how-to writing. First published in the Miami Herald *in 2004, these mangled directives make fun of overly simplified instructions for dealing with impossible situations "involving dangerous elements such as terrorists, kidnappers, robbers, rioters, or fans of the Oakland Raiders football team."*

WHEN I GOT INTO JOURNALISM, I expected to do many things. None of them involved standing on a colleague's groin. 1

But recently I learned that I might be called upon to do exactly that. I learned this in Fright School, which is known formally as Hostile Environment Training. This is a course, taught by corporate security consultants, that teaches you what to do if you find yourself in a situation involving dangerous elements such as terrorists, kidnappers, robbers, rioters, or fans of the Oakland Raiders. 2

I didn't think I needed this training, because I've lived for the past 20 years in a hostile environment, namely, Miami, where virtually everybody, including nuns, is packing heat.[1] But along with many other journalists, I was ordered by my company to attend Fright School because this summer I'm going to the Olympics and both political conventions. I'm writing this column before leaving for those events, and I sincerely hope that, by the time summer's over, we'll all be heaving large sighs of relief from knowing that nothing bad happened, and nobody had to actually stand on anybody's groin. 3

---

1. *Packing heat:* carrying a gun.

But just in case you ever find yourself in a hostile situation or, God forbid, a 4 Raiders home game, today I'm going to pass along the lessons I learned in Fright School, as recorded in my notes.

My first note says "cargo pants," because that's what the instructor was wearing. 5 He was a muscular, military-looking British guy who was quite cheerful, considering that he ended roughly every fourth sentence with: "And if THAT happens, you're going to die."

The instructor began by reviewing the various kinds of hostile situations we, as 6 journalists, might encounter. The three main points I got from that were:

1. A lot of things can happen.
2. All of these things can kill you.
3. So DON'T PANIC.

Among the specific threats we discussed were "dirty bombs," germ warfare, 7 mines, and booby traps. Because we took only the truncated one-day version of the course, the instructor couldn't go deeply into these threats, other than to note that they are all fatal. (He also pointed out that his company had the world's foremost authority on booby traps, and "he does a presentation that's quite entertaining.")

The most sensible way to avoid these threats, according to the instructor, is to 8 remain alert, use common sense, be inconspicuous, and avoid dangerous areas, such as the planet Earth. He also recommended that we carry the following items at all times: water, food, protective eyewear, protective headgear, an "escape hood" for gas attacks, a whistle, a personal alarm and a first-aid kit. He didn't say how you could look inconspicuous while carrying all these items: Maybe you could put them in your cargo pants and just pretend to have enormous thighs.

Here are a couple of other survival tips from the instructor that I wrote down: 9

"If you're going to use an escape rope, try to get some knots in it." 10

"Try to anticipate any strikes or blows." 11

Also, if you're going to get shot, the farther you are from the shooter, the better. 12 I learned that valuable tip during the first-aid section of our training. The instructor began this section by noting that some people are reluctant to attempt first aid. "But," he said, "if your colleague is dying, and you don't do anything, he's going to die, isn't he? And he's not going to thank you, is he?"

To which sports columnist Tom Powers replied: "He's not going to complain, 13 either."

In first-aid training, we learned about the Trimodal Death Distribution, with the 14 three Modes of Death being: Instant, Late and Delayed. The instructor said: "We're interested in the delayed diers."

I missed a lot of what he said next, because he was showing graphic color slides 15 of injuries, and one of them, entitled "Impaled Object," required me to put my head between my knees for several minutes. But I definitely recall hearing the instructor say, several times, that if your colleague is bleeding profusely from the femoral artery, you should stop it by standing on his groin. This may be solid advice, but before I follow it, I intend to confer with the colleague.

ME: Do you mind if I stand on your groin?

COLLEAGUE: Thanks, but I'd rather bleed to death.

ME (relieved): OK, then!

But we're talking worst-case scenarios, here. As I said, I'm hoping that nobody   16 needs any of this training, and that we all have a peaceful, hostility-free, and fun summer. Maybe I'll even see you at the conventions or Olympics! Assuming there are eye holes in my escape hood.

READING CLOSELY

1. Do you think Barry's "Fright School" instructor actually included planet Earth in his list of "dangerous areas" to be avoided (8)? Where else in this column does Barry seem to be exaggerating? Where does he seem to be reporting what really happened or was said?

2. Barry gives a number of survival "tips" in paragraphs 9–16. What do they all have in common, and why do you think he chose them for an essay on such a serious subject?

3. Why was Barry's instructor unable to go more deeply into some of the specific threats, such as germ warfare, that Barry and his fellow journalists might face?

STRATEGIES AND STRUCTURES

1. What is Barry's PURPOSE in writing this column? Is it to explain what he learned, to highlight the inadequacy of his training, to entertain readers and make them laugh? Some combination of these? How can you tell?

2. What process is Barry analyzing here? Is his analysis primarily explanatory or directive? Explain.

3. Where does Barry give the main steps of the process he is analyzing? How helpful are they? Where else in his essay does Barry include additional steps or directions?

4. Barry sometimes writes in the third-person, as when he says of his instructor, "He was a muscular, military-looking British guy" (5). Which personal pronoun (or pronouns) does Barry use more frequently, however? Why?

5. A solid process analysis presents the steps of the process in some orderly fashion with clear TRANSITIONS between each step. How well does Barry's analysis measure up to this standard? Explain.

6. *Other Methods.* Barry ends his column with a little DIALOGUE between himself and a fictional injured colleague. How does he prepare the way for this ending? Where else (and for what purposes) does Barry use other elements of NARRATIVE to support his analysis?

THINKING ABOUT LANGUAGE

1. A PARODY is a humorous imitation of a particular form of writing or behavior. What is Barry parodying here and why?

2. Barry's essay is about several "worst-case scenarios" (16). What is a *scenario* exactly, and why can these scenarios be analyzed as different *cases*?

3. What are the implications of Barry's nickname for the course in hostile environment training?

FOR WRITING

1. Write a paragraph or two analyzing one of the threats that Barry mentions in paragraph 7.

2. Write a parody of a process analysis in which you explain something you "learned" in a chemistry, math, writing, or some other class.

3. Citing Barry's column and other sources, write a set of instructions, either tongue-in-cheek or serious, explaining how to survive in a hostile environment.

MARCIA MULLER

Creating a Female Sleuth

Marcia Muller (b. 1944) wrote her first novel, a story about her dog, at the age of
twelve. Years later, however, a creative writing instructor at the University of Michigan
told her to forget about writing because she had "nothing to say." Muller persisted never-
theless, and in 1977, she published her first mystery novel, Edwin of the Iron Shoes.
Since then, she has written more than thirty novels, five collections of short stories, and
thirteen works of nonfiction, some of them co-authored with her husband, Bill
Pronzini.

Mystery novels, sometimes called "procedurals," are all about the process of solving
a crime. In "Creating a Female Sleuth," however, Muller analyzes the process of creat-
ing the crime solver herself. Notice how she usually works from character to plot—
rather than the other way around. Muller's analysis of her writing methods first
appeared in The Writer *magazine in October 1978.*

Several years ago, a friend handed me my first whodunit[1] as I was about to   1
embark on a long bus ride. I finished the book before I reached my destination and,
upon arrival, went straight to the paperback racks for another. I was hooked.

In the years that followed, my puzzle-prone friends and I noticed that one figure   2
was missing from the mystery scene. There were scores of male sleuths, both hard-
and soft-boiled. There were old ladies with knitting needles and noses for secrets.
There were even a few dedicated and hard-working policewomen. But nowhere, at
that time, could we find a female private eye.

Obviously, I decided, if I wanted to read about such a character, I would first   3
have to write about her.

The process of creating my sleuth, Sharon McCone, and plotting her first case—   4
Edwin of the Iron Shoes—presented a number of technical problems. Because
female sleuths are in themselves a rarity, my imaginary friend could not be too
unusual or too much of a super-woman if modern readers—both male and
female—were to identify with her. She also needed to have a background that
would make her choice of profession believable.

On the other hand, like all detectives, she had to be somewhat larger than life.   5
She had to be the sort of person who would do things you and I might never dream

---

1. *Whodunit*: colloquial name for the literary genre that deals with solving a crime, usually a
murder.

of: stalk her quarry through the highways and byways of the city; stand her ground with hostile cops; grapple hand-to-hand with dangerous criminals.

In order to reconcile these seeming opposites, I chose to give Sharon a normal, 6 perhaps pedestrian, family background and upbringing that produced a well-adjusted, uncomplicated adult. Sharon's problems are those we've all experienced at one time: an affectionate but nosy mother who, fortunately, lives 500 miles away; the frustration of not finding a decent job after graduating from college with a sociology major; the lack of an interesting man in one's life; too high a rent for too small a studio apartment.

Marital status, which affects a female investigator's freedom of movement far 7 more than a male's, was easy to decide, particularly when the police lieutenant in charge of Sharon's first murder case turned out to be attractive, if a bit of a smart-aleck. Sharon is single.

For the background that would qualify her for a career as a private investigator, 8 I chose department-store security, a relatively easy field to break into. Where else could a nice girl learn to fire a .38 Special or flip a grown man over with a judo hold? I decided that Sharon was bored with guarding dresses on the sales floor, had gone off to college, and then returned to investigative work when she realized the demand for sociologists was nil. Further training with a big security agency equipped her for a position as staff investigator at a San Francisco legal cooperative in time for her first big case.

With this plausible basis for my sleuth's choice of occupation and a number of 9 down-to-earth character traits, I gave my imagination free rein. I wanted to make Sharon's physical attributes stand out in the reader's mind, and at the same time to avoid the old, overused mirror-on-the-wall device ("As I stood before the mirror and brushed my hair, I thought about the case and noticed gray strands among the black.") Therefore, I decided to make Sharon a person with Scotch-Irish ancestry, whose one-eighth Shoshone Indian blood dominates her appearance. Her unusual looks, coupled with her name, cause people to comment, "McCone? But you look like an Indian!"—and this enabled me to dispense with a great deal of description.

Larger Than Life

Now I was really getting into the larger-than-life qualities, or, more accurately, the 10 larger-than-author traits. Sharon is much taller than I, so she can more easily wrestle with criminals. She never has to worry about her weight, presumably because she does not sit at a typewriter all day. She is more independent than the average soul, delights in asserting herself, and, of course, is much braver.

These admirable qualities were all very well to list, but the next problem was how 11 to express them in action. When I began writing up her first case, I found my heroine in a given situation and asked myself: "All right, what would *I* do?" The answer, inevitably, was something like "Run." Since this was not working out, I conditioned myself to think of what I would do if I were brave, tall, an expert at judo, and so on, each time taking it a step farther. I discovered it was better to have Sharon act ridiculously brave, even foolhardy, and moderate her actions later, than to start off timidly, because a timid response to a situation was more difficult to correct in a rewrite.

Touchier yet was the problem of emotional balance: how was Sharon to deal   12
with the rough situations that came up in the course of her work without sacrificing her femininity? The qualities of empathy and intuition would be great assets to her, because as a woman she might realize or even be told things that ordinary investigative methods would not turn up. Still, she couldn't cry at every bump and bruise, or lose her gun in her purse at the crucial moment. Again, I constantly had to consider what I would do if I were a trained professional, how I would condition and curb my natural responses. I constantly made adjustments for this balance in every draft of the novel, and am still making adjustments now, as I guide my sleuth through her second case.

A mechanical aid in getting acquainted with my character was writing the bio-   13
graphical sketch, a detailed run-down on Sharon's history, preferences and opinions from her own point of view. I wrote this in the first person, as if she were standing up to introduce herself to a group. Throughout the writing process, this "biography" was there to help refresh my memory as to details. It was no substitute, however, for getting to know my character through writing about her.

Two Rules for Plotting

Now that I had my sleuth, the next question was what kind of case she should   14
solve. In short, what was my plot to be?

I had a setting I wanted to explore: an enclave of antique and junk shops, loosely   15
based on several such areas in San Francisco, and I wanted to center on one particular shop containing an assortment of strange objects, including a department store mannequin named Edwin, who wore a pair of ornate iron shoes. I also had a problem for Sharon to solve: the dead body of the proprietor on the floor of the shop, with Edwin as the only witness to the murder.

With this in mind, I began to play the game of "what if." I started with the very   16
obvious questions: What if the proprietor had a fortune in antiques hidden in the shop? What if she had a jealous lover? What if several powerful real-estate syndicates were after the land the shop was on? What if, beneath her ordinary exterior, the victim hid some criminal secret? The answers to these and other often laughable questions gave the basis for my solution.

Knowing my solution was the real key to a plot that held together. I needed to   17
have some ending, however tentative, in mind at all times, or I couldn't plant clues

or make my suspects act properly suspicious. Without a solution, I didn't know what the clues pointed to or why my characters needed to behave strangely. This has become my first unbreakable rule of plotting.

My second unbreakable rule, to keep the plot as flexible as possible, may sound like a direct contradiction to the first. I found, however, that I had to be willing to modify my original solution or even throw it out and replace it with another when characters and events indicated this was necessary.

For example, I reached a point in my whodunit where all the loose ends were tying up nicely. Everything pointed to my chosen killer, his motives were coming clear, and my sleuth had won over the nasty police lieutenant by her clever use of logic. Elated, I took a breath to count pages and realized that I was only halfway through the book!

This is the kind of situation in which you need all the flexibility you can muster. I looked over what I had written and concluded that this would be not only a very short book, but also a very boring one. Everything pointed clearly to the killer. His motives were too pat and ordinary. I began once more to play "what if."

What if, at the height of his bedazzlement with Sharon's logic, the police lieutenant receives a phone call, and then smugly announces to her that the supposed murderer himself was dead? That he was knifed in his own apartment, in fact, and that the apartment had been searched?

Of course, the answer was that I had to get myself a new killer. What if the sleazy bail bondsman that the victim had been consorting with . . . ? The new solution was more interesting all around, and it gave me the extra pages I needed.

Plot Control

This experience taught me the difficulty of keeping the plot of a whodunit in hand even after you think you know what it is. I had to keep track of events that happened weeks, even years, before my opening action, all of which led up to the initial crime. There were also facts that had to be withheld from the reader as long as possible, and clues the reader had to be given. A number of characters were engaged in suspicious activities that may or may not have had something to do with the murder. How was I to keep track of all this?

Several mechanical devices helped. The first, a sketch of what really happened, was like a well-detailed short story. I started at the beginning of my mystery, two years before the murder, when the antique shop proprietor needed a great deal more money than her shop could bring in. I followed the course of events from there to the day she ended up dead on the shop floor, and finally ended the sketch with the arrest of her killer. The sketch was available for reference as my plot unfolded and the past was explained. And, in accordance with the flexibility rule, it was discarded and rewritten when the solution changed.

A second device was the sketch of each main character. While not as detailed as   25
the biography of the heroine, it contained much the same types of information:
background, important life events, outstanding physical and personality traits.
These sketches helped me keep the characters' motivations in mind and to keep
details about their lives consistent.

The most useful device for plot control was my time chart. It took the form of a   26
grid, with major characters plotted across the top and chapters or time frames plotted down the side; it covered the same period as the sketch of what really happened.

In the squares under each character on the chart, I noted what he or she was   27
doing during every time period. In this way, I avoided such embarrassing situations
as finding that the murderer was really with my detective when he was supposed to
have been doing in his second victim. I usually plotted only three to five chapters
ahead at a time, finding that the things characters said and did often suggested new
complications or scenes. However, I imagine this type of chart could be adapted
nicely to complete pre-planning as well.

The rewrite was my final check of how well my plot hung together. This was   28
when I went back and inserted clues I had forgotten, brought out necessary facets
of a suspect's character, and smoothed over inconsistencies and cut and cleaned up
style. My experience with rewrites has been rewarding: the wicked-looking bone-
handled knife which, as the murder weapon, plays a large part in my whodunit,
didn't even exist until the rewrite, when a critic friend pointed out that a small par-
ing knife made a pretty silly instrument of violent death.

During the final typing of the manuscript, I checked and rechecked my clues. I   29
believe in playing fair with the reader, and I wanted to make sure I'd given him
every clue Sharon came across in solving the case. Rather than have Sharon say: "I
realized something that told me who the killer was," I had her carry on a mental
conversation with Edwin, the heavy-footed mannequin. At its end, she says:
"Edwin, why didn't you tell me?" The conversation provides the reader with all the
clues he needs to solve the murders along with Sharon. And I will be delighted to
hear of readers who solve my whodunit ahead of my sleuth!

Reading Closely

1. Why did Marcia Muller decide to create a female private investigator in the first
   place? How did this decision affect her character's attributes?

2. What early "technical problems" did Muller face in creating her detective, and
   how did she solve them (4, 11)? What were some of the other important steps in
   the process of creating her sleuth?

3. How did making a time chart help Muller to organize and keep track of what was happening to her detective?

4. In the rewrite of her first whodunit, what sort of changes did Muller make (28)? What did they contribute to the overall process of writing the book (28)?

Strategies and Structures

1. Most of the events in Muller's analysis are arranged in chronological order. Point out some of the TRANSITIONS she uses to connect these events in time.

2. Early in her essay, Muller refers to "the process of creating my sleuth, Sharon McCone, and plotting her first case" (4). If we look at this process as having two distinct phases, which events in Muller's analysis make up the first phase?

3. Muller turns to the second phase when she asks, "In short, what was my plot to be?" (14). What are the main steps in *this* phase of her writing process?

4. Muller's analysis of how she created Sharon McCone sounds a lot like a detective solving a case. Why? What is Muller's purpose, besides explaining how she did it, in writing this analysis of her process?

5. Muller asks RHETORICAL QUESTIONS throughout her essay. Point out several, and explain how and why she answers then.

6. *Other Methods.* Any one of the activities that make up the writing process can be repeated at almost any time during the process. Where and how does Muller give EXAMPLES of this aspect of her own writing?

Thinking about Language

1. What does Muller mean by "larger-than-life" (10)? Why must her female detective meet this qualification?

2. In what sense is Muller using the word "express" (11) to refer to her character and plot?

3. What is the etymology of "whodunit" (1)?

For Writing

1. Write a paragraph or two analyzing the process that Muller went through to create her first female detective.

2. Write an essay analyzing the process you typically go through when you write an essay.

3. Write an analysis of the process by which one of your favorite detectives—from Monsieur Auguste Dupin or Sherlock Holmes to Sam Spade, Monk, Horatio Caine, or V. I. Warshawski—typically solves a mystery.

ROBERT CONNORS

How in the World Do You Get
a Skunk Out of a Bottle?

Robert Connors (1951–2000) was a writing teacher at the University of New Hampshire. As a scholar, he focused on the history of writing and writing instruction. The author of Composition-Rhetoric: Backgrounds, Theory, and Pedagogy *(1997), Connors published many influential journal articles on topics ranging from the comments teachers make on student papers to the history of citation systems. In 1981, Connors received the Braddock Award for his article on the modes of discourse—a study of the very methods taught in this book. When his life was abruptly ended by a motorcycle accident in 2000, the University of New Hampshire named its writing center for him—a center Connors himself had established there a decade earlier.*

"How in the World Do You Get a Skunk Out of a Bottle?" first appeared in Yankee *magazine; it is not about writing but about the author's zest for life and nature. A personal narrative of his encounter with a trapped animal, it includes a detailed analysis of the delicate procedure by which he set the creature free.*

THE SANDY DIRT of Canterbury Road is just right as I pant my way past John- 1
son's hayfield. The air cool enough for delight but not cold enough for long johns
and stocking cap, the early sun slanting low. No sound but my labored breathing
and the chunking noise of sneakers on dirt. Just another morning. Or so I think.

Then I see him, off to my right. Twenty-five feet or so from the road in a cut- 2
over hayfield. A skunk. One of the kind that are mostly white, with the black
mainly on their sides. From the corner of my eye I watch him turn, move. I detour
to the other side of the road.

But something seems wrong, in the way that he moves or the way that he looks. 3
Some glint of strangeness. I slow my pace, looking over my right shoulder. The
skunk moves through the stubble toward the road. I stop and shade my eyes against
the low sunlight. The skunk comes closer. And then I see it.

A glass jar. About $4\frac{1}{2}$ inches long, about three inches in diameter, with a 4
pinched-in neck—a large baby-food jar, perhaps. It is jammed over the skunk's
head, completely covering it past the ears. Unable to hear or smell, the skunk raises
his head in a clumsy, unnatural way. His dim eyes catch sight of my bright purple
warm-up jacket. He begins, slowly but unmistakably, to come toward me.

As you probably know, this is not what skunks or any wild animals typically do. 5
But as I stand on the bright, hard-packed road, this skunk is clearly coming toward
me. More, I can't help but feel that he is coming *to* me.

I begin to talk to him. Only later does it occur to me that he is probably unable 6
to hear anything with the jar on his head, but the talk is more for my sake anyway.

"Oh, boy," I say, as the skunk trundles closer, "if you aren't a textbook case in 7
conservation ethics, I've never seen one." I back away a step. What if he's rabid? He
lifts his head, feebly, to the right, to the left. I can see the long white silky hairs of
his back, the fogged translucence of the glass jar.

I have a sudden desire to turn, go, keep running, get home. 8

By this time the skunk has reached the high grass at the edge of the road. And 9
there he stops. His sides heave; the tight neck of the jar can hardly admit any air,
and each breath is a struggle of seven or eight seconds' duration. The skunk is shivering as well, slight tremors running through his whole body as he crouches,
watching me. Clearly, the skunk is going to die and not of starvation. He is suffo-
cating as I watch.

"What do you want me to do?" I say. "You've got to come to me. I can't come to 10
you. Who knows what mental state you're in?" The skunk looks at me. "Look, I'd
love to help you. But the covered end of you isn't the end I'm worried about." The
skunk wags his head slightly, tries to breathe. "What were you looking for in there
anyway, you dumb-head? That jar's been out here empty for years."

By now I realize that this skunk is my responsibility. The police would probably 11
kill him in order to save him. Getting someone from Fish and Game would take
hours. I am the one here, now.

Maybe I can throw a big rock and break the jar. Not get close enough to be 12
sprayed, but break the glass. Let the skunk breathe.

No. Any rock heavy enough to break the glass from a distance couldn't be 13
thrown accurately. It might hit the skunk and injure him. Even if the glass broke,
the edges might slash the skunk's face or get into his eyes. And with that kind of jar,
the neck might not break with the bottle part, leaving the skunk with a jagged
necklace of razor-edged glass that would sooner or later kill him. No, the rock idea
is out.

Perhaps I can find something to throw over him—a coat or a blanket so he can't 14
spray me—and grab the jar. But all I have is this warm-up jacket—too small to
cover him and too light to keep him from turning.

"I don't know, old skunkoid," I say, moving slightly closer to where he sits, 15
motionless except for the shivering. "There's no way that I'm just going to go over
to you and pull that jar off." One step closer. I have no idea what I *am* going to do.
Hunkering down, I keep on talking. "You understand my position. I have to go
teach college today. If you spray me, you will seriously undercut my efficiency." He
is still not moving. Stand up, move one step closer. Squat down again.

"I'm not going to hurt you. I present no threat. I'm scared to death of you, and 16
you probably are of me." Stand up, one step closer, squat down.

I can see the bloody scratches along the skunk's neck where he tried with claws 17 to free himself from the jar. I keep on talking, just to make noise, piling nonsense on nonsense.

Stand, step, squat, and I am three feet from the skunk. He regards me. Deep 18 breath. Then, very slowly, I reach out with my right hand. "Don't worry now, bubba.[1] I'm not here to hurt you. This jar is the problem." Slowly, slowly, reaching, the skunk still quiet, then *got it!* My hand clamps down on the warm rigidity of the jar.

Suddenly the skunk, until now motionless, is galvanized. He pulls back in panic, 19 his paws scrabbling at the grass; at my hand. I pull hard on the jar. Now it will come off and he will run away. One way or another, this is it.

But this is not it. Pulling hard, I find I am dragging the skunk, who pushes fran- 20 tically backward, onto the dirt road. His head is *impacted* into the jar. It will not come out.

"Oh, boy, come *on.*" The skunk is now completely in the road, struggling furi- 21 ously to get away, twisting and turning as I hold the jar tight. The one good thing at this point is that he is so completely wedged that he can't turn and fire, although there is little doubt that he regrets this keenly. As long as I have his head, I'm safe. I pull again and am only able to drag the skunk farther. "Oh, *great.* Now I get to take you home." He grunts audibly, pulls again, scrabbling up packed dirt.

There's nothing for it. I have to grab him with one hand and try to pull the jar 22 off with the other. With my left hand, I grasp him around the shoulder blades. His hair is soft. He would be nice to stroke. "Come on come on come on. . . ." I twist the jar hard to the left, and his head inside assumes a crazy angle, but he stops struggling. I pull hard on the jar. It does not move. "Come on, you. . . ." The jar is *really* socked onto his neck, which has swollen in some way. Grabbing hard at his shoulder blades, I twist and pull harder.

I am exerting all my strength now. And I see the threads of the jar turn, slowly, 23 then more quickly. "OK, something moving, heads up," then more movement, an upward sliding, and then with an audible *pop* the jar is off.

Without any thought except *escape,* I jump up, whirl, run. Unscathed. Un- 24 sprayed. At a safe distance, I stop and look back. The skunk stands in the middle of the road. He breathes deeply, several times, shakes himself from stem to stern, takes a few tottering steps across the road.

On the other side, he halts, then turns to look at me. I look back. For perhaps 25 30 seconds, we regard each other with great benignity. Then I hold up my index finger in a tutorial fashion.

---

1. *Bubba:* a common regional nickname for a boy or man.

"Next time you see me," I say, "don't spray me." He watches me gravely a   26
moment more, then turns and plods off into a cemetery across the road.

There is something in my hand. An empty jar. Starting to run up the long hill to   27
Main Street, I pitch it as hard as I can, sidearm, way out into a swamp. I hear it
splash as I run on up the hill into a sunny morning whose colors are joy, joy, joy.

Reading Closely

1. Naturally enough, Connors has "a sudden desire to turn, go, keep running, get
   home" when he sees the skunk coming toward him (8). Why does he stick
   around instead of following this instinct?

2. Do you think Connors is correct to assume that the skunk has "benign" feelings
   toward him (26)? Why or why not?

3. Connors is explaining how to do something most of his readers will never need
   to do. Why? What is his purpose in analyzing how to get a skunk out of a bottle?

Strategies and Structures

1. Why do you think Connors casts his title in the form of a question? What is his
   purpose in answering it?

2. Once Connors decides that the skunk is his "responsibility," he begins the
   process of extracting it from the bottle (11). That process ends in paragraph 24
   when the jar finally pops off. What are the main steps that Connors takes in
   between to achieve this end result?

3. Connors analyzes the process of freeing the skunk in chronological order. What
   transitions does he use to organize and connect the various steps of the
   process?

4. How would Connors' analysis be different if he were actually giving instructions
   for freeing a trapped animal?

5. *Other Methods.* Connors begins his essay with a description of the morning air
   and light. Where else does he describe the scene, and how do these descriptive
   elements contribute to his analysis of the process of meeting and dealing with
   an animal in trouble?

Thinking about Language

1. Why does Connors change "toward" to "to" in paragraph 5?

2. What does Connors mean by the phrase "conservation ethics" (7)? How does his essay address this idea?

3. Why does Connors hold up his finger in "tutorial fashion" when he bids good-bye to the skunk (26)?

4. We don't normally think of joy as a "color" (28). What has happened to Connors's senses on this crisp, cool morning as a result of his encounter with the skunk?

For Writing

1. Write a paragraph or two explaining the process you would have told Connors to go through if he had asked you how to remove the jar from the skunk's head.

2. One answer to the question raised by Connors' title might be, "Very carefully." Going beyond this obvious first step, write an essay analyzing how to deal with a difficult situation the reader might encounter in the woods, at work, in an airport, or while traveling in an unfamiliar city or country.

DIANE ACKERMAN

Why Leaves Turn Color in the Fall

Diane Ackerman (b. 1948) is a poet whose work reveals a scientist's close, accurate observation of nature; she is also a naturalist whose essays are suffused with a poet's wonder at the beauty and mystery of the world. Her five collections of verse include Jaguar of Sweet Laughter: New and Selected Poems *(1991) and* Animal Sense *(2003), an illustrated volume of poems for children. Among her many works of nonfiction are* The Whale by Moonlight *(1991),* A Natural History of Love *(1994), and* An Alchemy of Mind *(2004), which she describes as "a poetics of the brain based on the latest neuroscience." Of her many awards and accolades, she may be proudest of the molecule named for her—the dianackerone.*

"Why Leaves Turn Color in the Fall" demonstrates that the analysis of a natural process can be both scientifically accurate and also delightful, sensuous, even soulful. This essay first appeared in A Natural History of the Senses *(1990), the essay collection for which she is best known and which inspired a five-part PBS series, hosted by Ackerman herself.*

THE STEALTH OF AUTUMN catches one unaware. Was that a goldfinch perching in the early September woods, or just the first turning leaf? A red-winged blackbird or a sugar maple closing up shop for the winter? Keen-eyed as leopards, we stand still and squint hard, looking for signs of movement. Early-morning frost sits heavily on the grass, and turns barbed wire into a string of stars. On a distant hill, a small square of yellow appears to be a lighted stage. At last the truth dawns on us: Fall is staggering in, right on schedule, with its baggage of chilly nights, macabre holidays, and spectacular, heart-stoppingly beautiful leaves. Soon the leaves will start cringing on the trees, and roll up in clenched fists before they actually fall off. Dry seedpods will rattle like tiny gourds. But first there will be weeks of gushing color so bright, so pastel, so confettilike, that people will travel up and down the East Coast just to stare at it—a whole season of leaves. 1

Where do the colors come from? Sunlight rules most living things with its golden edicts. When the days begin to shorten, soon after the summer solstice on June 21, a tree reconsiders its leaves. All summer it feeds them so they can process sunlight, but in the dog days of summer the tree begins pulling nutrients back into its trunk and roots, pares down, and gradually chokes off its leaves. A corky layer of cells forms at the leaves' slender petioles, then scars over. Undernourished, the leaves stop producing the pigment chlorophyll, and photosynthesis ceases. Animals can migrate, hibernate, or store food to prepare for winter. But where can a tree 2

243

go? It survives by dropping its leaves, and by the end of autumn only a few fragile threads of fluid-carrying xylem hold leaves to their stems.

A turning leaf stays partly green at first, then reveals splotches of yellow and red   3 as the chlorophyll gradually breaks down. Dark green seems to stay longest in the veins, outlining and defining them. During the summer, chlorophyll dissolves in the heat and light, but it is also being steadily replaced. In the fall, on the other hand, no new pigment is produced, and so we notice the other colors that were always there, right in the leaf, although chlorophyll's shocking green hid them from view. With their camouflage gone, we see these colors for the first time all year, and marvel, but they were always there, hidden like a vivid secret beneath the hot glowing greens of summer.

The most spectacular range of fall foliage occurs in the northeastern United   4 States and in eastern China, where the leaves are robustly colored, thanks in part to a rich climate. European maples don't achieve the same flaming reds as their American relatives, which thrive on cold nights and sunny days. In Europe, the warm, humid weather turns the leaves brown or mildly yellow. Anthocyanin, the pigment that gives apples their red and turns leaves red or red-violet, is produced by sugars that remain in the leaf after the supply of nutrients dwindles. Unlike the carotenoids, which color carrots, squash, and corn, and turn leaves orange and yellow, anthocyanin varies from year to year, depending on the temperature and amount of sunlight. The fiercest colors occur in years when the fall sunlight is strongest and the nights are cool and dry (a state of grace scientists find vexing to forecast). This is also why leaves appear dizzyingly bright and clear on a sunny fall day: The anthocyanin flashes like a marquee.

Not all leaves turn the same colors. Elms, weeping willows, and the ancient   5 ginkgo all grow radiant yellow, along with hickories, aspens, bottlebrush buckeyes, cottonweeds, and tall, keening poplars. Basswood turns bronze, birches bright gold. Water-loving maples put on a symphonic display of scarlets. Sumacs turn red, too, as do flowering dogwoods, black gums, and sweet gums. Though some oaks yellow, most turn a pinkish brown. The farmlands also change color, as tepees of cornstalks and bales of shredded-wheat-textured hay stand drying in the fields. In some spots, one slope of a hill may be green and the other already in bright color, because the hillside facing south gets more sun and heat than the northern one.

An odd feature of the colors is that they don't seem to have any special purpose.   6 We are predisposed to respond to their beauty, of course. They shimmer with the colors of sunset, spring flowers, the tawny buff of a colt's pretty rump, the shuddering pink of a blush. Animals and flowers color for a reason—adaptation to their environment—but there is no adaptive reason for leaves to color so beautifully in the fall any more than there is for the sky or ocean to be blue. It's just one of the haphazard marvels the planet bestows every year. We find the sizzling colors thrilling, and in a sense they dupe us. Colored like living things, they signal death and disintegration. In time, they will become fragile and, like the body, return to dust. They are as we hope our own fate will be when we die: Not to vanish, just to sublime from one beautiful state into another. Though leaves lose their green life, they bloom with urgent colors, as the woods grow mummified day by day, and Nature becomes more carnal, mute, and radiant.

We call the season "fall," from the Old English *feallan*, to fall, which leads back   7 through time to the Indo-European *phol*, which also means to fall. So the word and the idea are both extremely ancient, and haven't really changed since the first of our kind needed a name for fall's leafy abundance. As we say the word, we're reminded of that other Fall, in the garden of Eden, when fig leaves never withered and scales fell from our eyes. Fall is the time when leaves fall from the trees, just as spring is when flowers spring up, summer is when we simmer, and winter is when we whine from the cold.

Children love to play in piles of leaves, hurling them into the air like confetti,   8 leaping into soft unruly mattresses of them. For children, leaf fall is just one of the odder figments of Nature, like hailstones or snowflakes. Walk down a lane over-hung with trees in the never-never land[1] of autumn, and you will forget about time and death, lost in the sheer delicious spill of color. Adam and Eve concealed their nakedness with leaves, remember? Leaves have always hidden our awkward secrets.

But how do the colored leaves fall? As a leaf ages, the growth hormone, auxin,   9 fades, and cells at the base of the petiole divide. Two or three rows of small cells, lying at right angles to the axis of the petiole, react with water, then come apart, leaving the petioles hanging on by only a few threads of xylem. A light breeze, and the leaves are airborne. They glide and swoop, rocking in invisible cradles. They are all wing and may flutter from yard to yard on small whirlwinds or updrafts, swivel-ing as they go. Firmly tethered to earth, we love to see things rise up and fly—soap bubbles, balloons, birds, fall leaves. They remind us that the end of a season is capricious, as is the end of life. We especially like the way leaves rock, careen, and swoop as they fall. Everyone knows the motion. Pilots sometimes do a maneuver called a "falling leaf," in which the plane loses altitude quickly and on purpose, by slipping first to the right, then to the left. The machine weighs a ton or more, but in one pilot's mind it is a weightless thing, a falling leaf. She has seen the motion before, in the Vermont woods where she played as a child. Below her the trees radi-

---

1. *Never-never land:* a place in J. M. Barrie's 1904 play *Peter Pan* where Peter Pan and his friends lived and never had to grow up. In current U.S. usage, a never-never land can be a fantasy land of the imagination or, as Ackerman uses it here, any enchanting place where time seems to stand still.

ate gold, copper, and red. Leaves are falling, although she can't see them fall, as she falls, swooping down for a closer view.

At last the leaves leave. But first they turn color and thrill us for weeks on end. 10 Then they crunch and crackle underfoot. They *shush*, as children drag their small feet through leaves heaped along the curb. Dark, slimy mats of leaves cling to one's heels after a rain. A damp, stuccolike mortar of semidecayed leaves protects the tender shoots with a roof until spring, and makes a rich humus. An occasional bulge or ripple in the leafy mounds signals a shrew or a field mouse tunneling out of sight. Sometimes one finds in fossil stones the imprint of a leaf, long since disintegrated, whose outlines remind us how detailed, vibrant, and alive are the things of this earth that perish.

Reading Closely

1. According to Diane Ackerman, why do trees "choke off" their leaves in autumn by depriving them of nutrients (2)?

2. The spectacular colors of leaves changing in the fall, says Ackerman, "don't seem to have any special purpose" (6). Why does she find this "odd" in any sort of process, particularly a natural one (6)?

3. Ackerman tells us not only how leaves turn color but why. What reasons does she give?

4. In what sense do dying leaves "dupe" us, according to Ackerman (6)?

Strategies and Structures

1. Is Ackerman's process analysis more explanatory or directive? Why? Explain.

2. In which paragraph does Ackerman identify the first step in the color-changing process? What is it? What are the other steps?

3. What process does Ackerman analyze in paragraphs 9–10? The analysis begins with a technical explanation, and then drifts into a poetical one. How is Ackerman preparing us for her conclusion?

4. *Other Methods.* Ackerman describes the onset of autumn in paragraph 1. To which of the reader's senses does she appeal most here? Elsewhere in her essay? What dominant impression of autumn do these descriptive passages create, and how do they contribute to Ackerman's analysis?

Thinking about Language

1. When autumn comes "staggering in," Ackerman writes, the leaves "cringe" on the trees and "roll up in clenched fists" from the cold (1). Why do you think Ackerman, a poet as well as a science writer, begins her analysis by PERSONIFY-ING nature in this way? Point out other examples of her use of FIGURES OF SPEECH in the essay.

2. Why do you think Ackerman uses the technical botanical term "petiole" (9) instead of just referring to the central *stalk* or *shaft* that runs down the middle of a leaf? Where else does she use scientific language like this, and why?

3. Why does Ackerman point out that the word "fall" is "extremely ancient" (7)?

4. Ackerman writes that fallen leaves "shush" when children walk through them (10). What does she mean by "shush," and which particular sense does it appeal to?

For Writing

1. Write a paragraph analyzing a relatively simple natural process, such as evaporation or condensation.

2. Write an essay analyzing a more complicated natural process, such as photosynthesis, lightning, or the lunar cycle.

VICTOR POLLACI

Exposure, Latency, Responsibility

As a junior in engineering at Cornell University, Victor Pollaci wrote "Exposure, Latency, Responsibility" for a cross-disciplinary seminar in expository writing. The assignment was to describe the natural world as seen through a particular lens, a topic that Pollaci, an accomplished photographer, took both literally and figuratively. At the urging of Sean Serrell, his instructor for English 288, Pollaci submitted the finished paper to an essay contest sponsored by Cornell's Knight Institute for Writing in the Disciplines; it won first prize and was published in the Fall 2003 issue of Discoveries, *the institute's literary journal.*

"Exposure, Latency, Responsibility" analyzes the technical process of taking artful photographs, particularly under conditions of low light. Composing through the lens of a camera has three basic aspects, according to Pollaci. "Exposure," for example, is the balance the photographer strikes between light and time by adjusting the aperture size and shutter speed of the camera. As Pollaci goes "deeper into the process," however, he compares it to hunting. In this broader analysis, mastering the fundamentals of photography requires a mixture of technical skill and such personal qualities as patience and an instinct for the "decisive moment."

As WE DROVE SOUTH, back to Los Angeles, the heat proved too much for our little U-Haul that could.[1] The desert landscape of Interstate 5 was altogether too warm for the worn and abused Toyota to handle, and I was going to be a day late for my flight back to New Jersey. Parked in a gas station, we doused the engine with water, checked the radiator, and decided that the situation was an excuse for one last adventure on the way home from California. I adjusted my flight plans, and we once again headed West, to the Pacific Coast Highway, cooler weather, and Hearst Castle.[2] I suppose there really was a range of things that we could have done, but this seemed the least stressful, and it had so far been a fairly stressful trip. I had been taking pictures the whole time, but the highway along the ocean provided me with the first true technical and ethical difficulty.

Since photography has become a serious endeavor of mine, I have tried to make

---

1. *Little U-Haul that could*: a reference to a children's book—*The Little Engine That Could*—that has been popular in the United States since its first publication in 1930. The story teaches optimism, determination, and believing in oneself.

2. *Hearst Castle*: the California estate of newspaper magnate William Randolph Hearst (1863–1951).

shooting under adverse lighting my specialty, but there's little to do when it's just dark. We pulled into a small town that survived off of passing traffic. There were a few beachfront hotels and restaurants, and we stopped, ate, and got a room to stay in. We went out after getting settled in, and walked along the beach. It was cool outside, and the sand was already gray, only lingering light remaining from the already hidden sun. The sea too was mostly gray and suggested a blue, total monochrome for which I believe color photography is best suited. However, composing in the lens, I was certain that the only value in the picture was compositional. The light was so low that I couldn't hope for much contrast or saturation, and the necessary shutter speed to expose one or two stops over normal was in excess of an eighth of a second, nowhere near the appropriate speed to freeze water coming in along jutting rock.

Faced with this sort of situation, the only available option is to prioritize. The idea is to select a few aspects of the exposure that are compatible in the given situation and use those to set a kind of trap for the image. Exposure is a balance of light and time (aperture size and shutter speed, respectively). At odds with the darkness, I chose to allow the length of the exposure to exceed what I knew to be necessary to stop motion without a flash, compromising clarity for the sake of contrast and whatever color there was to be pulled from the scene. With time, color becomes stronger, and more saturated, so while photos exposed longer are less sharp, they are more colorful. I closed the aperture to bring as much of the scene into focus as possible, matched the shutter speed, and finally increased the length of the exposure by two steps or "stops." But even with all of this thought going into the taking of the photo, I still had no idea what to expect outside of what my eyes showed in front of me. Despite that blindness, and without my trusty, leg-warmer-equipped tripod, I put the camera on a convenient wooden post and panned until I found a usable angle, opened the shutter, and left the rest to light and time.

As sometimes happens, I was surprised with the shot when I returned the film. There were subtle red hues and strong, blue tones as well. In fact the grays were nonexistent, and only the purely latent color remained.

In the darkroom, after exposing photo paper to the image on a negative, there is little to conclude immediately. While the image has been recorded on the paper, it is called latent, as it is not visible to the naked eye. It's the same way before you even open the shutter: the natural negative is there, but you need to capture it. Before the lens is an arrangement and exposure never before recorded. Usually, you see it, but sometimes, you don't.

During the Spanish Civil War in 1936, one of the first generation of "street photographers" was shooting with a group of soldiers bogged down behind a hill. One of the soldiers got up to charge over the hill, and the photographer, Robert Capa, took his picture. In the fraction of a second that the shutter was open, a bullet struck the soldier in the head, producing a bright explosion when the photo was developed. The caption under the photo reads, "Death of a Loyalist Soldier" (*Face to Face*). It's a famous picture now, and I believe that it is even ranked among *Life* magazine's greatest photos of the century. But Capa was highly criticized for it, and many of his contemporaries wondered about the motives of such an otherwise lucky shot. Specifically, Capa's audience had to wonder whether he was planning on seeing a man die, or whether it just happened in front of his already accomplished lens.

Exposures like Capa's are the ones that shake the confidence you have in your work. From behind the lens, these seemingly accidental triumphs make you question yourself and your skill. You have to wonder how much ownership the simple push of a shutter implies or imputes, and you start wondering how long your luck will hold out. It is a question of responsibility for what happens in front of a lens, and precisely how deliberate a photograph has to be before you can call it your own. It happened to me at the Museum of Modern Art in New York City, when I was there taking pictures of the patrons. While I was lying in wait, eyes open on the moment, something unexpected wandered across my lens.

The best way to approach a discreet project like this is to find a place to sit, plain view is fine, and stay there for a long time, camera in bag and wait for people to forget about you. I had been patiently studying a sculpture integrated with the escalator, when a German family came along into view a floor below me. They stood there for a moment, conversing, and then they put the old man's wheelchair in park and left him there.

He was facing a large bay window the height of the building. Beyond the window, a backhoe was digging a deep trench in the torn ground, and as I took the picture, the backhoe's shovel cast a ghost-like reflection on the glass. The old, wheelchair-bound man was looking at the digging of his own grave so late in life, despite my not having seen the reflection in the viewfinder. It is one of my best photos, and took the $500 prize for best in show at the Phillips Mill Photographic Exhibition in New Hope, Pennsylvania. But can I take credit for a latency that I was not aware of?

The answer may lie deeper in the process. Photography, like hunting, is a waiting game with the subject; whoever blinks first loses. The photographer misses an opportunity, or an elusive moment is captured on film. So along with waiting, one must know where to wait and what to look for. Success, in this respect, is a mixture of patience, technical skill, and experience.

When hunting, some birds utilize "search images" of their prey. These mental images allow the birds to focus their attention on the prey that they are looking for, and become more efficient hunters. Impressions are made in the birds' minds as they gain more experience locating a specific type or group of targets. Repeat

Excavation (2001). When Victor Pollaci took this photograph, he did not see the reflection of the backhoe in his viewfinder. "Can I take credit for a latency that I was not aware of?" he asks.

encounters allow the predators to sharpen the search image of a prospective meal in their minds, and use that image to notice prey in the future. This form of perception is especially important when the speed required to maintain flight is considered. The bird has only a short time to recognize its prey, especially well-camouflaged prey. Search images are most useful in situations where the target of the search is inconspicuous, and therefore demands a focusing of attention to spot it. As the search image improves, the necessary amount of attention committed to observation decreases, and even hidden prey become more apparent (Tartner).

Like birds, photographers must develop and use their own search images, but at a higher level than simple recognition. A search image is, to the photographer, a higher concept rooted in intuition. Instead of identifying what is present, we must identify opportunities. We must leave room in the frame for the striking of a bullet or the arm of a backhoe, and those latent elements must be positioned correctly in the frame so as to allow the image to develop into the full potential of the moment. This is the exercise of composition; and in dark and difficult situations where perception is challenged, the full force of attention must be focused, since the latencies in those scenes are especially inconspicuous. 12

The photographer concerns himself with dimensions beyond the spatial. In the same way that he locates the frame in space, he must also position it in time. Release the shutter too early or too late, and a latency's moment is lost. There is 13 no way for a negative to sit and wait for the right instant; film cannot expose for-ever. The window of opportunity can be only a fraction of a second that must be placed in the stream of motion at just the right point, like a falcon choosing when to dive.

These aspects come together in the theory of Henri Cartier-Bresson, one of the 14
early great street photographers. He coined a term for his shooting theory called "The Decisive Moment." Bresson believed that in every motion or movement there is a single moment in which the scene achieves a kind of natural balance and rhythm. The skill of the photographer is to take full advantage of his equipment to capture that moment. And so, good photographers have an eye open to decisive moments, and are able to compose in a way that holds on to them. It is a technique that requires a heightened intuition for timing and composition.

To the photographer, light and time are the most mysterious and fascinating ele- 15
ments of nature. They are beyond man's grasp and unstoppable. That we freeze them is a lie. They are integrals of life over time, moments per second. With every stop faster, the photographer comes closer and closer to recording his instanta-neous impressions. The instant is unachievable, but we can strive for it, and that is what keeps us shooting: an unattainable goal that will last us a lifetime. We can't ask ourselves to do the impossible, but we can chase after it, and there can be no fault in the chase.

The photo that I took in California showed me a new concept revealed in 16
nature, and alerted me to the fact that there is something beyond what my eyes record, what is there if they were to expose a little longer. The shutter is only open for a few brief moments, but it is long enough to serve host to the unexpected. Those unplanned exposures are not faults of the photographer; rather they are the product of his honed intuition and the reflection of the latencies forever present in nature. They occur because nature is teeming with latent exposures waiting to be uncovered. They are recorded because photographers know when to identify them, and where to set their traps. The only thing, however, that separates a photogra-pher from anyone else is his camera. All who open their eyes to the possibilities contained latently in the world are free to expose them in their own mind and add them to their own experience.

Works Cited

Face to Face with the Spanish Revolution: A Rare Exhibition of Photographs by Robert Capa. World Socialist Web Site. International Committee of the Fourth Inter-national, 1 Apr. 1999. Web. 9 Apr. 2009.

Tartner, Paul. *Birds: 25 Behaviour (3).* Biological Sciences Department, University of Paisley, n.d. Web. 26 Sept. 2002. <http://www-biol.paisley.ac.uk/courses/Tartner/biomedia/units/bird25.htm>.

READING CLOSELY

1. Photography, says Victor Pollaci, "has become a serious endeavor of mine" (2). How and how well does his essay illustrate this point?

2. What does Pollaci mean when he says that "only" the camera "separates the photographer from anyone else" (16)?

3. What are some of the "technical and ethical" difficulties that serious photographers encounter during the process of taking photographs, according to Pollaci (1)?

4. Do you think it was luck or skill that allowed the "street photographer" Robert Capa to photograph a soldier being killed in the Spanish Civil War (6)? To what extent was the photographer ethically responsible for taking advantage of such a situation? Explain.

5. In what way was Pollaci's act of photographing the man in the wheelchair similar to Capa's when he photographed a soldier being killed? What steps did Pollaci take to make that shot possible, and how "responsible" is he for it?

STRATEGIES AND STRUCTURES

1. His specialty as a photographer, says Pollaci, is "shooting under adverse lighting" (2). What are some of the main steps in this process as he explains it in paragraphs 2–9?

2. In explaining how to take serious photographs, Pollaci is also explaining how to think like a serious photographer. According to him, what are some of the main steps in *that* process?

3. How does Pollaci use PROCESS ANALYSIS to answer the question he raises at the end of paragraph 9: "But can I take credit for a latency that I was not aware of?"

4. What is the point of Pollaci's analysis, and when does he state it most clearly?

5. *Other Methods.* How does Pollaci use the photographs he took on the beach in California and in the museum in New York as EXAMPLES of what he has to say about "latent" images and latency in general (5)?

THINKING ABOUT LANGUAGE

1. Why do you think Pollaci uses such ABSTRACT terms in his title? Is it a good title for this essay? Why or why not?

2. Where and how does Pollaci DEFINE "latency"? What does he mean when he says, "It's the same way before you open the shutter" (5)?

3. Where and how does Pollaci define the other two key terms in his title—"exposure" and "responsibility"? How do these definitions, along with that of latency, help to tie his essay together?

4. How does Pollaci define "ownership" (7), and how does this definition fit in with his discussion of responsibility?

5. Who first defined the "Decisive Moment" in photography and what does it mean (14)?

FOR WRITING

1. Write a paragraph DEFINING one of the key terms in Pollaci's title as you understand it from reading his essay.

2. Write a paragraph or two COMPARING photography or some other creative process to hunting or some other sport.

3. Write an essay about an "accidental triumph" you have experienced, whether in a sport or game or in human relationships. Analyze the process by which you set the "trap" for the triumph (3, 6).

EMILY DICKINSON

The Way I read a Letter's—this—

Emily Dickinson (1830–1886) led an intensely private life that has become the stuff of literary legend. Born to a well-to-do family in Amherst, Massachusetts, Dickinson grew up among books and lively conversation, and—except for less than a year at the Mount Holyoke Female Seminary—she resided in the family home near Amherst College all her life. Over time, Dickinson become more and more reclusive, dressing mainly in white, seeing few visitors outside the family, and working on her poems—nearly eighteen hundred in all, only a handful of which were published during her lifetime. After Dickinson's death, her sister discovered among the poet's papers forty booklets of poems bound with string and unbound copies of almost four hundred poems.

"The Way I read a Letter's—this—" explains how the poet typically opened and read a letter from a correspondent with whom she was spiritually, but probably not physically, intimate. Dickinson scholars disagree on the identity of that correspondent, but the person with whom she exchanged the largest number of highly personal letters was her sister-in-law Susan Gilbert Dickinson. The "You" to whom Dickinson refers is probably the reader of the poem, as opposed to the author of the letter.

The Way I read a Letter's—this— 1
'Tis first—I lock the Door—
And push it with my fingers—next—
For transport it be sure—

And then I go the furthest off 5
To counteract a knock—
Then draw my little Letter forth
And slowly pick the lock—

Then—glancing narrow, at the Wall—
And narrow at the floor 10
For firm Conviction of a Mouse
Not exorcised before—

Peruse how infinite I am
To no one that You—know—
And sigh for lack of Heaven—but not 15
The Heaven God bestow—

READING CLOSELY

1. Dickinson is explaining how to read an intimate letter. How can you tell?

2. Why does the author of the letter comment on "how infinite" the reader is (13)?

3. To what "Heaven" is Dickinson referring if not to the one that "God bestow" (16)? Explain.

STRATEGIES AND STRUCTURES

1. Dickinson breaks the process of reading her letter into six steps. What are they?

2. Why does the speaker in Dickinson's poem go through the first five steps before she actually "peruses" the contents of the letter (13)?

3. For whom is Dickinson ANALYZING THIS PROCESS, and what is the effect of her using the personal pronoun "You" to address her audience (14)?

4. *Other Methods.* In addition to explaining how she reads a letter, Dickinson also shows the emotional EFFECT of the process. What is this effect, and what is its CAUSE?

THINKING ABOUT LANGUAGE

1. What "lock" is Dickinson picking in line 8? Why does she use this METAPHOR, and how does the first step in her analysis prepare the way for it?

2. "Exorcised" (12) is a word usually reserved for demons and evil spirits. Why does Dickinson use it here?

3. What are the CONNOTATIONS of "peruse" (13), and why does Dickinson use this term instead of the more common *read*?

FOR WRITING

1. Write a paragraph analyzing how *you* read a letter.

2. Write an essay explaining the process you go through when you read this or any poem.

CHAPTER 7
Comparison and Contrast

<hr>

When you compare apples to apples, our repair center represents the
pick of the crop. —FRANK'S AUTO BODY

When you take a shower, assuming you live in the Western hemisphere and it's a
weekday, you probably want to get clean as quickly and efficiently as you can. If
you bathe in a tub, you may soak a little longer; but chances are you will still be the
first (and last) to use the water you bathe in. Not so in Japan.

By comparison with the Western way of bathing, the Japanese way is drawn out
and ritualistic. Preferring the tub to the shower, the Japanese like to bathe slowly
and deliberately, even when they are in a hurry. Often whole families soak in the
same warm water, with the male head-of-household going first. This togetherness
is more a means of establishing family and social unity than of conserving water,
however. Getting clean is just as important to the Japanese as to their Western
counterparts. So before stepping into the communal tub, each Japanese bather
washes thoroughly from a bucket provided for that purpose.

Japanese and Western cultures have something else in common, besides a deep
respect for cleanliness. No matter how we draw our baths, we draw comparisons
when we think—and write—about the similarities and differences between two or
more subjects.

Defining Comparison:
Finding Similarities and Differences

When we COMPARE or CONTRAST anything—two people, two ways of bathing, two
cultures—we look at both the similarities (comparison) and the differences (con-

trast) between them. Which of these we emphasize in an essay depends, in part, on what we are comparing. In the case of the Japanese bath as compared to the Western version, for example, the differences are more numerous and striking than the similarities.

Consider this passage from a book on the subject:

> In the West, a bath is a place where one goes to cleanse the body; in Japan, it is where one goes to cleanse the soul. . . . When one bathes in Japan, it is about much more than cleanliness, though cleanliness is important. It is about family and community, the washing of each other's backs before bathing; about time to be alone and contemplative—time to watch the moon rise above the garden. . . . Unlike in America, where speed and efficiency are valued, . . . the Japanese make bathing a ritual—a prescribed order of rinsing, washing, and soaking that is passed down from one generation to the next, becoming an integral part of the society at large.
> —Bruce Smith and Yoshiko Yamamoto, *The Japanese Bath*

This passage is mostly contrast; that is, it stresses the differences between the two activities being compared. They *are* still being compared, however: comparisons are about relationships, whether of sameness and difference. In this chapter, therefore, we will use the word *comparison* both for drawing similarities between two related subjects *and* for pointing out their differences. (The word *contrast* will be reserved for discussing differences only.) We will also look more deeply into when and why we compare things, how to make effective comparisons, and how to organize an entire essay around common strategies of comparison and contrast that good writers use all the time.

Why Do We Compare?

Whether you live in America or Japan, one form of comparison is almost as familiar to you as bathing—comparison shopping. The reason you compare before you buy, of course, is so you can select the best product for your needs at the best price. For this purpose you may consult a buying guide, such as *Consumer Reports* magazine.

In a recent issue, the professional comparers at *Consumer Reports* compared similar makes, models, and brands of running shoes, peanut butter, home alarm systems, satellite digital radio services, binoculars, dishwashers, and baby wipes—all so consumers can be aware of the differences among them.

One of the main reasons we compare things—and not just consumer products—is to discover differences between two subjects that we would otherwise expect to be similar. For example, on a botany exam you might compare the leaf structure of two related species of ferns. Or, in literature, you might compare two Shakespearean sonnets.

We also make comparisons in order to find similarities between subjects that we might otherwise consider to be entirely different, as in this opening paragraph from a book on what happens to the human body after death:

> The way I see it, being dead is not terribly far off from being on a cruise ship. Most of your time is spent lying on your back. The brain has shut down. The flesh begins to soften. Nothing much new happens, and nothing is expected of you. —MARY ROACH, *Stiff*

We don't normally think of being dead and taking a cruise as being very much alike. By pointing out similarities between the two that we may not have thought of, however, Roach enables us to see both of these subjects—particularly the grimmer one—in a new light. This particular kind of comparison between two seemingly unrelated subjects is called an ANALOGY: it explains a less-familiar subject by comparing it to something we are likely to know more about.

Composing an Essay That Compares and Contrasts

The root meaning of the word *compare* is "to put with equals," and so the first thing you need to do when composing a comparison essay is to choose subjects that are truly comparable—apples to apples, oranges to oranges.

If two subjects are different in every way, there is little point in comparing them. The same is true if they are entirely alike. Your subjects should have enough in common, however, to provide a solid basis of comparison. A train and a jetliner, for instance, are very different machines; but both are modes of transportation, and that shared characteristic can become the basis for comparing them.

When you look for shared characteristics in your subjects, don't stretch your comparison too far, however. You don't want to make the logical blunder that the Duchess commits in Lewis Carroll's *Alice in Wonderland*:

> "Very true," said the Duchess: "flamingos and mustard both bite. And the moral of that is—'Birds of a feather flock together.'"
> "Only mustard isn't a bird," Alice remarked.
> "Right as usual," said the Duchess: "what a clear way you have of putting things."

Flamingos and mustard both bite, but not in ways that are similar enough to make them truly comparable. So beware what you compare. Before you bring two subjects together as equals in an essay, make sure they are "birds of a feather" by looking carefully at the characteristics that make them different from others but similar to each other. Those characteristics should be significant enough to form a solid basis of comparison. In Wonderland, you might compare turtles and tanks, for example, on the grounds that both move relatively slowly and have hard outer coverings. In the real world, however, don't bring two subjects together when the differences between them are far more significant than the similarities. Better to compare mustard and ketchup, or flamingos and roseate spoonbills—unless, of course, you plan to show just how much two apparently dissimilar subjects (being dead and going on a cruise, skyscrapers and airplanes) actually have in common.

Thinking about Purpose and Audience

Suppose that you are comparing running shoes for the simple purpose of buying a new pair to replace your old ones. In this case, you are comparing them in order to evaluate them—to decide which shoe fits your needs best, so you can choose the right one. However, if you were writing a comparison of several kinds of running shoes for *Consumer Reports*, you would be comparing your subjects in order to inform readers about them. Instead of evaluating the shoes and choosing a pair to fit your needs, your purpose would be to give readers the information they need to choose for themselves.

With comparisons, as with shoes, one size does not fit all. Whether you're writing a comparison to inform, evaluate, or for some other purpose, always keep the specific needs of your audience in mind. How much do your readers already know about your topic? Why should they want or need to know more? What distinctions can you make that they haven't already thought of?

If you are comparing running shoes for a runner's magazine or a shoe catalogue, for example, your readers are probably running enthusiasts who already know a good bit about your subject; so you should distinguish carefully among the different brands or models you're discussing. Thus you might point out that both the New Balance models 901 and 816 are durable, lightweight training shoes. The 901, however, is meant for the runner who is (in the words of the manufacturer) "looking for greater stability from heel to toe," while the 816 offers "a deeper toe box for runners needing more space in the forefoot."

A comparison like this is geared toward readers who are experienced runners and have highly specialized needs. Such fine distinctions would be lost on readers who are simply looking for the cheapest running shoe available, or the most expensive one, or the most stylish. So before you compare, size up your readers, and tailor your comparison to fit their specific needs.

Generating Ideas: Asking How Two Things Are Alike or Different

BRAINSTORMING and LISTING can help as you think about your comparison. Once you have a clear basis for comparing two subjects—flamingos and roseate spoonbills are both large pink birds; trains and jetliners are modes of mass transportation; NB 901s and 816s are medium-priced running shoes—the next step is to look for specific points of comparison between them. So ask yourself the key questions that any comparison raises: How, specifically, are your two subjects alike? How do they differ?

As you probe for similarities and differences between your subjects, make a point-by-point list like the following:

DIFFERENCES

American bath	Japanese bath
fast and efficient	slow and contemplative
usually solitary	often communal, even public
bather scrubs own back	family members scrub one another's backs
about getting clean	about family and community
mundane	ritualistic
stare at ceramic tile	watch the moon rise
concerned with the body	concerned with the soul

SIMILARITIES

American bath	Japanese bath
cleanliness is important	cleanliness is important

Listing the main ways in which two subjects are alike or different will help you to determine whether they're actually worth comparing—and will also help you to get the similarities and differences straight in your own mind before attempting to explain them to an audience.

Notice that in the lists above, each point on the American side matches the point on the Japanese side. If the point on the American side is "stare at ceramic tile," the point on the Japanese side is also about what you look at while bathing: "watch the moon rise." When you draw up your list, make sure you look at the same elements in both subjects. If you talk about the communal aspect of the Japanese bath, you need to mention whether American baths are communal or solitary—or your comparison will be incomplete.

Organizing and Drafting a Comparison

Once you have a list of the specific ways in which your two subjects are alike or different, you're ready to organize, and then to begin drafting your comparison. Make sure, however, that your main points of comparison deal with significant character-istics of your two subjects and that you draw a sufficient number of them. The tips on p. 265 can help you get started.

CHOOSING A METHOD OF ORGANIZATION

There are fundamentally two ways of organizing a comparison essay: you can go point by point or subject by subject. Let's look at the point-by-point method at work in a comparison of the career patterns of two ambitious women:

> Both Cleo and Alice are hard-driving workers; both are achievers; both spend so much time working that they have very little left for traditional leisure pursuits. The fundamental difference between Alice and Cleo is that they define work differently. Cleo is working *for* her company. Alice works *through* her company while working for herself. Cleo is a stabilizer. Alice is a scrambler. Most of us fall into one of these two camps. To make the most of your own career and psych out the people around you, it's essential to be able to tell them apart. —ELWOOD CHAPMAN, *Working Woman*

With a POINT-BY-POINT organization like this, you discuss each point of compari-son (or contrast) between your two subjects before going on to the next point. Here is Chapman's point-by-point comparison in outline form:

1. Kind of workers

   Cleo is hard-driving, an achiever.
   Alice is hard-driving, an achiever.

2. Time spent working

   Cleo spends all her time working.
   Alice spends all her time working.

3. How they define work

   Cleo works for her company.
   Alice works for herself.

4. How they affect their coworkers.

   Cleo is a stabilizer.
   Alice is a scrambler.

After using the point-by-point method to compare the two workers in the first paragraph of his essay, Chapman switches to the subject-by-subject method in the next two paragraphs:

> Cleo is a classic workaholic. She works from dawn till dusk (more than five days a week as necessary) with a major utility. She earns a good salary, is

highly esteemed by her bosses for her loyalty and reliability, and enjoys extraordinary job security (it probably would cost her employer at least 20 percent more than she earns to replace her).

Alice, a mid-management person in a financial institution, also works overtime, though she rarely spends more than 35 to 40 hours a week on actual work assignments. The rest of her time is given over to company information-gathering, checking out opportunities with competing firms, image building and similar activities.

The SUBJECT-BY-SUBJECT method discusses each subject individually, making a number of points about one subject and then covering more or less the same points about the other subject. Here is an outline of Chapman's subject-by-subject comparison:

Cleo

workaholic
earns a good salary
respected for her loyalty and reliability
enjoys extraordinary job security

Alice

workaholic
rarely spends all her time on work assignments
rest of time spent on career building

Which method of organization should you use? Any method that presents your points of comparison and contrast clearly and simply to the reader is a good method of organization. However, you will probably find that the point-by-point method works best for beginning and ending an essay, while the subject-by-subject method serves you well for longer stretches in the main body of your essay.

One reason for using the subject-by-subject method to organize most of your essay is that the point-by-point method, when relentlessly applied, can make the reader a little seasick: stabilizers give time, scramblers steal time; stabilizers avoid stress, scramblers seek it; stabilizers hate change, scramblers use it; stabilizers want job security, scramblers switch jobs with every opportunity; stabilizers are humble, scramblers trust themselves to the brink of disaster. And so on.

With the point-by-point method, you make more or less the same number of points for both subjects. With the subject-by-subject method, on the other hand, you can make as many points as you like on each subject. You do not have to give equal weight to both. The subject-by-subject method is, thus, indispensable for treating a subject in depth, whereas the point-by-point method is an efficient way of presenting a balanced comparison. Because it touches on both subjects more or less equally, the point-by-point method can also help you convince readers that two subjects are, indeed, fundamentally alike (or dissimilar).

The point-by-point method, in other words, is particularly useful for establishing a basis of comparison at the beginning of an essay, for reminding readers along the way why two subjects are being compared, and for summing up. Thus, after treating Cleo and Alice separately throughout most of his essay, Chapman comes back to the point-by-point method in the final paragraph:

> Alice is already ahead of Cleo in income and career status. Alice also receives a very genuine if different sort of esteem—the sort of wary respect the fox gets from the rabbit. And although Alice does not have the traditional job security that Cleo clings to, she has a different and far more valuable kind: she knows that whatever may happen in her current job, she can find another easily.

Like the fox and the rabbit, says Chapman, "scramblers" usually get ahead in their careers, while "stabilizers" tend to lag a little behind. Chapman is not recommending Alice over Cleo as a career model, however. He's simply highlighting the differences between them because his main point in comparing the two women is to argue that most workers fall into the "two camps" they represent.

STATING YOUR POINT

Your main point in drawing a comparison will determine whether you emphasize the similarities or the differences between your subjects. If you are comparing coaches you had in high school, for instance, you might focus on their differences in order to show the reader what constitutes a good (or bad) coach. If you're comparing two good blind dates to explain what makes for a successful one, however, you would focus on the similarities.

Whatever the main point of your comparison might be, make it clear right away in the form of an explicit thesis statement, and tell the reader which you are going to emphasize—the similarities or the differences between your subjects. Then, in the body of your essay, draw a sufficient number of specific points of comparison to prove your main point.

PROVIDING SUFFICIENT POINTS OF COMPARISON

No matter how you organize a comparison essay, you will have to provide a sufficient number of points of comparison between your subjects to demonstrate that they are truly comparable, and to justify your reasons for comparing them. How many points of comparison are enough to do the job?

Sufficiency isn't strictly a matter of numbers. It depends, in part, on just how

TIPS AND TEMPLATES FOR DRAFTING

When you begin to draft a comparison, you need to identify your subjects, state the basis on which you're comparing them, and indicate whether you plan to emphasize their similarities or their differences. These moves are fundamental to any comparison. See how Gitangeli Sapra makes such moves near the beginning of her essay in this chapter:

> Even if Western middle-class men are growing more faithful, forty percent of "marriages made for love" still end in divorce. By contrast, the rate of break-ups of arranged marriages in the Asian community is far lower.   —GITANGELI SAPRA, "I'm Happy with an Arranged Marriage"

Sapra identifies her two subjects ("marriages made for love," arranged marriages), states the basis on which she's comparing them ("rate of break-ups"), and indicates that she is planning to emphasize the differences (forty percent in divorce, "far lower"). Here is one more example from this chapter:

> They were two strong men, these oddly different generals, and they represented the strengths of two conflicting currents that, through them, had come into final collision.
> —BRUCE CATTON, "Grant and Lee: A Study in Contrasts"

The following templates can help you make some of these basic moves in your own writing. But don't take these as formulas where you just have to fill in the blanks. There are no easy formulas for good writing, but these templates can serve as starting points.

- ▶ *X* and *Y* can be compared on the grounds that both are _____.
- ▶ Like *X*, *Y* is also _____, _____, and _____.
- ▶ Although *X* and *Y* are both _____, the differences between them far outweigh the similarities. For example, *X* is _____, _____, and _____, while *Y* is _____, _____, and _____.
- ▶ Unlike *X*, *Y* is _____.
- ▶ Despite their obvious differences, *X* and *Y* are basically alike in that _____.
- ▶ At first glance, *X* and *Y* seem _____; however, a closer look reveals _____.
- ▶ In comparing *X* and *Y*, we can clearly see that _____.

inclined your audience is to accept (or reject) the main point your comparison is intended to make.

If you are comparing subjects that your readers are not familiar with, you may have to give more reasons for drawing the parallel than you would if your readers alaready know a lot about your subjects. In comparing dying to going on a cruise, for example, Mary Roach compares the two on the humorous basis that they are both forms of leisure, and she draws five points of comparison between them: (1) much of the time is spent lying on your back; (2) the brain shuts down; (3) the flesh begins to soften; (4) nothing new happens; (5) not much is expected of you. Roach might have gone on to make additional points of comparison, such as (6) you don't go anywhere in particular and (7) there's not much room in the cabin. Five points, however, are probably enough to persuade the reader that the two subjects are worth comparing, and any more than that would be going over-board.

To determine how many points of comparison you need to make, follow Roach's example: give a sufficient number to get your larger point across, but not so many that you run the comparison into the ground. In other words, whether your points of comparison are sufficient to support your thesis is not determined so much by how many you give as by how persuasive they seem to the reader. So consider your intended readers, and choose points of comparison you think they will find useful, interesting, or otherwise convincing.

USING OTHER METHODS

Comparison deals with subjects that have something significant in common, so CLASSIFICATION and DEFINITION can be useful in writing that compares. The following paragraph, for example, uses both methods to establish a firm basis for comparing writing to other ways of using language:

> Writing represents a unique mode of learning—not merely valuable, not merely special, but unique. That will be my contention in this paper. . . . Traditionally, the four language processes of listening, talking, reading, and writing are paired in either of two ways. The more informative seems to be the division many linguists make between first-order and second-order processes with talking and listening characterized as first-order processes; reading and writing, as second-order.   —JANET EMIG, "Writing as a Mode of Knowing"

The author of this passage, from a formal academic paper in linguistics and language acquisition, is comparing writing to other "language processes," particularly talking. Her main point in making the comparison is to argue that, among all the ways in which humans learn to use language, writing is unique.

To support this point and develop her comparison, Emig uses a number of other methods besides comparison and contrast. First, she classifies writing as a "second-order" use of language, and the more natural process of talking as a "first-order" use. Then, elsewhere in her introduction, Emig defines these two basic kinds of language activities: first-order language skills, such as talking, are learned *without* formal instruction, whereas second-order language skills, such as writing, are learned only *with* formal instruction.

Not every linguist would agree that writing is unique among human language activities. But it would be difficult to contest Emig's point that learning to write well takes a special, perhaps unique, form of language instruction by knowledgeable teachers who are dedicated to a difficult task. How else, but through highly specialized training, could we learn to draw formal written comparisons and contrasts in such academic disciplines as history, geography, sociology—and linguistics?

Reading a Comparison Essay with a Critical Eye

Once you've drafted a comparison essay, ask someone else to look over your draft and tell you how effective he or she finds your basic comparison—and why. Then read it over yourself, too, with a critical eye. Here are some questions that you and any other readers might ask when checking over a comparison:

SUBJECTS OF COMPARISON. What specific subjects does this essay compare? Are those subjects really similar enough to justify the comparison? On what basis are they compared? Does the text emphasize the similarities or the differences between them? Or does it give equal weight to both?

PURPOSE AND AUDIENCE. Who are the intended readers, and what is the general purpose of the comparison—To inform? To evaluate? Some other purpose? Does the comparison achieve this purpose? If not, what changes might help? What background information is included, and is it sufficient for the intended readers to fully understand the text? Are there any key terms that readers might not be familiar with and that need to be defined?

THE POINT. What is the main point of the essay, and has it been made clear to the reader? Is there an explicit thesis statement? If not, should there be?

ORGANIZATION. How is the essay organized? Where does it use the point-by-point method of organization? The subject-by-subject method? Whichever method is used, is it effective? When comparing subjects point by point, does the essay give more or less equal weight to each subject? When treating first one subject and then the other, does the essay follow more or less the same order in laying out the points of comparison for each subject?

POINTS OF COMPARISON. What are the specific points of comparison in the essay? Are they sufficient to convince the reader that the comparison is valid? Do the points of comparison cover the same elements in both subjects? Have any important points of comparison been omitted—and if so, what are they?

OTHER METHODS. What other methods are used besides comparison and contrast? Does the essay CLASSIFY subjects? DEFINE them? Make an ARGUMENT about them? What other methods might support the comparison?

Editing for Common Errors in Comparisons

As with other kinds of writing, comparisons use distinctive patterns of language and punctuation—and thus invite some common mistakes. The following tips will help you check your writing for errors that often crop up in comparisons.

Be sure that all comparisons are complete.

Remember that all comparisons examine at least two items; check to see that both are mentioned. Readers need to understand what is being compared.

INCOMPLETE When you take a bath, it is always better to relax.

COMPLETE   When you take a bath, it is always better to relax than to hurry.

INCOMPLETE Most hot tubs are not as hot.

COMPLETE   Most hot tubs are not as hot as typical Japanese baths.

Be sure that all comparisons are logically consistent.

Check to be sure that you've compared things that are alike. See how the first example below illogically compares a bath with a country.

ILLOGICAL   U.S. baths tend to be much less ritualistic than Japan.

LOGICAL   U.S. baths tend to be much less ritualistic than those in Japan.

Be sure that all comparisons are clear, that readers will understand what is being compared.

UNCLEAR Fumio taught me more than Sam.

CLEAR   Fumio taught me more than Sam did.

CLEAR   Fumio taught me more than he taught Sam.

Check for common usage errors.

GOOD, WELL, BETTER

Good is an adjective; *well* is the adverb form. *Better* is both adjective and adverb.

▶ Hilary is a *good* musician; she plays the violin as *well* as Tom does and *better* than I do.

BETWEEN, AMONG

Use *between* when you're comparing two items; use *among* when you're comparing three or more.

▶ *Between* Britain and France, France has the better health care system.

▶ *Among* all the countries of Europe, France has the best health care system.

"Car Talk"

When we compare and contrast two things, we note their similarities and differences. In this "Car Talk" column, the Magliozzi brothers and their correspondent compare two different ways of shifting gears in an old car. One is Sallie's way; the other is her psychoanalyst husband's. Which way is right for their aging Saturn? When we make comparisons in our daily lives, it is often for the purpose of choosing between alternatives. The specific choices we make, however, will depend upon our specific needs. In this case, Sallie's husband wants to get maximum power out of the car. Sallie, on the other hand, wants the engine "to last at least another five years." Given Sallie's objective, say Tom and Ray, her husband is "just nuts." The first thing Sallie is going to do with this professional opinion, of course, is show it to her husband. Will he be convinced? He may—if Tom and Ray have drawn their comparison properly. In a written comparison, you tell the reader why you're drawing the comparison—for example, to solve a problem or resolve a dispute ("Here's the problem"). Then, taking the readers' needs into account ("You two clearly want different things out of your vehicles"), you lay out the similarities and differences in your subjects that you consider to be most significant ("as much power as possible," "greatest longevity"). Even if you're making a personal evaluation, however, you don't just choose one alternative over the other. You give your readers the information they need in order to make intelligent decisions for themselves. In this case, Tom and Ray draw points of comparison that are probably sufficient in number and quality to convince Sallie's husband to let her drive the way she wants.

EVERYDAY COMPARISON

Dear Tom and Ray: I hope you can help settle an issue between me and my psychoanalyst husband. It's about how to drive my 1993 Saturn SL2. My hubby went out and bought a BMW motorcycle this past spring. Since then, he's announced that we've been driving the Saturn wrong for the past 10 years. He thinks we should wait until the engine reaches at least 4,000 rpm to shift into the next higher gear. ("The red zone isn't until 6,500 rmp!") He supports this assertion with talk of driving with the power curve, so that he can have optimal acceleration, or something like that. When I point out that the panel shows the orange arrow suggesting that he shift up at about 2,000 rpm, he calls it an "idiot light." I want this engine to last at least another five years. I'm afraid, though, that he might kill the engine or transmission. Or, from the way the engine sounds when he drives, that he might take off and fly into space —and since we live near Washington, D.C., he might be shot down as a potential terrorist. Help!—Sallie

RAY: Well, if you really want this engine to last another five years, you need to go to the Saturn dealer and have him change the ignition key. And then don't give your husband a copy of the new one.

TOM: Yeah. I'm kind of surprised that, as a psychoanalyst, he doesn't recognize that he's going through some sort of midlife crisis. I mean, the BMW motorcycle, the power curves . . . it can't get much more obvious, Sallie. I'd keep my eye out for hidden copies of Naked Coed Adventure Travel magazine if I were you.

RAY: Here's the problem, Your husband is not wrong. He's just nuts. You two clearly want different things out of your vehicles. He wants to get as much power as possible out of the engine (ask the analyst why he feels he's lacking in power, Sallie). And if he wants maximum power out of his engine, he's right; you shift near the top of the power curve, which is probably around 4,000 rpm in this car.

TOM: But if you want the best fuel economy, the greatest longevity from an engine or the fewest dirty looks from friends, neighbors and other drivers, you drive it gently and shift much earlier, like you do, Sallie.

RAY: So until the crisis of his passes, let him take out his power-curve aggressions on his motorcycle (provided you have good life insurance for him). But when the two of you take your car, you drive, and let him sit in the passenger seat and go "vroom, vroom."

GITANGELI SAPRA

I'm Happy with an Arranged Marriage

Gitangeli Sapra (b. 1979) studied journalism at London's Harrow College while work-
ing as a reporter at the Watford Observer. *She later took a day job as a marketing*
director while pursuing her freelance writing career at night. This dedication to writing
has paid off—Sapra's work has appeared in some of Britain's most prestigious dailies,
including The Telegraph *and* The Times.

   The compare-and-contrast approach that Sapra uses in "I'm Happy with an
Arranged Marriage" is one that she comes by naturally. Growing up in Britain, Sapra
has had to balance contemporary European social norms with the traditions of her
family's native India. Nowhere is the contrast between these different cultures more
pronounced than in their attitudes toward marriage. "I'm Happy with an Arranged
Marriage" first appeared in the Sunday London Times *in May 2003.*

Nᴜᴍʙᴇʀ sᴇᴠᴇɴ was preceded by his breath. Number three did not open his   1
mouth, his mother talked for him. I never actually saw prospective husband number eight: his mother preferred that I keep my gaze averted, Bollywood style.[1]

As the dance of modern-day arranged marriage, at least as I, a 24-year-old   2
Hindu born in Britain, have experienced it. Although so far it has been a series of
meetings with unsuitable suitors, I am not at all dismayed.

As Dame Elizabeth Butler-Sloss, president of the family division, said last week: 3
"I support the concept of an arranged marriage. It seems it has many advantages."

Even if Western middle-class men are growing more faithful, as some experts   4
suggest, 40% of "marriages made for love" still end in divorce. By contrast, the rate
of break-ups of arranged marriages in the Asian community is far lower.

This may be because arranged unions are based on mutual interests and similar   5
levels of education rather than physical attraction. The involvement of both families is also a deterrent to affairs—who would want to risk the wrath of their
mother, mother-in-law, brother and grandfather, as well as their wife, for a few
hours of fun?

Nor is the system as draconian as many might imagine. Arranged marriages are   6
simply introductions—the element of choice remains. True, initial meetings
between would-be brides and grooms take place in front of their families, but sub-

---

1. *Bollywood*: a blending of "Bombay" (the city now called Mumbai) and "Hollywood." In India
there is a thriving movie industry that makes hundreds of mostly Hindi-language films each year. The
industry, the place, and the films themselves are often referred to as Bollywood.

sequent "dates" are usually unchaperoned. And you are not expected to make any decisions until at least the sixth meeting.

A wild rush? I know of couples who agreed to marry after only the second meet- 7 ing. Several children later, the initial attraction has developed into an abiding love and respect. One friend even said yes on the first meeting, despite her intended turning up with his mother, aunt, uncle, three brothers and the dog. Eight years and two children later, she has no regrets.

Some marriages that are forced do still take place—perhaps 1,000 a year among 8 Pakistanis born in Britain. But the distinction is clear. As Butler-Sloss said: "Forced marriage is as unacceptable in the Indian subcontinent among those who understand the sharia (law) as in the Western world."

Nor is it just young Asians who see the benefits of arranged unions. Steven 9 Brown, chief executive of the Jewish Marriage Council, which runs its own matchmaking service, said: "The latest thing is shidduch dating, where a matchmaker introduces couples who go out unchaperoned to a Jewish restaurant four or five times to see if they have anything in common.

"Among the orthodox, arranged marriages are very much the done thing. The 10 degree of people remaining married after meeting like this is higher than in other cases."

Even Western women, post–Bridget Jones[2] and single, are keen on exploring the 11 idea. After all, the union of the Prince of Wales and Diana Spencer[3] was as orchestrated as any Delhi marriage.

Claire Oswald, 38, a writer who is white, Western, and single, recently lamented 12 in the Asian women's magazine *Memsahib* that no system of arranged marriage was available to her.

"I would love to have an arranged marriage," she wrote. "It's great that there is 13 so much family involvement and that the people who care about you help you to find a husband."

I am soon to meet number 12—a doctor, as my mother keeps telling everyone. 14 There is no pressure. But as I hurtle towards 25—middle-aged for an arranged marriage—I hope this one works out.

2. *Bridget Jones*: the heroine of best-selling novels by Helen Fielding about the trials of dating in London; *Bridget Jones's Diary* (1996) and *Bridget Jones: The Edge of Reason* (1999) were both made into movies.

3. *Prince of Wales and Diana Spencer*: Charles, the Prince of Wales, and Princess Diana, formerly Lady Diana Spencer; they were divorced in 1996.

Reading Closely

1. Gitangeli Sapra is comparing arranged marriages with those "made for love" (4). What main advantages and disadvantages does she find in each type?

2. Are you convinced by Sapra's ARGUMENT that arranged marriages are superior to "marriages made for love" (4)? Why or why not?

3. Sapra does not approve of all arranged marriages. What kind does she still find unacceptable? Why? What do you think?

Strategies and Structures

1. Sapra is a British citizen of Indian ancestry. Is she writing for readers with her own ethnic background, or for someone else? How do you know?

2. Are Sapra's points of comparison between the two types of marriage sufficient to support her claim that one is superior to the other? Why or why not?

3. How convincing do you find Sapra's EXAMPLES? Are there any that do her case more harm than good? If so, which ones?

4. *Other Methods.* According to Sapra, what is the main CAUSE of the lower percentage of divorces among arranged marriages as compared to "love" marriages? How convincing do you find this analysis?

Thinking about Language

1. In Hebrew, a "shidduch" is a "match" (9). Why does Sapra use this term to DESCRIBE the kind of marriage she advocates?

2. Is "made for love" (4) an adequate label of the kind of marriage that Sapra is contrasting with arranged marriages? Why or why not? What term would you suggest?

For Writing

1. Write a paragraph outlining the advantages of "marriage for love."

2. Write an essay comparing dates on your own with dates arranged for you, at least in part, by somebody else. Be sure to comment on the advantages and disadvantages of each.

NINA BERNSTEIN

French Sissies vs. German He-Men

Nina Bernstein is a journalist who has worked for the Milwaukee Journal, *the* Des Moines Register and Tribune, New York Newsday, *and, since 1995, the* New York Times. *Her first book,* The Lost Children of Wilder: The Epic Struggle to Change Foster Care *(2002), grew out of her 1994* Newsday *story about an abused runaway and earned Bernstein a National Book Award nomination.*

In "French Sissies vs. German He-Men," which first appeared in the New York Times *in 2003, Bernstein compares and contrasts the strikingly different reactions that many Americans felt toward France and Germany when both nations opposed going to war against Iraq. The prejudice against "feminine" France, she finds, plays into a much older rivalry.*

It WAS ON DISPLAY AGAIN LAST WEEK, that old double standard. On camera, 1 Germany's chancellor got a muscular handshake from America's president and a meeting that let bygones be bygones. France's president got the official cold shoulder and columnists' heated denunciations.

Yet France and Germany had taken the same position on the Bush administra- 2 tion's policies in Iraq. Both were offering to help train Iraqi security forces, but not to send soldiers. Both argued that only accelerated Iraqi sovereignty and a larger United Nations role could secure peace.

Apparently, it sounded different in French. Somehow, to American ears, it 3 always does. And at this point in strained trans-Atlantic relations, an obvious explanation comes to mind: in the American imagination, France is a woman, and Germany is just another guy.

The French themselves depict La Belle France as a bare-breasted "Marianne"[1] 4 on the barricades. They export high fashion, cosmetics, fine food—delicacies traditionally linked to a woman's pleasure, if not her boudoir. And French has always been Hollywood's language of love.

Germany, meanwhile, is the Fatherland, its spike helmets retooled into the sleek 5 insignia of cars like the Mercedes and BMW. It also exports heavy machinery and strong beer—products linked to manliness. And notwithstanding Goethe, Schiller

---

1. *Marianne:* the national emblem of France. She is not a historical figure but an idealized image that represents Liberty and Reason. Traditionally, she wears a cap of the type worn by freed Roman slaves and is thus a powerful symbol of freedom and liberty. She is often depicted as leading the battles of the French Revolution.

and Franka Potente, German is Hollywood's language of war, barked to the beat of combat boots in half a century of movies.[2]

Such images simply overpower facts that do not fit the picture—like decades of German pacifism and French militarism since World War II. So what if France was fighting in Vietnam, Algeria and Africa, and deploying a force of 36,000 troops around the world, while Germans held peace vigils and invented Berlin's Love Parade. For Americans, it seems, World War II permanently inoculated Germans against "the wimp factor" and branded the French indelibly as sissies.   6

Sure, both countries were dubbed members of the "Axis of Weasel"[3] and dissed as Old Europe for opposing the war in Iraq. But no one poured schnapps down the toilet, renamed sauerkraut or made prime-time jokes denigrating German manhood. Only France can evoke that kind of frat-boy frenzy.   7

"It's in the way we view both countries," said Irwin M. Wall, a historian of French-American relations. "We view Germany as producing iron and steel, and we view France as producing perfume and haute couture. You'll never get America out of this stereotype that France is a feminine country."   8

Of course, Mr. Wall added, when Secretary of State Colin L. Powell refers to America and France as having been in marriage counseling for 225 years, "you know darn well he means we're the male partner."   9

American officials have long used sexist stereotyping as diplomatic strategy. Franklin Roosevelt once declared that Charles de Gaulle knew no more about economics "than a woman knows about a carburetor." In 1953, *Life* magazine likened the French government to "a big can-can chorus" and France itself to a showgirl slipping a billion-dollar bill's worth of American aid into her stocking.   10

Frank Costigliola, a historian at the University of Connecticut, gives many such examples in his book *France and the United States: The Cold Alliance Since World War II*. He contends that giving France negative "feminine" traits has always served to delegitimize French points of view.   11

"Associated with France as a woman is France as hysterical, or France as crazy," he said. "It really is a knee-jerk reaction."   12

Robert O. Paxton, an emeritus professor of history at Columbia University, agreed. "It's an American stereotype and an American strategy," he stressed. "There   13

2. *Franka Potente* (b. 1974): German actress whose films include *Run, Lola, Run* (1998), *Blow* (2001), and *The Bourne Identity* (2002). *Johann Wolfgang von Goethe* (1749–1832) and *Friedrich Schiller* (1759–1805): celebrated writers of the Romantic movement.

3. *Axis of Weasel*: a play on the phrase "axis of evil," which was used by President George W. Bush in his 2002 State of the Union address to refer to three nations that he believed were sponsors of terror: Iraq, Iran, and North Korea. Bush's phrase is intended to recall the United States' foes in World War II, known collectively in English as the Axis powers. In U.S. popular culture, weasels are associated with deviousness, insincerity, and guile.

are elements in our culture that the Bush people can play on in stereotyping France as feminine."

The paradox, added Mr. Paxton, the author of *Vichy France*, is that the French 14 hold a mirror stereotype about America. "They believe the American male has been completely emasculated, and American women rule the roost."

Others use similar categories to explain why France, not Germany, rubs Americans so raw. "I haven't used male and female, but I've used cat countries and dog countries," said Walter Russell Mead, the author of *Special Providence: American Foreign Policy and How It Changed the World*. 15

Mr. Mead sees France as a cat country, while Germany—like America and 16 Britain—is a dog country, "the underdog baring its throat."

To the film critic Molly Haskell, it seems that France has been cast as the femme 17 fatale, "the seductress who's leading all Europe away from us."

"It's this insidious evil woman," she continued, "and the others are probably 18 good guys who are just being led astray."

What doesn't fit that script is forgotten—like Chancellor Gerhard Schröder's 19 pre-emptive election promise that Germany would not take part in a war against Saddam Hussein even if the United Nations authorized it. Or the fact that in his youth, President Jacques Chirac of France made banana splits at Howard Johnson's[4] in the United States before serving as a French Army officer.

"The Germans are getting away with it because we are so eager to tar and 20 feather France," said Ann Douglas, a cultural historian at Columbia University and the author of *The Feminization of American Culture*. "The constant need to denigrate France—and feminization has always been the way to go—is because France has always maintained a separate voice."

A female France, seen as the bastion of sensual pleasure and elite cultural 21 refinement, is a made-to-order enemy for the Texan in the White House, Ms. Douglas contended. With a sagging American economy, and the fear of appearing weak that often underlies aggressive masculinity, she said, French-bashing has new political appeal. "I think George Bush is carrying around a tremendous amount of anger," Ms. Douglas added, "and a lot of men are tapping into that."

But under Bill Clinton, reflexive animosity also flowed between Washington 22 and Paris, recalled Charles A. Kupchan, who was a security adviser on Europe in the Clinton years. "When the French sent dispatches about operations in Kosovo, people would just throw them away," he said. "The attitude was, if it's from France, it must be to undermine American power."

Still, said Mr. Kupchan, now a professor of international affairs at Georgetown 23

---

4. *Howard Johnson's*: an American restaurant and hotel chain that reached the height of its popularity in the 1950s; today nearly all the restaurants have gone out of business.

University: "Deep down inside, Americans feel deeper affinity for France than Germany. If France is female, there's also an attraction, a lure, a romance."

Maybe that's the rub. "The well-built iron-pumping male is being laughed at, 24
or poked fun at by the woman with attitude—that resonates with me," Mr.
Kupchan acknowledged. "It creates that mix of anger and indignation, that 'How
dare you?' "

READING CLOSELY

1. Nina Bernstein is not comparing the French and the Germans; she is comparing different American attitudes toward the two countries. Why? What is her main point in making this comparison?

2. Is Bernstein's comparison justified, in your opinion? Do Americans really apply a double standard when they think about France and Germany (1)? Explain.

3. What support does Bernstein offer for the idea that the French are far from "sissies" and that Germans are genuine pacifists? Why, then, do these stereotypes of the two countries still persist in America?

4. If Americans actually feel a "deeper affinity" for France than for Germany, why, according to Bernstein, are some Americans more offended by the actions and policies of the French than those of the Germans (23)?

STRATEGIES AND STRUCTURES

1. Does Bernstein's COMPARISON discover likeness where we might expect difference, or difference where we might expect similarity? Or both? Explain.

2. On what basis is Bernstein drawing her comparison? That is, what do her subjects have in common, fundamentally, despite their differences? Where and how does she make her basis of comparison clear to the reader?

3. Where and why does Bernstein use the point-by-point method of comparison? Where and why does she use the subject-by-subject method?

4. *Other Methods.* How does her comparison help Bernstein to ANALYZE THE CAUSES of American attitudes toward Europe, particularly the French?

THINKING ABOUT LANGUAGE

1. "He-men" and "sissies" are old-fashioned, almost quaint CLASSIFICATIONS of masculine and feminine behavior. Why do you think Bernstein uses such outmoded terms for her comparison?

2. What PARADOX is Bernstein describing in paragraph 14? Why is it paradoxical?

3. "Ay, there's the rub," says Hamlet in his "To be, or not to be" soliloquy in Act 3 of Shakespeare's play. Contemplating suicide, Hamlet compares death to a seductive sleep in which his troubles are forgotten. But "in that sleep of death," he fears, "what dreams may come?" Why do you think Bernstein ALLUDES to this debilitating combination of repulsion and desire in paragraph 24?

For Writing

1. Make a list of the similarities and differences you find most striking between the French and the Germans (or the people of two other countries) as depicted in American popular culture, particularly movies and television.

2. Write an essay comparing and contrasting the products and services you associate with Canada, France, Germany, or some other country with those you associate with the United States. Use the comparison to explain broader cultural similarities and differences between the two nations.

BRUCE CATTON

Grant and Lee: A Study in Contrasts

Bruce Catton (1899–1978), grew up in Benzonia, Michigan, listening to the stories told by Union army veterans and reenacting the battles of the Civil War. After serving briefly in the U.S. Navy during World War I, Catton worked as a reporter until the outbreak of World War II, during which he served as director of information for the War Production Board. A founding editor of American Heritage *magazine, he wrote many volumes about the Civil War, including* A Stillness at Appomattox *(1954), which won a Pulitzer Prize and a National Book Award. In 1976 Catton was honored with a Presidential Medal of Freedom as America's foremost historian of the Civil War.*

"Grant and Lee: A Study in Contrasts" was first published in The American Story *(1955), a collection of essays by leading historians. Catton compares the U.S. Civil War generals Ulysses S. Grant, who led the Union army, and Robert E. Lee, who led the forces of the Confederacy.*

WHEN ULYSSES S. GRANT and Robert E. Lee met in the parlor of a modest 1 house at Appomattox Court House, Virginia, on April 9, 1865, to work out the terms for the surrender of Lee's Army of Northern Virginia, a great chapter in American life came to a close, and a great new chapter began.

These men were bringing the Civil War[1] to its virtual finish. To be sure, other 2 armies had yet to surrender, and for a few days the fugitive Confederate government would struggle desperately and vainly, trying to find some way to go on living now that its chief support was gone. But in effect it was all over when Grant and Lee signed the papers. And the little room where they wrote out the terms was the scene of one of the poignant, dramatic contrasts in American history.

They were two strong men, these oddly different generals, and they represented 3 the strengths of two conflicting currents that, through them, had come into final collision.

Back of Robert E. Lee was the notion that the old aristocratic concept might 4 somehow survive and be dominant in American life.

---

1. *Civil War* (1861–1865): the war fought between those states and territories of the United States that remained loyal to the federal government in Washington under President Abraham Lincoln ("the Union") and the slave-holding Southern states that formed a separate government led by Jefferson Davis ("the Confederacy").

Lee was tidewater Virginia,[2] and in his background were family, culture, and tra- 5
dition . . . the age of chivalry transplanted to a New World which was making its
own legends and its own myths. He embodied a way of life that had come down
through the age of knighthood and the English country squire. America was a land
that was beginning all over again, dedicated to nothing much more complicated
than the rather hazy belief that all men had equal rights and should have an equal
chance in the world. In such a land Lee stood for the feeling that it was somehow
of advantage to human society to have a pronounced inequality in the social structure. There should be a leisure class, backed by ownership of land; in turn, society
itself should be keyed to the land as the chief source of wealth and influence. It
would bring forth (according to this ideal) a class of men with a strong sense of
obligation to the community; men who lived not to gain advantage for themselves,
but to meet the solemn obligations which had been laid on them by the very fact
that they were privileged. From them the country would get its leadership; to them
it could look for the higher values—of thought, of conduct, of personal deport-
ment—to give it strength and virtue.

Lee embodied the noblest elements of this aristocratic ideal. Through him, the 6
landed nobility justified itself. For four years, the Southern states had fought a desperate war to uphold the ideals for which Lee stood. In the end, it almost seemed
as if the Confederacy fought for Lee; as if he himself was the Confederacy . . . the
best thing that the way of life for which the Confederacy stood could ever have to
offer. He had passed into legend before Appomattox. Thousands of tired, underfed,
poorly clothed Confederate soldiers, long since past the simple enthusiasm of the
early days of the struggle, somehow considered Lee the symbol of everything for
which they had been willing to die. But they could not quite put this feeling into
words. If the Lost Cause, sanctified by so much heroism and so many deaths, had a
living justification, its justification was General Lee.

Grant, the son of a tanner on the Western frontier, was everything Lee was not. 7
He had come up the hard way and embodied nothing in particular except the eternal toughness and sinewy fiber of the men who grew up beyond the mountains. He
was one of a body of men who owed reverence and obeisance to no one, who were
self-reliant to a fault, who cared hardly anything for the past but who had a sharp
eye for the future.

These frontier men were the precise opposites of the tidewater aristocrats. Back 8
of them, in the great surge that had taken people over the Alleghenies[3] and into the

---

2. *Tidewater Virginia*: the coastal plain region of eastern Virginia where rivers flow inland from the
Chesapeake Bay. The region is geographically and culturally distinct. The first English colony in North
America, Jamestown, settled in 1607, is in the Tidewater area.

3. *Alleghenies*: the Allegheny Mountains, which run from northern Pennsylvania to southwestern
Virginia.

opening Western country, there was a deep, implicit dissatisfaction with a past that had settled into grooves. They stood for democracy, not from any reasoned conclusion about the proper ordering of human society, but simply because they had grown up in the middle of democracy and knew how it worked. Their society might have privileges, but they would be privileges each man had won for himself. Forms and patterns meant nothing. No man was born to anything, except perhaps to a chance to show how far he could rise. Life was competition.

Yet along with this feeling had come a deep sense of belonging to a national 9 community. The Westerner who developed a farm, opened a shop, or set up in business as a trader, could hope to prosper only as his own community prospered—and his community ran from the Atlantic to the Pacific and from Canada down to Mexico. If the land was settled, with towns and highways and accessible markets, he could better himself. He saw his fate in terms of the nation's own destiny. As its horizons expanded, so did his. He had, in other words, an acute dollars-and-cents stake in the continued growth and development of his country.

And that, perhaps, is where the contrast between Grant and Lee becomes most 10 striking. The Virginia aristocrat, inevitably, saw himself in relation to his own region. He lived in a static society which could endure almost anything except change. Instinctively, his first loyalty would go to the locality in which that society existed. He would fight to the limit of endurance to defend it, because in defending it he was defending everything that gave his own life its deepest meaning.

The Westerner, on the other hand, would fight with an equal tenacity for the 11 broader concept of society. He fought so because everything he lived by was tied to growth, expansion, and a constantly widening horizon. What he lived by would survive or fall with the nation itself. He could not possibly stand by unmoved in the face of an attempt to destroy the Union. He would combat it with everything he had, because he could only see it as an effort to cut the ground out from under his feet.

So Grant and Lee were in complete contrast, representing two diametrically 12 opposed elements in American life. Grant was the modern man emerging; beyond him, ready to come on the stage, was the great age of steel and machinery, of crowded cities and a restless burgeoning vitality. Lee might have ridden down from the old age of chivalry, lance in hand, silken banner fluttering over his head. Each man was the perfect champion of his cause, drawing both his strengths and his weaknesses from the people he led.

Yet it was not all contrast, after all. Different as they were—in background, in 13 personality, in underlying aspiration—these two great soldiers had much in common. Under everything else, they were marvelous fighters. Furthermore, their fighting qualities were really very much alike.

Each man had, to begin with, the great virtue of utter tenacity and fidelity. 14

Grant fought his way down the Mississippi Valley in spite of acute personal discouragement and profound military handicaps. Lee hung on in the trenches at Petersburg after hope itself had died. In each man there was an indomitable quality . . . the born fighter's refusal to give up as long as he can still remain on his feet and lift his two fists.

Daring and resourcefulness they had, too; the ability to think faster and move 15 faster than the enemy. These were the qualities which gave Lee the dazzling campaigns of Second Manassas and Chancellorsville and won Vicksburg for Grant.

Lastly, and perhaps greatest of all, there was the ability, at the end, to turn 16 quickly from war to peace once the fighting was over. Out of the way these two men behaved at Appomattox came the possibility of a peace of reconciliation. It was a possibility not wholly realized, in the years to come, but which did, in the end, help the two sections to become one nation again . . . after a war whose bitterness might have seemed to make such a reunion wholly impossible. No part of either man's life became him more than the part he played in this brief meeting in the McLean house at Appomattox. Their behavior there put all succeeding generations of Americans in their debt. Two great Americans, Grant and Lee—very different, yet under everything very much alike. Their encounter at Appomattox was one of the great moments of American history.

Reading Closely

1. According to Bruce Catton, Grant and Lee represented two distinct "currents" in American life and history (3). What were those currents, and what CONTRASTING qualities and ideals does Catton associate with each man?

2. Even though they were "in complete contrast," says Catton, Grant and Lee also "had much in common" (12, 13). In what ways were the two men alike?

3. Although Grant and Lee were both "great Americans," as Catton says, they were deadly enemies. Why did each man take the side he did?

4. Why, according to Catton, are all future generations of Americans "in their debt" (16)? Do you agree? Why or why not?

Strategies and Structures

1. On what basis is Catton comparing his two subjects? Where does he tell the reader what that basis of comparison is?

2. Why does Catton emphasize the differences between the two men he is comparing? For what audience and purpose is he drawing such a strong contrast?

3. Catton uses the subject-by-subject method through most of his essay. When and why does he switch to the point-by-point method?

4. *Other Methods.* Besides comparing and contrasting the two generals, Catton's study also ANALYZES THE CAUSES AND EFFECTS of the American Civil War. How does this analysis support and clarify his comparison?

THINKING ABOUT LANGUAGE

1. What view of history—and Grant's and Lee's roles in it—is suggested by Catton's use of METAPHORS from the theater in paragraphs 2 and 16?

2. Why do you think Catton capitalizes "Lost Cause" in paragraph 6?

3. "Obeisance" (7) means homage of the sort paid to a king. Why might Catton choose this term instead of the more familiar *obedience* when describing General Grant?

4. What are the CONNOTATIONS of "sinewy fiber" (7), and how does Catton's general DESCRIPTION of Grant justify the use of this phrase?

FOR WRITING

1. Make an outline of the key points you would make in a comparison and contrast of two other people—famous generals, Olympic athletes, favorite aunts, etc.

2. Write an essay comparing and contrasting two present-day public figures—for example, two U.S. presidents—whose actions, you feel, will put all succeeding generations of Americans in their debt.

ADAM GOODHEART

The Skyscraper and the Airplane

Adam Goodheart (b. 1970) is an essayist and a member of the editorial board of the
American Scholar, *the journal of the Phi Beta Kappa organization. His topics range
from radio sound effects to the Andaman Islands and Italian manners, from Romantic
poetry to Civil War battlefields. Goodheart's work has appeared in the* Atlantic
Monthly, *the* New York Times, Outside, *and other publications.*

*Though both penetrate the sky, skyscrapers and airliners aren't usually considered
as having much in common. In "The Skyscraper and the Airplane," however, Adam
Goodheart argues that the terrible conjunction of these two behemoths in the airspace
above New York City on September 11, 2001, should have come as no surprise because
they actually have many elements in common, both in structure and "in our collective
unconscious." This essay was originally published in 2002 in the* American Scholar.

> *And as the smart ship grew*
> *In stature, grace, and hue,*
> *In shadowy silent distance grew the Iceberg too.*
> —Thomas Hardy, "The Convergence of the Twain" (1912)

BEFORE THE FIRE, before the ash, before the bodies tumbling solitary through 1
space, one thin skin of metal and glass met another. Miles apart only moments
before, then feet, and then, in an almost inconceivable instant, only a fraction of an
inch. Try to imagine them there, suspended: two man-made behemoths joined in a
fatal kiss.

Fatal, fated: perhaps even long foreseen. The skyscraper and the airplane were 2
born side by side, and ever since then have occupied adjacent rooms in our collective unconscious. To call September 11th a nightmare is to be clinically precise
about it, for like all true nightmares, it was grafted together out of preexisting elements, fragments of our waking lives and our imaginations.

Nearly a century ago, just five years after the first scrawny aircraft left the 3
ground at Kitty Hawk,[1] a widely circulated illustration by a Manhattan publisher
named Moses King—"King's Dream of New York," he titled it—showed a fantasy
cityscape in which biplanes buzzed among the downtown office towers and a vast

---

1. *Kitty Hawk*: town in North Carolina where in 1903 Orville and Wilbur Wright made the first successful airplane flight.

dirigible brushed the uppermost cupola. In that same year, 1908, E. M. Forster[2] wrote a short story envisioning a world of the future where humans lived in huge structures composed of tiny, airless chambers, each one "like the cell of a bee," leaving them to travel in airships that crisscrossed the globe (though the earth had become so drably uniform, he observed, that "what was the good of going to Pekin[3] when it was just like Shrewsbury?"). In the last paragraph of the story, "The Machine Stops," Forster imagined this world coming to an end: "The whole city was broken like a honeycomb. An air-ship . . . crashed downwards, exploding as it went, rending gallery after gallery with its wings of steel."

Skyscraper and airplane: fragile containers for even-more-fragile flesh and   4 blood. Each an artificial shell of our own manufacture—or not quite of our own manufacture, since, strictly speaking, very few of us, as individuals, have any direct involvement in their creation. Each a capsule of recycled air, with windows sealed shut against the blue. Each an innovation that, in Forsterian terms, has made Pekin more and more like Shrewsbury. Each a honeycomb that traps us side by side with strangers. Each a rig that suspends us far above the ground, half-willing aerialists, and then whispers: *Trust me.* Each a machine that teaches us, in similar ways, how to be modern.

What keeps it up? What, that is to say, keeps *us* up? Perhaps one person in a thou-   5 sand really knows, understanding coolly why it is that the contraption doesn't plummet back to earth under our weight. For the rest of us, the precise functioning of wing and girder, the mathematical intricacies of gravitational thrust and counterthrust, remain life-long mysteries. Our animal selves, quite sensibly, would rather stick close to solid ground. But this is where we must steel ourselves to be something more than animals. We must summon up the will to trust—not so much in the metal armature beneath us as in the faceless experts who designed and built it, in the corporations that own and maintain it, in the armature of civilization and science. No wonder we sometimes get dizzy.

The cultural critic Marshall Berman, in selecting a title for his 1982 treatise on   6 the experience of modernity, borrowed a newly resonant phrase from Karl Marx: *All That Is Solid Melts Into Air.* "To be modern," he wrote, "is to find ourselves in an environment that promises us adventure, power, joy, growth, transformation of ourselves and the world—and, at the same time, that threatens to destroy everything we have, everything we know, everything we are." It is to ride atop a sky-

---

2. *E. M. Forster* (1879–1970): British novelist Edward Morgan Forster is also the author of *Howards End* (1908), *A Room with a View* (1910), and *A Passage to India* (1924).

3. *Pekin:* the preferred English spelling, in Forster's era, of the capital city of China. Today the preferred and most common spelling is Beijing; you may also encounter Peking.

scraper, to soar in an airplane. And both threatened us with such destruction, not just on that machine-bright morning in September, but long before.

Both sprang from the late nineteenth century, and from the American Middle 7 West (Louis Sullivan's Chicago, the Wright Brothers' Ohio[4])—a place where earth and sky were blank canvases waiting to be filled with movement and form. Yet both had deeper roots as well. In England in the 1780s, the decade in which the Montgolfiers took to the air in their balloons, and the young Wordsworth and Coleridge[5] sharpened their pens at grammar school, the Duke of Bedford owned an exceptionally large racehorse that one of his grooms named Skyscraper—the first recorded appearance of the word. (The mare finished first at the Epsom Derby in 1789.) In the years that followed, *skyscraper* was used to describe the uppermost sail on a ship's rigging (1794), a high hat or bonnet (1800), or simply a very tall person (1857). After crossing the Atlantic, it was used by American sportswriters as early as the 1860s to describe a towering fly ball. Like so many of the next century's most important words (*computer, rocket, network*), *skyscraper* jostled around indecisively for a while, hesitating between one meaning and another before settling into its ultimate niche. However they used the word, people were clearly grasping toward the sky, toward something up there that they could almost brush with their fingertips—and that they were determined to reach by one contrivance or another.

When the earliest buildings to be called skyscrapers appeared, in the 1870s and 8 1880s, they sprang into shape so suddenly as to seem born in a single piece. The pioneering architects of Chicago, one recent historian has written, "learned almost everything of importance that would be known a century later about how to build skyscrapers." Yet the skyscraper was not, as it seems to us now, a single unified invention, but rather many inventions knit into one.

First and foremost, of course, was the ability to produce cheap, high-quality 9 structural steel—the first truly revolutionary architectural innovation since the Romans invented the arch and the dome two millennia before. One nineteenth-century engineer couched this development in almost Darwinian terms: For the first time, he explained, tall buildings were designed as vertebrates instead of crustaceans. For the first time, their loads and stresses could be carried not by massive carapaces of masonry but by a web of slender struts and braces whose strength lay in its interconnectedness: a prototypical modern form, destined to be replicated in everything from computer chips to international airline routes. Louis Sullivan

---

4. *Wright Brothers' Ohio*: although their famous first flight was in Kitty Hawk, North Carolina, the Wright brothers lived and worked in Dayton, Ohio. *Louis Sullivan's Chicago*: American architect Louis Sullivan (1856–1924) was instrumental in creating many famous skyscrapers in Chicago.

5. *William Wordsworth* (1770–1850) and *Samuel Taylor Coleridge* (1772–1834): influential English Romantic poets. *Montgolfiers*: French brothers who invented the hot air balloon in 1783.

might have boasted of his buildings' pure functionalism, but in fact the skyscraper's exterior was merely its skin, its only function (besides shelter from the elements) to provide a kind of movie screen onto which the architect could project any embellishment he chose: rich Gothic traceries, Art Deco's silvery sheen, or, eventually, the stern theatrics of high modernism.

Still, if architects had had only steel to work with, the interiors of their sky- 10 scrapers would have just been little more than dark and dreary warrens. Office towers of ten and twenty stories required, for their basic functioning, a whole list of innovations that are now taken for granted, but that were still brand new in the second half of the nineteenth century: electric lights and central heating, passenger elevators and fire escapes, telephones and flush toilets. As fate had it, all of these appeared on the American scene at approximately the same time. And all of them, moreover, required a wholly new type of city to support them: one with reliable, centrally managed electric and gas companies, sewer systems, water mains, fire departments, elevator inspectors, telephone operators, trash collectors. Did the modern city give birth to the skyscraper, or vice versa? The answer, probably, is a bit of both.

Of all these varied accoutrements, none was more critical to the skyscraper's 11 development than the passenger elevator. At New York's Crystal Palace exposition in 1854, a Yonkers mechanic named Elisha Graves Otis[6] would periodically ascend high above the crowds on an open platform of wrought iron. As the machine creaked up to its zenith, the inventor gestured to an assistant, who cut through the hoisting rope with a hatchet. The spectators gasped in horror—but instead of plummeting to the ground, the elevator merely settled back into its ratcheted safety lock. "All safe, gentlemen, all safe," Otis announced.

Otis's words would become the constant refrain of the dawning era. In the nine- 12 teenth century, for the first time in human history, millions of ordinary people would be required to entrust their lives, on a daily basis, to technologies whose inner workings remained a mystery. They were a generation of pioneers, the men and women of New York and Chicago, no less than the settlers of the Great Plains. The odd thing, in retrospect, is how easily they seem to have taken the changes in stride. When the architect Bradford Gilbert, in 1888, topped off his Tower Building at eleven stories, many New York pedestrians avoided that block of Broadway, certain that the structure would topple in the first stiff breeze. But Gilbert, in an Otis-like show of confidence, moved his own office onto the uppermost floor; the

---

6. *Elisha Graves Otis* (1811–1861): inventor of the safety brake for elevators and founder of the Otis Elevator Company, the largest elevator company in the world. *Crystal Palace*: an iron-and-glass structure built to house the 1853 World's Fair, which showcased technological innovations from around the world.

building withstood a hurricane soon after, and before long was taken for granted. Barely two decades later, when the Metropolitan Life Building reached a record fifty stories, the only question was who would try for sixty. (It would be the retailing magnate Frank Woolworth, who began planning his skyscraper a few weeks after the Metropolitan tower opened.)

Even more remarkable, the mythology of the skyscraper was born full-fledged 13 with the building itself. Here is the earliest recorded appearance of the word in its contemporary sense, from an 1883 issue of *American Architect and Building News*: "This form of sky-scraper gives that peculiar refined, independent, self-contained, daring, bold, heaven-reaching, erratic, piratic, Quixotic, American thought." (Those were the days when even trade journals waxed Whitmanesque.)

A century earlier, Thomas Jefferson, proclaiming American exceptionalism in 14 his *Notes on Virginia*, cited the extraordinary size of native bears and elk, caverns and waterfalls. (He even vigorously defended American Indians against a French naturalist's insinuation that their "organs of generation" were smaller than average.) But the skyscraper rendered all of Jefferson's examples irrelevant. Here was the final proof of America's towering stature, in a tower raised not by God but by its citizens.

Before long, the race to scrape the sky lifted off the ground. And like the sky- 15 scraper's, the airplane's infancy was shortlived, its full maturity quick to arrive: Orville Wright would live to see the era of inflight movies. Strut and brace, spar and rib formed the bones of the plane as they did of the skyscraper, stiffening an outer shell designed to cut through hostile wind. And the airplane, too, would become a sort of capsule of human amenities, but to an even greater degree: a mobile life-support system, no less than a spaceship would be.

And yet, after nearly a century aloft, we have never learned to occupy planes as 16 comfortably as we do skyscrapers. Antoine de Saint-Exupéry,[7] in the 1930s, predicted that within a generation or two, the airplane would come to seem a perfectly commonplace thing, "an object as natural as a pebble polished by the waves." Instead, it still seems the very epitome of what is artificial and mechanical. Stepping aboard one, even the most habitual of flyers must exercise a small act of conscious will. The passenger never forgets that he is wagering his life on the journey, even if he knows that the odds in this type of roulette are relatively good.

Air travel is a unique experience in modern life, the sociologist Mark Gottdiener 17 recently wrote, "because, deep down inside us, it is a 'near death' experience. It is the most common way individuals surrender control and voluntarily place them-

---

7. *Antoine de Saint-Exupéry* (1900–1944): French writer and airplane pilot, author of *The Little Prince* (1943).

selves in harm's way in contemporary society. If they drive, they are also at risk, but they remain in control behind the wheel." Strapped into our seats, waiting on the runway, staring out the window at the stained frailty of the wing, we toy with fantasies of annihilation. We look at our fellow travelers and wonder what it would be like to face death alongside these strangers. A terribly intimate, terribly modern way to go: so close to one another in these well-lit rows, so far from family and home.

In a seminar for phobic flyers offered by American Airlines, participants spend   18
ten consecutive hours being lectured by pilots, flight attendants, mechanics, and psychologists, who repeat this phrase like a mantra: "Airplanes do not drop, dive, plummet, or fall." In doing so, they merely voice the silent chant of every airborne congregation. For flying requires an act of almost religious faith, the surrender of oneself, in absolute trust, to the wisdom and benevolent expertise of corporations, pilots, governments, engineers—the whole apparatus of modernity. In this setting, the smallest acts take on ritual significance: the pantomimed instructions of flight attendants, the dimming of lights, the serving of food. Airline meals, tiny and perfectly formed, are like the Japanese tea ceremony, in which gesture is more important than nourishment. In giving us food, the airline offers us a promise of sustenance; in eating, we accept. All of us know one or two stiff-necked dissenters who refuse to fly at all, and they irritate us more than their mild neurosis would warrant, as if they had renounced their citizenship in the commonwealth of flight.

If the skyscraper, with its crudely phallic thrust, is male, the airplane is female.   19
Entering, we pass into a place that promises—if rarely quite delivering—all the amenities of the womb: shelter, nourishment, warmth, dimness, sleep. The earliest flight attendants, in the 1920s, were men, but airlines quickly discovered that passengers preferred to be cared for by women, and before long they were openly competing with one another to provide the most beautiful and provocatively clad stewardesses. Erotic currents move among the passengers as well. Skyscrapers place us alongside strangers and demand that we work; airplanes seat us side by side and whisper idle fantasies of sex. This is the double face of modern alienation: the limitless pain of loneliness, the limitless promise of random encounters. Proximity, anonymity: the world of skyscrapers and airplanes is one in which terrorists stalk freely among their prey.

The architect of the World Trade Center, Minoru Yamasaki, was afraid of heights.   20
He once wrote that in a world of perfect freedom, he'd have created nothing but one-story buildings overlooking fields of flowers. He designed the Trade Center with narrow windows framed by vertical columns like prison bars, close enough together that he could steady himself against them when looking out. Instead of one-story buildings overlooking fields of flowers, he built gargantuan monoliths

overlooking a windswept plaza. Their scale was brutal, unsoftened by the slightest hint of stylishness. Only at a great distance did they impress, jutting like a double bowsprit from the prow of Manhattan, from the prow of America itself. Or, if you preferred, like a pair of middle fingers, raised against the hostile vastness of the Atlantic Ocean.

But to take in this view you had to stand far away: in Hoboken, or Hamburg, or   21
Kabul. (Or to observe the towers through a lens. Like so many twentieth-century creations, they seemed designed to be seen not in person but on film, as though the cinematic eye were the only one that mattered.) Standing at the base of the towers and looking up, the human observer had the sense mostly not of their height, but of their immense weight. They were two mountains of trapped kinetic energy, perpetually poised at the brink of release. The irony of architecture, all architecture, is that we create structures to shelter ourselves, yet in building them, we set ourselves at risk. The surest way to stay safe from fires, earthquakes, and bombs is never to go indoors. The surest way not to fall is to stay on the ground.

In *Anna Karenina*,[8] Levin is terrified by the birth of his first child, for he realizes   22
that he has brought into the world a new means for him to be hurt beyond all previous imagining. Tolstoy recognized that every act of creation has its shadow double, a coequal act of destruction. When Yamasaki created buildings on an unprecedented scale, he also created the potential for disaster on an unprecedented scale, a nightmare knit into every cubic inch of glass and steel. (The man who would eventually engineer their destruction understood this: he came from a family of builders.) They fascinated us, as airplanes do, because part of us always imagined them falling. It is the same part of us that loves our children because we can imagine them dying.

And when the towers did fall, we watched with the horror of witnesses to a   23
death half foreseen, in dreams and shadowy portents. They buckled, released their long-held burden, and wearily sank to earth.

The authors of the catastrophe—who can doubt it?—created something terrible   24
and permanent: an image that will stand for as long as any tower. In a thousand years, anyone who knows anything at all about us, the ancient Modern Americans, will probably know about the skyscraper and the airplane, and about the bright September morning that welded them together.

Eight days after the collapse, I stood on lower Broadway near where the sky-   25
scrapers had been. The destruction was all strangely contained behind chain-link fences and squads of stolid cops: all the familiar markers of a Situation Under Control. The mounded ruins poured out a thick column of white smoke, its innards

---

8. *Anna Karenina*: novel by Russian writer Leo Tolstoy published in installments during the 1870s.

glowing sickly yellow under the slanting rays of late-afternoon sun. It looked exactly as if the crater of a volcano had somehow opened up among the downtown office buildings, and now was being probed and monitored by businesslike teams of geologists and seismologists, lest it erupt again without warning. I was reminded of being atop Mount Etna,[9] and peering alongside other tourists into the gassy abyss of the caldera, looking fruitlessly for some deep-buried source of smoke and heat. Above everything, above the place where the towers had stood, a helicopter whirred, miraculously suspended, riding on a column of newly liberated air.

9. *Mount Etna*: a large active volcano in Italy.

READING CLOSELY

1. When and where did the earliest skyscrapers appear in America? What conditions, social and otherwise, were necessary to bring them about?

2. Why was the invention of the elevator so important to the development of the modern skyscraper? Why, when exhibiting it, did the inventor cut the hoisting rope and declare, "All safe, gentlemen. All safe" (11)?

3. Why, according to Adam Goodheart, does so much modern technology require an act of faith and trust from the ordinary user? How are airplanes unique in this regard (17)?

4. How and why was America's faith in the machine betrayed on September 11, 2001? In what ways, according to Goodheart, was that event and the ensuing destruction "fatal, fated: perhaps even long foreseen" (2)?

5. What is the significance of the fact that the "engineer" of the 9/11 catastrophe came from a family of builders (22)?

6. Does Goodheart convince you that his two subjects are truly comparable? Why or why not?

STRATEGIES AND STRUCTURES

1. On what basis does Goodheart COMPARE the skyscraper and the airplane in paragraph 2? In paragraphs 4, 15, and 22?

2. What is Goodheart's larger purpose in comparing his two subjects—to explain what caused 9/11? To DEFINE "modernity" (18)? Both? Something else? Explain.

3. On what basis does Goodheart compare the architecture of modern buildings with that of computer chips and airplane routes (9)? Is this a firm basis of comparison in your opinion? Why or why not?

4. To organize his essay, does Goodheart use primarily the subject-by-subject method or the point-by-point method? That is, does he make most of his points about the skyscraper first, and then about the airplane; or does he go point by point from one subject to the other? Why do you think he uses the method he does?

5. *Other Methods.* Goodheart's comparison is also a CAUSE-AND-EFFECT ANALYSIS. What are some of the causes and effects he mentions? In his view, what will be the most lasting effect of 9/11?

THINKING ABOUT LANGUAGE

1. Why does Goodheart ALLUDE to the description of an airship in E. M. Forster's short story, "The Machine Stops" (3)?

2. How does Goodheart's capsule history of the word *skyscraper* contribute to the broader history lesson offered by his essay?

3. One meaning of *armature* is "framework for a sculpture." According to Goodheart, what does this kind of "metal armature" have in common with "the armature of civilization and science" (5)?

4. What's the difference between a "contraption" (5) and a machine? Why does Goodheart use the word here?

5. What are the implications of "machine-bright morning" in paragraph 6 and "welded" in paragraph 24?

FOR WRITING

1. In a paragraph or two, compare and contrast two images, one that comes to mind when you think of 9/11 and one that comes to mind when you think of another catastrophe, war, or natural disaster.

2. Write an essay comparing the technology and spirit of an old-fashioned building, machine, car, boat, factory, business, village, or town with that of a more modern equivalent. For example, you might compare a country store, a typewriter, or a canoe with a shopping mall, a laptop, or a Jet Ski.

DAVID SEDARIS

Remembering My Childhood
on the Continent of Africa

*David Sedaris (b. 1956) made a name for himself as an elf in "Santaland," the story
about working with the Santas at Macy's he told on National Public Radio's* Morning
Edition *in 1992. His hilarious autobiographical tales have been an NPR staple ever
since, and his numerous book-length collections, from* Barrel Fever *(1994) to* When
You Are Engulfed in Flames *(2008), have all been best-sellers. In 2001 Sedaris won
the Thurber Prize for American Humor and was named "Humorist of the Year" by*
Time *magazine.*

*Lopsided comparisons have always been a rich source of comedy. In "Remembering
My Childhood on the Continent of Africa," taken from his collection* Me Talk Pretty
One Day *(2000), Sedaris juxtaposes his own "unspeakably dull" childhood in
Raleigh, North Carolina, with that of his partner, Hugh Hamrick, a diplomat's son who
grew up in Africa.*

WHEN HUGH WAS IN THE FIFTH GRADE, his class took a field trip to an   1
Ethiopian slaughterhouse. He was living in Addis Ababa at the time, and the
slaughterhouse was chosen because, he says, "it was convenient."

This was a school system in which the matter of proximity outweighed such   2
petty concerns as what may or may not be appropriate for a busload of eleven-year-
olds. "What?" I asked. "Were there no autopsies scheduled at the local morgue?
Was the federal prison just a bit too far out of the way?"

Hugh defends his former school, saying, "Well, isn't that the whole point of a   3
field trip? To see something new?"

"Technically yes, but . . ."   4

"All right then," he says. "So we saw some new things."   5

One of his field trips was literally a trip to a field where the class watched a   6
wrinkled man fill his mouth with rotten goat meat and feed it to a pack of waiting
hyenas. On another occasion they were taken to examine the bloodied bedroom
curtains hanging in the palace of the former dictator. There were tamer trips, to
textile factories and sugar refineries, but my favorite is always the slaughterhouse.
It wasn't a big company, just a small rural enterprise run by a couple of brothers
operating out of a low-ceilinged concrete building. Following a brief lecture on the
importance of proper sanitation, a small white piglet was herded into the room, its
dainty hooves clicking against the concrete floor. The class gathered in a circle to
get a better look at the animal, who seemed delighted with the attention he was

getting. He turned from face to face and was looking up at Hugh when one of the brothers drew a pistol from his back pocket, held it against the animal's temple, and shot the piglet, execution-style. Blood spattered, frightened children wept, and the man with the gun offered the teacher and bus driver some meat from a freshly slaughtered goat.

When I'm told such stories, it's all I can do to hold back my feelings of jealousy. 7 An Ethiopian slaughterhouse. Some people have all the luck. When I was in elementary school, the best we ever got was a trip to Old Salem or Colonial Williamsburg, one of those preserved brick villages where time supposedly stands still and someone earns his living as a town crier. There was always a blacksmith, a group of wandering patriots, and a collection of bonneted women hawking corn bread or gingersnaps made "the ol'-fashioned way." Every now and then you might come across a doer of bad deeds serving time in the stocks, but that was generally as exciting as it got.

Certain events are parallel, but compared with Hugh's, my childhood was 8 unspeakably dull. When I was seven years old, my family moved to North Carolina. When he was seven years old, Hugh's family moved to the Congo. We had a collie and a house cat. They had a monkey and two horses named Charlie Brown and Satan. I threw stones at stop signs. Hugh threw stones at crocodiles. The verbs are the same, but he definitely wins the prize when it comes to nouns and objects. An eventful day for my mother might have involved a trip to the dry cleaner or a conversation with the potato-chip deliveryman. Asked one ordinary Congo afternoon what she'd done with her day, Hugh's mother answered that she and a fellow member of the Ladies' Club had visited a leper colony on the outskirts of Kinshasa. No reason was given for the expedition, though chances are she was staking it out for a future field trip.

Due to his upbringing, Hugh sits through inane movies never realizing that 9 they're often based on inane television shows. There were no poker-faced sitcom martians in his part of Africa, no oil-rich hillbillies or aproned brides trying to wean themselves from the practice of witchcraft.[1] From time to time a movie would arrive packed in a dented canister, the film scratched and faded from its slow trip around the world. The theater consisted of a few dozen folding chairs arranged before a bedsheet or the blank wall of a vacant hangar out near the airstrip. Occasionally a man would sell warm soft drinks out of a cardboard box, but that was it in terms of concessions.

When I was young, I went to the theater at the nearby shopping center and 10 watched a movie about a talking Volkswagen. I believe the little car had a taste for

---

1. *Martians . . . practice of witchcraft*: references to *My Favorite Martian, The Beverly Hillbillies*, and *Bewitched*, popular U.S. TV shows in the 1960s.

mischief but I can't be certain, as both the movie and the afternoon proved unre-markable and have faded from my memory. Hugh saw the same movie a few years after it was released. His family had left the Congo by this time and were living in Ethiopia. Like me, Hugh saw the movie by himself on a weekend afternoon. Unlike me, he left the theater two hours later, to find a dead man hanging from a tele-phone pole at the far end of the unpaved parking lot. None of the people who'd seen the movie seemed to care about the dead man. They stared at him for a moment or two and then headed home, saying they'd never seen anything as crazy as that talking Volkswagen. His father was late picking him up, so Hugh just stood there for an hour, watching the dead man dangle and turn in the breeze. The death was not reported in the newspaper, and when Hugh related the story to his friends, they said, "You saw the movie about the talking car?"

I could have done without the flies and the primitive theaters, but I wouldn't have minded growing up with a houseful of servants. In North Carolina it wasn't unusual to have a once-a-week maid, but Hugh's family had houseboys, a word that never fails to charge my imagination. They had cooks and drivers, and guards who occupied a gatehouse, armed with machetes. Seeing as I had regularly petitioned my parents for an electric fence, the business with the guards strikes me as the last word in quiet sophistication. Having protection suggests that you are important. Having that protection paid for by the government is even better, as it suggests your safety is of interest to someone other than yourself.

Hugh's father was a career officer with the U.S. State Department, and every morning a black sedan carried him off to the embassy. I'm told it's not as glamorous as it sounds, but in terms of fun for the entire family, I'm fairly confident that it beats the sack race at the annual IBM picnic. By the age of three, Hugh was already carrying a diplomatic passport. The rules that applied to others did not apply to him. No tickets, no arrests, no luggage search: he was officially licensed to act like a brat. Being an American, it was expected of him, and who was he to deny the world an occasional tantrum?

They weren't rich, but what Hugh's family lacked financially they more than made up for with the sort of exoticism that works wonders at cocktail parties, lead-ing always to the remark "That sounds fascinating." It's a compliment one rarely receives when describing an adolescence spent drinking Icees at the North Hills Mall. No fifteen-foot python ever wandered onto my school's basketball court. I begged, I prayed nightly, but it just never happened. Neither did I get to witness a military coup in which forces sympathetic to the colonel arrived late at night to assas-sinate my next-door neighbor. Hugh had been at the Addis Ababa teen club when the electricity was cut off and soldiers arrived to evacuate the building. He and his friends had to hide in the back of a jeep and cover themselves with blankets during the ride home. It's something that sticks in his mind for one reason or another.

Among my personal highlights is the memory of having my picture taken with   14
Uncle Paul, the legally blind host of a Raleigh children's television show. Among
Hugh's is the memory of having his picture taken with Buzz Aldrin on the last leg
of the astronaut's world tour. The man who had walked on the moon placed his
hand on Hugh's shoulder and offered to sign his autograph book. The man who led
Wake County schoolchildren in afternoon song turned at the sound of my voice
and asked, "So what's your name, princess?"

When I was fourteen years old, I was sent to spend ten days with my maternal   15
grandmother in western New York State. She was a small and private woman
named Billie, and though she never came right out and asked, I had the distinct
impression she had no idea who I was. It was the way she looked at me, squinting
through her glasses while chewing on her lower lip. That, coupled with the fact
that she never once called me by name. "Oh," she'd say, "are you still here?" She
was just beginning her long struggle with Alzheimer's disease, and each time I
entered the room, I felt the need to reintroduce myself and set her at ease. "Hi, it's
me. Sharon's boy, David. I was just in the kitchen admiring your collection of
ceramic toads." Aside from a few trips to summer camp, this was the longest I'd
ever been away from home, and I like to think I was toughened by the experience.

About the same time I was frightening my grandmother, Hugh and his family   16
were packing their belongings for a move to Somalia. There were no English-
speaking schools in Mogadishu, so, after a few months spent lying around the family compound with his pet monkey, Hugh was sent back to Ethiopia to live with a
beer enthusiast his father had met at a cocktail party. Mr. Hoyt installed security
systems in foreign embassies. He and his family gave Hugh a room. They invited
him to join them at the table, but that was as far as they extended themselves. No
one ever asked him when his birthday was, so when the day came, he kept it to
himself. There was no telephone service between Ethiopia and Somalia, and letters
to his parents were sent to Washington and then forwarded on to Mogadishu,
meaning that his news was more than a month old by the time they got it. I suppose it wasn't much different than living as a foreign-exchange student. Young people do it all the time, but to me it sounds awful. The Hoyts had two sons about
Hugh's age who were always saying things like "Hey that's *our* sofa you're sitting on"
and "Hands off that ornamental stein. It doesn't belong to you."

He'd been living with these people for a year when he overheard Mr. Hoyt tell a   17
friend that he and his family would soon be moving to Munich, Germany, the beer
capital of the world.

"And that worried me," Hugh said, "because it meant I'd have to find some other   18
place to live."

Where I come from, finding shelter is a problem the average teenager might   19
confidently leave to his parents. It was just something that came with having a

mom and a dad. Worried that he might be sent to live with his grandparents in Kentucky, Hugh turned to the school's guidance counselor, who knew of a family whose son had recently left for college. And so he spent another year living with strangers and not mentioning his birthday. While I wouldn't have wanted to do it myself, I can't help but envy the sense of fortitude he gained from the experience. After graduating from college, he moved to France knowing only the phrase "Do you speak French?"—a question guaranteed to get you nowhere unless you also speak the language.

While living in Africa, Hugh and his family took frequent vacations, often in the   20 company of their monkey. The Nairobi Hilton, some suite of high-ceilinged rooms in Cairo or Khartoum: these are the places his people recall when gathered at a common table. "Was that the summer we spent in Beirut or, no, I'm thinking of the time we sailed from Cyprus and took the *Orient Express* to Istanbul."

Theirs was the life I dreamt about during my vacations in eastern North Car-   21 olina. Hugh's family was hobnobbing with chiefs and sultans while I ate hush puppies at the Sanitary Fish Market in Morehead City, a beach towel wrapped like a hijab around my head.[2] Someone unknown to me was very likely standing in a muddy ditch and dreaming of an evening spent sitting in a clean family restaurant, drinking iced tea and working his way through an extra-large seaman's platter, but that did not concern me, as it meant I should have been happy with what I had. Rather than surrender to my bitterness, I have learned to take satisfaction in the life that Hugh has led. His stories have, over time, become my own. I say this with no trace of a kumbaya.[3] There is no spiritual symbiosis; I'm just a petty thief who lifts his memories the same way I'll take a handful of change left on his dresser. When my own experiences fall short of the mark, I just go out and spend some of his. It is with pleasure that I sometimes recall the dead man's purpled face or the report of the handgun ringing in my ears as I studied the blood pooling beneath the dead white piglet. On the way back from the slaughterhouse, we stopped for Cokes in the village of Mojo, where the gas-station owner had arranged a few tables and chairs beneath a dying canopy of vines. It was late afternoon by the time we returned to school, where a second bus carried me to the foot of Coffeeboard Road. Once there, I walked through a grove of eucalyptus trees and alongside a bald pasture of starving cattle, past the guard napping in his gatehouse, and into the waiting arms of my monkey.

2. *Hijab*: a veil worn by Muslim women. *Hush puppies*: small, deep-fried balls of dough.

3. *Kumbaya*: the title and refrain of an African American folk song that originated as a spiritual sung by slaves in the Gullah-speaking Sea Islands of Georgia and South Carolina. The Gullah "kumbaya" means "come by here" in standard English. The song was a popular hit in the 1960s and was associated with the civil rights movement. Currently it is sung by many youth organizations, and the word has come to be associated with unity and closeness.

READING CLOSELY

1. As children in school, both David Sedaris and Hugh took occasional field trips. What is Sedaris's point in comparing their experiences? Broadly speaking, how do they compare?

2. Why did Sedaris find the movie about a talking Volkswagen to be "unremarkable" (10)? How did Hugh react to it, and why was his experience so different?

3. Instead of surrendering to his "bitterness," Sedaris has learned "to take satisfaction" from Hugh's account of his childhood (21). Why does Sedaris claim to be bitter, and how seriously are we supposed to take his claim?

4. Besides satisfaction and loose change, what else has Sedaris learned to "take" from Hugh's past life?

5. Whose childhood would you prefer to remember having lived, Sedaris's or Hugh's? Why?

STRATEGIES AND STRUCTURES

1. In comparing the early lives of himself and his partner, Sedaris emphasizes the differences. On what basis does he compare their experiences nevertheless? What did their childhoods have in common?

2. In paragraph 8, Sedaris uses the point-by-point method to organize his comparison. What would have been the result if he had kept on alternating like this between his two subjects throughout the rest of the essay? Explain.

3. How sufficient do you find Sedaris's main points of comparison for explaining his jealousy of Hugh's childhood (7)? How and how well do they prepare us for the ending, in which Sedaris takes over his friend's memories?

4. *Other Methods.* Sedaris's comparison includes many elements of personal NARRATIVE. What are some of them? (Cite specific examples from the text.) How would the essay be different without any narrative?

THINKING ABOUT LANGUAGE

1. His life and Hugh's shared the same verbs, says Sedaris, but different nouns and objects (8). What does Sedaris mean by this, and why is he comparing the lives of two boys to the grammatical parts of speech?

2. Among the "personal highlights" of his childhood, says Sedaris, is "the memory of having my picture taken with Uncle Paul, the legally blind host of a Raleigh children's television show" (14). How is Sedaris using IRONY here?

3. A "hijab" is a veil (21). What sort of hijab does Sedaris wear in the Sanitary Fish Market in Morehead City?

4. Sedaris describes himself as a "petty thief" (21). What is he stealing in this essay, and what has caused him to sink to this level?

For Writing

1. Ask a friend or family member to write down his or her recollections of an important event that you have both experienced. You do the same. Then, in a paragraph or so, compare and contrast the two versions.

2. In an essay, compare your childhood with that of someone whose early experience was very different from your own. Your counterpart can be someone you know personally or someone you don't, as long as you're familiar with details of his or her childhood.

JAMIE GULLEN

Self-Discovery and the Danish Way of Life

Jamie Gullen is a native of New York City. While an undergraduate at Cornell University, she spent several months in Copenhagen as a participant in the Danish Institute for Study Abroad (DIS). At first, Gullen expected her host country to be "culturally similar" to the one she had left behind. Comparing the two cultures during her months abroad, however, Gullen soon realized how much she had to learn—about herself as well as her hosts. "Self-Discovery and the Danish Way of Life" is the result of that comparative process. It won a prize in the DIS student essay contest in the spring of 2006.

As my final weeks in Copenhagen began drawing to a close, I was surprised 1 to find myself waiting patiently at a red light even though there were no cars or bikes in the near vicinity. As a New York City native, this observation was cause for a significant pause and some serious self-reflection. My thoughts settled on my first month in Copenhagen when I was having a discussion with a fellow DIS student. She was saying she had expected to feel some significant change in who she was from being abroad, but so far she felt like the same person she had always been. This got me thinking about whether or not I had experienced a significant change of self from being abroad in a culture totally different from the one in which I grew up. At that time, I did not have a good response to that question, but as I stood waiting for the green light on a spring night in Copenhagen, I found I had stumbled upon some important insights.

The answer I came to is that the very core of who I am and the things that matter 2 most to me have remained very much the same. But rather than viewing this in a negative light as some kind of stagnation or lack of personal growth, I realized it was exactly the opposite. Study abroad doesn't change who you are; it helps you discover who you are. By removing the immediate cultural environment in which I was immersed from the day I was born, I was able to discern which values and habits were really central to who I am as a person and which were merely the results of the influences of my family, friends, school, city, country, and cultural surroundings.

Before I came to Denmark, I expected it to be fairly culturally similar to the 3 United States. It is a democratic Western country where English is widely spoken and where American culture pervades television and movies, and the Danish government is very closely aligned with the American government. I was shocked to find out that the Danish way of life couldn't be more different from what I was expecting. The biggest difference I experienced originates with the Danish word *hygge*. This word has no direct translation into English, and when I asked a Danish person to define it for me, it took her five minutes just to begin to touch upon what the word signifies. That is because it is much more than a word; it is a way of life. What she told me was that *hygge* is most closely translated as the English word *cozy* and that it is experienced socially. It is a closeness and intimacy between friends, enjoyment of food and wine; it is dinner that lasts for four hours because of good conversation; and it is décor with dim lighting and candles everywhere. While I have experienced *hygge* during my stay in Denmark both with Danes and my fellow DIS students, it took some time for me to process the true significance of the word.

The turning point, in my understanding of both *hygge* and myself, was on my   4 program's short study tour in western Denmark. As I discussed everything from Danish politics to local Danish soccer teams with some natives in the small town of Kolding, the conversation casually turned to differences between the Danish and the American way of life. I was noting that many Danish people I have met view their careers as a way to provide for themselves financially and to engage in fields that interest them intellectually, but their conception of self-worth is not tied up in the prestige of their jobs or the number of hours worked each week or the amount of the paycheck they bring home in comparison to their peers. It was through this observation that I realized the true importance of *hygge*; it recognizes the human-ness of life and the individuality of the person. It is an appreciation of what really matters: friends, family, love, intimacy, and happiness.

Growing up, I lived in a fast-paced city, attended a rigorous high school and col-   5 lege, was surrounded by career-driven highly motivated peers, and was encouraged by my parents to put academics first. Coming to Denmark and experiencing *hygge* and the Danish way of life and learning served as a jolt to the immediate cultural world that had shaped me. I was forced to consider life from another angle. What I found is that deep down I have always held the *hygge* values to be of importance, and I have always wanted to be engaged in helping other people find a happy and peaceful way of life. It is just easier now to see how my external cultural eviron-ment has impacted and shaped these values and my sense of DIS, Danish, and my international self.

When I arrive home in New York City, it will no doubt take very little time for   6 me to join in with the throngs of jaywalkers marching defiantly across Madison Avenue, but what I have learned from being abroad in Denmark about who I am and what matters most to me will be knowledge that stays with me forever.

READING CLOSELY

1. What was the biggest difference between Danish and American culture that Jamie Gullen experienced while studying abroad in Denmark?

2. According to Gullen, how do the Danes approach their jobs and careers as compared with their American counterparts?

3. Gullen says that "study abroad doesn't change who you are" (2). What does it do, in her view? How?

4. What important lesson did Gullen learn from her period of study abroad?

STRATEGIES AND STRUCTURES

1. How does Gullen use the NARRATIVE device of waiting for a traffic light to help structure her entire essay?

2. In her introduction, Gullen says she "stumbled upon some important insights" as an American studying in Denmark (1). Gullen does not specify what those insights are, however, until after she compares the two countries in the main body of her essay. Should she have done so earlier? Why or why not?

3. How did the act of making comparisons lead Gullen to a "turning point" in her understanding of both her host country and herself (4)? Does her comparison emphasize the similarities between the two cultures, or their differences, or both? Explain.

4. Gullen sums up what she learned from her Danish experience in paragraph 5. Why doesn't she end there? What does paragraph 6 add to her comparison?

5. *Other Methods.* The "biggest difference" between Denmark and America that she encountered during her study abroad, says Gullen, can be summed up in the Danish word *hygge* (3). How does Gullen use an extended DEFINITION of this term to support her comparison of the two countries?

THINKING ABOUT LANGUAGE

1. The Danes, says Gullen, usually translate *hygge* as the English word *cozy* (3). Judging from Gullen's definition of the term, how would you translate it?

2. What are the CONNOTATIONS of "stumbled" (1) and "natives" (4)?

3. A "turning point" (4) implies an irreversible change. What, if anything, is irreversible about Gullen's experience as a student in Denmark?

FOR WRITING

1. Write a paragraph DEFINING what you see as a key difference between the culture of mainstream America and that of some other country or group.

2. Think of another country you would like to visit (or have already visited). Write an essay that compares that culture and your own. What do you expect (or what did you find) to be the main similarities and differences between them?

LIAM SHAKESPEARE

nnet 130

William Shakespeare (1554–1616) is not only English literature's greatest dramatist but also one of its greatest poets. Plays performed on the Elizabethan stage were rich with poetry for both practical reasons (there were few elaborate sets or special effects, so a play's setting had to be conjured almost entirely through words) and reasons of convention (audiences expected poetry, not realistic dialogue). Shakespeare's reputation as a great poet would be assured even if he had written nothing but dramas. In 1592, however, an outbreak of plague led authorities to close the theaters for two years, and the playwright turned to the composition of verse narratives. In 1609 the first edition of Shakespeare's sonnets was published. These sonnets were immediately recognized—and have been regarded ever since—as supreme expressions of the sonnet form. Sonnet 130 is about two ways of drawing comparisons.

My mistress' eyes are nothing like the sun;   1
Coral is far more red, than her lips red:
If snow be white, why then her breasts are dun;
If hairs be wires, black wires grow on her head.
I have seen roses damasked, red and white,   5
But no such roses see I in her cheeks;
And in some perfumes is there more delight
Than in the breath that from my mistress reeks.
I love to hear her speak, yet well I know
That music hath a far more pleasing sound: 10
I grant I never saw a goddess go,
My mistress, when she walks, treads on the ground:
And yet by heaven, I think my love as rare,
As any she belied with false compare.

READING CLOSELY

1. The speaker of Shakespeare's poem can find no similarities between the brightness of his lady's eyes and that of the sun, or the color of her cheeks and the pink (damask), white, or red of the rose. Why not?

2. What kind of lover *would* make such comparisons?

3. What is Shakespeare's speaker assuming about the character of his "mistress" and what will please her (1)? Explain.

STRATEGIES AND STRUCTURES

1. Who, do you suppose, is the intended AUDIENCE for Shakespeare's love poem: a particular lady, ladies in general, or readers of traditional love poetry, whether male or female? Some combination of these? Why do you think so?

2. Shakespeare's poem emphasizes the differences between the lady and the lovely things to which he COMPARES her. What is his purpose in avoiding the extravagant praise found in so many love poems of the period?

3. The English (or Shakespearean) sonnet consists of three quatrains followed by a couplet. Each group of four lines presents a different aspect of a subject, and the final two lines tie the whole together in some way. If the first four lines of Sonnet 130 deal with various sights, what is compared in lines 5–8? Lines 9–12?

4. How (and how well) do the final two lines of Shakespeare's poem resolve the tension generated by the rest of the comparison? Explain.

5. *Other Methods.* The woman in Sonnet 130 appears in many other Shakespearean sonnets, where she is known as "the dark lady." How does the DESCRIPTION of her in this poem fit this general characterization?

THINKING ABOUT LANGUAGE

1. Besides signifying general drabness, "dun" (3) is a mousey brown color. Is Shakespeare saying that the lady's skin is this color, or is he countering one HYPERBOLE with another? Explain.

2. To the reader of Shakespeare's day, "wires" (4) would have called to mind fine threads of beaten gold used in jewelry or embroidery. What is supposed to be shocking here is the color of the lady's hair. Why?

3. The meaning of "reeks" has changed since Shakespeare's time. Originally, the word meant "to emit smoke" rather than "to stink." How does this meaning fit in with Shakespeare's DESCRIPTION, especially in line 12, of the lady as a down-to-earth creature?

FOR WRITING

1. In line 14, "any she" may mean "any woman." With this in mind, translate the last two lines of Shakespeare's poem into modern English.

2. Write a paragraph summarizing the main points of comparison that Shakespeare makes in Sonnet 130.

CHAPTER 8

Classification

> You can divide your whole life into two basic categories. You're either
> staying in or going out. —JERRY SEINFELD, *Seinlanguage*

Let's say you live near the coast of Florida or Louisiana or the Carolinas, and you have just survived a hurricane. The power is back on; so is the water. The roof, however, is not. What kind of roof did you have? Which kinds held up well in the storm? What kind should you put back on your house? These are all questions of CLASSIFICATION.

Defining Classification:
Breaking a Subject into Categories

When you DESCRIBE something, you say what its characteristics are: "My old roof was a tasteful gray with green ridge caps." Classification is concerned with characteristics, too: "This is not my roof in your front yard. This is a metal roof, the kind they have across the lake. My roof was tile." When you classify something (a roof, an aquatic mammal, someone's personality), however, you say what category it belongs to—metal, asphalt, tile; dolphin, manatee, whale; introverted, extroverted —based on the characteristics of each category. There are basically two ways to classify.

When we classify individuals, we sort them into groups: this dog is a hound, that one is a terrier. When we classify groups—dogs, bicycles—we divide them into subgroups—hounds, terriers, retrievers; street bikes, mountain bikes, racing bikes. In this chapter, we will learn what constitutes a category (or significant group), how to devise a valid classification system, and how to use that system to construct an essay. Throughout the chapter, we will use the term *classification* to refer to both sorting and dividing, since, in either case, we are always going to be organizing a subject into categories.

Why Do We Classify Things?

We classify things in order to choose the kinds that best meet our needs. The hurricane was a direct hit, and neither tile nor asphalt roofs stood up well. What other kinds are there, and which kind is most likely to survive the next high wind?

Choosing among similar kinds of objects or ideas is only one reason for using classification in our thinking and writing, however. We classify people and things for many purposes: to evaluate (good dog, bad dog); to determine causes (mechanical failure, weather, or pilot error?); to conduct experiments (test group, control group), and to measure results (winners, losers, and runners-up).

We also classify in order to make sense of the world, grouping individuals according to the common traits that tell us the most about them. Consider the duckbill platypus. Even though it has a bill and lays eggs, biologists classify the platypus as a mammal with bird-like characteristics rather than a bird with mammalian ones. Why?

It's not simply that the platypus has mostly mammalian traits, such as hair, milk glands, and a neocortex region in the brain. Among all living mammals, only the platypus and the spiny anteater retain a few of the bird-like characteristics once common to many mammals. That these creatures are in a class by themselves tells us that, far from being a bird, the platypus simply branched off early from the family tree, before other mammals lost their bird-like traits in the course of evolution.

So if you're ever inclined to think of classification systems as mere catalogues, remember the platypus. By accurately classifying this strange mammal and other apparent anomalies, we can discover not only where each one belongs in the scheme of things, we can learn more about the basis of the natural order itself.

Composing a Classification Essay

Classification is a way of ordering the world and of organizing a piece of writing, whether a list, an essay, or even a whole book. In this chapter we will focus on how to use classification to organize an essay.

Whether you are writing about animals, people, machines, movies, or political movements, the first step in composing a classification essay is to divide your subject into appropriate categories. Those categories will be determined by the various attributes of your subject, of course; but they will also depend on your PRINCIPLE OF CLASSIFICATION—the basis on which you are classifying your subject. Dogs, for example, can be classified on the basis of breed, size, or some other principle. If you're classifying dogs by size, your categories might be small, medium, and large. But if breed is your principle of classification, then your categories would be golden retriever, greyhound, poodle, Irish setter, and so on.

Thinking about Purpose and Audience

In order to classify anything accurately, you have to examine all its important attributes. The specific traits you focus on and the categories you divide your subject into, however, will be determined largely by your purpose and audience. Consider the example of the roof that blew off in a hurricane. If your purpose is to determine—and write an article for your neighborhood newsletter explaining—what kind of roof will stay on best in the next hurricane, you're going to look closely at such traits as weight and wind resistance. And you are going to pay less attention to other traits, such as color or energy efficiency or even cost, that you might consider more closely if you had a different purpose in mind.

Once you've determined the kind of roof that has the highest wind rating, you probably are not going to have a hard time convincing these readers (many of whom also lost their roofs) that this is the kind to buy. They may expect you to prove that the kind you are recommending does in fact have the characteristics you claim for it (superior resistance to wind), but they are not likely to question the importance of those characteristics or the validity of focusing on them in your article. However, since your audience of homeowners may not be experts in roofing materials, you'll want to make sure you define any technical terms and use language they'll be familiar with. You won't always be able to assume your readers will appreciate the way you choose to classify a subject. So be prepared to explain why your audience should accept the criteria you use to classify your subject and the weight you place on particular attributes.

Generating Ideas: Considering What Categories There Are

There are many techniques—CLUSTERING, LOOPING, LISTING, and more—that can help you generate ideas. Once you have a subject in mind and a reason for classifying it, you will need to consider what categories there are and choose the ones that best suit your purpose and audience. Let's say your purpose is to evaluate different kinds of movies. Movies can be classified by genre—drama, comedy, romance, horror, thriller, musical. This might be a good classification system to use if you are analyzing movies for a film course. For the purpose of reviewing movies for a campus audience, however, a different set of categories would be more appropriate.

Let's say you are reviewing movies in the school newspaper. In this case, your principle of classification would be their quality, and you would divide them into, say, five categories: "must see," "excellent," "good," "mediocre," and "to be avoided at all costs." If you were reviewing some of those same movies for a parenting magazine, however, you might use different categories: "good for all ages," "pre-school," "six and up," and "not suitable for children."

When you're coming up with categories for a classification essay, then, make sure your categories are appropriate to your purpose and audience.

Organizing and Drafting a Classification Essay

The backbone of a classification essay is the classification system you create by dividing your subject into appropriate categories. Once you have a classification system in mind, you need to determine exactly how many categories to use. And you'll want to make sure that your categories are inclusive but don't overlap—and that they deal with significant aspects of your subject that are directly relevant to the point you're making. Be sure to state that point clearly, perhaps in a thesis statement. Also think about other methods of development you might want to use in addition to classification. The tips on p. 310 can help you get started.

ORGANIZING A CLASSIFICATION ESSAY

In the opening paragraphs of your essay, tell the reader what you're classifying and why, and explain your classification system, because the rest of your essay will be organized around that system. If you were writing an essay classifying bicycles, for example, something like this might make a good introduction:

> If you are buying or renting a bicycle, you need to know which features to look for in order to meet your needs. Bikes can best be divided into the following categories: mountain bikes, racing bikes, messenger bikes, touring bikes, and stunt bikes. If you understand these six basic types and the differences among them, you can make an informed decision, whether you're choosing a bicycle for a lifetime or just for the afternoon.

Not only does an introduction like this tell the reader what you're classifying and why, it provides a solid outline for organizing the rest of the essay.

Typically, the body of a classification essay is devoted to a point-by-point discussion of each of the categories that make up your classification system. Thus if you are

TIPS AND TEMPLATES FOR DRAFTING

When you begin to draft a classification essay, you need to identify your subject and explain the basis on which you're classifying it. These moves are fundamental to any classification. See how Deborah Tannen makes such moves in the beginning of her essay in this chapter:

> Unfortunately, men and women often have different ideas about what's appropriate, different ways of speaking. . . . Here [are] the biggest areas of miscommunication.
> —DEBORAH TANNEN, "But What Do You Mean?"

Tannen identifies her subject ("areas of miscommunication") and explains the basis on which she's classifying them (differences between men and women). Here is one more example from this chapter:

> Language is the tool of my trade. And I use them all—all the Englishes I grew up with. —AMY TAN, "Mother Tongue"

The following templates can help you make some of these basic moves in your own writing. But don't take these as formulas where you just have to fill in the blanks. There are no easy formulas for good writing, but these templates can serve as starting points.

▶ X can be classified on the basis of _____.

▶ Classified on the basis of _____, some of the most common types of X are _____, _____, and _____.

▶ X can be divided into two basic types, _____ or _____.

▶ Experts in the field typically divide X into _____, _____, and _____.

▶ Some other, less common types of X are _____, _____, and _____.

▶ This particular X clearly belongs in the _____ categeory, since it is _____, _____, and _____.

▶ _____, _____, and _____ are examples of this type of X.

▶ By classifying X in this way, we can see _____.

classifying bicycles into mountain bikes, racing bikes, messenger bikes, touring bikes, and stunt bikes, you would spend a paragraph, or at least several sentences, explaining the most important characteristics of each type. Depending upon the complexity of your subject, there will be more or fewer categories to explain; but remember that you must have at least two categories—vertebrates and invertebrates, good movies and bad movies—if you are to have a viable classification system.

Once you've laid out, in some detail, the categories that make up your classification system, remind the reader what your principle of classification is, and what point you are making by classifying your subject this way. The point of classifying bicycles by function, for example, is to inform the reader what categories of bicycles exist and which type is best suited to the reader's needs—climbing mountains, racing, delivering packages, doing tricks, or just cruising around.

STATING YOUR POINT

Classification isn't an end in itself, but a way of relating objects and ideas to each other within an orderly framework. So when you compose a classification essay, ask yourself not only what categories your subject can be divided into, but also what you can learn about that subject by classifying it in that way. Then tell the reader in a THESIS STATEMENT what your main point is and why you're dividing up your subject as you do. Usually, you'll want to state your main point in the introduction of your essay as you explain your classification system. Occasionally, your thesis statement may not come until the end, after you've thoroughly explained how your classification system works.

Let's look at a classification essay in which the point of the classification is not obvious. Here is the main introductory paragraph:

> I have moved more often than I care to remember. However, one thing always stays the same no matter where I have been. There is always a house next door, and that house contains neighbors. Over time, I have begun putting my neighbors into one of four categories: too friendly, unsociable, irritable, and just right. —JONATHAN R. GOULD JR., "The People Next Door"

Having introduced his subject and outlined his four-part classification system at the beginning of his essay, Gould devotes a paragraph to each of the four categories, taking them in order and looking at particular neighbors who fit each one—the "overly friendly" neighbor who had to be told that his house was on fire "in an attempt to make him leave," the "unsociable" neighbor who looked at the fresh-baked apple pie offered by Gould's wife "as if she intended to poison them," and so on. But what is Gould's point in classifying his neighbors according to this scheme?

In addition to making us smile, Gould's point in classifying his neighbors into these four categories is to make an observation about human nature. Here's the last paragraph of his essay:

> I have always felt it was important to identify the types of neighbors that were around me. Then I am better able to maintain a clear perspective on our relationship and understand their needs. After all, people do not really change; we just learn how to live with both the good and the bad aspects of their behavior.

Gould could have explained his point at the beginning of his essay, but he chose to build up to it instead. In a humorous essay, this can be an effective strategy—part of the fun is wondering where the game is headed and how it's going to end. When you have a more serious purpose in mind, however, you're better off making your main point clear in the beginning of your essay and then, in the conclusion, saying how what you've just written proves that point.

CHOOSING SIGNIFICANT CHARACTERISTICS

Whatever classification system you use, base your categories on the most significant characteristics of your subject—ones that explain something important about it. All neighbors, for example, have at least one thing in common: they are people who live near by. This trait, however, doesn't tell us much about them. Proximity may be an essential trait in DEFINING neighbors, but it is not a very useful characteristic for classifying them. For the same reason, you probably would not discuss such attributes as color or decoration when classifying bicycles. Whether a bicycle is blue with red racing stripes or red with blue stripes may be important aesthetically, but these attributes do not tell the reader what kind it is, since all different kinds of bicycles come in all different colors. Color, in other words, while important for classifying wine and laundry, isn't significant when it comes to bicycles. So as you choose your categories, make sure they're based on significant characteristics that actually help the reader to distinguish one type from another.

With bicycles, these would be such attributes as weight, strength, configuration of the handlebars, and thickness of the tires. Thick, knobby tires, heavy frames, and strong cross-braced handlebars that protect the rider from sudden jolts are significant characteristics of mountain bikes. Thin, smooth tires, lightweight frames, and dropped handlebars that put the rider in a more streamlined position are typical of racing bikes. Wide but relatively smooth tires, raised (but not cross-braced) handlebars, and sturdy, medium-weight frames—not to mention large padded seats—indicate touring bikes. And so on.

Citing significant characteristics is even more essential when you have a two-part classification system, also called a binary system. A binary system has the advantage of being very inclusive. All people can be divided into the living and the dead, for instance. Binary classification systems, however, potentially sacrifice depth for breadth. That is, you can use a binary system to classify a lot of people or things, but it may not necessarily tell the reader much about them. Pointing out that Shakespeare, for example, belongs in the "dead" category doesn't tell readers nearly as much about him as explaining that he was a playwright, a poet, and an actor.

CHOOSING CATEGORIES THAT ARE INCLUSIVE AND DON'T OVERLAP

Classifying can be intellectually challenging work. Not only must you divide your subject into categories that are truly distinctive, those categories must be inclusive enough to cover most cases, and they must not overlap.

Classifying ice cream into chocolate and vanilla alone isn't very useful because this system leaves out several other important kinds, such as strawberry, pistachio, and rum raisin. The categories in a good classification system include all kinds: for instance, no-fat, low-fat, and full-fat ice cream. And they should not overlap. Thus, chocolate, vanilla, homemade, and Ben and Jerry's do not make a good classification system because the same scoop of ice cream could fit into more than one category.

BREAKING CATEGORIES INTO SUBCATEGORIES

The categories in a classification essay should be broadly inclusive; but if your categories start to become too broad to be useful, try dividing them into narrower subcategories. Suppose you were drafting an essay on the Great Depression of the 1930s for a history class, and you were focusing on "tramps," the itinerant men (and occasionally women) who took to the road—especially the railroads—in search of food and work. In the lingo of the day, those tramps who begged, you would point out, were classified as "dings," and those who worked for a living were called "working stiffs." A third kind, who neither begged nor worked, were called "nose divers."

"Nose divers" designated a relatively narrow category of tramp—those who attended church and worshipped or prayed ("nose dived") in order to partake of meals and beds provided by the church. "Working stiffs," on the other hand, could get their living by almost any means; and to classify them accurately, you would need to divide this broad, general kind into subtypes—harvest tramp, tramp miner, fruit tramp, construction tramp, and sea tramp. Your essay would then go on to specify the chief characteristics of each of these narrower categories.

USING OTHER METHODS

DEFINITION can be especially useful when you classify something because you will need to define your categories (and any subcategories) according to their

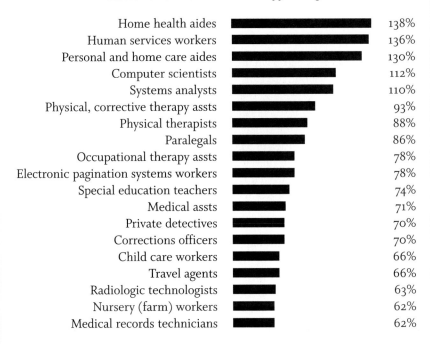

CLASSIFYING INFORMATION VISUALLY

Fastest Growing Occupations 1992–2005

Occupation	Percentage
Home health aides	138%
Human services workers	136%
Personal and home care aides	130%
Computer scientists	112%
Systems analysts	110%
Physical, corrective therapy assts	93%
Physical therapists	88%
Paralegals	86%
Occupational therapy assts	78%
Electronic pagination systems workers	78%
Special education teachers	74%
Medical assts	71%
Private detectives	70%
Corrections officers	70%
Child care workers	66%
Travel agents	66%
Radiologic technologists	63%
Nursery (farm) workers	62%
Medical records technicians	62%

Graph by U.S. Department of the Interior; based on statistics provided by the U.S. Census Bureau.

Statistical graphics, such as this bar graph, allow readers to grasp complex classification systems at a glance. This one, compiled by the U.S. Department of the Interior, classifies nineteen different occupations according to their rates of growth over a thirteen-year period. Which occupations grew the fastest between 1992 and 2005? By what percentages did their numbers increase? Which occupations grew at a lesser rate? How much did a particular occupation—private detectives, for example—grow in relation to the other occupations? Sometimes, questions like these are best answered by presenting your data visually.

distinguishing characteristics. You will also need to DESCRIBE those characteristics. Sometimes you may have reason to analyze the CAUSES of certain characteristics, or what EFFECTS they may have. The author of the following passage uses all three methods (and more) to classify the ailments of horses confined to their stalls:

> In his natural state the horse is a range animal. If he cannot roam a reasonable territory, he may express his frustration by developing some unpleasant or even health-threatening habits. Chewing on fences or stall boards may be followed by cribbing and wind-sucking, vices in which the horse bites down on a hard surface and swallows air at the same time, to the accompaniment of little grunts. (Some will argue that cribbing is a genetically acquired habit, but it is rarely seen in a horse at liberty.)
>
> Further, a continually stabled horse may become a weaver, swaying from side to side in a restless, compulsive pattern. To me, this is as sad a scenario as watching a caged tiger pace back and forth behind bars. Cribbers and weavers, for obvious reasons, frequently develop digestive problems. The message is clear, then: as much turnout for as many hours as possible.
>
> —MAXINE KUMIN, *Women, Animals, and Vegetables*

In this passage, Kumin classifies overly confined horses as "cribbers and weavers." Defining the behaviors of both kinds as "unpleasant or even health-threatening habits," she then describes the characteristics that distinguish each kind: the cribber "bites down on a hard surface and swallows air at the same time," whereas the weaver sways "from side to side in a restless, compulsive pattern."

Kumin is so concerned about the welfare of overly confined horses, however, that she does more than simply classify, define, and describe their ailments. She analyzes the cause of those ailments and ARGUES for a particular remedy. Cribbing and weaving are not genetic conditions, says Kumin; they are acquired behaviors caused by the confinement itself. Her point, therefore, is clear: horse owners should let their animals range more freely, instead of confining them to the stable.

Reading a Classification Essay with a Critical Eye

The most important part of any classification essay is the classification system itself. Does yours have one? How many categories does it include? What are they? Once you've drafted your essay, ask someone else to read your draft and tell you how well he or she thinks your classification system supports your point—and how it might be improved. Should any categories be redefined or omitted? Should any new ones be added? The following are some basic guidelines for checking over a classification essay:

PURPOSE AND AUDIENCE. Is there a good reason for classifying this particular subject this way? Who is the intended audience of the essay? Does the essay give sufficient background information for the audience to understand (and accept) the proposed classification? Are key terms defined, especially ones that might be unfamiliar to some readers?

THE POINT. Is the main point of the essay clearly laid out in a THESIS STATEMENT? How and how well does the classification itself support the main point?

THE CLASSIFICATION SYSTEM AND THE CATEGORIES. Is the classification system appropriate for the subject and purpose of the essay? What is the PRINCIPLE OF CLASSIFICATION? Should that principle be revised in any way? If so, how? Do the categories suit the essay's purpose and audience?

SIGNIFICANT CHARACTERISTICS. Do the characteristics that make up the categories tell the reader something important about the subject? Does the essay demonstrate that the things being classified actually have these characteristics?

DO ANY CATEGORIES OVERLAP? Can any individual item fit into more than one of the categories that make up the classification system? If so, how might the principle of classification be revised so as to avoid this problem?

ARE THE CATEGORIES INCLUSIVE? If not, what new categories need to be added in order to make the classification system complete?

SUBCATEGORIES. Would any of the basic categories that make up the classification system be clearer or easier to explain if they were divided into subgroups?

OTHER METHODS. Does the essay use other methods of development besides classification? For instance, does it clearly DEFINE all the basic categories and subcategories in the classification system? Does it fully DESCRIBE the distinctive attributes of each category? Does it ANALYZE what CAUSED those attributes, or what EFFECTS they might have?

Editing for Common Errors in a Classification Essay

Classification invites certain kinds of errors. Here are some tips for checking your writing for these errors—and editing any that you find.

If you've listed categories in a single sentence, make sure they are parallel in form—all nouns, all adjectives, all phrases, and so on.

NOT A horse can be nervous, aggressive, or calmly accept a saddle.

BUT A horse can be nervous, aggressive, or calm.

NOT Some say work can be divided into two categories. We're either working too hard or it's a waste of time.

BUT Some say work can be divided into two categories. We're either working too hard or wasting time.

Check that adjectives are in the following order: size, age, color.

Adjectives identify characteristics, so you'll probably use at least some adjectives when you write a classification essay.

NOT old brown big boots

BUT big old brown boots

A Gas Station Sign

When we classify something, we divide it into different categories based on the distinguishing features of each category. Like most service stations, Tom's Shell Station in Madison, Wisconsin, classifies the gasoline it sells into three grades—regular, plus, and premium. The different grades are distinguished by their different "octane" ratings, a measure of the anti-knock properties of each grade. The higher the octane, the higher the price of the gasoline. Prices are a common form of classification, too. The large sign in front of Tom's Shell uses both of these classification systems, putting a high price on plus and premium gas. His purpose in creating the sign, however, says owner Tom Jones, was not just to distinguish the different grades of the product he sells. It was to make customers smile, even in the face of today's high prices at the pump. That way, Tom figured, they might forget their suffering for a moment, complain less—and buy more gas.

EVERYDAY CLASSIFICATION

STEPHANIE ERICSSON

The Ways We Lie

Stephanie Ericsson (b. 1953) was two months pregnant with her first child when her husband suddenly died. Already an author of screenplays and two books about addiction, Ericsson poured her grief into her journals, which were excerpted in the Utne Reader *and then collected in a volume of essays,* Companion Through the Darkness: Inner Dialogues on Grief *(1993). The book struck a chord with both critics and readers.*

"There are many ways to lie," writes Ericsson in this essay from Companion Through the Darkness. *Beginning with a broad definition of* lie, *"The Ways We Lie" identifies some of the most common kinds, including the falsehoods we tell ourselves as well as those we inflict upon other people.*

THE BANK CALLED TODAY and I told them my deposit was in the mail, even though I hadn't written a check yet. It'd been a rough day. The baby I'm pregnant with decided to do aerobics on my lungs for two hours, our three-year-old daughter painted the living-room couch with lipstick, the IRS put me on hold for an hour, and I was late to a business meeting because I was tired.

I told my client the traffic had been bad. When my partner came home, his haggard face told me his day hadn't gone any better than mine, so when he asked, "How was your day?" I said, "Oh, fine," knowing that one more straw might break his back. A friend called and wanted to take me to lunch. I said I was busy. Four lies in the course of a day, none of which I felt the least bit guilty about.

We lie. We all do. We exaggerate, we minimize, we avoid confrontation, we spare people's feelings, we conveniently forget, we keep secrets, we justify lying to the big-guy institutions. Like most people, I indulge in small falsehoods and still think of myself as an honest person. Sure I lie, but it doesn't hurt anything. Or does it?

I once tried going a whole week without telling a lie, and it was paralyzing. I discovered that telling the truth all the time is nearly impossible. It means living with some serious consequences: The bank charges me $60 in overdraft fees, my partner keels over when I tell him about my travails, my client fires me for telling her I didn't feel like being on time, and my friend takes it personally when I say I'm not hungry. There must be some merit to lying.

But if I justify lying, what makes me any different from slick politicians or the corporate robbers who raided the S&L industry?[1] Saying it's okay to lie one way and not another is hedging. I cannot seem to escape the voice deep inside me that tells me: When someone lies, someone loses.

What far-reaching consequences will I, or others, pay as a result of my lie? Will   6
someone's trust be destroyed? Will someone else pay *my* penance because I ducked out? We must consider the *meaning of our actions*. Deception, lies, capital crimes, and misdemeanors all carry meanings. *Webster's* definition of *lie* is specific:

1. a false statement or action especially made with the intent to deceive;

2. anything that gives or is meant to give a false impression.

A definition like this implies that there are many, many ways to tell a lie. Here are just a few.

The White Lie

> A man who won't lie to a woman has very little consideration for her feelings.
> —Bergen Evans

The white lie assumes that the truth will cause more damage than a simple, harm-   7
less untruth. Telling a friend he looks great when he looks like hell can be based on a decision that the friend needs a compliment more than a frank opinion. But, in effect, it is the liar deciding what is best for the lied to. Ultimately, it is a vote of no confidence. It is an act of subtle arrogance for anyone to decide what is best for someone else.

Yet not all circumstances are quite so cut-and-dried. Take, for instance, the ser-   8
geant in Vietnam who knew one of his men was killed in action but listed him as missing so that the man's family would receive indefinite compensation instead of the lump-sum pittance the military gives widows and children. His intent was hon-orable. Yet for twenty years this family kept their hopes alive, unable to move on to a new life.

Facades

> Et tu, Brute?
> —Caesar

We all put up facades to one degree or another. When I put on a suit to go to see a   9
client, I feel as though I am putting on another face, obeying the expectation that

---

1. *S&L industry:* savings and loan (S&L) associations accept savings deposits from consumers and issue home mortgage loans. In the S&L crisis of the 1980s, more than a thousand independent savings and loan institutions in America collapsed, costing the U.S. government an estimated $125 billion and probably contributing to the economic recession of the early 1990s.

serious businesspeople wear suits rather than sweatpants. But I'm a writer. Normally, I get up, get the kid off to school, and sit at my computer in my pajamas until four in the afternoon. When I answer the phone, the caller thinks I'm wearing a suit (though the UPS man knows better).

But facades can be destructive because they are used to seduce others into an illusion. For instance, I recently realized that a former friend was a liar. He presented himself with all the right looks and the right words and offered lots of new consciousness theories, fabulous books to read, and fascinating insights. Then I did some business with him, and the time came for him to pay me. He turned out to be all talk and no walk. I heard a plethora of reasonable excuses, including in-depth descriptions of the big break around the corner. In six months of work, I saw less than a hundred bucks. When I confronted him, he raised both eyebrows and tried to convince me that I'd heard him wrong, that he'd made no commitment to me. A simple investigation into his past revealed a crowded graveyard of disenchanted former friends.

Ignoring the Plain Facts

Well, you must understand that Father Porter is only human. . . .
—A MASSACHUSETTS PRIEST

In the '60s, the Catholic Church in Massachusetts began hearing complaints that Father James Porter was sexually molesting children. Rather than relieving him of his duties, the ecclesiastical authorities simply moved him from one parish to another between 1960 and 1967, actually providing him with a fresh supply of unsuspecting families and innocent children to abuse. After treatment in 1967 for pedophilia, he went back to work, this time in Minnesota. The new diocese was aware of Father Porter's obsession with children, but they needed priests and recklessly believed treatment had cured him. More children were abused until he was relieved of his duties a year later. By his own admission, Porter may have abused as many as a hundred children.

Ignoring the facts may not in and of itself be a form of lying, but consider the context of this situation. If a lie is *a false action done with the intent to deceive*, then the Catholic Church's conscious covering for Porter created irreparable consequences. The church became a co-perpetrator with Porter.

Deflecting

When you have no basis for an argument, abuse the plaintiff.　—CICERO

I've discovered that I can keep anyone from seeing the true me by being selectively blatant. I set a precedent of being up-front about intimate issues, but I never bring up the things I truly want to hide; I just let people assume I'm revealing everything. It's an effective way of hiding.

Any good liar knows that the way to perpetuate an untruth is to deflect attention from it. When Clarence Thomas[2] exploded with accusations that the Senate hearings were a "high-tech lynching," he simply switched the focus from a highly charged subject to a radioactive subject. Rather than defending himself, he took the offensive and accused the country of racism. It was a brilliant maneuver. Racism is now politically incorrect in official circles—unlike sexual harassment, which still rewards those who can get away with it. 14

Some of the most skillful deflectors are passive-aggressive people who, when accused of inappropriate behavior, refuse to respond to the accusations. This you-don't-exist stance infuriates the accuser, who, understandably, screams something obscene out of frustration. The trap is sprung and the act of deflection successful, because now the passive-aggressive person can indignantly say, "Who can talk to someone as unreasonable as you?" The real issue is forgotten and the sins of the original victim become the focus. Feeling guilty of name-calling, the victim is fully tamed and crawls into a hole, ashamed. I have watched this fighting technique work thousands of times in disputes between men and women, and what I've learned is that the real culprit is not necessarily the one who swears the loudest. 15

Omission

The cruelest lies are often told in silence.   —R. L. STEVENSON

Omission involves telling most of the truth minus one or two key facts whose absence changes the story completely. You break a pair of glasses that are guaranteed under normal use and get a new pair, without mentioning that the first pair broke during a rowdy game of basketball. Who hasn't tried something like that? But what about omission of information that could make a difference in how a person lives his or her life? 16

For instance, one day I found out that rabbinical legends tell of another woman in the Garden of Eden before Eve. I was stunned. The omission of the Sumerian goddess Lilith from Genesis—as well as her demonization by ancient misogynists as an embodiment of female evil—felt like spiritual robbery. I felt like I'd just found out my mother was really my stepmother. To take seriously the tradition that Adam was created out of the same mud as his equal counterpart, Lilith, redefines all of Judeo-Christian history. 17

2. *Clarence Thomas*: U.S. Supreme Court justice who was accused of sexual harassment during his 1991 Senate confirmation hearings. Thomas's "high-tech lynching" statement referred to the lynching of blacks in the late nineteenth and early twentieth centuries.

Some renegade Catholic feminists introduced me to a view of Lilith that had   18
been suppressed during the many centuries when this strong goddess was seen
only as a spirit of evil. Lilith was a proud goddess who defied Adam's need to control her, attempted negotiations, and when this failed, said adios and left the Garden of Eden.

This omission of Lilith from the Bible was a patriarchal strategy to keep women   19
weak. Omitting the strong-woman archetype of Lilith from Western religions and
starting the story with Eve the Rib has helped keep Christian and Jewish women
believing they were the lesser sex for thousands of years.

Stereotypes and Clichés

> Where opinion does not exist, the status quo becomes stereotyped and all
> originality is discouraged.   —BERTRAND RUSSELL

Stereotype and cliché serve a purpose as a form of shorthand. Our need for vast   20
amounts of information in nanoseconds has made the stereotype vital to modern
communication. Unfortunately, it often shuts down original thinking, giving
those hungry for the truth a candy bar of misinformation instead of a balanced
meal. The stereotype explains a situation with just enough truth to seem unquestionable.

All the "isms"—racism, sexism, ageism, et al.—are founded on and fueled by the   21
stereotype and the cliché, which are lies of exaggeration, omission, and ignorance.
They are always dangerous. They take a single tree and make it a landscape. They
destroy curiosity. They close minds and separate people. The single mother on welfare is assumed to be cheating. Any black male could tell you how much of his
identity is obliterated daily by stereotypes. Fat people, ugly people, beautiful people, old people, large-breasted women, short men, the mentally ill, and the homeless all could tell you how much more they are like us than we want to think. I
once admitted to a group of people that I had a mouth like a truck driver. Much to
my surprise, a man stood up and said, "I'm a truck driver, and I never cuss." Needless to say, I was humbled.

Groupthink

> Who is more foolish, the child afraid of the dark, or the man afraid of the
> light?   —MAURICE FREEHILL

Irving Janis, in *Victims of GroupThink*, defines this sort of lie as a psychological phe-   22
nomenon within decision-making groups in which loyalty to the group has become
more important than any other value, with the result that dissent and the appraisal
of alternatives are suppressed. If you've ever worked on a committee or in a corpo-

ration, you've encountered groupthink. It requires a combination of other forms of lying—ignoring facts, selective memory, omission, and denial, to name a few.

The textbook example of groupthink came on December 7, 1941. From as early as   23
the fall of 1941, the warnings came in, one after another, that Japan was preparing for a massive military operation. The Navy command in Hawaii assumed Pearl Harbor was invulnerable—the Japanese weren't stupid enough to attack the United States' most important base. On the other hand, racist stereotypes said the Japanese weren't smart enough to invent a torpedo effective in less than 60 feet of water (the fleet was docked in 30 feet); after all, U.S. technology hadn't been able to do it.

On Friday, December 5, normal weekend leave was granted to all the command-   24
ers at Pearl Harbor, even though the Japanese consulate in Hawaii was busy burning papers. Within the tight, good-ole-boy cohesiveness of the U.S. command in Hawaii, the myth of invulnerability stayed well entrenched. No one in the group considered the alternatives. The rest is history.

Out-and-Out Lies

The only form of lying that is beyond reproach is lying for its own sake.
                                                                —OSCAR WILDE

Of all the ways to lie, I like this one the best, probably because I get tired of trying   25
to figure out the real meanings behind things. At least I can trust the bald-faced lie. I once asked my five-year-old nephew, "Who broke the fence?" (I had seen him do it.) He answered, "The murderers." Who could argue?

At least when this sort of lie is told it can be easily confronted. As the person   26
who is lied to, I know where I stand. The bald-faced lie doesn't toy with my perceptions—it argues with them. It doesn't try to refashion reality, it tries to refute it. *Read my lips.*[3] . . . No sleight of hand. No guessing. If this were the only form of lying, there would be no such thing as floating anxiety or the adult-children of alcoholics movement.

Dismissal

Pay no attention to that man behind the curtain! I am the Great Oz!
                                                            —THE WIZARD OF OZ

Dismissal is perhaps the slipperiest of all lies. Dismissing feelings, perceptions, or   27
even the raw facts of a situation ranks as a kind of lie that can do as much damage to a person as any other kind of lie.

---

3. *Read my lips*: a phrase made especially famous during President George H. W. Bush's 1988 election campaign. He emphatically said, "Read my lips: no new taxes." Once in office, he did raise taxes.

The roots of many mental disorders can be traced back to the dismissal of real- 28
ity. Imagine that a person is told from the time she is a tot that her perceptions are
inaccurate. *"Mommy, I'm scared."* "No, you're not, darling." *"I don't like that man next
door, he makes me feel icky."* "Johnny, that's a terrible thing to say, of course you like
him. You go over there right now and be nice to him."

I've often mused over the idea that madness is actually a sane reaction to an 29
insane world. Psychologist R. D. Laing supports this hypothesis in *Sanity, Madness
& the Family*, an account of his investigations into families of schizophrenics. The
common thread that ran through all of the families he studied was a deliberate,
staunch dismissal of the patient's perceptions from a very early age. Each of the
patients started out with an accurate grasp of reality, which, through meticulous
and methodical dismissal, was demolished until the only reality the patient could
trust was catatonia.

Dismissal runs the gamut. Mild dismissal can be quite handy for forgiving the 30
foibles of others in our day-to-day lives. Toddlers who have just learned to manipulate their parents' attention sometimes are dismissed out of necessity. Absolute
attention from the parents would require so much energy that no one would get to
eat dinner. But we must be careful and attentive about how far we take our "necessary" dismissals. Dismissal is a dangerous tool, because it's nothing less than a lie.

Delusion

> We lie loudest when we lie to ourselves. —ERIC HOFFER

I could write the book on this one. Delusion, a cousin of dismissal, is the tendency 31
to see excuses as facts. It's a powerful lying tool because it filters out information
that contradicts what we want to believe. Alcoholics who believe that the problems
in their lives are legitimate reasons for drinking rather than results of the drinking
offer the classic example of deluded thinking. Delusion uses the mind's ability to
see things in myriad ways to support what it wants to be the truth.

But delusion is also a survival mechanism we all use. If we were to fully contem- 32
plate the consequences of our stockpiles of nuclear weapons or global warming, we
could hardly function on a day-to-day level. We don't want to incorporate that
much reality into our lives because to do so would be paralyzing.

Delusion acts as an adhesive to keep the status quo intact. It shamelessly 33
employs dismissal, omission, and amnesia, among other sorts of lies. Its most cunning defense is that it cannot see itself.

> The liar's punishment . . . is that he cannot believe anyone else. —GEORGE BERNARD SHAW

These are only a few of the ways we lie. Or are lied to. As I said earlier, it's not 34
easy to entirely eliminate lies from our lives. No matter how pious we may try to

be, we will still embellish, hedge, and omit to lubricate the daily machinery of living. But there is a world of difference between telling functional lies and living a lie. Martin Buber once said, "The lie is the spirit committing treason against itself." Our acceptance of lies becomes a cultural cancer that eventually shrouds and reorders reality until moral garbage becomes as invisible to us as water is to a fish.

How much do we tolerate before we become sick and tired of being sick and   35 tired? When will we stand up and declare our *right* to trust? When do we stop accepting that the real truth is in the fine print? Whose lips do we read this year when we vote for president? When will we stop being so reticent about making judgments? When do we stop turning over our personal power and responsibility to liars?

Maybe if I don't tell the bank the check's in the mail I'll be less tolerant of the   36 lies told me every day. A country song I once heard said it all for me: "You've got to stand for something or you'll fall for anything."

READING CLOSELY

1. According to Ericsson, what basic characteristics do all lies have in common? How and how well do the kinds of lies she lists fit this basic DEFINITION?

2. Ericsson classifies lies into ten different categories. Which kinds of lies does she herself admit to committing? Who does she say commits the other kinds?

3. Some kinds of lies, says Ericsson, are more serious than others. Which kinds does she find least harmful? Which kinds do the most damage, in her view? How?

4. Why can't Ericsson get more worked up about "out-and-out" (or "bald-faced") lies (25–26)?

5. "We lie," says Ericsson. "We all do" (3). Do you agree? Why or why not?

6. "We must consider the *meaning of our actions*," says Ericsson (6). Why? What reasons does she give for taking responsibility for our lies? Do you agree with Ericsson's ARGUMENT, especially with what she says about "trust" (25, 35)? Why or why not?

STRATEGIES AND STRUCTURES

1. Throughout her essay, Ericsson admits that she tells lies. Why do you think she adopts this "confessional" strategy? How effective do you find it? Why?

2. Why is Ericsson CLASSIFYING lies in this essay? Where does she state her main point in doing so most directly?

3. Ericsson identifies the main characteristics, as she sees them, of each category of lie that she discusses. How significant do you find these characteristics?

4. Ericsson says that some kinds of lies, such as "groupthink," are made up of "a combination of other forms of lying" (22). Does this sort of "overlapping" invalidate her system? Why or why not?

5. Ericsson warns against stereotyping in paragraphs 20–21. On what basis does she object to stereotypes? Can she be accused of engaging in this practice at any point in her essay? Explain your answer by referring to specific kinds of lies and their characteristics.

6. *Other Methods.* Ericsson gives EXAMPLES of each of the different categories of lies. Which examples do you find most effective? Least effective? Explain.

THINKING ABOUT LANGUAGE

1. What are the differences between a "white lie" and an "out-and-out lie"? What are the connotations of each expression?

2. How can lying be committed in silence?

3. Ericsson writes that "our acceptance of lies becomes a cultural cancer" (34). Why do you think she uses the expression "cultural cancer"?

FOR WRITING

1. Have you ever lied in one or more of the ways that Ericsson cites? Write a paragraph or two on each kind of lie you've told giving examples from your own experience but classifying them according to Ericsson's categories.

2. Write a classification essay on the ways people do one of the following: tell the truth, avoid work, make friends, break with friends, find a job, quit a job, or delude themselves.

DEBORAH TANNEN

But What Do You Mean?

Deborah Tannen (b. 1945) is a professor of linguistics at Georgetown University. Best known for her studies of how men and women communicate, she is the author of twenty books and more than 100 articles, including You Just Don't Understand: Men and Women in Conversation *(1990) and* You're Wearing *That?* Understanding Mothers and Daughters in Conversation *(2006).*

"But What Do You Mean?" first appeared in Redbook *magazine in 1994 and summarizes much of Tannen's best-selling book* Talking from 9 to 5: Women and Men at Work *(1994). In this essay, Tannen classifies the most common ways in which men and women miscommunicate in the workplace.*

CONVERSATION IS A RITUAL. We say things that seem obviously the thing to say, without thinking of the literal meaning of our words, any more than we expect the question "How are you?" to call forth a detailed account of aches and pains. 1

Unfortunately, women and men often have different ideas about what's appropriate, different ways of speaking. Many of the conversational rituals common among women are designed to take the other person's feelings into account, while many of the conversational rituals common among men are designed to maintain the one-up position, or at least avoid appearing one-down. As a result, when men and women interact—especially at work—it's often women who are at the disadvantage. Because women are not trying to avoid the one-down position, that is unfortunately where they may end up. 2

Here, the biggest areas of miscommunication. 3

1. Apologies

Women are often told they apologize too much. The reason they're told to stop doing it is that, to many men, apologizing seems synonymous with putting oneself down. But there are many times when "I'm sorry" isn't self-deprecating, or even an apology; it's an automatic way of keeping both speakers on an equal footing. For example, a well-known columnist once interviewed me and gave me her phone number in case I needed to call her back. I misplaced the number and had to go through the newspaper's main switchboard. When our conversation was winding down and we'd both made ending-type remarks, I added, "Oh, I almost forgot—I lost your direct number, can I get it again?" "Oh, I'm sorry," she came back instantly, even though she had nothing wrong and *I* was the one who'd lost 4 the number. But I understood she wasn't really apologizing; she was just automati-cally reassuring me she had no intention of denying me her number.

Even when "I'm sorry" *is* an apology, women often assume it will be the first 5
step in a two-step ritual: I say "I'm sorry" and take half the blame, then you take the other half. At work, it might go something like this:

> A: When you typed this letter, you missed this phrase I inserted.
> B: Oh, I'm sorry. I'll fix it.
> A: Well, I wrote it so small it was easy to miss.

When both parties share blame, it's a mutual face-saving device. But if one per- 6
son, usually the woman, utters frequent apologies and the other doesn't, she ends up looking as if she's taking the blame for mishaps that aren't her fault. When she's only partially to blame, she looks entirely in the wrong.

I recently sat in on a meeting at an insurance company where the sole woman, 7
Helen, said "I'm sorry" or "I apologize" repeatedly. At one point she said, "I'm thinking out loud. I apologize." Yet the meeting was intended to be an informal brainstorming session, and *everyone* was thinking out loud.

The reason Helen's apologies stood out was that she was the only person in the 8
room making so many. And the reason I was concerned was that Helen felt the annual bonus she had received was unfair. When I interviewed the colleagues, they said that Helen was one of the best and most productive workers—yet she got one of the smallest bonuses. Although the problem might have been outright sexism, I suspect her speech style, which differs from that of her male colleagues, masks her competence.

Unfortunately, not apologizing can have its price too. Since so many women use 9
ritual apologies, those who don't may be seen as hard-edged. What's important is to be aware of how often you say you're sorry (and why), and to monitor your speech based on the reaction you get.

2. Criticism

A woman who cowrote a report with a male colleague was hurt when she read a 10
rough draft to him and he leapt into a critical response—"Oh, that's too dry! You have to make it snappier!" She herself would have been more likely to say, "That's a really good start. Of course, you'll want to make it a little snappier when you revise."

Whether criticism is given straight or softened is often a matter of convention. 11
In general, women use more softeners. I noticed this difference when talking to an editor about an essay I'd written. While going over changes she wanted to make, she said, "There's one more thing. I know you may not agree with me. The reason I noticed the problem is that your other points are so lucid and elegant." She went

on hedging for several more sentences until I put her out of her misery: "Do you want to cut that part?" I asked—and of course she did. But I appreciated her tentativeness. In contrast, another editor (a man) I once called summarily rejected my idea for an article by barking, "Call me when you have something new to say."

Those who are used to ways of talking that soften the impact of criticism may find it hard to deal with the right-between-the-eyes style. It has its own logic, however, and neither style is intrinsically better. People who prefer criticism given straight are operating on an assumption that feelings aren't involved: "Here's the dope. I know you're good; you can take it."   12

3. Thank-Yous

A woman manager I know starts meetings by thanking everyone for coming, even though it's clearly their job to do so. Her "thank-you" is simply a ritual.   13

A novelist received a fax from an assistant in her publisher's office; it contained suggested catalog copy for her book. She immediately faxed him her suggested changes and said, "Thanks for running this by me," even though her contract gave her the right to approve all copy. When she thanked the assistant, she fully expected him to reciprocate: "Thanks for giving me such a quick response." Instead, he said, "You're welcome." Suddenly, rather than an equal exchange of pleasantries, she found herself positioned as the recipient of a favor. This made her feel like responding, "Thanks for nothing!"   14

Many women use "thanks" as an automatic conversation starter and closer; there's nothing literally to say thank you for. Like many rituals typical of women's conversation, it depends on the goodwill of the other to restore the balance. When the other speaker doesn't reciprocate, a woman may feel like someone on a seesaw whose partner abandoned his end. Instead of balancing in the air, she has plopped to the ground, wondering how she got there.   15

4. Fighting

Many men expect the discussion of ideas to be a ritual fight—explored through verbal opposition. They state their ideas in the strongest possible terms, thinking that if there are weaknesses someone will point them out, and by trying to argue against those objections, they will see how well their ideas hold up.   16

Those who expect their own ideas to be challenged will respond to another's ideas by trying to poke holes and find weak links—as a way of *helping*. The logic is that when you are challenged you will rise to the occasion: Adrenaline makes your mind sharper; you get ideas and insights you would not have thought of without the spur of battle.   17

But many women take this approach as a personal attack. Worse, they find it   18 impossible to do their best work in such a contentious environment. If you're not used to ritual fighting, you begin to hear criticism of your ideas as soon as they are formed. Rather than making you think more clearly, it makes you doubt what you know. When you state your ideas, you hedge in order to fend off potential attacks. Ironically, this is more likely to *invite* attack because it makes you look weak.

Although you may never enjoy verbal sparring, some women find it helpful to [19] learn how to do it. An engineer who was the only woman among four men in a small company found that as soon as she learned to argue she was accepted and taken seriously. A doctor attending a hospital staff meeting made a similar discovery. She was becoming more and more angry with a male colleague who'd loudly disagreed with a point she'd made. Her better judgment told her to hold her tongue, to avoid making an enemy of this powerful senior colleague. But finally she couldn't hold it in any longer, and she rose to her feet and delivered an impassioned attack on his position. She sat down in a panic, certain she had permanently damaged her relationship with him. To her amazement, he came up to her afterward and said, "That was a great rebuttal. I'm really impressed. Let's go out for a beer after work and hash out our approaches to this problem."

5. Praise

A manager I'll call Lester had been on his new job six months when he heard that [20] the women reporting to him were deeply dissatisfied. When he talked to them about it, their feelings erupted; two said they were on the verge of quitting because he didn't appreciate their work, and they didn't want to wait to be fired. Lester was dumbfounded: He believed they were doing a fine job. Surely, he thought, he had said nothing to give them the impression he didn't like their work. And indeed he hadn't. That was the problem. He had said *nothing*—and the women assumed he was following the adage "If you can't say something nice, don't say anything." He thought he was showing confidence in them by leaving them alone.

Men and women have different habits in regard to giving praise. For example, [21] Deirdre and her colleague William both gave presentations at a conference. Afterward, Deirdre told William, "That was a great talk!" He thanked her. Then she asked, "What did you think of mine?" and he gave her a lengthy and detailed critique. She found it uncomfortable to listen to his comments. But she assured herself that he meant well, and that his honesty was a signal that she, too, should be honest when he asked for a critique of his performance. As a matter of fact, she had noticed quite a few ways in which he could have improved his presentation. But she never got a chance to tell him because he never asked—and she felt put down. The worst part was that it seemed she had only herself to blame, since she *had* asked what he thought of her talk.

But had she really asked for his critique? The truth is, when she asked for his   22
opinion, she was expecting a compliment, which she felt was more or less required
following anyone's talk. When he responded with criticism, she figured, "Oh, he's
playing 'Let's critique each other' "—not a game she'd initiated, but one which she
was willing to play. Had she realized he was going to criticize her and not ask her
to reciprocate, she would never have asked in the first place.

It would be easy to assume that Deirdre was insecure, whether she was fishing   23
for a compliment or soliciting a critique. But she was simply talking automatically,
performing one of the many conversational rituals that allow us to get through the
day. William may have sincerely misunderstood Deirdre's intention—or may have
been unable to pass up a chance to one-up her when given the opportunity.

6. Complaints

"Troubles talk" can be a way to establish rapport with a colleague. You complain   24
about a problem (which shows that you are just folks) and the other person
responds with a similar problem (which puts you on equal footing). But while such
commiserating is common among women, men are likely to hear it as a request to
solve the problem.

One woman told me she would frequently initiate what she thought would be   25
pleasant complaint-airing sessions at work. She'd talk about situations that bothered her just to talk about them, maybe to understand them better. But her male
office mate would quickly tell her how she could improve the situation. This left
her feeling condescended to and frustrated. She was delighted to see this very
impasse in a section in my book *You Just Don't Understand*, and showed it to him.
"Oh," he said, "I see the problem. How can we solve it?" Then they both laughed,
because it had happened again: He short-circuited the detailed discussion she'd
hoped for and cut to the chase of finding a solution.

Sometimes the consequences of complaining are more serious: A man might   26
take a woman's lighthearted griping literally, and she can get a reputation as a
chronic malcontent. Furthermore, she may be seen as not up to solving the problems that arise on the job.

7. Jokes

I heard a man call in to a talk show and say, "I've worked for two women and nei-   27
ther one had a sense of humor. You know, when you work with men, there's a lot of
joking and teasing." The show's host and guest (both women) took his comment at
face value and assumed the women this man worked for were humorless. The
guest said, "Isn't it sad that women don't feel comfortable enough with authority to
see the humor?" The host said, "Maybe when more women are in authority roles,

they'll be more comfortable with power." But although the women this man worked for *may* have taken themselves too seriously, it's just as likely that they each had a terrific sense of humor, but maybe the humor wasn't the type he was used to. They may have been like the woman who wrote to me: "When I'm with men, my wit or cleverness seems inappropriate (or lost!) so I don't bother. When I'm with my women friends, however, there's no hold on puns or cracks and my humor is fully appreciated."

The types of humor women and men tend to prefer differ. Research has shown   28
that the most common form of humor among men is razzing, teasing, and mock-hostile attacks, while among women it's self-mocking. Women often mistake men's teasing as genuinely hostile. Men often mistake women's mock self-deprecation as truly putting themselves down.

Women have told me they were taken more seriously when they learned to   29
joke the way the guys did. For example, a teacher who went to a national conference with seven other teachers (mostly women) and a group of administrators (mostly men) was annoyed that the administrators always found reasons to leave boring seminars, while the teachers felt they had to stay and take notes. One evening, when the group met at a bar in the hotel, the principal asked her how one such seminar had turned out. She reported, "As soon as you left, it got much better." He laughed out loud at her response. The playful insult appealed to the men—but there was a trade-off. The women seemed to back off from her after this. (Perhaps they were put off by her using joking to align herself with the bosses.)

There is no "right" way to talk. When problems arise, the culprit may be style   30
differences—and *all* styles will at times fail with others who don't share or understand them, just as English won't do you much good if you try to speak to someone who knows only French. If you want to get your message across, it's not a question of being "right"; it's a question of using language that's shared—or at least understood.

READING CLOSELY

1. In this essay, what principle of classification is Deborah Tannen using to classify "different ways of speaking" (2)?

2. In what fundamental way do the "conversational rituals" of men and women differ, according to Tannen (2)? Do you think she's right? Why or why not?

3. Tannen says she is classifying the "different ways" in which men and women speak (2). What else is she classifying?

4. Women, says Tannen, tend to apologize more often than men do. Why? She also finds that women often say "thank-you" when they don't really mean it (13). What *do* they often mean by "thank-you"?

5. In Tannen's view, when women complain, they are often trying to "establish rapport" (24). How does she say most men respond to this technique?

6. Women, says Tannen, often see "verbal opposition" as a direct attack (16). How does she say that men see it?

STRATEGIES AND STRUCTURES

1. "Although you may never enjoy verbal sparring, some women find it helpful to learn how to do it" (19). To whom is Tannen speaking here? Can you find other evidence that indicates the identity of her intended audience?

2. What is Tannen's underlying purpose in classifying the verbal behavior of men and women in terms of the workplace? How can you tell?

3. Tannen divides her subject into seven main "areas" (3). Are these categories based on significant characteristics? Are they mutually exclusive? Do they cover all kinds of communication? Explain.

4. Tannen breaks "jokes" into the "the types of humor women and men tend to prefer" (28). Why does she use subcategories here and not elsewhere in her classification?

5. How and how well does Tannen use classification to structure her ARGUMENT about women in the workplace?

6. *Other Methods.* Much of Tannen's evidence is anecdotal—that is, she tells brief stories to make her points. How effective do you find these NARRATIVE elements of her essay? Explain.

THINKING ABOUT LANGUAGE

1. "Conversation," says Tannen, "is a ritual" (1). What is "ritual" behavior, and why do you think Tannen uses this term?

2. What are the CONNOTATIONS of "hard-edged" when it's applied to women (9)? What are its connotations when applied to men?

3. What is "right-between-the-eyes style" (12)? What two things are being compared in this METAPHOR?

4. Tannen accuses a man of "barking" (11) and several women of allowing their emotions to "erupt" (20). How do these choices of words confirm or contradict her assertions about the way men and women communicate?

FOR WRITING

1. Can you think of any "areas of miscommunication" (3) between men and women that Tannen has overlooked? Write a paragraph on each kind, providing specific examples.

2. Write an essay about the different ways in which one of the following groups of people communicate (or miscommunicate) with each other: siblings, children and parents, students and teachers, engineers and liberal arts majors, old people and young people, or some other group or groups.

AMY TAN

Mother Tongue

Amy Tan (b. 1952) was born in Oakland, California, to Chinese immigrants. She earned an M.A. in linguistics from San Jose State University and worked on programs for disabled children before becoming a freelance business writer. In 1987 she visited China for the first time. Upon returning to the United States, she set to work on a collection of interconnected stories about Chinese American mothers and daughters. The Joy Luck Club *(1989) was an international success, and was translated into seventeen languages (including Chinese). Since then Tan has published several novels, including* The Kitchen God's Wife *(1991),* The Bonesetter's Daughter *(2001), and* Saving Fish from Drowning *(2005)—in addition to two children's books and a book of nonfiction,* The Opposite of Fate: A Book of Musings *(2003), which explores lucky accidents, choice, and memory.*

In her essay "Mother Tongue," which first appeared in the Threepenny Review, *a literary magazine, in 1990, Tan classifies various forms of the English language, from her mother's "broken English" (a term she dislikes) to the complex prose of academia. "And I use them all," she writes—"all the Englishes I grew up with."*

I AM NOT A SCHOLAR OF ENGLISH or literature. I cannot give you much more than personal opinions on the English language and its variations in this country or others.

I am a writer. And by that definition, I am someone who has always loved language. I am fascinated by language in daily life. I spend a great deal of my time thinking about the power of language—the way it can evoke an emotion, a visual image, a complex idea, or a simple truth. Language is the tool of my trade. And I use them all—all the Englishes I grew up with.

Recently, I was made keenly aware of the different Englishes I do use. I was giving a talk to a large group of people, the same talk I had already given to half a dozen other groups. The nature of the talk was about my writing, my life, and my book, *The Joy Luck Club.* The talk was going along well enough, until I remembered one major difference that made the whole talk sound wrong. My mother was in the room. And it was perhaps the first time she had heard me give a lengthy speech, using the kind of English I have never used with her. I was saying things like, "The intersection of memory upon imagination" and "There is an aspect of my fiction that relates to thus-and-thus"—a speech filled with carefully wrought grammatical phrases, burdened, it suddenly seemed to me, with nominalized forms, past perfect tenses, conditional phrases, all the forms of standard English that I had learned in school and through books, the forms of English I did not use at home with my mother.

Just last week, I was walking down the street with my mother, and I again found myself conscious of the English I was using, the English I do use with her. We were talking about the price of new and used furniture and I heard myself saying this: "Not waste money that way." My husband was with us as well, and he didn't notice any switch in my English. And then I realized why. It's because over the twenty years we've been together I've often used the same kind of English with him, and sometimes he even uses it with me. It has become our language of intimacy, a different sort of English that relates to family talk, the language I grew up with.

So you'll have some idea of what this family talk I heard sounds like, I'll quote what my mother said during a recent conversation which I videotaped and then transcribed. During this conversation, my mother was talking about a political gangster in Shanghai who had the same last name as her family's, Du, and how the gangster in his early years wanted to be adopted by her family, which was rich by comparison. Later, the gangster became more powerful, far richer than my mother's family, and one day showed up at my mother's wedding to pay his respects. Here's what she said in part:

"Du Yusong having business like fruit stand. Like off the street kind. He is Du like Du Zong—but not Tsung-ming Island people. The local people call putong, the river east side, he belong to that side local people. That man want to ask Du Zong father take him in like become own family. Du Zong father wasn't look down on him, but didn't take seriously, until that man big like become a mafia. Now important person, very hard to inviting him. Chinese way, came only to show respect, don't stay for dinner. Respect for making big celebration, he shows up. Mean gives lots of respect. Chinese custom. Chinese social life that way. If too important won't have to stay too long. He come to my wedding. I didn't see, I heard it. I gone to boy's side, they have YMCA dinner. Chinese age I was nineteen."

You should know that my mother's expressive command of English belies how much she actually understands. She reads the *Forbes*[1] report, listens to *Wall Street Week*, converses daily with her stockbroker, reads all of Shirley MacLaine's books with ease—all kinds of things I can't begin to understand. Yet some of my friends tell me they understand 50 percent of what my mother says. Some say they understand 80 to 90 percent. Some say they understand none of it, as if she were speaking pure Chinese. But to me, my mother's English is perfectly clear, perfectly natural. It's my mother tongue. Her language, as I hear it, is vivid, direct, full of

1. *Forbes*: a business-oriented periodical that focuses on stocks, bonds, business trends, and other items of interest to investors.

observation and imagery. That was the language that helped shape the way I saw things, expressed things, made sense of the world.

Lately, I've been giving more thought to the kind of English my mother speaks. 8 Like others, I have described it to people as "broken" or "fractured" English. But I wince when I say that. It has always bothered me that I can think of no way to describe it other than "broken," as if it were damaged and needed to be fixed, as if it lacked a certain wholeness and soundness. I've heard other terms used, "limited English," for example. But they seem just as bad, as if everything is limited, including people's perceptions of the limited English speaker.

I know this for a fact, because when I was growing up, my mother's "limited" 9 English limited *my* perception of her. I was ashamed of her English. I believed that her English reflected the quality of what she had to say. That is, because she expressed them imperfectly her thoughts were imperfect. And I had plenty of empirical evidence to support me: the fact that people in department stores, at banks, and at restaurants did not take her seriously, did not give her good service, pretended not to understand her, or even acted as if they did not hear her.

My mother has long realized the limitations of her English as well. When I was 10 fifteen, she used to have me call people on the phone to pretend I was she. In this guise, I was forced to ask for information or even to complain and yell at people who had been rude to her. One time it was a call to her stockbroker in New York. She had cashed out her small portfolio and it just so happened we were going to go to New York the next week, our very first trip outside California. I had to get on the phone and say in an adolescent voice that was not very convincing, "This is Mrs. Tan."

And my mother was standing in the back whispering loudly, "Why he don't send 11 me check, already two weeks late. So mad he lie to me, losing me money."

And then I said in perfect English, "Yes, I'm getting rather concerned. You had 12 agreed to send the check two weeks ago, but it hasn't arrived."

Then she began to talk more loudly. "What he want, I come to New York tell 13 him front of his boss, you cheating me?" And I was trying to calm her down, make her be quiet, while telling the stockbroker, "I can't tolerate any more excuses. If I don't receive the check immediately, I am going to have to speak to your manager when I'm in New York next week." And sure enough, the following week there we were in front of this astonished stockbroker, and I was sitting there red-faced and quiet, and my mother, the real Mrs. Tan, was shouting at his boss in her impeccable broken English.

We used a similar routine just five days ago, for a situation that was far less 14 humorous. My mother had gone to the hospital for an appointment, to find out about a benign brain tumor a CAT scan had revealed a month ago. She said she had spoken very good English, her best English, no mistakes. Still, she said, the hospital did not apologize when they said they had lost the CAT scan and she had come for nothing. She said they did not seem to have any sympathy when she told them she was anxious to know the exact diagnosis, since her husband and son had both died of brain tumors. She said they would not give her any more information until the next time and she would have to make another appointment for that. So she said she would not leave until the doctor called her daughter. She wouldn't budge. And when the doctor finally called her daughter, me, who spoke in perfect English—lo and behold—we had assurances the CAT scan would be found, promises that a conference call on Monday would be held, and apologies for any suffering my mother had gone through for a most regrettable mistake.

I think my mother's English almost had an effect on limiting my possibilities in 15
life as well. Sociologists and linguists probably will tell you that a person's developing language skills are more influenced by peers. But I do think that the language spoken in the family, especially in immigrant families which are more insular, plays a large role in shaping the language of the child. And I believe that it affected my results on achievement tests, IQ tests, and the SAT. While my English skills were never judged as poor, compared to math, English could not be considered my strong suit. In grade school I did moderately well, getting perhaps B's, sometimes B-pluses, in English and scoring perhaps in the sixtieth or seventieth percentile on achievement tests. But those scores were not good enough to override the opinion that my true abilities lay in math and science, because in those areas I achieved A's and scored in the ninetieth percentile or higher.

This was understandable. Math is precise; there is only one correct answer. 16
Whereas, for me at least, the answers on English tests were always a judgment call, a matter of opinion and personal experience. Those tests were constructed around items like fill-in-the-blank sentence completion, such as, "Even though Tom was _____, Mary thought he was _____." And the correct answer always seemed to be the most bland combinations of thoughts, for example, "Even though Tom was shy, Mary thought he was charming," with the grammatical structure "even though" limiting the correct answer to some sort of semantic opposites, so you wouldn't get answers like, "Even though Tom was foolish, Mary thought he was ridiculous." Well, according to my mother, there were very few limitations as to what Tom could have been and what Mary might have thought of him. So I never did well on tests like that.

The same was true with word analogies, pairs of words in which you were sup- 17
posed to find some sort of logical, semantic relationship—for example, "*Sunset* is to *nightfall* as _____ is to _____." And here you would be presented with a list of four possible pairs, one of which showed the same kind of relationship: *red* is to

stoplight, bus is to *arrival, chills* is to *fever, yawn* is to *boring*. Well, I could never think that way. I knew what the tests were asking, but I could not block out of my mind the images already created by the first pair, "*sunset* is to *nightfall*"—and I would see a burst of colors against a darkening sky, the moon rising, the lowering of a curtain of stars. And all the other pairs of words—red, bus, stoplight, boring—just threw up a mass of confusing images, making it impossible for me to sort out something as logical as saying: "A sunset precedes nightfall" is the same as "a chill precedes a fever." The only way I would have gotten that answer right would have been to imagine an associative situation, for example, my being disobedient and staying out past sunset, catching a chill at night, which turns into feverish pneumonia as punishment, which indeed did happen to me.

I have been thinking about all this lately, about my mother's English, about 18
achievement tests. Because lately I've been asked, as a writer, why there are not more Asian Americans represented in American literature. Why are there few Asian Americans enrolled in creative writing programs? Why do so many Chinese students go into engineering? Well, these are broad sociological questions I can't begin to answer. But I have noticed in surveys—in fact, just last week—that Asian students, as a whole, always do significantly better on math achievement tests than in English. And this makes me think that there are other Asian-American students whose English spoken in the home might also be described as "broken" or "limited." And perhaps they also have teachers who are steering them away from writing and into math and science, which is what happened to me.

Fortunately, I happen to be rebellious in nature and enjoy the challenge of dis- 19
proving assumptions made about me. I became an English major my first year in college, after being enrolled as pre-med. I started writing nonfiction as a freelancer the week after I was told by my former boss that writing was my worst skill and I should hone my talents toward account management.

But it wasn't until 1985 that I finally began to write fiction. And at first I wrote 20
using what I thought to be wittily crafted sentences, sentences that would finally prove I had mastery over the English language. Here's an example from the first draft of a story that later made its way into *The Joy Luck Club*, but without this line: "That was my mental quandary in its nascent state." A terrible line, which I can barely pronounce.

Fortunately, for reasons I won't get into today, I later decided I should envision 21
a reader for the stories I would write. And the reader I decided upon was my mother, because these were stories about mothers. So with this reader in mind— and in fact she did read my early drafts—I began to write stories using all the Englishes I grew up with: the English I spoke to my mother, which for lack of a better

term might be described as "simple"; the English she used with me, which for lack of a better term might be described as "broken"; my translation of her Chinese, which could certainly be described as "watered down"; and what I imagined to be her translation of her Chinese if she could speak in perfect English, her internal language, and for that I sought to preserve the essence, but neither an English nor a Chinese structure. I wanted to capture what language ability tests can never reveal: her intent, her passion, her imagery, the rhythms of her speech and the nature of her thoughts.

Apart from what any critic had to say about my writing, I knew I had succeeded   22 where it counted when my mother finished reading my book and gave me her verdict: "So easy to read."

READING CLOSELY

1. Amy Tan classifies the various "Englishes" that she uses into two basic categories. What are they, and what are the main characteristics of each kind?

2. How many different types of English did Tan learn from talking with her mother, a native speaker of Chinese? What are the different attributes of each type?

3. According to Tan, what are the essential attributes of "standard" English (3)? How did she learn to use this kind of English?

4. Which kinds of English does Tan use most often as a writer? Why?

STRATEGIES AND STRUCTURES

1. "So you'll have some idea of what this family talk I heard sounds like, I'll quote what my mother said during a recent conversation" (5). Here and elsewhere in her essay Tan addresses the reader directly as "you." Why do you think she does this?

2. Why is Tan classifying the different kinds of English she knows and uses? Is she, for example, conveying information, arguing a point, telling an entertaining story—some other purpose? Explain.

3. Should Tan have laid out her classification system more fully at the beginning of her essay instead of waiting to the end? Why or why not?

4. In paragraphs 15–18, Tan advances an ARGUMENT about IQ and achievement tests. What's her point here, and how does she use classification to support it?

5. *Other Methods.* Tan classifies "all the Englishes" she grew up with in paragraph 21, near the end of her essay. How well does this classification system fit the specific EXAMPLES she has cited earlier? Explain.

Thinking about Language

1. Explain the PUN in Tan's title. How does it prepare us for the rest of her essay?

2. Tan does not want to use "broken" or "fractured" as names for the kind of English her mother speaks (8). Why not?

3. Tan never gives a name to the kind of English she uses to represent her mother's "internal language" (21). What would you call it? Why?

For Writing

1. In a paragraph or two, give several examples of "standard" (or "nonstandard") English, and explain why they belong in this category.

2. How many different kinds of English, or other languages, do you use at home, at school, or among friends? Write an essay classifying them, and explaining how and when you use each type.

DAVID BROOKS

People Like Us

David Brooks (b. 1961) was born in Toronto and grew up in New York City. Soon after graduating from the University of Chicago with a degree in history, he began his journalism career as a police reporter for a newspaper wire service. Brooks next spent nine years at the Wall Street Journal, *first as a book-review editor and then as a foreign correspondent. In 1995 he joined the staff of the* Weekly Standard, *a publication of the emerging neoconservative movement; he appears regularly as a political analyst on PBS television and National Public Radio, and contributes a regular column to the Op-Ed page of the* New York Times. *Brooks has authored two books of social commentary,* Bobos in Paradise: The New Upper Class and How They Got There *(2000) and* On Paradise Drive: How We Live Now (And Always Have) in the Future Tense *(2004).*

"People Like Us" first appeared in 2003 in The Atlantic, *a magazine devoted mainly to political science and foreign affairs. Although the essay focuses on the various principles of classification by which people sort themselves according to a simple binary system—them and us—Brooks also contemplates a number of alternate "groupings." Classification is thus a method of development in the essay as well as its main subject.*

MAYBE IT'S TIME to admit the obvious. We don't really care about diversity all 1 that much in America, even though we talk about it a great deal. Maybe somewhere in this country there is a truly diverse neighborhood in which a black Pentecostal minister lives next to a white anti-globalization activist, who lives next to an Asian short-order cook, who lives next to a professional golfer, who lives next to a postmodern-literature professor and a cardiovascular surgeon. But I have never been to or heard of that neighborhood. Instead, what I have seen all around the country is people making strenuous efforts to group themselves with people who are basically like themselves.

Human beings are capable of drawing amazingly subtle social distinctions and 2 then shaping their lives around them. In the Washington, D.C., area Democratic lawyers tend to live in suburban Maryland, and Republican lawyers tend to live in suburban Virginia. If you asked a Democratic lawyer to move from her $750,000 house in Bethesda, Maryland, to a $750,000 house in Great Falls, Virginia, she'd look at you as if you had just asked her to buy a pickup truck with a gun rack and to shove chewing tobacco in her kid's mouth. In Manhattan the owner of a $3 million SoHo loft would feel out of place moving into a $3 million Fifth Avenue apartment.

A West Hollywood interior decorator would feel dislocated if you asked him to move to Orange County. In Georgia a barista from Athens would probably not fit in serving coffee in Americus.

It is a common complaint that every place is starting to look the same. But in the information age, the late writer James Chapin once told me, every place becomes more like itself. People are less often tied down to factories and mills, and they can search for places to live on the basis of cultural affinity. Once they find a town in which people share their values, they flock there, and reinforce whatever was distinctive about the town in the first place. Once Boulder, Colorado, became known as congenial to politically progressive mountain bikers, half the politically progressive mountain bikers in the country (it seems) moved there; they made the place so culturally pure that it has become practically a parody of itself.

But people love it. Make no mistake—we are increasing our happiness by segmenting off so rigorously. We are finding places where we are comfortable and where we feel we can flourish. But the choices we make toward that end lead to the very opposite of diversity. The United States might be a diverse nation when considered as a whole, but block by block and institution by institution it is a relatively homogeneous nation.

When we use the word "diversity" today we usually mean racial integration. But even here our good intentions seem to have run into the brick wall of human nature. Over the past generation reformers have tried heroically, and in many cases successfully, to end housing discrimination. But recent patterns aren't encouraging: according to an analysis of the 2000 census data, the 1990s saw only a slight increase in the racial integration of neighborhoods in the United States. The number of middle-class and upper-middle-class African-American families is rising, but for whatever reasons—racism, psychological comfort—these families tend to congregate in predominantly black neighborhoods.

In fact, evidence suggests that some neighborhoods become more segregated over time. New suburbs in Arizona and Nevada, for example, start out reasonably well integrated. These neighborhoods don't yet have reputations, so people choose their houses for other, mostly economic reasons. But as neighborhoods age, they develop personalities (that's where the Asians live, and that's where the Hispanics live), and segmentation occurs. It could be that in a few years the new suburbs in the Southwest will be nearly as segregated as the established ones in the Northeast and the Midwest.

Even though race and ethnicity run deep in American society, we should in theory be able to find areas that are at least culturally diverse. But here, too, people show few signs of being truly interested in building diverse communities: If you run a retail company and you're thinking of opening new stores, you can choose among dozens of consulting firms that are quite effective at locating your potential customers. They can do this because people with similar tastes and preferences tend to congregate by ZIP code.

The most famous of these precision marketing firms is Claritas, which breaks 8 down the U.S. population into sixty-two psycho-demographic clusters, based on such factors as how much money people make, what they like to read and watch, and what products they have bought in the past. For example, the "suburban sprawl" cluster is composed of young families making about $41,000 a year and living in fast-growing places such as Burnsville, Minnesota, and Bensalem, Pennsylvania. These people are almost twice as likely as other Americans to have three-way calling. They are two and a half times as likely to buy Light n' Lively Kid Yogurt. Members of the "towns & gowns" cluster are recent college graduates in places such as Berkeley, California, and Gainesville, Florida. They are big consumers of Dove Bars and *Saturday Night Live*. They tend to drive small foreign cars and to read *Rolling Stone* and *Scientific American*.

Looking through the market research, one can sometimes be amazed by how 9 efficiently people cluster—and by how predictable we all are. If you wanted to sell imported wine, obviously you would have to find places where rich people live. But did you know that the sixteen counties with the greatest proportion of imported-wine drinkers are all in the same three metropolitan areas (New York, San Francisco, and Washington, D.C.)? If you tried to open a motor-home dealership in Montgomery County, Pennsylvania, you'd probably go broke, because people in this ring of the Philadelphia suburbs think RVs are kind of uncool. But if you traveled just a short way north, to Monroe County, Pennsylvania, you would find yourself in the fifth motor-home-friendliest county in America.

Geography is not the only way we find ourselves divided from people unlike us. 10 Some of us watch Fox News, while others listen to NPR. Some like David Letterman, and others—typically in less urban neighborhoods—like Jay Leno. Some go to charismatic churches; some go to mainstream churches. Americans tend more and more often to marry people with education levels similar to their own, and to befriend people with backgrounds similar to their own.

My favorite illustration of this latter pattern comes from the first, noncontroversial chapter of *The Bell Curve*.[1] Think of your twelve closest friends, Richard J. 11 Hernstein and Charles Murray write. If you had chosen them randomly from the American population, the odds that half of your twelve closest friends would be college graduates would be six in a thousand. The odds that half of the twelve would have advanced degrees would be less than one in a million. Have any of your twelve closest friends graduated from Harvard, Stanford, Yale, Princeton, Caltech,

---

1. *The Bell Curve* (1994): a book about the role of intelligence in social and economic success that controversially connected race and intelligence.

MIT, Duke, Dartmouth, Cornell, Columbia, Chicago, or Brown? If you chose your friends randomly from the American population, the odds against your having four or more friends from those schools would be more than a billion to one.

Many of us live in absurdly unlikely groupings, because we have organized our   12
lives that way.

It's striking that the institutions that talk the most about diversity often practice   13
it the least. For example, no group of people sings the diversity anthem more frequently and fervently than administrators at just such elite universities. But elite
universities are amazingly undiverse in their values, politics, and mores. Professors
in particular are drawn from a rather narrow segment of the population. If faculties
reflected the general population, 32 percent of professors would be registered
Democrats and 31 percent would be registered Republicans. Forty percent would
be evangelical Christians. But a recent study of several universities by the conservative Center for the Study of Popular Culture and the American Enterprise Institute found that roughly 90 percent of those professors in the arts and sciences who
had registered with a political party had registered Democratic. Fifty-seven professors at Brown were found on the voter-registration rolls. Of those, fifty-four
were Democrats. Of the forty-two professors in the English, history, sociology, and
political-science departments, all were Democrats. The results at Harvard, Penn
State, Maryland, and the University of California at Santa Barbara were similar to
the results at Brown.

What we are looking at here is human nature. People want to be around others   14
who are roughly like themselves. That's called community. It probably would be
psychologically difficult for most Brown professors to share an office with someone
who was pro-life, a member of the National Rifle Association, or an evangelical
Christian. It's likely that hiring committees would subtly—even unconsciously—
screen out any such people they encountered. Republicans and evangelical Christians have sensed that they are not welcome at places like Brown, so they don't
even consider working there. In fact, any registered Republican who contemplates
a career in academia these days is both a hero and a fool. So, in a semi-self-selective
pattern, brainy people with generally liberal social mores flow to academia, and
brainy people with generally conservative mores flow elsewhere.

The dream of diversity is like the dream of equality. Both are based on ideals we   15
celebrate even as we undermine them daily. (How many times have you seen
someone renounce a high-paying job or pull his child from an elite college on the
grounds that these things are bad for equality?) On the one hand, the situation is
appalling. It is appalling that Americans know so little about one another. It is
appalling that many of us are so narrow-minded that we can't tolerate a few people
with ideas significantly different from our own. It's appalling that evangelical
Christians are practically absent from entire professions, such as academia, the

media, and filmmaking. It's appalling that people should be content to cut themselves off from everyone unlike themselves.

The segmentation of society means that often we don't even have arguments   16
across the political divide. Within their little validating communities, liberals and
conservatives circulate half-truths about the supposed awfulness of the other side.
These distortions are believed because it feels good to believe them.

On the other hand, there are limits to how diverse any community can or   17
should be. I've come to think that it is not useful to try to hammer diversity into
every neighborhood and institution in the United States. Sure, Augusta National[2]
should probably admit women, and university sociology departments should probably hire a conservative or two. It would be nice if all neighborhoods had a good
mixture of ethnicities. But human nature being what it is, most places and institutions are going to remain culturally homogeneous.

It's probably better to think about diverse lives, not diverse institutions. Human   18
beings, if they are to live well, will have to move through a series of institutions and
environments, which may be individually homogeneous but, taken together, will
offer diverse experiences. It might also be a good idea to make national service a
rite of passage for young people in this country: it would take them out of their
narrow neighborhood segment and thrust them in with people unlike themselves.
Finally, it's probably important for adults to get out of their own familiar circles. If
you live in a coastal, socially liberal neighborhood, maybe you should take out a
subscription to *The Door*, the evangelical humor magazine; or maybe you should
visit Branson, Missouri. Maybe you should stop in at a megachurch. Sure, it would
be superficial familiarity, but it beats the iron curtains that now separate the
nation's various cultural zones.

Look around at your daily life. Are you really in touch with the broad diversity of   19
American life? Do you care?

2. *Augusta National*: a prestigious golf club in Augusta, Georgia, that is the site of a major professional golf event, the Masters' Tournament. Augusta National excludes women from becoming members. Because the club is home to a sporting event with widespread public interest and attention, there
has been public debate on the issue in recent years and pressure on the club to change its policy.

READING CLOSELY

1. What prevents Americans from achieving true diversity, according to Brooks?
   In his view, what main criterion do we all use for dividing ourselves into
   groups?

2. What principle of classification do marketing firms such as Claritas use to classify people (8)? What is the purpose of their classifications?

3. How useful is economic data for classifying people in social and political ways? That is, how much does what people buy tell us about who they are? Explain.

4. According to Brooks, how likely is it that Americans will reshuffle themselves into a more diverse population? What has CAUSED our homogeneous society, in his view, and what does he think can be done to correct it?

5. What does Brooks mean when he says, "It's probably better to think about diverse lives, not diverse institutions" (18)? Do you agree? Why or why not?

STRATEGIES AND STRUCTURES

1. "Look around at your daily life," Brooks admonishes (19). To what AUDIENCE is he speaking here? What kinds of readers might be most likely to resist Brooks's claim that the lack of diversity in American society is "obvious" (1)?

2. What is the main principle of classification in the first half of Brooks's essay? How and how well does Brooks use it to support his point about the lack of diversity in America?

3. What principle of classification is Brooks illustrating when he refers to *The Bell Curve* (11)? When he refers to several "elite universities" (13)?

4. Most of the ways in which Americans group themselves, says Brooks, are "absurdly unlikely" (12). Which of his many EXAMPLES do you find particularly strong—or weak? Why?

5. Throughout his essay, Brooks proposes a number of alternative ways to group people. What are some of them? On what principle of classification are they based? How do they support what Brooks says about diversity?

6. *Other Methods.* Brooks is using classification to support an ARGUMENT about classification. How so? Is this an effective strategy? Why or why not?

THINKING ABOUT LANGUAGE

1. Brooks uses a number of synonyms for *segregate* and *segregation*. What are some of them? Why doesn't he simply adopt the more familiar term instead?

2. The word "diversity" comes up throughout Brooks's essay. How and where does he DEFINE it?

3. In reasoning why people prefer to be around their peers, Brooks states: "That's called community" (14). Is he being IRONIC here? Explain.

4. "Iron curtains" (18) is a phrase from the days of America's cold war with the former Soviet Union. Why do you think Brooks uses it in an essay about cultural divisions at home?

FOR WRITING

1. Write a paragraph enumerating the types of people you would expect to find in an ideally diverse neighborhood.

2. Write a classification essay in which you respond to the statement that "we don't really care about diversity all that much in America" (1). You can agree or disagree, but prove your point by dividing Americans into a number of categories that show their similarities or differences.

MICHELLE WATSON

Shades of Character

*Michelle Watson was a student at Roane State Community College in eastern Ten-
nessee when she wrote this classification essay for an English class. "Shades of Character" is based on Watson's research in child psychology and education, particularly her
study of typical childhood personalities. Watson's instructor, Jennifer Jordan-Henley,
chose the essay for publication on the website of the college's Online Writing Lab.*

*Citing the work of several experts, Watson classifies children's personalities accord-
ing to commonly recognized types. This classification system provides a framework for
organizing the entire essay, which discusses each type in turn, paying close attention to
the significant attributes that distinguish one "shade" of behavior from another. Watson documents her sources using the MLA style.*

ANYONE WHO HAS SPENT TIME around children will notice that each one has   1
a special personality all his or her own. Children, like adults, have different traits
that make up their personalities. Experts have researched these traits in detail, and
they classify children into different categories. Some experts have named more
than three categories, but Dr. Peter L. Mangione[1] has chosen three that most
experts agree with. These categories are "flexible," "fearful," and "feisty." Children
generally may have similar interests, but the way they interact and deal with these
interests displays their personality types.

The flexible personality is the most common of the three types. About "forty per-   2
cent of all children fall into the flexible or easy group" (Mangione). These children
usually handle feelings of anger and disappointment by becoming only mildly upset.
This does not mean that they do not feel mad or disappointed, they just choose to
react mildly. These actions mean the flexible child is easy to take care of and be
around. According to Mangione, such children usually "adapt to new situations and
activities quickly, are toilet-trained easily, and are generally cheerful." Flexible children are subtle in their need for attention. Instead of yelling and demanding it, they
will slowly and politely let their caregivers know about the need. If they do not get
the attention right away, they "seldom make a fuss." They patiently wait, but they
still make it known that they need the attention. These children also are easygoing,
so routines like feeding and napping are regular (Mangione).

Flexible children may be referred to as "good as gold" because of their cheerful   3

1. *Dr. Peter L. Mangione*: a child psychologist and co-director of the Center for Child and Family
Studies in Sausalito, California. He is the content developer and writer of the video *Flexible, Fearful, or
Feisty: The Different Temperaments of Infants and Toddlers* (1990), produced by the California Depart-
ment of Education. All quotations from Dr. Mangione are from this video.

attitudes. Since these are well-behaved children, the caregiver needs to make sure the child is getting the attention he or she needs. The caregiver should "check in with the flexible child from time to time" (Mangione). By checking in with the child regularly, the caregiver will be more knowledgeable about when the child needs attention and when he or she does not.

The next temperament is the fearful type. These are the more quiet and shy chil-   4 dren. This kind makes up about 15 percent of all children, according to Mangione. They adapt slowly to new environments and take longer than flexible children when warming up to things. When presented with a new environment, fearful children often cling to something or someone familiar, whether it be the main caregiver or a material object such as a blanket. The fearful child will cling until he or she feels comfortable with the new situation. This can result in a deep attachment of the child to a particular caregiver or object. Fearful children may also withdraw when pushed into a new situation too quickly (Mangione). They may also withdraw when other children are jumping into a new project or situation they are not comfortable with. These children may tend to play alone rather than with a group.

In dealing with fearful children, caregivers find they need more attention than   5 flexible children. A good technique for helping these children is having "a sequence of being with, talking to, stepping back, remaining available, and moving on" (Mangione). The caregiver can also help fearful children by giving them "extra soothing combined with an inch-by-inch fostering of independence and assertiveness" (Viorst 174). One of the most effective techniques is just taking everything slowly and helping the child to become more comfortable with his or her surroundings.

The third temperament type is called feisty. About "10 percent" of children fit   6 into this category (Mangione). Feisty children express their opinions in a very intense way. Whether they are happy or mad, everyone around them will know how they feel. These children remain active most of the time, and this causes them to be very aggressive. Feisty children often have a tendency toward "negative persistence" and will go "on and on nagging, whining and negotiating" if there is something they particularly want ("Facts About Temperament"). Unlike flexible children, feisty children are irregular in their napping and feeding times, but they do not adapt well to changes in their routines. They get "used to things and won't give them up" ("Facts About Temperament"). Anything out of the ordinary can send them into a fit. If these children are not warned of a change, they may react very negatively (Mangione). Feisty children also tend to be very sensitive to their surrounding environment. As a result, they may have strong reactions to their surroundings.

When dealing with feisty children, the caregiver should know strategies that   7 receive positive results when different situations arise. Mangione supports the "redirection technique" to calm feisty children. This method helps when the child is reacting very negatively to a situation. According to Mangione, to properly implement the redirection technique, the caregiver should begin by recognizing and empathizing with the feelings of the feisty child and placing firm limits on any unacceptable behavior. This response lets the child know that both his or her desire for the toy and feelings of anger when denied the toy are acceptable to the caregiver. At the same time, the caregiver should clearly communicate to the child that expressing anger through hurtful or disruptive behavior is not acceptable. The child will probably need time to experience his or her emotions and settle down. Then offer an alternative toy or activity that may interest the child, who is then given time to consider the new choice and to accept or reject it.

Caregivers should consider that these children generally do not have regular 8 feeding and napping times. The caregiver should be flexible when working with these children and should try to conform more to the desires of the child (Mangione). If there is going to be a change in a child's routine, the caregiver has an easier time when the child has been warned of the change.

Generally speaking, children can be divided into three groups, but caregivers 9 must not forget that each child is an individual. Children may have the traits of all three of the personality groups, but they are categorized into the one they are most like. Whatever their temperament, children need to be treated according to their individual needs. When these needs are met appropriately the child will be happier, and those around the child will feel better also. Knowing the general personality types and how to react to them will help to make the caregiver's job much easier and aid in the relief of unnecessary stress.

Works Cited

"Facts About Temperament." *Temperamentproject*. Australian Temperament Project, n.d. Web. 25 Oct. 2000. < http://www.temperamentproject.bc.ca/html/facts/html >.

Mangione, Peter L., cont. dev./writ. *Flexible, Fearful, or Feisty: The Different Temperaments of Infants and Toddlers*. Prod. J. Ronald Lally. Cont. dev. S. Signer and J. Ronald Lally. Dir. Janet Poole. Media Services Unit, California Dept. of Education, 1990. Videocassette.

Viorst, Judith. "Is Your Child's Personality Set at Birth?" *Redbook* Nov. 1995: 174+. *Academic OneFile*. Web. 23 Oct. 2000.

READING CLOSELY

1. According to Michelle Watson, experts in child psychology agree on at least three basic types when classifying the personalities of young children: "flexible," "fearful," and "feisty" (1). What are the main characteristics of each type?

2. If every child has "a special personality all his or her own," how is it that Watson and the experts she cites can group them into personality types (1)? Explain.

3. "Feisty children," says Watson, "express their opinions in a very intense way" (6). What specific techniques does she offer for dealing with such children?

STRATEGIES AND STRUCTURES

1. Watson not only identifies "the general personality types" of young children; she explains "how to react to them" (9). Why? Who is her intended audience, and what is her main point in classifying infants and toddlers as she does?

2. Watson lays out her classification system in the opening paragraph of her essay. What is her principle of classification? Why does she use this principle instead of classifying children by sex, height, weight, or some other physical characteristic?

3. In what order does Watson present the personality types in her classification system? Is this arrangement logical? Why or why not?

4. How significant are the characteristics that Watson uses to define her three personality types? Does she always describe the same kind of behavior, such as how a child reacts to objects, when defining each type? Should she? Explain.

5. *Other Methods.* In the conclusion of her essay, Watson reminds the reader that "children can be divided into three groups" (9). What ARGUMENT is she also making here? How and how well does her classification of children support that argument?

THINKING ABOUT LANGUAGE

1. What are the CONNOTATIONS of "feisty" (1)? What other terms might experts have chosen for this personality type, and why do you think they settled on this one?

2. Watson speaks of "caregivers" throughout her essay. Why do you think she uses this term instead of *parents* or *family members*?

3. How would you DEFINE "negative persistence" (6)?

FOR WRITING

1. Which of Watson's three personality types were you as a child? Write a paragraph using your early behavior as an EXAMPLE of the type.

2. Using the three-part system that Watson discusses, write an essay classifying you and your siblings, or several other children you have known, into each of the various types.

GABRIEL GARCÍA MÁRQUEZ

A Very Old Man with Enormous Wings

*Gabriel García Márquez (b. 1928) grew up in Aracataca, a remote town near Colum-
bia's Caribbean coast. After studying law at the University of Bogotá, he worked as a
journalist in Latin America, Europe, and the United States; he now resides in Mexico
City. A renowned novelist, García Márquez received the Nobel Prize for Literature in
1982. Perhaps his most famous work is* One Hundred Years of Solitude *(1967), a
novel that fuses realism and fantasy to create a microcosm of modern Latin America in
six generations of one family.*

*"A Very Old Man with Enormous Wings" is from García Márquez's first collection of
short stories,* Leaf Storm *(1955; translated by Gregory Rabassa and published in English in 1971). The story is typical of his "magical realism," a style that treats marvelous
occurrences as ordinary events and commonplace events as marvels.*

ON THE THIRD DAY OF RAIN they had killed so many crabs inside the house   1
that Pelayo had to cross his drenched courtyard and throw them into the sea,
because the newborn child had a temperature all night and they thought it was due
to the stench. The world had been sad since Tuesday. Sea and sky were a single ash-
gray thing and the sands of the beach, which on March nights glimmered like pow-
dered light, had become a stew of mud and rotten shellfish. The light was so weak
at noon that when Pelayo was coming back to the house after throwing away the
crabs, it was hard for him to see what it was that was moving and groaning in the
rear of the courtyard. He had to go very close to see that it was an old man, a very
old man, lying face down in the mud, who, in spite of his tremendous efforts,
couldn't get up, impeded by his enormous wings.

Frightened by that nightmare, Pelayo ran to get Elisenda, his wife, who was put-   2
ting compresses on the sick child, and he took her to the rear of the courtyard.
They both looked at the fallen body with mute stupor. He was dressed like a rag-
picker. There were only a few faded hairs left on his bald skull and very few teeth
in his mouth, and his pitiful condition of a drenched great-grandfather had taken
away any sense of grandeur he might have had. His huge buzzard wings, dirty and
half-plucked, were forever entangled in the mud. They looked at him so long and
so closely that Pelayo and Elisenda very soon overcame their surprise and in the
end found him familiar. Then they dared speak to him, and he answered in an
incomprehensible dialect with a strong sailor's voice. That was how they skipped
over the inconvenience of the wings and quite intelligently concluded that he was
a lonely castaway from some foreign ship wrecked by the storm. And yet, they

called in a neighbor woman who knew everything about life and death to see him, and all she needed was one look to show them their mistake.

"He's an angel," she told them. "He must have been coming for the child, but the poor fellow is so old that the rain knocked him down." 3

On the following day everyone knew that a flesh-and-blood angel was held captive in Pelayo's house. Against the judgment of the wise neighbor woman, for whom angels in those times were the fugitive survivors of a celestial conspiracy, they did not have the heart to club him to death. Pelayo watched over him all afternoon from the kitchen, armed with his bailiff's club, and before going to bed he dragged him out of the mud and locked him up with the hens in the wire chicken coop. In the middle of the night, when the rain stopped, Pelayo and Elisenda were still killing crabs. A short time afterward the child woke up without a fever and with a desire to eat. Then they felt magnanimous and decided to put the angel on a raft with fresh water and provisions for three days and leave him to his fate on the high seas. But when they went out into the courtyard with the first light of dawn, they found the whole neighborhood in front of the chicken coop having fun with the angel, without the slightest reverence, tossing him things to eat through the openings in the wire as if he weren't a supernatural creature but a circus animal. 4

Father Gonzaga arrived before seven o'clock, alarmed at the strange news. By that time onlookers less frivolous than those at dawn had already arrived and they were making all kinds of conjectures concerning the captive's future. The simplest among them thought that he should be named mayor of the world. Others of sterner mind felt that he should be promoted to the rank of five-star general in order to win all wars. Some visionaries hoped that he could be put to stud in order to implant on earth a race of winged wise men who could take charge of the universe. But Father Gonzaga, before becoming a priest, had been a robust woodcutter. Standing by the wire, he reviewed his catechism in an instant and asked them to open the door so that he could take a close look at that pitiful man who looked more like a huge decrepit hen among the fascinated chickens. He was lying in a corner drying his open wings in the sunlight among the fruit peels and breakfast leftovers that the early risers had thrown him. Alien to the impertinences of the world, he only lifted his antiquarian eyes and murmured something in his dialect when Father Gonzaga went into the chicken coop and said good morning to him in Latin. The parish priest had his first suspicion of an imposter when he saw that he did not understand the language of God or know how to greet His ministers. Then he noticed that seen close up he was much too human: he had an unbearable smell of the outdoors, the back side of his wings was strewn with parasites and his main feathers had been mistreated by terrestrial winds, and nothing about him measured up to the proud dignity of angels. Then he came out of the chicken coop and in a brief sermon warned the curious against the risks of being ingenuous. He reminded them that the devil had the bad habit of making use of 5 carnival tricks in order to confuse the unwary. He argued that if wings were not the essential element in determining the difference between a hawk and an airplane, they were even less so in the recognition of angels. Nevertheless, he promised to write a letter to his bishop so that the latter would write to his primate so that the latter would write to the Supreme Pontiff in order to get the final verdict from the highest courts.

His prudence fell on sterile hearts. The news of the captive angel spread with 6
such rapidity that after a few hours the courtyard had the bustle of a marketplace and they had to call in troops with fixed bayonets to disperse the mob that was about to knock the house down. Elisenda, her spine all twisted from sweeping up so much marketplace trash, then got the idea of fencing in the yard and charging five cents admission to see the angel.

The curious came from far away. A traveling carnival arrived with a flying acro- 7
bat who buzzed over the crowd several times, but no one paid any attention to him because his wings were not those of an angel but, rather, those of a sidereal bat. The most unfortunate invalids on earth came in search of health: a poor woman who since childhood had been counting her heartbeats and had run out of num- bers; a Portuguese man who couldn't sleep because the noise of the stars disturbed him; a sleepwalker who got up at night to undo the things he had done while awake; and many others with less serious ailments. In the midst of that shipwreck disorder that made the earth tremble, Pelayo and Elisenda were happy with fatigue, for in less than a week they had crammed their rooms with money and the line of pilgrims waiting their turn to enter still reached beyond the horizon.

The angel was the only one who took no part in his own act. He spent his time 8
trying to get comfortable in his borrowed nest, befuddled by the hellish heat of the oil lamps and sacramental candles that had been placed along the wire. At first they tried to make him eat some mothballs, which, according to the wisdom of the wise neighbor woman, were the food prescribed for angels. But he turned them down, just as he turned down the papal lunches[1] that the penitents brought him, and they never found out whether it was because he was an angel or because he was an old man that in the end he ate nothing but eggplant mush. His only super- natural virtue seemed to be patience. Especially during the first days, when the hens pecked at him, searching for the stellar parasites that proliferated in his wings, and the cripples pulled out feathers to touch their defective parts with, and even the most merciful threw stones at him, trying to get him to rise so they could see him standing. The only time they succeeded in arousing him was when they burned his side with an iron for branding steers, for he had been motionless for so many hours that they thought he was dead. He awoke with a start, ranting in his hermetic language and with tears in his eyes, and he flapped his wings a couple of

---

1. *Papal lunches:* food given in the name of the pope.

times, which brought on a whirlwind of chicken dung and lunar dust and a gale of panic that did not seem to be of this world. Although many thought that his reaction had been one not of rage but of pain, from then on they were careful not to annoy him, because the majority understood that his passivity was not that of a hero taking his ease but that of a cataclysm in repose.

Father Gonzaga held back the crowd's frivolity with formulas of maidservant 9 inspiration while awaiting the arrival of a final judgment on the nature of the captive. But the mail from Rome showed no sense of urgency. They spent their time finding out if the prisoner had a navel, if his dialect had any connection with Aramaic, how many times he could fit on the head of a pin, or whether he wasn't just a Norwegian with wings. Those meager letters might have come and gone until the end of time if a providential event had not put an end to the priest's tribulations.

It so happened that during those days, among so many other carnival attrac- 10 tions, there arrived in town the traveling show of the woman who had been changed into a spider for having disobeyed her parents. The admission to see her was not only less than the admission to see the angel, but people were permitted to ask her all manner of questions about her absurd state and to examine her up and down so that no one would ever doubt the truth of her horror. She was a frightful tarantula the size of a ram and with the head of a sad maiden. What was most heart-rending, however, was not her outlandish shape but the sincere affliction with which she recounted the details of her misfortune. While still practically a child she had sneaked out of her parents' house to go to a dance, and while she was coming back through the woods after having danced all night without permission, a fearful thunderclap rent the sky in two and through the crack came the lightning bolt of brimstone that changed her into a spider. Her only nourishment came from the meatballs that charitable souls chose to toss into her mouth. A spectacle like that, full of so much human truth and with such a fearful lesson, was bound to defeat without even trying that of a naughty angel who scarcely deigned to look at mortals. Besides, the few miracles attributed to the angel showed a certain mental disorder, like the blind man who didn't recover his sight but grew three new teeth, or the paralytic who didn't get to walk but almost won the lottery, and the leper whose sores sprouted sunflowers. Those consolation miracles, which were more like mocking fun, had already ruined the angel's reputation when the woman who had been changed into a spider finally crushed him completely. That was how Father Gonzaga was cured forever of his insomnia and Pelayo's courtyard went back to being as empty as during the time it had rained for three days and crabs walked through the bedrooms.

The owners of the house had no reason to lament. With the money they saved 11 they built a two-story mansion with balconies and gardens and high netting so that crabs wouldn't get in during the winter, and with iron bars on the windows so that angels wouldn't get in. Pelayo also set up a rabbit warren close to town and gave up his job as bailiff for good, and Elisenda bought some satin pumps with high heels and many dresses of iridescent silk, the kind worn on Sunday by the most desirable women in those times. The chicken coop was the only thing that didn't receive any attention. If they washed it down with creolin and burned tears of myrrh[2] inside it every so often, it was not in homage to the angel but to drive away the dungheap stench that still hung everywhere like a ghost and was turning the new house into an old one. At first, when the child learned to walk, they were careful that he not get too close to the chicken coop. But then they began to lose their fears and got used to the smell, and before the child got his second teeth he'd gone inside the chicken coop to play, where the wires were falling apart. The angel was no less standoffish with him than with other mortals, but he tolerated the most ingenious infamies with the patience of a dog who had no illusions. They both came down with chicken pox at the same time. The doctor who took care of the child couldn't resist the temptation to listen to the angel's heart, and he found so much whistling in the heart and so many sounds in his kidneys that it seemed impossible for him to be alive. What surprised him most, however, was the logic of his wings. They seemed so natural on that completely human organism that he couldn't understand why other men didn't have them too.

When the child began school it had been some time since the sun and rain had caused the collapse of the chicken coop. The angel went dragging himself about here and there like a stray dying man. They would drive him out of the bedroom with a broom and a moment later find him in the kitchen. He seemed to be in so many places at the same time that they grew to think that he'd been duplicated, that he was reproducing himself all through the house, and the exasperated and unhinged Elisenda shouted that it was awful living in that hell full of angels. He could scarcely eat and his antiquarian eyes had also become so foggy that he went about bumping into posts. All he had left were the bare cannulae of his last feathers. Pelayo threw a blanket over him and extended him the charity of letting him sleep in the shed, and only then did they notice that he had a temperature at night, and was delirious with the tongue twisters of an old Norwegian. That was one of the few times they became alarmed, for they thought he was going to die and not even the wise neighbor woman had been able to tell them what to do with dead angels.

And yet he not only survived his worst winter, but seemed improved with the first sunny days. He remained motionless for several days in the farthest corner of the courtyard, where no one would see him, and at the beginning of December

12

13

---

2. *Myrrh*: a resin that is burned as incense; one of the gifts of the Magi to the infant Jesus. *Creolin*: a general-purpose deodorizing disinfectant.

some large, stiff feathers began to grow on his wings, the feathers of a scarecrow, which looked more like another misfortune of decrepitude. But he must have known the reason for those changes, for he was quite careful that no one should notice them, that no one should hear the sea chanteys that he sometimes sang under the stars. One morning Elisenda was cutting some bunches of onions for lunch when a wind that seemed to come from the high seas blew into the kitchen. Then she went to the window and caught the angel in his first attempts at flight. They were so clumsy that his fingernails opened a furrow in the vegetable patch and he was on the point of knocking the shed down with the ungainly flapping that slipped on the light and couldn't get a grip on the air. But he did manage to gain altitude. Elisenda let out a sign of relief, for herself and for him, when she saw him pass over the last houses, holding himself up in some way with the risky flapping of a senile vulture. She kept watching him even when she was through cutting the onions and she kept on watching until it was no longer possible for her to see him, because then he was no longer an annoyance in her life but an imaginary dot on the horizon of the sea.

READING CLOSELY

1. At the beginning of García Márquez's story, "the wise neighbor woman" classifies the man with wings as a fallen angel, who like the rest of his kind is a "fugitive survivor of a celestial conspiracy" (4). So why does she advise Pelayo and Elisenda to club the angel to death? Why don't they follow her advice?

2. Besides wings, what other characteristics of angels does the very old man exhibit? Which of his attributes, if any, are essentially human?

3. Why does Father Gonzaga attempt to speak to the angel in Latin?

4. The inferior miracles attributed to the angel and the competition of the spider woman contribute to the decline of his reputation among the curious. But what single aspect of the angel's character does more than anything else to cause the mortals in the story to lose interest in him? What does this say about the character of mortals?

5. The angel's new feathers begin to grow in December. Why not May or June or some other time of the year?

STRATEGIES AND STRUCTURES

1. What principle of classification is Pelayo using when he locks the old man up with the hens in the chicken coop?

2. Father Gonzaga, we are told, "argued that if wings were not the essential element in determining the difference between a hawk and an airplane, they were

even less so in the recognition of angels" (5). If wings are not "essential" in dividing angels from mortals, what characteristics would be?

3. Are the villagers right or wrong to ignore Father Gonzaga's ARGUMENT that wings are not the defining characteristic of angels? Why do you think so?

4. When the doctor sees the angel, he is surprised at "the logic of his wings" (11). Why? How is the doctor tempted to classify angels? Mortals?

5. Why do you think García Márquez's story ends with Elisenda looking up at the angel instead of the angel looking down on her? Were you at all surprised by what the angel does (or doesn't do) in the ending? Why or why not? What characteristics and behaviors would you use to classify angels?

6. *Other Methods.* When we first see the old man, "his huge buzzard wings" are "dirty and half-plucked" and "forever entangled in the mud" (2). How does García Márquez use these and other physical DESCRIPTIONS of the old man to help explain why the villagers ultimately classify (or misclassify) him as a species of fowl?

THINKING ABOUT LANGUAGE

1. The villagers eventually see the fallen angel as "a cataclysm in repose" (8). What does this METAPHOR imply about the angel's power?

2. Explain the IRONY of putting an angel in the same category as chickens and other barnyard fowl.

3. Explain the IRONY of the old angel's coming down with the chicken pox at the same time as the child.

4. The hens search for "stellar" parasites among the angel's ruffled feathers, which scatter "lunar" dust along with more terrestrial kinds when the angel flaps his wings (8). How do such adjectives help García Márquez to establish the true identity of the visitor?

FOR WRITING

1. Pelayo and Elisenda make a simple error in classification. To avoid that mistake, write a paragraph explaining some of the essential characteristics you would use to distinguish angels from mortals.

2. "We know on the authority of Scripture," said Pope Gregory (who also identified the seven deadly sins) "that there are nine orders of angels." Write an essay dividing elves, fairies, trolls, giants, dragons, robots or other supernatural or nonhuman creatures into their various subcategories. Be sure to give the significant characteristics of each subcategory.

CHAPTER 9

Definition

A guy with a twelve-inch arm can have much more noticeable muscles than a guy with an eighteen-inch arm because he has better definition.

—PETE SISCO, *Train Smart*

Y**ou** know what getting ripped off is. How about "getting ripped"? According to bodybuilder Pete Sisco, "getting ripped" refers to muscle definition: You build up your muscles so they stick out and are easier to see. Likewise, when you DEFINE something—from bodybuilding to high-definition electronics—you make its fundamental nature sharp and clear.

In her essay "So, You Want to Be a Writer," novelist Allegra Goodman defines a writer as someone who is truly at home with "peace and quiet," qualities which she then goes on to define as follows: *Quiet*, says Goodman—using the technique of defining something by telling what it is not—is simply the absence of noise. *Peace*, however, she notes, is more difficult to grasp. "Peace is not the same as quiet," Goodman writes. "Peace means you avoid checking your email every ten seconds. Peace means you are willing to work offline, screen calls, and forget your to-do list for an hour."

In a broader definition, *peace* might be defined as the absence of war, or as a state of contentment and inner serenity. Goodman, however, is defining her subject from the perspective of the frazzled writer who is striving to avoid distractions and concentrate on her own thoughts and words. For her intended readers (those who want to be writers), Goodman chooses a relatively narrow definition of her subject, one that suits both her audience and purpose.

Defining Definition:
Telling What Something Is

A DEFINITION explains what something is—and is not—by identifying the characteristics that set it apart from all others like it. An accomplished writer, for example, is a person who habitually deals with words and ideas, often in electronic form. The same is true of any chronic browser of the Internet. Unlike the chronic Internet user, however, the writer—at least in Allegra Goodman's definition—must be willing and able to disconnect from the Web (and any other source of distraction) when it threatens to destroy his or her concentration.

Or take athletes. Bodybuilders, runners, and swimmers can all be defined as athletes who need to keep their body fat under control and to build up muscle strength. Consequently, their muscles are often sharply defined. Among these three types of athletes, however, only bodybuilders train primarily for muscle definition and bulk. In other words, training for muscle definition and bulk is a characteristic that *defines* bodybuilders alone. Runners and swimmers may want and need strong muscles, too, but what defines them is their speed on the track and in the pool, not the size or look of their muscles on the beach. Definitions set up boundaries; they say, in effect: "This is the territory occupied by my subject, and everything outside these boundaries is something else." Definition can also be a method of developing a subject in writing, and in this chapter we will see how to organize an entire essay around a definition.

Basic dictionary definitions have two parts: the general class to which the term belongs, and the specific characteristics that distinguish the term from other terms in that class. This is the pattern that definitions have followed since Dr. Samuel Johnson compiled the *Dictionary of the English Language* more than 250 years ago. For example, Johnson's famous definition of a "lexicographer," or dictionary maker, as "a harmless drudge" fits this pattern: *drudge* is the general class, and *harmless* is a characteristic that distinguishes the lexicographer from other kinds of drudges.

Here are a few more current examples of basic definitions:

Term being defined	General class	Distinguishing characteristic(s)
writer	user of words	requires peace and quiet
muscle	body tissue	fibrous, capable of contracting
osprey	hawk	fish-eating

Because basic definitions like these help to explain the fundamental nature of a subject, they can be useful for beginning almost any kind of essay. When you want to define a subject in depth, however, you will need an EXTENDED DEFINITION. An extended definition includes all the parts of a basic definition—the term you're defining, its general class, and its essential distinguishing characteristics. Unlike a basic definition, however, an extended definition doesn't stop there. It goes on to discuss other important distinguishing characteristics of the subject as well. For instance, if the basic definition of a bodybuilder is "an athlete who trains for muscle definition and bulk," an extended definition of a bodybuilder might look at a bodybuilder's focus and motivation, training regimen, bodybuilding competitions, and so on. Extended definitions also use many of the other methods of development discussed in this book, such as NARRATION, DESCRIPTION, and EXAMPLE.

In this chapter, we will not only see how to write basic definitions that are sharp and clear, we will learn how to construct an extended definition and make it the backbone of a complete essay. We will consider how to use SYNONYMS and ETYMOLOGIES in a definition, and how to use other methods of development.

Why Do We Define Things?

Being naturally curious, human beings define in order to understand the fundamental nature of things. For example, if you were defining *abolitionism* on an exam in U.S. history, you might first give a brief dictionary definition—"advocacy of the abolishment of slavery in the United States"—but you would move on to discuss the abolition movement before the Civil War and the legal abolishment of slavery by President Lincoln's Emancipation Proclamation. Writing about this term would thus help you make sense of history, in this case the history of an important social and political movement in American culture.

Sometimes, however, understanding a definition can be personally enlightening. The great anti-slavery orator Frederick Douglass escaped from slavery as a young man. In 1845, he wrote about how he came to learn the meaning of *abolition*:

> If a slave ran away and succeeded in getting clear . . . or did anything very wrong in the mind of a slaveholder, it was spoken of as the fruit of *abolition*. Hearing the word in this connection very often, I set about learning what it meant. The dictionary afforded me little or no help. I found it was "the act of abolishing"; but then I did not know what was to be abolished. Here I was perplexed. I did not dare to ask anyone about the meaning, for I was satisfied that it was something they wanted me to know very little about. After a patient waiting, I got one of our city papers, containing an account . . . of the slave trade between the States. From this time I understood the words *abolition* and *abolitionist*, and always drew near when that word was spoken, expecting to hear something of importance to myself and fellow-slaves. The light broke in upon me by degrees.   —FREDERICK DOUGLASS, *Narrative*

Such is the power and purpose of definitions: without them, we're in the dark about many things of importance to us. Before he could write so powerfully about the concept of *abolition*, young Douglass first had to learn what it meant in common usage. Defining, then, is ultimately a process of exploration. We extend our definitions in order to extend our horizons—and those of our readers.

Composing a Definition Essay

When you compose a definition essay, your first challenge is to find a topic worth defining. That topic may be complex, like relativity or Marxism or capitalism. Or, sometimes, you may devote an entire essay to a definition because you are arguing that a word or concept means something that others might not have thought of, or might disagree with. For example, if you were defining *intelligent design* in an essay you might want to say, at some length, not only what intelligent design is but why the reader should (or should not) believe in it. Definitions that require a whole essay often deal with terms that are open to debate or controversy. For example: What constitutes *racism* or *sexual harassment*? When does a *fetus* becomes a viable human being? What characterizes *friendship*?

Dictionary definitions will help you begin to think about such questions, but to write an essay that defines something fully—especially if it's something complicated or controversial—you will need to construct an extended definition and probably to call upon other methods of development. That is, you may need to DESCRIBE the subject, give EXAMPLES of it, analyze what CAUSED it or how it works, or COMPARE it with others. Take the concept of *longitude*, for example. Longitude can be defined as "distance measured east and west on the earth's surface." This basic definition doesn't fully define the subject, however. To extend such a definition, you might describe the place from which longitude is measured (the Royal Observatory in Greenwich, England, just outside of London on a steep hill), analyze how it's measured (in minutes and degrees from the prime meridian), and compare it with *latitude* (distance on the earth's surface as measured north and south of the equator).

Thinking about Purpose and Audience

When you define something, your general purpose is to say what it is, but you may have any number of specific reasons for doing this. You may be conveying useful information to someone, demonstrating that you understand the meaning of an important term or concept, arguing for a particular definition, or just entertaining the reader. Keep your purpose in mind as you construct your definition, and adapt the tone of your essay to fit that purpose—objective when you want to inform, persuasive when you are arguing in favor of a particular definition, humorous when you want the reader to smile.

Whatever your specific purpose for constructing a definition, you need to consider why your audience might want (or be reluctant) to know more about it and what it means. Also think about how the reader might already define the term. What information can you supply to make it easier for the reader to understand your definition, or be more receptive to it?

For example, if you were defining longitude in a manual for would-be sailors, you would compare it with latitude and explain how each measures different directions on the globe. You would also point out that determining longitude requires an accurate timepiece—if not a Global Positioning System—whereas latitude can be estimated just by eyeballing the angle of the sun or stars above the horizon. Since you're defining longitude for navigational purposes, you won't need to point out that, in the days before accurate clocks, measuring (or mismeasuring) longitude posed a grave danger to sailors on the high seas. However, such historical information—though irrelevant in a sailing manual—might be of vital interest if you were constructing a broad definition of longitude for a general audience, as in this passage from an entire book on the subject:

> Here lies the real, hard-core difference between latitude and longitude. . . . The zero-degree parallel of latitude [the equator] is fixed by the laws of nature, while the zero-degree meridian of longitude shifts like the sands of time. This difference makes finding latitude child's play, and turns the determination of longitude, especially at sea, into an adult dilemma—one that stumped the wisest minds of the world for the better part of human history.
> —DAVA SOBEL, *Longitude*

In *Longitude*, Sobel defines her subject as a scientific, political, and philosophical concept. In an essay, rather than a book, you can't define longitude or any other subject on such a global scale, but you can focus on those aspects of your subject that best suit your purpose and that your audience is most likely to find interesting and useful.

Generating Ideas:
Asking What Something Is—and Is Not

LISTING, CLUSTERING, BRAINSTORMING, and many other techniques can help you generate ideas for a definition. But in order to define a subject, you need to know what its distinguishing characteristics are—what makes it different from other things in the same general class. How do you know which characteristics are essential to your definition? Start by thinking about the characteristics that tell us the most about it. For instance, suppose we wanted to define what an engineer is. We know that engineers often use tools and have specialized knowledge about how things are built. But these characteristics also apply to carpenters and burglars. What characteristics tell us the most about engineers?

According to one expert, these characteristics are all *essential* to engineers:

- They are fascinated with the physical world.
- They value utility over beauty or knowledge.
- They have a thorough understanding of mathematics and science.
- They are trained to apply that knowledge to physical objects and systems.
- Their purpose in doing so is to remake the world by shaping it to practical use.

—MICHAEL DAVIS, "Defining 'Engineer' "

As you come up with a list of essential distinguishing characteristics for your subject, you should also ask what your subject is *not*. Here is how Michael Davis answers that question when defining engineers:

- Engineers are not pure scientists. They may generate knowledge, but that knowledge is not an end in itself, as it can be for a mathematician or physicist.
- Though they may produce beautiful structures, such as bridges or towers, engineers are not artists (in the way that architects are).
- Engineers are not primarily interested in rules (lawyers) or money (accountants) or people (managers).
- Engineers must write reports that are both clear and accurate, but they are not primarily writers either.

The essential distinguishing characteristics that you list—the traits that make your subject what it is—will form the foundation of your definition essay.

Organizing and Drafting a Definition Essay

When you have a clear idea of your purpose and audience—and a solid list of distinguishing characteristics for your subject—you are ready to start organizing and drafting your essay. First you will need to construct a basic definition of your subject—and then to extend that definition. There are a number of techniques that can help, including the other methods of development discussed in this book. The tips and templates on p. 368 can help you get started.

TIPS AND TEMPLATES FOR DRAFTING

When you begin to draft a definition, you need to identify your subject, assign it to a general class, and specify particular characteristics that distinguish it from others in that same class. These moves are fundamental to any definition. See how Fatima Mernissi makes such moves in her essay in this chapter:

> Harem was the place where a man sheltered his family, his wife or wives, and children and relatives. It could be a house or a tent, and it referred both to the space and to the people who lived within it.
> —FATIMA MERNISSI, "The Harem Within"

Mernissi identifies her subject ("harem"), assigns it to a general class (places), and specifies the particular characteristic ("where a man sheltered his family") that distinguishes it from others in that class. Here is one more example from this chapter:

> H. is unique in that she is both a dead person *and* a patient on the way to surgery. She is what's known as a "beating-heart cadaver," alive and well everywhere but her brain.
> —MARY ROACH, "How to Know If You're Dead"

The following templates can help you make some of these basic moves in your own writing. But don't take these as formulas where you just have to fill in the blanks. There are no easy formulas for good writing, but these templates can serve as starting points.

▶ In general, X can be defined as a kind of _____.

▶ What specifically distinguishes X from others in this category is _____.

▶ X is usually a _____; but it can also be a _____, or even a _____.

▶ X is often used to mean _____, but a better synonym would be _____ or _____.

▶ One way to define X is as the opposite of _____, the distinguishing features of which are _____, _____, and _____.

▶ If we define X as _____, we can then define Y as _____.

▶ By defining X in this way, we can see that _____.

STATING YOUR POINT

By itself, an extended definition does not constitute a well-organized essay; you need to explain the point your definition is intended to make. A THESIS STATEMENT—usually made in the introduction and perhaps repeated with variations at the end—is a good way to do this. Here is a thesis for an extended definition of a farmer, written by Craig Schafer, an Ohio State student who grew up on a farm in the Midwest: "By definition, a farmer is someone who tills the soil for a living, but I define a true farmer according to his or her attitudes toward the land." This is a good thesis statement because it both defines the subject and says something more about that subject that gives the reader reason to read the rest of your definition.

SPECIFYING ADDITIONAL DISTINGUISHING CHARACTERISTICS

Of all the ways you can extend a basic definition, perhaps the most effective is simply to specify additional characteristics that set your subject apart. Thus, to support his definition of a farmer as a person with certain attitudes toward the land, Schafer goes on to specify what those attitudes are, devoting a paragraph to each:

- A farmer is a born optimist. He plants his crops with no assurance that nature will cooperate or that markets will be favorable.
- A farmer is devoted to the soil. He enjoys letting it sift through his fingers or just sniffing the fresh clean aroma of a newly plowed field.
- A farmer is self-denying. His barn is often better planned and sometimes more modern than his house.
- A farmer is independent. Unions have found it impossible to organize him.

As you identify other distinguishing characteristics, make sure that they are sufficient to define your subject thoroughly and completely.

USING SYNONYMS

Another way to extend a definition is by offering SYNONYMS. If you can substitute a more familiar word for the term you are defining, the reader may be more likely to understand and accept your definition. For example, if you were defining a *blog* for readers unfamiliar with the Internet, you might say that it is an electronic journal or diary. You could then go on to say which particular characteristics of journals apply to blogs and which ones don't. Both blogs and journals, you might point out, record the personal thoughts of their authors; but blogs, unlike journals, typically include links to other sites and blogs, and invite response.

USING DEFINITION TO FRAME AN ARGUMENT

"In this world," said Benjamin Franklin, "nothing is certain but death and taxes." No matter what you think of taxes, they won't kill you—literally. By putting taxes and death in the same framework, however, Franklin humorously asserts that the two terms belong in the same general class with the same distinguishing characteristic (both are "certain"). This sort of framing is a clever way of implying that two terms have other characteristics in common as well, in this case negative ones.

Suppose you were the mayor of a small town and you wanted to build a recreation center. How might you convince the citizens of your town that a tax increase (to pay for the new recreation center) was a good thing?

The linguist George Lakoff has pondered such questions. If you consider taxes, for instance, to be a necessary evil, Lakoff suggests, you might present them as "dues." Then you would be defining them as what you pay to live in a civilized society where there are services that have been paid for by previous taxpayers. Defined this way, Lakoff argues, paying taxes becomes an act of patriotism.

Defining a term (*taxes*) by associating it with other terms (*dues*) that carry CONNOTATIONS (patriotism) you want to "rub off" on your key term is a strategy of ARGUMENTATION that Lakoff and others call "framing." In the following passage, for example, Gretel Ehrlich defines (or redefines) what it means to be a cowboy—normally framed in masculine terms—by framing her subject in feminine terms:

> Cowboys are perhaps the most misunderstood group of workers anywhere. Romanticized in the movies and on billboards as handsome, macho loners always heading off into the sunset, they are more likely to be homebodies or social misfits too shy to work with people. Their work has more to do with mothering and nurturing than with exhibitions of virility. A cowboy can bottle-feed a calf around the clock, forecast weather, use a sewing machine, make anything out of canvas or leather, and serve as midwife to any animal.

Marlboro Man or midwife? The frame of reference in which you define a subject can predispose your readers to accept not only your definition but the larger point your definition is intended to make.

USING ETYMOLOGIES

Often you can usefully extend the definition of a term by tracing its history, or ETY-MOLOGY. This is what an engineer at the University of Houston did when he asked, "Who are we who have been calling ourselves *engineers* since the early nineteenth century?" Here's part of his answer:

> The word *engineering* probably derives from the Latin word *ingeniatorum*. In 1325 a contriver of siege towers was called by the Norman word *engynours*. By 1420 the English were calling a trickster an *yngynore*. By 1592 we find the word *enginer* being given to a designer of phrases—a wordsmith. The Oxford English Dictionary gets to the first use of the modern word engineer in 1635, but you might not be crazy about its use. Someone is quoted as calling the devil—"that great engineer, Satan."
> —JOHN H. LIENHARD, "The Polytechnic Legacy"

Although few people today would use the word *engineer* to describe Satan, knowing the history of the word and its earlier variations can help us define what an engineer is, namely one who devises things with cleverness and ingenuity, whether it's a siege tower or a carefully crafted piece of writing. You can find the etymology of a word in most dictionaries, alongside the definition.

USING OTHER METHODS

As you draft a definition essay, draw on the other methods in this book to round out your definition and support your thesis. Let's say you are defining *cowboy*. You could note that the cowboy is a vital part of the cattle industry and an iconic figure in American culture who is usually thought to be "the rugged silent type." You could ARGUE that this is a misconception, founded on equating him too often with the likes of the Marlboro Man. Then you could go on to DESCRIBE the attitudes and daily work of the cowboy as you define him.

This is what Gretel Ehrlich, a writer who lives on a ranch in Wyoming, does in her extended definition of the American cowboy. Ehrlich's thesis is that "in our hellbent earnestness to romanticize the cowboy we've ironically disesteemed his true character." What is that true character? Ehrlich is going to define it for us, beginning with this basic definition: "A cowboy is someone who loves his work."

Ehrlich might have started with the standard dictionary definition of a cowboy as "a man, usually on horseback, who herds and tends cattle on a ranch, especially in the western U.S." By choosing "loves his work" from among all the other characteristics that might be said to define a cowboy, however, she introduces a distinguishing characteristic of her subject that the reader may not have thought of. She then goes on to extend her definition by using a number of other methods of development, as shown in several examples below from her book, *The Solace of Open Spaces*. First she DESCRIBES the work that is the key distinguishing characteristic of her subject.

> A cowboy is someone who loves his work. Since the hours are long—ten to fifteen hours a day—and the pay is $30 he has to. What's required of him is an odd mixture of physical vigor and maternalism. His part of the beef-raising industry is to birth and nurture calves and take care of their mothers. For the most part his work is done on horseback and in a lifetime he sees and comes to know more animals than people.

Next, Ehrlich ANALYZES THE PROCESS of how a cowboy does some of his work:

> If a cow is stuck in a boghole he throws a loop around her neck, takes his dally (a half hitch around the saddle horn), and pulls her out with horse-power. If a calf is born sick, he may take her home, warm her in front of the kitchen fire, and massage her legs until dawn.

Then Ehrlich introduces a little NARRATIVE of a particular cowboy saving a horse:

> One friend, whose favorite horse was trying to swim a lake with hobbles on, dove under water and cut her legs loose with a knife, then swam her to shore, his arm around her neck lifeguard-style, and saved her from drowning.

Because Ehrlich is using her definition to make an argument about the "true character" of the cowboy, an important part of her definition is devoted to COMPARING AND CONTRASTING her idea of a cowboy with that of the cowboy as he is typically (or stereotypically) defined.

> Instead of the macho, trigger-happy man our culture has perversely wanted him to be, the cowboy is more apt to be convivial, quirky, and soft-hearted.

Ehrlich also analyzes the actual CAUSES AND EFFECTS of the cowboy's behavior as she sees them—all in the service of defining what a true cowboy is to her.

> If he's "strong and silent" it's because there is probably no one to talk to. If he "rides away into the sunset" it's because he's been on horseback since four in the morning moving cattle and he's trying, fifteen hours later, to get home to his family. If he's "a rugged individualist" he's also part of a team: ranch work is teamwork and even the glorified open range cowboys of the 1880s rode up and down the Chisholm Trail in the company of twenty or thirty other riders.

This definition does two things: it takes a fresh look at the characteristics usually attributed to the cowboy, and it introduces the author's own, more expansive characteristics. When you construct a new definition or rework an accepted one as

Ehrlich does, the new characteristics that you introduce do not have to outlaw the old ones. They just need to open up enough space for the reader to come over to your side of the fence. Thus, the cowboy can still be defined as "strong and silent" when he has to be—like a hero from a Western. But if the American cowboy is to be conceived as more than a cardboard figure, he can also be regarded as "convivial," "quirky," and "soft-hearted" at times.

Reading a Definition Essay with a Critical Eye

Once you have a draft of your definition essay, ask a friendly critic to read it and tell you what's working and what isn't. Then read it over yourself with an eye for what can be improved. Below are some questions that any reader, including yourself, should ask when checking over a definition essay:

PURPOSE AND AUDIENCE. For whom is this definition written? What is its purpose—to define something the reader probably doesn't know much about? To demonstrate knowledge to an already knowledgeable reader? How is the reader likely to define the subject being defined? Does the definition confirm a standard definition, or challenge or expand it in some way? How?

THE BASIC DEFINITION. Does the definition identify the general class to which the subject of the essay belongs, plus the distinguishing characteristics that separate that subject from others in the same class? If not, how might the definition be improved?

THE POINT. What is the main point of the definition? Is it stated as a thesis, preferably in the introduction of the essay? How might the main point be made even clearer to the reader?

DISTINGUISHING CHARACTERISTICS. How does the essay extend the basic definition? Does it introduce essential distinguishing characteristics of the subject? Are the characteristics sufficient to define the subject? Have any essential characteristics been left out? Which characteristics are most informative? Do any need to be sharpened or omitted? Does the definition say what the subject is not? Should it?

SYNONYMS AND ETYMOLOGIES. Are words with similar meanings or word histories used to help define key terms? If not, would either of these devices improve the definition?

OTHER METHODS. What other basic methods of development are used: DESCRIPTION? COMPARISON AND CONTRAST? Something else? If they are not used, how might such methods be incorporated into the definition?

Editing for Common Errors in Definitions

As with other kinds of writing, definition essays are prone to certain kinds of errors. The following tips will help you check over your drafts for these problems.

Check that any word referred to *as a word* is in italics.

▶ The term *cowboy* is easy to define, but the life of a cowboy is not so easy to characterize.

▶ Generally referred to as *abolitionism*, the movement to abolish slavery changed the course of U.S. history.

▶ Abolitionism was especially strong in the Northern states, but many Southerners were abolitionists, too.

Where *cowboy* and *abolitionism* are italicized in these sentences, they are being referred to as words. When they are not italicized, they are referring to concepts.

Check each basic definition to make sure it includes the class to which the term belongs.

NOT Engineering applies science for practical purposes.

BUT Engineering is a professional field that applies science for practical purposes.

NOT A Labrador retriever has a friendly disposition and is patient with children.

BUT A Labrador retriever is a breed of dog that has a friendly disposition and is patient with children.

Without *professional field* and *breed of dog*, the preceding sentences are statements about their subjects rather than definitions of them.

Check for common usage errors.

IS WHERE, IS WHEN

Where and *when* should not be used to introduce definitions.

NOT Engineering is where you put science to use.

BUT Engineering is the practice of putting science to use.

NOT   A recession is when prices go up and sales go down.

BUT   A recession is the economic condition in which prices go up and sales go down.

COMPRISE, COMPOSE

Comprise means "to consist of." *Compose* means "to make up." The whole *comprises* the parts; the parts *compose* the whole.

▸ American democracy comprises many divergent ideals.

▸ The United States comprises fifty states.

▸ American democracy is composed of many divergent ideals.

▸ The United States is composed of fifty states.

An Epitaph

When we define something (or someone), we say what its distinguishing characteristics are. In this cartoon by Roz Chast, a frequent contributor to the *New Yorker*, the deceased's entire life is defined by his verbal and math scores on a standardized test. Chast's purpose in penning the cartoon is to amuse the reader, but she is also making fun of overly narrow definitions. Test scores do not adequately define life—or death. For some people and institutions (such as college admissions offices), narrow definitions can run deep—too deep if they lose sight of the complexities of the person or thing they are defining. Like Mr. Jones' epitaph, good definitions require precision. But when you construct a definition, keep your (and the reader's) eye on the truly important distinguishing features of your subject.

EVERYDAY DEFINITION

BRYAN SYKES

So, What Is DNA and What Does It Do?

*Bryan Sykes (b. 1948) is an international celebrity in the usually obscure world of lab-
oratory science. A professor of genetics at Oxford University, Sykes first came to promi-
nence when he successfully retrieved DNA from archaeological remains. Thus was
born a whole new field, which Sykes calls "bioarchaeology"—the use of modern
genetic testing to help trace, for example, the lineage of an ancient warlord or the history of a family surname. Sykes is the author of two best-sellers that brought startling
scientific news to a popular audience. The Seven Daughters of Eve (2001), from
which the following selection is taken, argues that virtually all modern Europeans
descend from just seven women. Adam's Curse: A Future without Men (2004)
argues that the male-determining Y chromosome is a "graveyard of rotting genes that
will, in 125,000 years, render men unable to breed naturally."*

*Beginning with its title, "So, What Is DNA and What Does It Do?" illustrates how
the skillful use of definition can make a scientific idea accessible to nonscientist readers. Just as the complex DNA molecule is composed of simple parts, Sykes's definition of
DNA is constructed from simple ideas that he assembles into one of the "big ideas" of
modern science.*

ALL OF US ARE AWARE, as people must have been for millennia, that children   1
often resemble their parents and that the birth of a child follows nine months after
sexual intercourse. The mechanism for inheritance remained a mystery until very
recently, but that didn't stop people from coming up with all sorts of theories.
There are plenty of references in classical Greek literature to family resemblances,
and musing on the reasons for them was a familiar pastime for early philosophers.
Aristotle, writing around 335 BC, speculated that the father provided the pattern for
the unborn child and the mother's contribution was limited to sustaining it within
the womb as well as after birth. This idea made perfect sense to the patriarchal attitudes of Western civilization at the time. It was only reasonable that the father, the
provider of wealth and status, was also the architect of all his children's features
and nature. This was not to underestimate the necessity of choosing a suitable wife.
After all, seeds planted in a good soil always do better than those put into a poor
one. However, there was a problem and it was one that was to haunt women for a
long time to come.

If children are born with their father's design, how was it that men had daugh-   2
ters? Aristotle was challenged on this point during his lifetime, and his answer was
that all babies would be the same as their fathers in every respect, including being

male, unless they were somehow "interfered with" in the womb. This "interference" could be relatively minor, leading to such trivial variations as a child having red hair instead of black like his father; or it could be more substantial—leading to major ones such as being deformed or female. This attitude has had serious consequences for many women throughout history who have found themselves discarded and replaced because they failed to produce sons. This ancient theory developed into the notion of the *homunculus*, a tiny, preformed being that was inoculated into the woman during sexual intercourse. Even as late as the beginning of the eighteenth century the pioneer of microscopy, Anthony van Leewenhoek, imagined he could see tiny homunculi curled up in the heads of sperm.

Hippocrates, whose name is commemorated in the oath that newly qualified   3
doctors used to take (some still do), had a less extreme view than Aristotle which did give women a role. He believed that both men and women produced a seminal fluid, and that the characteristics of the baby were decided by which parts of the fluid prevailed when they mixed after copulation. A child might have its father's eyes or its mother's nose as a result of this process; if neither parent's fluid prevailed for a particular characteristic, the child might be somewhere in between, having, for example, hair of a color that was intermediate between the two parents.

This theory was much more obviously connected to most people's experience of   4
real life. "He's just like his father" or "She's got her mother's smile" and other similar observations are repeated millions of times every day throughout the world. The idea that the parents' characteristics are somehow blended in the offspring was the predominant belief among scientists until the end of the nineteenth century. Darwin certainly knew no better, and it was one reason why he could never find a suitable mechanism to explain his theory of natural selection; for anything new and favorable would be continually diluted out by the blending process at each generation. Even though geneticists today scoff at such apparent ignorance among their predecessors, I wouldn't mind betting that a theory of blending is, even now, a perfectly satisfactory explanation for what most people observe with their own eyes.

Eventually, two practical developments in the nineteenth century provided key   5
clues to what was really going on. One was the invention of new chemical dyes for the textile industry, and the other was a change in the way microscope lenses were ground which made big improvements in their performance. Greater magnification meant that individual cells were now easily visible; and their internal structure was revealed when they were stained with the new dyes. Now the process of fertilization, the fusion of a single large egg cell and a single small, determined sperm, could be observed. When cells divided, strange thread-like structures could be seen assembling and then separating equally into the two new cells. Because they stained very brightly with the new dyes these curious structures became

known as *chromosomes*—from Greek, meaning literally, "colored bodies"—years before anyone had a clue about what they did.

During fertilization, one set of these strange threads seemed to come from the father's sperm and another set from the mother's egg. This was just what had been predicted by the man universally acknowledged as the father of genetics, Gregor Mendel, a monk in the town of Brno in the Czech Republic who laid the foundation for the whole of genetics from his experimental breeding of peas in the monastery garden in the 1860s. He concluded that whatever it was that determined heredity would be passed on equally from both parents to their offspring. Unfortunately he died before he ever saw a chromosome; but he was right. With the important exception of mitochondrial DNA . . . and the chromosomes that determine sex, genes—specific pieces of genetic coding that occur in the chromosomes—are inherited equally from both sets of parents. The essential part played by chromosomes in heredity and the fact that they must contain within them the secrets of inheritance was already well established by 1903. But it took another fifty years to discover what chromosomes are made of and how they worked as the physical messengers of heredity. 6

In 1953 two young scientists working in Cambridge, James D. Watson and Francis Crick, solved the molecular structure of a substance which had been known about for a long time and largely thought of as dull and unimportant. As if to emphasize its obscurity, it was given a really long name, *deoxyribonucleic acid*, now happily abbreviated to DNA. Although a few experiments had implicated DNA in the mechanism of inheritance, the smart money was on proteins as the hereditary material. They were complicated, sophisticated, had twenty different components (the amino-acids) and could assume millions of different forms. Surely, the thinking went, only something really complicated could manage such a monumental task as programming a single fertilized egg cell to grow into a fully formed and functional human being. It couldn't possibly be this DNA, which had only four components. Admittedly it was in the right place, in the cell nucleus; but it probably did something very dull like absorbing water, rather like bran. 7

Despite the general lack of interest in this substance shown by most of their scientific contemporaries, Watson and Crick felt sure it held the key to the chemical mechanism of heredity. They decided to have a crack at working out its molecular structure using a technique that was already being used to solve the structure of the more glamorous proteins. This entailed making long crystalline fibers of purified DNA and bombarding them with X-rays. As the X-rays entered the DNA, most went straight through and out the other side. But a few collided with the atoms in the molecular structure and bounced off to one side where they were detected by sheets of X-ray film—the same kind of film that hospital radiographers still use to get an image of a fractured bone. The deflected X-rays made a regular pattern of 8 spots on the film, whose precise locations were then used to calculate the positions of atoms within the DNA.

After many weeks spent building different models with rods and sheets of card- 9
board and metal to represent the atoms within DNA, Watson and Crick suddenly found one which fitted exactly with the X-ray pattern. It was simple, yet at the same time utterly marvellous, and it had a structure that immediately suggested how it might work as the genetic material. As they put it with engaging self-confidence in the scientific paper that announced the discovery: "It has not escaped our notice that the specific pairings we have postulated immediately suggest a possible copying mechanism for the genetic material." They were absolutely right, and were rewarded by the Nobel Prize for Medicine and Physiology in 1962.

One of the essential requirements for the genetic material had to be that it 10
could be faithfully copied time and again, so that when a cell divides, both of the two new cells—the "daughter cells," as they are called—each receive an equal share of the chromosomes in the nucleus. Unless the genetic material in the chromosomes could be copied every time a cell divided it would very soon run out. And the copying had to be very high quality or the cells just wouldn't work. Watson and Crick had discovered that each molecule of DNA is made up of two very long coils, like two intertwined spiral staircases—a "double helix." When the time comes for copies to be made, the two spiral staircases of the double helix disengage. DNA has just four key components, which are always known by the first letters of their chemical names: A for adenine, C for cytosine, G for guanine and T for thymine. Formally they are known as *nucleotide bases*—"bases" for short. You can now forget the chemicals and just remember the four symbols "A," "C," "G" and "T."

The breakthrough in solving the DNA structure came when Watson and Crick 11
realized that the only way the two strands of the double helix could fit together properly was if every "A" on one strand is interlocked with a "T" directly opposite it on the other strand. Just like two jigsaw pieces, "A" will fit perfectly with "T" but not with "G" or "C" or with another "A." In exactly the same way, "C" and "G" on opposite strands can fit only with each other, not with "A" or "T." This way *both* strands retain the complementary coded sequence information. For example, the sequence "ATTCAG" on one strand has to be matched by the sequence "TAAGTC" on the other. When the double helix unravels this section, the cell machinery constructs a new sequence *"TAAGTC"* opposite "ATTCAG" on one of the old strands and builds up *"ATTCAG"* opposite "TAAGTC" on the other. The result is two new double helices identical to the original. Two perfect copies every time. Preserved during all this copying is the sequence of the four chemical letters. And what is the sequence? It is information pure and simple. DNA doesn't actually do anything itself. It doesn't help you breathe or digest your food. It just instructs other things how to do it. The cellular middle managers which receive the instructions and do

the work are, it turns out, the proteins. They might look sophisticated, and they are; but they operate under strict directions from the boardroom, the DNA itself.

Although the complexity of cells, tissues and whole organisms is breathtaking, 12 the way in which the basic DNA instructions are written is astonishingly simple. Like more familiar instruction systems such as language, numbers or computer binary code, what matters is not so much the symbols themselves but the order in which they appear. Anagrams, for example "derail" and "redial," contain exactly the same letters but in a different order, and so the words they spell out have completely different meanings. Similarly, 476,021 and 104,762 are different numbers using the same symbols laid out differently. Likewise, 001010 and 100100 have very different meanings in binary code. In exactly the same way the order of the four chemical symbols in DNA embodies the message. "ACGGTA" and "GACAGT" are DNA anagrams that mean completely different things to a cell, just as "derail" and "redial" have different meanings for us.

So, how is the message written and how is it read? DNA is confined to the chro- 13 mosomes, which never leave the cell nucleus. It is the proteins that do all the real work. They are the executives of the body. They are the enzymes which digest your food and run your metabolism; they are the hormones that coordinate what is happening in different parts of your body. They are the collagens of the skin and bone, and the hemoglobins of the blood. They are the antibodies that fight off infection. In other words, they do everything. Some are enormous molecules, some are tiny. What they all have in common is that they are made up of a string of sub-units, called amino-acids, whose precise order dictates their function. Amino-acids in one part of the string attract amino-acids from another part, and what was a nice linear string crumples up into a ball. But this is a ball with a very particular shape, that then allows the protein to do what it was made for: being a catalyst for biological reactions if it is an enzyme, making muscles if it is a muscle protein, trapping invading bacteria if it is an antibody, and so on. There are twenty amino-acids in all, some with vaguely familiar names like lysine or phenylalanine (one of the ingredients of the sweetener aspartame) and others most people haven't come across, like cysteine or tyrosine. The order in which these amino-acids appear in the protein precisely determines its final shape and function, so all that is required to make a protein is a set of DNA instructions which define this order. Somehow the coded information contained in the DNA within the cell nucleus must be relayed to the protein production lines in another part of the cell.

If you can spare one, pluck out a hair. The translucent blob on one end is the 14 root or follicle. There are roughly a million cells in each hair follicle, and their only purpose in life is to make hair, which is mainly made up of the protein keratin. As you pulled the hair out, the cells were still working. Imagine yourself inside one of these cells. Each one is busy making keratin. But how do they know how to do it?

The key to making any protein, including keratin, is just a matter of making sure that the amino-acids are put in the right order. What is the right order? Go and look it up in the DNA which is on the chromosomes in the cell nucleus. A hair cell, like every cell in the body, has a full set of DNA instructions, but you only want to know how to make keratin. Hair cells are not interested in how to make bone or blood, so all those sections of DNA are shut down. But the keratin instruction, the keratin *gene*, is open for consultation. It is simply the sequence of DNA symbols specifying the order of amino-acids in keratin.

The DNA sequence in the keratin gene begins like this: ATGACCTCCTTC . . . 15 (etc. etc.). Because we are not used to reading this code it looks like a random arrangement of the four DNA symbols. However, while it might be unintelligible to us, it is not so to the hair cell. This is a small part of the code for making keratin, and it is very simple to translate. First the cell reads the code in groups of three symbols. Thus ATGACCTCCTTC becomes ATG–ACC–TCC–TTC. Each of these groups of three symbols, called a triplet, specifies a particular amino-acid. The first triplet ATG is the code for the amino-acid methionine, ACC stands for threonine, TCC for serine, TTC for phenylalanine and so on. This is the genetic code which is used by all genes in the cell nuclei of all species of plants and animals.

The cell makes a temporary copy of this code, as if it were photocopying a few 16 pages of a book, then dispatches it to the protein-making machinery in another part of the cell. When it arrives here, the production plant swings into action. It reads the first triplet and decodes it as meaning the amino-acid methionine. It takes a molecule of methionine off the shelf. It reads the second triplet for the amino-acid threonine, takes a molecule of threonine down and joins it to the methionine. The third triplet means serine, so a molecule of serine gets tacked on to the threonine. The fourth triplet is for phenylalanine, so one of these is joined to the serine. Now we have the four amino-acids specified by the DNA sequence of the keratin gene assembled in the correct order: methionine–threonine–serine–phenylalanine. The next triplet is read, and the fifth amino-acid is added, and so on. This process of reading, decoding and adding amino-acids in the right order continues until the whole instructions have been read through to the end. The new keratin molecule is now complete. It is cut loose and goes to join hundreds of millions of others to form part of one of the hairs that are growing out of your scalp. Well, it would if you had not pulled it out.

READING CLOSELY

1. The THESIS of the book from which this chapter is taken is that variations in the human genome indicate that all humans presently living on Earth descended from only seven individual females. How does Sykes's DEFINITION of "the mechanism for inheritance" tie in with that thesis (1)?

2. According to Sykes, why did early theories assume that the father "provided the pattern" of characteristics inherited in the offspring (1)?

3. In the nineteenth century, how did the invention of chemical dyes for the textile industry and improvements in the microscope challenge the old theories of genetics?

4. The father of modern genetics, Gregor Mendel, "died before he ever saw a chromosome" (6). Nevertheless, what basic principle of inherited traits did Mendel rightly predict?

5. Before Watson and Crick "solved the molecular structure" of DNA in 1954, most researchers were betting on proteins as "the hereditary material" (7). Why were proteins the front runners?

6. How does Sykes DEFINE DNA, and how does DNA work with proteins? What does he mean when he says, "DNA doesn't actually do anything itself" (11)?

STRATEGIES AND STRUCTURES

1. Sykes's chapter is constructed around a series of interlocking DEFINITIONS, beginning with those of genes and chromosomes in paragraph 6. Why do you think he organizes his piece this way—before defining DNA itself?

2. Sykes uses a conversational TONE to help him keep his audience interested in scientific concepts. Where and why do you find this strategy—including his use of humor—particularly effective?

3. In paragraphs 14–16, Sykes uses the extended EXAMPLE of a strand of hair—to illustrate what? How does this example also help bring the entire selection to a satisfying close?

4. *Other Methods.* Besides giving basic DEFINITIONS of key genetic components, Sykes also draws on PROCESS ANALYSIS to explain what each of the components does. Which processes in particular does he analyze, and how do they work?

THINKING ABOUT LANGUAGE

1. In paragraph 5, how does Sykes use the ETYMOLOGY, or historical meaning, of *chromosomes* to help him define the term?

2. What does DNA stand for, and why is it "happily abbreviated" as such (7)?

3. An *anagram* is a word or phrase formed by reordering the letters of another word or phrase. What is the purpose of Syke's extended example of the anagrams "derail" and "redial" (12)?

4. Sykes uses the ANALOGY of a manufacturing company to define the role of each genetic component in the process of making new cells. DNA constitutes top management—"the boardroom" (11). Who are the middle managers, executives, and workers on the factory floor? How and how well does this extended analogy help to explain what each component does and how all the components work together?

5. When Sykes says, "Hair cells are not interested in how to make bone or blood," he is using the technique of PERSONIFICATION (14). Where else does he use personification to get his message across?

FOR WRITING

1. Write a paragraph or two defining a double helix and what it does.

2. Write an essay defining mitochondrial DNA and its role in genetic inheritance.

3. Write an essay explaining how DNA testing is currently used in medicine, police work, language study, or some other application. Be sure to document any sources.

GEOFFREY NUNBERG

The War of Words: "Terror" and "Terrorism"

Geoffrey Nunberg, a professor at the University of California at Berkeley and chair of the usage panel of the American Heritage Dictionary, *has devoted his career to examining the words we use and what they reveal. "There has never been an age as wary as ours," he writes, "of the tricks words can play, obscuring distinctions and smoothing over the corrugations of the actual world." Nunberg has examined those tricks not only in scholarly works but also in countless articles for the general reader. He writes a regular feature on words for the* New York Times, *and his voice is familiar to listeners of the National Public Radio program* Fresh Air. *Many of Nunberg's commentaries on language, culture, and politics have been collected in* The Way We Talk Now (2001) *and* Going Nucular (2004).*

In "The War of Words: 'Terror' and 'Terrorism,' " Nunberg illustrates how the definitions of words have become one more weapon in our political battles, helping to shape perceptions and influence policy. This article first appeared in the New York Times *in 2004.*

"THE LONG-TERM DEFEAT OF TERROR will happen when freedom takes hold in   1
the broader Middle East," President George W. Bush said on June 28, [2004,] as he announced the early transfer of sovereignty to the Iraqis.

The "defeat of terror"—the wording suggests that much has changed since   2
Sept. 11, 2001. In his speech on that day, Bush said, "We stand together to win the war against terrorism," and over the next year the White House described the enemy as terrorism twice as often as terror. But in White House speeches over the past year, those proportions have been reversed. And the shift from "terrorism" to "terror" has been equally dramatic in major newspapers, according to a search of several databases.

Broad linguistic shifts such as these usually owe less to conscious decisions by   3
editors or speechwriters than to often-unnoticed changes in the way people perceive their world. Terrorism may itself be a vague term, as critics have argued. But terror is still more amorphous and elastic, and alters the understanding not just of the enemy but of the war against it.

True, phrases like "terror plots" or "terror threat level" can make terror seem   4
merely a headline writer's shortening of the word terrorism. But even there, "terror" draws on a more complex set of meanings. It evokes both the actions of terrorists and the fear they are trying to engender.

"Do we cower in the face of terror?" Bush asked on Irish television a few days   5
before the handover in Iraq, with "terror" doing double work.

And unlike "terrorism," "terror" can be applied to states as well as to insurgents,   6
as in the president's frequent references to Saddam Hussein's "terror regime." Even
if Saddam can't actually be linked to the attacks of Sept. 11, "terror" seems to connect them etymologically.

The modern senses of "terror" and "terrorism" go back to a single historical   7
moment: "la Terreur," Robespierre's Reign of Terror[1] in 1793 and 1794. "Terror,"
Robespierre said, "is nothing other than justice, prompt, severe, inflexible; it is
therefore an emanation of virtue."

It was the ruthless severity of that emanation that moved Edmund Burke[2] to   8
decry "those hell-hounds called terrorists," in one of the first recorded uses of "terrorist" in English.

For Robespierre and his contemporaries, "terror" conveyed the exalted emotion   9
people may feel when face to face with the absolute. That was what led Albert
Camus[3] to describe terror as the urge that draws people to the violent certainties of
totalitarianism, where rebellion hardens into ideology.

With time, though, the word's aura of sublimity faded. By 1880, "holy terror"   10
was only a jocular name for an obstreperous child and "terrible" no longer suggested the sense of awe it had in "terrible swift sword." By the Jazz Age, "terrific"
was just a wan superlative. Terror was still a name for intense fear, but it no longer
connoted a social force.

"Terrorism," too, has drifted since its origin. By modern times, the word could   11
refer only to the use of violence against a government, not on its behalf—though
some still claimed the "terrorist" designation proudly.

It wasn't until the beginning of the post-colonial period[4] that all groups rejected   12
the terrorist label in favor of names such as freedom fighters or mujahadeen. By
then, "terrorism" was no longer a genuine -ism, but the name for a reprehensible

---

1. *Reign of Terror*: period from September 1793 to July 1794 during which the government established by the French Revolution executed tens of thousands of its critics. *Maximilien Robespierre*
(1758–1794): an attorney who became one of the most powerful and bloodthirsty leaders of the French
Revolution.

2. *Edmund Burke* (1729–1797): British statesman and orator who supported the American Revolution but opposed the revolution in France because of its violence.

3. *Albert Camus* (1913–1960): French writer and philosopher known for blending Christianity and
existentialism.

4. *Post-colonial period*: the decades immediately after World War II in which many African and
other countries gained independence from their nineteenth-century colonial rulers. In general, *post-
colonialism* refers to the many issues, such as creating a national identity, that countries face after their
former colonizers have withdrawn.

strategy, often extended as a term of abuse for anyone whose methods seemed ruthless.

But the recent uses of "terror" seem to draw its disparate, superseded senses 13 back together in a way that Burke might have found familiar. Today, it is again a name that encompasses both the dark forces that threaten "civilization" and the fears they arouse.

The new senses of the noun are signaled in another linguistic shift in the press 14 and in White House speeches. Just as "terrorism" has been replaced by "terror," so "war" is much more likely now to be followed by "on" rather than "against."

That "war on" pattern dates from the turn of the 20th century, when people 15 adapted epidemiological metaphors to describe campaigns against social evils such as alcohol, crime and poverty—endemic conditions that could be mitigated but not eradicated.

"The war on terror," too, suggests a campaign aimed not at human adversaries 16 but at a pervasive social plague. At its most abstract, terror comes to seem as persistent and inexplicable as evil itself, without raising any inconvenient theological qualms. And in fact, the White House's use of "evil" has declined by 80 percent over the same period that its use of "terror" has been increasing.

Like wars on ignorance and crime, a "war on terror" suggests an enduring state 17 of struggle—a "never-ending fight against terror and its relentless onslaughts," as Albert Camus put it in *The Plague*, his 1947 allegory of the rise and fall of Fascism.

It is as if the language is girding itself for the long haul. 18

READING CLOSELY

1. The word *terror,* says Geoffrey Nunberg, "draws on a more complex set of meanings" than the word *terrorism* (4). What are some of those differences in meaning between the two terms as Nunberg DEFINES them?

2. During the French Revolution, according to Nunberg, how did the traditional definition of *terror* change? What important element did the Revolution introduce into the modern meaning of the term?

3. According to Nunberg, how has the meaning of *terrorism* changed (11)?

4. Why is Nunberg concerned with changes in how words are defined? What is his THESIS, or main point, about such changes?

STRATEGIES AND STRUCTURES

1. Nunberg begins with a specific EXAMPLE (of "broad linguistic shifts") before he explains what he is DEFINING (3). How effective do you find this strategy? Why?

2. "Even if Saddam can't actually be linked to the attacks of Sept. 11, 'terror' seems to connect them etymologically" (6). What issue is Nunberg raising here? Does he ARGUE a position on that issue, or does he remain more or less objective? Explain.

3. How does Nunberg himself use ETYMOLOGIES to make connections in his essay? Is this an effective strategy? Why or why not?

4. *Other Methods.* In the body of his essay, Nunberg is COMPARING and CONTRASTING the definitions, old and new, of *terror* and *terrorism.* Explain how he extends these comparisons in the last quarter of his essay.

THINKING ABOUT LANGUAGE

1. What is the purpose of Nunberg's ALLUSION to Albert Camus's ideas in paragraphs 9 and 17?

2. What does Nunberg mean when he says that "war on" is an "epidemiological" metaphor (15)?

3. Why, according to Nunberg, has the use of the word *evil* in American political discourse declined by 80 percent in recent years (16)?

4. "Girding" (as in "girding one's loins") is what a warrior typically does in preparation for battle (18). Why do you think Nunberg ends his essay with this METAPHOR? Who or what is embattled?

FOR WRITING

1. Write a paragraph or two DEFINING "long haul" (18) by explaining its history as a transportation term.

2. What significant changes—in politics, priorities, and preoccupations—do you think have affected the meanings of basic English words, especially since 9/11? Citing Nunberg's examples and any others you want to draw on, write an essay explaining and defining some of those new meanings.

FATIMA MERNISSI

The Harem Within

*Fatima Mernissi (b. 1940) was born and raised in a traditional Moroccan household—
a harem. Mernissi's female relatives, however, insisted that she receive the education
that they had been denied. Her interest in political science eventually led her to the
Sorbonne in Paris, Brandeis University in Boston, where she earned her doctorate, and
the University of Mohammed V in Morocco, where she taught sociology. Above all,
Mernissi has devoted her career to examining—and challenging—the strictures placed
upon women in traditional Islamic societies. Her publications include* The Veil and
the Male Elite: A Feminist Interpretation of Islam *(1988);* Doing Daily Battle:
Interviews with Moroccan Women *(1991); and* Islam and Democracy: Fear of the
Modern World *(1992).*

"The Harem Within" first appeared as a chapter in Mernissi's memoir Dreams of
Trespass: Tales of a Harem Girlhood *(1995).*

O∪R HAREM IN FEZ was surrounded by high walls and, with the exception of   1
the little square chunk of sky that you could see from the courtyard below, nature
did not exist. Of course, if you rushed like an arrow up to the terrace, you could see
that the sky was larger than the house, larger than everything, but from the courtyard, nature seemed irrelevant. It had been replaced by geometric and floral
designs reproduced on tiles, woodwork, and stucco. The only strikingly beautiful
flowers we had in the house were those of the colorful brocades which covered the
sofas and those of the embroidered silk drapes that sheltered the doors and windows. You could not, for example, open a shutter to look outside when you wanted
to escape. All the windows opened onto the courtyard. There were none facing the
street.

Once a year, during springtime, we went on a *nzaha*, or picnic, at my uncle's   2
farm in Oued Fez, ten kilometers from the city. The important adults rode in cars,
while the children, divorced aunts, and other relatives were put into two big trucks
rented for the occasion. Aunt Habiba and Chama always carried tambourines, and
they would make such a hell of a noise along the way that the truck driver would go
crazy. "If you ladies don't stop this," he would shout, "I'm going to drive off the road
and throw everyone into the valley." But his threats always came to nothing,
because his voice would be drowned out by the tambourines and hand clapping.

On picnic day, everyone woke up at dawn and buzzed around the courtyard as if   3
it were a religious festival day with groups of people organizing food here, drinks
there, and putting drapes and carpets into bundles everywhere. Chama and Mother

took care of the swings. "How can you have a picnic without swings?" they would argue whenever Father suggested they forget about them for once, because it took so much time to hang them from the trees. "Besides," he would add, just to provoke Mother, "swings are fine for children, but when heavy grownups are involved, the poor trees might suffer." While Father talked and waited for Mother to get angry, she would just keep on packing up the swings and the ropes to tie them with, without a single glance in his direction. Chama would sing aloud, "If men can't tie the swings / women will do it / Lallallalla," imitating the high-pitched melody of our national anthem "Maghribuna watanuna" (Our Morocco, Our Homeland). Meanwhile, Samir and I would be feverishly looking for our espadrilles,[1] for there was no help to be had from our mothers, so involved were they in their own projects, and Lalla Mani would be counting the number of glasses and plates "just to evaluate the damage, and see how many will be broken by the end of the day." She could do without the picnic, she often said, especially since as far as tradition was concerned, its origin was dubious. "There's no record of it in the Hadith,"[2] she said, "It might even be counted as a sin on Judgment Day."

We would arrive on the farm in mid-morning, equipped with dozens of carpets 4 and light sofas and *khanouns*.[3] Once the carpets had been unfolded, the light sofas would be spread out, the charcoal fires lit, and the shish kebabs grilled. The tea-kettles would sing along with the birds. Then, after lunch, some of the women would scatter into the woods and fields, searching for flowers, herbs, and other kinds of plants to use in their beauty treatments. Others would take turns on the swings. Only after sunset would we make the journey back to the house, and the gate would be closed behind us. And for days after that, Mother would feel miserable. "When you spend a whole day among trees," she would say, "waking up with walls as horizons becomes unbearable."

You could not get into our house, except by passing through the main gate controlled by Ahmed the doorkeeper. But you could get out a second way, by using the roof-level terrace. You could jump from our terrace to the neighbors' next door, and then go out to the street through their door. Officially, our terrace key was kept in Lalla Mani's possession, with Ahmed turning off the lights to the stairs after sunset. But because the terrace was constantly being used for all kinds of domestic activities throughout the day, from retrieving olives that were stored in big jars up there,

---

1. *Espadrille*: a type of lightweight women's shoes made of canvas and hemp rope. The shoes and their name have their origin in France; their use by Mernissi and her family may reflect Morocco's history as a French colony.

2. *Hadith*: a written collection of the sayings and traditions associated with Muhammad and his companions.

3. *Khanouns*: portable metal or pottery fire containers used for grilling food over charcoal.

to washing and drying clothes, the key was often left with Aunt Habiba, who lived in the room right next to the terrace.

The terrace exit route was seldom watched, for the simple reason that getting 6 from it to the street was a difficult undertaking. You needed to be quite good at three skills: climbing, jumping, and agile landing. Most of the women could climb up and jump fairly well, but not many could land gracefully. So, from time to time, someone would come in with a bandaged ankle, and everyone would know just what she'd been up to. The first time I came down from the terrace with bleeding knees, Mother explained to me that a woman's chief problem in life was figuring out how to land. "Whenever you are about to embark on an adventure," she said, "you have to think about the landing. Not about the takeoff. So whenever you feel like flying, think about how and where you'll end up."

But there was also another, more solemn reason why women like Chama and 7 Mother did not consider escaping from the terrace to be a viable alternative to using the front gate. The terrace route had a clandestine, covert dimension to it, which was repulsive to those who were fighting for the principle of a woman's right to free movement. Confronting Ahmed at the gate was a heroic act. Escaping from the terrace was not, and did not carry with it that inspiring, subversive flame of liberation.

None of this intrigue applied, of course, to Yasmina's farm. The gate had hardly 8 any meaning, because there were no walls. And to be in a harem, I thought, you needed a barrier, a frontier. That summer, when I visited Yasmina, I told her what Chama had said about how harems got started. When I saw that she was listening, I decided to show off all my historical knowledge, and started talking about the Romans and their harems, and how the Arabs became the sultans of the planet thanks to Caliph Harun al-Rashid's one thousand women, and how the Christians tricked the Arabs by changing the rules on them while they were asleep. Yasmina laughed a lot when she heard the story, and said that she was too illiterate to evaluate the historical facts, but that it all sounded very funny and logical too. I then asked her if what Chama had said was true or false, and Yasmina said that I needed to relax about this right-and-wrong business. She said that there were things which could be both, and things which could be neither. "Words are like onions," she said. "The more skins you peel off, the more meanings you encounter. And when you start discovering multiplicities of meanings, then right and wrong becomes irrelevant. All these questions about harems that you and Samir have been asking are all fine and good, but there will always be more to be discovered." And then she added, "I am going to peel one more skin for you now. But remember, it is only one among others."

The word "harem," she said, was a slight variation of the word *haram*, the forbid- 9 den, the proscribed. It was the opposite of *halal*, the permissible. Harem was the

place where a man sheltered his family, his wife or wives, and children and relatives. It could be a house or a tent, and it referred both to the space and to the people who lived within it. One said "Sidi So-and-So's harem," referring both to his
family members and to his physical home. One thing that helped me see this more
clearly was when Yasmina explained that Mecca, the holy city, was also called
Haram. Mecca was a space where behavior was strictly codified. The moment you
stepped inside, you were bound by many laws and regulations. People who entered
Mecca had to be pure: they had to perform purification rituals, and refrain from
lying, cheating, and doing harmful deeds. The city belonged to Allah and you had to
obey his *shariᶜa*, or sacred law, if you entered his territory. The same thing applied
to a harem when it was a house belonging to a man. No other men could enter it
without the owner's permission, and when they did, they had to obey his rules. A
harem was about private space and the rules regulating it. In addition, Yasmina
said, it did not need walls. Once you knew what was forbidden, you carried the
harem within. You had it in your head, "inscribed under your forehead and under
your skin." That idea of an invisible harem, a law tattooed in the mind, was fright-
fully unsettling to me. I did not like it at all, and I wanted her to explain more.

The farm, said Yasmina, was a harem, although it did not have walls. "You only 10
need walls, if you have streets!" But if you decided, like Grandfather, to live in the
countryside, then you didn't need gates, because you were in the middle of the
fields and there were no passersby. Women could go freely out into the fields,
because there were no strange men hovering around, peeping at them. Women
could walk or ride for hours without seeing a soul. But if by chance they did meet
a male peasant along the way, and he saw that they were unveiled, he would cover
his head with the hood of his own *djellaba*⁴ to show that he was not looking. So in
this case, Yasmina said, the harem was in the peasant's head, inscribed somewhere
under his forehead. He knew that the women on the farm belonged to Grandfather
Tazi, and that he had no right to look at them.

This business of going around with a frontier inside the head disturbed me, and 11
discreetly I put my hand to my forehead to make sure it was smooth, just to see if
by any chance I might be harem-free. But then, Yasmina's explanation got even
more alarming, because the next thing she said was that any space you entered had
its own invisible rules, and you needed to figure them out. "And when I say space,"
she continued, "It can be any space—a courtyard, a terrace, or a room, or even the
street for that matter. Wherever there are human beings, there is a *qaᵓida*, or invisible rule. If you stick to the *qaᵓida*, nothing bad can happen to you." In Arabic, she
reminded me, *qaᵓida* meant many different things, all of which shared the same
basic premise. A mathematical law or a legal system was a *qaᵓida*, and so was the

---

4. *Djellaba*: a traditional Moroccan robe.

foundation of a building. *Qaʾida* was also a custom, or a behavioral code. *Qaʾida* was everywhere. Then she added something which really scared me: "Unfortunately, most of the time, the *qaʾida* is against women."

"Why?" I asked. "That's not fair, is it?" And I crept closer so as not to miss a   12 word of her answer. The world, Yasmina said, was not concerned about being fair to women. Rules were made in such a manner as to deprive them in some way or another. For example, she said, both men and women worked from dawn until very late at night. But men made money and women did not. That was one of the invisible rules. And when a woman worked hard, and was not making money, she was stuck in a harem, even though she could not see its walls. "Maybe the rules are ruthless because they are not made by women," was Yasmina's final comment. "But why aren't they made by women?" I asked. "The moment women get smart and start asking that very question," she replied, "instead of dutifully cooking and washing dishes all the time, they will find a way to change the rules and turn the whole planet upside down." "How long will that take?" I asked, and Yasmina said, "A long time."

I asked her next if she could tell me how to figure out the invisible rule or   13 *qaʾida*, whenever I stepped into a new space. Were there signals, or something tangible that I could look for? No, she said, unfortunately not, there were no clues, except for the violence after the fact. Because the moment I disobeyed an invisible rule, I would get hurt. However, she noted that many of the things people enjoyed doing most in life, like walking around, discovering the world, singing, dancing, and expressing an opinion, often turned up in the strictly forbidden category. In fact, the *qaʾida*, the invisible rule, often was much worse than walls and gates. With walls and gates, you at least knew what was expected from you.

At those words, I almost wished that all rules would suddenly materialize into   14 frontiers and visible walls right before my very eyes. But then I had another uncomfortable thought. If Yasmina's farm was a harem, in spite of the fact that there were no walls to be seen, then what did *hurriya*, or freedom, mean? I shared this thought with her, and she seemed a little worried, and said that she wished I would play like other kids, and stop worrying about walls, rules, constraints, and the meaning of *hurriya*. "You'll miss out on happiness if you think too much about walls and rules, my dear child," she said. "The ultimate goal of a woman's life is happiness. So don't spend your time looking for walls to bang your head on." To make me laugh, Yasmina would spring up, run to the wall, and pretend to pound her head against it, screaming, "*Aie, aie!* The wall hurts! The wall is my enemy!" I exploded with laughter, relieved to learn that bliss was still within reach, in spite of it all. She looked at me and put her finger to her temple, "You understand what I mean?"

Of course I understood what you meant, Yasmina, and happiness did seem   15 absolutely possible, in spite of harems, both visible and invisible. I would run to hug her, and whisper in her ear as she held me and let me play with her pink pearls. "I love you Yasmina. I really do. Do you think I will be a happy woman?"

"Of course you will be happy!" she would exclaim. "You will be a modern, edu-   16 cated lady. You will realize the nationalists' dream. You will learn foreign languages, have a passport, devour books, and speak like a religious authority. At the very least, you will certainly be better off than your mother. Remember that even I, as illiterate and bound by tradition as I am, have managed to squeeze some happiness out of this damned life. That is why I don't want you to focus on the frontiers and the barriers all the time. I want you to concentrate on fun and laughter and happiness. That is a good project for an ambitious young lady."

READING CLOSELY

1. How does the house in which Mernissi grew up differ from a typical American or other Western home? Consider the physical characteristics of the house as well as the "spiritual" ones.

2. Why does Mernissi pay so much attention to the two possible exits from the house—the main one through the front gate and a "clandestine" one through the terrace (7)?

3. Why do you think Mernissi mentions her father only briefly, when she is DESCRIBING the preparations for the annual family picnic? What is the role of Ahmed the doorkeeper in the family harem?

4. In paragraphs 2–4, Mernissi describes the family's annual picnic, or *nzaha*, in some detail. How is the *nzaha* like a *harem*, and how is it different?

5. Why do you think Mernissi is so interested in the DEFINITION of a harem? What advice does her aunt give her about her preoccupation with this term? Does this advice seem to be the main point of this selection? Why or why not?

STRATEGIES AND STRUCTURES

1. According to Mernissi, a harem is a kind of "private space" (9). What additional characteristics do she and Aunt Yasmina introduce in order to extend and refine this basic definition?

2. How and where does Aunt Yasmina use ETYMOLOGIES and ANTONYMS to help explain what a harem is?

3. Aunt Yasmina introduces an "alarming" synonym for *harem* in paragraph 11. What is it, and how does her use of the term help young Mernissi to understand what is being explained to her?

4. How effective, finally, do you find "illiterate" Aunt Yasmina as an interpreter of meanings and definer of words (8)? What is Mernissi's main point in quoting so many of her aunt's definitions? Is there anything subversive about Yasmina's role? Explain.

5. *Other Methods.* How do the events of Mernissi's NARRATIVE—such as the conflict with the bus driver, Chama's singing about the swings, and the conversation with Yasmina—help to support her definition of "the harem within" and other key terms?

THINKING ABOUT LANGUAGE

1. Why does Mernissi use the word "escape" when describing her family home (1)? How does her description of the place fit in with what she says about nature?

2. The dictionary definition of a *harem* is "the section of a house reserved for women in a Muslim household." What are the CONNOTATIONS of *harem* as Mernissi uses the term?

3. Mernissi's mother tells her that a woman's main problem in life is "figuring out how to land" (6). What does she mean by this METAPHOR?

4. Defining words, says Aunt Yasmina, is like peeling onions (8). Why does she use this ANALOGY? Is the comparison accurate? Why or why not?

5. A harem is not only a physical place, says Mernissi, but an idea "inscribed under your forehead," "a law tattooed in the mind" (9). What are the implications of *inscribed* and *tattooed* in this definition?

FOR WRITING

1. In a paragraph or two, DEFINE what you thought a harem was before you read Mernissi's essay, and explain how you would define the term now.

2. Write a definition essay about an idea or place that significantly affected your childhood in a positive or negative way. Include a COMPARISON of your perspective on that idea or place today with your perspective back then.

3. Write a NARRATIVE about some unwritten rules that you have encountered. Include an interpreter, like Aunt Yasmina, who defines the rules for you, or at least makes you aware of them.

MARY ROACH

How to Know If You're Dead

Mary Roach is a San Francisco–based journalist whose first book, Stiff: The Curious Lives of Human Cadavers *(2003), propelled her to the forefront of popular science writers; one reviewer called her "the funniest science writer in the country." When asked how she came to write a best-seller about a subject most readers would regard as morbid, Roach replied, "Good question. It's possible that I'm a little strange." In fact, a glance at a few of the articles she's written gives one a sense of Roach's wide-ranging, quirky sensibilities: "Don't Jump!" ("Exactly what happens when a person leaps off the Golden Gate Bridge?"); "Turning Orange" ("Raw carrot abuse is nothing to laugh at"); "How to Feel Better about Falling Apart" ("Here's how I cope with my disgusting, sagging middle-aged body"). Roach's book* Spook: Science Tackles the Afterlife *(2005) takes up where* Stiff *leaves off, and her most recent book,* Bonk: The Curious Coupling of Science and Sex *(2007), tackles another of life's mysteries.*

In "How to Know If You're Dead," which first appeared in Stiff, *Roach explores the meaning of* dead *and finds, surprisingly, that the definition is a subject of disagreement among doctors, lawyers, and would-be spiritualists. Despite the jaunty tone of her prose, Roach is meticulous in her scientific reporting; the meaning of death, she finds, casts more than a little light on the meaning of life.*

A PATIENT ON THE WAY TO SURGERY travels at twice the speed of a patient on the way to the morgue. Gurneys that ferry the living through hospital corridors move forward in an aura of purpose and push, flanked by caregivers with long strides and set faces, steadying IVs, pumping ambu bags, barreling into double doors. A gurney with a cadaver commands no urgency. It is wheeled by a single person, calmly and with little notice like a shopping cart.

For this reason, I thought I would be able to tell when the dead woman was wheeled past. I have been standing around at the nurses' station on one of the surgery floors of the University of California at San Francisco Medical Center, watching gurneys go by and waiting for Von Peterson, public affairs manager of the California Transplant Donor Network, and a cadaver I will call H. "There's your patient," says the charge nurse. A commotion of turquoise legs passes with unexpected forward-leaning urgency.

H is unique in that she is both a dead person *and* a patient on the way to surgery. She is what's known as a "beating-heart cadaver," alive and well everywhere but her brain. Up until artificial respiration was developed, there was no such entity; without a functioning brain, a body will not breathe on its own. But hook it up to a res-

1

2

3

397

pirator and its heart will beat, and the rest of its organs will, for a matter of days, continue to thrive.

H doesn't look or smell or feel dead. If you leaned in close over the gurney, you   4
could see her pulse beating in the arteries of her neck. If you touched her arm, you would find it warm and resilient, like your own. This is perhaps why the nurses and doctors refer to H as a patient, and why she makes her entrance to the OR at the customary presurgery clip.

Since brain death is the legal definition of death in this country, H the person is   5
certifiably dead. But H the organs and tissues is very much alive. These two seemingly contradictory facts afford her an opportunity most corpses do not have: that of extending the lives of two or three dying strangers. Over the next four hours, H will surrender her liver, kidneys, and heart. One at a time, surgeons will come and go, taking an organ and returning in haste to their stricken patients. Until recently, the process was known among transplant professionals as an "organ harvest," which had a joyous, celebratory ring to it, perhaps a little too joyous, as it has been of late replaced by the more businesslike "organ recovery."

In H's case, one surgeon will be traveling from Utah to recover her heart, and   6
another, the one recovering both the liver and the kidneys, will be taking them two floors down. UCSF is a major transplant center, and organs removed here often remain in house. More typically, a transplant patient's surgeon will travel from UCSF to a small town somewhere to retrieve the organ—often from an accident victim, someone young with strong, healthy organs, whose brain took an unexpected hit. The doctor does this because typically there is no doctor in that small town with experience in organ recovery. Contrary to rumors about surgically trained thugs cutting people open in hotel rooms and stealing their kidneys,[1] organ recovery is tricky work. If you want to be sure it's done right, you get on a plane and go do it yourself.

Today's abdominal recovery surgeon is named Andy Posselt. He is holding an   7
electric cauterizing wand, which looks like a cheap bank pen on a cord but functions like a scalpel. The wand both cuts and burns, so that as the incision is made, any vessels that are severed are simultaneously melted shut. The result is that there is a good deal less bleeding and a good deal more smoke and smell. It's not a bad smell, but simply a seared-meat sort of smell. I want to ask Dr. Posselt whether he likes it, but I can't bring myself to, so instead I ask whether he thinks it's bad that I like the smell, which I don't really, or maybe just a little. He replies that it is neither bad nor good, just morbid.

---

1. *Rumors . . . stealing their kidneys*: reference to a persistent urban legend about people getting drunk at parties, passing out, and waking up in a hotel room bathtub surrounded in ice and finding that one or both of their kidneys had been removed. These stories are always presented as true and as coming from a reputable but distant source ("it happened to my neighbor's cousin's wife's coworker's son").

I have never before seen major surgery, only its scars. From the length of them, 8
I had imagined surgeons doing their business, taking things out and putting them
in, through an opening maybe eight or nine inches long, like a woman poking
around for her glasses at the bottom of her purse. Dr. Posselt begins just above
H's pubic hair and proceeds a good two feet north, to the base of her neck. He's
unzipping her like a parka. Her sternum is sawed lengthwise so that her rib cage
can be parted, and a large retractor is installed to pull the two sides of the incision
apart so that it is now as wide as it is long. To see her this way, held open like a
Gladstone bag,[2] forces a view of the human torso for what it basically is: a large,
sturdy container for guts.

On the inside, H looks very much alive. You can see the pulse of her heartbeat 9
in her liver and all the way down her aorta. She bleeds where she is cut and her
organs are plump and slippery-looking. The electronic beat of the heart monitor
reinforces the impression that this is a living, breathing, thriving person. It is
strange, almost impossible, really, to think of her as a corpse. When I tried to
explain beating-heart cadavers to my stepdaughter Phoebe yesterday, it didn't make
sense to her. But if their heart is beating, aren't they still a person? she wanted to
know. In the end she decided they were "a kind of person you could play tricks on
but they wouldn't know." Which, I think, is a pretty good way of summing up most
donated cadavers. The things that happen to the dead in labs and ORs are like gossip passed behind one's back. They are not felt or known and so they cause no pain.

The contradictions and counterintuitions of the beating-heart cadaver can exact 10
an emotional toll on the intensive care unit (ICU) staff, who must, in the days preceding the harvest, not only think of patients like H as living beings, but treat and
care for them that way as well. The cadaver must be monitored around the clock
and "life-saving" interventions undertaken on its behalf. Since the brain can no
longer regulate blood pressure or the levels of hormones and their release into the
bloodstream, these things must be done by ICU staff, in order to keep the organs
from degrading. Observed a group of Case Western Reserve University School of
Medicine physicians in a *New England Journal of Medicine* article entitled "Psy-
chosocial and Ethical Implications of Organ Retrieval": "Intensive care unit personnel may feel confused about having to perform cardiopulmonary resuscitation
on a patient who has been declared dead, whereas a 'do not resuscitate' order has
been written for a living patient in the next bed."

. . .

The modern medical community is on the whole quite unequivocal about the brain 11
being the seat of the soul, the chief commander of life and death. It is similarly
unequivocal about the fact that people like H are, despite the hoochy-koochy going
on behind their sternums, dead. We now know that the heart keeps beating on its

2. *Gladstone bag*: an early suitcase, hinged to open in the middle and lie flat.

own not because the soul is in there, but because it contains its own bioelectric power source, independent of the brain. As soon as H's heart is installed in someone else's chest and that person's blood begins to run through it, it will start beating anew—with no signals from the recipient's brain.

The legal community took a little longer than the physicians to come around to the concept of brain death. It was 1968 when the *Journal of the American Medical Association* published a paper by the Ad Hoc Committee of the Harvard Medical School to Examine the Definition of Brain Death advocating that irreversible coma be the new criterion for death, and clearing the ethical footpath for organ transplantation. It wasn't until 1974 that the law began to catch up. What forced the issue was a bizarre murder trial in Oakland, California. 12

The killer, Andrew Lyons, shot a man in the head in September 1973 and left him brain-dead. When Lyons's attorneys found out that the victim's family had donated his heart for transplantation, they tried to use this in Lyons's defense: If the heart was still beating at the time of surgery, they maintained, then how could it be that Lyons had killed him the day before? They tried to convince the jury that, technically speaking, Andrew Lyons hadn't murdered the man, the organ recovery surgeon had. According to Stanford University heart transplant pioneer Norman Shumway, who testified in the case, the judge would have none of it. He informed the jury that the accepted criteria for death were those set forth by the Harvard committee, and that that should inform their decision. (Photographs of the victim's brains "oozing from his skull," to quote the *San Francisco Chronicle*, probably didn't help Lyons's case.) In the end, Lyons was convicted of murder. Based on the outcome of the case, California passed legislation making brain death the legal definition of death. Other states quickly followed suit. 13

Andrew Lyons's defense attorney wasn't the first person to cry murder when a transplant surgeon removed a heart from a brain-dead patient. In the earliest days of heart transplants, Shumway, the first U.S. surgeon to carry out the procedure, was continually harangued by the coroner in Santa Clara County, where he practiced. The coroner didn't accept the brain-death concept of death and threatened that if Shumway went ahead with his plans to remove a beating heart from a brain-dead person and use it to save another person's life, he would initiate murder charges. Though the coroner had no legal ground to stand on and Shumway went ahead anyway, the press gave it a vigorous chew. New York heart transplant surgeon Mehmet Oz recalls the Brooklyn district attorney around that time making the same threat. "He said he'd indict and arrest any heart transplant surgeon who went into his borough and harvested an organ." 14

The worry, explained Oz, was that someday someone who wasn't actually brain-dead was going to have his heart cut out. There exist certain rare medical conditions that can look, to the untrained or negligent eye, a lot like brain death, and the 15 legal types didn't trust the medical types to get it right. To a very, very small degree, they had reason to worry. Take, for example, the condition known as "locked-in state." In one form of the disease, the nerves, from eyeballs to toes, suddenly and rather swiftly drop out of commission, with the result that the body is completely paralyzed, while the mind remains normal. The patient can hear what's being said but has no way of communicating that he's still in there, and that no, it's definitely not okay to give his organs away for transplant. In severe cases, even the muscles that contract to change the size of the pupils no longer function. This is bad news, for a common test of brain death is to shine a light in the patient's eyes to check for the reflexive contraction of the pupils. Typically, victims of locked-in state recover fully, provided no one has mistakenly wheeled them off to the OR to take out their heart.

Like the specter of live burial that plagued the French and German citizenry in the 1800s, the fear of live organ harvesting is almost completely without foundation. A simple EEG will prevent misdiagnosis of the locked-in state and conditions like it. 16

On a rational level, most people are comfortable with the concept of brain death and organ donation. But on an emotional level, they may have a harder time accepting it, particularly when they are being asked to accept it by a transplant counselor who would like them to okay the removal of a family member's beating heart. Fifty-four percent of families asked refuse consent. "They can't deal with the fear, however irrational, that the true end of their loved one will come when the heart is removed," says Oz. That they, in effect, will have killed him. 17

Even heart transplant surgeons sometimes have trouble accepting the notion that the heart is nothing more than a pump. When I asked Oz where he thought the soul resided, he said, "I'll confide in you that I don't think it's all in the brain. I have to believe that in many ways the core of our existence is in our heart." Does that mean he thinks the brain-dead patient isn't dead? "There's no question that the heart without a brain is of no value. But life and death is not a binary system." It's a continuum. It makes sense, for many reasons, to draw the legal line at brain death, but that doesn't mean it's really a line. "In between life and death is a state of near-death, or pseudo-life. And most people don't want what's in between." 18

. . .

The harvesting of H is winding down. The last organs to be taken, the kidneys, are being brought up and separated from the depths of her open torso. Her thorax and abdomen are filled with crushed ice, turned red from blood. "Cherry Sno-Kone," I write in my notepad. It's been almost four hours now, and H has begun to look more like a conventional cadaver, her skin dried and dulled at the edges of the incision. 19

The kidneys are placed in a blue plastic bowl with ice and perfusion fluid. A relief surgeon arrives for the final step of the recovery, cutting off pieces of veins 20 and arteries to be included, like spare sweater buttons, along with the organs, in case the ones attached to them are too short to work with. A half hour later, the relief surgeon steps aside and the resident comes over to sew H up.

As he talks to Dr. Posselt about the stitching, the resident strokes the bank of fat 21 along H's incision with his gloved hand, then pats it twice, as though comforting her. When he turns back to his work, I ask him if it feels different to be working on a dead patient.

"Oh, yes," he answers. "I mean, I would never use this kind of stitch." He has 22 begun stitching more widely spaced, comparatively crude loops, rather than the tight, hidden stitches used on the living.

I rephrase the question: Does it feel odd to perform surgery on someone who 23 isn't alive?

His answer is surprising. "The patient *was* alive." I suppose surgeons are used to 24 thinking about patients—particularly ones they've never met—as no more than what they see of them: open plots of organs. And as far as that goes, I guess you could say H *was* alive. Because of the cloths covering all but her opened torso, the young man never saw her face, didn't know if she was male or female.

While the resident sews, a nurse picks stray danglies of skin and fat off the oper- 25 ating table with a pair of tongs and drops them inside the body cavity, as though H were a handy wastebasket. The nurse explains that this is done intentionally: "Anything not donated stays with her." The jigsaw puzzle put back in its box.

The incision is complete, and a nurse washes H off and covers her with a blan- 26 ket for the trip to the morgue. Out of habit or respect, he chooses a fresh one. The transplant coordinator, Von, and the nurse lift H onto a gurney. Von wheels H into an elevator and down a hallway to the morgue. The workers are behind a set of swinging doors, in a back room. "Can we leave this here?" Von shouts. H has become a "this." We are instructed to wheel the gurney into the cooler, where it joins five others. H appears no different from the corpses already here.[3]

But H *is* different. She has made three sick people well. She has brought them 27 extra time on earth. To be able, as a dead person, to make a gift of this magnitude is phenomenal. Most people don't manage this sort of thing while they're alive. Cadavers like H are the dead's heros.

It is astounding to me, and achingly sad, that with eighty thousand people on 28 the waiting list for donated hearts and livers and kidneys, with sixteen a day dying

---

3. Unless H's family is planning a naked open-casket service, no one at her funeral will be able to tell she's had organs removed. Only with tissue harvesting, which often includes leg and arm bones, does the body take on a slightly altered profile, and in this case PVC piping or dowels are inserted to normalize the form and make life easier for mortuary staff and others who need to move the otherwise somewhat noodle-ized body. [Author's note.]

there on that list, that more than half of the people in the position H's family was in will say no, will choose to burn those organs or let them rot. We abide the surgeon's scalpel to save our own lives, our loved ones' lives, but not to save a stranger's life. H has no heart, but heartless is the last thing you'd call her.

READING CLOSELY

1. A "beating-heart cadaver," says Mary Roach, is "both a dead person and a patient on the way to surgery" (3). How is this possible? What are some of the "contradictions and counterintuitions" posed by a beating-heart cadaver (10)?

2. What is the legal DEFINITION of death in the United States, according to Roach? What was the role of the Andrew Lyons case in establishing this definition (13)?

3. Define the condition known as "locked-in state" (15). Why do such medical conditions worry some people in regard to organ transplants?

4. How is the legal and medical definition of death complicated by Roach's conversation with Dr. Oz in paragraph 18?

STRATEGIES AND STRUCTURES

1. What ARGUMENT is Roach making on the basis of her extended DEFINITION? What is her main point? Where does she state it?

2. Fifty-four percent of the families whom doctors ask for permission to retrieve the organs of brain-dead patients, says Roach, refuse permission (17). As she notes later, that's "more than half" (28). Do you think such facts bolster Roach's argument? In what way?

3. Roach uses a number of direct quotations from physicians, nurses, and others. Is this an effective strategy? Support your answer with several examples from the selection.

4. *Other Methods.* How does the EXAMPLE of patient H contribute to Roach's definition of death? How does it contribute to her ARGUMENT?

THINKING ABOUT LANGUAGE

1. Why, according to Roach, did the medical community change its terminology from "harvesting" organs to "recovering" them (5)? What do you think of the change?

2. Roach uses many nonmedical terms and SIMILES in her essay, such as "like a shopping cart" (1), "hoochy-koochy" (11), and "Cherry Sno-Kone" (19). Point out other examples. Given the seriousness of her subject, do you find such informal language appropriate or inappropriate? Explain your reaction.

3. What cleared "the ethical footpath for organ transplantation," says Roach, was a report published in 1968 in the *Journal of the American Medical Association* (12). What are the implications of this "footpath" METAPHOR?

4. In paragraph 14, while talking about the press coverage of the case, Roach uses the CONCRETE image "vigorous chew" rather than an ABSTRACT phrase such as "good coverage." Which do you prefer, and why?

5. Is Von, the transplant coordinator, right to refer to patient H as "this" (26)? Why or why not?

For Writing

1. Write a paragraph giving the legal DEFINITION of death as doctors and lawyers have come to define it since 1968.

2. Write a paragraph defining death according to some criterion other than "irreversible coma" (12).

3. In paragraph 18, Roach asks Dr. Oz where he thinks the soul resides. Write a definition essay addressing this question. Be sure to deal with the implications of the physician's observation that death isn't "really a line" (18).

GAIL BABILONIA

The Celebrity Chef

Gail Babilonia was an undergraduate at Rutgers when she wrote "The Celebrity Chef" as a research paper for an English course. It was one of twelve student essays selected for publication in the 2004 issue of Dialogues@RU: A Journal of Undergraduate Research.

"The Celebrity Chef" is a study in communications theory that does more than define a new kind of cook. Using various communications models, this essay also defines a new brand of celebrity whose audience, in turn, can be understood as participants, spectators, or targets.

WHEN WE HEAR THE WORD *CHEF*, we imagine a nameless Frenchman dressed in an all-white apron and a tall white hat with ownership rights to a fancy, upscale restaurant. However, today the chef at a well-known restaurant may no longer be hidden in the kitchen; well-known chefs can be seen every day on television. The celebrity chef is a recent addition to both the culinary and media worlds. Not too long ago, there were only a few: Julia Child was the most famous, and remains an icon today. Now, however, there are many more chefs to watch on the Food Network. Emeril Lagasse is the most popular, and demonstrates the role that celebrity chefs currently play in our lives. Although a recent addition, celebrity chefs have had a great influence on our culture: they have changed our ideas about celebrity and about the social status of the chef; they have redefined the kind of food ordinary people can have, and transformed the way men feel about cooking. However, the impact of the celebrity chef is one that most of us barely recognize.

Few students in a culinary institute expect to use their certification to become a "celebrity chef" or a Food Network television personality. There is far too much hard work involved in becoming a trained chef to have time to think about being a famous one. Tania Ralli, a student currently enrolled at the French Culinary Institute in New York City, explains: "[W]e were cooking five hours a night, three nights a week, after full days at our regular jobs. The cost, $28,000 in tuition and fees, signaled the depth of our commitment" (Ralli 4). Because tuition and fees are so high, many students must work full time and attend school in addition to their jobs. In their classes, the students cook recipes over and over in preparation for a final exam in which they cook two recipes randomly selected from among the hundreds that they have learned. However, Ralli claims, "cooking school was more than learning about technique. From developing heat-resistant hands to managing temperamental personalities, we developed the stamina necessary in a professional kitchen" (4). The students are critiqued based on their efficiency and speed, and on the taste and presentation of their food; they are not trained to be charismatic, friendly, or photogenic. Students focus on surviving in professional kitchens, not on cooking under studio lights. Becoming famous is not a priority for most would-be chefs: students enter the culinary world in hopes of having more practical things like job security, benefits, and decent pay. By and large, they are too sensible to daydream about becoming the next Emeril, which is fortunate because becoming a celebrity chef is beyond their control: becoming a famous chef really depends on the media and the audience.

What makes a chef a "celebrity chef"? According to David Giles, an author who   3 explored the psychology of fame and celebrity, "the defining characteristic of a celebrity is that there is essentially a media production" (2) on television, radio, or in the movies through which a personality is exposed to the public. Actors are celebrities because their media productions are the movies and television shows that they appear in. The celebrity chef receives wide exposure through the media and is well known because of the media; the celebrity chef's own show, and frequent appearances on popular daytime talk shows are his media productions. Without media attention and publicity, a celebrity chef loses the defining characteristic that distinguishes him from a restaurant chef. In connection with celebrity, Giles discusses the differences between two groups of accomplished people, athletes and academics, one exposed to the public more than the other:

> The priorities of the media or the dominant culture determines which spheres of activity are most likely to yield fame to the people within them. In Britain . . . there are huge numbers of footballers [soccer players] who are famous to the general public regardless of our interest in football. . . . Generally speaking, academics are not likely to be as famous as sports people; unless we appear regularly on television, our activities simply aren't visible enough, important enough, or as photogenic as the activities of people working in other fields. (6)

The celebrity chef, of course, corresponds to the famous athlete who is recog-   4 nized even by people who may not follow sports, and the chef hidden away in a restaurant corresponds to the invisible and unphotogenic academic who receives little public recognition. Celebrity chefs have status because they are exposed to the general public, and are "visible enough" to keep the public's attention directed toward them (Giles 6). Both a chef in a restaurant and a celebrity chef have had proper training in fine culinary schools and have worked for years alongside great chefs as their mentors. However, a celebrity chef is exposed to the public through the media, especially through television, constantly appearing outside the restaurant kitchen as a guest on popular talk shows and on packages of his own line of kitchenware. The public is continuously exposed to what celebrity chefs have to offer, but we are exposed to the great restaurant chefs only when we are actually at their restaurant, or read about them (if we follow the culinary world) in publications like *Gourmet* and *Food and Wine*. The point is that celebrity chefs are exposed through mass media—we know of them because we have no control over when we will stumble upon them on our favorite morning talk show or at the kitchenware section of department stores.

The epitome of the celebrity chef is Emeril Lagasse. No other chefs on the Food   5
Network have shows or audiences like he has, and his show is a true media production. First of all, the set of *Emeril Live* breaks away from traditional instructive cooking shows: instead of having Emeril demonstrating and speaking into the camera, the show has a talk-show format with a live audience and music provided by Doc Gibbs and the *Emeril Live* Band. The band defines Emeril as "essentially (part of) a media production" (Giles 2). On no other cooking show is the chef accompanied by a live band, which connects *Emeril Live* to entertainment shows like *The Tonight Show*[1] rather than to other cooking shows (Emeril even has conversations with his bandleader Doc Gibbs just as Jay Leno does with his band leader, Kevin Eubanks). Moreover, Emeril's show is unique in that it both serves to teach people how to cook and to entertain them, which is what makes him different from any other chef and what makes him a true celebrity.

Aside from the elements of Emeril's show that are a product of set designers,   6
producers, and other creative television production executives, the response of the audience sets Emeril apart. Denis McQuail, a professor emeritus of communication at the University of Amsterdam, Netherlands, describes what he calls an "audience-sender relationship" which can be broken down into three categories: the audience as a target, the audience as participants, and the audience as spectators (40). These categories can help us to understand the rapport that Emeril has with his audience, which makes him a celebrity. Emeril enters from the back of the set, shakes everyone's hands, and makes small-talk with some of the audience members before reaching his place behind the studio's stove. From his entrance, we see how Emeril establishes a relationship with the audience; he could simply start his show by entering from backstage without greeting the audience members, but in doing so, he makes the audience what McQuail calls "participants":

> Communication is defined in terms of sharing and participation, increasing the commonality between sender and receiver, rather than in changing "receivers" in line with the purpose of the "sender"; . . . communication is

---

1. *The Tonight Show/Jay Leno: The Tonight Show*, a television institution, is a one-hour program that is broadcast on the NBC network after the late news. Jay Leno has hosted the show since 1992.

not instrumental or utilitarian, and the attitude of the audience is likely to be
playful or personally . . . committed in one way or another. Audience members are essentially participants. (41)

When he makes contact with the audience, Emeril receives a response that is   7
both "playful" and "personally committed"; he receives this type of feedback
because he takes a relaxed and laid-back approach to instructive cooking, constantly including his audience so that they do not feel intimidated by the complicated dishes that he prepares. Furthermore, he gives the audience the opportunity
to participate by echoing his notorious sound effect "BAM!" and by being able to
taste the food that he has cooked before them. In the way he approaches the audience, he "increases the commonality between the sender [himself] and the
receiver [the audience]." He makes himself approachable and down to earth, which
makes the audience feel comfortable with him. In addition to being participants,
the audience of *Emeril Live* also functions as what McQuail calls the "audience as
spectators" (41). Since Emeril has already established the audience as participants,
this affects how his audience responds as spectators, which in turn affects Emeril's
status as a celebrity:

> The [audience as spectator] arises in a model of communication in which the
> source . . . simply capture[s] the attention of the audience, regardless of com-
> municative effect. Audience attention is what is measured by ratings and
> thus cashable in the form of subscriptions, box office receipts, and payments
> from advertisers. It is also cashable in terms of status and influence within
> the media and in society generally. Fame and celebrity are more likely to
> result from sheer amount of public exposure than from measured "effects" or
> from measures of audience "appreciation." (41–42)

This model can be seen in the way that Emeril "captures" the attention of the   8
audience by entertaining them with funny sound effects and facial expressions
while he cooks. Because Emeril has already engaged his audience into his show as
participants, he receives this loyalty of his audience as spectators as measured, by
his ratings, and by the attendance at his sold-out *Emeril Live* personal appearances.
Through these appearances, moreover, Emeril increases his "cashable" status of
fame and celebrity through frequent "public exposure."

We have to keep in mind that Emeril's character is a production of the media   9
that is aimed toward a particular audience. McQuail's model of the "audience as a
target" explains that "the communication process is considered primarily as the
sending of signals or messages over time for the purposes of control or influence.
The receiver, and thus the audience, is perceived as a *destination* or *target* for the
purposeful transfer or meaning" (41). Emeril's production executives target a spe-

cific audience, and control his popularity by giving *Emeril Live* primetime spots on the Food Network, daily at 8 P.M. and 11 P.M., and Emeril's other show *The Essence of Emeril*, at 4 P.M., giving him constant visibility in terms of a specific audience. Emeril's "destination" or "target" seems to be working-class Americans, since the shows air at times when working Americans would be arriving home or settling down to watch television after dinner or at bedtime. This scheduling ensures that Emeril is able to gain the audience's loyalty by making his "media production" available at the times when most of his target audience is watching, and "control" the audience's attention by strategically choosing the most advantageous times to air his shows, which in turn increases his celebrity.

McQuail's audience-response models suggest that Emeril has a great responsi-   10
bility to his audience in order to maintain his image as a celebrity chef. Although Emeril gains his audience by being charismatic, friendly, and approachable, at the same time, he is creating an illusion by having the audience believe that there is only one way in which he can behave. Richard Dyer, a lecturer in film at the University of Warwick, writing about stars (we can use the terms "stars" and "celebrities" interchangeably since both refer to public figures), claims that

> the roles and/or performance of a star in a film were taken as revealing the personality of the star. . . . What was only sometimes glimpsed and seldom brought out by Hollywood or the stars was that personality was itself a construction known and expressed only through films, stories, publicity. (22–23)

The public sometimes has a difficult time separating the actor's true character from the character he plays, but is aware of the difference. However, with Emeril there is a different situation because Emeril is part of a media production: there is a constructed public persona that Emeril projects to the audience, and Emeril's funny character is designed to create an illusion that there is only one Emeril. His fans forget that as they watch this chef demonstrate how to prepare food, they are also watching him "cook up" an appealing character, because the audience is unable to differentiate Emeril's persona on television from his identity off camera. Since there is a media production and Emeril is the celebrity-product, the producers have to make sure that Emeril maintains his persona. Convincing the audience that Emeril has only one personality changes the traditional idea of celebrity, since with movie stars, for example, people identify with the characters who are being played rather than with the actors themselves. The audience does not see Emeril "acting" while he is cooking on his television show, and since Emeril projects only one persona, people feel that they are able to identify with him.

As a teacher, Emeril also changes the traditional idea of celebrity. Usually,   11
celebrities are admired for being photogenic or skillful; however, these qualities are not something that people can learn or apply to their own lives. Observing the

audience at the show, we see the audience waiting attentively, ready to learn, as if they are waiting for a miracle to happen before their eyes. But that's the thing. Emeril emphasizes how "EASY" it is to prepare these dishes. He constantly uses phrases such as "it's as simple as that" and "it's not rocket science" to encourage the audience to try to cook the dishes themselves. By introducing a recipe as "easy to make," Emeril instills the desire to cook, and the confidence to cook, the kind of food that is usually only served in expensive and intimidating restaurants. Consequently, Emeril's instruction helps to democratize fine food. People may not be able to dine in upscale restaurants because they lack the time or the money, but Emeril changes the idea that fine food is only available at expensive restaurants. By making great food available, Emeril reaches out to those who ordinarily would not experience exquisitely prepared food, and emphasizes that it is not hard for people to cook well themselves. This shows us the difference between a "celebrity" and a "celebrity chef": where celebrities are usually simply entertainers, celebrity chefs are inspirations, teachers, and leaders. The audience is able to connect with the celebrity chef because each show has a lesson that the audience can take home and use. The audiences of movies and television can only watch and admire what the actors do; they can not take home instructions on how to act; however, the celebrity chef can give the audience the knowledge necessary to cook an elaborate meal at home, which ultimately has a greater impact than a movie has on a person's life.

The celebrity chef also challenges our gender stereotypes. For many years, food in the home has been associated with the women of the household. Traditionally, women have cooked for the family and taken charge of the food served at every meal. Ironically, however, men dominate the culinary world—professional cooking and *haute cuisine* are mostly associated with male chefs and restaurateurs, and industrial kitchens are filled with male chefs. Susan Gregory, a researcher in the sociology of food and the sociology of the family attributes women's dominance of the kitchens at home and the household in general to the nurture factor (Bowlby, Gregory, and McKie 62): cooking at home is part of care and nurturing, and therefore associated with women. That Emeril changes this idea is evident in the people who attend the tapings of *Emeril Live*. Emeril's show attracts men to his audience because in many ways he makes cooking both masculine and possible for them. Recently, when he taped an episode of *Emeril Live* at an Air Force base, the audience was predominately male, and this is, in turn, seen by his television audience. Whenever he sprinkles a spice or garnishes a dish, he utters his notorious sound effect, "BAM!" which seems to appeal to the noisy little boy in the men in his audience. The fact that Emeril is a *male* celebrity chef is what gives him the power to redefine the cooking boundaries in the American household. Emeril is a celebrity, accomplished and qualified, but above all, he helps men feel more comfortable with cooking because he presents himself as someone that guys can relate to, and makes men "participants" in the show.

With the growing popularity of food in the media, celebrity chefs have had an 13 enormous impact on food in our lives. However, not everyone feels that chefs deserve all this media attention. Stephen Bayley, a British media journalist, concludes that it is

> Time, I think, to bury the celebrity chef in all his annoying forms . . . Chefs are artisans who should be confined to their workplace: what they should have in their hands is a spatula and a skillet, not a media schedule. They should be sweating brutally over hot stoves, not perspiring elegantly under the television lights. . . . There he goes, preening and strutting, discommoding the credulous gluttons who pay his salary. (82)

Bayley sums up certain class-based objections to celebrity chefs—that chefs are artisans, not stars, and should stay in the kitchen and serve us, not perform for us. However, as a celebrity chef, Emeril Lagasse has used his status as a chef and a celebrity to encourage his audiences to cook food that is usually reserved for the famous and wealthy, and by instilling in them the confidence to go home and cook his dishes themselves. Most important, Emeril is able to reach out to ordinary men and reassure them that his kind of cooking is not just for the women of the household, or the chefs of the wealthy. By providing entertainment with cooking, Emeril gives the men of his audience the confidence to approach cooking with a different perspective. Moreover, he has changed the culinary and media worlds by fusing them together and adding "BAM!"

Works Cited

Bayley, Stephen. "The Celebrity Chef." *New Statesman* 17 Dec. 2001: 82. Print.

Bowlby, Sophia, Susan Gregory, and Linda McKie. *Gender, Power and the Household*. New York: St. Martin's Press, 1999. Print.

Dyer, Richard. *Stars*. London: British Film Institute, 1979. Print.

Emeril Live. Perf. Emeril Lagasse. Food Network. 8 Nov. 2003. Television.

Emeril Live. Perf. Emeril Lagasse. Food Network. 23 Nov. 2003. Television.

The Essence of Emeril. Perf. Emeril Lagasse. Food Network. 21 Aug. 2004. Television.

Giles, David. *Illusions of Immortality*. New York: St. Martin's Press, 2000. Print.

Lewis, Robert C. "Restaurant Advertising Appeals and Consumers' Intentions." *Journal of Advertising Research* 21.5 (1981): 69–74. Print.

McQuail, Denis. *Audience Analysis*. Thousand Oaks, CA: Sage Publications, 1997. Print.

Ralli, Tania. "Learning to Saute in a Melting Pot." *New York Times* 23 Sept. 2003: F-4. Print.

Reading Closely

1. How does Gail Babilonia DEFINE a "celebrity chef"?

2. According to Babilonia, what makes Emeril Lagasse a perfect EXAMPLE of a celebrity chef?

3. How has Lagasse made cooking an "acceptable" activity for men (12)?

4. How do chefs like Lagasse use their celebrity status to change our ideas and attitudes about food?

5. What is Babilonia's main point in defining a celebrity chef rather than some other kind of celebrity?

Strategies and Structures

1. Babilonia's entire essay is built on a single extended example, that of Emeril Lagasse. Is this one case, as she develops it, sufficient to define her subject? Why or why not?

2. What is the purpose of Babilonia's frequent references to the work of David Giles, a professor who has written about the psychology of celebrity (3)? How effective do you find this and Babilonia's other references to experts?

3. Babilonia is defining a celebrity chef. To what extent is she also defining what makes a celebrity? Explain.

4. *Other Methods.* Not only does Babilonia explain how chefs are trained, she analyzes how celebrities are made and how Lagasse, in particular, goes about being a celebrity. How and how well do these forays into PROCESS ANALYSIS serve to support her definition? Point to passages that you find particularly instructive.

Thinking about Language

1. How does Babilonia use the stereotype of the "nameless Frenchman dressed in an all-white apron" to advance her definition of a celebrity chef (1)?

2. Why do you think cooking schools refer to themselves as *culinary institutes* rather than as *cooking schools* (2)?

3. What is the purpose of Babilonia's ANALOGY between a chef hidden away in the kitchen and an "unphotogenic academic" (4)?

4. Stephen Bayley, a British journalist, thinks its time to "bury" the celebrity chef (13). Why has he chosen such a harsh term?

5. What is "BAM" and how did Lagasse "add" it to both cooking and his show (13)? What's his recipe for success?

For Writing

1. "A celebrity is a person who is famous for being famous." Write a paragraph defining celebrity that *contradicts* this famous definition, attributed to, among others, the artist Andy Warhol and the American historian Daniel J. Boorstin. (Boorstin actually said a celebrity is "a person who is known for his well-knowness," while Warhol spoke of everyone's "fifteen minutes of fame").

2. Write a paragraph defining one of the following: heroism, fame, notoriety, repute, infamy.

3. Write an essay defining what a chef traditionally is and does. Be sure to explain how chefs get to be chefs.

FLANNERY O'CONNOR

A Good Man Is Hard to Find

Mary Flannery O'Connor (1925–1964) was born in Savannah, Georgia, studied at the Georgia State College for Women, and earned an MFA at the Writer's Workshop of the University of Iowa. Soon afterward, she was diagnosed with lupus, a painful auto-immune disorder that would trouble her for the rest of her brief life. Eight years after she died of the disease, her posthumously collected Complete Stories *won the 1972 National Book Award. She wrote two novels,* Wise Blood *(1952) and* The Violent Bear It Away *(1960), but she's best known for her witty, sharply observed, darkly ironic, and sometimes shockingly violent short stories—the epitome of what is known as "Southern Gothic."*

Above all, O'Connor's fiction is marked by her obsessions with morality and mortality, as well as her unwillingness to accept simplistic explanations for life's mysteries. "A Good Man Is Hard to Find," the title story in her 1955 collection, culminates in a kind of debate over the definition of "goodness"—is it a quality deep inside every human heart, something that can be awakened at any time, in the Christian sense of "redemption"? Or are there some people in whom no goodness resides, people who are simply irredeemable? O'Connor provides no easy answer.

THE GRANDMOTHER didn't want to go to Florida. She wanted to visit some of 1 her connections in east Tennessee and she was seizing at every chance to change Bailey's mind. Bailey was the son she lived with, her only boy. He was sitting on the edge of his chair at the table, bent over the orange sports section of the *Journal.* "Now look here, Bailey," she said, "see here, read this," and she stood with one hand on her thin hip and the other rattling the newspaper at his bald head. "Here this fellow that calls himself The Misfit is aloose from the Federal Pen and headed toward Florida and you read here what it says he did to these people. Just you read it. I wouldn't take my children in any direction with a criminal like that aloose in it. I couldn't answer to my conscience if I did."

Bailey didn't look up from his reading so she wheeled around then and faced the 2 children's mother, a young woman in slacks, whose face was as broad and innocent as a cabbage and was tied around with a green head-kerchief that had two points on the top like rabbit's ears. She was sitting on the sofa, feeding the baby his apricots out of a jar. "The children have been to Florida before," the old lady said. "You all ought to take them somewhere else for a change so they would see different parts of the world and be broad. They never have been to east Tennessee."

The children's mother didn't seem to hear her but the eight-year-old boy, John 3

Wesley, a stocky child with glasses, said, "If you don't want to go to Florida, why dontcha stay at home?" He and the little girl, June Star, were reading the funny papers on the floor.

"She wouldn't stay at home to be queen for a day," June Star said without raising 4 her yellow head.

"Yes and what would you do if this fellow, The Misfit, caught you?" the grand- 5 mother asked.

"I'd smack his face," John Wesley said. 6

"She wouldn't stay at home for a million bucks," June Star said. "Afraid she'd 7 miss something. She has to go everywhere we go."

"All right, Miss," the grandmother said. "Just remember that the next time you 8 want me to curl your hair."

June Star said her hair was naturally curly. 9

The next morning the grandmother was the first one in the car, ready to go. She 10 had her big black valise that looked like the head of a hippopotamus in one corner, and underneath it she was hiding a basket with Pitty Sing, the cat, in it. She didn't intend for the cat to be left alone in the house for three days because he would miss her too much and she was afraid he might brush against one of the gas burners and accidentally asphyxiate himself. Her son, Bailey, didn't like to arrive at a motel with a cat.

She sat in the middle of the back seat with John Wesley and June Star on either 11 side of her. Bailey and the children's mother and the baby sat in front and they left Atlanta at eight forty-five with the mileage on the car at 55890. The grandmother wrote this down because she thought it would be interesting to say how many miles they had been when they got back. It took them twenty minutes to reach the outskirts of the city.

The old lady settled herself comfortably, removing her white cotton gloves and 12 putting them up with her purse on the shelf in front of the back window. The children's mother still had on slacks and still had her head tied up in a green kerchief, but the grandmother had on a navy blue straw sailor hat with a bunch of white violets on the brim and a navy blue dress with a small white dot in the print. Her collars and cuffs were white organdy trimmed with lace and at her neckline she had pinned a purple spray of cloth violets containing a sachet. In case of an accident, anyone seeing her dead on the highway would know at once that she was a lady.

She said she thought it was going to be a good day for driving, neither too hot 13 nor too cold, and she cautioned Bailey that the speed limit was fifty-five miles an hour and that the patrolmen hid themselves behind billboards and small clumps of trees and sped out after you before you had a chance to slow down. She pointed out interesting details of the scenery: Stone Mountain; the blue granite that in some places came up to both sides of the highway; the brilliant red clay banks slightly streaked with purple; and the various crops that made rows of green lace-work on the ground. The trees were full of silver-white sunlight and the meanest of them sparkled. The children were reading comic magazines and their mother had gone back to sleep.

"Let's go through Georgia fast so we won't have to look at it much," John Wesley   14 said.

"If I were a little boy," said the grandmother, "I wouldn't talk about my native   15 state that way. Tennessee has the mountains and Georgia has the hills."

"Tennessee is just a hillbilly dumping ground," John Wesley said, "and Georgia is   16 a lousy state too."

"You said it," June Star said.   17

"In my time," said the grandmother, folding her thin veined fingers, "children   18 were more respectful of their native states and their parents and everything else. People did right then. Oh look at the cute little pickaninny!" she said and pointed to a Negro child standing in the door of a shack. "Wouldn't that make a picture, now?" she asked and they all turned and looked at the little Negro out of the back window. He waved.

"He didn't have any britches on," June Star said.   19

"He probably didn't have any," the grandmother explained. "Little niggers in the   20 country don't have things like we do. If I could paint, I'd paint that picture," she said.

The children exchanged comic books.   21

The grandmother offered to hold the baby and the children's mother passed him   22 over the front seat to her. She set him on her knee and bounced him and told him about the things they were passing. She rolled her eyes and screwed up her mouth and stuck her leathery thin face into his smooth bland one. Occasionally he gave her a faraway smile. They passed a large cotton field with five or six graves fenced in the middle of it, like a small island. "Look at the graveyard!" the grandmother said, pointing it out. "That was the old family burying ground. That belonged to the plantation."

"Where's the plantation?" John Wesley asked.   23

"Gone With the Wind," said the grandmother. "Ha. Ha."   24

When the children finished all the comic books they had brought, they opened   25 the lunch and ate it. The grandmother ate a peanut butter sandwich and an olive and would not let the children throw the box and the paper napkins out the window. When there was nothing else to do they played a game by choosing a cloud and making the other two guess what shape it suggested. John Wesley took one the shape of a cow and June Star guessed a cow and John Wesley said, no, an automobile, and June Star said he didn't play fair, and they began to slap each other over the grandmother.

The grandmother said she would tell them a story if they would keep quiet.   26

When she told a story, she rolled her eyes and waved her head and was very dramatic. She said once when she was a maiden lady she had been courted by a Mr. Edgar Atkins Teagarden from Jasper, Georgia. She said he was a very good-looking man and a gentleman and that he brought her a watermelon every Saturday afternoon with his initials cut in it, E. A. T. Well, one Saturday, she said, Mr. Teagarden brought the watermelon and there was nobody at home and he left it on the front porch and returned in his buggy to Jasper, but she never got the watermelon, she said, because a nigger boy ate it when he saw the initials, E. A. T.! This story tickled John Wesley's funny bone and he giggled and giggled but June Star didn't think it was any good. She said she wouldn't marry a man that just brought her a watermelon on Saturday. The grandmother said she would have done well to marry Mr. Teagarden because he was a gentleman and had bought Coca-Cola stock when it first came out and that he had died only a few years ago, a very wealthy man.

They stopped at The Tower for barbecued sandwiches. The Tower was a part 27 stucco and part wood filling station and dance hall set in a clearing outside of Timothy. A fat man named Red Sammy Butts ran it and there were signs stuck here and there on the building and for miles up and down the highway saying, TRY RED SAMMY'S FAMOUS BARBECUE. NONE LIKE FAMOUS RED SAMMY'S! RED SAM! THE FAT BOY WITH THE HAPPY LAUGH. A VETERAN! RED SAMMY'S YOUR MAN!

Red Sammy was lying on the bare ground outside The Tower with his head 28 under a truck while a gray monkey about a foot high, chained to a small chinaberry tree, chattered nearby. The monkey sprang back into the tree and got on the highest limb as soon as he saw the children jump out of the car and run toward him.

Inside, The Tower was a long dark room with a counter at one end and tables at 29 the other and dancing space in the middle. They all sat down at a board table next to the nickelodeon and Red Sam's wife, a tall burnt-brown woman with hair and eyes lighter than her skin, came and took their order. The children's mother put a dime in the machine and played "The Tennessee Waltz," and the grandmother said that tune always made her want to dance. She asked Bailey if he would like to dance but he only glared at her. He didn't have a naturally sunny disposition like she did and trips made him nervous. The grandmother's brown eyes were very bright. She swayed her head from side to side and pretended she was dancing in her chair. June Star said play something she could tap to so the children's mother put in another dime and played a fast number and June Star stepped out onto the dance floor and did her tap routine.

"Ain't she cute?" Red Sam's wife said, leaning over the counter. "Would you like 30 to come be my little girl?"

"No I certainly wouldn't," June Star said. "I wouldn't live in a broken-down place 31 like this for a million bucks!" and she ran back to the table.

"Ain't she cute?" the woman repeated, stretching her mouth politely.   32

"Arn't you ashamed?" hissed the grandmother.   33

Red Sam came in and told his wife to quit lounging on the counter and hurry up   34
with these people's order. His khaki trousers reached just to his hip bones and his
stomach hung over them like a sack of meal swaying under his shirt. He came over
and sat down at a table nearby and let out a combination sigh and yodel. "You can't
win," he said. "You can't win," and he wiped his sweating red face off with a gray
handkerchief. "These days you don't know who to trust," he said. "Ain't that the
truth?"

"People are certainly not nice like they used to be," said the grandmother.   35

"Two fellers come in here last week," Red Sammy said, "driving a Chrysler. It   36
was a old beat-up car but it was a good one and these boys looked all right to me.
Said they worked at the mill and you know I let them fellers charge the gas they
bought? Now why did I do that?"

"Because you're a good man!" the grandmother said at once.   37

"Yes'm,¹ I suppose so," Red Sam said as if he were struck with this answer.   38

His wife brought the orders, carrying the five plates all at once without a tray,   39
two in each hand and one balanced on her arm. "It isn't a soul in this green world
of God's that you can trust," she said. "And I don't count nobody out of that, not
nobody," she repeated, looking at Red Sammy.

"Did you read about that criminal, The Misfit, that's escaped?" asked the grand-   40
mother.

"I wouldn't be a bit surprised if he didn't attact this place right here," said the   41
woman. "If he hears about it being here, I wouldn't be none surprised to see him. If
he hears it's two cent in the cash register, I wouldn't be a tall surprised if he . . ."

"That'll do," Red Sam said. "Go bring these people their Co'-Colas," and the   42
woman went off to get the rest of the order.

"A good man is hard to find," Red Sammy said. "Everything is getting terrible. I   43
remember the day you could go off and leave your screen door unlatched. Not no
more."

He and the grandmother discussed better times. The old lady said that in her   44
opinion Europe was entirely to blame for the way things were now. She said the
way Europe acted you would think we were made of money and Red Sam said it
was no use talking about it, she was exactly right. The children ran outside into the
white sunlight and looked at the monkey in the lacy chinaberry tree. He was busy
catching fleas on himself and biting each one carefully between his teeth as if it
were a delicacy.

---

1. *Yes'm/Nome*: O'Connor's way of representing the southern pronunciation of "yes, ma'am" and
"no, ma'am."

They drove off again into the hot afternoon. The grandmother took cat naps and 45
woke up every few minutes with her own snoring. Outside of Toombsboro she
woke up and recalled an old plantation that she had visited in this neighborhood
once when she was a young lady. She said the house had six white columns across
the front and that there was an avenue of oaks leading up to it and two little
wooden trellis arbors on either side in front where you sat down with your suitor
after a stroll in the garden. She recalled exactly which road to turn off to get to it.
She knew that Bailey would not be willing to lose any time looking at an old house,
but the more she talked about it, the more she wanted to see it once again and find
out if the little twin arbors were still standing. "There was a secret panel in this
house," she said craftily, not telling the truth but wishing that she were, "and the
story went that all the family silver was hidden in it when Sherman came through
but it was never found . . ."

"Hey!" John Wesley said. "Let's go see it! We'll find it! We'll poke all the wood- 46
work and find it! Who lives there? Where do you turn off at? Hey Pop, can't we
turn off there?"

"We never have seen a house with a secret panel!" June Star shrieked. "Let's go 47
to the house with the secret panel! Hey Pop, can't we go see the house with the
secret panel!"

"It's not far from here, I know," the grandmother said. "It wouldn't take over 48
twenty minutes."

Bailey was looking straight ahead. His jaw was as rigid as a horseshoe. "No," he 49
said.

The children began to yell and scream that they wanted to see the house with 50
the secret panel. John Wesley kicked the back of the front seat and June Star hung
over her mother's shoulder and whined desperately into her ear that they never
had any fun even on their vacation, that they could never do what THEY wanted to
do. The baby began to scream and John Wesley kicked the back of the seat so hard
that his father could feel the blows in his kidney.

"All right!" he shouted and drew the car to a stop at the side of the road. "Will 51
you all shut up? Will you all just shut up for one second? If you don't shut up, we
won't go anywhere."

"It would be very educational for them," the grandmother murmured. 52

"All right," Bailey said, "but get this: this is the only time we're going to stop for 53
anything like this. This is the one and only time."

"The dirt road that you have to turn down is about a mile back," the grand- 54
mother directed. "I marked it when we passed."

"A dirt road," Bailey groaned. 55

After they had turned around and were headed toward the dirt road, the grand- 56
mother recalled other points about the house, the beautiful glass over the front

doorway and the candle-lamp in the hall. John Wesley said that the secret panel was probably in the fireplace.

"You can't go inside this house," Bailey said. "You don't know who lives there." 57

"While you all talk to the people in front, I'll run around behind and get in a 58 window," John Wesley suggested.

"We'll all stay in the car," his mother said. 59

They turned onto the dirt road and the car raced roughly along in a swirl of pink 60 dust. The grandmother recalled the times when there were no paved roads and thirty miles was a day's journey. The dirt road was hilly and there were sudden washes in it and sharp curves on dangerous embankments. All at once they would be on a hill, looking down over the blue tops of trees for miles around, then the next minute, they would be in a red depression with the dust-coated trees looking down on them.

"This place had better turn up in a minute," Bailey said, "or I'm going to turn 61 around."

The road looked as if no one had traveled on it in months. 62

"It's not much farther," the grandmother said and just as she said it, a horrible 63 thought came to her. The thought was so embarrassing that she turned red in the face and her eyes dilated and her feet jumped up, upsetting her valise in the corner. The instant the valise moved, the newspaper top she had over the basket under it rose with a snarl and Pitty Sing, the cat, sprang onto Bailey's shoulder.

The children were thrown to the floor and their mother, clutching the baby, was 64 thrown out the door onto the ground; the old lady was thrown into the front seat. The car turned over once and landed right-side-up in a gulch off the side of the road. Bailey remained in the driver's seat with the cat—gray-striped with a broad white face and an orange nose—clinging to his neck like a caterpillar.

As soon as the children saw they could move their arms and legs, they scram- 65 bled out of the car, shouting, "We've had an ACCIDENT!" The grandmother was curled up under the dashboard, hoping she was injured so that Bailey's wrath would not come down on her all at once. The horrible thought she had had before the accident was that the house she had remembered so vividly was not in Georgia but in Tennessee.

Bailey removed the cat from his neck with both hands and flung it out the win- 66 dow against the side of a pine tree. Then he got out of the car and started looking for the children's mother. She was sitting against the side of the red gutted ditch, holding the screaming baby, but she only had a cut down her face and a broken shoulder. "We've had an ACCIDENT!" the children screamed in a frenzy of delight.

"But nobody's killed," June Star said with disappointment as the grandmother 67 limped out of the car, her hat still pinned to her head but the broken front brim standing up at a jaunty angle and the violet spray hanging off the side. They all sat down in the ditch, except the children, to recover from the shock. They were all shaking.

"Maybe a car will come along," said the children's mother hoarsely   68

"I believe I have injured an organ," said the grandmother, pressing her side, but   69 no one answered her. Bailey's teeth were clattering. He had on a yellow sport shirt with bright blue parrots designed in it and his face was as yellow as the shirt. The grandmother decided that she would not mention that the house was in Tennessee.

The road was about ten feet above and they could see only the tops of the trees   70 on the other side of it. Behind the ditch they were sitting in there were more woods, tall and dark and deep. In a few minutes they saw a car some distance away on top of a hill, coming slowly as if the occupants were watching them. The grandmother stood up and waved both arms dramatically to attract their attention. The car continued to come on slowly, disappeared around a bend and appeared again, moving even slower, on top of the hill they had gone over. It was a big black battered hearse-like automobile. There were three men in it.

It came to a stop just over them and for some minutes, the driver looked down   71 with a steady expressionless gaze to where they were sitting, and didn't speak. Then he turned his head and muttered something to the other two and they got out. One was a fat boy in black trousers and a red sweat shirt with a silver stallion embossed on the front of it. He moved around on the right side of them and stood staring, his mouth partly open in a kind of loose grin. The other had on khaki pants and a blue striped coat and a gray hat pulled down very low, hiding most of his face. He came around slowly on the left side. Neither spoke.

The driver got out of the car and stood by the side of it, looking down at them.   72 He was an older man than the other two. His hair was just beginning to gray and he wore silver-rimmed spectacles that gave him a scholarly look. He had a long creased face and didn't have on any shirt or undershirt. He had on blue jeans that were too tight for him and was holding a black hat and a gun. The two boys also had guns.

"We've had an ACCIDENT!" the children screamed.   73

The grandmother had the peculiar feeling that the bespectacled man was some-   74 one she knew. His face was as familiar to her as if she had known him all her life but she could not recall who he was. He moved away from the car and began to come down the embankment, placing his feet carefully so that he wouldn't slip. He had on tan and white shoes and no socks, and his ankles were red and thin. "Good afternoon," he said. "I see you all had you a little spill."

"We turned over twice!" said the grandmother.   75

"Oncet," he corrected. "We seen it happen. Try their car and see will it run,   76 Hiram," he said quietly to the boy with the gray hat.

"What you got that gun for?" John Wesley asked. "Whatcha gonna do with that 77 gun?"

"Lady," the man said to the children's mother, "would you mind calling them 78 children to sit down by you? Children make me nervous. I want all you all to sit down right together there where you're at."

"What are you telling US what to do for?" June Star asked. 79

Behind them the line of woods gaped like a dark open mouth. "Come here," said 80 their mother.

"Look here now," Bailey began suddenly, "we're in a predicament! We're in . . ." 81

The grandmother shrieked. She scrambled to her feet and stood staring. "You're 82 The Misfit!" she said. "I recognized you at once!"

"Yes'm," the man said, smiling slightly as if he were pleased in spite of himself to 83 be known, "but it would have been better for all of you, lady, if you hadn't of reck-ernized me."

Bailey turned his head sharply and said something to his mother that shocked 84 even the children. The old lady began to cry and The Misfit reddened.

"Lady," he said, "don't you get upset. Sometimes a man says things he don't 85 mean. I don't reckon he meant to talk to you thataway."

"You wouldn't shoot a lady, would you?" the grandmother said and removed a 86 clean handkerchief from her cuff and began to slap at her eyes with it.

The Misfit pointed the toe of his shoe into the ground and made a little hole and 87 then covered it up again. "I would hate to have to," he said.

"Listen," the grandmother almost screamed, "I know you're a good man. You 88 don't look a bit like you have common blood. I know you must come from nice peo-ple!"

"Yes mam," he said, "finest people in the world." When he smiled he showed a 89 row of strong white teeth. "God never made a finer woman than my mother and my daddy's heart was pure gold," he said. The boy with the red sweat shirt had come around behind them and was standing with his gun at his hip. The Misfit squatted down on the ground. "Watch them children, Bobby Lee," he said. "You know they make me nervous." He looked at the six of them huddled together in front of him and he seemed to be embarrassed as if he couldn't think of anything to say. "Ain't a cloud in the sky," he remarked, looking up at it. "Don't see no sun but don't see no cloud neither."

"Yes, it's a beautiful day," said the grandmother. "Listen," she said, "you shouldn't 90 call yourself The Misfit because I know you're a good man at heart. I can just look at you and tell."

"Hush!" Bailey yelled. "Hush! Everybody shut up and let me handle this!" He 91 was squatting in the position of a runner about to sprint forward but he didn't move.

"I pre-chate that, lady," The Misfit said and drew a little circle in the ground 92
with the butt of his gun.

"It'll take a half a hour to fix this here car," Hiram called, looking over the raised 93
hood of it.

"Well, first you and Bobby Lee get him and that little boy to step over yonder 94
with you," The Misfit said, pointing to Bailey and John Wesley. "The boys want to
ast you something," he said to Bailey. "Would you mind stepping back in them
woods there with them?"

"Listen," Bailey began, "we're in a terrible predicament! Nobody realizes what 95
this is," and his voice cracked. His eyes were as blue and intense as the parrots in
his shirt and he remained perfectly still.

The grandmother reached up to adjust her hat brim as if she were going to the 96
woods with him but it came off in her hand. She stood staring at it and after a second she let it fall on the ground. Hiram pulled Bailey up by the arm as if he were
assisting an old man. John Wesley caught hold of his father's hand and Bobby Lee
followed. They went off toward the woods and just as they reached the dark edge,
Bailey turned and supporting himself against a gray naked pine trunk, he shouted,
"I'll be back in a minute, Mamma, wait on me!"

"Come back this instant!" his mother shrilled but they all disappeared into the 97
woods.

"Bailey Boy!" the grandmother called in a tragic voice but she found she was 98
looking at The Misfit squatting on the ground in front of her. "I just know you're a
good man," she said desperately. "You're not a bit common!"

"Nome, I ain't a good man," The Misfit said after a second as if he had consid- 99
ered her statement carefully, "but I ain't the worst in the world neither. My daddy
said I was a different breed of dog from my brothers and sisters. 'You know,' Daddy
said, 'it's some that can live their whole life out without asking about it and it's others has to know why it is, and this boy is one of the latters. He's going to be into
everything!' " He put on his black hat and looked up suddenly and then away deep
into the woods as if he were embarrassed again. "I'm sorry I don't have on a shirt
before you ladies," he said, hunching his shoulders slightly. "We buried our clothes
that we had on when we escaped and we're just making do until we can get better.
We borrowed these from some folks we met," he explained.

"That's perfectly all right," the grandmother said. "Maybe Bailey has an extra 100
shirt in his suitcase."

"I'll look and see terrectly," The Misfit said. 101

"Where are they taking him?" the children's mother screamed. 102

"Daddy was a card himself," The Misfit said. "You couldn't put anything over on 103
him. He never got in trouble with the Authorities though. Just had the knack of
handling them."

"You could be honest too if you'd only try," said the grandmother. "Think how 104
wonderful it would be to settle down and live a comfortable life and not have to
think about somebody chasing you all the time."

The Misfit kept scratching in the ground with the butt of his gun as if he were 105
thinking about it. "Yes'm, somebody is always after you," he murmured.

The grandmother noticed how thin his shoulder blades were just behind his hat 106
because she was standing up looking down on him. "Do you ever pray?" she asked.

He shook his head. All she saw was the black hat wiggle between his shoulder 107
blades. "Nome," he said.

There was a pistol shot from the woods, followed closely by another. Then 108
silence. The old lady's head jerked around. She could hear the wind move through
the tree tops like a long satisfied insuck of breath. "Bailey Boy!" she called.

"I was a gospel singer for a while," The Misfit said. "I been most everything. 109
Been in the arm service, both land and sea, at home and abroad, been twict married, been an undertaker, been with the railroads, plowed Mother Earth, been in a
tornado, seen a man burnt alive oncet," and he looked up at the children's mother
and the little girl who were sitting close together, their faces white and their eyes
glassy; "I even seen a woman flogged," he said.

"Pray, pray," the grandmother began, "pray, pray . . ." 110

"I never was a bad boy that I remember of," The Misfit said in an almost dreamy 111
voice, "but somewheres along the line I done something wrong and got sent to the
penitentiary. I was buried alive," and he looked up and held her attention to him by
a steady stare.

"That's when you should have started to pray," she said. "What did you do to get 112
sent to the penitentiary that first time?"

"Turn to the right, it was a wall," The Misfit said, looking up again at the cloud- 113
less sky. "Turn to the left, it was a wall. Look up it was a ceiling, look down it was a
floor. I forget what I done, lady. I set there and set there, trying to remember what
it was I done and I ain't recalled it to this day. Oncet in a while, I would think it was
coming to me, but it never come."

"Maybe they put you in by mistake." the old lady said vaguely. 114

"Nome," he said. "It wasn't no mistake. They had the papers on me." 115

"You must have stolen something," she said. 116

The Misfit sneered slightly. "Nobody had nothing I wanted," he said. "It was a 117
head-doctor at the penitentiary said what I had done was kill my daddy but I
known that for a lie. My daddy died in nineteen ought nineteen of the epidemic flu
and I never had a thing to do with it. He was buried in the Mount Hopewell Baptist churchyard and you can go there and see for yourself."

"If you would pray," the old lady said, "Jesus would help you." 118

"That's right," The Misfit said.   119

"Well then, why don't you pray?" she asked trembling with delight suddenly.   120

"I don't want no hep," he said. "I'm doing all right by myself."   121

Bobby Lee and Hiram came ambling back from the woods. Bobby Lee was drag-   122
ging a yellow shirt with bright blue parrots in it.

"Thow me that shirt, Bobby Lee," The Misfit said. The shirt came flying at him   123
and landed on his shoulder and he put it on. The grandmother couldn't name what
the shirt reminded her of. "No, lady," The Misfit said while he was buttoning it up,
"I found out the crime don't matter. You can do one thing or you can do another,
kill a man or take a tire off his car, because sooner or later you're going to forget
what it was you done and just be punished for it."

The children's mother had begun to make heaving noises as if she couldn't get   124
her breath. "Lady," he asked, "would you and that little girl like to step off yonder
with Bobby Lee and Hiram and join your husband?"

"Yes, thank you," the mother said faintly. Her left arm dangled helplessly and   125
she was holding the baby, who had gone to sleep, in the other. "Hep that lady up,
Hiram," The Misfit said as she struggled to climb out of the ditch, "and Bobby Lee,
you hold onto that little girl's hand."

"I don't want to hold hands with him," June Star said. "He reminds me of a pig."   126

The fat boy blushed and laughed and caught her by the arm and pulled her off   127
into the woods after Hiram and her mother.

Alone with The Misfit, the grandmother found that she had lost her voice.   128
There was not a cloud in the sky nor any sun. There was nothing around her but
woods. She wanted to tell him that he must pray. She opened and closed her mouth
several times before anything came out. Finally she found herself saying, "Jesus.
Jesus," meaning, Jesus will help you, but the way she was saying it, it sounded as if
she might be cursing.

"Yes'm," The Misfit said as if he agreed. "Jesus thown everything off balance. It   129
was the same case with Him as with me except He hadn't committed any crime
and they could prove I had committed one because they had the papers on me. Of
course," he said, "they never shown me my papers. That's why I sign myself now. I
said long ago, you get you a signature and sign everything you do and keep a copy
of it. Then you'll know what you done and you can hold up the crime to the punishment and see do they match and in the end you'll have something to prove you ain't
been treated right. I call myself The Misfit," he said, "because I can't make what all
I done wrong fit what all I gone through in punishment."

There was a piercing scream from the woods, followed closely by a pistol report.   130
"Does it seem right to you, lady, that one is punished a heap and another ain't punished at all?"

"Jesus!" the old lady cried. "You've got good blood! I know you wouldn't shoot a   131
lady! I know you come from nice people! Pray! Jesus, you ought not to shoot a lady.
I'll give you all the money I've got!"

"Lady," The Misfit said, looking beyond her far into the woods, "there never was   132
a body that give the undertaker a tip."

There were two more pistol reports and the grandmother raised her head like a   133
parched old turkey hen crying for water and called, "Bailey Boy, Bailey Boy!" as if
her heart would break.

"Jesus was the only One that ever raised the dead," The Misfit continued, "and   134
He shouldn't have done it. He thown everything off balance. If He did what He
said, then it's nothing for you to do but thow away everything and follow Him, and
if He didn't, then it's nothing for you to do but enjoy the few minutes you got left
the best way you can—by killing somebody or burning down his house or doing
some other meanness to him. No pleasure but meanness," he said and his voice had
become almost a snarl.

"Maybe He didn't raise the dead," the old lady mumbled, not knowing what she   135
was saying and feeling so dizzy that she sank down in the ditch with her legs
twisted under her.

"I wasn't there so I can't say He didn't," The Misfit said. "I wisht I had of been   136
there," he said, hitting the ground with his fist. "It ain't right I wasn't there because
if I had of been there I would of known. Listen lady," he said in a high voice, "if I
had of been there I would of known and I wouldn't be like I am now." His voice
seemed about to crack and the grandmother's head cleared for an instant. She saw
the man's face twisted close to her own as if he were going to cry and she murmured, "Why you're one of my babies. You're one of my own children!" She
reached out and touched him on the shoulder. The Misfit sprang back as if a snake
had bitten him and shot her three times through the chest. Then he put his gun
down on the ground and took off his glasses and began to clean them.

Hiram and Bobby Lee returned from the woods and stood over the ditch, look-   137
ing down at the grandmother who half sat and half lay in a puddle of blood with
her legs crossed under her like a child's and her face smiling up at the cloudless sky.

Without his glasses, The Misfit's eyes were red-rimmed and pale and defenseless-   138
looking. "Take her off and thow her where you thown the others," he said, picking
up the cat that was rubbing itself against his leg.

"She was a talker, wasn't she?" Bobby Lee said, sliding down the ditch with a   139
yodel.

"She would of been a good woman," The Misfit said, "if it had been somebody   140
there to shoot her every minute of her life."

"Some fun!" Bobby Lee said.   141

"Shut up, Bobby Lee," The Misfit said. "It's no real pleasure in life."   142

READING CLOSELY

1. How did The Misfit in Flannery O'Connor's story get his name?

2. Why does The Misfit think that Jesus "thrown everything off balance" by raising the dead (134)? Why is he concerned with matters of religious faith at all?

3. How religious is the grandmother in O'Connor's story? When she mentions Jesus, why does it sound "as if she might be cursing" (128)?

4. At the end of the story, when she *is* dead, the grandmother has "her legs crossed under her like a child's" (137). Where else in the story is the grandmother COM-PARED to a child? How does she compare in character and personality with June Star and John Wesley, the actual children in the story?

5. What is the grandmother doing when The Misfit shoots her? Why is he so upset at that particular moment?

STRATEGIES AND STRUCTURES

1. "A good man is hard to find," says Red Sammy Butts, proprietor of the Tower restaurant (43). Yet the grandmother has just called him a good man simply because he has allowed some travellers to charge their gas (37). How are the two of them DEFINING goodness? What is O'Connor's point in introducing different definitions of goodness just before The Misfit appears in her narrative?

2. When, in an attempt to save herself, the grandmother calls The Misfit a good man, he replies, "I ain't a good man" (99). The Misfit is correct: he is, after all, a pathological killer who ruthlessly murders an entire family, including a baby. However, does The Misfit display any characteristics that might be defined as "good" if he weren't otherwise so evil?

3. "She would of been a good woman," The Misfit says to Bobby Lee, "if it had been somebody there to shoot her every minute of her life" (140). What does The Misfit mean by this? How has the grandmother (or *grand mother*) been truly "good" just before she is shot?

4. The grandmother dies with "her face smiling up at the cloudless sky," presumably toward heaven (137). Is there any sense in which The Misfit could be defined as her savior?

5. The Misfit defines pleasure as "meanness" (134). Yet at the end of the story he tells Bobby Lee, "It's no real pleasure in life" (142). Why not? Why can't the Misfit enjoy being murderously mean? What definition of the good life throws him off balance? Why does he take it to heart?

6. *Other Methods.* From whose perspective is this story NARRATED? Whose story is this? The Misfit's? The grandmother's? Explain.

THINKING ABOUT LANGUAGE

1. "A good man is hard to find" is the first line of the chorus in a popular song recorded by blues singer Bessie Smith in 1927. The next line in the original recording is, "You always get another kind." How well does this prediction fit O'Connor's story? Why would she name such a dark story after a popular song?

2. One reviewer of their first album says that the post-punk band Pitty Sing is named after "an evil cat in a Flannery O'Connor short story." It's not the cat's fault that someone lets it out of the bag. Who is the guilty party, and how does this PUN—"letting the cat out of the bag"—resonate throughout the story?

3. The cat Pitty Sing is named for a character in the *Mikado*, a comic opera by William S. Gilbert and Arthur Sullivan. "Pitty Sing" (10) is baby talk for "Pretty Thing." What does the cat's name tell you about the maturity level of some of the characters in the story?

4. Why does O'Connor describe The Misfit as reacting "as if a snake had bitten him" when the grandmother touches his shoulder (136)? What's the ALLUSION?

FOR WRITING

1. A psychiatrist would probably diagnose O'Connor's Misfit as a *psychopath*. Write a paragraph or two defining this neurosis as exemplified by O'Connor's villain.

2. Write an essay analyzing how conventional definitions of good and evil are called into question by O'Connor's classic story.

CHAPTER 10

Cause and Effect

For want of a nail the shoe was lost; for want of a shoe the horse was lost, and for want of a horse the rider was lost, being overtaken and slain by the enemy, all for want of care about a horse-shoe nail.

—BENJAMIN FRANKLIN, *The Way to Wealth*

Suppose you place leftover lasagna in a stainless-steel container, cover it with aluminum foil, and store it in the refrigerator. When you come back a few days later to reheat the dish, you notice tiny holes in the aluminum. Why, you ask? Even more pressing: can you safely eat your leftovers? What would be the effect on your body if you did? With these questions, you have just launched into an analysis of CAUSE AND EFFECT.

Defining Cause and Effect:
Analyzing Why Things Happen—or Might Happen

When we analyze something, we take it apart to see how the pieces fit together. A common way in which things fit together, especially in the physical universe, is that one causes the other. In the case of your leftover lasagna, for example, the aluminum foil deteriorates because it is touching the tomato sauce as well as the stainless-steel bowl. "When aluminum metal is in simultaneous contact with a different metal," writes the food critic Robert L. Wolke, who is also a professor of chemistry, the combination "constitutes an electric battery"—if there is also present "an electrical conductor such as tomato sauce."

When we analyze causes and effects, we not only explain why something happened (what caused the holes in the foil), we predict what might happen—for example, if you eat the lasagna anyway.

In this chapter, we will discuss how to analyze causes and effects; how to tell causation from coincidence; how to distinguish probable causes from merely possible ones; and how to organize a cause-and-effect essay by tracing events in chronological order from cause to effect—or backward in time from effect to cause.

Why Do We Analyze Causes and Effects?

According to the British philosopher David Hume in his *Enquiry Concerning Human Understanding*, much of the thinking that human beings do is "founded on the relation of cause and effect." Like Adam and Eve when they discovered fire (Hume's example), we analyze causes and effects in order to learn how things relate to each other in the physical world. Also, when we know what causes something, we can apply that knowledge to our future behavior and that of others: Don't put your hand in the fire because it will burn. Don't cover your leftover lasagna with aluminum foil because if the foil touches the sauce, you'll get metal in your food.

Hume was not just speaking of the knowledge we gain from experience, however. By using research and our powers of reasoning in addition to those of direct observation, we can also analyze the causes and effects of things that we cannot experience directly, such as the causes of the Civil War, or the effects of AIDS on the social and political future of Africa, or what will happen to the U.S. economy if the health care system is (or is not) reformed. Thus the analysis of cause-and-effect relationships is just as important in the study of history, politics, economics, and many other fields as in the sciences.

Composing a Cause-and-Effect Analysis

You'll often have occasion to write a whole essay analyzing causes or effects (or both)—to analyze the causes of an event in history, to predict the effects of a proposed government policy, and so on. Such analysis is not easy, but you'll find that it can be an effective way to organize an essay, for it offers a way of thinking about events or trends that are not easily explained—and a method for trying to explain what caused them or to predict what their effects might be. But keep in mind that even simple effects can have complex causes—as in our tomato sauce example. Technically speaking, the holes in the aluminum foil were caused by the transfer of electrons from the foil to the steel bowl *through* the tomato sauce. What caused the corrosive sauce to touch the foil in the first place? Clearly, yet another cause is in play here—human error, as indicated in the diagram on p. 431.

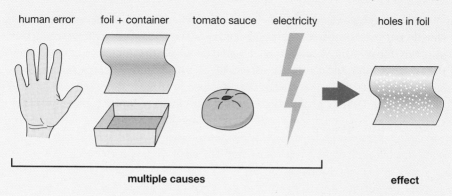

If relatively simple effects—such as the holes in the aluminum foil—can have multiple causes like these, just think how many causes you will need to identify as you analyze and explain more complex effects, such as the French Revolution, World War II, or why married men, on average, make more money than unmarried men.

Fortunately, as we shall see, even the most daunting array of causes can be reduced to a few basic causes. And thinking about the order in which they occur in time and their importance in producing a given effect, in turn, can provide you with a solid basis for organizing your essay.

Thinking about Purpose and Audience

As a professor of chemistry, Wolke fully understands the complexities of the chemical reaction he is analyzing, but the tomato sauce example here comes from *What Einstein Told His Cook*, a book he wrote to explain "kitchen science" to a general audience. So Wolke largely avoids the technical vocabulary of the laboratory and assumes no specialized knowledge on the part of the reader. Instead, he uses everyday language and offers practical applications for his scientific findings: store your leftovers in any kind of container you like, Wolke concludes, "just make sure that the foil isn't in contact with the sauce." When you write a cause-and-effect analysis, keep your readers in mind—use language appropriate for your audience and define any terms they may not know.

Wolke's purpose is to instruct his readers, and his topic is one that is easy to explain, at least for a chemist. Often, however, you will find yourself analyzing causes or effects that cannot be explained easily, and then you will actually need to argue for possible causes or effects—to persuade your readers that a cause is plausible or an effect is likely.

Let's say you are taking Chemistry 101, and when you go to the campus bookstore to buy your textbook, you find that it costs $139. Your first thought is to write an article for the school newspaper accusing the bookstore of highway robbery, but then you stop to think: *why* is the price so high? You do some research and discover some of the causes: the increasing costs of paper, printing, and transportation; the costs of running a bookstore; the fact that authors need to be compensated for their work, and that publishers and bookstores are businesses that need to produce some kind of profit. Perhaps you'll still want to write an angry article, but at least you'll be able to show that you've *analyzed the causes* of the problem.

And let's say you decide to suggest in your article that students buy only used books. But then you'd need to *consider the effects* of that solution. Since publishers and authors receive no payment for used books, buying them exclusively could mean that there would soon be no other kind available. That's an effect that would be attractive to an audience of used book dealers—but that might not be so appealing to students.

As with all kinds of writing, when you analyze causes or effects, you need to think about your larger purpose for writing and the audience you want to reach.

Generating Ideas:
Asking Why and What If

There are lots of ways to generate ideas for a cause-and-effect analysis—BRAIN-STORMING, CLUSTERING, and more. The essential question to ask when you want to figure out what CAUSED something, however, is *why*. Why does your gravy have lumps in it? Why did you fail the chemistry final? Why does a curve ball drop as it crosses home plate? Why was Napoleon defeated in his march on Russia in 1812? Why did terminal 2E collapse at the Paris airport?

If, on the other hand, you want to figure out what the EFFECTS of something are, then the basic question to ask is not why but *what*, or *what if*. What if you don't study for the chemistry exam? What are the results likely to be? What will happen if the curve ball fails to drop? What effect did the weather have on Napoleon's campaign? What if you eat your leftover lasagna even though it might now contain invisible bits of aluminum?*

As you pursue answers to the basic questions *why* and *what if*, keep in mind that a single effect may have multiple causes. If you were to ask why the U.S. financial system almost collapsed in the fall of 2008, for example, you would need to consider a number of possible causes, such as the following:

---

*Nothing much will happen, except that your lasagna may taste slightly metallic. You won't get sick from the metal because the hydrochloric acid in your stomach will dissolve the aluminum.

- greed and corruption on Wall Street
- vastly inflated real estate values
- subprime mortgage loans offered to unqualified borrowers
- massive defaults when those borrowers could no longer make their mortgage payments
- a widespread credit crunch and drying up of money for new loans.

As you probe more deeply into the causes of a major event like the financial crisis of 2008, you will discover that such effects not only have multiple causes; those causes are also interconnected. That is, they occur in chains—as in the proverb about a kingdom lost "all for the want of a horseshoe nail." When it comes time to organize your essay, you may find that following the chain of events in chronological order from cause to effect—or backward in time from effect to cause—is an excellent way to organize a cause-and-effect analysis.

Organizing and Drafting a Cause-and-Effect Analysis

Once you've asked yourself *why* or *what if* and you've identified the causes or the effects of a cause, you're ready to start organizing and drafting. You'll want to choose a method of organization, state your point clearly, and distinguish main causes from contributing causes and immediate causes from remote causes. You'll also want to distinguish between true causes and mere coincidences. You might also think about using visuals and other methods of development, like NARRATIVE and PROCESS ANALYSIS, in your cause-and-effect analysis. The tips and templates on p. 434 can help you get started.

STATING YOUR POINT

As you draft a cause-and-effect analysis, you can start with effects and then examine their causes; or you can start with causes and go on to examine their effects. In either case, tell the reader right away which you are going to focus on and why—what your main point, or THESIS, is.

For example, if you are analyzing the causes of the financial meltdown in the United States in 2008, you might signal the main point of your analysis in a statement like this one:

> The main cause of the financial meltdown in the United States in 2008 was the freezing of credit, which made it impossible for anyone to borrow money.

Once you've told the reader whether you're focusing on causes or effects and what your thesis is, you're ready to present your analysis.

TIPS AND TEMPLATES FOR DRAFTING

When you begin to draft a cause-and-effect analysis, you need to identify what you're analyzing and to indicate whether you plan to emphasize its causes or its effects. These moves are fundamental to any cause-and-effect analysis. See how Henry L. Roediger III makes these moves at the beginning of his essay in this chapter:

> What reasons are given for the high price of textbooks? . . . If I had to bet, the root cause is a feature of the marketplace that has changed greatly over the years and fundamentally reshaped the textbook market: sale of used books.
> —HENRY L. ROEDIGER III, "Why Are Textbook So Expensive?"

Roediger identifies what he's analyzing ("the high price of textbooks") and indicates that he is going to focus on the causes of this phenomenon ("the root cause is"). Here is one more example from this chapter:

> If those first farmers could have foreseen the consequences of adopting food production, they might not have opted to do so. Why, unable to foresee the result, did they nevertheless make that choice?
> —JARED DIAMOND, "To Farm or Not to Farm"

The following templates can help you make some of these basic moves in your own writing. But don't take these as formulas where you just have to fill in the blanks. There are no easy formulas for good writing, but these templates can serve as starting points.

▶ The main cause / effect of X is _____.

▶ X would also seem to have a number of contributing causes, including _____, _____, and _____.

▶ Some additional effects of X are _____, _____, and _____.

▶ Among the most important remote causes / effects of X are _____, _____, and _____.

▶ Although the causes of X are not known, we can speculate that a key factor is _____.

▶ X cannot be attributed to mere chance or coincidence because _____.

▶ Once we know what causes X, we are in a position to _____.

DISTINGUISHING BETWEEN THE MAIN CAUSE AND CONTRIBUTING CAUSES

To help your reader fully understand how a number of causes work together to produce a single effect, you can distinguish the main cause of the effect from the contributing causes. Consider the partial collapse of terminal 2E at the Paris airport on the morning of May 23, 2004. One factor in the disaster was gravity. However, the problem with gravity as an explanation for the collapse is that it doesn't really tell us much that we don't already know. If we're really going to figure out why the building fell down, we're going to have to look at both the main and contributing causes.

The main cause is the one that has the greatest power to produce the effect. It must be both necessary to cause the effect and sufficient to do so. As it turns out, the main cause of the terminal collapse was faulty design. As Christian Horn writes in *Architecture Week*, "The building was not designed to support the stress it was put under."

A contributing cause is a secondary cause, one that is necessary to produce the effect but not sufficient to do it alone. An important contributing cause to the collapse of terminal 2E was weak concrete. Another was the increased stress on the concrete roof shell due to the rapid expansion and contraction of the metal support structure. Still another was the wild fluctuation in temperature in the days leading up to the collapse, which contributed to the stress on the metal.

If terminal 2E had been properly designed, however, no combination of contributing causes would have been sufficient to bring it down. Contributing causes are necessary to produce an effect, but even taken together they are not sufficient to cause it.

CAUSES BEHIND THE COLLAPSE OF TERMINAL 2E

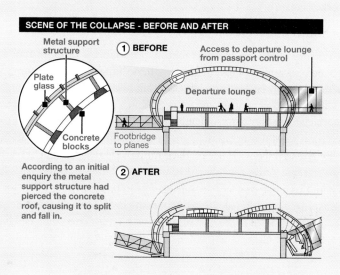

SCENE OF THE COLLAPSE - BEFORE AND AFTER

Metal support structure
Plate glass
Concrete blocks

① BEFORE
Access to departure lounge from passport control
Departure lounge
Footbridge to planes

According to an initial enquiry the metal support structure had pierced the concrete roof, causing it to split and fall in.

② AFTER

DISTINGUISHING BETWEEN IMMEDIATE AND REMOTE CAUSES

As you look into the various causes of a particular effect, be sure to consider immediate and remote causes. This will require you to distinguish mechanical details in the causal chain from more theoretical causes. Benjamin Franklin, you'll notice, did not say that the main cause of the rider's death was the loss of a horseshoe nail. He said the main cause was a "want of care" about such nitty-gritty details.

The most nitty-gritty link in any causal chain—the one closest in time and most directly responsible for producing the effect—is the immediate cause. In the case of the financial meltdown of 2008, the immediate cause was the drying up of credit that made it almost impossible to get loans. Credit oils the wheels of commerce; when credit dries up, the wheels cease to turn and the financial engine stops.

Remote causes, by contrast with immediate ones, are less apparent to the observer and more distant in time from the observed effect. A remote cause of the financial meltdown of 2008 was the "subprime" lending to borrowers who, eventually, could not meet their mortgage payments. A more remote cause of the meltdown was the burst of the housing bubble: as the supply of available housing exceeded demand, housing values fell, and many borrowers found that their homes were worth less than their mortgages.

Recklessness on Main Street was not the most remote cause of the eventual meltdown, however. The most remote cause was greed on Wall Street. Subprime loans were risky—but they were very profitable. The lender took his profit and then, to trim his risks, packaged the bad loans with good ones and sold the package to unwary investors. When investors finally figured out what they had bought, fear trumped greed, and even banks were afraid to lend money to each other. Hence the drying up of credit—until the federal government intervened.

DISTINGUISHING BETWEEN CAUSATION AND COINCIDENCE

It is well documented that married men as a group make more money—somewhere between 10 and 50 percent more—than unmarried men as a group. Does being married actually *cause* this wage difference, or is it merely a coincidence?

As you link together causes and effects, don't confuse causation with coincidence. Just because one event (getting married) happens *before* another (making more money), it does not necessarily mean the first event actually caused the second. To conclude that it always does is to commit the logical blunder of reasoning *post hoc, ergo propter hoc* (Latin for "after this, therefore because of this"). Most superstitions are based on such *post hoc* reasoning. Mark Twain's Huck Finn, for example, commits this fallacy when he sees a spider burning in a candle: "I didn't need anybody to tell me that that was an awful bad sign and would fetch me some bad luck." Huck is going to encounter all sorts of troubles, but the burning spider isn't the cause.

In our marriage and money example, being married is a necessary condition for earning the "marital wage premium." That is, statistics show that married men as a group *always* earn more money than single men. Is being married sufficient to make men wealthier? Or is it merely a matter of coincidence rather than causation? Most married people are older than unmarried people, and most older people earn more money than younger people. Could age be the real cause behind the "marital wage premium"? Or is it simply another correlation? Before you assert that something is a cause, make sure you've considered whether it could be a coincidence.

ORGANIZING A CAUSE-AND-EFFECT ANALYSIS

Causes always precede effects in time. Thus a natural way to present the effects of a given cause is by arranging them in chronological order. If you were tracing the effects of the financial meltdown of 2008, for example, you would start with the crisis and then proceed chronologically, detailing its effects in the order in which they occurred, namely:

- banks and other financial institutions collapse as mortgage holders default
- the stock market plummets
- the federal government steps in with a massive bailout, providing a steady stream of much-needed credit to markets
- confidence is restored on Wall Street and Main Street

Reverse chronological order, in which you begin with a known effect and work backward through the possible causes, can also be effective for organizing a cause-and-effect analysis. In the case of the 2008 financial crisis, you would again begin with the crisis itself (the known effect): the financial engine stops because it has run out of credit. Then you would work backward in time through all the possible causes you could think of—presenting them in reverse chronological order:

- credit dries up because banks stop lending money to one another
- banks stopped lending because borrowers defaulted on existing loans
- borrowers defaulted because the values of their homes went down
- banks made risky loans on overvalued homes because Wall Street could easily sell those loans to investors
- Wall Street packaged bad loans and sold them to investors in order to increase profits and executive bonuses

You can also organize your analysis around the various types of causes, exploring the immediate cause before moving on to the remote causes (or vice versa) or exploring the contributing causes before the main cause (or vice versa).

USING VISUALS TO CLARIFY CAUSAL RELATIONSHIPS

Illustrations and images can help your reader to understand what caused a complicated effect—or the complicated causes behind a simple effect. Take, for instance, the famous map showing Napoleon's campaign in Russia in 1812 (see p. 439). This map shows the progress of Napoleon's army. The advance toward Moscow is shown by a light-colored line, while the retreat is represented by the darker line below it. The thickness of the lines represents the number of soldiers in Napoleon's army— the thicker the line, the more troops in the army. At the bottom of the map are temperatures for certain dates during the retreat. As the army retreats from Moscow and the line representing the army gets thinner (showing that the army has fewer and fewer troops), the temperatures get colder.*

The map conveys a mass of data that would take many words to write out: dates, temperatures, troop movements, numbers of troops, not to mention distances and the locations of rivers and cities. All this information is crucial in analyzing why so many of Napoleon's soldiers died in their retreat from Moscow in 1812. If you're analyzing the causes of the French retreat, you might want to include a map like this, and then connect the dots between the data it shows: one cause of the casualties on Napoleon's retreat from Moscow was the freezing temperatures.

A graph showing the relationship between temperature and number of troops would also make the point that the cold winter caused the deaths of many soldiers.

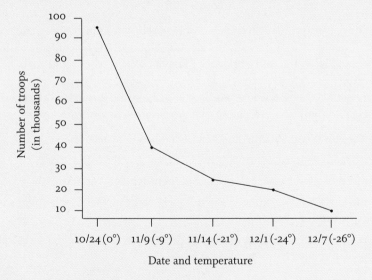

*Nov. 9, perhaps 40,000 troops, -9°. Nov. 14, about 25,000 troops, -21°. Dec. 7, 8,000 troops, -26°. (Since the map was made by the French engineer Charles Minard in 1861, the temperatures are in the French Réaumur: -9° Réaumur is approximately 11.75° Fahrenheit; -26° Réaumur is approximately -26.5° Fahrenheit.)

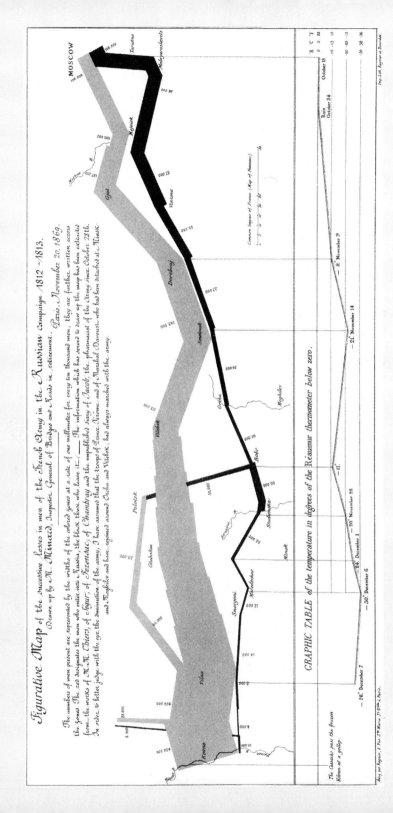

Figurative Map of the successive losses in men of the French Army in the Russian campaign 1812–1813.

Drawn up by M. Minard, Inspector General of Bridges and Roads in retirement. Paris, November 20, 1869.

The numbers of men present are represented by the widths of the colored zones at a rate of one millimetre for every ten thousand men; they are further written across the zones. The red designates the men who enter into Russia, the black those who leave it. — The information which has served to draw up the map has been extracted from the works of M.M. Thiers, of Segur, of Fezensac, of Chambray and the unpublished diary of Jacob, the pharmacist of the Army since October 28th. In order to better judge with the eye the diminution of the army, I have assumed that the troops of Prince Jérôme and of Marshal Davoust, who had been detached at Minsk and Mogilev and have rejoined around Orcha and Vitebsk, had always marched with the army.

GRAPHIC TABLE of the temperature in degrees of the Réaumur thermometer below zero.

The Cossacks pass the frozen Niemen at a gallop.

Auto. par Regnier, 8 Pas. S.te Marie St. Gain, à Paris.

Imp. Lith. Regnier et Dourdet.

If you decide to include visuals, be sure that they actually illuminate your analysis, and don't merely decorate it. Remember to label each part of a chart or graph, and position visuals as close as possible to your discussion of the topic they address.

USING OTHER METHODS

It is hard to explain *why* something happened without first explaining *what* happened and *how* it happened. So when you analyze causes and effects, consider using NARRATION to help explain the what:

> Recently, a young man by the name of Benny Paret was killed in the ring. The killing was seen by millions; it was on television.

And use PROCESS ANALYSIS to help explain the how:

> In the twelfth round, he was hit hard in the head several times, went down, was counted out, and never came out of the coma.

These are the words of Norman Cousins in a classic cause-and-effect analysis. Having set up his analysis by using other methods, Cousins then turns to the causes of Benny Paret's death. The immediate cause, obviously, was the fist that hit him. The main cause, Cousins explains, was something else:

> The primary responsibility lies with the people who pay to see a man hurt. The referee who stops a fight too soon from the crowd's viewpoint can expect to be booed. The crowd wants the knockout; it wants to see a man stretched out on the canvas. This is the supreme moment in boxing.
> —NORMAN COUSINS, "Who Killed Benny Paret?"

Cousins's essay was written in 1962. Yet another fighter was killed in the boxing ring as recently as 2007. Cousins's essay may not have achieved the effect he hoped for—getting professional boxing thrown out of the ring of legitimate sport—but the impact of his words is still clear: "No one doubts that many people enjoy prize fighting and will miss it if it should be thrown out. And that is precisely the point." The point is also that good writers like Cousins often use cause-and-effect analysis to make a point when they are constructing ARGUMENTS, yet another method of development that goes hand-in-hand with cause-and-effect analysis.

Reading a Cause-and-Effect Analysis with a Critical Eye

Once you have written a draft (or two or three) of your essay, it's always wise to ask someone else to look over what you have written. Ask readers where they find your analysis clear and convincing, what specific evidence they find good or bad, and where they think you need more (or less) explanation. Here are some key questions that can help you or someone else check over a cause-and-effect analysis.

PURPOSE AND AUDIENCE. Why is the reader being asked to consider these particular causes or effects? Is the intended audience likely to find the analysis plausible as well as useful? What additional information might readers need?

THE POINT. What is the analysis intended to show? Is the point made clearly in a thesis statement? How and how well does the analysis support the point?

CHRONOLOGICAL ORDER. Does the essay analyze causes and effects in chronological order where appropriate? Does it consistently link cause to effect and effect to cause?

REVERSE CHRONOLOGICAL ORDER. Where effects are known but causes are uncertain, it is clear what chain of events most likely led to the effect(s) in question? If not, how can the order of events be clarified?

TYPES OF CAUSES. How well are the significant causes analyzed—the main cause, the most important contributing causes, the immediate cause, and the most important remote causes? What other causes (or effects) should be considered?

CAUSE OR COINCIDENCE? At any point, is a coincidence mistaken for a cause? Are all of the causes necessary to produce the indicated effects? Do they have the power to produce those effects?

VISUALS. Are charts, graphs, or diagrams included to clarify causal relationships? If not, would they be helpful? Are all visuals clearly and appropriately labeled?

USING OTHER METHODS. Does the essay use other methods of development besides cause-and-effect analysis? For instance, does it use NARRATION to present some of the events being analyzed? Or does it use PROCESS ANALYSIS to show how—in addition to why—a particular effect came about? Does the analysis ARGUE that one cause or effect is more likely than another?

Editing for Common Errors in a Cause-and-Effect Analysis

Writing about causes and effects generally calls for certain words and verb forms—words like *because* or *as a result*, verbs like *caused* or *will result in*. Here are some items to check for when you edit your analysis.

Check all connectors to be sure they're logical and precise.

Words like *because* or *since* connect the "cause" part of a sentence to the "effect" part (or the reverse). Be sure the connectors you use make the causal link absolutely clear.

UNCLEAR Since the concrete deteriorated, the roof collapsed.

PRECISE Because the concrete deteriorated, the roof collapsed.

Since has two meanings, "for the reason that" and "after the time that," so it does not make clear whether the roof collapsed after the concrete deteriorated or because it deteriorated. *Because* is the more precise term.

UNCLEAR The concrete deteriorated, and consequently the roof collapsed.

PRECISE The concrete deteriorated, and as a result the roof collapsed.

Consequently can mean "subsequently" or "as a result." The editing makes the causal link clear.

Check your verbs to make sure they clearly express cause and effect.

Some verbs clearly express causation, whereas others only imply that one thing causes another.

VERBS THAT EXPRESS CAUSATION	VERBS THAT IMPLY CAUSATION
account for	follow
bring about	happen
cause	imply
effect	involve
make	implicate
result	take place

VAGUE The partial collapse of terminal 2E involved weak concrete.

PRECISE Weak concrete caused the partial collapse of terminal 2E.

Check for common usage errors.

AFFECT, EFFECT

Affect is a verb meaning "influence." *Effect* is usually a noun meaning "result," but it can also be a verb meaning "bring about."

▸ Getting married did not affect his wages.

▸ Getting married did not have the effect of increasing his wages.

▸ Getting married did not effect a change in his wages.

REASON IS BECAUSE, REASON WHY

Avoid using these expressions; both are redundant. In the first case, use *that* instead of *because*. In the second, use *reason* alone.

NOT The reason the roof collapsed is because the concrete deteriorated.

BUT The reason the roof collapsed is that the concrete deteriorated.

NOT Weakened concrete is the reason why the roof collapsed.

BUT Weakened concrete is the reason the roof collapsed.

A Rube Goldberg Pencil Sharpener

This whimsical drawing by American cartoonist Rube Goldberg (1883–1970) illustrates how causes and effects typically operate—in chains of linked events, with the effect of one event becoming the cause of another. For example, the *immediate* cause is the one closest to the end result—in this case, the actions of the woodpecker. The previous events (flying the kite, burning the pants, smoking out the possum) are the *contributing* causes. Goldberg's designs for elaborate machines and systems to perform simple tasks have inspired many imitators. Each year, for example, engineering students at Purdue University sponsor a national Rube Goldberg contest. The 2005 winner of the Purdue competition, a model of "complexity and inefficiency," was a contraption that took 125 steps to replace the batteries in a flashlight and turn it on.

EVERYDAY CAUSE AND EFFECT

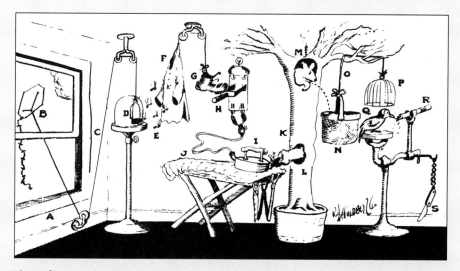

The Professor gets his think-tank working and evolves the simplified pencil sharpener.

Open window (**A**), and fly kite (**B**). String (**C**) lifts small door (**D**), allowing moths (**E**) to escape and eat red flannel shirt (**F**). As weight of shirt becomes less, shoe (**G**) steps on switch (**H**), which heats electric iron (**I**) and burns hole in pants (**J**). Smoke (**K**) enters hole in tree (**L**), smoking out opossum (**M**), which jumps into basket (**N**), pulling rope (**O**) and lifting cage (**P**), allowing woodpecker (**Q**) to chew wood from pencil (**R**), exposing lead. Emergency knife (**S**) is always handy in case opossum or the woodpecker gets sick and can't work.

HAL R. VARIAN

Analyzing the Marriage Gap

Hal R. Varian (b. 1947) is a professor of business and economics at the University of California at Berkeley, specializing in the economics of information technology. Co-author of Information Rules: A Strategic Guide to the Network Economy *(1998), Varian says in that book that movies, music, software, stock quotations, and other "information goods" have supplanted industrial goods "as the key drivers of world markets."*

In the labor market, say many economists, a key driver is marriage. "Analyzing the Marriage Gap" was first published in 2004 as one of Varian's regular business columns in the New York Times. *In it, Varian investigates the claim that married men make more money than unmarried men. There is no doubt that marriage has this effect, says Varian; "the question is why." As he analyzes the most likely causes for the wage gap between married and unmarried men, Varian also looks at the nature of causation in general.*

MARRIED MEN MAKE MORE MONEY than single men—a lot more. Labor econ- 1
omists estimate that even when you control for age, education and other demographic effects, the "marriage wage premium" is 10 percent to 50 percent.

The question is why. 2

There are two broad classes of explanation. One view holds that marriage causes 3
men to receive higher wages. The other view is that higher wages are simply correlated with, but not caused by, marital status.

There are a variety of reasons that marriage might cause higher wages. It might 4
be that employers prefer married men to single men because they are more productive. After all, they have spouses who share responsibility for household chores
and provide other sorts of support and assistance. Single men just have that empty
apartment.

On the other hand, it could be that employers have an irrational prejudice for 5
married men. Employers might view them as more productive, more reliable and
more committed, whether or not these things are true.

Whether there really is an employer preference for married men is irrelevant. 6
Marriage has a causal effect: single men who choose to marry will tend to receive
higher wages.

The other class of theories holds that being married is simply correlated with 7
higher wages. It may be that women are attracted to stable, hardworking men.
Employers also find such men attractive, so they want to hire and promote them. If

this is true, then we would see married men having higher wages. But it isn't that marriage caused those higher wages—rather, the same things that caused marriage caused the higher wages.

Such a correlation could also arise from irrelevant characteristics. Maybe   8 women prefer good-looking guys, and employers also like handsome men, even when appearance has nothing to do with job productivity. In this case we would also observe that the same men who are more likely to be married are also more likely to be employed and have higher wages.

In the correlation explanations of the marriage premium, the same factors that   9 caused the men to marry caused them to get higher wages—but there is no direct causal link between marriage and high wages. To drive this point home, suppose Hamlet is considering proposing to Ophelia,[1] but is consumed with doubts. "To be married or not to be married, that is the question."

If the causal theories are correct, then if Hamlet proposes and Ophelia accepts,   10 his future wages would be higher on average than if he stayed single. If the correlation theories are correct, then choosing to marry would have no effect on Hamlet's future wages, and he may as well remain single.

Recently, two economists, Kate Antonovics of the University of California at San   11 Diego and Robert Town of the University of Minnesota, have come up with a clever way to decide between the causal and the correlation theories. Their paper, "Are All the Good Men Married? Uncovering the Sources of the Marital Wage Premium," was published in the May 2004 issue of *The American Economic Review*.

Their approach is based on looking at monozygotic, or identical, twins. The   12 authors argue that twins have the same genetic endowment and (usually) the same upbringing. Since twins have the same underlying physical and mental capabilities, they should have similar productivity. Even if employers are biased toward certain irrelevant characteristics, monozygotic twins should be affected by such biases equally.

Hence differences in wages between married and unmarried twins should be   13 free of most of the effects that might cause a spurious correlation between marriages and wages. If a married twin has a higher wage than his single brother, the difference is probably caused by marriage, not just correlated with it.

The economists drew on a unique data set, the Minnesota Twins Registry,   14 which tracked most twins born in Minnesota between 1936 and 1955. In the mid-1990's, the Registry sent the twins a questionnaire asking about their socio-economic status. Using this data, the researchers were able to construct a sample

---

1. *Hamlet and Ophelia*: in Shakespeare's play, Hamlet is the son of the recently murdered king of Denmark, and Ophelia is the daughter of the king's advisor. Hamlet is well known for his indecision, and his "To be or not to be" soliloquy is one of Shakespeare's most famous.

of 136 pairs of monozygotic twins, of whom 85 percent were married. In 23 percent of the cases, one twin was married, the other wasn't.

They extracted data from the survey on the hourly wages, weeks worked a year, 15 age and educational attainment of the men in their sample and compared these with figures for all American males. The results implied that their sample was reasonably representative of the nation's population.

Consistent with other studies, they found a significant marriage premium. Con- 16 trolling for education, age and other variables, the married men in their sample earned about 19 percent more than unmarried men. They then examined just the wage differences between twins, while still controlling for education. They found that married twins had 26 percent higher wages than their unmarried siblings. Hence, even among very similar men, those who are married earn substantially more.

The authors found essentially the same results if they factored in divorced or 17 widowed status, or added variables like a spouse's work experience, number of children and wage history.

This result suggests that marriage really does have a causal impact on wages. Of 18 course, it is not conclusive. After all, maybe the married twin really is different in some way from his brother, and that difference is important to both potential spouses and employers. Still, it is suggestive evidence.

So, here's the advice Hamlet would get from a labor economist: put your doubts 19 aside and marry Ophelia. Stop moping around and go get a job. You may not be any happier, but at least you'll make more money.

READING CLOSELY

1. What possible CAUSES for the marriage gap does Varian cite? Which ones do you find most plausible? Why?

2. In addition to discussing specific causes of the marriage gap, what general questions does Varian raise about the nature of cause and effect?

3. The twins study, according to Varian, "should be free of most of the effects that might cause a spurious correlation between marriages and wages" (13). What are some of those EFFECTS? Why should a study based on identical twins be free of them?

4. What do you think is the main point of Varian's essay? How serious do you consider his advice to the Hamlets of the world to be—or not to be?

STRATEGIES AND STRUCTURES

1. How does Varian's EXAMPLE of the twins study by Antonovics and Town in paragraphs 11–18 support his analysis of the causes of the marriage gap?

2. The evidence of the twins study is "suggestive," says Varian, but "not conclusive" (18). Throughout his essay, how and how well does Varian distinguish between probable and possible causes? Explain.

3. *Other Methods.* Before he considers specific causes for the marriage gap, Varian COMPARES and CONTRASTS "two broad classes of explanation" (3). What are they, and how do they differ from each other?

THINKING ABOUT LANGUAGE

1. Look up *spurious*, a word often applied to ARGUMENTS (13). Why does Varian use it in the context of a cause-and-effect analysis?

2. Explain Varian's ALLUSION to Shakespeare's *Hamlet*. What happens to Lady Ophelia in the play? How appropriate is the allusion, in your opinion?

3. *Zygotes* are fertilized ova. So what would "monozygotic" twins be, and why would they be "identical" (12, 14)?

4. In a research experiment, what is meant by "control[ling] for" (1, 16)?

FOR WRITING

1. Do you think the marriage wage premium is caused by marriage? Write a hypothetical email to Varian questioning or agreeing with his evidence and analysis.

2. Women, in general, still earn less than men for the same work. Write an essay analyzing the causes of the gender pay gap.

3. "Irregular" workers—such as students, some military personnel, migrant laborers, and other immigrants—typically earn less than "regular" members of the civilian work force. Why? Analyze the causes in a particular case you know about, whether of an individual worker (including yourself) or a group.

HENRY LOUIS GATES JR.

The Way to Reduce Black Poverty in America

Henry Louis Gates Jr. (b. 1950) is the W. E. B. Du Bois Professor of the Humanities and chair of the Department of African and African American Studies at Harvard. A graduate of Yale, Gates earned his Ph.D. in English literature from Cambridge University. Gates's memoir, Colored People *(1994), won the Heartland Prize for nonfiction. His best-known scholarly work,* The Signifying Monkey *(1987), examines various forms of language play by which people in a position of weakness trick people in power. He is coeditor (with Anthony Appiah) of the encyclopedia* Encarta Africana *(1999) and general editor of the* Norton Anthology of African American Literature *(second edition, 2003). "The Way to Reduce Black Poverty in America" appeared in August 2004 on the Op-Ed page of the* New York Times.

GO INTO ANY INNER-CITY NEIGHBORHOOD, Barack Obama said in his keynote address to the Democratic National Convention,[1] "and folks will tell you that government alone can't teach kids to learn. They know that parents have to parent, that children can't achieve unless we raise their expectations and eradicate the slander that says a black youth with a book is acting white." In a speech filled with rousing applause lines, it was a line that many black Democratic delegates found especially galvanizing. Not just because they agreed, but because it was a home truth they'd seldom heard a politician say out loud.

Why has it been so difficult for American black leaders to say such things in public, without being pilloried for "blaming the victim"? Why the huge flap over Bill Cosby's[2] insistence that black teenagers do their homework, stay in school, master standard English and stop having babies? Any black person who frequents a barbershop or beauty parlor in the inner city knows that Cosby was only echoing sentiments widely shared in the black community.

"If our people studied calculus like we studied basketball," my father, age 91, once remarked, "we'd be running MIT." When my brother and I were growing up in the 1950s, our parents convinced us that the "blackest" thing that we could be was a doctor or a lawyer.

---

1. *Barack Obama . . . Convention:* Barack Obama, then a state senator from Illinois and a candidate for the U.S. Senate, was the keynote speaker at the 2004 Democratic National Convention.

2. *Bill Cosby:* an African American stand-up comic and actor (b. 1937). He's perhaps best known for his program the *Cosby Show,* which ran from 1984 to 1992 and portrayed an affluent, highly educated African American family in everyday middle-class situations.

Yet in too many black neighborhoods today, academic achievement has actually 4
come to be stigmatized. "We are worse off than we were before *Brown v. Board*,"[3]
says Dr. James Comer, a child psychiatrist at Yale. "And a large part of the reason
for this is that we have abandoned our own black traditional core values, values
that sustained us through slavery and Jim Crow segregation."[4]

Making it, as Obama told me, "requires diligent effort and deferred gratifica- 5
tion. Everybody sitting around their kitchen table knows that."

"Americans suffer from anti-intellectualism, starting in the White House," 6
Obama went on. "Our people can least afford to be anti-intellectual." Too many of
our children have come to believe that it's easier to become a black professional
athlete than a doctor or lawyer.

Reality check: According to the 2000 census, there were more than 31,000 7
black physicians and surgeons, 33,000 black lawyers and 5,000 black dentists.
Guess how many black athletes are playing professional basketball, football and
baseball combined. About 1,400.

"We talk about leaving no child behind," says Dena Wallerson, a sociologist at 8
Connecticut College. "The reality is that we are allowing our own children to be
left behind." Nearly a third of black children are born into poverty. The question is:
why?

Scholars like my Harvard colleague William Julius Wilson say that the causes of 9
black poverty are both structural and behavioral. Think of structural causes as "the
devil made me do it," and behavioral causes as "the devil is in me." Structural
causes are faceless systemic forces, like the disappearance of jobs. Behavioral
causes are self-destructive life choices and personal habits. To break the conspiracy
of silence, we have to address both of these factors.

It's important to talk about life chances—about the constricted set of opportuni- 10
ties that poverty brings. But to treat black people as if they're helpless rag dolls
swept up and buffeted by vast social trends—as if they had no say in the shaping of
their lives—is a supreme act of condescension. Only 50 percent of all black Americans graduate from high school; an estimated 64 percent of black teenage girls will
become pregnant.

Are white racists forcing black teenagers to drop out of school or to have babies? 11

Cosby got a lot of flak for complaining about children who couldn't speak stan- 12
dard English. Yet it isn't a derogation of the black vernacular—a marvelously rich

3. *Brown v. Board*: in the landmark civil rights case *Brown v. Board of Education* (1954), the U.S.
Supreme Court ruled that racial segregation in public schools denies students the equal protection
under the law guaranteed by the Constitution. This decision overturned the doctrine of "separate but
equal" facilities for black Americans established in *Plessy v. Ferguson*.

4. *Jim Crow segregation*: reference to racist laws of the late nineteenth and early twentieth centuries that kept blacks and whites separated in public facilities.

and inventive tongue—to point out that there's a language of the marketplace, too, and learning to speak that language has generally been a precondition for economic success, whoever you are. When we let black youth become monolingual, we've limited their imaginative and economic possibilities.

These issues can be ticklish, no question, but they're badly served by silence or 13
squeamishness. We can't talk about the choices people have without talking about the choices people make.

Reading Closely

1. Poverty among black Americans is the main EFFECT that Gates is analyzing. According to his analysis, what are the chief CAUSES of that effect?

2. In paragraph 9, Gates speaks of a "conspiracy of silence." What conspiracy is he talking about?

3. What is Gates's main point about how to reduce black poverty in America? How effective do you find his solution? Explain.

4. In addition to income levels, what other social issues does Gates address? Give examples, and explain their relationship to his main argument.

Strategies and Structures

1. Gates begins his analysis by referring to Barack Obama and Bill Cosby. How do their public remarks EXEMPLIFY what he says about a "conspiracy of silence" (9)? Why would Gates, or any writer, refer to a (then) up-and-coming politician and a famous comedian when making a controversial point?

2. "The question is: why?" is a RHETORICAL QUESTION because Gates intends to answer it himself (8). Where does Gates ask other rhetorical questions, some of which require no answer at all? Try rewriting one of these questions as a statement. How does this change affect his argument?

3. Gates uses statistics in paragraphs 7 and 10. How do these facts and figures support his position?

4. Gates concludes his essay by linking speaking with doing: "We can't talk about the choices people have without talking about the choices people make" (13). Why do you think he ends this way? How else might he have concluded?

5. *Other Methods.* Gates CLASSIFIES "the causes of black poverty" into two types, "structural" and "behavioral" (9). How does he DEFINE each type?

THINKING ABOUT LANGUAGE

1. A "vernacular" is the informal spoken language of a group of people (12). Where does Gates himself use vernacular language in his essay? Why does he do so?

2. What is "standard English" (12)? What, according to Gates, is the role of standard English? Of vernacular English?

3. What are the implications of Gates's "rag doll" METAPHOR (10)?

FOR WRITING

1. Gates's article was written for the Op-Ed page of the *New York Times*, a page opposite the editorial page that's devoted to opinion pieces, usually on controversial issues of the day. Write a letter to the editor responding to Gates.

2. AIDS, sexually transmitted diseases, genocide, mental illness, the Holocaust, birth control, and divorce are taboo topics for various people and communities. Write an essay analyzing the effects that continued silence on one of these topics, or some other controversial subject, is likely to have on individuals and society.

3. "Anti-intellectualism," say Gates and Barack Obama, is not limited to a particular community; Americans in general "suffer" from it (6). Write an essay agreeing or disagreeing with this position.

JARED DIAMOND

To Farm or Not to Farm

Jared Diamond (b. 1937) is a professor of geography at the University of California, Los Angeles. Diamond's research focuses on biological membranes, ecology, and evolutionary biology, but he is also interested in the broad patterns in human history and the history of science. A speaker of twelve languages, he is the author of hundreds of articles and two best-selling books, Collapse: How Societies Choose to Fail or Succeed *(2004) and* Guns, Germs, and Steel: The Fates of Human Societies *(1997). "To Farm or Not to Farm" is a chapter from* Guns, Germs, and Steel, *which won the Pulitzer Prize for nonfiction.*

Why did it take so long for the indigenous hunter-gatherers of the Fertile Crescent to settle down and begin to farm? Why did some native peoples in parts of Australia, South Africa, and North America never do so indigenously? Since not all of the effects of agriculture were beneficial, why did the shift from hunter-gatherers to farmers occur at all? "To Farm or Not to Farm" addresses these and many other questions about the causes and effects, over the last ten thousand years, of one of the most important social and economic changes in the evolution of human societies.

FORMERLY, ALL PEOPLE ON EARTH were hunter-gatherers. Why did any of them adopt food production at all? Given that they must have had some reason, why did they do so around 8500 B.C. in Mediterranean habitats of the Fertile Crescent,[1] only 3,000 years later in the climatically and structurally similar Mediterranean habitats of southwestern Europe, and never indigenously in the similar Mediterranean habitats of California, southwestern Australia, and the Cape of South Africa? Why did even people of the Fertile Crescent wait until 8500 B.C., instead of becoming food producers already around 18,500 or 28,500 B.C.?

From our modern perspective, all these questions at first seem silly, because the drawbacks of being a hunter-gatherer appear so obvious. Scientists used to quote a phrase of Thomas Hobbes's in order to characterize the lifestyle of hunter-gatherers as "nasty, brutish, and short."[2] They seemed to have to work hard, to be driven by

1. *Fertile Crescent:* historical region of Mesopotamia extending from the Mediterranean on the west to the Tigris and Euphrates rivers on the east. This region includes modern-day Israel, the West Bank, Jordan, Lebanon, Syria, and Iraq, and has long been the site of human settlements.

2. *"Nasty, brutish, and short":* the phrase is from *Leviathan* (1651), in which the British political philosopher is analyzing the "natural condition" of humankind. In that state, says Hobbes (1588–1679), people are in universal competition and are "apt to invade and destroy one another." Only laws and social contracts can resolve this condition.

the daily quest for food, often to be close to starvation, to lack such elementary material comforts as soft beds and adequate clothing, and to die young.

In reality, only for today's affluent First World citizens, who don't actually do the work of raising food themselves, does food production (by remote agribusinesses) mean less physical work, more comfort, freedom from starvation, and a longer expected lifetime. Most peasant farmers and herders, who constitute the great majority of the world's actual food producers, aren't necessarily better off than hunter-gatherers. Time budget studies show that they may spend more rather than fewer hours per day at work than hunter-gatherers do. Archaeologists have demonstrated that the first farmers in many areas were smaller and less well nourished, suffered from more serious diseases, and died on the average at a younger age than the hunter-gatherers they replaced. If those first farmers could have foreseen the consequences of adopting food production, they might not have opted to do so. Why, unable to foresee the result, did they nevertheless make that choice?

There exist many actual cases of hunter-gatherers who did see food production practiced by their neighbors, and who nevertheless refused to accept its supposed blessings and instead remained hunter-gatherers. For instance, Aboriginal hunter-gatherers of northeastern Australia traded for thousands of years with farmers of the Torres Strait Islands, between Australia and New Guinea. California Native American hunter-gatherers traded with Native American farmers in the Colorado River valley. In addition, Khoi herders west of the Fish River of South Africa traded with Bantu farmers east of the Fish River, and continued to dispense with farming themselves. Why?

Still other hunter-gatherers in contact with farmers did eventually become farmers, but only after what may seem to us like an inordinately long delay. For example, the coastal peoples of northern Germany did not adopt food production until 1,300 years after peoples of the Linearbandkeramik culture introduced it to inland parts of Germany only 125 miles to the south. Why did those coastal Germans wait so long, and what led them finally to change their minds?

Before we can answer these questions, we must dispel some misconceptions about the origins of food production and then reformulate the question. What actually happened was not a *discovery* of food production, nor an *invention*, as we might first assume. There was often not even a conscious choice between food production and hunting-gathering. Specifically, in each area of the globe the first people who adopted food production could obviously not have been making a conscious choice or consciously striving toward farming as a goal, because they had never seen farming and had no way of knowing what it would be like. Instead, as we shall see, food production *evolved* as a by-product of decisions made without awareness of their consequences. Hence the question that we have to ask is why food production did evolve, why it evolved in some places but not others, why at different times in different places, and why not instead at some earlier or later date.

. . .

. . . Even in the cases of the most rapid independent development of food pro- 7
duction from a hunting-gathering lifestyle, it took thousands of years to shift from
complete dependence on wild foods to a diet with very few wild foods. In early
stages of food production, people simultaneously collected wild foods *and* raised
cultivated ones, and diverse types of collecting activities diminished in importance
at different times as reliance on crops increased.

The underlying reason why this transition was piecemeal is that food produc- 8
tion systems evolved as a result of the accumulation of many separate decisions
about allocating time and effort. Foraging humans, like foraging animals, have only
finite time and energy, which they can spend in various ways. We can picture an
incipient farmer waking up and asking: Shall I spend today hoeing my garden (predictably yielding a lot of vegetables several months from now), gathering shellfish
(predictably yielding a little meat today), or hunting deer (yielding possibly a lot of
meat today, but more likely nothing)? Human and animal foragers are constantly
prioritizing and making effort-allocation decisions, even if only unconsciously.
They concentrate first on favorite foods, or ones that yield the highest payoff. If
these are unavailable, they shift to less and less preferred foods.

Many considerations enter into these decisions. People seek food in order to sat- 9
isfy their hunger and fill their bellies. They also crave specific foods, such as
protein-rich foods, fat, salt, sweet fruits, and foods that simply taste good. All other
things being equal, people seek to maximize their return of calories, protein, or
other specific food categories by foraging in a way that yields the most return with
the greatest certainty in the least time for the least effort. Simultaneously, they
seek to minimize their risk of starving: moderate but reliable returns are preferable
to a fluctuating lifestyle with a high time-averaged rate of return but a substantial
likelihood of starving to death. One suggested function of the first gardens of
nearly 11,000 years ago was to provide a reliable reserve larder as insurance in case
wild food supplies failed.

Conversely, men hunters tend to guide themselves by considerations of prestige: 10
for example, they might rather go giraffe hunting every day, bag a giraffe once a
month, and thereby gain the status of great hunter, than bring home twice a
giraffe's weight of food in a month by humbling themselves and reliably gathering
nuts every day. People are also guided by seemingly arbitrary cultural preferences,
such as considering fish either delicacies or taboo. Finally, their priorities are heavily influenced by the relative values they attach to different lifestyles—just as we
can see today. For instance, in the 19th-century U.S. West, the cattlemen, sheepmen, and farmers all despised each other. Similarly, throughout human history

farmers have tended to despise hunter-gatherers as primitive, hunter-gatherers have despised farmers as ignorant, and herders have despised both. All these elements come into play in people's separate decisions about how to obtain their food.

As we already noted, the first farmers on each continent could not have chosen 11 farming consciously, because there were no other nearby farmers for them to observe. However, once food production had arisen in one part of a continent, neighboring hunter-gatherers could see the result and make conscious decisions. In some cases the hunter-gatherers adopted the neighboring system of food production virtually as a complete package; in others they chose only certain elements of it; and in still others they rejected food production entirely and remained hunter-gatherers.

For example, hunter-gatherers in parts of southeastern Europe had quickly 12 adopted Southwest Asian cereal crops, pulse crops,[3] and livestock simultaneously as a complete package by around 6000 B.C. All three of these elements also spread rapidly through central Europe in the centuries before 5000 B.C. Adoption of food production may have been rapid and wholesale in southeastern and central Europe because the hunter-gatherer lifestyle there was less productive and less competitive. In contrast, food production was adopted piecemeal in southwestern Europe (southern France, Spain, and Italy), where sheep arrived first and cereals later. The adoption of intensive food production from the Asian mainland was also very slow and piecemeal in Japan, probably because the hunter-gatherer lifestyle based on seafood and local plants was so productive there.

Just as a hunting-gathering lifestyle can be traded piecemeal for a food- 13 producing lifestyle, one system of food production can also be traded piecemeal for another. For example, Indians of the eastern United States were domesticating local plants by about 2500 B.C. but had trade connections with Mexican Indians who developed a more productive crop system based on the trinity of corn, squash, and beans. Eastern U.S. Indians adopted Mexican crops, and many of them discarded many of their local domesticates, piecemeal; squash was domesticated independently, corn arrived from Mexico around A.D. 200 but remained a minor crop until around A.D. 900, and beans arrived a century or two later. It even happened that food-production systems were abandoned in favor of hunting-gathering. For instance, around 3000 B.C. the hunter-gatherers of southern Sweden adopted farming based on Southwest Asian crops, but abandoned it around 2700 B.C. and reverted to hunting-gathering for 400 years before resuming farming.

---

3. *Pulse crops*: the edible seeds of pod-bearing plants, such as peas and beans. *Cereal crops*: grains, such as rice.

. . . We should not suppose that the decision to adopt farming was made in a vac-   14
uum, as if the people had previously had no means to feed themselves. Instead, we
must consider food production and hunting-gathering as *alternative strategies* competing with each other. Mixed economies that added certain crops or livestock to
hunting-gathering also competed against both types of "pure" economies, and
against mixed economies with higher or lower proportions of food production. Nevertheless, over the last 10,000 years, the predominant result has been a shift from
hunting-gathering to food production. Hence we must ask: What were the factors
that tipped the competitive advantage away from the former and toward the latter?

That question continues to be debated by archaeologists and anthropologists.   15
One reason for its remaining unsettled is that different factors may have been decisive in different parts of the world. Another has been the problem of disentangling
cause and effect in the rise of food production. However, five main contributing
factors can still be identified; the controversies revolve mainly around their relative importance.

One factor is the decline in the availability of wild foods. The lifestyle of hunter-   16
gatherers has become increasingly less rewarding over the past 13,000 years, as
resources on which they depended (especially animal resources) have become less
abundant or even disappeared. . . . Most large mammal species became extinct in
North and South America at the end of the Pleistocene,[4] and some became extinct
in Eurasia and Africa, either because of climate changes or because of the rise in
skill and numbers of human hunters. While the role of animal extinctions in eventually (after a long lag) nudging ancient Native Americans, Eurasians, and Africans
toward food production can be debated, there are numerous incontrovertible cases
on islands in more recent times. Only after the first Polynesian settlers had exterminated moas[5] and decimated seal populations on New Zealand, and exterminated
or decimated seabirds and land birds on other Polynesian islands, did they intensify
their food production. For instance, although the Polynesians who colonized Easter
Island around A.D. 500 brought chickens with them, chicken did not become a
major food until wild birds and porpoises were no longer readily available as food.
Similarly, a suggested contributing factor to the rise of animal domestication in the
Fertile Crescent was the decline in abundance of the wild gazelles that had previously been a major source of meat for hunter-gatherers in that area.

A second factor is that, just as the depletion of wild game tended to make   17
hunting-gathering less rewarding, an increased availability of domesticable wild

4. *Pleistocene*: the geologic period—from about 2 million to 11,000 years ago—during which modern humans evolved.
5. *Moas*: large, flightless, ostrich-like birds.

plants made steps leading to plant domestication more rewarding. For instance, climate changes at the end of the Pleistocene in the Fertile Crescent greatly expanded the area of habitats with wild cereals, of which huge crops could be harvested in a short time. Those wild cereal harvests were precursors to the domestication of the earliest crops, the cereals wheat and barley, in the Fertile Crescent.

Still another factor tipping the balance away from hunting-gathering was the cumulative development of technologies on which food production would eventually depend—technologies for collecting, processing, and storing wild foods. What use can would-be farmers make of a ton of wheat grains on the stalk, if they have not first figured out how to harvest, husk, and store them? The necessary methods, implements, and facilities appeared rapidly in the Fertile Crescent after 11,000 B.C., having been invented for dealing with the newly available abundance of wild cereals. 18

Those inventions included sickles of flint blades cemented into wooden or bone handles, for harvesting wild grains; baskets in which to carry the grains home from the hillsides where they grew; mortars and pestles,[6] or grinding slabs, to remove the husks; the technique of roasting grains so that they could be stored without sprouting; and underground storage pits, some of them plastered to make them waterproof. Evidence for all of these techniques becomes abundant at sites of hunter-gatherers in the Fertile Crescent after 11,000 B.C. All these techniques, though developed for the exploitation of wild cereals, were prerequisites to the planting of cereals as crops. These cumulative developments constituted the unconscious first steps of plant domestication. 19

A fourth factor was the two-way link between the rise in human population density and the rise in food production. In all parts of the world where adequate evidence is available, archaeologists find evidence of rising densities associated with the appearance of food production. Which was the cause and which the result? This is a long-debated chicken-or-egg problem: did a rise in human population density force people to turn to food production, or did food production permit a rise in human population density? 20

In principle, one expects the chain of causation to operate in both directions. . . . Food production tends to lead to increased population densities because it yields more edible calories per acre than does hunting-gathering. On the other hand, human population densities were gradually rising throughout the late Pleistocene anyway, thanks to improvements in human technology for collecting and processing wild foods. As population densities rose, food production became 21

---

6. *Mortars and pestles*: a set of grinding implements, usually made of stone or wood, consisting of a bowl (mortar) and a rounded club (pestle).

increasingly favored because it provided the increased food outputs needed to feed all those people.

That is, the adoption of food production exemplifies what is termed an auto- 22 catalytic process—one that catalyzes itself in a positive feedback cycle, going faster and faster once it has started. A gradual rise in population densities impelled people to obtain more food, by rewarding those who unconsciously took steps toward producing it. Once people began to produce food and become sedentary, they could shorten the birth spacing and produce still more people, requiring still more food. This bidirectional link between food production and population density explains the paradox that food production, while increasing the quantity of edible calories per acre, left the food producers less well nourished than the hunter-gatherers whom they succeeded. That paradox developed because human population densities rose slightly more steeply than did the availability of food.

Taken together, these four factors help us understand why the transition to food 23 production in the Fertile Crescent began around 8500 B.C., not around 18,500 or 28,500 B.C. At the latter two dates hunting-gathering was still much more rewarding than incipient food production, because wild mammals were still abundant; wild cereals were not yet abundant; people had not yet developed the inventions necessary for collecting, processing, and storing cereals efficiently; and human population densities were not yet high enough for a large premium to be placed on extracting more calories per acre.

A final factor in the transition became decisive at geographic boundaries 24 between hunter-gatherers and food producers. The much denser populations of food producers enabled them to displace or kill hunter-gatherers by their sheer numbers, not to mention the other advantages associated with food production (including technology, germs, and professional soldiers). In areas where there were only hunter-gatherers to begin with, those groups of hunter-gatherers who adopted food production outbred those who didn't.

As a result, in most areas of the globe suitable for food production, hunter- 25 gatherers met one of two fates: either they were displaced by neighboring food producers, or else they survived only by adopting food production themselves. In places where they were already numerous or where geography retarded immigration by food producers, local hunter-gatherers did have time to adopt farming in prehistoric times and thus to survive as farmers. This may have happened in the U.S. Southwest, in the western Mediterranean, on the Atlantic coast of Europe, and in parts of Japan. However, in Indonesia, tropical Southeast Asia, most of sub-equatorial Africa, and probably in parts of Europe, the hunter-gatherers were replaced by farmers in the prehistoric era, whereas a similar replacement took place in modern times in Australia and much of the western United States.

Only where especially potent geographic or ecological barriers made immigra- 26 tion of food producers or diffusion of locally appropriate food-producing techniques very difficult were hunter-gatherers able to persist until modern times in areas suitable for food production. The three outstanding examples are the persistence of Native American hunter-gatherers in California, separated by deserts from the Native American farmers of Arizona; that of Khoisan hunter-gatherers at the Cape of South Africa, in a Mediterranean climate zone unsuitable for the equatorial crops of nearby Bantu farmers; and that of hunter-gatherers throughout the Australian continent, separated by narrow seas from the food producers of Indonesia and New Guinea. Those few peoples who remained hunter-gatherers into the 20th century escaped replacement by food producers because they were confined to areas not fit for food production, especially deserts and Arctic regions. Within the present decade, even they will have been seduced by the attractions of civilization, settled down under pressure from bureaucrats or missionaries, or succumbed to germs.

READING CLOSELY

1. According to Diamond, what is the "underlying reason" that it took so long for humans to become farmers instead of hunter-gatherers (8)? Do you think this reason supports his main point? Explain.

2. How does Diamond DEFINE "mixed economies," and why did they exist (14)?

3. Beginning in paragraph 16, Diamond analyzes the major CAUSES, over the last ten thousand years, of the shift from hunting-gathering to farming. What five main factors does he mention?

4. What are the main advantages, according to Diamond, of farming as opposed to hunting and gathering? Why did some peoples nonetheless retain (or revert to) the older economy?

5. Under what conditions did a few indigenous peoples remain hunter-gatherers into the twentieth century?

STRATEGIES AND STRUCTURES

1. Do you think Diamond is writing for an AUDIENCE of geographers, archaeologists, and historians, or for a more general audience? Support your opinion with evidence from the text.

2. Throughout his analysis, Diamond asks *why* or *what if* a number of times. Many of these are RHETORICAL QUESTIONS—Diamond answers them himself or implies the answer—but others are left unanswered. Why? Explain by referring to specific questions.

3. What is the nature of the problem in causation that Diamond raises in paragraph 20? How does he solve this problem in his own analysis?

4. *Other Methods.* What is Diamond EXEMPLIFYING in paragraphs 4–5? How do these examples fit in with his analysis of cause and effect?

Thinking about Language

1. In paragraph 14 and the discussion that follows, why does Diamond speak of "factors" instead of "causes"?

2. What does the METAPHOR of "tipping the balance" mean in paragraph 18? Why do you think Diamond uses it?

3. Look up *catalyst* in a dictionary. How does a catalytic process differ from an "autocatalytic process" (22)?

4. A *paradox* is an apparent contradiction that may still be true or valid (22). To what specific PARADOX is Diamond referring, and how does he resolve it?

For Writing

1. Choose one of the following causes: bureaucrats, politicians, missionaries, germs. Write a paragraph or two analyzing one effect of your cause on a particular place or group of people.

2. Find out about a family farm or small business in your community that is still operating despite pressures to sell out or close. Either interview the people involved to collect data or do some local research. Then write an essay that gives the reasons the farm or business has survived.

3. The family farm is said to be disappearing in America. Why? After doing some research, write an essay that analyzes the main causes of this effect.

HENRY L. ROEDIGER III

Why Are Textbooks So Expensive?

Henry L. Roediger III (b. 1947) is a professor of psychology at Washington University in St. Louis. Roediger is a specialist in memory and human learning, and the author or coauthor of many articles and psychology textbooks. What caused him to specialize in the psychology of memory? Roediger attributes his choice to an event in his childhood—the death of his mother when he was five years old. "That event changed my life drastically," says Roediger. "I was determined to hold on to my memories of her, to relive the past by remembering them. At a very early age, I spent a lot of time thinking about memory and how it works."

"Why Are Textbooks So Expensive?" appeared in 2005 in The Observer, *a journal published by the American Psychological Society, of which Roediger is a past president.*

NEWSLETTERS AND OTHER MISSIVES that I receive seem filled with stories about textbooks and textbook prices, with many wringing their hands over why textbooks are so expensive now relative to the more distant past (usually when the author of the article was in college). I suspect some articles arise from middle-aged parents who suddenly must pay for their own children's college textbooks and they recoil when they see a bill of $500 a semester or thereabouts.

What reasons are given for the high price of textbooks? Of course, there's general inflation, but evidence points to textbook prices outpacing inflation. Others point their fingers at the bright colors in many books (relative to older black and white models) and argue that production costs are needlessly pushed up by color. (A quick check of my own bookstore shows that many books without color are more expensive than those with color, probably due to the number of books in the print run.) Another suggested hypothesis is textbook publishers simply seek greater profit margins now than they did in the past. After all, the market used to be dominated by rather genteel textbook companies that really cared about scholarly texts and not so much about being wildly profitable. A comfortable, modest profit line was fine in the old days. Those days are now gone, because traditional textbook companies have been bought up by gigantic conglomerates that look only to the bottom line and seek huge profits. For these companies, so the theory goes, textbooks are just one more product line, no different from detergent or tires or toilet paper, on which to make a profit. The fact that many formerly independent textbook companies are being bought up and merged under the same corporate umbrella could also be partly responsible, if this process reduces competition through having fewer companies. Another facet of the debate is the frequent revision schedule of basic textbooks. Most introductory psychology textbooks are revised every three years, some every two years. Doesn't this constant revision drive up the prices?

Although the reasons listed above may have some merit, I don't think any of them is fundamental to why textbook prices are so high. In fact, I suspect that most of the properties described above are effects and not causes. What is the cause? If I had to bet, the root cause is a feature of the marketplace that has changed greatly over the years and fundamentally reshaped the textbook market: sale of used books.

The organized used book market represents the great change in the landscape of higher education publishing, but one that has gone relatively unnoticed.

Let us go back in time to what educational historians refer to as the later Paleolithic era in higher education, that is, the late 1960s, when I was in college. Here was how the used book market worked then. I was a psychology major and was about to take a course in history of psychology. A psychology major in my fraternity, Dave Redmond (now a big-time lawyer in Richmond, Virginia) was going on to law school and wanted to sell some of his psychology textbooks. He asked if I wanted to buy Edna Heidbreder's *Seven Psychologies*, for a dollar. I said OK. The book had cost him $2.95, which is still listed in my copy. . . .

. . . This was how the used book market worked in my day. One student sold books to another student on a hit or miss basis. Books didn't cost much. Oh, also, most students kept their books and started building a personal library. (This is another idea that seems to have faded with time. Personal library? Today's students assume everything they need to know is on the Internet.)

Let's fast forward to 1981. I was teaching at Purdue University and was considering (with Betty Capaldi and several others) writing an introductory psychology textbook, since textbook companies were wooing us to do so. However, neither Betty nor I had ever even taught introductory psychology, so we decided to teach independent sections one semester. We examined a lot of books and decided to use Phil Zimbardo's textbook, *Psychology and Life.* . . . Betty and I were each to teach a section of 475 students, so we ordered 950 books. Nine hundred fifty books was, and is, a big textbook order. Think of the profits to the company and the author!

A few days before classes were to begin, I happened by one of the three Purdue bookstores to buy something. I decided to go see the hundreds of copies of the book I had ordered, gleaming at me on the shelves. I found them, all right, but I was shocked at my discovery. Every single book on the shelf was a used copy! I went through many of them, disbelieving, and saw that quite a few were in poor condition (marked up, spines damaged, etc.), yet the prices were still substantial. How could this be? Zimbardo's book had never been used at Purdue before recent times. Where did all these used copies come from? I decided to walk to the other two bookstores and discovered exactly the same situation; every book for sale was a used book in the other two stores. There wasn't a new book to be found.

The organized used book market represents the great change in the landscape of higher education publishing, but one that has gone relatively unnoticed by most academics (unless they are textbook authors). The implications are huge. Consider the situation in today's dollars (although I am estimating). A single author of a textbook might make a 15 percent royalty on the net price of the book (sometimes a bit more); the net price is the price the bookstore pays the textbook company for the book and the list price is the price set by the bookstore to sell to the student. The net price of an introductory psychology textbook today might be $65 (before the bookstore marks it up), so the author would make $9.75 per book. However, that is only if the book is bought from the company; if the student buys used books, the author makes nothing and neither does the company. If 950 used books are sold, the author would lose (be cheated out of?) $9,262, and the textbook company would perhaps lose a similar or larger amount. (Profit margins probably differ from company to company and book to book. They are a closely guarded secret.) Of course, at Purdue in 1981 the figures would have been smaller, but the principle the same. The fact of modern campus life is that used book companies buy up textbooks on one campus, warehouse them, and ship them to wherever the book is being adopted, and therefore prevent sales of new books.

Consider what this means. The textbook company that invested hundreds of thousands of dollars—maybe millions for introductory textbooks—to sign, develop, review, produce, market, and distribute a book over several years is denied its just profits. The author or authors who wrote the book over many years are denied their royalties. Meanwhile, huge profits are made by the used book companies who did nothing whatsoever to create the product. They are true parasites, deriving profits with no investment (and no value added to the product) while damaging their hosts. The issue here is similar to that in the movie and recording industries for pirated products that are sold very cheaply, denying the companies and the artists their profits. One major dissimilarity in these cases is that pirated movies and music are illegal whereas the used textbook market is legal. (There have been proposals to change this state of affairs. For example, one idea is that when used book companies resell texts they would pay the original textbook company and author a royalty.)

The high price of textbooks is the direct result of the used book market. A textbook is customarily used for one semester and (unlike the old days) students rarely keep their books now but sell them back to the bookstore (more on that anon). Therefore, the same text might be used by three to four students, but the textbook company and author profit the first time a book is sold and not thereafter. It stands to reason that textbooks must be priced aggressively, because the profits from the repeated sales will not go to the authors and companies that actually wrote and produced the books, but rather to the companies that specialize in buying and selling used books. Further, the reason textbooks are revised so frequently is to combat the used book market, which further drives up the company's costs. Frequent revisions also add wear and tear on the authors who must perpetually revise their books. (I've sometimes wanted to have two somewhat different versions of my textbooks and then alternate them.) Most fields of psychology hardly move at such a swift pace as to justify two- to three-year revision cycles of introductory textbooks. The famous textbooks of the 1950s and 1960s were revised every eight to 10 years or so, but after the used textbook market gained steam, revisions became frequent. Moreover, because of the used book market, profitability of many companies was hurt and they became ripe for takeovers, which further consolidated the market. That is why I said in the third paragraph that many factors used to "explain" the high prices of books are probably effects, with the cause being the organized used book companies that prey parasitically on the host publishing companies and threaten to destroy them.

Other changes have also affected the market. College and university bookstores 12 used to be owned by the school and operated as a service to the students and the faculty, but those days are past on most campuses. Now the bookstores are operated by large companies (Follett's, Barnes and Noble, and others), often the same ones who operate used book operations. Most "bookstores" have turned into carnivals where emphasis is placed on selling sweatshirts, trinkets, souvenirs and snacks and, oh, incidentally (used) books.

Another pernicious trend: After universities relinquished their hold on book- 13 stores, the bookstores aggressively raised the percentage markup on the net price paid to the publisher on new books. Thirty years ago a standard rate of markup was 20 percent and publishers provided list prices on their books (because markups were standard). I can recall the great hue and cry that arose when textbook stores started marking up books by 25 percent. However, a 25 percent markup for today's bookstores would look like chump change. Publishing companies now sell the bookstore the books based on a net price and the bookstore decides on the list price, often marking up the books 30 to 40 percent in the process. The profits go to the company owning the store and the company pays the college or university for the right to have a monopoly business on campus. However, many students have now learned that it is cheaper and (given the huge lines) sometimes easier to buy textbooks from other sources like Amazon.com.

Let me give you a concrete example. Last summer the eighth edition of my text- 14 book (with Barry Kantowitz and David Elmes), *Experimental Psychology: Understanding Psychological Research*, was published by Wadsworth Publishing Company.

The net price (the price the bookstore pays the [publisher] for a new book) the first time the book is sold is $73.50. The authors receive 15 percent royalties on the book, so we would split the $11 royalty three ways. However, at the Washington University bookstore, the list price of the book is $99.75, a markup of $26.25 (or 35.7 percent)! Yes, that's right, the authors who wrote the book get $11.02 for their years of hard work whereas the bookstore that ordered the books, let them sit on the shelves for a couple of weeks, and sold them, gets $26.25 per book. (If books are not sold, they are returned to the [publisher] for a full price refund. It's a no-risk business.)

Yet the story gets even worse because of the used book problem. After the stu- 15 dent uses the book (and if it is in pretty good condition), the bookstore will buy it back from the student at a greatly marked down price, somewhere between 25 and 50 percent. Let's assume that *Experimental Psychology* is bought back for 40 percent of the list price (which is probably a generous assumption at most bookstores). That would be $39.90. After buying it, the bookstore will mark it back up dramatically and resell the book. Suppose the used book is sold for $75, which sounds like a bargain relative to the new book price of $99.75, and it is. However, notice that the profit markup for the bookstore on this used book would then be $35.10, which is higher than the (still very large) profit made on the new book ($26.25). In fact, the primary reason bookstores prefer selling used books to new books is the much higher profit margins on used books. So, on the second (and third and fourth, etc.) sales of the same book, the bookstore and used book company make huge cumulative profits. The textbook company that invested large sums into developing the book (and the authors who invested time and energy and research into writing it) receive exactly zero on these resold books.

If this sounds bad, it actually gets worse. Another insidious influence in the text- 16 book industry is the problem of sales of complimentary copies. In order to market their wares to professors, it is customary for textbook companies to give out free copies of their books. [Everyone] who teach[es] basic courses in the psychology curriculum receive[s] such books. This is just another price of doing business for the book companies. However, many of these books find their way into the used book market because some professors sell books to scavengers from the used book companies who search through university campuses seeking to buy complimentary copies. Now these companies are soliciting professors to sell their complimentary copies by e-mail. I never sell my complimentary books, of course, because I believe it unethical to sell for profit something I was given by a company in good faith. However, apparently many professors do sell their books. Now the textbook company gets hit by a double whammy: The book they produced to give to a professor for possible adoption enters the market and takes away a new book sale in the marketplace!

Is it any wonder that textbook prices are so high? The wonder is that they aren't 17
higher.

. . .

The textbook companies themselves have few alternatives in dealing with this 18
problem. They can and do raise the price of the books so that they try to recoup
their investment on the first sale (hence the high price of textbooks). They can
revise the book frequently, which renders the previous edition obsolete. They can
try to bundle in or shrink-wrap some additional item (a workbook, a CD) with the
new text, so that students will need to buy new books to get the free item. This
strategy can work, but some bookstores will just unbundle the book from the study
guide and sell both! (So, a study guide the bookstore received free can be sold for,
say, $15.) Unless and until laws are changed to prevent the organized sale of used
books, you can expect textbook prices to keep increasing. . . .

READING CLOSELY

1. Roediger analyzes several of the usual reasons given for the steep rise in the
   prices of college textbooks (2), as well as what he says is the main or "root"
   CAUSE (3). What are the usual reasons and what does he claim to be the main
   cause?

2. What is the point of the brief NARRATIVE that Roediger tells in paragraphs 5–6
   about buying his undergraduate psychology book from a classmate? How about
   the narrative he tells in paragraphs 7–8? How do these stories relate to his main
   point? Where does he state it?

3. According to Roediger, what specific EFFECTS has the used-book market had on
   the authors and publishers of textbooks? On the consumers of those books?

4. How and why, according to Roediger, do college bookstores sell used copies of
   textbooks that have never been used on their campuses?

STRATEGIES AND STRUCTURES

1. Where and how does Roediger shift from analyzing CAUSES to analyzing
   EFFECTS? Where does he switch back? How effective do you find this strategy?
   Why?

2. What is the purpose of the EXAMPLE that Roediger gives in paragraph 14? Why
   does he refer to it as a CONCRETE example? List some other concrete examples
   he uses. For what purposes does he use them?

3. As an author of textbooks himself, Roediger has a stake in his analysis that purchasers of textbooks do not have. Does that stake necessarily invalidate his claims? Why or why not?

4. *Other Methods.* Besides analyzing causes and effects, what ARGUMENT is Roediger making? What conclusions does he come to?

THINKING ABOUT LANGUAGE

1. In paragraphs 10 and 11, Roediger uses a biological ANALOGY. What is he comparing to what? How helpful do you find the comparison?

2. Roediger calls campus bookstores "carnivals" (12). Why?

3. How does Roediger DEFINE the "net price" of a newly published book (9)? How about the "profit margin" (9)?

4. Roediger uses HYPERBOLE, or exaggeration, when he calls the 1960s "the later Paleolithic era" (5). Why does he use hyperbole here? What does it contribute to the ARGUMENT he is making?

FOR WRITING

1. Write a paragraph or two analyzing some effects of rising textbook costs from your own standpoint as a consumer.

2. Have you ever purchased a textbook that is labeled "free examination copy" or "not for resale"? If, as Roediger contends, the sale of such books contributes to the high cost of textbooks, what if anything do you think should be done about teachers and stores selling free copies they received from the publisher for review? Write an opinion piece for your campus newspaper (in other words, for an audience of students) ARGUING for or against this practice.

3. As intellectual property, books are similar to music. Do you agree or disagree with this statement? Write an essay in which you COMPARE AND CONTRAST the sale of used books with the practice of obtaining music using Napster, Grutella, Grokster, or another file-sharing technology.

PAULA T. KELSO

Behind the Curtain: The Body, Control, and Ballet

Paula T. Kelso teaches at Lewis and Clark Community College in Godfrey, Illinois. Trained as a ballerina, Kelso has danced professionally in the Midwest, New York, North Carolina, and California. In the spring of 2002, as an undergraduate majoring in sociology at Southern Illinois University, Edwardsville, Kelso chose "Body Obsession in Ballet" as the topic for her senior seminar. The resulting paper earned an A, and she presented it the following October at a meeting of the Illinois Sociology Association. In 2003, Kelso's study, which follows the documentation style of the American Psychological Association (APA), was published in Edwardsville Journal of Sociology.*

"Behind the Curtain" is an insider's view of the destructive physical and psychological effects female dancers endure because of a professional culture of enforced starvation. Under the influence of legendary choreographer George Balanchine and his successors, Kelso argues, ballet in America adopted an impossible (and dangerous) ideal of female beauty.*

MANY YOUNG GIRLS and their parents are attracted to the ballet because of the applauding audiences, the lights, the sequins and feathers, the colorful, elaborate tutus, and satin pointe shoes. Where else can a young girl dream of becoming a princess, a swan, a dancing snowflake or flower, a sugarplum, or lilac fairy? Where else can she be a character right out of a fairy tale like Cinderella or Sleeping Beauty? Where else can she be rescued by and collapse into the arms of her handsome prince? Ballet is the magical world where these dreams can come true. Young girls and women can be all of these things, characters that symbolize femininity in a society that teaches young girls to be and want everything pink and pretty. However, in the shadows of the spotlight lurks an abusive world of eating disorders, verbal harassment, fierce competition, and injured, fatigued, and malnourished dancers. This world of fantasy is just that: fantasy and make-believe. 1

The Problem

Body image is defined as the way in which people see themselves in the mirror every day: the values, judgments, and ideas that they attach to their appearance. Benn and Walters (2001) argue that these judgments and ideas come from being socialized into particular ways of thinking, mainly from society's ideas of what beauty is, shown especially in the current media and consumer culture (p. 140). The average person is inundated with 3,000 advertisements daily (Kilbourne, 2

2002). In these advertisements, women are shown in little clothing and in stereo-typical roles. These women are not real (Kilbourne, 2002). They have been altered by computer airbrushing, retouching, and enhancing, and in many cases, several women are used to portray the same model (Kilbourne, 2002). The cultural idea of what is beautiful has changed over the years. In the 1950s, Marilyn Monroe, who wore a size 16 at one point in her career, was considered the epitome of sexiness and beauty (Jhally, 1995). Contrast this with more recent examples such as Court-ney Cox and Jennifer Aniston from the television show *Friends*, who are considered beautiful. They wear a size 2 (Jhally, 1995). While models and celebrities have become thinner, the average woman is heavier today. This makes an even larger difference between the real and the ideal.

Like the rest of society, dancers' appearances have also changed over the years.   3
In the 1930s and 1940s, ballerinas were considered thin at the time but, as can be seen in photographs, looked very healthy (Gordon, 1983). Since dancers have gen-erally been slimmer than ideal, these dancers' becoming even thinner for today's ideal is a problem. As one renowned ballet teacher said it: "It is a reflection of soci-ety, everything has become more streamlined" (Benn & Walters, 2001, p. 146).

In order to understand the pressures that dancers face to be thin, it is necessary   4
to explore the ideas behind the practice of ballet. Women who become dancers are not exempt from cultural expectations that tell them in order to be successful and beautiful, they must also be very thin. They live with the same pressures as the rest of society, however, they also have to deal with the risk of unemployment if they gain any amount of weight or their bodies do not look a certain way (Gordon, 1983). In a career where education is discouraged because of the time it would take away from a dancer's most successful years, many professional dancers are not attending college and in some cases are even dropping out of high school (Gordon, 1983). These dancers are putting all of their resources into their body and its appearance. If a dancer does gain weight, develops an eating disorder, or becomes injured, she is left out of work with relatively few choices for the future. Most pro-fessional companies have "appearance clauses" in their contracts, which usually state that if the dancer gains any noticeable amount of weight, she is eligible to lose her position in the company (Gordon, 1983; Saint Louis Ballet, 1993). These clauses also state that tattoos, piercings, and changing hair color are not permitted (Gordon, 1983). Haircuts are discouraged, and usually only allowed with the per-mission of the director.

Almost everyone credits George Balanchine, the renowned dancer, teacher, and   5
choreographer, with the current aesthetic of ballet in the West, referred to by most as the "Balanchine body," or the "anorexic look" (Gordon, 1983). He has promoted the skeletal look by his costume requirements and his hiring practices, as well as the treatment of his dancers (Gordon, 1983). The ballet aesthetic currently consists

of long limbs, and a skeletal frame, which accentuates the collarbones and length of the neck, as well as absence of breasts and hips (Benn & Walters, 2001; Gordon, 1983; Kirkland, 1986). Balanchine was known to throw out comments to his dancers, such as: "eat nothing" and "must see the bones" (Kirkland, 1986, p. 56).

If Balanchine has created this aesthetic, other choreographers have followed   6
and adopted it as the norm. Mikhail Baryshnikov, star dancer and former director of American Ballet Theatre, did not tolerate any body type but the Balanchine one (Gordon, 1983). During rehearsal and without any warning, he fired a corps de ballet member because she was too "fat" in his opinion (Gordon, 1983, p. 150). He said that he "couldn't stand to see her onstage anymore" (Gordon, 1983, p. 150). Fortunately, management intervened and the dancer was rehired. However, Baryshnikov and the rest of his management were known to have had meetings with their dancers in order to emphasize the importance of weight loss (Gordon, 1983). Obviously, dancers need to be fit and trim in order to be successful in their occupation, and no one should argue that staying fit is not helpful in order to see a dancer's body line; however, it is the extreme skeletal goal that is cause for so much concern.

It is not uncommon for a dancer to walk into what she thinks will be her daily   7
ballet class and find a scale set up in the center of the dance studio instead (Gordon 1983). These weigh-ins are arranged ahead of time and kept secret from the dancers. A director from American Ballet Theatre explained that warning the dancers would defeat the purpose. As one former dancer put it: "A forewarned dancer is a forestarved dancer"[1] (Gordon 1983, p. 43). Not only are the dancers' weights recorded but many times are read aloud to the entire class. Even the youngest dancers, at one pre-professional academy, at age eleven "gasped in horror" as the teacher read their weights aloud at 50 to 60 pounds (Gordon 1983, p. 43). Public humiliation is not uncommon in the ballet world (Benn & Walters, 2001; Hamilton, 1998). Directors and teachers are known to make hateful comments and even resort to name-calling in some cases (Gordon, 1983). One director told one of his dancers to "drop the weight in three weeks. I don't care how you do it" (Benn & Walters, 2001, p. 145). When she did in fact drop the weight by basically not eating, she was rewarded with a role in the performance that the company was rehearsing. Dancers learn at an early age that rewards and punishments are based upon weight. If a dancer loses weight, she is praised and rewarded with a role in a ballet. If she does not, she is punished by not being cast at all (Gordon, 1983). It seems that directors and teachers perceive how thin a dancer becomes as a sign of dedication to the art and is often times rewarded (Benn & Walters, 2001). Suzanne Gordon (1983) accompanied several members of an elite advanced pre-

---

1. *Forewarned/forestarved*: a word play on the English proverb, "forewarned is forearmed."

professional academy to a professional audition. She witnessed hundreds of dancers asked to walk across the floor of the studio, where many of them were then asked to leave. After fifteen or more years of professional training, these dancers were not allowed to even audition. Apparently, they did not have the right "look." This practice is used by most professional companies across the United States (Gordon, 1983).

Directors and company managers are not the only ones who put pressure on dancers to stay thin. Ballet critics often refer to body sizes when writing reviews of a performance (Benn & Walters, 2001). This can be a nightmare for a dancer, particularly if a negative body shape statement is printed next to her name for anyone to read in the morning paper. For example, two critics wrote reviews after seeing a company perform a Balanchine Ballet (a ballet in which the dancers wear nothing but tights and leotards). One said he witnessed, "an awful lot of wobbling bottoms on display" and the other claimed that this particular company had "rejected the starved-greyhound look in ballerinas—but now things have gone too far the other way. Bonnard legs and Ingres bottoms[2] are all very well, but not on stage, and particularly not in Balanchine" (Benn & Walters, 2001, p. 149). These reviews were taken to heart by the company directors, who threatened to fire members of the corps de ballet if they did not lose the weight fast. So they did, by not eating (Benn & Walters, 2001).

According to research conducted by Benn and Walters (2001), dancers studied were found to only consume 700 to 900 calories per day. Many of the subjects were consuming less than 700. Surveys conducted in the United States, China, Russia, and Western Europe by Hamilton (1998) found that female dancers' weights were 10 to 15 percent below the ideal weight for their height. According to the American Psychiatric Association's official criteria for anorexia nervosa, the number one factor for diagnosis is if the person's weight is more than 15 percent below the ideal weight for height. This is dangerously close to most dancers! Another factor for diagnosing anorexia nervosa is if the person has developed amenorrhea, that is, if they have missed three consecutive menstrual cycles (Hamilton, 1998). According to Suzanne Gordon's research (1983), many dancers have ceased menstruating or have many cycle irregularities. Once someone stops menstruating, she may lose 4 percent of her bone mass annually for the next three to four years (Hamilton, 1998). This causes another set of problems: injury and osteoporosis. If dancers are not consuming enough calories, many times they are nutritionally deficient, which Hamilton (1998) supports in her arguments. If dancers are malnourished and continue to heavily exert themselves through dance,

2. *Bonnard/Ingres*: French painters of the nineteenth and eighteenth centuries, respectively. They each painted women more round and plump than dancers today are supposed to be.

stress fractures, a common injury among dancers, are unavoidable (Gordon, 1983; Hamilton, 1998). Also, osteoporosis is common. One dancer took a bone density test and at 21 years old found she had the bones of a 70 year old (Hamilton, 1998). Dancers are not receiving crucial health and nutrition information, and they may not realize the harm they are inflicting on their bodies until it is too late. Benn and Walters (2001) found that only 18% of current dancers had received proper nutritional education.

Many people believe the myth that female dancers must be skeletal because of 10 the male dancers who have to partner and lift them. This is simply not true. Gordon (1983) interviewed several professional male dancers, who said that they preferred to partner heavier dancers rather than dancers who fit the "anorexic look." Patrick Bissell, a well-renowned dancer, says that "it's not easy to partner very thin dancers . . . they scream out all of a sudden because you pick them up . . . it makes you very tentative about how you touch them" (Gordon, 1983, p. 151). Another famous dancer, Jeff Gribler, agrees. He says that "It's easy to bruise a woman when you partner anyway, and if she seems too frail, you don't want to grip too hard. It can be really painful for her to be partnered" (Gordon, 1983, p. 152). Vane Vest, another dancer, says "these anorexic ballerinas—I can't bear to touch them . . . you partner a woman and lift her at the waist and you want to touch something. These skinny ballerinas, it's awful . . . how can you do a *pas de deux* with one of those girls?" (Gordon, 1983, p. 152). Gordon found in her research that ballerinas in Europe and elsewhere weigh more than North American ballerinas, yet male dancers do not seem to have a problem partnering them (Gordon, 1983).

Another myth is that this unhealthy "Balanchine body" is the only body capable 11 of the technical feats that ballet requires. People also believe that if dancers were not this thin, audiences would not come to the ballet. However some of the most famous and successful companies are located in Europe and elsewhere. European companies, even with dancers who are not emaciated, are very successful. Gordon (1983) found that in European companies, particularly the Royal Swedish Ballet, dancers look somewhat different. She noticed older dancers in their late thirties and forties, and also that dancers were not nearly as thin as American dancers (Gordon, 1983). These dancers were definitely thin, but they looked healthy. They had breasts, hips, and curves, and actually looked womanly. During a gala performance for American Ballet Theatre, Gordon sat next to a New York ballet critic. When guest artist Zhandra Rodriguez from Ballet de Caracas, Venezuela came on stage, Gordon immediately noticed that she had visible breasts. When she mentioned this to the critic, the critic retorted, "she can't be an American" (Gordon, 1983, p. 151).

. . .

Analyses: Two Theories about the World of Ballet

Subculture Theory

Many wonder why dancers and their parents continue to take part in the ballet   12
world after learning about some of its negative aspects. Subculture theory can
explain why dancers continue to dance, even in the face of major internal and external obstacles and criticism. Subculture theory has mainly been used to explain
deviance and crime in the past; however, it works well in analyzing ballet as a
unique world of its own with different norms and values from the rest of society.

A subculture can be defined as a group of people who share a common identity   13
through a unique set of characteristics common to the entire group, yet not
entirely distinct from the rest of the society in which the group lives (Farley, 1998).
The subculture is a part of the larger society, yet it has certain ideas, beliefs, behaviors, and values that set it apart in some way. Farley (1998) states that individuals
with a common interest and occupation commonly form subcultures. Ballet is
truly an entire world all to its own. It functions within society, but it is a distinct
group that should be recognized as such. The world of ballet has its own ideas of
what the body should look like that are more extreme than the rest of society; however, the current ballet aesthetic would not be popular if dancers lived in a culture
that did not value extreme thinness. All ballet companies across the world value
thinness; however, it seems that only North American companies, especially the
United States, have this dangerous goal of skeletal thinness.

Dancers are raised in this subculture of ballet, many from as young as three   14
years of age. They spend every night in this world among directors, teachers, and
other students who help to normalize ballet's ideas and values, and they internalize
these messages. Dancers rely on their teachers for support and guidance, but also
for approval and selection of parts in ballets. This leads to a generalized fear
instilled in the dancers.

. . .

Ideas of beauty and health are different in the ballet world than in the larger   15
society. Many dancers believe themselves to be healthy because they form "their
ideas of healthy and normal . . . according to the norms and values of the ballet
world" (Benn & Walters, 2001, p. 142). Because dancers are surrounded by eating
disorders, many believe themselves to be healthy because they do not deny themselves food completely and they do not binge and purge. Many dancers may look
healthy enough, but in reality they are not. They would not be diagnosed as med-
ically anorexic, but they are staying thin by means of "gentle starvation," meaning
not consuming enough calories and being nutritionally deficient (Benn & Walters,
2001, p. 142).

Another aspect of the ballet world, which helps to define its subculture, is the   16
idea of control. There is an authoritarian power culture in the ballet world that
forces conformity to harmful behaviors. Dancers have become accustomed to abusive treatment; it becomes a normal part of life in the subculture. Dancers' acceptance of such treatment has been referred to as "silent conformity" for the
"unquestioning, subservient way in which . . . [dancers accept] abuse and unreasonable behavior" (Stinson, 1998; cited by Benn & Walters, 2001, p. 140). This
is one reason why ballet has been compared to a cult in some of the literature
(Benn & Walters, 2001; Gordon, 1983; Smith, 1998). Directors and management
have the power, and they exert it over the dancers, who must obey certain rules if
they intend to continue dancing.

. . .

Paradox Theory

In *Women and the Knife: Cosmetic Surgery and the Colonization of Women's Bodies*   17
(1991), Kathryn Morgan discusses four paradoxes inherent in the choice to
undergo cosmetic surgery. The structure of her argument works well with the paradoxes inherent in the ballet world.

PARADOX ONE: ART?

Ballet is known as a performing *art*. Art implies a creative process through which   18
the artist can express her innermost thoughts and feelings to an audience. Many
dancers dance because they learn to express themselves through movement. However, all of ballet looks the same with cookie-cut out dancers expressing themselves
in the same ways to the same music. There is no individual creativity to be explored here; only the creativity of the director is seen. The director's feelings are
then described to the dancer and the dancer's job is to express that feeling to the
audience. Creativity tends to be quashed in the classroom by focusing only on technique, which trains bodies to be a vehicle for someone else's creativity. Gelsey
Kirkland (1986), a world-renowned ballerina, says in her autobiography that Balanchine had a "monopoly on taste and creative control" at New York City Ballet (p.
49). She also says that the dancers relied on him for "ideas and psychological motivation" (cited by Benn & Walters, 2001, p. 148). Michelle Benash, another dancer,
says that "you have to lose your personality; your movement, your style are dictated
to you" (Gordon, 1983, p. 112). A former New York City Ballet dancer puts it this
way: Balanchine believed "that women should provide the inspiration that triggers
men's creativity" (Gordon, 1983, p. 173). Dancers, then, merely become puppets for
someone else's creativity and emotion.

PARADOX TWO: CONTROL?

All dancers must have control over their bodies in order to master the technique 19
required to perform professionally. Dancers start training young so that their hips
will form a certain way in order to have the required "turn out." They also must
spend years training their leg, feet, and abdomen muscles in order to jump, balance, and dance on pointe properly. These skills require intense years of training
and hard work in order to establish the right strength. One would imagine that
dancers would have plenty of control over their own bodies; however, management
takes over this control by exerting power over the bodies' appearance. Having the
right technique and strength is not nearly enough to dance professionally, one
must also exhibit the right "look." This look, as discussed previously, is unhealthy
and almost impossible to achieve.

PARADOX THREE: THE WONDERS OF THE HUMAN FORM

Ballet is supposed to showcase what the human body is capable of physically 20
accomplishing. Audiences come to see ballet because of the feats that they will
likely see at the performance. Amazing jumps, turns, and tricks are fan favorites.
However, ballet is not showcasing what the human form can accomplish, it is
merely showcasing what one, almost impossible, body type may be capable of exe-
cuting. Dancers are supposed to make these feats look effortless, but it is doubtful
that anyone leaving the theatre feels as if they could mimic these steps without the
required body.

PARADOX FOUR: THE LOOK

Dancers are usually referred to as beautiful and graceful creatures, capable of 21
accomplishing extraordinary feats on stage. Off stage, these dancers resemble broken young children. They oftentimes look emaciated and injured, collapsing off-
stage after performances or limping to their dressing rooms. Dancers are artists, but
they are also athletes who train their bodies every day. Athletes are usually considered to be the epitome of the human form and very physically fit. One look backstage and these are not the thoughts that would come to mind of the dance world.
Most dancers are very unhealthy physically and oftentimes emotionally as well.

Conclusion

The dangerous aesthetic of the ballet world is an area that needs much more atten- 22
tion and further research. Artistic directors of companies do not like to discuss or
acknowledge problems with the current ballet aesthetic, which can be seen in their
reluctance to talk about these issues and the lack of available research on the topic.

. . . Aside from a few current journal articles that discuss eating habits, no one has really attempted to see if the abusive world Gordon exposed in her book has changed at all since her research in the 1980s. *Off Balance: The Real World of Ballet* alerted us to the fact that ballet was not so lovely and magical backstage. . . . I can attest to experiencing all of the aspects of ballet, in my pre-professional training and in my professional dancing, that Gordon showed. I also know from fellow dancers in the Midwest, New York, North Carolina, and San Francisco that their experiences are and have been very similar to what Gordon portrays in her book. There have . . . been recent examples in the media, which suggest that not much has changed since the 1980s. For example, the Boston Ballet ballerina who died at 22 due to complications from an eating disorder (Segal, 2002). Management had told the dancer that she was "chunky" and that she needed to lose weight before she developed anorexia (Segal, 2002). Another example occurred in San Francisco, where nine-year-old Fredrika Keefer was denied admission to San Francisco Ballet School because she was considered too short and chunky by administration. . . . A fictitious example can be seen in the [2000] movie *Center Stage*, where dancers at a highly competitive pre-professional school deal with eating disorders, weight issues, and competition. This film also addressed a director's control of his company, albeit briefly and sentimentalized. . . . Further research is important to assess the current situation in the dance world and to see if the aesthetic and treatment of dancers has improved at all since the dance community and the public have been made aware of the dangers.

The health and sanity of dancers are being sacrificed for this art form. Until 23 dancers, audiences, and management accept a new, healthier paradigm, dancers will continue to suffer. Segal (2001) articulates it best when he writes:

> What we accept as the "tradition" of extreme thinness is arguably just a mid-to-late 20th century whim of the white ballet establishment. And it needs to stop, for the health of the art form and the women dedicated to it, before ballet training becomes a symbol, like Chinese foot binding, of a society's cruel subjugation of women to a crippling, inhuman illusion. (p. 2)

References

Benn, T., & Walters, D. (2001). Between Scylla and Charybdis. Nutritional education versus body culture and the ballet aesthetic: The effects on the lives of female dancers. *Research in Dance Education, 2*(2), 139–154.

Farley, J. (1998). *Sociology* (4th ed.). Upper Saddle River, NJ: Prentice-Hall.

Gordon, S. (1983). *Off balance: The real world of ballet.* New York: Pantheon.

Hamilton, L. (1998). *Advice for dancers: Emotional counsel and practical strategies.* San Francisco: Jossey-Bass.

Jhally, S. (Producer). (1995). *Slim hopes: Advertising and the obsession with thinness* [Motion picture].

Kilbourne, J. (2002, February). *The naked truth: Advertising's image of women.* Presentation to Principia College, Elsah, IL.

Kirkland, G. (1986). *Dancing on my grave.* Garden City, NY: Doubleday.

Morgan, K. P. (1991). Women and the knife: Cosmetic surgery and the colonization of women's bodies. In L. Richardson, V. Taylor, and N. Whittier (Eds.), *Feminist frontiers* (pp. 116–127). New York: McGraw-Hill.

Saint Louis Ballet. (1993). Employment contract. St. Louis, MO: Saint Louis Ballet.

Segal, L. (2001, April 1). The shape of things to come. *Los Angeles Times.* Retrieved from http://www.latimes.com

Smith, C. (1998). On authoritarianism in the dance classroom. In S. B. Shapiro (Ed.), *Dance, power, and difference* (pp. 123–146). Leeds, UK: Human Kinetics.

Stinson, S. W. (1998). Seeking a feminist pedagogy for children's dance. In S. B. Shapiro (Ed.), *Dance, power, and difference* (pp. 23–48). Leeds, UK: Human Kinetics.

Reading Closely

1. According to Paula Kelso, where and how does American society get its ideals of female beauty? What is "not real" about them (2)? Why are ballerinas particularly susceptible to those ideals?

2. In Kelso's view, what was the role of choreographer George Balanchine and his followers in promoting "the skeletal look" among American ballerinas (5)? How convincing do you find Kelso's evidence?

3. One reason, supposedly, that ballerinas need to be thin is so that male dancers can lift them. How and how well does Kelso address this "myth" (10)? What other myths does she explore?

4. From their directors, teachers, and fellow students, says Kelso, young girls who aspire to become ballerinas often pick up a "generalized fear" (14). Of what? How and why is this fear "instilled" in them (14)?

Strategies and Structures

1. Why does Kelso begin her essay with a brief DESCRIPTION of the "magical" aspects of ballet (1)? What CONTRAST is she setting up? How effective do you find this opening strategy?

2. The IMMEDIATE CAUSE of anorexia nervosa is not eating enough calories to sustain life and health. What are some of the REMOTE CAUSES, especially among ballerinas, according to Kelso?

3. Of all the possible causes Kelso cites, which would you say is the MAIN CAUSE of the problems that plague ballerinas? Explain.

4. To support her analysis, Kelso uses a variety of brief EXAMPLES from outside sources, including stratified data about health issues, opinions from experts, and questions from ballerinas. Jot down five or six examples that you find particularly effective.

5. *Other Methods.* Kelso's analysis of causes and effects in the "abusive world" of professional ballet could be the basis of an ARGUMENT (1). What is her main PURPOSE in conducting the analysis, and how might she use the results to argue her point?

Thinking about Language

1. What are the CONNOTATIONS of *lurks* and *shadow* (1)?

2. Explain the specialized meanings, in a sociology paper, of the following terms: *socialized* (2), *normalize* (14), and *internalize* (14).

3. How and how effectively does Kelso use the "broken young children" SIMILE to develop her analysis (21)?

4. A PARADOX is an apparent contradiction that may, nonetheless, be true or valid. What is paradoxical about the observations that Kelso makes in paragraphs 17–21? What do they show about the culture of ballet in America?

For Writing

1. In a culture obsessed with thinness, why are so many Americans overweight? Draft the opening paragraph of the essay you might write if you were analyzing the causes of this phenomenon.

2. Write an essay that analyzes the causes and effects of a common eating disorder.

3. Swimmers have bodies distinctive to their sports. So do wrestlers, gymnasts, and cyclists. Write an analysis of a particular sport and the typical effects, psychological as well as physical, that it has upon the athlete. Don't forget to say how the "culture" of the sport contributes to these effects.

YANN MARTEL

How Pi Got His Name

*Yann Martel is a Canadian writer who was born in Spain in 1963. His parents were
civil servants, so the family moved often—to Alaska, Costa Rica, Mexico, France.
Martel attended college in Canada, graduating from Trent University as a philosophy
major. It was on top of a big boulder outside Bombay that the idea came to him to write
a novel in which religion intermingles with zoology. The result was the best-selling
book The Life of Pi (2002). "How Pi Got His Name" is a complete chapter from that
novel. Elsewhere in the book, Martel explains that his main character—who grows up
in India with the common family name Patel—is given his unusual first name, Piscine,
because his father has fond memories of a French swimming pool.*

*In this piece, the boys at Piscine Molitor Patel's English-speaking school in
Pondicherry, India, cruelly corrupt Pi's name. As a result of their mocking and teasing,
Pi eventually takes on a new name, thus asserting his own identity.*

M Y NAME ISN'T THE END OF THE STORY about my name. When your name is   1
Bob no one asks you, "How do you spell that?" Not so with Piscine Molitor Patel.[1]

Some thought it was P. Singh and that I was a Sikh,[2] and they wondered why I   2
wasn't wearing a turban.

In my university days I visited Montreal once with some friends. It fell to me to   3
order pizzas one night. I couldn't bear to have yet another French speaker guffaw-
ing at my name, so when the man on the phone asked, "Can I 'ave your name?" I
said, "I am who I am." Half an hour later two pizzas arrived for "Ian Hoolihan."

It is true that those we meet can change us, sometimes so profoundly that we are   4
not the same afterwards, even unto our names. Witness Simon who is called Peter,
Matthew also known as Levi, Nathaniel who is also Bartholomew, Judas, not Iscariot,
who took the name Thaddeus, Simeon who went by Niger, Saul who became Paul.[3]

My Roman soldier[4] stood in the schoolyard one morning when I was twelve. I   5

---

1. *Piscine Molitor Patel*: Patel is a common name in India and Pakistan. *Piscine* is the French word
for "swimming pool," and Piscine Molitor is the name of a famous public swimming pool in Paris,
France, that is in the process of being restored to its former glory.

2. *Sikh*: a follower of Sikhism, a monotheistic religion that was founded in India in 1469. Sikh men
wear turbans as a symbol of holiness.

3. *Simon/Peter . . . Saul/Paul*: Figures from early Christian history who were known by more than
one name after their encounters with Jesus.

4. *Roman soldier*: an allusion to the crucifixion of Jesus, when Roman soldiers placed a crown of
thorns on his head and mocked his title of "King of the Jews."

had just arrived. He saw me and a flash of evil genius lit up his dull mind. He raised his arm, pointed at me and shouted, "It's *Pissing* Patel!"

In a second everyone was laughing. It fell away as we filed into the class. I   6
walked in last, wearing my crown of thorns.

The cruelty of children comes as news to no one. The words would waft across   7
the yard to my ears, unprovoked, uncalled for: "Where's Pissing? I've got to go." Or: "You're facing the wall. Are you Pissing?" Or something of the sort. I would freeze or, the contrary, pursue my activity, pretending not to have heard. The sound would disappear, but the hurt would linger, like the smell of piss long after it has evaporated.

Teachers started doing it too. It was the heat. As the day wore on, the geography   8
lesson, which in the morning had been as compact as an oasis, started to stretch out like the Thar Desert;[5] the history lesson, so alive when the day was young, became parched and dusty; the mathematics lesson, so precise at first, became muddled. In their afternoon fatigue, as they wiped their foreheads and the backs of their necks with their handkerchiefs, without meaning to offend or get a laugh, even teachers forgot the fresh aquatic promise of my name and distorted it in a shameful way. By nearly imperceptible modulations I could hear the change. It was as if their tongues were charioteers driving wild horses. They could manage well enough the first syllable, the *Pea*, but eventually the heat was too much and they lost control of their frothy-mouthed steeds and could no longer rein them in for the climb to the second syllable, the *seen*. Instead they plunged hell-bent into *sing*, and next time round, all was lost. My hand would be up to give an answer, and I would be acknowledged with a "Yes, Pissing." Often the teacher wouldn't realize what he had just called me. He would look at me wearily after a moment, wondering why I wasn't coming out with the answer. And sometimes the class, as beaten down by the heat as he was, wouldn't react either. Not a snicker or a smile. But I always heard the slur.

I spent my last year at St. Joseph's School feeling like the persecuted prophet   9
Muhammad in Mecca, peace be upon him. But just as he planned his flight to Medina, the Hejira that would mark the beginning of Muslim time, I planned my escape and the beginning of a new time for me.[6]

After St. Joseph's, I went to Petit Séminaire, the best private English-medium   10

---

5. *Thar Desert*: a desert in southeastern Pakistan and northwestern India that covers seventy-seven thousand square miles. It is the seventh largest desert in the world and the largest on the Indian subcontinent.

6. *Muhammad . . . new time for me*: Muhammad was the prophet who founded Islam. He was born in Mecca, a city in present-day Saudi Arabia, in about 570 C.E. Muhammad was persecuted in Mecca for his religious beliefs, causing him to leave for the oasis of Yathrib (later the city of Medina) in about 622 C.E. This migration from Mecca to Medina became known as the Hejira.

secondary school in Pondicherry. Ravi was already there, and like all younger brothers, I would suffer from following in the footsteps of a popular older sibling. He was the athlete of his generation at Petit Séminaire, a fearsome bowler and a powerful batter, the captain of the town's best cricket[7] team, our very own Kapil Dev. That I was a swimmer made no waves; it seems to be a law of human nature that those who live by the sea are suspicious of swimmers, just as those who live in the mountains are suspicious of mountain climbers. But following in someone's shadow wasn't my escape, though I would have taken any name over "Pissing", even "Ravi's brother". I had a better plan than that.

I put it to execution on the very first day of school, in the very first class. Around   11
me were other alumni of St. Joseph's. The class started the way all new classes start, with the stating of names. We called them out from our desks in the order in which we happened to be sitting.

"Ganapathy Kumar," said Ganapathy Kumar.   12

"Vipin Nath," said Vipin Nath.   13

"Shamshool Hudha," said Shamshool Hudha.   14

"Peter Dharmaraj," said Peter Dharmaraj.   15

Each name elicited a tick on a list and a brief mnemonic stare from the teacher.   16
I was terribly nervous.

"Ajith Giadson," said Ajith Giadson, four desks away . . .   17

"Sampath Saroja," said Sampath Saroja, three away . . .   18

"Stanley Kumar," said Stanley Kumar, two away . . .   19

"Sylvester Naveen," said Sylvester Naveen, right in front of me.   20

It was my turn. Time to put down Satan. Medina, here I come.   21

I got up from my desk and hurried to the blackboard. Before the teacher could   22
say a word, I picked up a piece of chalk and said as I wrote:

$$\textit{My name is}$$
$$\textit{Piscine Molitor Patel,}$$
$$\textit{known to all as}$$

—I double underlined the first two letters of my given name—

$$\textit{Pi Patel}$$

7. *Cricket*: a British game something like baseball. Instead of a pitcher, cricket has a bowler; instead of bases, it has wickets. The game is popular in India and Pakistan as well as in Britain.

For good measure I added

$$\pi = 3.14$$

and I drew a large circle, which I then sliced in two with a diameter, to evoke that basic lesson of geometry.

There was silence. The teacher was staring at the board. I was holding my breath. Then he said, "Very well, Pi. Sit down. Next time you will ask permission before leaving your desk." 23

"Yes, sir." 24

He ticked my name off. And looked at the next boy. 25

"Mansoor Ahamad," said Mansoor Ahamad. 26

I was saved. 27

"Gautham Selvaraj," said Gautham Selvaraj. 28

I could breathe. 29

"Arun Annaji," said Arun Annaji. 30

A new beginning. 31

I repeated the stunt with every teacher. Repetition is important in the training not only of animals but also of humans. Between one commonly named boy and the next, I rushed forward and emblazoned, sometimes with a terrible screech, the details of my rebirth. It got to be that after a few times the boys sang along with me, a crescendo that climaxed, after a quick intake of air while I underlined the proper note, with such a rousing rendition of my new name that it would have been the delight of any choirmaster. A few boys followed up with a whispered, urgent "Three! Point! One! Four!" as I wrote as fast as I could, and I ended the concert by slicing the circle with such vigour that bits of chalk went flying. 32

When I put my hand up that day, which I did every chance I had, teachers granted me the right to speak with a single syllable that was music to my ears. Students followed suit. Even the St. Joseph's devils. In fact, the name caught on. Truly we are a nation of aspiring engineers: shortly after, there was a boy named Omprakash who was calling himself Omega, and another who was passing himself off as Upsilon, and for a while there was a Gamma, a Lambda and a Delta. But I was the first and the most enduring of the Greeks at Petit Séminaire. Even my brother, the captain of the cricket team, that local god, approved. He took me aside the next week. 33

"What's this I hear about a nickname you have?" he said. 34

I kept silent. Because whatever mocking was to come, it was to come. There was no avoiding it. 35

"I didn't realize you liked the color yellow so much." 36

The color yellow? I looked around. No one must hear what he was about to say, 37 especially not one of his lackeys. "Ravi, what do you mean?" I whispered.

"It's all right with me, brother. Anything's better than 'Pissing'. Even 'Lemon 38 Pie'."

As he sauntered away he smiled and said, "You look a bit red in the face." 39

But he held his peace. 40

And so, in that Greek letter that looks like a shack with a corrugated tin roof, in 41 that elusive, irrational number with which scientists try to understand the universe, I found refuge.

Reading Closely

1. What is Pi's real name? How does he get his first, unwanted nickname?

2. How does Pi establish his new, preferred nickname? What are the main steps in the PROCESS?

3. Young Pi has learned a useful lesson about people from his father, who is a zookeeper. What is the lesson, and how does Pi use it to his advantage?

4. Why "Pi"? There is the sound, but what other aspects of this mysterious Greek letter cause the young man to take "refuge" in it (41)?

5. The main "theme" of the entire book from which this piece is taken, says Martel, is "that reality is a story and we can choose our story and so why not pick 'the better story.' " How and how well does the story of Pi's name illustrate this main point?

Strategies and Structures

1. Names can have profound EFFECTS on personal identity. How do the EXAMPLES in paragraphs 2–4 illustrate this principle?

2. *How* Pi got his new name is also an account of *why* he had to change the old one. What are the main psychological CAUSES (or motives) for Pi's actions, as Martel tells the story?

3. Much of Pi's story consists of naming names. What technique does Martel use to keep the roster of names from becoming a mere list?

4. *Other Methods.* Martel uses two NARRATIVES in this cause-and-effect piece. What happens in each story? Try rewriting this material and just explaining how Pi's name came about—without using the stories. What are the advantages and disadvantages of giving the information directly, without the narratives?

THINKING ABOUT LANGUAGE

1. The cruel PUN, or play on words, on Piscine's first name requires that we know how to pronounce it properly in the first place. Where and how does Martel help his audience solve this little problem?

2. Martel uses METAPHORS from Christian, Muslim, and Sikh traditions. What are some of them, and how do they help identify the causes of Pi's actions and emotions?

3. Why does Pi describe the Greek letter from which he takes his name as a "shack" (41)?

FOR WRITING

1. Write a paragraph or two about how you or someone you know acquired a name or nickname. Be sure to set up the situation in terms of cause(s) and effect(s).

2. "The cruelty of children," says Pi, "comes as news to no one" (7). Write an essay agreeing or disagreeing with this statement. Analyze specific behaviors and the effects they have in a particular case or cases.

3. What's in a name? Shakespeare and others have posed the question and attempted to answer it. Write an essay ARGUING that names and other labels are (or are not) very significant.

CHAPTER II

Argument

Come now, and let us reason together . . .   —ISAIAH 1:18

Well, do you want to have just one argument, or were you thinking of taking a course?
                                                    —*Monty Python's Flying Circus*

For the sake of argument, let's assume that you are a parent, and you want your children to grow up in a safe and healthy environment. Consequently, you install a swimming pool in the backyard so they can learn to swim and get lots of good exercise.

No sooner has the concrete dried on your new pool when your next-door neighbor comes over and says, "Nice pool."

"Yeah," you reply, "we want our children to be healthy and strong—swimming is great exercise. Also, we want them to be safe; most of the earth's covered in water, you know, and they should learn how to swim."

"Right," says your neighbor. "But a pool like that's not a good idea for little kids. In fact, it's a safety hazard. Don't you know that far more children drown each year than die from gunshot wounds? Your kids would be much safer if you tore out that pool and bought a gun."

You disagree with your neighbor's belief that guns are safer than backyard swimming pools. Now you and your neighbor can *have* an argument—the kind that might degenerate into a shouting match—or you can rationally question your neighbor's claim and calmly state your own position on the matter. This second, more rational sort of argument is the subject of this chapter.

Defining Argument:
Making and Supporting a Claim

When you construct an argument, you take a position on an issue and you support that position with evidence. Suppose you believe that swimming pools are safe so long as they are properly fenced. This is your *claim*, and you can cite facts and figures, examples, expert testimony, or personal experience to support it.

In this chapter, we are going to examine how to make a claim and support it with evidence and logical reasoning. There are times, however, when logic isn't enough, so we will also learn how to appeal to our readers' emotions and how to establish our own credibility.

Why Do We Argue?

When we argue, we express our opinions and ideas in a way that gets others to take them seriously. Unlike statements of fact, opinions are not necessarily correct or incorrect. The ultimate purpose of a good argument is not to convince others that your claim is absolutely right or wrong. It is to demonstrate that it is plausible—worth listening to, and maybe even acting upon. Many arguments, in fact, ask the reader to *explore* an issue, not just accept or reject a particular claim. Exploratory arguments are intended to open up discussion, to help us gain new knowledge, and even to lead to some kind of consensus.

Composing an Argument

Writing that *argues* a claim and asks readers to agree with it is sometimes distinguished from writing that seeks to *persuade* readers to take action. In this chapter, however, we will use the terms *argue* and *persuade* more or less interchangeably, because there's not much point in arguing that a claim is correct if you can't also persuade the reader that it's worth acting on.

Any claim worth arguing about has more than one side, however; rational people can disagree with it. We can all agree that backyard swimming pools can be dangerous under certain circumstances. We might reasonably disagree, however, on what those circumstances are and what to do about them.

When you make a claim, it should be arguable in this sense of being debatable. Some claims cannot reasonably be argued. For instance:

- *Matters of taste*: I hate broccoli.
- *Matters of faith*: And on the third day He arose.
- *Matters of fact*: In 1996, 742 children under age 10 drowned in the United States.

Matters of fact can be contested, of course. You might, for instance, know of a case of drowning that went unreported, and so you would point out that the figure ought to be 743 instead of 742. But a claim like this does not leave much room for debate. It can be established simply by checking the facts. An argument can collapse if its facts are wrong, but a good argument does not just state the facts. It argues something significant *about* the facts.

So when you compose a written argument, make sure your claim is arguable, or open to opinion—and that it's one you actually have a stake in. If you don't really care much about your topic, your reader probably won't either.

Thinking about Purpose and Audience

When you compose an argument, your purpose is to persuade other people to hear you out, to listen thoughtfully to what you have to say—even if they don't completely accept your views. Whatever your claim, your argument is more likely to appeal to your audience if it is tailored to their particular needs and interests.

For example, your next-door neighbor might be more inclined to accept a swimming pool in your backyard if, in addition to addressing the safety issue, you also argued that a nice pool would increase property values in the neighborhood. On the other hand, if you need to persuade the city planning department to issue you a permit so that you can build a pool, you'd be better off telling them that, because there is no public pool within a reasonable distance from your house, children in your neighborhood must now travel too far just to enjoy a swim during the summer.

So as you compose an argument, think about what your readers' views on the particular issue are likely to be. Of all the evidence you might present in support of your case, what kind would your intended readers most likely find reasonable and, thus, convincing?

Generating Ideas: Finding Effective Evidence

You can start generating ideas by using the same techniques that you use with other kinds of writing, like LISTING and BRAINSTORMING.

The most important question to ask as you think about your argument is *why*— why should your audience accept your claim? What evidence—facts, figures, examples, and so on—can you provide to convince your readers that your claim is true? Let's look at some of the most effective types of evidence.

Suppose you want to argue that the SAT is unfair because it is biased in favor of certain socioeconomic groups. To support a claim like this effectively, you can use *facts, statistics, examples, personal experience,* and *expert testimony.*

Facts. Because facts can be verified, they make good evidence for persuading readers to accept your point of view. In an essay arguing that the SAT favors the wealthy, for example, you might cite facts about the cost of tutors for the test:

> In New York City, a company called Advantage charges $500 for 50 minutes of coaching with their most experienced tutors, and $165 for the same amount of time with their least experienced tutors.

Statistics. A particularly useful form of evidence when you want to show a tendency or trend is statistics. This type of evidence is also verifiable and, thus, convincing to many readers. You could, for example, support your claim that the SAT favors the wealthy by citing statistics about income and test scores:

> On the 1992 SAT, test takers with family incomes over $70,000 scored an average of 1000 points out of a possible 1600. On the same SAT, test takers with family incomes of less than $10,000 scored an average of 767 points out of a possible 1600.

Examples. Good examples make an argument more concrete and specific—and thus more likely to be understood and accepted by your audience. The following question, from an actual SAT exam, might be a good example of how the SAT favors wealthy students. The question asks the test taker to select a pair of words that matches the relationship expressed by the first pair:

RUNNER : MARATHON

(A) envoy : embassy

(B) martyr : massacre

(C) oarsman : regatta

(D) referee : tournament

(E) horse : stable

The correct answer is C: an oarsman competes in a regatta, an organized boat race, in much the same way as a runner competes in a marathon. But because regattas are, by and large, a pursuit of the wealthy, you could argue that the question favors the wealthy test taker—and so is a good example of socioeconomic bias in the SAT.

Expert testimony. One of the most effective kinds of evidence is the direct testimony of experts in the field you are writing about. For example, to make a serious case against the SAT, you might quote a statement like this by Richard Atkinson, former president of the University of California: "Anyone involved in education should be concerned about how overemphasis on the SAT is distorting educational priorities and practices, how the test is perceived by many as unfair, and how it can have a devastating impact on the self-esteem and aspirations of young students. . . . There is widespread agreement that overemphasis on the SAT harms American education."

Personal experience. Often you can effectively cite personal experience to support an argument, as with the following anecdote about how the SAT favors certain socioeconomic groups:

> No one in my family ever participated in a regatta—as a high school student, I didn't even know the meaning of the word. The only time I ever acted as an oarsman was in a leaky rowboat on Quarry Lake. So when I took the SAT a few years ago and encountered analogy questions that referred to regattas and other unfamiliar things, I barely broke 600 on the verbal aptitude section. Kenyon took me anyway, maybe because I play the violin. I graduated in the top ten percent of my class—with a combined major in music and English.

Many readers find personal testimony like this to be particularly moving, but be sure that any personal experience you cite as evidence is actually pertinent to the claim you're making.

No matter what type of evidence you present—whether facts and figures, examples, expert testimony, or personal experience—it must be pertinent to your argument and convince your audience that your claim is plausible and worth taking seriously.

Organizing and Drafting an Argument

Once you have a claim and evidence to support it, you're ready to start organizing and drafting your argument: to state your claim; appeal to your readers' needs and interests; and present yourself as trustworthy and reliable. You'll also need to anticipate and respond to likely objections. Finally, you'll want to think about which other methods of development, such as NARRATION and DEFINITION, might be useful in your argument. The tips on p. 493 can help you get started.

ORGANIZING AN ARGUMENT

Claim and support. Any well-constructed argument is organized around these two basic elements. Let's consider an argument by an economist who teaches at the

University of Chicago. In an editorial in the *Chicago Sun-Times* entitled "Pools More Dangerous Than Guns," Steven D. Levitt writes that "when it comes to children," a swimming pool in the backyard is more deadly than a gun in the house. This is Levitt's *claim*.

Levitt states this claim at the beginning of his argument, then gives evidence to support it in the next seven paragraphs of his essay. Most of his evidence is statistical: 742 drownings in one year, approximately 550 of those in residential pools; 6 million pools in the United States; 175 deaths as a result of guns; 200 million guns; one death per one million guns.

Levitt's evidence shows that approximately one child dies for every 11,000 pools in the United States, whereas one child dies for every one million guns. This is roughly a ratio of one hundred to one. Levitt concludes by connecting the dots for his readers when he says, "Thus, on average, the swimming pool is about 100 times more likely to kill a child than the gun is."

Levitt's argument follows a straightforward organization—claim, evidence, conclusion—that is effective for any argument:

1. State your claim clearly in your introduction.

2. In the main body of your argument, present evidence in support of your claim.

3. Develop the body of your argument until you have offered good reasons and sufficient evidence to support your claim.

4. In the conclusion, restate your claim and sum up how the evidence supports that claim.

STATING YOUR CLAIM

State your claim clearly and directly at the beginning of your argument—and take care not to claim more than you can possibly prove. As an arguable claim, "swimming pools are more dangerous than guns" is too broad. More dangerous for whom, we might ask? Under what circumstances?

We need to narrow this claim if we want to write an essay-length argument. We would do better to restate our claim as follows: "For young children who can't swim, swimming pools are more dangerous than guns." We have narrowed our claim to apply to a particular group, young children who do not yet know how to swim. Our claim could be still more restricted, however. In addition to narrowing it to a particular group, we could limit it to a particular kind of hazard. Thus we might write, "For young children who can't swim, *unprotected* swimming pools are more dangerous than guns." Because it is narrower, this is a more supportable claim than the one we started with.

TIPS AND TEMPLATES FOR DRAFTING

When you begin to draft an argument, you need to identify your subject and state the basic claim you plan to make about that subject. These moves are fundamental to any argument. See how Barack Obama makes these moves in his speech on "A More Perfect Union":

> [W]e cannot solve the challenges of our time unless we solve them together—unless we perfect our union by understanding that we may have different stories, but we hold common hopes; that we may not look the same and we may not have come from the same place, but we all want to move in the same direction—towards a better future for our children and our grandchildren.
>
> —BARACK OBAMA, "A More Perfect Union"

Obama identifies the subject of his argument ("the challenges of our time") and states his basic claim about that subject (that we must solve them together). Here is one more example from this chapter:

> Some have criticized the RIAA for going after students. But I would argue that it is entirely right—both legally and morally—for them to do so.
>
> —MARCI A. HAMILTON, "Why Suing College Students for Illegal Music Downloading Is Right"

The following templates can help you make some of these basic moves in your own writing. But don't take these as formulas where you just have to fill in the blanks. There are no easy formulas for good writing, but these templates can serve as starting points.

- ▶ In this argument about X, the main point I want to make is _____.
- ▶ Others may say _____, but I would argue that _____.
- ▶ My contention about X is supported by the fact that _____.
- ▶ Additional facts that support this view of X are _____, _____, and _____.
- ▶ My own experience with X shows that _____.
- ▶ My view of X is supported by _____, who says that X is _____.
- ▶ What you should do about X is _____.

USING LOGICAL REASONING: INDUCTION AND DEDUCTION

When Steven Levitt writes "Thus, on average, the swimming pool is about 100 times more likely to kill a child than the gun is," he is using logical reasoning. For certain purposes—such as convincing a toddler to stay clear of an unguarded swimming pool—logic is not very effective. In many writing situations, however, logical reasoning is indispensable for persuading others that your ideas and opinions are valid.

There are two main kinds of logical reasoning, *induction* and *deduction*. Induction is reasoning from particular evidence to a general conclusion. You reason inductively when you observe the cost of a gallon of gas at half-a-dozen service stations and conclude that the price of gas is uniformly high. Levitt uses induction in his argument about guns and swimming pools. He looks at the number of children who drowned in residential swimming pools in a particular year—550—and the number of children who died from gunshot wounds in the same year—175. Reasoning inductively from these particular cases, Levitt reaches his conclusion that pools are more dangerous than guns to young children.

Inductive reasoning is based on probability—it draws a conclusion from a limited number of specific cases. When you argue inductively, you are not claiming that a conclusion is certain but that it is likely. Even relatively few cases can provide you with the basis of a good inductive argument—if they are truly representative of a larger group. Exit polls of a few hundred people, for example, can often predict the outcome of an election involving thousands of voters. If it's truly representative, even a small sampling is sometimes enough. You would need only one or two cases of cholera on a high school swimming team, for instance, to infer that the pool in the gym is probably contaminated and that the whole school is in danger. Unless you take into account every possible individual case, though, inductive reasoning is never 100 percent certain: it usually requires an "inductive leap" at the end, as when you move from the individual cases of cholera on the team to the general inference that the school as a whole is threatened.

By contrast with induction, deduction moves from general principles to a particular conclusion. You reason deductively when your car stops running and— knowing that cars in general need fuel to run on and recalling that you started with half a tank and have been driving all day—you conclude that you are out of gas. Deductive arguments can be stated as SYLLOGISMS, which have a major premise, a minor premise, and a conclusion. For example:

Major premise: All unguarded swimming pools are dangerous.

Minor premise: This pool is unguarded.

Conclusion: This pool is dangerous.

This is a valid syllogism, meaning that the conclusion follows logically from the premises.

The great advantage of deduction over induction is that it deals with logical certainty rather than mere probability. As long as the premises you begin with are true and the syllogism is properly constructed, the conclusion must be true. But you can run into trouble when one or more of the premises are false, or when the syllogism isn't constructed properly.

In a properly constructed syllogism, the conclusion links the first part of the minor premise ("this pool") to the second part of the major premise ("dangerous"). One of the most common mistakes that people make in constructing syllogisms is simply repeating, in the minor premise, the trait named at the end of the major premise, as in the following example:

AN INVALID SYLLOGISM

Major premise: All planets are round.

Minor premise: My head is round.

Conclusion: My head is a planet.

Being round is a characteristic that "planets" and "my head" share, but many other things are round, too. A diagram can help us see why this syllogism doesn't work:

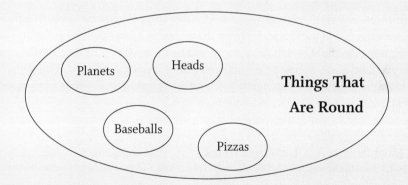

As this diagram illustrates, just being round doesn't mean that planets and heads have much else in common; in fact, they belong to entirely separate categories within the larger one of things that are round.

Advertisers use this kind of faulty reasoning all the time to try to convince you that you must buy their products if you want to be a cool person. Such reasoning is faulty because even if you accept the premise that, for example, all people who buy motorcycles are cool, there are lots of cool people who don't buy motorcycles—as indicated by the following diagram:

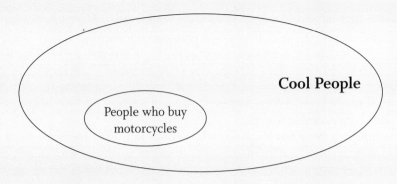

PROPERLY CONSTRUCTED SYLLOGISMS

Major premise: All planets are round.

Minor premise: Earth is a planet.

Conclusion: Earth is round.

Major premise: All people who buy motorcycles are cool.

Minor premise: Susan has bought a motorcycle.

Conclusion: Susan is cool.

Not so sure about this second example? Both of these syllogisms are valid—that is, the conclusion follows logically from the premises. A syllogism can be logically valid, however, and the conclusion may still be false—if one or more of the premises are false. (Not everyone would agree, for example, with the premise that all motorcycle owners are cool.) Study the following obvious example of a properly constructed syllogism with a false premise.

A PROPERLY CONSTRUCTED SYLLOGISM WITH A FALSE PREMISE

Major premise: All spiders have six legs.

Minor premise: The black widow is a spider.

Conclusion: The black widow has six legs.

The conclusion that black widows have six legs is logical, given the premises of this argument. However, since the major premise of the argument is wrong—spiders actually have eight legs—the conclusion of the argument is also wrong.

When you use deduction in your writing, your reader is less likely to question your reasoning if your argument follows the logic of a properly constructed syllogism or other model argument. Be prepared, however, to defend your premises if they are not as self-evident as "spiders have eight legs" or "all humans are mortal."

If you are arguing, for example, that intelligent design should be taught in science classes, you might structure your basic argument like this:

Major premise: All scientific theories should be taught in science classes.

Minor premise: Intelligent design is scientific theory.

Conclusion: Intelligent design should be taught in science classes.

This is a well-constructed deductive argument. As long as your readers accept the premises—particularly the minor premise about the scientific nature of intelligent design—they will probably accept your conclusion. If you believe, however, that some readers may disagree with the premises of your argument—and you still hope to convince them—you should provide strong evidence to support those premises. Or, if necessary, you should consider how you might rework your premises.

USING INDUCTION AND DEDUCTION IN VARIOUS ACADEMIC FIELDS

Because it draws upon observation and the analysis of particular data, induction is the method you are most likely to use when you construct an argument in the fields of engineering and the applied sciences. In the humanities and social sciences, induction is also particularly useful for analyzing specific written texts (the poems of Rita Dove, the letters of John Adams, a set of questionnaires) and for drawing general conclusions about them. You also use inductive reasoning when you cite personal experience as evidence, because you are arguing that something you observed or experienced personally has general significance for others.

Deductive reasoning is particularly useful for constructing arguments in the fields of philosophy, ethics, theology, and the more theoretical sciences, such as mathematics and physics, where particular cases tend to be subject to universal principles (such as $E=MC^2$). For example, the argument that a large round object recently discovered in the night sky should be classified as a planet because it meets all the criteria that define planets in general would be a deductive argument.

AVOIDING LOGICAL FALLACIES

Logical fallacies are errors in logical reasoning. Though they can seem plausible and even persuasive, they lead to wrong-headed conclusions. Here are some of the most common logical fallacies to watch out for when you write (and read).

Post hoc, ergo propter hoc. Latin for "after this, therefore because of this," this kind of faulty reasoning assumes that just because one event (such as rain) comes after another event (a rain dance), it occurs *because* of the first event. For example: "Soon after the country declared war, the divorce rate increased. War is harmful to marriages." Just because the country declared war before the divorce rate went up doesn't mean the declaration caused the increase.

THE TOULMIN METHOD

In a formal deductive argument, we begin with two general principles and draw a conclusion based on the logical relationship between them. In practical arguments, however, as the British philosopher Stephen Toulmin recognized, we often begin with a conclusion and look around for evidence to support it. Recognizing this less formal kind of deduction, Toulmin devised a system of argument that combines both logic and observation.

In Toulmin's system, an argument is made up of three basic parts: the *claim*, the *grounds*, and the *warrant*. For example:

Claim: Steven Spielberg is the greatest director in the history of film.
Grounds: His films have grossed more than those of any other director.
Warrant: The best measure of a film's quality is financial success.

The claim is the main point the argument is intended to prove. The grounds are the evidence on which that claim is based. And the warrant is the reason that the grounds justify the claim.

In a Toulmin argument, the grounds can be facts, statistics, examples, expert testimony, personal experience, or other kinds of evidence. It is an observable fact, for instance, that Spielberg has grossed approximately $8 billion at the box office—more than any other director in film history.

Though they constitute grounds for a claim, facts and other data are not alone sufficient, in Toulmin's view, to support that claim completely. It takes logic as well: a warrant is needed to explain how and why the grounds logically justify the claim. In this case, the warrant for accepting the claim about Spielberg as the world's greatest filmmaker is the assumption that films and directors are best judged by how much money they make.

Not everyone would agree with this assumption, of course. Most real-life arguments, in fact, are about the assumptions on which the argument is based. But breaking an argument down into Toulmin's three parts can be especially useful for spotting faulty or unstated assumptions—so you can strengthen them in your own arguments or question them in the arguments of others.

Non sequitur. Latin for "does not follow," a non sequitur is a statement that has little or no logical connection to the preceding statement: "The early Egyptians were masters of architecture and geometry. Thus they created a vast network of trade and commerce throughout the ancient world." Since mastering architecture and geometry has little to do with trade, this second statement is a non sequitur.

Begging the question. An argument that begs the question takes for granted what it is supposed to prove: "Americans should be required to carry ID cards because Americans need to be prepared to prove their identity." This statement assumes that Americans should have to prove their identity.

Appeal to doubtful authority. This is the fallacy of citing as expert testimony the opinions of people who do not necessarily have special knowledge of the issue: "According to Jay Leno, the candidate who takes South Carolina will win the election." Leno isn't an expert on politics, so citing his opinion on political matters to support an argument is an appeal to doubtful authority.

Ad hominem. This fallacy attacks the person making an argument instead of addressing the actual issue: "She's the head of the union, and she's crazy. Don't pay any attention to her views on the economy." Saying she's the head of a union and calling her crazy focuses on her as a person rather than on her views of the issue.

Either/or reasoning. This fallacy, sometimes called a "false dilemma," treats a complicated issue as if it had only two sides: "Either you believe that God created the universe according to His plan, which is the view of religion; or you believe that the universe evolved randomly, which is the view of science." This statement doesn't allow for beliefs outside of these two options.

Hasty generalization. This fallacy draws a conclusion based on far too little evidence: "In all four of the stories by Edgar Allan Poe that we read for English 201, the narrator is mentally ill. Poe himself must have been mad." There is not nearly enough evidence here to determine Poe's mental health.

False analogy. This fallacy is committed when an argument is based on a faulty comparison: "Children are like dogs. A happy dog is a disciplined dog, and a happy child is one who knows the rules and is taught to obey them." Dogs and children aren't alike enough to assume that what is good for one is good for the other.

APPEALING TO YOUR READER'S EMOTIONS

Sound logical reasoning is hard to refute, but sometimes, in order to persuade readers to accept your claim, it will help to appeal to their emotions as well.

As an economist writing for a general audience, Steven Levitt knows that people often find numbers dry and unmoving, so after citing statistics, he goes on to appeal to the emotions and feelings of readers, especially those who are parents.

USING ROGERIAN ARGUMENT

The psychologist Carl Rogers recognized that people are much more likely to listen to someone they feel is listening to them. If you want to persuade others to accept your views, Rogers reasoned, it is better to treat them as colleagues rather than adversaries. Instead of an "I'm right and you're wrong" approach, therefore, Rogers recommended using "win-win" strategies of argument that invite collaboration and consensus rather than confrontation and conflict. In other words, instead of *having* an argument, the Rogerian approach says, with Isaiah, "Come let us reason together."

To use Rogerian methods of argument in your own writing, you need to show your audience that you are well aware that the issue at hand can be viewed in different lights and that you have thoughtfully considered viewpoints other than your own. To do this, summarize opposing viewpoints carefully and accurately, and acknowledge their merit. Then introduce your views and look for common ground between them and the views of others. Explain how your views address these common concerns and what additional advantages they have, and give evidence in support of your point of view.

For example, suppose that you are in favor of greater gun-control legislation. Instead of lashing out at all gun owners, however, you decide to try a more conciliatory, Rogerian approach. You might begin by acknowledging that the U.S. Constitution guarantees certain rights to individuals, in particular the right to self-defense and to protect personal property. You might also acknowledge that many people, including hunters and target shooters, look upon certain types of guns as gear or sporting goods. Others view them as collectibles and are interested in their history and manufacture.

Once you have shown your genuine concern and respect for the rights and enthusiasms of gun owners, you could look for ways in which gun-control legislation may actually serve their interests. For example, you might point out that strict licensing and training in the proper handling of firearms can help reduce injury and death among those who use guns for sport. In the event of theft, you might note, enforced registration of guns would also help collectors and other owners of valuable firearms to retrieve their stolen property. You might even concede that stricter gun-control legislation probably is not necessary in the case of people who already abide by existing gun-control laws, own guns legally, and use them responsibly. Having established as much common ground as you can among the parties in the gun-control debate, you are now ready to introduce and explain your position.

You favor stricter gun controls, even to the point of banishing firearms altogether. Why? You believe that guns are inherently dangerous and that they can fall into the hands of people who do not abide by the rules. Also, they can be *accidentally* misused. Wouldn't society as a whole be better off, you wonder, if guns were all but impossible to obtain—even if that meant curtailing the rights of some individuals? You realize that not everyone will agree with this position; but having made clear that you understand and sympathize with the views of the other side, you can reasonably expect that those who might otherwise dismiss your claims out of hand will be more inclined to listen to you. And you can even hope that readers who are not committed to either point of view will be more likely to adopt yours.

Levitt says his purpose is not to promote guns but to "focus parents on an even greater threat to their children," observing that it takes only thirty seconds for a child to drown, that child drownings are "typically silent," and that as a parent, if you let your guard down for an instant, a pool (or even a bucket of water) "may steal your child's life."

Steal is a carefully chosen word here. It implies evil intent—the pool lies in wait for the child, like a thief. We are well beyond logic and statistics now. Evil that is quick and silent demands an ever-watchful parent: "Simply stated, keeping your children safe around water is one of the single most important things a parent can do to protect a child."

Emotional? Of course. But this is emotionalism in a good cause, carefully applied to support a well-reasoned argument. And often, the best way to urge your readers to action is by tugging at their heartstrings. When you appeal to the reader's emotions, however, be careful to avoid sensationalism and alarmism—they can undermine your argument. So after sounding the alarm, Levitt calmly directs readers to the website of the U.S. Consumer Products Safety Commission, which "offers a publication detailing some simple steps for safeguarding pools."

ESTABLISHING YOUR OWN CREDIBILITY

When you construct an argument, you can demonstrate with irrefutable logic that what you have to say is valid and true. And you can appeal to the reader's emotions with genuine fervor. Your words may still fall on deaf ears, however, if your readers don't fully trust you. What makes Levitt's argument so credible in the end is that he himself has lost a child.

Levitt's first child, Andrew, did not drown. When the boy was just over a year old, he came down with meningitis and, within two days, died in the hospital. Levitt wrote his essay, in part, to channel a father's grief, which gives him an emotional and ethical authority that nothing else could. "As a father who has lost a son," Levitt writes, "I know first-hand the unbearable pain that comes with a child's death."

Levitt's loss is different in one crucial regard from that of the parent whose child dies in an unguarded swimming pool. "Amidst my grief," he says, "I am able to take some small solace in the fact that everything possible was done to fight the disease that took my son's life." Having said this, the grieving father closes with a final appeal to the reader, whom he addresses directly in the second person: "If my son had died in a backyard pool due to my own negligence, I would not even have that to cling to. . . . Parents who have lost children would do anything to get their babies back. . . . Safeguard your pool so you don't become one of us." You don't need to have children or a swimming pool to recognize the power of such an argument. Nor do you need such a close, personal tie to your subject in order to establish your own credibility.

There are many less dramatic ways to establish your credibility when you construct an argument. Readers are more likely to trust you, for example, if they feel you are presenting the issues objectively. So acknowledge opposing points of view, and treat them fairly and accurately.

If you have experience or special expertise in your subject, let your readers know. For instance, if you're arguing that American ballet companies require their dancers to be too thin and you danced with a professional ballet company for three years, tell your readers that. Also, pay close attention to the tone of your argument. Whether you come across as calm and reasonable or full of righteous anger, your tone will say much about your own values and motives for writing—and about you as a person. Nothing does more to establish your credibility with your readers than to persuade them that they are listening to the words of a moral and ethical person who shares their values and understands their concerns.

ANTICIPATING OTHER ARGUMENTS

As you construct an argument, it's important to consider viewpoints other than your own, including objections that others might raise to your argument. Anticipating other arguments, in fact, is yet another way to establish your credibility and win the reader's confidence. Readers are more likely to see you as trustworthy if, instead of ignoring an opposing argument, you state it fairly and accurately and then refute it—by showing that the reasoning is faulty or that the evidence is insufficient or that the argument fails to consider some key aspect of the subject.

For instance, suppose you think that private ownership of firearms is a deterrent to crime and you oppose stricter gun-control laws. Some of your readers, however, may believe that private ownership of guns actually *increases* crime, and they may be prepared to cite studies showing that there are more homicides in places where there are more guns.

Anticipating this argument, you might refute it by saying, "Proponents of stricter gun-control legislation are right when they cite studies showing that more homi-cides occur in places where more people have guns. However, such studies refer, by and large, to 'loose' firearms. The situation is different where guns are protected—kept under lock and key where a child or intruder can't get to them. Responsible gun ownership actually reduces crime." Proponents of stricter gun controls still may not be entirely convinced, but they are far more likely to listen to your argument because you readily admit that guns can be dangerous and you address, head-on, a major point of opposition to your views.

Even when you do not have a ready response to an opposing argument, you'll still want to acknowledge it in order to show that you've thought carefully about all aspects of the issue.

USING OTHER METHODS

Each method of writing discussed in chapters 3–10 can be useful when you con-struct an argument. If you are arguing for (or against) stricter gun-control laws, for example, you will need to DEFINE the present rules and what you mean by "stricter" ones. You may also need to use CAUSE-AND-EFFECT ANALYSIS to explain what good (or harm) new laws would do. Or you may want to COMPARE AND CON-TRAST the old laws with the new ones; or draw on PROCESS ANALYSIS to explain how the new laws will be enforced.

Reading an Argument with a Critical Eye

Once you have a draft of your argument, ask someone to read it and tell you where your case seems particularly convincing and where it seems to break down. Then read the argument again critically yourself. Here are some questions to guide you (and any other readers) as you assess a written argument:

PURPOSE AND AUDIENCE.   What is the basic purpose of the argument—To inform? To move the reader to action? Some other purpose? How well does the argument achieve its purpose? How might it be revised to do so better? Who is the intended audience? What will they know about the topic, and will they need any additional background information? What are their views likely to be on the topic?

THE CLAIM.   What is the claim? Is it stated clearly and directly in a thesis statement? If not, should it be? Is it arguable—could reasonable people disagree about it? Is the claim limited enough to be covered well? If not, how could it be narrowed down fur-ther? Is it clear why this claim is significant, and why the reader should care about it?

EVIDENCE.   What evidence is given to support the claim? Is it factually correct? If personal experience is cited as evidence, is it pertinent? Is the evidence sufficient to support the claim, or is additional evidence needed? What kind?

LOGICAL REASONING.   How well do the parts of the essay hold together? What kind of reasoning connects the evidence with the claim—Inductive? Deductive? Both? In general, how *convincing* is the argument? How could it be strengthened?

EMOTIONAL APPEALS.   Does the argument appeal to readers' emotions? If so, to what end—to evoke readers' concerns, to move them to action? Is any emotional appeal sufficiently restrained? Is it convincing? If there's no emotional appeal, should there be?

CREDIBILITY.   What kind of person does the author of this argument seem to be? Does he or she come across as an ethical person of good character who shares and respects readers' values? If not, what changes could convey that credibility? What special experience or knowledge, if any, does the author bring to this particular issue? In sum, does the author seem trustworthy?

ANTICIPATING OTHER ARGUMENTS.   What other arguments might someone make about the topic? What objections might they raise to the claim? Are other arguments respectfully acknowledged and, where possible, refuted?

OTHER METHODS.   What other methods of development does the argument use? For example, does it DEFINE the issues clearly? Does it ANALYZE CAUSES AND EFFECTS? Does it give specific EXAMPLES? If other methods are not used, where might they be helpful?

Editing for Common Errors in Arguments

Certain grammatical errors are common in arguments. The following guidelines will help you check for such problems—and edit them as needed.

Check your punctuation with subordinating conjunctions such as *if, therefore, thus, consequently, however, nevertheless,* and *because.*

When the subordinating conjunction comes at the beginning of a sentence and links it to an earlier statement, the conjunction should be followed by a comma:

▶ Therefore, the minimum legal drinking age should not be lowered to age 18.

▶ Consequently, stronger immigration laws will be unnecessary.

When the subordinating conjunction comes at the beginning of a sentence and is part of an introductory clause—a group of words that includes a subject and verb—the entire clause should be followed by a comma:

▸ Because guest workers will be legally registered, stronger immigration laws will be unnecessary.

▸ If acting legally is just as easy as acting illegally, most people will choose the legal course of action.

When a subordinating conjunction joins two independent clauses—groups of words that can stand alone as complete sentences—the conjunction is preceded by a semicolon and followed by a comma:

▸ Many of the best surgeons have the highest rates of malpractice; thus, the three-strikes-and-you're-out rule for taking away a doctor's license may do more harm than good.

When the subordinating conjunction comes in the middle of an independent clause, it should be set off by commas:

▸ A physician who removes the wrong leg, however, clearly deserves a much harsher penalty than one who forgets to remove a sponge.

Check for common usage errors.

HOWEVER, NEVERTHELESS

Use *however* when you acknowledge a different argument but want to minimize its consequence:

▸ The surgeon may have been negligent; however, he should not lose his license because the patient lied about the dosage he was taking.

Use *nevertheless* when you acknowledge a different argument but wish to argue for a harsher consequence anyway:

▸ The surgeon may not have been negligent; nevertheless, he should lose his license because the patient died.

IMPLY, INFER

Use *imply* when you mean "to state indirectly":

▸ The coach's speech implied that he expected the team to lose the game.

Use *infer* when you mean "to draw a conclusion":

▸ From the coach's speech, the audience inferred that the team would lose the game.

Life Is Good

An argument makes a claim—in the example here, that "life is good"—and supports it with facts, figures, and other evidence, including the testimony of experts. In the case of the "Life is good" brand of clothing and accessories, the main evidence that the company offers to back up this sweeping claim is Jake, the broadly smiling stick-figure in a beret who appears on many of their products. In 1994, Bert and John Jacobs, the founders of the company, chose Jake as their spokesperson because he was "a symbol about what was right in the world." Since then, Jake has symbolized the good life on millions of tee-shirts and coffee mugs—a projected $135 million worth in 2008 alone. Whether he's plinking his guitar, kicking back in a beach chair, or roasting marshmallows with his dog Rocket, Jake beams the message that happiness lies in the simple pleasures of life and is thus within the grasp of just about anyone. Such an argument appeals more to an audience's feelings and emotions, of course, than to its reason and logic. But so moving is the personal testimony of the cheerful Jake, apparently, that his smiling image has not only convinced consumers to accept his company's optimistic premise about life, but to wear it on their sleeves—and hats and dog collars.

EVERYDAY ARGUMENT

THOMAS JEFFERSON

The Declaration of Independence

Thomas Jefferson (1743–1826) was born to a wealthy landowning family in colonial Virginia and studied mathematics and political philosophy at William and Mary College. He became a lawyer and was elected to the Virginia legislature in 1769, where he was a leading spokesman for the cause of American independence. During the Revolutionary War, he served as governor of Virginia; afterward, he became the nation's first Secretary of State. He served as John Adams's vice-president and was elected president himself in 1800. Jefferson was also one of the leading architects of his day, and an inventor, naturalist, archeologist, violinist, horticulturist, and patron of the arts.

Jefferson stipulated that his epitaph would mention only three of his many achievements: author of Virginia's Statute of Religious Freedom, founder of the University of Virginia, and author of the Declaration of Independence. In its form and intent, the Declaration of Independence is primarily an argument—a point-by-point justification for American independence. Lawyerly in tone, it is essentially a legal brief addressed to both the British throne and the court of world opinion. The Declaration lists the colonists' grievances against the British king and concludes that Americans are left with no recourse but full independence. The document's ratification by the Continental Congress on July 4, 1776, marked the birth of the United States.

WHEN IN THE COURSE OF HUMAN EVENTS, it becomes necessary for one people 1 to dissolve the political bands which have connected them with another, and to assume among the powers of the earth, the separate and equal station to which the Laws of Nature and of Nature's God entitle them, a decent respect to the opinions of mankind requires that they should declare the causes which impel them to the separation.

We hold these truths to be self-evident, that all men are created equal, that they 2 are endowed by their Creator with certain unalienable Rights, that among these are Life, Liberty and the pursuit of Happiness. That to secure these rights, Governments are instituted among Men, deriving their just powers from the consent of the governed. That whenever any Form of Government becomes destructive of these ends, it is the Right of the People to alter or to abolish it, and to institute new Government, laying its foundation on such principles and organizing its powers in such form, as to them shall seem most likely to effect their Safety and Happiness. Prudence, indeed, will dictate that Governments long established should not be changed for light and transient causes; and accordingly all experience hath shewn, that mankind are more disposed to suffer, while evils are sufferable, than to right themselves by abolishing the forms to which they are accustomed. But when a long train of abuses and usurpations pursuing invariably the same Object evinces a design to reduce them under absolute Despotism, it is their right, it is their duty, to throw off such Government, and to provide new Guards for their future security. Such has been the patient sufferance of these Colonies; and such is now the necessity which constrains them to alter their former Systems of Government. The history of the present King of Great Britain[1] is a history of repeated injuries and usurpations, all having in direct object the establishment of absolute Tyranny over these States. To prove this, let Facts be submitted to a candid world.

He has refused his Assent to Laws, the most wholesome and necessary for the public good.　3

He has forbidden his Governors to pass Laws of immediate and pressing importance, unless suspended in their operation till his Assent should be obtained; and when so suspended, he has utterly neglected to attend to them.　4

He has refused to pass other Laws for the accommodation of large districts of people, unless those people would relinquish the right of Representation in the Legislature, a right inestimable to them and formidable to tyrants only.　5

He has called together legislative bodies at places unusual, uncomfortable, and distant from the depository of their public Records, for the sole purpose of fatiguing them into compliance with his measures.　6

He has dissolved Representative Houses repeatedly, for opposing with manly firmness his invasions on the rights of the people.　7

He has refused for a long time, after such dissolutions, to cause others to be elected; whereby the Legislative powers, incapable of Annihilation, have returned to the People at large for their exercise; the State remaining in the mean time exposed to all the dangers of invasion from without, and convulsions within.　8

He has endeavoured to prevent the population of these States; for that purpose obstructing the Laws of Naturalization of Foreigners; refusing to pass others to encourage their migration hither, and raising the conditions of new Appropriations of Lands.　9

He has obstructed the Administration of Justice, by refusing his Assent to Laws for establishing Judiciary powers.　10

He has made Judges dependent on his Will alone, for the tenure of their offices, and the amount and payment of their salaries.　11

He has erected a multitude of New Offices, and sent hither swarms of Officers to harass our people, and eat out their substance.　12

He has kept among us, in time of peace, Standing Armies without the Consent of our legislatures.　13

---

1. *The present King of Great Britain*: George III (1738–1820), who ruled from 1760 to 1820.

He has affected to render the Military independent of and superior to the Civil 14
power.

He has combined with others to subject us to a jurisdiction foreign to our con- 15
stitution, and unacknowledged by our laws; giving his Assent to their acts of pretended Legislation:

For Quartering large bodies of armed troops among us: 16

For protecting them, by a mock Trial, from punishment for any Murders which 17
they should commit on the Inhabitants of these States:

For cutting off our Trade with all parts of the world: 18

For imposing Taxes on us without our Consent: 19

For depriving us in many cases, of the benefits of Trial by Jury: 20

For transporting us beyond the Seas to be tried for pretended offenses: 21

For abolishing the free System of English Laws in a neighbouring Province, 22
establishing therein an Arbitrary government, and enlarging its Boundaries so as to
render it at once an example and fit instrument for introducing the same absolute
rule into these Colonies:

For taking away our Charters, abolishing our most valuable Laws, and altering 23
fundamentally the Forms of our Governments:

For suspending our own Legislatures, and declaring themselves invested with 24
power to legislate for us in all cases whatsoever.

He has abdicated Government here, by declaring us out of his Protection and 25
waging War against us.

He has plundered our seas, ravaged our Coasts, burnt our towns and destroyed 26
the lives of our people.

He is at this time transporting large Armies of foreign Mercenaries to compleat 27
the works of death, desolation and tyranny, already begun with circumstances of
Cruelty & perfidy scarcely paralleled in the most barbarous ages, and totally unwor-
thy the Head of a civilized nation.

He has constrained our fellow Citizens taken Captive on the high Seas to bear 28
Arms against their Country, to become the executioners of their friends and
Brethren, or to fall themselves by their Hands.

He has excited domestic insurrections amongst us, and has endeavoured to 29
bring on the inhabitants of our frontiers, the merciless Indian Savages, whose
known rule of warfare, is an undistinguished destruction of all ages, sexes and conditions.

In every stage of these Oppressions We have Petitioned for Redress in the most 30
humble terms: Our repeated Petitions have been answered only by repeated injury.
A Prince, whose character is thus marked by every act which may define a Tyrant,
is unfit to be the ruler of a free people.

Nor have We been wanting in attentions to our British brethren. We have 31 warned them from time to time of attempts by their legislature to extend an unwarrantable jurisdiction over us. We have reminded them of the circumstances of our emigration and settlement here. We have appealed to their native justice and magnanimity, and we have conjured them by the ties of our common kindred to disavow these usurpations, which would inevitably interrupt our connections and correspondence. They too have been deaf to the voice of justice and of consanguinity. We must, therefore acquiesce in the necessity, which denounces our Separation, and hold them, as we hold the rest of mankind, Enemies in War, in Peace Friends.

We, therefore, the Representatives of the United States of America, in General   32
Congress, Assembled, appealing to the Supreme Judge of the world for the rectitude of our intentions, do, in the Name, and by Authority of the good People of these Colonies, solemnly publish and declare, That these United Colonies are, and of Right ought to be Free and Independent States; that they are Absolved from all Allegiance to the British Crown, and that all political connection between them and the State of Great Britain, is and ought to be totally dissolved; and that as Free and Independent States, they have full Power to levy War, conclude Peace, contract Alliances, establish Commerce, and to do all other Acts and Things which Independent States may of right do. And for the support of this Declaration, with a firm reliance on the protection of divine Providence, we mutually pledge to each other our Lives, our Fortunes and our sacred Honor.

READING CLOSELY

1. According to Thomas Jefferson (and the other signers of the Declaration of Independence) what is the purpose of government?

2. What claim is Jefferson making on the basis that King George's government has not fulfilled the purpose of government? What remedy is he calling for?

3. Of the many "injuries and usurpations" that Jefferson attributes to the British king, which seem most intolerable to you (2)? Why?

STRATEGIES AND STRUCTURES

1. "We hold these truths to be self-evident" (2). Another name for self-evident truths stated at the beginning of an ARGUMENT is *premises*. On what specific premises is Jefferson's argument based? Which ones are most critical to his case?

2. Is the underlying logic of the Declaration basically inductive or deductive? Or both? Explain.

3. Paragraph 31 seems to be a digression from Jefferson's main line of argument. Why do you think he includes it?

4. Jefferson and the other signers of the Declaration made their case for independence on logical grounds. Many of the issues they addressed, however, were highly emotional. Where and how does the Declaration appeal to the emotions of its audience as well as their sense of reason?

5. How does the Declaration present the authors as men of good character who want to do what is morally right? Refer to paragraph numbers in your response.

6. *Other Methods.* Jefferson says that King George has committed "every act which may define a Tyrant" (30). How does Jefferson use this DEFINITION to support his argument that the king is unfit to rule a free people?

Thinking about Language

1. In modern English, "unalienable" (2) should be *inalienable*. Why do you think a person of Jefferson's intelligence and education would make this error?

2. Why does Jefferson begin so many of his sentences with the personal pronoun *he*, referring to King George?

3. What is "consanguinity" (31)? How can it be said to have a "voice"?

4. According to your dictionary, do most of the following words derive from Latin or Anglo-Saxon? Why do you think the signers of the Declaration used such a vocabulary to address the king of England?

transient (2)	*usurpations* (2)	*evinces* (2)
despotism (2)	*constrains* (2)	*candid* (2)
abdicated (25)	*perfidy* (27)	*redress* (30)
magnanimity (31)	*acquiesce* (31)	*rectitude* (32)?

For Writing

1. You are King George, and you've just received the Declaration of Independence, a direct challenge to your authority over the American colonies. Compose a few paragraphs replying to Jefferson's charges and defending your actions and policies toward the colonies. Assume that the Declaration accurately describes those actions—don't base your argument on a denial.

2. Compose an essay arguing that "the pursuit of Happiness" (2) is unwise, that happiness cannot be guaranteed, and that the excessive pursuit of anything can lead to chaos in the life of the individual and in the state. Or, alternatively, defend Jefferson's claim that the pursuit of happiness is an inalienable right.

CHIEF SEATTLE

Reply to the U.S. Government

Chief Seattle (1786–1866) rose to leadership of the Suquamish and Duwamish Indian tribes through his prowess as a warrior, but he is remembered mainly as a man of peace. When his eldest son was killed in a fight with a rival tribe, he sought consolation from nearby Roman Catholic missionaries and was baptized in 1848. Though broken-hearted by the loss of the traditional Indian way of life, Seattle believed that the influx of white immigrants into his native Puget Sound region was unstoppable and that only by accommodating them could his people survive. The settlers reciprocated by naming their new city after him.

Seattle's reputation as an orator is legendary—literally so, because no authentic record exists of Seattle's words in his own language, Lushootseed. In 1854, the territorial governor of the Pacific Northwest, Isaac I. Stevens, presented Seattle with a formal U.S. government offer to buy over two million acres of Indian land around Puget Sound. Seattle responded with an impassioned speech—which was first published thirty-three years later in the Seattle Sunday Star, *"translated" by Dr. Henry A. Smith, who indeed had been present at the speech but who spoke no Lushootseed. In any case, the text we have of Seattle's speech rings true as an eloquent assertion of the rights and dignity of his people.*

YONDER SKY that has wept tears of compassion upon my people for centuries untold, and which to us appears changeless and eternal may change. Today is fair. Tomorrow may be overcast with clouds. My words are like the stars that never change. Whatever Seattle says the great chief at Washington can rely upon with as much certainty as he can upon the return of the sun or the seasons. The White Chief says that Big Chief at Washington sends us greetings of friendship and good-will. That is kind of him for we know he has little need of our friendship in return. His people are many. They are like the grass that covers vast prairies. My people are few. They resemble the scattering trees of a storm-swept plain. The great, and—I presume—good, White Chief sends us word that he wishes to buy our lands but is willing to allow us enough to live comfortably. This indeed appears just, even generous, for the Red Man no longer has rights that he need respect, and the offer may be wise also, as we are no longer in need of an extensive country. . . . I will not dwell on, nor mourn over, our untimely decay, nor reproach our paleface brothers with hastening it, as we too may have been somewhat to blame.

Youth is impulsive. When our young men grow angry at some real or imaginary wrong, and disfigure their faces with black paint, it denotes that their hearts are black, and then they are often cruel and relentless, and our old men and old women are unable to restrain them. Thus it has ever been. Thus it was when the white men first began to push our forefathers further westward. But let us hope that the hostilities between us may never return. We would have everything to lose and nothing to gain. Revenge by young men is considered gain, even at the cost of their own lives, but old men who stay at home in times of war, and mothers who have sons to lose, know better.

Our good father at Washington—for I presume he is now our father as well as   3
yours, since King George[1] has moved his boundaries further north—our great good father, I say, sends us word that if we do as he desires he will protect us. His brave warriors will be to us a bristling wall of strength, and his wonderful ships of war will fill our harbors so that our ancient enemies far to the northward—the Hydas and Tsimpsians[2]—will cease to frighten our women, children, and old men. Then in reality will he be our father and we his children. But can that ever be? Your God is not our God! Your God loves your people and hates mine. He folds his strong and protecting arms lovingly about the paleface and leads him by the hand as a father leads his infant son—but He has forsaken His red children—if they really are his. Our God, the Great Spirit, seems also to have forsaken us. Your God makes your people wax strong every day. Soon they will fill the land. Our people are ebbing away like a rapidly receding tide that will never return. The white man's God cannot love our people or He would protect them. They seem to be orphans who can look nowhere for help. How then can we be brothers? How can your God become our God and renew our prosperity and awaken in us dreams of returning greatness? If we have a common heavenly father He must be partial—for He came to his paleface children. We never saw Him. He gave you laws but He had no word for His red children whose teeming multitudes once filled this vast continent as stars fill the firmament. No; we are two distinct races with separate origins and separate destinies. There is little in common between us.

To us the ashes of our ancestors are sacred and their resting place is hallowed   4
ground. You wander far from the graves of your ancestors and seemingly without regret. Your religion was written upon tablets of stone[3] by the iron finger of your God so that you could not forget. The Red Man could never comprehend nor remember it. Our religion is the traditions of our ancestors—the dreams of our old

---

1. *King George*: George IV (1762–1830), king of England from 1820 to 1830. As the border with Canada (a British colony) moved north, more of Washington state became part of the United States.

2. *Hydas and Tsimpsians*: Native American tribes of British Columbia, Canada; "Hyda" is more commonly spelled "Haida."

3. *Written upon tables of stone*: a reference to the Ten Commandments, which according to the Hebrew Bible were written by God and given to Moses on stone tablets.

men, given them in solemn hours of night by the Great Spirit; and the visions of our sachems;[4] and it is written in the hearts of our people.

Your dead cease to love you and the land of their nativity as soon as they pass 5 the portals of the tomb and wander way beyond the stars. They are soon forgotten and never return. Our dead never forget the beautiful world that gave them being.

Day and night cannot dwell together. The Red man has ever fled the approach of 6 the White Man, as the morning mist flees before the morning sun. However, your proposition seems fair and I think that my people will accept it and will retire to the reservation you offer them. Then we will dwell apart in peace, for the words of the Great White Chief seem to be the words of nature speaking to my people out of dense darkness.

It matters little where we pass the remnant of our days. They will not be many. 7 A few more moons; a few more winters—and not one of the descendants of the mighty hosts that once moved over this broad land or lived in happy homes, protected by the Great Spirit, will remain to mourn over the graves of a people once more powerful and hopeful than yours. But why should I mourn at the untimely fate of my people? Tribe follows tribe, and nation follows nation, like the waves of the sea. It is the order of nature, and regret is useless. Your time of decay may be distant, but it will surely come, for even the White Man whose God walked and talked with him as friend with friend, cannot be exempt from the common destiny. We may be brothers after all. We will see.

We will ponder your proposition, and when we decide we will let you know. But 8 should we accept it, I here and now make this condition that we will not be denied the privilege without molestation of visiting at any time the tombs of our ancestors, friends and children. Every part of this soil is sacred in the estimation of my people. Every hillside, every valley, every plain and grove, has been hallowed by some sad or happy event in days long vanished. . . . The very dust upon which you now stand responds more lovingly to their footsteps than to yours, because it is rich with the blood of our ancestors and our bare feet are conscious of the sympathetic touch. . . . Even the little children who lived here and rejoiced here for a brief season will love these somber solitudes and at eventide they greet shadowy returning spirits. And when the last Red Man shall have perished, and the memory of my tribe shall have become a myth among the White Men, these shores will swarm with the invisible dead of my tribe, and when your children's children think themselves alone in the field, the store, the shop, upon the highway, or in the silence of the pathless woods, they will not be alone. . . . At night when the streets of your cities and villages are silent and you think them deserted, they will throng

---

4. *Sachems*: high-level tribal leaders.

with the returning hosts that once filled and still love this beautiful land. The White Man will never be alone.

Let him be just and deal kindly with my people, for the dead are not powerless. 9 Dead, did I say? There is no death, only a change of worlds.

READING CLOSELY

1. According to Chief Seattle, why did the young men of his tribe go to war (2)? What was their mood, and what was the significance of their painted faces?

2. The proposition that Seattle promises to think over at the end of his speech is the government's offer to buy over two million acres of Indian land. What condition does he place on accepting it?

3. Seattle doubts that the White Man and the Red Man will ever be brothers. Why? In what sense does he think they may be "brothers after all" (7)?

4. What does he say will happen "when the last Red Man shall have perished" (8)?

5. What does Seattle mean by "a change of worlds" (9)? How does his view of life after death differ from Christian ideas of heaven?

STRATEGIES AND STRUCTURES

1. What personal qualities would you attribute to Seattle after reading his speech? Point out specific statements and phrases that help to characterize him. How does paragraph 2 in particular show Seattle's character?

2. In general, do you think Seattle sounds trustworthy? Why or why not?

3. How and why does Seattle show his respect for the "Big Chief at Washington" (1)? How does the defeated chief show that he is not cowed by the Big Chief?

4. What reasons does Seattle give for why the Big Chief at Washington should grant his condition that the Duwamish people be allowed "without molestation" to visit their homeland (8)?

5. *Other Methods.* In the second half of his speech, Seattle COMPARES AND CONTRASTS "your dead" and "our dead" (5). What are some of the differences? How do those differences support his claim that "the dead are not powerless" (9)?

Thinking about Language

1. Seattle refers to the Big Chief at Washington as "our good father" (3). Why do you think he draws this ANALOGY between a head of state and the patriarch of a family?

2. The conquering whites, says Seattle, are like "the grass that covers vast prairies," and Native Americans are like "scattering trees" or a "receding tide," though they were once like the "stars" (1, 3). How do these nature METAPHORS fit in with Seattle's references to physical decay and the cycle of the seasons?

3. What does he mean when he says, "Day and night cannot dwell together" (6)?

4. In what sense is the translator using the word *sympathetic* when he reports Seattle as saying that "our bare feet are conscious of the sympathetic touch" (8)?

5. According to the translator of his speech, who wrote about the occasion in the *Seattle Sunday Star*, Seattle "arose with all the dignity of a senator" and spoke in "solemn and impressive tones." How does the language and style of this translation help to convey that dignity and solemnity? Include examples in your response.

For Writing

1. You have been given the task of introducing Seattle before he stands up to give his speech. Write a paragraph or two for the occasion.

2. On behalf of the Big Chief at Washington, compose a reply to Seattle's speech in which you try to convince him to accept Washington's proposal.

3. A class you want to take has reached its enrollment capacity, and the instructor asks you to explain in writing why she should let you in. Make the case for yourself as a good and valuable addition to the class.

MARTIN LUTHER KING JR.

I Have a Dream

Martin Luther King Jr. (1929–1968) was born in Atlanta, Georgia, at a time when racial discrimination was routine and institutionalized, especially in the South. King attended segregated schools and earned his B.A. in sociology from Morehouse College in 1948. Already an ordained Baptist minister, he then studied at Crozer Theological Seminary and at Boston University, where he received his Ph.D. in systematic theology. In 1953, King became the pastor of Dexter Avenue Baptist Church in Montgomery, Alabama, just as the civil rights movement was beginning to crystallize. He won national recognition for leading a black boycott of Montgomery's segregated bus system and, in 1957, was elected president of a new organization, the Southern Christian Leadership Conference (SCLC), which combined King's Christian principles with a commitment to nonviolent protest. The SCLC's tireless campaign of marches, demonstrations, and civil disobedience gradually caught the public imagination. Inspired by King, President John F. Kennedy initiated the legislation that would become the Civil Rights Act of 1964. That same year, King was awarded the Nobel Prize for Peace. Though he won the love and admiration of millions, he was also subjected to arrests, political harrassment, and threats of violence. On April 4, 1968, he was assassinated as he stood on a hotel balcony in Memphis.

One dramatic moment of King's career came in 1963 when he stood on the steps of the Lincoln Memorial to address a crowd of a quarter-million people who had heeded King's call for a March on Washington for Jobs and Freedom. King's "I Have a Dream" speech, steeped in the cadences of the Bible, the Declaration of Independence, and the Gettysburg Address, is a classic invocation of moral authority, a stirring call to "open the doors of opportunity to all of God's children."

FIVE SCORE YEARS AGO, a great American, in whose symbolic shadow we stand,[1] signed the Emancipation Proclamation. This momentous decree came as a great beacon light of hope to millions of Negro slaves who had been seared in the flames of withering injustice. It came as a joyous daybreak to end the long night of captivity.

---

1. *In whose symbolic shadow we stand*: King's speech was delivered in front of the Lincoln Memorial. *A great American*: reference to President Abraham Lincoln. *Five score years ago*: an echo of the opening line of Lincoln's 1863 Gettysburg Address, in which he dedicated a cemetery for fallen Civil War soldiers: "Four score and seven years ago our fathers brought forth, upon this continent, a new nation, conceived in liberty, and dedicated to the proposition that all men are created equal."

But one hundred years later, we must face the tragic fact that the Negro is still [2] not free. One hundred years later, the life of the Negro is still sadly crippled by the manacles of segregation and the chains of discrimination. One hundred years later, the Negro lives on a lonely island of poverty in the midst of a vast ocean of material prosperity. One hundred years later, the Negro is still languishing in the corners of American society and finds himself an exile in his own land. So we have come here today to dramatize an appalling condition.

In a sense we have come to our nation's capital to cash a check. When the archi- [3] tects of our republic wrote the magnificent words of the Constitution and the Declaration of Independence, they were signing a promissory note to which every American was to fall heir. This note was a promise that all men would be guaranteed the inalienable rights of life, liberty, and the pursuit of happiness.

It is obvious today that America has defaulted on this promissory note insofar as [4] her citizens of color are concerned. Instead of honoring this sacred obligation, America has given the Negro people a bad check which has come back marked "insufficient funds." But we refuse to believe that the bank of justice is bankrupt. We refuse to believe that there are insufficient funds in the great vaults of opportunity of this nation. So we have come to cash this check—a check that will give us upon demand the riches of freedom and the security of justice. We have also come to this hallowed spot to remind America of the fierce urgency of *now*. This is no time to engage in the luxury of cooling off or to take the tranquilizing drug of gradualism. *Now* is the time to rise from the dark and desolate valley of segregation to the sunlit path of racial justice. *Now* is the time to open the doors of opportunity to all of God's children. *Now* is the time to lift our nation from the quicksands of racial injustice to the solid rock of brotherhood.

It would be fatal for the nation to overlook the urgency of the moment and to [5] underestimate the determination of the Negro. This sweltering summer of the Negro's legitimate discontent will not pass until there is an invigorating autumn of freedom and equality. Nineteen sixty-three is not an end, but a beginning. Those who hope that the Negro needed to blow off steam and will now be content will have a rude awakening if the nation returns to business as usual. There will be neither rest nor tranquility in America until the Negro is granted his citizenship rights. The whirlwinds of revolt will continue to shake the foundations of our nation until the bright day of justice emerges.

But there is something that I must say to my people who stand on the warm [6] threshold which leads into the palace of justice. In the process of gaining our rightful place we must not be guilty of wrongful deeds. Let us not seek to satisfy our thirst for freedom by drinking from the cup of bitterness and hatred.

We must forever conduct our struggle on the high plane of dignity and disci- [7] pline. We must not allow our creative protest to degenerate into physical violence.

Again and again we must rise to the majestic heights of meeting physical force with soul force. The marvelous new militancy which has engulfed the Negro community must not lead us to distrust of all white people, for many of our white brothers, as evidenced by their presence here today, have come to realize that their destiny is tied up with our destiny and their freedom is inextricably bound to our freedom. We cannot walk alone.

And as we walk, we must make the pledge that we shall march ahead. We cannot turn back. There are those who are asking the devotees of civil rights, "When will you be satisfied?" We can never be satisfied as long as our bodies, heavy with the fatigue of travel, cannot gain lodging in the motels of the highways and the hotels of the cities. We cannot be satisfied as long as the Negro's basic mobility is from a smaller ghetto to a larger one. We can never be satisfied as long as a Negro in Mississippi cannot vote and a Negro in New York believes he has nothing for which to vote. No, no, we are not satisfied, and we will not be satisfied until justice rolls down like waters and righteousness like a mighty stream. 8

I am not unmindful that some of you have come here out of great trials and tribulations. Some of you have come fresh from narrow cells. Some of you have come from areas where your quest for freedom left you battered by the storms of persecution and staggered by the winds of police brutality. You have been the veterans of creative suffering. Continue to work with the faith that unearned suffering is redemptive. 9

Go back to Mississippi, go back to Alabama, go back to Georgia, go back to Louisiana, go back to the slums and ghettos of our northern cities, knowing that somehow this situation can and will be changed. Let us not wallow in the valley of despair. 10

I say to you today, my friends, that in spite of the difficulties and frustrations of the moment, I still have a dream. It is a dream deeply rooted in the American dream. 11

I have a dream that one day this nation will rise up and live out the true meaning of its creed: "We hold these truths to be self-evident: that all men are created equal." 12

I have a dream that one day on the red hills of Georgia the sons of former slaves and the sons of former slaveowners will be able to sit down together at a table of brotherhood. 13

I have a dream that one day even the state of Mississippi, a desert state, sweltering with the heat of injustice and oppression, will be transformed into an oasis of freedom and justice. 14

I have a dream that my four children will one day live in a nation where they will not be judged by the color of their skin but by the content of their character. 15

I have a dream today. 16

I have a dream that one day the state of Alabama, whose governor's lips are 17 presently dripping with the words of interposition and nullification, will be transformed into a situation where little black boys and black girls will be able to join hands with little white boys and white girls and walk together as sisters and brothers.

I have a dream today. 18

I have a dream that one day every valley shall be exalted, and every hill and 19 mountain shall be made low, the rough places will be made plain, and the crooked places will be made straight, and the glory of the Lord shall be revealed and all flesh shall see it together.

This is our hope. This is the faith that I go back to the South with. With this 20 faith we will be able to hew out of the mountain of despair a stone of hope. With this faith we will be able to transform the jangling discords of our nation into a beautiful symphony of brotherhood. With this faith we will be able to work together, to pray together, to struggle together, to go to jail together, to stand up for freedom together, knowing that we will be free one day.

This will be the day, this will be the day when all of God's children will be able 21 to sing with new meaning "My country 'tis of thee, sweet land of liberty, of thee I sing. Land where my fathers died, land of the Pilgrim's pride, from every mountainside, let freedom ring!"

And if America is to be a great nation, this must become true. And so let freedom 22 ring from the prodigious hilltops of New Hampshire. Let freedom ring from the mighty mountains of New York! Let freedom ring from the heightening Alleghenies of Pennsylvania!

Let freedom ring from the snow-capped Rockies of Colorado! 23

Let freedom ring from the curvaceous slopes of California! 24

But not only that; let freedom ring from Stone Mountain of Georgia! 25

Let freedom ring from Lookout Mountain of Tennessee! 26

Let freedom ring from every hill and molehill of Mississippi. 27

From every mountainside, let freedom ring. 28

And when this happens, and when we allow freedom to ring—when we let it 29 ring from every village and every hamlet, from every state and every city, we will be able to speed up that day when all of God's children—black men and white men, Jews and Gentiles, Protestants and Catholics—will be able to join hands and sing in the words of the old Negro spiritual: "Free at last! Free at last! Thank God Almighty, we are free at last!"

READING CLOSELY

1. The "great American" (1) to whom Martin Luther King Jr. refers in the first paragraph of his speech is, of course, Abraham Lincoln. Why does King begin by invoking Lincoln and the Emancipation Proclamation, which Lincoln signed in January 1863?

2. What is the "appalling condition" that King seeks "to dramatize" (2) to the quarter of a million civil rights activists who gathered around the Lincoln Memorial in Washington to hear his speech?

3. What does King admonish the multitude to do about the condition he is calling to their attention? Was he wise to insist that their actions not "degenerate into physical violence" (7)? Why or why not?

4. What is King's dream? When and how does he envision its becoming a reality?

STRATEGIES AND STRUCTURES

1. King takes it for granted that the condition of many African Americans in 1963 is "appalling" (2). Is he committing the logical fallacy of begging the question? Explain.

2. In the third part of his speech (20–29), King says, "When we allow freedom to ring, . . . we will be able to speed up that day when all of God's children . . . will be able to join hands" (29). If we conceive of King's entire speech as a logical ARGUMENT, how does this statement logically connect King's dream in paragraphs 11 to 19 to the reality he describes in paragraphs 1 to 10?

3. Though he uses logical reasoning, King's chief strategy in this speech, perhaps, is to appeal to his audience's sense of moral justice, beginning with the evocation of President Lincoln in the opening line. What other sources of authority does he refer to throughout the speech? How do these sources help King give the impression that he himself is a man of good character who deserves to be listened to and trusted?

4. Where and how does King appeal to his audience's emotions? Point out several examples that you find particularly persuasive.

5. What evidence can you find in the text of King's speech to indicate that it was written to be delivered orally instead of laid out on the printed page? Consider such elements as the length of his sentences, his choice of words, and the repetition of such phrases as, "I have a dream." How might King's experience as a minister have helped him to compose such a moving oration?

6. *Other Methods.* In the "I have a dream" part of his speech (11–19), King describes a future condition that is contrary to present fact. How does that condition COMPARE AND CONTRAST with the "appalling condition" he has described earlier?

THINKING ABOUT LANGUAGE

1. King's speech is full of METAPHORS ("the flames of withering injustice"); SIMILES ("righteousness like a mighty stream"); and other figures of speech. How does such figurative language help him, throughout his oration, to balance his call for action with his call for nonviolence?

2. Why does King begin his speech with the phrase "five score years ago" instead of simply saying "a hundred years ago"?

3. Explain the "bad check" metaphor in paragraphs 3–4 of King's speech. Why might he choose this particular metaphor for this particular audience?

4. Why does King speak of "the Negro" throughout his speech, instead of "African Americans" or "blacks"?

5. Why do you think King ends his speech with an ALLUSION to an "old Negro spiritual" (29)? How effective do you find this ending?

FOR WRITING

1. King was not just speaking to the activists who joined him in Washington on that August day in 1963. He was mindful of a wider audience, including the press. Write a paragraph or two analyzing how King's speech anticipates the objections of those who might disagree with, or even be hostile to, his dream.

2. Write an essay describing and analyzing King's use of logical reasoning, his appeal to emotion, or the way he establishes his credibility. Whichever you choose, be sure to discuss how King's language supports it.

3. Write an essay in which you argue that nonviolent protest is the best way to achieve change—or that violence is sometimes necessary to change things. Refer to historical examples in your essay, like the civil rights movement, India's struggle for independence led by Mahatma Gandhi, or the war in Afghanistan.

BARACK OBAMA

A More Perfect Union

> *Barack Obama (b. 1961), the son of a black father from Kenya and a white mother*
> *from Kansas, grew up mostly in Hawaii. A graduate of Columbia University and Har-*
> *vard Law School, Obama served in the Illinois State Senate from 1997 to 2004, when*
> *he was elected to the U.S. Senate. As the Democratic presidential nominee in the 2008*
> *election, Obama sought to avoid making race a key issue in the campaign, preferring*
> *to run on his political platform, his record in the Senate, and his reputation for bring-*
> *ing together politicians of opposing parties and conflicting viewpoints. In March 2008,*
> *however, Obama faced a growing controversy triggered by the sermons of the Reverend*
> *Jeremiah Wright, his pastor for more than twenty years at Trinity United Church of*
> *Christ in Chicago. Wright, a former Marine, accused the U.S. government of fostering*
> *racism and claimed that it "lied about inventing the HIV virus as a means of genocide*
> *against people of color."*
>
> *"A More Perfect Union," a speech delivered in Philadelphia on March 18, 2008, was*
> *Obama's response to the controversy. Condemning Wright's remarks but putting them*
> *in the historical context of the black experience in America, it soon became known as*
> *Obama's speech on race. The speech takes its title from the preamble to the United*
> *States Constitution.*

"**W**E THE PEOPLE, in order to form a more perfect union."[1]   1

Two hundred and twenty-one years ago, in a hall that still stands across the   2
street,[2] a group of men gathered and, with these simple words, launched America's
improbable experiment in democracy. Farmers and scholars, statesmen and patriots who had traveled across an ocean to escape tyranny and persecution finally
made real their declaration of independence at a Philadelphia convention that
lasted through the spring of 1787.[3]

The document they produced was eventually signed but ultimately unfinished.   3
It was stained by this nation's original sin of slavery, a question that divided the
colonies and brought the convention to a stalemate until the founders chose to

1. *We the people . . .* : the beginning of the preamble to the United States Constitution.
2. *Hall that still stands across the street*: a reference to Constitution Hall in Philadelphia, Pennsylvania, where the Constitution was created. Obama delivered his speech in the National Constitution
Center in Philadelphia.
3. *Through the spring of 1787*: the Constitutional Convention of 1787 was convened to address problems with the Articles of Confederation, which united the American colonies under one government.
At the convention, the founding fathers created a new document, the United States Constitution.

allow the slave trade to continue for at least twenty more years, and to leave any final resolution to future generations.

Of course, the answer to the slavery question was already embedded within our Constitution—a Constitution that had at its very core the ideal of equal citizenship under the law; a Constitution that promised its people liberty, and justice, and a union that could be and should be perfected over time.

And yet words on a parchment would not be enough to deliver slaves from bondage, or provide men and women of every color and creed their full rights and obligations as citizens of the United States. What would be needed were Americans in successive generations who were willing to do their part—through protests and struggle, on the streets and in the courts, through a civil war and civil disobedience and always at great risk—to narrow that gap between the promise of our ideals and the reality of their time.

This was one of the tasks we set forth at the beginning of this campaign—to continue the long march of those who came before us, a march for a more just, more equal, more free, more caring and more prosperous America. I chose to run for the presidency at this moment in history because I believe deeply that we cannot solve the challenges of our time unless we solve them together—unless we perfect our union by understanding that we may have different stories, but we hold common hopes; that we may not look the same and we may not have come from the same place, but we all want to move in the same direction—towards a better future for our children and our grandchildren.

This belief comes from my unyielding faith in the decency and generosity of the American people. But it also comes from my own American story.

I am the son of a black man from Kenya and a white woman from Kansas. I was raised with the help of a white grandfather who survived a Depression to serve in Patton's army during World War II and a white grandmother who worked on a bomber assembly line at Fort Leavenworth[4] while he was overseas. I've gone to some of the best schools in America and lived in one of the world's poorest nations. I am married to a black American who carries within her the blood of slaves and slaveowners—an inheritance we pass on to our two precious daughters. I have brothers, sisters, nieces, nephews, uncles, and cousins, of every race and every hue, scattered across three continents, and for as long as I live, I will never forget that in no other country on Earth is my story even possible.

It's a story that hasn't made me the most conventional candidate. But it is a story

---

4. *Fort Leavenworth*: a U.S. Army fort in Leavenworth, Kansas. *Depression*: the Great Depression was a severe economic downturn that began in the United States after the stock market crashed in 1929 and ended around the beginning of World War II in 1939. *Patton's army*: a reference to General George S. Patton (1885–1945), a leading American general during World War II.

that has seared into my genetic makeup the idea that this nation is more than the sum of its parts—that out of many, we are truly one.

Throughout the first year of this campaign, against all predictions to the con- 10
trary, we saw how hungry the American people were for this message of unity. Despite the temptation to view my candidacy through a purely racial lens, we won commanding victories in states with some of the whitest populations in the country. In South Carolina, where the Confederate flag[5] still flies, we built a powerful coalition of African Americans and white Americans.

This is not to say that race has not been an issue in the campaign. At various 11
stages in the campaign, some commentators have deemed me either "too black" or "not black enough." We saw racial tensions bubble to the surface during the week before the South Carolina primary. The press has scoured every exit poll for the latest evidence of racial polarization, not just in terms of white and black, but black and brown as well.

And yet, it has only been in the last couple of weeks that the discussion of race 12
in this campaign has taken a particularly divisive turn.

On one end of the spectrum, we've heard the implication that my candidacy is 13
somehow an exercise in affirmative action; that it's based solely on the desire of wide-eyed liberals to purchase racial reconciliation on the cheap. On the other end, we've heard my former pastor, Reverend Jeremiah Wright, use incendiary language to express views that have the potential not only to widen the racial divide, but views that denigrate both the greatness and the goodness of our nation; that rightly offend white and black alike.

I have already condemned, in unequivocal terms, the statements of Reverend 14
Wright that have caused such controversy. For some, nagging questions remain. Did I know him to be an occasionally fierce critic of American domestic and foreign policy? Of course. Did I ever hear him make remarks that could be considered controversial while I sat in church? Yes. Did I strongly disagree with many of his political views? Absolutely—just as I'm sure many of you have heard remarks from your pastors, priests, or rabbis with which you strongly disagreed.

But the remarks that have caused this recent firestorm weren't simply contro- 15
versial. They weren't simply a religious leader's effort to speak out against perceived injustice. Instead, they expressed a profoundly distorted view of this country—a view that sees white racism as endemic, and that elevates what is wrong with America above all that we know is right with America; a view that sees

5. *Confederate flag*: the flag that represents the southern Confederate states that seceded during the Civil War. Because the states that seceded relied on slave labor and were opposed to ending slavery, today the Confederate flag is controversial—some see it as a symbol of racism, while others see it as a celebration of the South and Southern culture.

the conflicts in the Middle East as rooted primarily in the actions of stalwart allies like Israel, instead of emanating from the perverse and hateful ideologies of radical Islam.

As such, Reverend Wright's comments were not only wrong but divisive, divisive 16 at a time when we need unity; racially charged at a time when we need to come together to solve a set of monumental problems—two wars, a terrorist threat, a falling economy, a chronic health care crisis and potentially devastating climate change; problems that are neither black or white or Latino or Asian, but rather problems that confront us all.

Given my background, my politics, and my professed values and ideals, there 17 will no doubt be those for whom my statements of condemnation are not enough. Why associate myself with Reverend Wright in the first place, they may ask? Why not join another church? And I confess that if all that I knew of Reverend Wright were the snippets of those sermons that have run in an endless loop on the television and YouTube, or if Trinity United Church of Christ conformed to the caricatures being peddled by some commentators, there is no doubt that I would react in much the same way.

But the truth is, that isn't all that I know of the man. The man I met more than 18 twenty years ago is a man who helped introduce me to my Christian faith, a man who spoke to me about our obligations to love one another; to care for the sick and lift up the poor. He is a man who served his country as a U.S. Marine; who has studied and lectured at some of the finest universities and seminaries in the country, and who for over thirty years led a church that serves the community by doing God's work here on Earth—by housing the homeless, ministering to the needy, providing day care services and scholarships and prison ministries, and reaching out to those suffering from HIV/AIDS.

In my first book, *Dreams from My Father*, I described the experience of my first 19 service at Trinity:

> People began to shout, to rise from their seats and clap and cry out, a forceful wind carrying the reverend's voice up into the rafters. . . . And in that single note—hope—I heard something else; at the foot of that cross, inside the thousands of churches across the city, I imagined the stories of ordinary black people merging with the stories of David and Goliath, Moses and Pharaoh, the Christians in the lion's den, Ezekiel's field of dry bones.[6] Those

---

6. *David and Goliath . . . field of dry bones*: all are references to the Hebrew Bible. David defeated the giant Goliath with a slingshot. Moses defied the Pharoah by leading the Israelites out of Egypt, where they were enslaved. "The Christians in the lion's den" combines two different stories. In the Bible, Daniel was thrown into a lions' den for praying, which was against the law; God saved him by shutting the lions' mouths. In the Roman Empire in the early days of Christianity, Christians were often

stories—of survival, and freedom, and hope—became our story, my story; the blood that had spilled was our blood, the tears our tears; until this black church, on this bright day, seemed once more a vessel carrying the story of a people into future generations and into a larger world. Our trials and triumphs became at once unique and universal, black and more than black; in chronicling our journey, the stories and songs gave us a means to reclaim memories that we didn't need to feel shame about . . . memories that all people might study and cherish—and with which we could start to rebuild.

That has been my experience at Trinity. Like other predominantly black churches 20 across the country, Trinity embodies the black community in its entirety—the doctor and the welfare mom, the model student and the former gang-banger. Like other black churches, Trinity's services are full of raucous laughter and sometimes bawdy humor. They are full of dancing, clapping, screaming and shouting that may seem jarring to the untrained ear. The church contains in full the kindness and cruelty, the fierce intelligence and the shocking ignorance, the struggles and successes, the love and, yes, the bitterness and bias that make up the black experience in America.

And this helps explain, perhaps, my relationship with Reverend Wright. As 21 imperfect as he may be, he has been like family to me. He strengthened my faith, officiated at my wedding, and baptized my children. Not once in my conversations with him have I heard him talk about any ethnic group in derogatory terms, or treat whites with whom he interacted with anything but courtesy and respect. He contains within him the contradictions—the good and the bad—of the community that he has served diligently for so many years.

I can no more disown him than I can disown the black community. I can no 22 more disown him than I can my white grandmother—a woman who helped raise me, a woman who sacrificed again and again for me, a woman who loves me as much as she loves anything in this world, but a woman who once confessed her fear of black men who passed by her on the street, and who on more than one occasion has uttered racial or ethnic stereotypes that made me cringe.

These people are a part of me. And they are a part of America, this country that 23 I love.

Some will see this as an attempt to justify or excuse comments that are simply 24 inexcusable. I can assure you it is not. I suppose the politically safe thing would be to move on from this episode and just hope that it fades into the woodwork. We can dismiss Reverend Wright as a crank or a demagogue, just as some have dis-

---

persecuted by being fed to lions. Ezekiel, a Hebrew prophet, had a vision of a field of dry bones that he made come together and grow flesh.

missed Geraldine Ferraro,[7] in the aftermath of her recent statements, as harboring some deep-seated racial bias.

But race is an issue that I believe this nation cannot afford to ignore right now. [25] We would be making the same mistake that Reverend Wright made in his offending sermons about America—to simplify and stereotype and amplify the negative to the point that it distorts reality.

The fact is that the comments that have been made and the issues that have surfaced over the last few weeks reflect the complexities of race in this country that we've never really worked through—a part of our union that we have yet to perfect. [26] And if we walk away now, if we simply retreat into our respective corners, we will never be able to come together and solve challenges like health care, or education, or the need to find good jobs for every American.

Understanding this reality requires a reminder of how we arrived at this point. [27] As William Faulkner once wrote, "The past isn't dead and buried. In fact, it isn't even past." We do not need to recite here the history of racial injustice in this country. But we do need to remind ourselves that so many of the disparities that exist in the African-American community today can be directly traced to inequalities passed on from an earlier generation that suffered under the brutal legacy of slavery and Jim Crow.[8]

Segregated schools were, and are, inferior schools; we still haven't fixed them, [28] fifty years after *Brown v. Board of Education*,[9] and the inferior education they provided, then and now, helps explain the pervasive achievement gap between today's black and white students.

Legalized discrimination—where blacks were prevented, often through violence, from owning property, or loans were not granted to African-American business owners, or black homeowners could not access FHA mortgages[10] or blacks [29] were excluded from unions, or the police force, or fire departments—meant that black families could not amass any meaningful wealth to bequeath to future gener-

---

7. *Geraldine Ferraro*: a member of the U.S. House of Representatives from 1978 to 1984, Ferraro ran for vice president alongside presidential candidate Walter Mondale in 1984. In March 2008, Ferraro, a supporter of Hillary Clinton, told a Torrance, California, newspaper that "If Obama was a white man, he would not be in this position. And if he was a woman (of any color), he would not be in this position. He happens to be very lucky to be who he is. And the country is caught up in the concept."

8. *Jim Crow*: refers to the laws that segregated blacks and whites in public facilities like schools, public transportation, and restaurants.

9. *Brown v. Board of Education*: the 1954 Supreme Court case that ended legal racial segregation in public schools.

10. *FHA mortgages*: the Federal Housing Administration insures private mortgages, reducing the risk to mortgage lenders and allowing those who might not otherwise qualify for a mortgage to obtain one.

ations. That history helps explain the wealth and income gap between black and white, and the concentrated pockets of poverty that persists in so many of today's urban and rural communities.

A lack of economic opportunity among black men, and the shame and frustra- 30 tion that came from not being able to provide for one's family, contributed to the erosion of black families—a problem that welfare policies for many years may have worsened. And the lack of basic services in so many urban black neighborhoods— parks for kids to play in, police walking the beat, regular garbage pick-up and building code enforcement—all helped create a cycle of violence, blight, and neglect that continues to haunt us.

This is the reality in which Reverend Wright and other African Americans of 31 his generation grew up. They came of age in the late fifties and early sixties, a time when segregation was still the law of the land and opportunity was systematically constricted. What's remarkable is not how many failed in the face of discrimination, but rather how many men and women overcame the odds; how many were able to make a way out of no way for those like me who would come after them.

But for all those who scratched and clawed their way to get a piece of the Amer- 32 ican Dream, there were many who didn't make it—those who were ultimately defeated, in one way or another, by discrimination. That legacy of defeat was passed on to future generations—those young men and increasingly young women who we see standing on street corners or languishing in our prisons, without hope or prospects for the future. Even for those blacks who did make it, questions of race, and racism, continue to define their worldview in fundamental ways. For the men and women of Reverend Wright's generation, the memories of humiliation and doubt and fear have not gone away; nor has the anger and the bitterness of those years. That anger may not get expressed in public, in front of white co-workers or white friends. But it does find voice in the barbershop or around the kitchen table. At times, that anger is exploited by politicians, to gin up votes along racial lines, or to make up for a politician's own failings.

And occasionally it finds voice in the church on Sunday morning, in the pulpit 33 and in the pews. The fact that so many people are surprised to hear that anger in some of Reverend Wright's sermons simply reminds us of the old truism that the most segregated hour in American life occurs on Sunday morning. That anger is not always productive; indeed, all too often it distracts attention from solving real problems; it keeps us from squarely facing our own complicity in our condition, and prevents the African-American community from forging the alliances it needs to bring about real change. But the anger is real; it is powerful; and to simply wish it away, to condemn it without understanding its roots, only serves to widen the chasm of misunderstanding that exists between the races.

In fact, a similar anger exists within segments of the white community. Most 34
working- and middle-class white Americans don't feel that they have been particularly privileged by their race. Their experience is the immigrant experience—as far
as they're concerned, no one's handed them anything, they've built it from scratch.
They've worked hard all their lives, many times only to see their jobs shipped overseas or their pension dumped after a lifetime of labor. They are anxious about their
futures, and feel their dreams slipping away; in an era of stagnant wages and global
competition, opportunity comes to be seen as a zero sum game,[11] in which your
dreams come at my expense. So when they are told to bus their children to a school
across town; when they hear that an African American is getting an advantage in
landing a good job or a spot in a good college because of an injustice that they
themselves never committed; when they're told that their fears about crime in
urban neighborhoods are somehow prejudiced, resentment builds over time.

Like the anger within the black community, these resentments aren't always 35
expressed in polite company. But they have helped shape the political landscape for
at least a generation. Anger over welfare and affirmative action helped forge the
Reagan Coalition.[12] Politicians routinely exploited fears of crime for their own
electoral ends. Talk show hosts and conservative commentators built entire careers
unmasking bogus claims of racism while dismissing legitimate discussions of racial
injustice and inequality as mere political correctness or reverse racism.

Just as black anger often proved counterproductive, so have these white resent- 36
ments distracted attention from the real culprits of the middle class squeeze—a
corporate culture rife with inside dealing,[13] questionable accounting practices, and
short-term greed; a Washington dominated by lobbyists and special interests; economic policies that favor the few over the many. And yet, to wish away the resentments of white Americans, to label them as misguided or even racist, without
recognizing they are grounded in legitimate concerns—this too widens the racial
divide, and blocks the path to understanding.

This is where we are right now. It's a racial stalemate we've been stuck in for 37
years. Contrary to the claims of some of my critics, black and white, I have never
been so naïve as to believe that we can get beyond our racial divisions in a single
election cycle, or with a single candidacy—particularly a candidacy as imperfect as
my own.

---

11. *Zero sum game*: a situation in which one party's loss is the other party's benefit; it is impossible
for both sides to win.

12. *Reagan Coalition*: the group of voters, both Republican and Democratic, who elected Ronald
Reagan president in 1980 and 1984. Though a Republican himself, Reagan attracted members of both
major political parties.

13. *Inside dealing*: when individuals who have access to information not available to the general
public use that information to buy or sell stocks or otherwise profit.

But I have asserted a firm conviction—a conviction rooted in my faith in God and my faith in the American people—that working together we can move beyond some of our old racial wounds, and that in fact we have no choice if we are to continue on the path of a more perfect union.

For the African-American community, that path means embracing the burdens of our past without becoming victims of our past. It means continuing to insist on a full measure of justice in every aspect of American life. But it also means binding our particular grievances—for better health care, and better schools, and better jobs—to the larger aspirations of all Americans—the white woman struggling to break the glass ceiling, the white man who's been laid off, the immigrant trying to feed his family. And it means taking full responsibility for own lives—by demanding more from our fathers, and spending more time with our children, and reading to them, and teaching them that while they may face challenges and discrimination in their own lives, they must never succumb to despair or cynicism; they must always believe that they can write their own destiny.

Ironically, this quintessentially American—and yes, conservative—notion of self-help found frequent expression in Reverend Wright's sermons. But what my former pastor too often failed to understand is that embarking on a program of self-help also requires a belief that society can change.

The profound mistake of Reverend Wright's sermons is not that he spoke about racism in our society. It's that he spoke as if our society was static; as if no progress has been made; as if this country—a country that has made it possible for one of his own members to run for the highest office in the land and build a coalition of white and black, Latino and Asian, rich and poor, young and old—is still irrevocably bound to a tragic past. But what we know—what we have seen—is that America can change. That is true genius of this nation. What we have already achieved gives us hope—the audacity to hope—for what we can and must achieve tomorrow.

In the white community, the path to a more perfect union means acknowledging that what ails the African-American community does not just exist in the minds of black people; that the legacy of discrimination—and current incidents of discrimination, while less overt than in the past—are real and must be addressed. Not just with words, but with deeds—by investing in our schools and our communities; by enforcing our civil rights laws and ensuring fairness in our criminal justice system; by providing this generation with ladders of opportunity that were unavailable for previous generations. It requires all Americans to realize that your dreams do not have to come at the expense of my dreams; that investing in the health, welfare, and education of black and brown and white children will ultimately help all of America prosper.

In the end, then, what is called for is nothing more, and nothing less, than what all the world's great religions demand—that we do unto others as we would have them do unto us. Let us be our brother's keeper,[14] Scripture tells us. Let us be our sister's keeper. Let us find that common stake we all have in one another, and let our politics reflect that spirit as well.

For we have a choice in this country. We can accept a politics that breeds division, and conflict, and cynicism. We can tackle race only as spectacle—as we did in the O.J. trial—or in the wake of tragedy, as we did in the aftermath of Katrina[15]—or as fodder for the nightly news. We can play Reverend Wright's sermons on every channel, every day and talk about them from now until the election, and make the only question in this campaign whether or not the American people think that I somehow believe or sympathize with his most offensive words. We can pounce on some gaffe by a Hillary supporter as evidence that she's playing the race card,[16] or we can speculate on whether white men will all flock to John McCain in the general election regardless of his policies. 44

We can do that. 45

But if we do, I can tell you that in the next election, we'll be talking about some other distraction. And then another one. And then another one. And nothing will change. 46

That is one option. Or, at this moment, in this election, we can come together and say, "Not this time." This time we want to talk about the crumbling schools that are stealing the future of black children and white children and Asian children and Hispanic children and Native American children. This time we want to reject the cynicism that tells us that these kids can't learn; that those kids who don't look like us are somebody else's problem. The children of America are not those kids, they are our kids, and we will not let them fall behind in a twenty-first-century economy. Not this time. 47

This time we want to talk about how the lines in the Emergency Room are filled with whites and blacks and Hispanics who do not have health care, who don't have the power on their own to overcome the special interests in Washington, but who can take them on if we do it together. 48

This time we want to talk about the shuttered mills that once provided a decent life for men and women of every race, and the homes for sale that once belonged to 49

---

14. *Let us be our brother's keeper*: a reference to the story of Cain and Abel in the Hebrew Bible. Cain killed his brother Abel out of jealousy; when God asked Cain where Abel was, Cain replied, "Am I my brother's keeper?"

15. *Katrina*: Hurricane Katrina, which devastated New Orleans in 2005. The city has a large black population, and some criticized the slow and inadequate federal response as being motivated by racial prejudice. *O.J. trial*: the 1994 trial of O.J. Simpson, a black football star accused of murdering his white ex-wife, Nicole Brown Simpson, and her friend, Ronald Goldman.

16. *Playing the race card*: introducing the issue of race into an argument.

Americans from every religion, every region, every walk of life. This time we want to talk about the fact that the real problem is not that someone who doesn't look like you might take your job; it's that the corporation you work for will ship it overseas for nothing more than a profit.

This time we want to talk about the men and women of every color and creed 50 who serve together, and fight together, and bleed together under the same proud flag. We want to talk about how to bring them home from a war that never should've been authorized and never should've been waged, and we want to talk about how we'll show our patriotism by caring for them, and their families, and giving them the benefits they have earned.

I would not be running for president if I didn't believe with all my heart that 51 this is what the vast majority of Americans want for this country. This union may never be perfect, but generation after generation has shown that it can always be perfected. And today, whenever I find myself feeling doubtful or cynical about this possibility, what gives me the most hope is the next generation—the young people whose attitudes and beliefs and openness to change have already made history in this election.

There is one story in particular that I'd like to leave you with today—a story I 52 told when I had the great honor of speaking on Dr. King's[17] birthday at his home church, Ebenezer Baptist, in Atlanta.

There is a young, twenty-three-year-old white woman named Ashley Baia who 53 organized for our campaign in Florence, South Carolina. She had been working to organize a mostly African-American community since the beginning of this campaign, and one day she was at a round-table discussion where everyone went around telling their story and why they were there.

And Ashley said that when she was nine years old, her mother got cancer. And 54 because she had to miss days of work, she was let go and lost her health care. They had to file for bankruptcy, and that's when Ashley decided that she had to do something to help her mom.

She knew that food was one of their most expensive costs, and so Ashley con- 55 vinced her mother that what she really liked and really wanted to eat more than anything else was mustard and relish sandwiches. Because that was the cheapest way to eat.

She did this for a year until her mom got better, and she told everyone at the 56 round-table that the reason she joined our campaign was so that she could help the millions of other children in the country who want and need to help their parents too.

Now Ashley might have made a different choice. Perhaps somebody told her 57

---

17. *Dr. King*: Martin Luther King Jr. (1929–1968), the U.S. civil rights leader.

along the way that the source of her mother's problems were blacks who were on welfare and too lazy to work, or Hispanics who were coming into the country illegally. But she didn't. She sought out allies in her fight against injustice.

Anyway, Ashley finishes her story and then goes around the room and asks everyone else why they're supporting the campaign. They all have different stories and reasons. Many bring up a specific issue. And finally they come to this elderly black man who's been sitting there quietly the entire time. And Ashley asks him why he's there. And he does not bring up a specific issue. He does not say health care or the economy. He does not say education or the war. He does not say that he was there because of Barack Obama. He simply says to everyone in the room, "I am here because of Ashley."   58

"I'm here because of Ashley." By itself, that single moment of recognition between that young white girl and that old black man is not enough. It is not enough to give health care to the sick, or jobs to the jobless, or education to our children.   59

But it is where we start. It is where our union grows stronger. And as so many generations have come to realize over the course of the two hundred and twenty-one years since a band of patriots signed that document in Philadelphia, that is where the perfection begins.   60

Reading Closely

1. Barack Obama sums up the message of his speech (and his campaign) in a single word. What is it? In which paragraphs does it appear?

2. In addition to racial tension, what other important issues, according to Obama, does America face today?

3. What does Obama see as the best way to deal with the country's problems? What does he see as the greatest threat to solving them?

4. Why does Obama refuse to "disown" Reverend Wright (22)?

5. Why does Obama nevertheless find Wright's remarks "inexcusable" (24)?

Strategies and Structures

1. First delivered in Philadelphia, across the street from Independence Hall, Obama's speech takes its title from the Declaration of Independence and begins with a direct reference to the men who composed that document (2). Why do you think Obama connects his words to those of the Founding Fathers? Why is this an effective strategy—or if it's not, why not?

2. Who is Obama's intended audience, and what is his purpose in addressing them?

3. How does Obama anticipate objections to his speech, especially to how he characterizes his personal relationship with Reverend Wright? Refer to paragraph numbers in your response.

4. With regard to the issue of race, what is Obama's main claim? What evidence does he use to support that claim? How convincing is that evidence?

5. How does Obama draw on personal experience? How pertinent is this evidence to his argument? Refer to paragraph numbers in your response.

6. How and how well does Obama establish his credibility as a person who understands the needs and values of "every race and every hue" (8)? Explain.

7. Why do you think Obama ends his speech with the story of Ashley and the "elderly black man" (60)? Is this an effective way to conclude? Why or why not?

8. *Other Methods.* Obama ANALYZES THE CAUSES of "the anger and the bitterness" of Reverend Wright and his generation (32). What are some of them? What, according to Obama, are some of the potential EFFECTS of those feelings?

Thinking about Language

1. The word *perfect* is not normally used with *more* or *most*. The phrase "a more perfect union" is archaic and would be seen today as ungrammatical. How and where does Obama's speech play on this phrase?

2. A *story* is a NARRATIVE, an account of what happened to somebody in a particular time and place. The word can also mean the *material* for such a narrative— as in "that's the American story." Where and why does Obama use *story* in this second sense?

3. Obama refers to slavery as "this nation's original sin" (3). Theologists often use the phrase "original sin" to refer to the sins of Adam and Eve, which caused them to be thrown out of the Garden of Eden and which were passed down to all later generations. Why do you think Obama uses it in a speech about a controversy involving his former pastor?

4. How does Obama use the personal pronoun *we* throughout his speech? Why do you think he uses it this way?

5. What are the CONNOTATIONS of the following words and phrases?

stained (3)	*seared into my genetic makeup* (9)
scoured (11)	*divisive* (12, 16)
on the cheap (13)	*firestorm* (15)
distorted (15)	*disown* (22)

FOR WRITING

1. Write a paragraph or two analyzing how Obama's speech appeals to his audience's emotions. Refer to paragraph numbers in your response.

2. NARRATE a brief, true story about yourself or a relative or friend that could take place only in America, or that otherwise illustrates this "improbable experiment in democracy" (2).

3. Write an argument that supports or disagrees with the claim that "race is an issue . . . this nation cannot afford to ignore right now" (25). Be sure to demonstrate your credibility by taking into account the needs and values of various racial and ethnic communities.

ANDREW MARVELL

To His Coy Mistress

Andrew Marvell (1621–1678) was an English metaphysical poet, a follower of John Donne and George Herbert. In his own time, he was better known as a nimble politician of unquestionable integrity. He served as an assistant to poet John Milton, who was then serving as Latin secretary in Oliver Cromwell's republican government. Marvell was elected to Parliament in 1659, just a year before the monarchy was restored under Charles II.

"To His Coy Mistress" is essentially an argument: the speaker summons his formidable powers of seductive eloquence to persuade his sweetheart to yield herself to the passions of the moment.

Had we but world enough, and time,   1
This coyness, lady, were no crime.
We would sit down and think which way
To walk, and pass our long love's day;
Thou by the Indian Ganges' side   5
Shouldst rubies find; I by the tide
Of Humber[1] would complain. I would
Love you ten years before the Flood;
And you should, if you please, refuse
Till the conversion of the Jews.[2]   10
My vegetable love should grow
Vaster than empires, and more slow.
An hundred years should go to praise
Thine eyes, and on thy forehead gaze;
Two hundred to adore each breast,   15
But thirty thousand to the rest;
An age at least to every part,
And the last age should show your heart.
For, lady, you deserve this state,
Nor would I love at lower rate.   20

1. *Humber:* river running through Marvell's hometown of Hull in northern England.
2. *Conversion of the Jews:* in Marvell's time, Christians commonly believed that Christ would return and that all Jews would then convert to Christianity.

But at my back I always hear
Time's winged chariot hurrying near;
And yonder all before us lie
Deserts of vast eternity.
Thy beauty shall no more be found,   25
Nor, in thy marble vault, shall sound
My echoing song; then worms shall try
That long preserv'd virginity,
And your quaint honour turn to dust,
And into ashes all my lust.   30
The grave's a fine and private place,
But none I think do there embrace.

    Now therefore, while the youthful hue
Sits on thy skin like morning dew,
And while thy willing soul transpires   35
At every pore with instant fires,
Now let us sport us while we may;
And now, like am'rous birds of prey,
Rather at once our time devour,
Than languish in his slow-chapp'd power.   40
Let us roll all our strength, and all
Our sweetness, up into one ball;
And tear our pleasures with rough strife
Through the iron gates of life.
Thus, though we cannot make our sun   45
Stand still, yet we will make him run.

READING CLOSELY

1. To whom is the speaker in Marvell's poem addressing his "song" (27)? Why? What is he trying to convince her to do?

2. What seems to be the lady's position, so far, on the issue he raises? What evidence, if any, does Marvell cite to suggest that she may be eventually persuaded by her lover's ARGUMENT?

3. Why is the speaker in Marvell's poem so concerned with the passage of time?

STRATEGIES AND STRUCTURES

1. In stanza one, the lover describes a condition contrary to fact. What is it? Why do you think he begins his plea this way instead of just going straight to the point?

2. If they had enough space and time, Marvell's speaker tells his beloved, "This coyness, lady, were no crime" (2). What evidence does he introduce in stanza two to suggest that they don't?

3. "Now therefore" (33) and "thus" (45) signal the conclusion of the logical reasoning that holds Marvell's poem together. What ultimate claim is the speaker making in this final stanza?

4. Does the speaker in Marvell's poem use mostly inductive or deductive logic? Explain.

5. Why do you think Marvell relies so heavily on logic in a love poem? Does he ever appeal to the lady's emotions or her sense that he is a trustworthy person? If so, how and where?

6. *Other Methods.* Marvell's speaker offers two contrasting visions of the future. How do they COMPARE with each other—and with the present as the speaker characterizes it? How does he use these comparisons to support his argument?

THINKING ABOUT LANGUAGE

1. How does your dictionary define "coyness" (2)? Why do you think the lady in Marvell's poem is said to be "coy" instead of "shy" or "retiring"?

2. In what sense is Marvell using the word "complain" (7)?

3. In Marvell's day, it was thought that vegetables could grow indefinitely. What, then, are the implications of the phrase "vegetable love" (11)?

4. Explain the HYPERBOLE in her refusing "till the conversion of the Jews" (10).

5. Explain the PUN on *sun* in the final lines of Marvell's poem.

FOR WRITING

1. Write a paragraph explaining the logical reasoning that binds together the three stanzas of Marvell's poem. How valid and effective do you find it, and why?

2. Write an essay analyzing "To His Coy Mistress" as a poem on the theme of *carpe diem* (Latin for "seize the day"). To what extent does the argument of the poem reach beyond the sphere of the two lovers into the wider world?

Debating the Drinking Age

After the repeal of Prohibition, which outlawed alcohol from 1920 to 1933, most states set the minimal legal drinking age (MLDA) at 21. Between 1970 and 1975, however, as the minimum age fell for voting and other activities, twenty-nine states reduced the MLDA. As a result, some researchers contended, more teenagers were killed or seriously injured in automobile and other accidents. Over the next decade, under pressure from such advocacy groups as Mothers Against Drunk Driving (MADD), sixteen states increased their MLDAs; and in 1984, the federal government enacted the National Minimum Drinking Age Act, which cut federal funding for highways by ten percent to states with an MLDA under 21.

Today, all states comply with this act, which prohibits the purchase and public possession of alcohol by people under 21. The act does not ban the consumption of alcohol by young people, however. And in recent years, some lawmakers and educators have called for a reevaluation of the MLDA. In 2005, for example, the president of Middlebury College wrote in the *New York Times* that "the 21-year-old drinking age is bad social policy and terrible law" because, in his opinion, it promotes binge drinking and other forms of irresponsible or illegal behavior on college campuses.

Should the MLDA be lowered? In the texts presented here, a journalist, a professor, and a research scientist each discuss the legal, medical, and social consequences of the minimum legal age for the purchase and public consumption of alcohol:

Ruth Engs, "Why the Drinking Age Should Be Lowered," p. 542
Jack Hitt, "The Battle of the Binge," p. 545
Robert Voas, "There's No Benefit to Lowering the Drinking Age," p. 549

Questions about this group of readings can be found on p. 552.

RUTH C. ENGS

Why the Drinking Age Should Be Lowered:
An Opinion Based on Research

Ruth Clifford Engs is a professor of applied health science at Indiana University, where her work has concentrated mainly on the use, abuse, and regulation of alcohol. In particular, she has written extensively about the drinking patterns and drinking problems of college students.

"Why the Drinking Age Should Be Lowered" appears on Engs's website. The real issue, according to Engs, isn't underage drinking but irresponsible drinking. Elsewhere Engs has described her preferred approach to the problem—drinking permits modeled on driving permits. "How can we expect youth to know how to drink," she writes, "if they are not educated about sensible consumption?"

THE LEGAL DRINKING AGE should be lowered to about 18 or 19 and young adults allowed to drink in controlled environments such as restaurants, taverns, pubs and official school and university functions. In these situations responsible drinking could be taught through role modeling and educational programs. Mature and sensible drinking behavior would be expected. This opinion is based upon research that I have been involved in for over twenty years concerning college-age youth and the history of drinking in the United States and other cultures. 1

Although the legal purchase age is 21 years of age, a majority of college students under this age consume alcohol but in an irresponsible manner. This is because drinking by these youth is seen as an enticing "forbidden fruit," a "badge of rebellion against authority" and a symbol of adulthood. As a nation we have tried prohibition legislation twice in the past for controlling irresponsible drinking problems. This was during national prohibition in the 1920s and state prohibition during the 1850s. These laws were finally repealed because they were unenforceable and because the backlash towards them caused other social problems. Today we are repeating history and making the same mistakes that occurred in the past. Prohibition did not work then and prohibition for young people under the age of 21 is not working now. 2

The flouting of the current laws is readily seen among university students. Those under the age of 21 are more likely to be heavy—sometimes called "binge"— drinkers (consuming over 5 drinks at least once a week). For example, 22 percent of all students under 21 compared to 18 percent over 21 years of age are heavy drinkers. Among drinkers only, 32 percent of under age compared to 24 percent of legal age are heavy drinkers. 3

Research from the early 1980s until the present has shown a continuous 4
decrease in drinking and driving related variables which has paralleled the nation's,
and also university students', decrease in per capita consumption. However, these
declines started in 1980, before the national 1987 law that mandated states to have
21-year-old-alcohol-purchase laws.

The decrease in drinking and driving problems are the result of many factors 5
and not just the rise in purchase age or the decreased per capita consumption.
These include: education concerning drunk driving, designated driver programs,
increased seat belt and air bag usage, safer automobiles, lower speed limits, free
taxi services from drinking establishments, etc.

While there has been a decrease in per capita consumption and motor vehicle 6
crashes, unfortunately, during this same time period there has been an *increase* in
other problems related to heavy and irresponsible drinking among college-age
youth. Most of these reported behaviors showed little change until *after* the 21-
year-old law in 1987. For example from 1982 until 1987 about 46 percent of students reported "vomiting after drinking." This jumped to over 50 percent after the
law change. Significant increases were also found for other variables: "cutting class
after drinking" jumped from 9 percent to almost 12 percent; "missing class because
of hangover" went from 26 percent to 28 percent; "getting lower grades because of
drinking" rose from 5 percent to 7 percent; and "been in a fight after drinking"
increased from 12 percent to 17 percent. All of these behaviors are indices of irresponsible drinking. This increase in abusive drinking behavior is due to "underground drinking" outside of adult supervision in student rooms and apartments
where same-age individuals congregate and because of lack of knowledge of
responsible drinking behaviors.

Based upon the fact that our current prohibition laws are not working, alterna- 7
tive approaches from the experience of other, and more ancient cultures, who do
not have these problems, need to be tried. Groups such as Italians, Greeks, Chinese
and Jews, who have few drinking related problems, tend to share some common
characteristics. Alcohol is neither seen as a poison or a magic potion, there is little
or no social pressure to drink, irresponsible behavior is never tolerated, young people learn at home from their parents and from other adults how to handle alcohol
in a responsible manner, there is societal consensus on what constitutes responsible drinking. Because the 21-year-old-drinking-age law is not working, and is counterproductive, it behooves us as a nation to change our current prohibition law and
to teach responsible drinking techniques for those who choose to consume alcoholic beverages.

READING CLOSELY

1. What is Ruth Engs's claim? Where does she state it most clearly and directly?

2. Engs isn't arguing that people under 21 should drink more. So why does she think lowering the MLDA is a good idea? What specific reasons does she give?

3. Why do you think Engs refers to the drinking practices of "more ancient cultures" (7)?

4. Engs states that research has shown that both "drinking and driving related variables" and "per capita consumption" of alcohol have decreased since 1980 (4). Why doesn't she attribute these good results to the MLDA law? To what *does* she attribute these results?

STRATEGIES AND STRUCTURES

1. How does Engs establish her credibility on the subject of student drinking? Refer to specific places in the text in your response.

2. Who is her intended audience? What does Engs want them to do?

3. How and how well does Engs deal with potential objections to her argument?

4. What kind of evidence does Engs use to support her claim that the drinking age should be lowered?

5. *Other Methods.* Engs COMPARES the MLDA law to the prohibition laws of the 1920s, in which all alcohol was banned in the United States (2). Do you think this is an effective comparison? Why or why not? Is it a fair one? Explain.

THINKING ABOUT LANGUAGE

1. "Forbidden fruit" (2) is a reference to the Bible—Genesis 2:16–17. How does Engs use this ALLUSION to support her argument?

2. Engs refers to the MLDA laws as "our current prohibition law" (7). What are the CONNOTATIONS of the word *prohibition* in this context?

3. The word *flouting* (3) is frequently confused with *flaunting*. Why is *flouting* the correct choice here?

FOR WRITING

1. Engs claims that "ancient cultures . . . have few drinking related problems" (7). Outline the main points you would make in an argument addressing this claim. You might support it, refute it, or agree with some parts but not others.

2. Write an argument addressing the question of "how to handle alcohol in a responsible manner" (7).

JACK HITT

The Battle of the Binge

Jack Hitt (b. 1957) is a frequent contributor to such magazines as Harper's, GQ,
Mother Jones, *and* Outside. *As a reporter for the* New York Times Magazine, *he has
covered everything from the abortion debate and presidential politics to Internet spam
and featherless chickens. A familiar voice on National Public Radio's* This American
Life, *Hitt is also the author of* Off the Road: A Modern-Day Walk Down the Pilgrim's Route into Spain *(1994).*

*Raised and educated in an era when college students "strained to act intelligently
and comfortably while drinking with an elder," Hitt revisits his alma mater in "The
Battle of the Binge," first published in the* New York Times Magazine *in 1999. Largely
as a result of laws that raised the legal age to 21, Hitt argues, drinking on campus has
changed in ways that he finds both appalling and sobering.*

BACK IN THE 70's—my college time—an English professor I barely knew 1
named Ted Stirling spotted me on the quad and invited me to a small, informal
reading after supper. Maybe he felt sorry for me. I had marooned myself in the
French ghetto of *la litterature comparative*, and had further exiled myself in the cul-
de-sac between Latin and Spanish. So I went that night to sit on stuffed sofas
beneath scowling bishops in gilt frames and to discuss Wallace Stevens's poem
"Thirteen Ways of Looking at a Blackbird." Afterward, Stirling bought the students
a pitcher of beer at the pub, and we strained to act intelligently and comfortably
while drinking with an elder. ("Stevens an insurance agent! Surely you jest, Professor. Why, that would make poets the unacknowledged underwriters of the world,
wouldn't you agree?")

I started thinking about how I learned to drink at college—I went to Sewanee, 2
in Tennessee—when I read about a recent Harvard study that found that 43 percent, nearly half, of all college students today "binge drink," defined as regularly
pounding down four or five stiff ones in a row in order to get blasted. The pan-
demic is so severe that 113 college presidents united a few weeks ago to publicly
admit that a generation is in peril. They have also rolled out a public-service ad,
which employs that brand of sarcasm Madison Avenue thinks young people find
amusing. "Binge Beer," it says. "Who says falling off a balcony is such a bad thing?"
See, you're supposed to realize that falling off a balcony is, in fact, a bad thing.

Other educational tactics include dry rock concerts, abstinent fraternities, 3
"mock 'tail" parties, a Web site of course (www.nasulgc.org/bingedrink) and a new
CD-ROM called "Alcohol 101" and featuring a "virtual party" that segues into an

anatomical lecture about how quickly the bloodstream absorbs alcohol. Look out, Myst.[1]

What no one seems to have noticed is that the rise in binging has occurred at the very same time that the legal drinking age has been raised everywhere to 21. If you're 18 to 21, it's the 1920's again and a mini-Prohibition is in full swing. As a result, moderate drinking has almost vanished among students and, more tellingly, from school-sponsored events. How anachronistic it feels to describe what used to be routine college functions, like a Dizzy Gillespie concert or a Robert Penn Warren reading, followed by a reception, with drinks and hors d'oeuvres, at which students were expected to at least pretend to be cool about it, i.e., practice drinking. I frequently received dinner invitations from faculty members like Tom Spaccarelli, a Spanish professor who served up tapas while uncorking a Rioja for a few students. We handled the long stems of our wineglasses as confidently as a colt its legs.

And there was always another occasion. Sewanee had dozens of those inane college societies like Green Ribbon, a group whose invitation to membership I haughtily trashed after Professor Paschall, my sponsor, explained that the point was nothing more than "getting dressed up and having cocktails with some alumni."

But I began to see the point about 10 years after graduation when I returned to Sewanee to give a little talk. Afterward, I took some students to the pub where they sheepishly ordered cider. At first, I thought this new college life—clean and sober—was a good idea.

Then my nephew, a junior there at that time, explained the typical partygoer's schedule: drive off campus or hide in the woods (often alone), guzzle a pint of bourbon, eat a box of breath mints and then stumble into the dry sorority party serenely blotto. My nephew knew two students who had died—falling off a cliff, blood poisoning—and five others who had been paralyzed or seriously injured in car accidents because of binging. For a college with roughly 1,300 students, this constitutes a statistical massacre.

We drank wildly in the 70's, too. The Phi's had their seasonal Screaming Bull blowout. Kegs were easy to find on weekends. I have drunk tequila only once in my life, and this being a family newspaper, my account of that evening can proceed no further. I was a member of the Sewanee Temperance League, whose annual outdoor party pledged to "rid the world of alcohol by consuming it all ourselves." But all those events were crowded social occasions, almost always with professors and their spouses in attendance—not prowling alone in the woods with a pint. After college, when you got a job, Screaming Bull opportunities quickly tapered off; the

---

1. *Myst:* a popular computer game that was released in 1993.

working world was different yet, in time, quite familiar, like an evening with Ted Stirling or a dinner at Tom Spaccarelli's.

This year, Ohio University's zero-tolerance program has proudly outlawed empty beer cans in the dorm. Nearly 7 percent of the entire 16,000-student enrollment last year was disciplined for alcohol abuse, often handed over as criminals to the Athens Municipal Court. Despite all the tough bluster, the binge rate among students there hasn't budged from an astounding 60 percent. 9

For college students, booze has been subsumed into the Manichaean[1] battle of our drug war. It's either Prohibition or cave into the hippies' legalization schemes. And it seems fairly unreversible. Legislatures raised the drinking minimum in reaction to the raw emotion deployed by Mothers Against Drunk Driving. Then colleges were bullied by insurance companies that threatened to jack up liability rates if administrators didn't take aggressive action. The old days of looking the other way, when the police used to pick up toasted students and quietly drive them to their dorms, seems like collaboration in today's harsh light. 10

There probably is a way out of this, but it is going to require some larger cultural changes that will make us see the irony, even cruelty, of infantilizing certain young adults. The very people who have urged this situation into existence are too often the people who vent about the increasing lack of "responsibility" in our society (demanding, for example, that juvenile offenders be treated in court as adults). But for middle-class kids in college, they make responsibility an ever-receding ideal, never quite grasped in the pampered ease of an extended adolescence. 11

In the early 70's, the big political fight among college students was for the right to vote. The argument held that kids who were considered old enough to die for their country and order a drink in a bar should be able to choose their political leaders. It is back to two out of three again. But booze is not like the vote, which can be ignored to no one's immediate peril. Rather, alcohol consumption, like table manners or sexual behavior, is a socialized phenomenon, which if not taught, yields up a kind of wild child. By denying the obvious pleasure of drinking and not teaching it by example, is anyone really surprised that we've loosed upon the world a generation of feral drunks? 12

---

1. *Manichaean*: Manichaeanism is a dualistic religion named after a Persian prophet of the third century C.E. In everyday usage, "Manichaean" refers to a conflict of opposites, such as good and evil, light and darkness.

READING CLOSELY

1. When Hitt was in college, how and when did students consume alcohol? In his view, why has "moderate drinking" all but vanished among college students (4)?

2. What is Hitt's explanation for why the MLDA was raised to twenty-one in the first place? Why does he think this trend is "fairly unreversible" (10)?

3. Hitt thinks that a number of changes would have to occur before the MLDA is either lowered or ignored (11). What are some of those changes?

STRATEGIES AND STRUCTURES

1. Who is Hitt's intended audience, and how does he establish his credibility with them?

2. How and how well does Hitt deal with potential objections to his argument?

3. Hitt argues that "the rise in binging has occurred at the very same time that the legal drinking age has been raised everywhere to 21" (4). Do you think he effectively demonstrates a CAUSE-AND-EFFECT relationship between the two?

4. *Other Methods.* Hitt's evidence is mainly anecdotal. Cite several examples of his use of personal NARRATIVE, and explain how they support his argument.

THINKING ABOUT LANGUAGE

1. Hitt speaks of the "raw emotion" with which, he claims, Mothers Against Drunk Driving convinced legislators to raise the MLDA (10). What are the CONNOTATIONS of the term *deployed* in the same paragraph? Of *feral* (12)?

2. What are the implications of the SIMILE "as a colt its legs" (4)?

3. When Hitt speaks of cultural changes in paragraph 11, how is he DEFINING *culture*? How does this definition contribute to his argument?

FOR WRITING

1. Write a paragraph or two arguing that responsible drinking is a moral and ethical issue rather than (or as well as) a "socialized phenomenon" (12).

2. Although Hitt admits a drop in the MLDA is unlikely unless the federal government goes along, he doesn't deal directly with what it would cost individual states if they lowered the MLDA without federal approval—and therefore lost 10 percent of their federal funding for highways. Write an argument that claims the MLDA should or should not be lowered, taking into account the economic aspects of the issue.

ROBERT VOAS

There's No Benefit to Lowering the Drinking Age

Robert Voas is a senior research scientist at the Pacific Institute for Research and Eval-
uation in Calverton, Maryland. A former astronaut training officer for NASA, he holds
a Ph.D. in psychology from the University of California at Los Angeles. After leaving
NASA, Voas spent several years in the Peace Corps before joining the U.S. Department
of Transportation, where he served as director of the National Highway Traffic Safety
Administration's Office of Program Evaluation. A member of the national board of
Mothers Against Drunk Driving (MADD), Voas is the author of many articles on motor
vehicle accidents and alcohol abuse, particularly among teenagers.

    "There's No Benefit to Lowering the Drinking Age" first appeared in the Christian
Science Monitor *in 2006.*

$\mathbf{A}$FTER NEARLY FOUR DECADES of exacting research on how to save lives and 1
reduce injuries by preventing drinking and driving, there is a revanchist attempt
afoot to roll back one of the most successful laws in generations: the minimum
legal drinking age of 21.

This is extremely frustrating. While public health researchers must produce 2
painstaking evidence that's subjected to critical scholarly review, lower-drinking-
age advocates seem to dash off remarks based on glib conjecture and self-selected
facts.

It's startling that anybody—given the enormous bodies of research and data— 3
would consider lowering the drinking age. And yet, legislation is currently pending
in New Hampshire and Wisconsin to lower the drinking age for military personnel
and for all residents in Vermont. Just as bad are the arguments from think-tank
writers, various advocates, and even academics (including at least one former college president) that ignore or manipulate the real evidence and instead rely on
slogans.

I keep hearing the same refrains: "If you're old enough to go to war, you should 4
be old enough to drink," or "the drinking-age law just increases the desire for the
forbidden fruit," or "lower crash rates are due to tougher enforcement, not the
21 law," or "Europeans let their kids drink, so they learn how to be more responsible," or finally, "I did it when I was a kid, and I'm OK."

First, I'm not sure what going to war and being allowed to drink have in com- 5
mon. The military takes in youngsters particularly because they are not yet fully
developed and can be molded into soldiers. The 21 law is predicated on the fact
that drinking is more dangerous for youth because they're still developing mentally

549

and physically, and they lack experience and are more likely to take risks. Ask platoon leaders and unit commanders, and they'll tell you that the last thing they want is young soldiers drinking.

As for the forbidden fruit argument, the opposite is true. Research shows that 6 back when some states still had a minimum drinking age of 18, youths in those states who were under 21 drank more and continued to drink more as adults in their early 20s. In states where the drinking age was 21, teenagers drank less and continue to drink less through their early 20s.

And the minimum 21 law, by itself, has most certainly resulted in fewer acci- 7 dents, because the decline occurred even when there was little enforcement and tougher penalties had not yet been enacted. According to the National Highway Traffic Safety Administration, the 21 law has saved 23,733 lives since states began raising drinking ages in 1975.

Do European countries really have fewer youth drinking problems? No, that's 8 a myth. Compared to American youth, binge drinking rates among young people are higher in every European country except Turkey. Intoxication rates are higher in most countries; in Britain, Denmark, and Ireland they're more than twice the U.S. level. Intoxication and binge drinking are directly linked to higher levels of alcohol-related problems, such as drinking and driving.

But, you drank when you were a kid, and you're OK. Thank goodness, because 9 many kids aren't OK. An average of 11 American teens die each day from alcohol-related crashes. Underage drinking leads to increased teen pregnancy, violent crime, sexual assault, and huge costs to our communities. Among college students, it leads to 1,700 deaths, 500,000 injuries, 600,000 physical assaults, and 70,000 sexual assaults each year.

Recently, New Zealand lowered its drinking age, which gave researchers a good 10 opportunity to study the impact. The result was predictable: The rate of alcohol-related crashes among young people rose significantly compared to older drivers.

I've been studying drinking and driving for nearly 40 years and have been 11 involved in public health and behavioral health for 53 years. Believe me when I say that lowering the drinking age would be very dangerous; it would benefit no one except those who profit from alcohol sales.

If bars and liquor stores can freely provide alcohol to teenagers, parents will be 12 out of the loop when it comes to their children's decisions about drinking. Age 21 laws are designed to keep such decisions within the family where they belong. Our society, particularly our children and grandchildren, will be immeasurably better off if we not only leave the minimum drinking age law as it is, but enforce it better, too.

Reading Closely

1. What is Robert Voas's claim? Where does he articulate it in most clearly?

2. According to Voas, what is the basis for the "21 law" (5)?

3. What other consequences, besides an increase in traffic fatalities among teens, does Voas attribute to "underage drinking" (9)?

4. In Voas's opinion, who are the only people to benefit from a lower MLDA?

5. Why does Voas think that lowering the MLDA would keep parents "out of the loop" (12)?

Strategies and Structures

1. What is the main evidence that Voas provides to support his claim?

2. Who is Voas's intended audience? How does he appeal to their emotions?

3. How and how well does Voas establish his credibility as an expert?

4. Good writers anticipate the arguments that are most likely to be raised by people with different points of view. Voas makes this strategy the main organizing principle of his entire argument. How?

5. *Other Methods.* Voas finds little in common between "going to war and being allowed to drink" (5). Where else (and how effectively) does he use COMPARISON AND CONTRAST to support his argument?

Thinking about Language

1. Look up *revanchist* in a dictionary (1). What does it mean, and how does it fit the context in which it is used here?

2. Why does Voas refer to arguments for lowering the drinking age as "glib conjecture" (2)? How well does he succeed in showing that the phrase is justified?

3. "Refrains" (4) and "myth" (8) have to do with songs and stories. Why (and how effectively) does Voas use these terms?

For Writing

1. To the argument "you drank when you were a kid, and you're OK," Voas replies: "Thank goodness, because many kids aren't OK" (9). Is this retort logical, or does it "beg the question"? (See "Avoiding Logical Fallacies," p. 499.) Write a paragraph explaining your view.

2. "Age 21 laws," says Voas, "are designed to keep such decisions [about alcohol consumption] within the family where they belong" (12). Compose an argument refuting or supporting this claim.

Debating the Drinking Age

The following questions refer to the arguments on pp. 542–50.

READING ARGUMENTS

1. Among the participants in this debate on the MLDA, which writer focuses mainly on binge drinking as a form of unsophisticated social behavior? On binge drinking as a form of socially irresponsible behavior? On binge drinking as a form of dangerous behavior? Explain.

2. Which of the arguments in this debate do you think is most likely to appeal to the age group it talks about—that is, those under age 21? to parents and others responsible for the behavior of minors? to academics and health care professionals? Explain why in each case.

3. Which of the participants in this debate makes the most effective use of statistics? How so? Who uses facts and figures the least? Would that person's argument be stronger if it included more numbers? Why or why not?

4. To what extent would you say the language and general style of writing in each of these essays fits the viewpoint and profession of the author (professor of health sciences, journalist, public health researcher)? How would you describe these different prose styles?

FOR WRITING

1. Write a paragraph or two explaining which of the arguments in this debate you find strongest (or weakest)—and why.

2. Write an argument in which you take a position (and support it—with facts, statistics, expert testimony, and other evidence) on some aspect of the MLDA debate not fully covered by Engs, Hitt, or Voas.

Debating Intellectual Property Rights

Intellectual property refers to "labors of the mind"—including books, films, music, software, and architectural or mechanical designs—over which the author may be entitled to certain legal rights of ownership. Intellectual property rights originated with copyright, a legal concept that was established in the United States by the first U.S. Copyright Act, signed into law in 1790 by George Washington. The nation's founders believed that copyright laws encouraged individual creativity, but they also regarded ideas as public goods, and they placed strict limits—fourteen years, with one renewal—on how long someone could enjoy a monopoly on their own creations.

In 1909, however, Congress doubled the length of copyright. The Copyright Act of 1976 further extended the rights of authors to their own lifetime plus fifty years. And in 1998, copyrights held by individuals picked up another twenty years under the Sonny Bono Copyright Term Extension Act. This legislation is sometimes referred to as the "Mickey Mouse Protection Act" because it also extended (to almost a hundred years) the term of copyright on works of corporate authorship, including Disney cartoons. Because Mickey made his first appearance in 1928, he was scheduled to enter the public domain in 2003, to be followed soon after by Pluto, Goofy, and Donald Duck. Under the new law, however, early Disney characters—and thousands of other works—will remain private property until at least 2019.

Who should own the words, music, and other intellectual property created by individuals? In these texts, a journalist and two lawyers each explore the conflict between private property rights and the need for public access to intellectual property in the age of the Internet:

Ellen Goodman, "Who Owns Dr. King's Words?," p. 554
Marci A. Hamilton, "Why Suing College Students for Illegal Music Downloading Is Right," p. 557
Lawrence Lessig, "Free Culture," p. 562

Questions about this group of readings can be found on p. 567.

ELLEN GOODMAN

Who Owns Dr. King's Words?

Ellen Goodman (b. 1941) joined the Boston Globe *as a columnist in 1967, and readers soon warmed to the quietly serious voice she brought to American political discourse. Her columns are published in nearly four hundred newspapers around the country. Her books include six collections of her columns, most recently* Paper Trail: Common Sense in Uncommon Times *(2004). In 1980 she was awarded a Pulitzer Prize for Distinguished Commentary.*

In "Who Owns Dr. King's Words?," first published in the Boston Globe *in 1999, Goodman addresses the issue posed by her title: is an important speech a matter of public history, or is it private property? With characteristic even-handedness, she weighs the arguments over the ownership of a dream.*

At FIRST IT SOUNDS LIKE A QUESTION for a panel of philosophers: Who owns 1
a dream? What happens when a vision that's formed in the words of one person is released like a balloon into the air to be shared with everyone? Whose property is it then?

The dream in this case was described by Martin Luther King Jr. Standing before 2
a crowd of 200,000 at the Lincoln Memorial on that August day in 1963, he found the language to match the moment. "I Have a Dream," he told the country in a speech that became a part of our collective eloquence, as much a part of our heritage as the Gettysburg Address.[1]

Dr. King had a gift. Now people are wrangling over the value of that gift. 3

Today the question of dreamers and owners, words and property, history and 4
money, has been set before a panel of three judges in Atlanta. The King family is asking an appeals court to rule that CBS must pay them to use the dream speech in a documentary sold on videotape. They claim that they—not the public—own Dr. King's words.

For years, the King family has been protective or litigious—choose one or the 5
other. They sued and settled with Henry Hampton, who produced the "Eyes on the Prize" documentary. They sued and settled with *USA Today*. They regard themselves as keepers of the legacy . . . and the accounting books.

In 1963, no one would have believed there was money to be made from civil 6
rights history. In his lifetime Dr. King was interested in justice, not profit. His

---

1. *Gettysburg Address*: one of the most recognized and often-quoted speeches in U.S. history, delivered in 1863 by President Abraham Lincoln.

family at times lived on the salary of a $6,000-a-year minister. He contributed everything, even his Nobel Prize money, to the Southern Christian Leadership Conference.

When Dr. King was assassinated, the sum total of his estate was a $50,000 insurance policy bought for him by Harry Belafonte.[2] That, plus his words.   7

These words are what the family lawyers call "intellectual property." It's property that will soon be worth an estimated $50 million from multimedia deals, licensing, and real estate.   8

I do not mean to suggest that the family is in the protection racket solely for the money. Schools are granted the use of the "Dream Speech" freely. At the same time, one of the many lawsuits was against a company that wanted to use Dr. King's image on refrigerator magnets.   9

It's not surprising that the family would resist the trivialization of a man's magnetism into a refrigerator magnet. It's far too easy in our culture to slip from being a martyr on a pedestal to a pop icon on a T-shirt.   10

While we are talking about King and commercialism, it is fair to ask the difference between the family profit—much of which goes to the Center for Nonviolent Social Change in Atlanta—and CBS's profit.   11

But nevertheless there is still the little matter of public history and private property.   12

In the appeals court, the case will not be decided on the grounds of greed but of copyright law and free speech. On the one hand Dr. King gave the press advance copies of the speech; on the other hand, the most eloquent passages were extemporaneous. On the one hand he copyrighted the speech after it was given; on the other hand he characterized it as "a living petition to the public and the Congress."   13

Those of us who work with words for a living understand the desire to control our ephemeral "product." We are sensitive to the notion of intellectual property and do not take kindly to bootlegged editions of CDs or books or software that show up on black markets.   14

But Martin Luther King Jr. was not a rock star. Or a software designer. He was a preacher, a leader, a prophet, a martyr. He was, in every sense of the word, a public figure.   15

One day, 36 years ago, he gave voice to our collective idealism and words to our best collective yearnings: "I have a dream that my four little children will one day live in a nation where they will not be judged by the color of their skin but by the content of their character."   16

This is not a private dream. It doesn't belong to his family estate. It belongs to all of us.   17

---

2. *Harry Belafonte*: a musician and activist who was a friend of King's.

READING CLOSELY

1. In Goodman's view, who owns Martin Luther King's "I Have a Dream" speech, and where does she state her opinion most directly?

2. "There is still the little matter," Goodman says, "of public history and private property" (12). What conflicting interests is she referring to here?

3. How and where does Goodman explain the increase in value of Martin Luther King's "intellectual property" (8)?

4. Why is it "not surprising," according to Goodman, that King's family would be protective of his legacy, including his famous speech (10)?

STRATEGIES AND STRUCTURES

1. Who is Goodman's intended audience? How do you know?

2. How, and how well, does Goodman support her claim that King's words belong "to all of us" (17)? Refer to specific passages in the text in your response.

3. Goodman reminds us that she is among those "who work with words for a living" (14). How effective do you find this method of establishing her credibility?

4. Goodman contends that, because Martin Luther King Jr. was a "public figure," his dream "belongs to all of us" (15–17). Does this argument appeal primarily to the reader's reason or to his or her emotions? Why do you say so?

5. *Other Methods.* Goodman likens "I Have a Dream" to Lincoln's Gettysburg Address (2). How and how well does this COMPARISON support her argument?

THINKING ABOUT LANGUAGE

1. Goodman equates King's "I Have a Dream" speech with a "balloon" released into the air (1). Is this a good ANALOGY? Why or why not?

2. Goodman offers the reader a choice between "protective" and "litigious" (5). Why? What are the CONNOTATIONS of these different terms?

3. Explain the distinction that Goodman is making between being "on a pedestal" and being "on a T-shirt" (10).

FOR WRITING

1. Write a paragraph or two explaining how and why someone's words might (or might not) be considered a form of property.

2. Who does King's famous speech belong to in your opinion? Write an argument in which you take (and support) a position on this particular issue—and on the ownership of intellectual property in general.

MARCI A. HAMILTON

Why Suing College Students for Illegal Music Downloading Is Right

Marci A. Hamilton is a professor at Yeshiva University's Benjamin N. Cardozo School of Law, where she is also the founding director of the Intellectual Property Law Program. Over the course of her career she has clerked for U.S. Supreme Court Justice Sandra Day O'Connor, testified before Congress about constitutional law, and advised lawmakers in Europe and Africa on issues of religious freedom. Hamilton has published innumerable articles in legal journals, and she writes a regular column for FindLaw.com. Her most recent book is God vs. the Gavel: Religion and the Rule of Law *(2005).*

Hamilton's position on the issue of music file-sharing is evident even in the title of this 2003 FindLaw article. In Hamilton's view, copyright law serves an essential function in society; without it, "only the rich, or the government-sponsored, could be this culture's full-time creators."

Rᴇᴄᴇɴᴛʟʏ, ᴀɴᴅ ᴄᴏɴᴛʀᴏᴠᴇʀѕɪᴀʟʟʏ, the recording industry has switched tactics in its fight against illegal downloading. Despite fear of a public relations debacle, it is planning to sue student downloaders.   1

First, however, it must identify them, and gather evidence of their illegal activity. Toward this end, subpoenas have already been sent to a number of universities and Internet Service Providers. Hundreds more are expected in September, after school starts.   2

Meanwhile, the Recording Industry Association of America (RIAA) has not only led the fight for these lawsuits, but also joined together with campus administrators to educate students on the law and the consequences of violating it.   3

Some have criticized the RIAA and others in the music industry for going after students. But I will argue that it is entirely right—both legally and morally—for them to do so.   4

The enduring value of an enforceable copyright law

In a society that enjoys the benefit of a strong, enforceable copyright law, it is too easy to forget what life would be like without it.   5

While my son went to space camp[1] in Huntsville, Alabama, recently, the rest of   6

---

1. *Space camp:* a summer program for kids ages 9 to 11, where they learn about America's space program with activities in astronaut training, rocket building, robotics, and more.

us went to Nashville, the home of country music and the Country Music Hall of Fame. The museum is excellent at many different levels, but my favorite element was the film of television clips showing country music over the past 50 years. Now, my mother is from Wyoming and my father from Kentucky, so I was destined to be a country-western music fan. The film brought back a million childhood memories; it also reminded me why copyright is such an absolute necessity.

Was it not for copyright's ability to build fences around intangible goods such as lyrics and melodies, a performer like Loretta Lynn would not have been able to leave Butcher Holler, Kentucky, and share her gifts with the world. The list of country music stars that have come from humble beginnings is long, and the best country music never forgets its origins.

The world would have been a lesser place but for copyright's ability to pave the road for these stars to travel from rags to riches, from hillbilly country to the big lights. The Country Music Hall of Fame gives you a real taste of that story as it displays the humble beginnings of some, as well as the gold-plated piano Priscilla Presley gave to Elvis on their first wedding anniversary.

In a culture without copyright, only the rich, or the government-sponsored, could be this culture's full-time creators. Poor artists such as Loretta Lynn would have to flip burgers long into their music careers—and might even give up on music entirely.

For these reasons, imagining a world without copyright wouldn't just impoverish the musicians. It would also impoverish the museum, the culture and music itself.

If the class of creators were winnowed down to the rich and the government-sponsored, and the free market were thus to be replaced by a patronage system, the ability of art to speak to the American people would dwindle precipitously. Artistic works would cater to elites; classical music might survive, but rock and country would encounter grave difficulties.

In the end, then, there is no such thing as cost-free downloading. It may be fiscally free today, but it will cost society dearly in the future.

The advent of the anti-copyright culture

The simple, yet crucial reasons why we have copyright in the first place are easy to forget in the new Information Era. Its utopian early years led adults and students alike to believe that whatever came across their computer screen could be—and ought to be—downloaded cost-free. There was a moment of stunned disbelief: copyright seemed obsolete.

Some saw this simply as a technological reality; others viewed it as a positive social development as well. In fact, it turned out that it was neither. Still, an anti-copyright culture developed—to the shock of the recording industry.

At first, the industry—wary of alienating the young people who were often its best buyers—made a strategic decision to go after the big boys in court. That meant targeting Napster[2]—and soon the industry won its fight. 15

Nevertheless, the industry continued to hemorrhege, dropping approximately 8 percent in sales last year. The culprits may well be the new Web sites, such as KaZaa, which, unlike Napster, do not depend on centralized servers. These sites accordingly make it nearly impossible to identify the Web host or master. 16

The industry then had no choice but to go after users—which meant going after students—and it did. As soon as it made the decision, copyright didn't seem so obsolete, after all. 17

While technology did tend to facilitate illegal downloading, it did not pose infinite obstacles to figuring out who was committing these copyright crimes; universities and ISPs[3] alike tracked their users in certain ways. Although the industry will continue to work on improving the technological protection for works on the Web, for now, the courts will serve them quite well. 18

That goes to show that, with respect to copyright, new rules are not needed; just enforcement of the old. We were never living in a true legal vacuum, as the "Information Wants to Be Free" contingent suggested; we were living in an enforcement vacuum instead, and that is now changing, as violators are being hunted down. 19

Even the hunt itself has had a chilling effect. Knowing that one is committing a crime, and may be caught, is scary indeed. Students will back off of illegal copying once they learn that the free ride was an illusion; and if they don't, many parents will step in to ensure that their children don't earn a criminal record along with their college diploma. 20

Like shoplifting, illegal downloading can be reduced by monitoring and warning

In a lot of ways, downloading is more like shoplifting than it is like "piracy," the term often used for it. Pirates embrace a life of crime; shoplifters often see their activity (wrongly) as an exciting and slightly risky diversion—a relatively petty vice in an otherwise law-abiding life. 21

The more seriously society takes shoplifting, the more shoplifters will be deterred. The same is true, I believe, for illegal downloaders. Every law-breaking student has a diploma at stake, and only a scintilla of students is hardened criminals. Like the thrill of shoplifting, the thrill of illegal downloading may fade quickly in the face of serious penalties, and a real risk of getting caught. 22

2. *Napster:* an online file-sharing service that allowed users to download music files from other users' computers for free; it is now a legal, pay-per-download service.
3. *ISPs:* "Internet Service Providers," companies that provide access to the Web.

Of course, technological "locks" won't be perfect, and some level of crime will   23
remain. But here, again, the shoplifting analogy is instructive. Stores do not lock
up every item they offer to prevent shoplifting. Instead, they post signs saying
shoplifting is a crime, monitor their customers, and press charges against individual shoplifters. Despite all this, retail stores have had to build into their profit picture losses that will result from undetected shoplifting.

The recording industry will have to use similar tactics, and like retail stores,   24
they will have to live with a small loss from undetected stealing. But that loss can
be minimized, through warnings, monitoring, and enforcement. And word of
enforcement spreads. Few will be shoplifting from the store that famously pressed
charges against Winona Ryder.[4] Few students will keep downloading once their
classmates have famously gotten in deep trouble for doing just that. That is good
for them, but even better for us.

---

4. *Winona Ryder*: Hollywood actress who was caught shoplifting from the department store Saks
Fifth Avenue in 2001.

READING CLOSELY

1. According to Marci Hamilton, what is the legal basis for suing college students
   for downloading music?

2. Why does Hamilton think the recording industry is morally right to pursue students who download music illegally?

3. What technological changes make it necessary, in Hamilton's view, for the
   recording industry to go after individual students rather than "the big boys" like
   Napster (15)?

4. Hamilton argues that society benefits from "a strong, enforceable copyright
   law" (5). What specific benefits does she cite?

STRATEGIES AND STRUCTURES

1. In paragraph 24, Hamilton makes a distinction between "them" and "us." How
   does this distinction help to define her intended audience?

2. Why do you think Hamilton begins her essay by describing her trip to the Country Music Hall of Fame in Nashville? Is this an effective introduction to her
   argument? Why or why not?

3. Without strong copyright laws, Hamilton argues, "the ability of art to speak to the American people would dwindle" (11). Explain the logical reasoning behind this conclusion, particularly the premises (or assumptions) on which it is based. Is that reasoning valid? Explain.

4. "Knowing that one is committing a crime, and may be caught," says Hamilton, "is scary indeed" (20). Thus, she argues, "students will back off of illegal copying" once existing copyright laws are enforced (20). Is this a valid line of reasoning? Is it based more on logic or emotion, or does it appeal primarily to a sense of what is right and fair? Explain.

5. *Other Methods.* Hamilton argues that illegal downloading is "more like shoplifting" than piracy (21). How and how well does this COMPARISON contribute to her argument?

THINKING ABOUT LANGUAGE

1. It is not literally possible "to build fences around intangible goods" (7). How does this METAPHOR help Hamilton to define the legal concept of intellectual property?

2. Copyright laws, says Hamilton, "pave the road" for poor musicians "to travel from rags to riches" (8). In context, how might these CLICHÉS be justified?

3. Hamilton refers to "copyright crimes" and "violators" who are being "hunted down" (18, 19). Why do you think she uses such no-nonsense language?

FOR WRITING

1. Outline the main points you would make and the evidence you would cite to support the following claim in a speech or written argument: "Even in a society without copyright protection, popular music, such as rock and country, would survive and flourish."

2. Should students be sued for illegally downloading music and other intellectual property? Write an argument in which you take a position on this issue. Whether you argue for or against (or somewhere in between), be sure to anticipate other arguments and possible objections to your point of view.

LAWRENCE LESSIG

Free Culture

Lawrence Lessig (b. 1961), a professor at Stanford Law School, is committed to what he calls "free culture," in which ideas and creative notions freely circulate so that everyone can borrow from and build upon them—particularly in regard to emerging technologies. In The Future of Ideas *(2001), Lessig argues that antiquated notions of intellectual property are a hindrance to technological innovation and the free exchange of ideas, a claim that won him a place on* Scientific American's *list of the world's top fifty visionaries in 2002.*

The following argument is taken from Lessig's Free Culture: How Big Media Uses Technology and the Law to Lock Down Culture and Control Creativity *(2004). It deals with the conflict between an artist's right to get paid for his or her work and the demands of the Internet. Instead of going after college students, what the law should do in the case of such "killer apps" as music file-sharing, Lessig argues, is wait.*

IF YOU'RE LIKE I WAS A DECADE AGO, or like most people are when they first start thinking about these issues, then just about now you should be puzzled about something you hadn't thought through before.

We live in a world that celebrates "property." I am one of those celebrants. I believe in the value of property in general, and I also believe in the value of that weird form of property that lawyers call "intellectual property." A large, diverse society cannot survive without property; a large, diverse, and modern society cannot flourish without intellectual property.

But it takes just a second's reflection to realize that there is plenty of value out there that "property" doesn't capture. I don't mean "money can't buy you love," but rather, value that is plainly part of a process of production, including commercial as well as noncommercial production. If Disney animators had stolen a set of pencils to draw *Steamboat Willie*,[1] we'd have no hesitation in condemning that taking as wrong—even though trivial, even if unnoticed. Yet there was nothing wrong, at least under the law of the day, with Disney's taking from Buster Keaton or from the Brothers Grimm.[2] There was nothing wrong with the taking from Keaton because

---

1. *Steamboat Willie*: a 1928 Mickey Mouse cartoon, the first to be made with sound.

2. *Brothers Grimm*: Jakob Grimm (1785–1863) and Wilhelm Grimm (1786–1859), German brothers who collected and published folk tales and fairy tales such as "Snow White and the Seven Dwarfs," "Little Red Riding Hood," and "Hansel and Gretel." *Buster Keaton*: an early comic actor (1895–1966) best known for his silent films of the 1920s.

Disney's use would have been considered "fair." There was nothing wrong with the taking from the Grimms because the Grimms' work was in the public domain.

Thus, even though the things that Disney took—or more generally, the things taken by anyone exercising Walt Disney creativity—are valuable, our tradition does not treat those takings as wrong. Some things remain free for the taking within a free culture, and that freedom is good. . . .

It's the same with a thousand examples that appear everywhere once you begin to look. Scientists build upon the work of other scientists without asking or paying for the privilege. ("Excuse me, Professor Einstein, but may I have permission to use your theory of relativity to show that you were wrong about quantum physics?") Acting companies perform adaptations of the works of Shakespeare without securing permission from anyone. (Does *anyone* believe Shakespeare would be better spread within our culture if there were a central Shakespeare rights clearinghouse that all productions of Shakespeare must appeal to first?) And Hollywood goes through cycles with a certain kind of movie: five asteroid films in the late 1990s; two volcano disaster films in 1997.

Creators here and everywhere are always and at all times building upon the creativity that went before and that surrounds them now. That building is always and everywhere at least partially done without permission and without compensating the original creator. No society, free or controlled, has ever demanded that every use be paid for or that permission for Walt Disney creativity must always be sought. Instead, every society has left a certain bit of its culture free for the taking—free societies more fully than unfree, perhaps, but all societies to some degree.

The hard question is therefore not *whether* a culture is free. All cultures are free to some degree. The hard question instead is "*How* free is this culture?" How much, and how broadly, is the culture free for others to take and build upon? Is that freedom limited to party members? To members of the royal family? To the top ten corporations on the New York Stock Exchange? Or is that freedom spread broadly? To artists generally, whether affiliated with the Met[3] or not? To musicians generally, whether white or not? To filmmakers generally, whether affiliated with a studio or not?

Free cultures are cultures that leave a great deal open for others to build upon; unfree, or permission, cultures leave much less. Ours was a free culture. It is becoming much less so.

. . .

The battle that got this whole [copyright] war going was about music. . . . The appeal of file-sharing music was the crack cocaine of the Internet's growth. It drove demand for access to the Internet more powerfully than any other single applica-

---

3. *The Met*: could refer to either the Metropolitan Museum of Art or the Metropolitan Opera, both in New York City.

tion. It was the Internet's killer app[4]—possibly in two senses of that word. It no doubt was the application that drove demand for bandwidth. It may well be the application that drives demand for regulations that in the end kill innovation on the network.

The aim of copyright, with respect to content in general and music in particular, is to create the incentives for music to be composed, performed, and, most importantly, spread. The law does this by giving an exclusive right to a composer to control copies of her performance.

File-sharing networks complicate this model by enabling the spread of content for which the performer has not been paid. Today, file sharing is addictive. In ten years, it won't be. It is addictive today because it is the easiest way to gain access to a broad range of content. It won't be the easiest way to get access to a broad range of content in ten years. Today, access to the Internet is cumbersome and slow—we in the United States are lucky to have broadband service at 1.5 MBs, and very rarely do we get service at that speed both up and down.[5] Although wireless access is growing, most of us still get access across wires. Most only gain access through a machine with a keyboard. The idea of the always on, always connected Internet is mainly just an idea.

But it will become a reality, and that means the way we get access to the Internet today is a technology in transition. Policy makers should not make policy on the basis of technology in transition. They should make policy on the basis of where the technology is going. The question should not be, how should the law regulate sharing in this world? The question should be, what law will we require when the network becomes that network it is clearly becoming? That network is one in which every machine with electricity is essentially on the Net; where everywhere you are—except maybe the desert or the Rockies—you can instantaneously be connected to the Internet. Imagine the Internet as ubiquitous as the best cellphone service, where with the flip of a device, you are connected.

In that world, it will be extremely easy to connect to services that give you access to content on the fly—such as Internet radio, content that is streamed to the user when the user demands. Here, then, is the critical point: When it is *extremely* easy to connect to services that give access to content, it will be *easier* to connect to services that give you access to content than it will be to download and store content *on the many devices you will have for playing content*. It will be easier, in other

10

11

12

13

---

4. *Killer app*: short for "killer application"; a program so desirable that people will pay for the hardware or software it runs on just so they can use the application. In this instance, Lessig believes that file-sharing—sharing files between computers—is so desirable that people will obtain Internet access (necessary for file-sharing) just to be able to do it.

5. *Up and down*: uploading (from computer to Web) and downloading (from Web to computer).

words, to subscribe than it will be to be a database manager, as everyone in the download-sharing of Napster-like[6] technologies essentially is. Content services will compete with content sharing, even if the services charge money for the content they give access to.

This point about the future is meant to suggest a perspective on the present: It is emphatically temporary. The "problem" with file-sharing—to the extent there is a real problem—is a problem that will increasingly disappear as it becomes easier to connect to the Internet. And thus it is an extraordinary mistake for policy makers today to be "solving" this problem in light of a technology that will be gone tomorrow. . . .   14

But what if "piracy" doesn't disappear? What if there is a competitive market providing content at a low cost, but a significant number of consumers continue to "take" content for nothing? Should the law do something then?   15

Yes, it should. But again, what it should do depends upon how the facts develop. The real issue is not whether [the law] eliminates sharing in the abstract. The real issue is its effect on the market. Is it better (a) to have a technology that is 95 percent secure and produces a market of size x, or (b) to have a technology that is 50 percent secure but produces a market of five times x? Less secure might produce more unauthorized sharing, but it is likely to also produce a much bigger market in authorized sharing. The most important thing is to assure artists' compensation without breaking the Internet. Once that's assured, then it may well be appropriate to find ways to track down the petty pirates.   16

6. *Napster*: an online file-sharing service that allowed users to download music files from other users' computers for free; it is now a legal, pay-per-download service.

Reading Closely

1. Why does Lessig think the courts should not impose heavy restrictions on Internet file-sharing at the present time?

2. To what extent does Lessig believe in the right of individuals to own property, including intellectual property? Why does he feel this way? Refer to the text in your response.

3. How did the downloading of music stir up a copyright "war" (9)?

4. Why does Lessig think file-sharing and other forms of Internet "piracy" will disappear? How convincing do you find his evidence? Explain.

5. Lessig thinks artists should be compensated for their work, but "without breaking the Internet" (16). In Lessig's view, why is it as important to the cultural life

of the nation to have a strong Internet as it is to protect the rights of people whose intellectual property has already contributed to that culture?

STRATEGIES AND STRUCTURES

1. What is Lessig's main point, and where does he state it most directly?

2. Why do you think Lessig begins his argument by saying, "If you're like I was a decade ago" (1)? What assumptions is he making about his audience, and why, in particular, does he refer to the reader as "puzzled" (1)?

3. How and how well does Lessig establish his credibility as an ethical person who is looking out for the reader's best interests?

4. How and how well does Lessig justify "Walt Disney creativity" in the early days of animated cartoons (4)? Is his reasoning valid?

5. What general standard does Lessig adopt for judging whether or not the "taking" of intellectual property is ethical? Do you find this argument convincing? Why or why not?

6. *Other Methods.* Lessig defines a free culture as one "that leave[s] a great deal open for others to build upon" (8). How does this DEFINITION contribute to his argument about keeping some intellectual property free?

THINKING ABOUT LANGUAGE

1. Point out the different ways in which Lessig uses the word *free*. What are its various meanings at different places in his argument?

2. As applied to the copyright controversy, how appropriate do you find the word *war* (9)? Is this just HYPERBOLE, or is the issue important (and controversial) enough to justify the term? Explain your view.

3. Why does Lessig refer to "Walt Disney creativity" throughout his essay instead of using a phrase like "the limited taking of the intellectual property of others"?

4. What are the implications of Lessig's use of the word *addictive* (11)?

FOR WRITING

1. Write a few paragraphs exploring the idea that intellectual property is a form of private property that must be protected by law. You could defend this claim, challenge it, or agree in some ways but disagree in others.

2. In ten years, Lessig predicts, file-sharing won't be "the easiest way to get access to a broad range of content" on the Internet (11). Instead, he argues, it will be easier "to connect to services that give you access to content on the fly"—and to pay for those services (13). Write an argument defending or challenging this view of where Internet technology is headed.

Debating Intellectual Property Rights

The following questions refer to the arguments on pp. 554–65.

Reading Arguments

1. Which position, Goodman's on sharing Dr. King's words or Hamilton's on suing students for downloading music, is best supported by Lessig's argument for keeping intellectual culture free and open? Explain.

2. Who do you think makes the best use of logical reasoning to support his or her claim? Of facts and figures? Why do you say so?

3. How effective do you find Hamilton's EXAMPLE of Loretta Lynn and the Country Music Hall of Fame (6–10)? How about Lessig's references to Einstein, Shakespeare, and Hollywood (5)? Which is a better use of specific examples to support an argument? Explain.

4. Among the participants in this debate, which one uses the shortest sentences and the least abstract language? To what extent do you think this prose style (and that of the other writers in the debate) is influenced by his or her intended audience? Explain.

For Writing

1. Write a paragraph or two explaining which of the arguments in this debate you find strongest or weakest—and why.

2. Write an argument in which you take a position (and support it—with facts, statistics, expert testimony, and other evidence) on some aspect of the intellectual property debate not fully covered by Goodman, Hamilton, or Lessig.

Debating Ethics in a Commercial Culture

When Henry David Thoreau retreated to Walden Pond, he was not just looking for a quiet place to write. An astute observer and critic of his times, Thoreau was also protesting the creeping commercialism of American life. "The mass of men lead lives of quiet desperation," he wrote, because they are always "trying to get into business and trying to get out of debt." It was not a new theme, even in 1854.

In fact, the European conquest of North America had begun as a business venture financed by the Spanish monarchy. New Amsterdam, the oldest incorporated city in North America, was established as a Dutch trading center to promote the interests of the world's first multinational corporation, the Dutch East India Company. Although the Company went bankrupt in 1800—well before Thoreau wrote about the commercialization of American life—it had paid stockholders an annual dividend of 18 percent per year for almost two centuries. New Amsterdam itself survived to become New York, the financial capital of a nation founded in liberty and justice for all—and in stocks and bonds for those who could afford them. Thoreau's generation was perhaps the first to realize the extent to which business and commerce were shaping the values of the young nation. Today, even Walden Pond is threatened by development; the issue is no longer how to escape from commercialism but how to behave ethically in a culture that almost everyone now sees as highly commercialized at every level.

What constitutes ethical behavior—and how do we achieve it—in a fundamentally commercial culture? In these wide-ranging texts, a professor of history, a former U.S. secretary of labor, and two attorneys discuss ethics, morality, religion, and moneymaking in America:

Questions about this group of readings can be found on p. 583.

GARY CROSS

Toys for Saps

Gary Cross is a professor of history at Pennsylvania State University and a specialist in the field of commercial culture and its impact on children and family relations. The "abiding theme" of his scholarship, says Cross, is "the origins, uses, meanings, and consequences of affluence." Among many other books, he is the author of Kids' Stuff: Toys and the Changing World of American Childhood *(1997) and* Men to Boys: The Making of Modern Immaturity *(2008).*

"Toys for Saps" first appeared on the Op-Ed page of the New York Times *in 2007. It argues that the success of Mattel and other major toymakers provides "a superb model for business" but not "such a good way to raise children."*

THE CHIEF EXECUTIVE OF MATTEL,[1] Robert Eckert, has just apologized to 1
America's parents for allowing hundreds of thousands of Chinese-made toys decorated with leaded paint or containing powerful magnets into the country, exposing children to danger. This is admirable, as is the recall of these toys and the toy industry's request that Congress impose mandatory toy safety testing standards. But what Mr. Eckert and other major toy makers should also apologize for is the toys themselves and the way they are promoted.

When I looked at Mattel's list of recently recalled toys, it became obvious 2
that something more than our dependence on foreign goods or even the physical safety of children is at stake here. The problem is that the toys and the business model that creates them have so little to do with the needs of children and their parents.

On the list were 56 Polly Pocket sets (including a Lip Gloss Studio Playset), 3
11 Doggie Daycare toys, 4 Batman figures, 43 Sesame Street toys (not just Elmo Stacking Rings but Giggle Grabber Soccer Elmo and Grow Me Elmo Sprinkler), 10 Dora the Explorers and more than a score of assorted figures and cars. These are designed mostly for preschoolers; none encourage violence and many feature the cute and caring. But, a parent might ask, why 56 Polly Pocket sets? Wouldn't a half-dozen meet the needs of any child? And why teach 4-year-olds the fine points of cosmetics?

Yet most of us are not shocked by this list. Indeed, a business model that sells 4
endless additions to basic toys even when they have nothing to do with any recognized child-rearing ideal or even imaginative play seems natural.

---

1. *Mattel*: world's largest toy company by volume of sales.

This wasn't always the case. In the early 1970s, child advocates like Action for 5
Children's Television recognized that television ads for toys had a magical power
over children. They tried to ban these commercials to give parents, not toy companies, control over the desires of their offspring. In 1978, Michael Pertschuk, chairman of the Federal Trade Commission, argued that ads appealing to young children
were inherently "unfair."

The toy and candy industries, which advertised directly to children, mobilized 6
and accused the commission and child advocates of trying to restrict commercial-
free speech and of wanting a nanny state. In 1980, Congress complied by prohibit-
ing the commission from regulating ads aimed at children.

About the same time, toy makers noticed that their earnings from selling *Star* 7
Wars characters were more profitable than the movies themselves and fully
embraced character licensing. Aided by the early '80s deregulation of ads, Mattel,
Hasbro and others created cartoons that were essentially program-length commercials. These cartoons, like *He-Man and the Masters of the Universe* or *Care Bears*, promoted toy lines in their story plots and led to an endless wave of toys based on
television and movie characters.

At the same time, American toy makers outsourced production, mostly to 8
China, and concentrated on design and marketing, transforming a seasonal industry (mostly at Christmas) into wave after wave of movie-toy promotions. As a
result, in 1987, 60 percent of toys sold in the United States were based on licensed
characters, compared with about 10 percent in 1980. Toy sales increased from
$6.1 billion in 1982 to $12.5 billion in 1986.

This was a superb model for business success, but it hasn't been such a good way 9
to raise children. Since 1973, the Consumer Product Safety Commission has set
standards and recalled hazardous toys, protecting the physical safety of children.
But government does nothing to protect children's psychological needs. Sure,
youngsters want this stuff (after all, they see it on television every day) and they
find ways of playing with these toys, sometimes imaginatively abandoning the
commercial back story of the characters.

But the problem is that the fun built into the toy is mostly in receiving the latest 10
Polly Pocket[2] and adding it to a collection, rather than playing with it. Additive—if
not addictive—desire is created and satisfied by these toy lines. They serve little
positive purpose other than to teach children to be good consumers and want all
the Dora the Explorer[3] toys.

Many people might associate this selling tactic with violent action figures or 11
Barbie and Bratz dolls, but PBS Kids' cartoon characters and Children's Television

2. *Polly Pocket*: a line of small plastic dolls and their accessories.
3. *Dora the Explorer*: an animated television series for preschoolers and young children.

Workshop (now Sesame Workshop)[4] puppets have been licensed to the toy companies since 1971. How many toddlers do you know who are obsessed with anything
having to do with Elmo and Thomas the Tank Engine[5] toys?

Is it any surprise that children are running through their childhoods so quickly?   12
Not only do many of these licensed toys introduce young people to fashion and
consumerism before they have developed critical judgment, but we as parents give
them the stuff too early. And so much of it is junk.

Perhaps it's time to rethink the decision to allow the unrestricted advertising and   13
cartoon promotion of toy lines that has produced year-round marketing and piles of
plastic toys, bought and soon discarded. After all, we ought to be just as concerned
about the impact of character licensing and toy advertising on our children's psyche
as we are on protecting them from ingesting leaded paint and magnets.

4. *Children's Television Workshop / Sesame Workshop*: nonprofit organization that produces the educational television program *Sesame Street*. *PBS Kids*: refers to a number of programs for young children
produced by PBS. *Bratz*: a line of dolls created in 2001; more urban and modern than Barbie, they are
popular with school-age girls. *Barbie*: a line of dolls with adult figures, created in 1959; they also appeal
primarily to school-age girls.

5. *Thomas the Tank Engine*: an anthropomorphized train engine and the eponymous star of a children's television series. *Elmo*: one of the characters on TV's *Sesame Street*; he is particularly popular
with toddlers and preschoolers.

Reading Closely

1. Gary Cross thinks that the licensing and marketing of children's toys in America
   is unethical. What does he think the toy industry is doing wrong?

2. In Cross's view, what should children do with toys instead of merely collecting
   them?

3. According to Cross, how is the licensing and marketing of toys different today
   from a few decades ago?

4. What does Cross think should be done to protect children from the psychological ill effects of consuming too many "junk" toys (12)?

Strategies and Structures

1. What is Cross's purpose in criticizing "a superb model for business success" (9)?
   Where is it stated most directly? How and how well does his argument achieve
   that purpose?

2. How and how well does Cross demonstrate that he is not necessarily opposed to
   profits in business? Why would he want or need to demonstrate this?

3. Cross claims that the toy industry may be doing harm to "our children's psyche" (13). Who is the intended audience for this argument? Explain.

4. To what extent is Cross's argument aimed at his audience's rational faculties? Their emotions? Explain.

5. "We as parents give them the stuff too early," says Cross. "And so much of it is junk" (12). How and how well is Cross establishing his credibility here?

6. Why do you think Cross introduces and concludes his argument with a reference to the recall of toys that may be harmful to young children because of leaded paint and magnets? Is this an effective strategy? Why or why not?

7. *Other Methods.* Cross analyzes a number of changes in the marketing and design of toys in America. What are some of them, and what EFFECTS, according to Cross, have those changes had? How does this analysis support his argument about who should have "control over the desires" of young children (5)?

THINKING ABOUT LANGUAGE

1. How does Cross appeal to his audience's emotions by using the slang term *saps* in the title of his essay?

2. Explain the CONNOTATIONS of "the cute and caring" (3), "natural" (4), "additive" (10), and "stuff" (12).

3. Cross does not use the term *brainwashing* in his essay. Should he have?

FOR WRITING

1. Write a paragraph in which you give specific EXAMPLES of—and support or defend—the "business model that sells endless additions to basic toys" (4).

2. Do children ever learn useful lessons from toys? Write an argument in which you claim that some toys are educational or otherwise beneficial. Be sure to give sufficient evidence to support your claim.

ROBERT B. REICH

Don't Blame Wal-Mart

Robert B. Reich (b. 1946) is a professor of public policy at the University of California, Berkeley. From 1993 to 1997, he was U.S. secretary of labor under President Bill Clinton. As labor secretary, he was instrumental in the passing of the Family and Medical Leave Act, which ensures that workers can take unpaid leave for medical reasons or to care for family members. He also worked to end sweatshops and child labor, raise the minimum wage, and launch job training programs.

Reich's writing has appeared in the New Yorker, Washington Post, New York Times, Wall Street Journal, *and* Atlantic Monthly. *He is also the cofounder of the* American Prospect, *a political magazine. Reich's many books include* The Work of Nations: Preparing for 21st Century Capitalism *(1991),* Locked in the Cabinet *(1997), and* Reason: Why Liberals Will Win the Battle for America *(2004). In 2003, he was awarded the Dagmar and Václav Havel Foundation Vize 97 Prize for his work in social and economic thought.*

"Don't Blame Wal-Mart," which first appeared on the New York Times *Op-Ed page in 2005, argues that America's economy pits our natural inclinations as consumers (seeking the best deals) against our social ideals as citizens (seeking the best for our fellow workers and our communities).*

B OWING TO INTENSE PRESSURE from neighborhood and labor groups, a real 1 estate developer has just given up plans to include a Wal-Mart store in a mall in Queens, thereby blocking Wal-Mart's plan to open its first store in New York City. In the eyes of Wal-Mart's detractors, the Arkansas-based chain embodies the worst kind of economic exploitation: it pays its 1.2 million American workers an average of only $9.68 an hour, doesn't provide most of them with health insurance, keeps out unions, has a checkered history on labor law and turns main streets into ghost towns by sucking business away from small retailers.

But isn't Wal-Mart really being punished for our sins? After all, it's not as if Wal- 2 Mart's founder, Sam Walton, and his successors created the world's largest retailer by putting a gun to our heads and forcing us to shop there.

Instead, Wal-Mart has lured customers with low prices. "We expect our suppli- 3 ers to drive the costs out of the supply chain," a spokeswoman for Wal-Mart said. "It's good for us and good for them."

Wal-Mart may have perfected this technique, but you can find it almost every- 4 where these days. Corporations are in fierce competition to get and keep customers, so they pass the bulk of their cost cuts through to consumers as lower prices. Products are manufactured in China at a fraction of the cost of making them here, and American consumers get great deals. Back-office[1] work, along with computer programming and data crunching, is "offshored" to India, so our dollars go even further.

Meanwhile, many of us pressure companies to give us even better bargains. I look on the Internet to find the lowest price I can and buy airline tickets, books, merchandise from just about anywhere with a click of a mouse. Don't you? 5

The fact is, today's economy offers us a Faustian bargain:[2] it can give consumers deals largely because it hammers workers and communities. 6

We can blame big corporations, but we're mostly making this bargain with ourselves. The easier it is for us to get great deals, the stronger the downward pressure on wages and benefits. Last year, the real wages of hourly workers, who make up about 80 percent of the work force, actually dropped for the first time in more than a decade; hourly workers' health and pension benefits are in free fall. The easier it is for us to find better professional services, the harder professionals have to hustle to attract and keep clients. The more efficiently we can summon products from anywhere on the globe, the more stress we put on our own communities. 7

But you and I aren't just consumers. We're also workers and citizens. How do we strike the right balance? To claim that people shouldn't have access to Wal-Mart or to cut-rate airfares or services from India or to Internet shopping, because these somehow reduce their quality of life, is paternalistic tripe. No one is a better judge of what people want than they themselves. 8

The problem is, the choices we make in the market don't fully reflect our values as workers or as citizens. I didn't want our community bookstore in Cambridge, Mass., to close (as it did last fall) yet I still bought lots of books from Amazon.com. In addition, we may not see the larger bargain when our own job or community isn't directly at stake. I don't like what's happening to airline workers, but I still try for the cheapest fare I can get. 9

The only way for the workers or citizens in us to trump the consumers in us is through laws and regulations that make our purchases a social choice as well as a personal one. A requirement that companies with more than 50 employees offer their workers affordable health insurance, for example, might increase slightly the price of their goods and services. My inner consumer won't like that very much, but the worker in me thinks it a fair price to pay. Same with an increase in the min- 10

---

1. *Back-office:* the departments that are necessary to keep a company running but do not bring in revenue, such as accounting, data-entry, and human resources. The "front office," in contrast, refers to sales and other parts of a business that interact with customers.

2. *Faustian bargain:* in German legend, Dr. Faustus pledges his soul to the devil in exchange for knowledge and success; thus, in a "Faustian bargain," an advantage is acquired at great cost.

imum wage or a change in labor laws making it easier for employees to organize and negotiate better terms.

I wouldn't go so far as to re-regulate the airline industry or hobble free trade with China and India—that would cost me as a consumer far too much—but I'd like the government to offer wage insurance to ease the pain of sudden losses of pay. And I'd support labor standards that make trade agreements a bit more fair.

These provisions might end up costing me some money, but the citizen in me thinks they are worth the price. You might think differently, but as a nation we aren't even having this sort of discussion. Instead, our debates about economic change take place between two warring camps: those who want the best consumer deals, and those who want to preserve jobs and communities much as they are. Instead of finding ways to soften the blows, compensate the losers or slow the pace of change—so the consumers in us can enjoy lower prices and better products without wreaking too much damage on us in our role as workers and citizens—we go to battle.

I don't know if Wal-Mart will ever make it into New York City. I do know that New Yorkers, like most other Americans, want the great deals that can be had in a rapidly globalizing high-tech economy. Yet the prices on sales tags don't reflect the full prices we have to pay as workers and citizens. A sensible public debate would focus on how to make that total price as low as possible.

READING CLOSELY

1. According to Robert Reich, why shouldn't we blame Wal-Mart for paying low wages, skimping on health insurance for workers, resisting unions, violating labor law, and turning "main streets into ghost towns by sucking business away from small retailers" (1)?

2. Reich claims not to be arguing on the side of either consumers or workers in the highly competitive retail marketplace. Whose side *is* he on, then? Explain.

3. What first step does Reich propose for addressing the problem of the "economic exploitation" of workers and communities in a commercial culture (1)?

4. How, finally, does Reich hope the problem will be solved? What specific changes does he advocate?

STRATEGIES AND STRUCTURES

1. "I look on the Internet to find the lowest price I can," says Reich. "Don't you?" (5). Who is Reich's intended audience here? What is his purpose in speaking to them so directly?

2. How and how well does Reich establish his credibility with his audience?

3. What middle ground does Reich propose for bringing together "those who want the best consumer deals" and "those who want to preserve jobs and communities" (12)? Is this a good way to promote debate between "warring camps," or should Reich have come down firmly on one side or the other? Explain.

4. *Other Methods.* Reich uses Wal-Mart as his main EXAMPLE. How and how well does it represent the dilemma that he says the American consumer must wrestle with?

THINKING ABOUT LANGUAGE

1. Explain the IRONY in Reich's reference to "our sins" (2).

2. A "Faustian bargain" (6) is made at great cost to the soul. Is Reich justified in applying the term to the bargain hunters at Wal-Mart or on Amazon.com? Why or why not?

3. Explain the CONNOTATIONS of "tripe" (8) and "trump" (10).

FOR WRITING

1. In a paragraph or two, explain why it is (or is not) "paternalistic tripe" (8) to argue that outsourcing jobs to India or replacing them with Internet services reduces the quality of life for American consumers.

2. "Yet the prices on sales tags," Reich argues, "don't reflect the full prices we have to pay as workers and citizens" (13). Compose a well-supported argument agreeing or disagreeing with this claim.

BRUCE FROHNEN AND LEO CLARKE

Scandal in Corporate America: An Ethical, Not a Legal, Problem

Bruce Frohnen earned a doctorate in government at Cornell University and a law degree at Emory University before taking a position as resident scholar at the Heritage Foundation, a conservative think tank. He later spent five years as an aide to former U.S. Senator Spencer Abraham. Presently, Frohnen is a professor at Ave Maria School of Law, a Roman Catholic institution in Ann Arbor, Michigan. His books include Virtue and the Promise of Conservatism *(1993),* The New Communitarians and the Crisis of Modern Liberalism *(1996), and* American Conservatism: An Encyclopedia *(2006), co-written with Jeremy Beer and Jeffery O. Nelson.*

Leo Clarke, a graduate of both Stanford University and the UCLA School of Law, joined the law faculty at Ave Maria in 2001. The author of numerous scholarly articles on business law, Clarke teamed up with Frohnen to write a response to a wave of financial scandals plaguing American business at the turn of the twenty-first century. "Scandal in Corporate America: An Ethical, Not a Legal, Problem," which appeared in USA Today *in 2002, argues that "the answer to corporate skullduggery is not more or stronger law"; rather, by returning to "deep moral habits and our religious tradition," business leaders can create a lasting culture of corporate ethics.*

Scandals within some of America's largest corporations have brought about 1 some long-overdue soul-searching among people in business and government. Presidential speeches and Congressional bills set forth useful ideas and policies regarding heavier penalties for fraud and clearer standards for accounting practitioners. Nevertheless, it would be a mistake to think that some new regulations from Washington will make everything right with the business community. The answer to corporate skullduggery is not more or stronger law. Over 2,000 years of lawmaking and lawbreaking have demonstrated that laws are important, but cannot do the job by themselves.

Statutes will be effective only where the human spirit and will are already 2 attuned to the law's objectives. Law may solve a problem that stems from good-faith differences regarding particular public policies, but it cannot change the attitude that the law itself is something to be overcome as just one more obstacle to making the maximum amount of money in the minimum amount of time. As long as American business executives and their professional advisors believe in their hearts that greed is good and that the appearance of satisfying shareholders is more important than actually satisfying them, more law will be a futile response.

. . .

Honesty and ethical behavior are not just goods relevant to Sunday morning and   3
the Hereafter; they are critical to our economic well-being. We have often heard it
said that the vast majority of people in business are decent folk who try to act fairly
and honestly. This is as true of lawyers and accountants as it is of businesspeople.
Yet, what does it mean to act fairly and honestly? This should be an easy question
to answer. Don't lie, cheat, or steal, but, for instance, what does it mean to lie? This
seemingly simple question has become all but impossible for many of those in business and the professions to answer, just as it has for leading public servants. That is
the heart of our ethical dilemma.

We increasingly are losing our understanding of just what it means to act fairly   4
and honestly. To be sure, we have a multitude of laws on the books that say, in
essence, "Thou shalt not lie." However, the very number and complexity of these
laws, applied in different ways to almost every aspect of economic life, have
blurred the basic point: Lies are evil. The very complexity of our laws has encouraged many professionals and business people to find ways of conducting business
that arguably fit within the letter of the law while avoiding its true intent. The
game is not whether a statement is true, but whether it can be defended as not
knowingly false. Moreover, those accountants and lawyers who choose to game the
system are seldom caught and punished because their professional associations—
those who are supposed to police their conduct—no longer understand what it
really means to lie or tell the truth. We have become so tolerant of half-truths, hair-
splitting definitions, and the notion that truth is "subjective" that we have lost our
ability to enforce basic, commonsense honesty, even where it is crucial to our economic well-being.

Let us look in a very oversimplified way at some of the failings—one might say   5
crimes—the nation has seen recently. The two most notorious (and expensive)
cases are Enron and WorldCom.[1] The former encompassed a myriad of complex
transactions involving mysterious, gossamer partnerships that allowed Enron to
book huge corporate profits and payments to insiders, while ignoring any associated financial liabilities. Was there any real business reason to structure those
transactions in such a fashion? Of course not—unless one is attempting to make
something seem what it's not. Enron was just the New Century equivalent of putting sawdust in the Model T's transmission or changing the brand on cattle.[2]

---

1. *WorldCom*: large telecommunications company whose internal audit uncovered accounting
fraud in 2002. *Enron*: an energy producer and distributor whose fraudulent practices led to bankruptcy
in 2001.

2. *Changing the brand on cattle*: cattle are marked with a brand to show which ranch they belong
to; cattle thieves (rustlers) would change the brand so that the cattle couldn't be traced back to their
rightful owners. *Putting sawdust in the Model T's transmission*: this practice will make a car run
smoothly for a short time (long enough to sell the car, perhaps), but soon the transmission will be

WorldCom was not only bigger, but more surprising. Internal bookkeepers sim- 6
ply accounted for everyday spending (that should have been deducted from
income) as expenditures for "capital assets"—as if an appreciable number of pencils and paper clips bought today would still be in use a year from now. That simple
adjustment greatly overstated income because expenditures for capital assets are
spread over the life of the asset instead of being deducted 100% from income right
away. Sure, future reported income would be substantially reduced in the long run,
but those WorldCom Keynesians[3] figured that, in the long run, they would all be
dead. Unfortunately for stockholders, it was their investments that died.

How did such obvious lying occur? After all, in both cases, the corporate 7
employees and the outside auditors and counsel retained to support the reliability
of the internal accounting were all operating under rules that said, in effect, "Thou
shalt not lie"—that transactions are to be accounted for according to their substance, not just any seemingly defensible argument concerning how they might be
represented on a form.

Here is one answer to that simple question: We have become too sophisticated, 8
as individuals and as a society, to believe that God will punish us if we tell a lie, and
that answer is also our problem. Our facile confidence that there are no longer any
moral roles everyone must obey no matter what has led us to forget that bad behavior naturally brings bad consequences. It has encouraged more and more of us to
behave worse and worse without even realizing it. As author C. S. Lewis observed,
"Moral collapse follows upon spiritual collapse." Our refusal to teach our children—and our professionals—that they are answerable to their society and ultimately to God for their behavior has cost us our collective moral bearings. We have
lost our ability as a society to pass moral judgment on individual behavior. Indeed,
we condemn ethical judgments as just that—"judgmental."

· · ·

Our nation was founded by devoutly religious people convinced that they 9
should be a "city on a hill"[4] shining as an example to all nations of how well religious people would treat one another and of how good a community they could
build together. They brought with them the Christian religion and a determination
to make their political leaders answer to religious principles, a determination they
inherited from the Israelites, whose Ten Commandments they took, quite rightly,
to be the foundation of their system of law. These religious ancestors sought to

---

completely destroyed and beyond repair. A Model T was a popular and durable early automobile made
by Ford from 1908 to 1927.

3. *Keynesians*: named after British economist John Maynard Keynes (1883–1946), Keynesian economics calls for government intervention during times of economic crisis.

4. *City on a hill*: in his famous sermon "A Model of Christian Charity" (1630), John Winthrop
(1587/8–1649), the first governor of Massachusetts and a Puritan, describes an early Puritan settlement in the Massachusetts Bay Colony as "a city upon a hill."

build that city on the basis not merely of laws, but of individual habits and norms of behavior rooted in their religion. Yet, we forbid our children from learning about the Judeo-Christian roots of their nation, and of their way of life. This does not mean that other cultures have no valid truths, but only that this country was built on one ethical system and it will work only if we continually follow that system. Anyone who has ever tried to run a Windows-based program on a Mac should appreciate that point.

. . .

Changing Business Culture

So, how can we change business culture to make the truth both a cultural and eco-   10
nomic imperative? Certainly, we must start in primary schools with real values education, but we can also deprogram our current corps of executives, lawyers, and accountants. While the President and Congress would have us scare them into telling the truth, we think the problem will be resolved more quickly and completely with a simple two-step approach. First, those in business need to be assured that telling the truth is not only okay, it is what the people they are working for want. We are already seeing that message being conveyed in the market by investors who are punishing those firms that have been identified as having engaged in so-called "aggressive accounting." We see as well that firms that eschew aggressive accounting—such as Coca-Cola, which announced it will begin reporting stock options as expenses—are being rewarded by investors.

Merely reinforcing the fact that virtue is its own reward is not enough, though.   11
We must overcome two generations of moral relativism and teach executives, accountants, and attorneys how to recognize the truth. For instance, most professional licensing organizations require licensees to participate in continuing education, and a small portion of that requirement is generally satisfied at the end of a long day of "substantive" learning. Now, however, investors and clients are beginning to realize that ethics is a part of substantive business. Lawyers and accountants have so long viewed themselves as being mouthpieces for a particular spin on a client's business that they need to be taught the skills necessary for ferreting out the truth and evaluating the dynamics of business that might—and often do—lead to fraud. More than this, they need to be taught how to counsel their clients objectively and with a view toward helping them meet their obligations. In short, far more than preaching is needed. All players in the disclosure regime must be taught not only how to recognize the truth when they see it, but how to press their superiors and their clients until they find it.

This means very practical ethical training—teaching attorneys how to negotiate   12
honestly, teaching accountants what techniques do and do not accord with an honest balance statement, etc. Yet, even this is not enough. Business and professional schools across the country are making noises about "getting serious" about ethics,

but what will this mean in practice? Unless we reconnect with the source of our ethical precepts, grounding moral rules like "don't lie" in deep moral habits and our religious tradition, once the latest crisis of confidence passes, it will be business (and lying) as usual.

To give weight and meaning to seeming platitudes like "don't lie," we need our   13
religious institutions, families, and communities to speak more forcefully about the religious grounding of decent behavior. We need to develop a more positive attitude in our political institutions and public schools toward the religious tradition that is at the root of our system of ordered liberty, and what remains of our habits of moral behavior. We are not suggesting that public schools inculcate students into any particular religion. However, when we ban the Ten Commandments—the font of our legal and ethical system—from our courthouses and schools, we have lost contact with common sense. Does "Thou shalt not lie" become an impermissible command when its origin in religious experience is acknowledged? Does the prohibition against stealing become oppressive when we admit that, in every civilization on this planet, it stems from the religious belief that we owe a duty to our God to treat others as we would have them treat us?

In the appendix to *Mere Christianity*,[5] Lewis recounts moral strictures common   14
to every society on Earth. This moral code, which can be summed up in the Golden Rule or, more extensively, the Ten Commandments, is, in every instance, rooted in religious belief. Without that belief in God and a rational universe ordered by Him on moral principles, nothing makes sense finally, and everything is permitted. Divorced from the story of their origins, of the meaning and necessity of moral conduct, people cannot make sense of their lives and will fall back on selfishness and the will to dominate others. As we work to reestablish an ethical structure to business behavior, we had best remember our need for religious moorings. Otherwise, we will continue to see more Enrons and WorldComs, whether new laws are put on the books or not.

5. *Mere Christianity*: a book by C. S. Lewis in which he describes the fundamental tenets of Christianity and makes an argument for their truth.

READING CLOSELY

1. According to Bruce Frohnen and Leo Clarke, who or what is responsible for the unethical behavior they attribute to American business?

2. Frohnen and Clarke do not think "new regulations from Washington will make everything right with the business community" (1). What do they propose instead?

3. In fact, say Frohnen and Clarke, existing laws and regulations that are meant to make business more fair and ethical, actually make them less so. Why and how, in their opinion, is this the case?

4. According to Frohnen and Clarke, what did the founders of the nation take to be the "foundation of their system of law" (9)?

STRATEGIES AND STRUCTURES

1. To whom are Frohnen and Clarke referring when they say that "we have become too sophisticated" (8)? Who is their intended audience?

2. What evidence do Frohnen and Clarke give to support their claim that corporate America is morally and ethically bankrupt? Is that evidence sufficient to make their case? Why or why not?

3. How and how well do Frohnen and Clarke establish their credibility as judges of moral and ethical conduct?

4. *Other Methods.* "Divorced from the story of their origins," say Frohnen and Clarke, "people cannot make sense of their lives and will fall back on selfishness and the will to dominate others" (14). How and how well do Frohnen and Clarke use NARRATION to support this argument?

THINKING ABOUT LANGUAGE

1. When John Winthrop spoke of a "city upon a hill," he was reminding his parishioners not only to be righteous but that their actions would be highly visible: "So that if we shall deal falsely with our God in this work we have undertaken . . . we shall be made a story and a by-word throughout the world." To what extent, if any, does this context of keeping up appearances undermine Frohnen and Clarke's ALLUSION (9)?

2. In what humorous sense are Frohnen and Clarke referring to "those WorldCom Keynesians" who treated everyday expenses as money spent for enduring capital assets (6)?

3. Explain the CONNOTATIONS of *skullduggery* (1), *game* (4), and *judgmental* (8).

FOR WRITING

1. Write a paragraph or two in which you outline the specific moral and ethical principles that any business or corporation ought to follow.

2. "Honesty and ethical behavior are not just goods relevant to Sunday morning and the Hereafter; they are critical to our economic well-being" (3). Write an argument in which you support or challenge this claim.

Debating Ethics in a Commercial Culture

The following questions refer to the arguments on pp. 569–81.

READING ARGUMENTS

1. Reich feels that telling people what they should want is "paternalistic tripe" because "no one is a better judge of what people want than they themselves" (8). What would Frohnen and Clarke say to this argument? Explain.

2. Reich and Frohnen and Clarke appeal extensively to the reader's sense of honesty and fair play. Is this sufficient, or would specific points in their arguments be further strengthened by more extensive use of logical reasoning supported by data? Which points (if any)? Explain.

3. All of the participants in this debate believe that the commercialism of Anglo-American culture has had serious EFFECTS upon the ethics and morality of the culture. Which ones also ANALYZE THE CAUSES of that commercialism? How do they analyze these causes, and how well?

4. Among the voices in this debate, which ones seem most credible and trustworthy to you? Why? How do they establish that credibility?

FOR WRITING

1. In a paragraph or two, explain which of the arguments in this debate you find strongest or weakest—and why.

2. Write an argument in which you take a position (and support it—with facts, statistics, expert testimony, and other evidence) on some aspect of the debate about ethical behavior in a commercial culture that is not fully covered by Cross, Reich, or Frohnen and Clarke.

CHAPTER 12

Combining the Methods

The web of our life is of a mingled yarn. . . .
—WILLIAM SHAKESPEARE, *All's Well That Ends Well*

When you have a single, clear purpose in mind, you may be able to write a well-organized essay by using a single method of development. The yarns of life, however, are often mingled, as Shakespeare said, and when you're writing on a complex topic, you might actually end up using a number of different methods in the same essay. Professional writers do this all the time—as best-selling author Michael Lewis does in the first five pages of his 1989 book *Liar's Poker*. (All five pages are printed in their entirety at the end of this introduction.)

Trained in business and finance (as well as in literature), Lewis began his career as a bond salesman on Wall Street,[1] where he spent much of his time on the telephone. After a few years, Lewis decided he wanted to try his hand at a different kind of verbal communication and became a professional writer. In *Liar's Poker*, Lewis compares the economic climate of Wall Street to a high-stakes game.

Lewis isn't simply telling an amusing story about Wall Street and its pastimes. Like an anthropologist studying a strange tribe, he is giving an expert's view of an entire culture. To this more complicated end, Lewis draws on *all* the methods of development. He begins to develop his topic with a NARRATIVE of the day the head of the firm challenged one of the traders to play an office gambling game for a million dollars:

---

1. *Wall Street*: financial district of New York City where stocks and bonds are bought and sold. Stocks are actual shares in a company; bonds are promissory notes (IOUs) that pay interest.

It was sometime early in 1986, the first year of the decline of my firm, Salomon Brothers. Our chairman, John Gutfreund, left his desk at the head of the trading floor and went for a walk. . . . This day in 1986, however, Gutfreund did something strange. Instead of terrifying us all, he walked a straight line to the trading desk of John Meriwether, a member of the board of Salomon Inc. and also one of Salomon's finest bond traders. He whispered a few words. The traders in the vicinity eavesdropped. What Gutfreund said has become a legend at Salomon Brothers and a visceral part of its corporate identity. He said: "One hand, one million dollars, no tears."

Throughout his narrative, Lewis also weaves in a detailed DESCRIPTION of the field of play ("like an epileptic ward"), the spectators ("nerve-racked"), and the key players. First there is the challenger, John Gutfreund:

Gutfreund took the pulse of the place by simply wandering around it and asking questions of the traders. An eerie sixth sense guided him to wherever a crisis was unfolding. Gutfreund seemed able to smell money being lost.

Then there is the champ himself, as Lewis describes him:

John Meriwether had, in the course of his career, made hundreds of millions of dollars for Salomon Brothers. He had an ability, rare among people and treasured by traders, to hide his state of mind. . . . He wore the same blank half-tense expression when he won as he did when he lost. . . . People would say, "He's the best businessman in the place," or "the best risk taker I have ever seen," or "a very dangerous Liar's Poker player."

And what is Liar's Poker itself? To explain this, Lewis must weave in a PROCESS ANALYSIS:

In Liar's Poker a group of people—as few as two, as many as ten—form a circle. Each player holds a dollar bill close to his chest. The game is similar in spirit to the card game known as I Doubt It. Each player attempts to fool the others about the serial numbers printed on the face of his dollar bill. . . . The bidding escalates until all the other players agree to challenge a single player's bid. Then, and only then, do the players reveal their serial numbers and determine who is bluffing whom.

Why are Gutfreund, Meriwether, and the other grown men in the office of Salomon Brothers playing what looks, on the surface, like a child's game? Because they thought a good Liar's Poker player was also likely to be a good bond trader. Lewis, it would seem, is using the game as an EXAMPLE of how the trader's mind works:

The questions a Liar's Poker player asks himself are, up to a point, the same questions a bond trader asks himself. Is this a smart risk? Do I feel lucky? How cunning is my opponent? Does he have any idea what he's doing, and if not, how do I exploit his ignorance?

Now we know how Liar's Poker is played and, in general, why the men in Lewis's office played it. We don't, however, know why, on this particular day, Gutfreund challenged Meriwether to play the game for the unheard-of sum of a million dollars.

To provide this information, Lewis must do a CAUSE-AND-EFFECT ANALYSIS, in which he adds a COMPARISON AND CONTRAST of the two men; that comparison, in turn, is based on a CLASSIFICATION of the men according to their functions as managers or traders within the firm:

> Gutfreund was the King of Wall Street, but Meriwether was King of the Game. . . . Gutfreund had once been a trader, but that was as relevant as an old woman's claim that she was once quite a dish. . . . Compared with managing, trading was admirably direct. You made your bets and either you won or you lost. When you won, people—all the way up to the top of the firm—admired you, envied you, and feared you, and with reason: You controlled the loot. When you managed a firm, well, sure you received your quota of envy, fear, and admiration. But for all the wrong reasons. *You did not make the money for Salomon. You did not take the risk.*

Why (the causes) Gutfreund challenged Meriwether (the effect) on this particular day is now clear: "The single rash act of challenging the arbitrage[2] boss to one hand for a million dollars was Gutfreund's way of showing he was a player, too." But it is not yet clear why Meriwether felt obliged to accept the challenge. To explain *this*, Lewis adds a DEFINITION of the player's "code" of conduct:

> The code of the Liar's Poker player was something like the code of the gun-slinger.[3] It required a trader to accept all challenges. Because of the code—which was *his* code—John Meriwether felt obliged to play. But he knew it was stupid.

---

2. *Arbitrage*: buying stocks, bonds, and other securities for immediate resale to profit from price differences in different markets.

3. *Code of the gunslinger*: code of conduct rooted in the legendary Wild Wild West of the eighteenth- and nineteenth-century western United States. The phrase refers to a stoic, warrior-like way of life that required the gunslinger to accept all challenges.

Okay. So now we know how the game is played and why the chief manager of Salomon Brothers challenged the chief bond trader to play a hand of Liar's Poker for a million dollars. We also know why the arbitrage boss felt obliged to accept the challenge. (To see how Meriwether actually met the challenge, you will have to read the rest of the story.)

But what's the point? The story of the great Liar's Poker challenge may be interesting if you just want to know what happened one day in a big Wall Street firm when people were playing when they should have been working. But what's the significance of these people and their actions? Why should you as a reader want to know about them?

Lewis has already told us the significance of the game for the players. In order to tie all the threads together, however, he must also explain what it might mean to us, his readers and audience. He does so in what amounts to a thesis statement:

> The game has some of the feel of trading, just as jousting has some of the feel of war. . . . Each player seeks weakness, predictability, and pattern in the others and seeks to avoid it in himself. The bond traders of Goldman, Sachs, First Boston, Morgan Stanley, Merrill Lynch, and other Wall Street firms all play some version of Liar's Poker.

This is not a reassuring assessment of what goes on in America's financial centers. But it may be an accurate one—if you buy Lewis's line of argument. And making an ARGUMENT about an ethically murky region of American culture is Lewis's goal; all the narrative, description, and other methods he uses support that goal.

You won't always use every method of developing a topic in every essay you write, however. Depending on your main purpose in writing, one or two will usually dominate, as in most of the model essays in this book.

MICHAEL LEWIS

Liar's Poker

IT WAS SOMETIME EARLY IN 1986, the first year of the decline of my firm, Salomon Brothers. Our chairman, John Gutfreund, left his desk at the head of the trading floor and went for a walk. At any given moment on the trading floor billions of dollars were being risked by bond traders. Gutfreund took the pulse of the place by simply wandering around it and asking questions of the traders. An eerie sixth sense guided him to wherever a crisis was unfolding. Gutfreund seemed able to smell money being lost.

He was the last person a nerve-racked trader wanted to see. Gutfreund (pro-nounced *Good friend*) liked to sneak up from behind and surprise you. This was fun for him but not for you. Busy on two phones at once trying to stem disaster, you had no time to turn and look. You didn't need to. You felt him. The area around you began to convulse like an epileptic ward. People were pretending to be frantically busy and at the same time staring intently at a spot directly above your head. You felt a chill in your bones that I imagine belongs to the same class of intelligence as the nervous twitch of a small furry animal at the silent approach of a grizzly bear. An alarm shrieked in your head: Gutfreund! Gutfreund! Gutfreund!

Often as not, our chairman just hovered quietly for a bit, then left. You might never have seen him. The only trace I found of him on two of these occasions was a turdlike ash on the floor beside my chair, left, I suppose, as a calling card. Gutfre-und's cigar droppings were longer and better formed than those of the average Salomon boss. I always assumed that he smoked a more expensive blend than the rest, purchased with a few of the $40 million he had cleared on the sale of Salomon Brothers in 1981 (or a few of the $3.1 million he paid himself in 1986, more than any other Wall Street CEO).

This day in 1986, however, Gutfreund did something strange. Instead of terrify-ing us all, he walked a straight line to the trading desk of John Meriwether, a mem-ber of the board of Salomon Inc. and also one of Salomon's finest bond traders. He whispered a few words. The traders in the vicinity eavesdropped. What Gutfreund said has become a legend at Salomon Brothers and a visceral part of its corporate identity. He said: "One hand, one million dollars, no tears."

One hand, one million dollars, no tears. Meriwether grabbed the meaning instantly. The King of Wall Street, as *Business Week* had dubbed Gutfreund, wanted to play a single hand of a game called Liar's Poker for a million dollars. He played the game most afternoons with Meriwether and the six young bond arbitrage traders who worked for Meriwether and was usually skinned alive. Some traders said Gutfreund was heavily outmatched. Others who couldn't imagine John Gutfre-und as anything but omnipotent—and there were many—said that losing suited his purpose, though exactly what that might be was a mystery.

The peculiar feature of Gutfreund's challenge this time was the size of the stake. Normally his bets didn't exceed a few hundred dollars. A million was unheard of. The final two words of his challenge, "no tears," meant that the loser was expected to suffer a great deal of pain but wasn't entitled to whine, bitch, or moan about it. He'd just have to hunker down and keep his poverty to himself. But why? You might ask if you were anyone other than the King of Wall Street. Why do it in the first place? Why, in particular, challenge Meriwether instead of some lesser manag-ing director? It seemed an act of sheer lunacy. Meriwether was the King of the Game, the Liar's Poker champion of the Salomon Brothers trading floor.

On the other hand, one thing you learn on a trading floor is that winners like Gutfreund *always* have some reason for what they do; it might not be the best of reasons, but at least they have a concept in mind. I was not privy to Gutfreund's innermost thoughts, but I do know that all the boys on the trading floor gambled and that he wanted badly to be one of the boys. What I think Gutfreund had in mind in this instance was a desire to show his courage, like the boy who leaps from the high dive. Who better than Meriwether for the purpose? Besides, Meriwether was probably the only trader with both the cash and the nerve to play.

The whole absurd situation needs putting into context. John Meriwether had, in the course of his career, made hundreds of millions of dollars for Salomon Brothers. He had an ability, rare among people and treasured by traders, to hide his state of mind. Most traders divulge whether they are making or losing money by the way they speak or move. They are either overly easy or overly tense. With Meriwether you could never, ever tell. He wore the same blank half-tense expression when he won as he did when he lost. He had, I think, a profound ability to control the two emotions that commonly destroy traders—fear and greed—and it made him as noble as a man who pursues his self-interest so fiercely can be. He was thought by many within Salomon to be the best bond trader on Wall Street. Around Salomon no tone but awe was used when he was discussed. People would say, "He's the best businessman in the place," or "the best risk taker I have ever seen," or "a very dangerous Liar's Poker player."

Meriwether cast a spell over the young traders who worked for him. His boys ranged in age from twenty-five to thirty-two (he was about forty). Most of them had Ph.D.'s in math, economics, and/or physics. Once they got onto Meriwether's trading desk, however, they forgot they were supposed to be detached intellectuals. They became disciples. They became obsessed by the game of Liar's Poker. They regarded it as *their* game. And they took it to a new level of seriousness.

John Gutfreund was always the outsider in their game. That *Business Week* put his picture on the cover and called him the King of Wall Street held little significance for them. I mean, that was, in a way, the whole point. Gutfreund was the King of Wall Street, but Meriwether was King of the Game. When Gutfreund had been crowned by the gentlemen of the press, you could almost hear traders thinking: *Foolish names and foolish faces often appear in public places.* Fair enough, Gutfreund had once been a trader, but that was as relevant as an old woman's claim that she was once quite a dish.

At times Gutfreund himself seemed to agree. He loved to trade. Compared with managing, trading was admirably direct. You made your bets and either you won or you lost. When you won, people—all the way up to the top of the firm—admired you, envied you, and feared you, and with reason: You controlled the loot. When you managed a firm, well, sure you received your quota of envy, fear, and admiration. But for all the wrong reasons. *You did not make the money for Salomon. You did not take risk.* You were hostage to your producers. They took risk. They proved their superiority every day by handling risk better than the rest of the risk-taking world. The money came from risk takers such as Meriwether, and whether it came or not was really beyond Gutfreund's control. That's why many people thought that the single rash act of challenging the arbitrage boss to one hand for a million dollars was Gut-freund's way of showing he was a player, too. And if you wanted to show off, Liar's Poker was the only way to go. The game had a powerful meaning for traders. People like John Meriwether believed that Liar's Poker had a lot in common with bond trading. It tested a trader's character. It honed a trader's instincts. A good player made a good trader, and vice versa. We all understood it.

The Game: In Liar's Poker a group of people—as few as two, as many as ten—form a circle. Each player holds a dollar bill close to his chest. The game is similar in spirit to the card game known as I Doubt It. Each player attempts to fool the others about the serial numbers printed on the face of his dollar bill. One trader begins by making "a bid." He says, for example, "Three sixes." He means that all told the serial numbers of the dollar bills held by every player, including himself, contain at least three sixes.

Once the first bid has been made, the game moves clockwise in the circle. Let's say the bid is three sixes. The player to the left of the bidder can do one of two things. He can bid higher (there are two sorts of higher bids: the same quantity of a higher number [three sevens, eights, or nines] and more of any number [four fives, for instance]). Or he can "challenge"—that is like saying, "I doubt it."

The bidding escalates until all the other players agree to challenge a single player's bid. Then, and only then, do the players reveal their serial numbers and determine who is bluffing whom. In the midst of all this, the mind of a good player spins with probabilities. What is the statistical likelihood of there being three sixes within a batch of, say, forty randomly generated serial numbers? For a great player, however, the math is the easy part of the game. The hard part is reading the faces of the other players. The complexity arises when all players know how to bluff and double-bluff.

The game has some of the feel of trading, just as jousting has some of the feel of war. The questions a Liar's Poker player asks himself are, up to a point, the same questions a bond trader asks himself. Is this a smart risk? Do I feel lucky? How cunning is my opponent? Does he have any idea what he's doing, and if not, how do I exploit his ignorance? If he bids high, is he bluffing, or does he actually hold a strong hand? Is he trying to induce me to make a foolish bid, or does he actually have four of a kind himself? Each player seeks weakness, predictability, and pattern in the others and seeks to avoid it in himself. The bond traders of Goldman, Sachs, First Boston, Morgan Stanley, Merrill Lynch, and other Wall Street firms all play some version of Liar's Poker. But the place where the stakes run highest, thanks to John Meriwether, is the New York bond trading floor of Salomon Brothers.

The code of the Liar's Poker player was something like the code of the gunslinger. It required a trader to accept all challenges. Because of the code—which was *his* code—John Meriwether felt obliged to play. But he knew it was stupid. For him, there was no upside. If he won, he upset Gut-freund. No good came of this. But if he lost, he was out of pocket a million bucks. This was worse than upsetting the boss. Although Meriwether was by far the better player of the game, in a single hand anything could happen. Luck could very well determine the outcome. Meriwether spent his entire day avoiding dumb bets, and he wasn't about to accept this one.

"No, John," he said, "if we're going to play for those kind of numbers, I'd rather play for real money. Ten million dollars. No tears."

Ten million dollars. It was a moment for all players to savor. Meriwether was playing Liar's Poker before the game even started. He was bluffing. Gutfreund considered the counterproposal. It would have been just like him to accept. Merely to entertain the thought was a luxury that must have pleased him well. (It *was* good to be rich.)

On the other hand, ten million dollars was, and is, a lot of money. If Gutfreund lost, he'd have only thirty million or so left. His wife, Susan, was busy spending the better part of fifteen million dollars redecorating their Manhattan apartment (Meriwether knew this). And as Gutfreund *was* the boss, he clearly wasn't bound by the Meriwether code. Who knows? Maybe he didn't even know the Meriwether code. Maybe the whole point of his challenge was to judge Meriwether's response. (Even Gutfreund had to marvel at the king in action.) So Gutfreund declined. In fact, he smiled his own brand of forced smile and said, "You're crazy."

No, thought Meriwether, just very, very good.

A Book Cover

The basic methods of writing that good writers draw upon every day are sometimes used in combination with each other. This cover for a book about human cadavers, for example, employs a number of them all at once. The title, *Stiff*, is a DESCRIPTION of the physical condition of the human body after death, and the words at the top and bottom describe the book itself ("bestseller," "gross," "educational," "sidesplitting"). In everyday speech, however, the word *stiff* also refers to a dead person. Going beyond physical description, Roach's title is a name or label identifying an important aspect of her subject—the sometimes conflicting legal, moral, and medical DEFINITIONS of death itself. Good writers often kill even more than two birds with one stone, however. As you describe and define a subject, you may also tell a story about it, as this book cover does by combining elements of NARRATION with those of description and definition. We see just enough of the person pictured on the cover of Roach's book to know that he or she ended up in the morgue with a tag attached to the big toe. End of story—usually. For the human cadavers in Roach's book, however, death is only the beginning. Simultaneously grim and humorous, the image on the cover captures the first stages of this narrative. The later stages are implied in Roach's subtitle, *The Curious Lives of Human Cadavers*, which tells us that *Stiff* is a book about what happens to our bodies after we die.

EVERYDAY WRITING

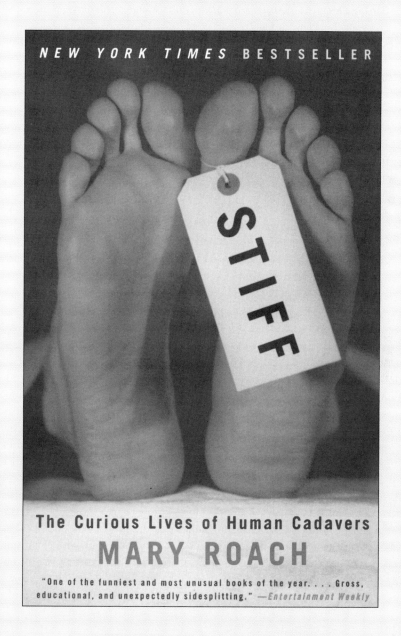

NEW YORK TIMES BESTSELLER

STIFF

The Curious Lives of Human Cadavers
MARY ROACH

"One of the funniest and most unusual books of the year. . . . Gross,
educational, and unexpectedly sidesplitting." —*Entertainment Weekly*

BARBARA EHRENREICH

Serving in Florida

Barbara Ehrenreich (b. 1941) is a native of Butte, Montana. She attended Reed College and earned a Ph.D. in biology from Rockefeller University. A reporter and prolific writer, Ehrenreich has published more than a dozen books, including Fear of Falling: The Inner Life of the Middle Class *(1989),* Nickel and Dimed: On (Not) Getting By in America *(2002), and* Bait and Switch: The (Futile) Pursuit of the American Dream *(2005). Ehrenreich has also written numerous essays for, among others,* The Progressive, New Republic, Mother Jones, *and the* Atlantic Monthly.

In 1998, on assignment from Harper's, *Ehrenreich went undercover as a low-wage worker, waiting tables and cleaning hotel rooms in Florida, working at a nursing home in Maine, and becoming a Wal-Mart "associate" in Minneapolis. The result of this intensive period of investigative reporting was* Nickel and Dimed, *which quickly became a best-seller. "Serving in Florida," a selection from that book, is a narrative of the "pink-collar" life in service jobs traditionally reserved for women. But it is a narrative in support of an argument: former welfare recipients, single mothers, and other workers earning the minimum wage (often even less), Ehrenreich argues, are not "getting by" in America. For many entry-level workers, she concludes, the land of opportunity has become a land of indentured servitude.*

Mostly out of laziness, I decide to start my low-wage life in the town nearest to where I actually live, Key West, Florida, which with a population of about 25,000 is elbowing its way up to the status of a genuine city. The downside of familiarity, I soon realize, is that it's not easy to go from being a consumer, thoughtlessly throwing money around in exchange for groceries and movies and gas, to being a worker in the very same place. I am terrified, especially at the beginning, of being recognized by some friendly business owner or erstwhile neighbor and having to stammer out some explanation of my project. Happily, though, my fears turn out to be entirely unwarranted: during a month of poverty and toil, no one recognizes my face or my name, which goes unnoticed and for the most part unuttered. In this parallel universe where my father never got out of the mines and I never got through college, I am "baby," "honey," "blondie," and, most commonly, "girl."

My first task is to find a place to live. I figure that if I can earn $7 an hour— which, from the want ads, seems doable—I can afford to spend $500 on rent or maybe, with severe economies, $600 and still have $400 or $500 left over for food and gas. In the Key West area, this pretty much confines me to flophouses and trailer homes—like the one, a pleasing fifteen-minute drive from town, that has no air-conditioning, no screens, no fans, no television, and, by way of diversion, only the challenge of evading the landlord's Doberman pinscher. The big problem with this place, though, is the rent, which at $675 a month is well beyond my reach. All right, Key West is expensive. But so is New York City, or the Bay Area, or Jackson, Wyoming, or Telluride, or Boston, or any other place where tourists and the wealthy compete for living space with the people who clean their toilets and fry their hash browns. Still, it is a shock to realize that "trailer trash" has become, for me, a demographic category to aspire to.

So I decide to make the common trade-off between affordability and convenience and go for a $500-a-month "efficiency" thirty miles up a two-lane highway from the employment opportunities of Key West, meaning forty-five minutes if there's no road construction and I don't get caught behind some sun-dazed Canadian tourists. I hate the drive, along a roadside studded with white crosses commemorating the more effective head-on collisions, but it's a sweet little place—a cabin, more or less, set in the swampy backyard of the converted mobile home where my landlord, an affable TV repairman, lives with his bartender girlfriend. Anthropologically speaking, the trailer park would be preferable, but here I have a gleaming white floor and a firm mattress, and the few resident bugs are easily vanquished.

The next piece of business is to comb through the want ads and find a job. I rule out various occupations for one reason or another: hotel front-desk clerk, for example, which to my surprise is regarded as unskilled and pays only $6 or $7 an hour, gets eliminated because it involves standing in one spot for eight hours a day. Waitressing is also something I'd like to avoid, because I remember it leaving me bone-tired when I was eighteen, and I'm decades of varicosities and back pain beyond that now. Telemarketing, one of the first refuges of the suddenly indigent, can be dismissed on grounds of personality. This leaves certain supermarket jobs, such as deli clerk, or housekeeping in the hotels and guest houses, which pays about $7 and, I imagine, is not too different from what I've been doing part-time, in my own home, all my life.

So I put on what I take to be a respectable-looking outfit of ironed Bermuda shorts and scooped-neck T-shirt and set out for a tour of the local hotels and supermarkets. Best Western, Econo Lodge, and HoJo's[1] all let me fill out application forms, and these are, to my relief, mostly interested in whether I am a legal resident of the United States and have committed any felonies. My next stop is Winn-Dixie, the supermarket, which turns out to have a particularly onerous application process, featuring a twenty-minute "interview" by computer since, apparently, no

---

1. *Best Western, Econo Lodge,* and *HoJo's*: inexpensive motel chains.

human on the premises is deemed capable of representing the corporate point of view. I am conducted to a large room decorated with posters illustrating how to look "professional" (it helps to be white and, if female, permed) and warning of the slick promises that union organizers might try to tempt me with. The interview is multiple-choice: Do I have anything, such as child care problems, that might make it hard for me to get to work on time? Do I think safety on the job is the responsibility of management? Then, popping up cunningly out of the blue: How many dollars' worth of stolen goods have I purchased in the last year? Would I turn in a fellow employee if I caught him stealing? Finally, "Are you an honest person?"

Apparently I ace the interview, because I am told that all I have to do is show up in some doctor's office tomorrow for a urine test. This seems to be a fairly general rule: if you want to stack Cheerios boxes or vacuum hotel rooms in chemically fascist America, you have to be willing to squat down and pee in front of a health worker (who has no doubt had to do the same thing herself).[2] The wages Winn-Dixie is offering—$6 and a couple of dimes to start with—are not enough, I decide, to compensate for this indignity. 6

I lunch at Wendy's, where $4.99 gets you unlimited refills at the Mexican part of the Super-bar, a comforting surfeit of refried beans and cheese sauce. A teenage employee, seeing me studying the want ads, kindly offers me an application form, which I fill out, though here, too, the pay is just $6 and change an hour. Then it's off for a round of the locally owned inns and guest houses in Key West's Old Town, which is where all the serious sightseeing and guzzling goes on, a couple of miles removed from the functional end of the island, where the discount hotels make their homes. At The Palms, let's call it, a bouncy manager actually takes me around to see the rooms and meet the current housekeepers, who, I note with satisfaction, look pretty much like me—faded ex-hippie types in shorts with long hair pulled back in braids. Mostly, though, no one speaks to me or even looks at me except to proffer an application form. At my last stop, a palatial B & B, I wait twenty minutes to meet "Max," only to be told that there are no jobs now but there should be one soon, since "nobody lasts more than a couple weeks." 7

Three days go by like this and, to my chagrin, no one from the approximately twenty places at which I've applied calls me for an interview. I had been vain enough to worry about coming across as too educated for the jobs I sought, but no one even seems interested in finding out how overqualified I am. Only later will I realize that the want ads are not a reliable measure of the actual jobs available at 8

2. Eighty-one percent of large employers now require preemployment drug testing, up from 21 percent in 1987. Among all employers, the rate of testing is highest in the South. The drug most likely to be detected—marijuana, which can be detected weeks after use—is also the most innocuous, while heroin and cocaine are generally undetectable three days after use. Alcohol, which clears the body within hours after ingestion, is not tested for. [Author's note.]

any particular time. They are, as I should have guessed from Max's comment, the employers' insurance policy against the relentless turnover of the low-wage work-force. Most of the big hotels run ads almost continually, if only to build a supply of applicants to replace the current workers as they drift away or are fired, so finding a job is just a matter of being in the right place at the right time and flexible enough to take whatever is being offered that day. This finally happens to me at one of the big discount chain hotels where I go, as usual, for housekeeping and am sent instead to try out as a waitress at the attached "family restaurant," a dismal spot looking out on a parking garage, which is featuring "Pollish sausage and BBQ sauce" on this 95-degree day. Phillip, the dapper young West Indian who introduces himself as the manager, interviews me with about as much enthusiasm as if he were a clerk processing me for Medicare, the principal questions being what shifts I can work and when I can start. I mutter about being woefully out of practice as a waitress, but he's already on to the uniform: I'm to show up tomorrow wearing black slacks and black shoes; he'll provide the rust-colored polo shirt with "Hearth-side," as we'll call the place, embroidered on it, though I might want to wear my own shirt to get to work, ha ha. At the word *tomorrow*, something between fear and indignation rises in my chest. I want to say, "Thank you for your time, sir, but this is just an experiment, you know, not my actual life."

So begins my career at the Hearthside, where for two weeks I work from 2:00 till 10:00 P.M. for $2.43 an hour plus tips.[3] Employees are barred from using the front door, so I enter the first day through the kitchen, where a red-faced man with shoulder-length blond hair is throwing frozen steaks against the wall and yelling, "Fuck this shit!" "That's just Billy," explains Gail, the wiry middle-aged waitress who is assigned to train me. "He's on the rag again"[4]—a condition occasioned, in this instance, by the fact that the cook on the morning shift had forgotten to thaw out the steaks. For the next eight hours, I run after the agile Gail, absorbing bits of instruction along with fragments of personal tragedy. All food must be trayed, and the reason she's so tired today is that she woke up in a cold sweat thinking of her boyfriend, who was killed a few months ago in a scuffle in an upstate prison. No refills on lemonade. And the reason he was in prison is that a few DUIs caught up with him, that's all, could have happened to anyone. Carry the creamers to the

9

---

3. According to the Fair Labor Standards Act, employers are not required to pay "tipped employ-ees," such as restaurant servers, more than $2.13 an hour in direct wages. However, if the sum of tips plus $2.13 an hour falls below the minimum wage, or $5.15 an hour, the employer is required to make up the difference. This fact was not mentioned by managers or otherwise publicized at either of the restaurants where I worked. [Author's note.]

4. *He's on the rag*: "on the rag" is a slang term for menstruation and is usually used to mean "ir-ritable."

table in a "monkey bowl," never in your hand. And after he was gone she spent several months living in her truck, peeing in a plastic pee bottle and reading by candlelight at night, but you can't live in a truck in the summer, since you need to have the windows down, which means anything can get in, from mosquitoes on up.

At least Gail puts to rest any fears I had of appearing overqualified. From the first day on, I find that of all the things that I have left behind, such as home and identity, what I miss the most is competence. Not that I have ever felt 100 percent competent in the writing business, where one day's success augurs nothing at all for the next. But in my writing life, I at least have some notion of *procedure*: do the research, make the outline, rough out a draft, etc. As a server, though, I am beset by requests as if by bees: more iced tea here, catsup over there, a to-go box for table 14, and where are the high chairs, anyway? Of the twenty-seven tables, up to six are usually mine at any time, though on slow afternoons or if Gail is off, I sometimes have the whole place to myself. There is the touch-screen computer-ordering system to master, which I suppose is meant to minimize server-cook contacts but in practice requires constant verbal fine-tuning: "That's gravy on the mashed, OK? None on the meatloaf," and so forth. Plus, something I had forgotten in the years since I was eighteen: about a third of a server's job is "side work" invisible to customers—sweeping, scrubbing, slicing, refilling, and restocking. If it isn't all done, every little bit of it, you're going to face the 6:00 P.M. dinner rush defenseless and probably go down in flames. I screw up dozens of times at the beginning, sustained in my shame entirely by Gail's support—"It's OK, baby, everyone does that sometime"—because, to my total surprise and despite the scientific detachment I am doing my best to maintain, I *care*. 10

The whole thing would be a lot easier if I could just skate through it like Lily Tomlin in one of her waitress skits, but I was raised by the absurd Booker T. Washingtonian[5] precept that says: If you're going to do something, do it well. In fact, "well" isn't good enough by half. Do it better than anyone has ever done it before. Or so said my father, who must have known what he was talking about because he managed to pull himself, and us with him, up from the mile-deep copper mines of Butte to the leafy suburbs of the Northeast, ascending from boiler-makers to martinis before booze beat out ambition. As in most endeavors I have encountered in my life, "doing it better than anyone" is not a reasonable goal. Still, when I wake up at 4 A.M. in my own cold sweat, I am not thinking about the writing deadlines I'm neglecting; I'm thinking of the table where I screwed up the order and one of the kids didn't get his kiddie meal until the rest of the family had moved on to their Key lime pies. That's the other powerful motivation—the customers, or "patients," 11

5. *Booker T. Washington* (1856–1915): African American educator and activist. *Lily Tomlin*: actress and comedian.

as I can't help thinking of them on account of the mysterious vulnerability that seems to have left them temporarily unable to feed themselves. After a few days at Hearthside, I feel the service ethic kick in like a shot of oxytocin, the nurturance hormone. The plurality of my customers are hardworking locals—truck drivers, construction workers, even housekeepers from the attached hotel—and I want them to have the closest to a "fine dining" experience that the grubby circumstances will allow. No "you guys" for me; everyone over twelve is "sir" or "ma'am." I ply them with iced tea and coffee refills; I return, midmeal, to inquire how everything is; I doll up their salads with chopped raw mushrooms, summer squash slices, or whatever bits of produce I can find that have survived their sojourn in the cold storage room mold-free.

There is Benny, for example, a short, tight-muscled sewer repairman who cannot even think of eating until he has absorbed a half hour of air-conditioning and ice water. We chat about hyperthermia and electrolytes until he is ready to order some finicky combination like soup of the day, garden salad, and a side of grits. There are the German tourists who are so touched by my pidgin "*Wilkommen*" and "*Ist alles gut?*" that they actually tip. (Europeans, no doubt spoiled by their trade union–ridden, high-wage welfare states, generally do not know that they are supposed to tip. Some restaurants, the Hearthside included, allow servers to "grat" their foreign customers, or add a tip to the bill. Since this amount is added before the customers have a chance to tip or not tip, the practice amounts to an automatic penalty for imperfect English.) There are the two dirt-smudged lesbians, just off from their shift, who are impressed enough by my suave handling of the fly in the piña colada that they take the time to praise me to Stu, the assistant manager. There's Sam, the kindly retired cop who has to plug up his tracheotomy hole with one finger in order to force the cigarette smoke into his lungs.

Sometimes I play with the fantasy that I am a princess who, in penance for some tiny transgression, has undertaken to feed each of her subjects by hand. But the nonprincesses working with me are just as indulgent, even when this means flouting management rules—as to, for example, the number of croutons that can go on a salad (six). "Put on all you want," Gail whispers, "as long as Stu isn't looking." She dips into her own tip money to buy biscuits and gravy for an out-of-work mechanic who's used up all his money on dental surgery, inspiring me to pick up the tab for his pie and milk. Maybe the same high levels of agape can be found throughout the "hospitality industry." I remember the poster decorating one of the apartments I looked at, which said, "If you seek happiness for yourself you will never find it. Only when you seek happiness for others will it come to you," or words to that effect—an odd sentiment, it seemed to me at the time, to find in the dank one-room basement apartment of a bellhop at the Best Western. At Hearthside, we utilize whatever bits of autonomy we have to ply our customers with the illicit calories that signal our love. It is our job as servers to assemble the salads and desserts, pour the dressings, and squirt the whipped cream. We also control the number of butter pats our customers get and the amount of sour cream on their baked potatoes. So if you wonder why Americans are so obese, consider the fact that waitresses both express their humanity and earn their tips through the covert distribution of fats.

Ten days into it, this is beginning to look like a livable lifestyle. I like Gail, who   14
is "looking at fifty," agewise, but moves so fast she can alight in one place and then another without apparently being anywhere between. I clown around with Lionel, the teenage Haitian busboy, though we don't have much vocabulary in common, and loiter near the main sink to listen to the older Haitian dishwashers' musical Creole, which sounds, in their rich bass voices, like French on testosterone. I bond with Timmy, the fourteen-year-old white kid who buses at night, by telling him I don't like people putting their baby seats right on the tables: it makes the baby look too much like a side dish. He snickers delightedly and in return, on a slow night, starts telling me the plots of all the *Jaws* movies (which are perennial favorites in the shark-ridden Keys): "She looks around, and the water-skier isn't there anymore, then SNAP! The whole boat goes . . ."

I especially like Joan, the svelte fortyish hostess, who turns out to be a militant   15
feminist, pulling me aside one day to explain that "men run everything—we don't have a chance unless we stick together." Accordingly, she backs me up when I get overpowered on the floor, and in return I give her a chunk of my tips or stand guard while she sneaks off for an unauthorized cigarette break. We all admire her for standing up to Billy and telling him, after some of his usual nastiness about the female server class, to "shut the fuck up." I even warm up to Billy when, on a slow night and to make up for a particularly unwarranted attack on my abilities, or so I imagine, he tells me about his glory days as a young man at "coronary school" in Brooklyn, where he dated a knockout Puerto Rican chick—or do you say "culinary"?

I finish up every night at 10:00 or 10:30, depending on how much side work I've   16
been able to get done during the shift, and cruise home to the tapes I snatched at random when I left my real home—Marianne Faithfull, Tracy Chapman, Enigma, King Sunny Adé, Violent Femmes—just drained enough for the music to set my cranium resonating, but hardly dead. Midnight snack is Wheat Thins and Monterey Jack, accompanied by cheap white wine on ice and whatever AMC has to offer. To bed by 1:30 or 2:00, up at 9:00 or 10:00, read for an hour while my uniform whirls around in the landlord's washing machine, and then it's another eight hours spent following Mao's central instruction, as laid out in the Little Red Book,[6] which was: Serve the people.

. . .

---

6. *Little Red Book*: a collection of quotations by China's Chairman Mao Zedong.

I could drift along like this, in some dreamy proletarian idyll, except for two things.   17
One is management. If I have kept this subject to the margins so far it is because I
still flinch to think that I spent all those weeks under the surveillance of men (and
later women) whose job it was to monitor my behavior for signs of sloth, theft,
drug abuse, or worse. Not that managers and especially "assistant managers" in
low-wage setting like this are exactly the class enemy. Mostly, in the restaurant
business, they are former cooks still capable of pinch-hitting in the kitchen, just as
in hotels they are likely to be former clerks, and paid a salary of only about $400 a
week. But everyone knows they have crossed over to the other side, which is,
crudely put, corporate as opposed to human. Cooks want to prepare tasty meals,
servers want to serve them graciously, but managers are there for only one reason—to make sure that money is made for some theoretical entity, the corporation,
which exists far away in Chicago or New York, if a corporation can be said to have
a physical existence at all. Reflecting on her career, Gail tells me ruefully that she
swore, years ago, never to work for a corporation again. "They don't cut you no
slack. You give and you give and they take."

Managers can sit—for hours at a time if they want—but it's their job to see that   18
no one else ever does, even when there's nothing to do, and this is why, for servers,
slow times can be as exhausting as rushes. You start dragging out each little chore
because if the manager on duty catches you in an idle moment he will give you
something far nastier to do. So I wipe, I clean, I consolidate catsup bottles and
recheck the cheesecake supply, even tour the tables to make sure the customer
evaluation forms are all standing perkily in their places—wondering all the time
how many calories I burn in these strictly theatrical exercises. In desperation, I
even take the desserts out of their glass display case and freshen them up with
whipped cream and bright new maraschino cherries; anything to look busy. When,
on a particularly dead afternoon, Stu finds me glancing at a *USA Today* a customer
has left behind, he assigns me to vacuum the entire floor with the broken vacuum
cleaner, which has a handle only two feet long, and the only way to do that without
incurring orthopedic damage is to proceed from spot to spot on your knees.

On my first Friday at Hearthside there is a "mandatory meeting for all restau-   19
rant employees," which I attend, eager for insight into our overall marketing strategy and the niche (your basic Ohio cuisine with a tropical twist?) we aim to
inhabit. But there is no "we" at this meeting. Phillip, our top manager except for an
occasional "consultant" sent out by corporate headquarters, opens it with a sneer:
"The break room—it's disgusting. Butts in the ashtrays, newspapers lying around,
crumbs." This windowless little room, which also houses the time clock for the
entire hotel, is where we stash our bags and civilian clothes and take our half-hour
meal breaks. But a break room is not a right, he tells us, it can be taken away. We
should also know that the lockers in the break room and whatever is in them

can be searched at any time. Then comes gossip; there has been gossip; gossip (which seems to mean employees talking among themselves) must stop. Off-duty employees are henceforth barred from eating at the restaurant, because "other servers gather around them and gossip." When Phillip has exhausted his agenda of rebukes, Joan complains about the condition of the ladies' room and I throw in my two bits about the vacuum cleaner. But I don't see any backup coming from my fellow servers, each of whom has slipped into her own personal funk; Gail, my role model, stares sorrowfully at a point six inches from her nose. The meeting ends when Andy, one of the cooks, gets up, muttering about breaking up his day off for this almighty bullshit.

Just four days later we are suddenly summoned into the kitchen at 3:30 P.M., even though there are live tables on the floor. We all—about ten of us—stand around Phillip, who announces grimly that there has been a report of some "drug activity" on the night shift and that, as a result, we are now to be a "drug-free" workplace, meaning that all new hires will be tested and possibly also current employees on a random basis. I am glad that this part of the kitchen is so dark because I find myself blushing as hard as if I had been caught toking up in the ladies' room myself: I haven't been treated this way—lined up in the corridor, threatened with locker searches, peppered with carelessly aimed accusations— since at least junior high school. Back on the floor, Joan cracks, "Next they'll be telling us we can't have *sex* on the job." When I ask Stu what happened to inspire the crackdown, he just mutters about "management decisions" and takes the opportunity to upbraid Gail and me for being too generous with the rolls. From now on there's to be only one per customer and it goes out with the dinner, not with the salad. He's also been riding the cooks, prompting Andy to come out of the kitchen and observe—with the serenity of a man whose customary implement is a butcher knife—that "Stu has a death wish today." 20

Later in the evening, the gossip crystallizes around the theory that Stu is himself the drug culprit, that he uses the restaurant phone to order up marijuana and sends one of the late servers out to fetch it for him. The server was caught and she may have ratted out Stu, at least enough to cast some suspicion on him, thus accounting for his pissy behavior. Who knows? Personally, I'm ready to believe anything bad about Stu, who serves no evident function and presumes too much on our common ethnicity, sidling up to me one night to engage in a little nativism directed at the Haitian immigrants: "I feel like I'm the foreigner here. They're taking over the country." Still later that evening, the drug in question escalates to crack. Lionel, the busboy, entertains us for the rest of the shift by standing just behind Stu's back and sucking deliriously on an imaginary joint or maybe a pipe. 21

The other problem, in addition to the less-than-nurturing management style, is that this job shows no sign of being financially viable. You might imagine, from a 22 comfortable distance, that people who live, year in and year out, on $6 to $10 an hour have discovered some survival stratagems unknown to the middle class. But no. It's not hard to get my coworkers talking about their living situations, because housing, in almost every case, is the principal source of disruption in their lives, the first thing they fill you in on when they arrive for their shifts. After a week, I have compiled the following survey:

Gail is sharing a room in a well-known downtown flophouse for $250 a week. Her roommate, a male friend, has begun hitting on her, driving her nuts, but the rent would be impossible alone.

Claude, the Haitian cook, is desperate to get out of the two-room apartment he shares with his girlfriend and two other, unrelated people. As far as I can determine, the other Haitian men live in similarly crowded situations.

Annette, a twenty-year-old server who is six months pregnant and abandoned by her boyfriend, lives with her mother, a postal clerk.

Marianne, who is a breakfast server, and her boyfriend are paying $170 a week for a one-person trailer.

Billy, who at $10 an hour is the wealthiest of us, lives in the trailer he owns, paying only the $400-a-month lot fee.

The other white cook, Andy, lives on his dry-docked boat, which, as far as I can tell from his loving descriptions, can't be more than twenty feet long. He offers to take me out on it once it's repaired, but the offer comes with inquiries as to my marital status, so I do not follow up on it.

Tina, another server, and her husband are paying $60 a night for a room in the Days Inn. This is because they have no car and the Days Inn is in walking distance of the Hearthside. When Marianne is tossed out of her trailer for subletting (which is against trailer park rules), she leaves her boyfriend and moves in with Tina and her husband.

Joan, who had fooled me with her numerous and tasteful outfits (hostesses wear their own clothes), lives in a van parked behind a shopping center at night and showers in Tina's motel room. The clothes are from thrift shops.[7]

7. I could find no statistics on the number of employed people living in cars or vans, but according to a 1997 report of the National Coalition for the Homeless, "Myths and Facts about Homelessness," nearly one-fifth of all homeless people (in twenty-nine cities across the nation) are employed in full- or part-time jobs. [Author's note.]

It strikes me, in my middle-class solipsism, that there is gross improvidence in   23
some of these arrangements. When Gail and I are wrapping silverware in napkins—the only task for which we are permitted to sit—she tells me she is thinking
of escaping from her roommate by moving into the Days Inn herself. I am
astounded: how she can even think of paying $40 to $60 a day? But if I was afraid
of sounding like a social worker, I have come out just sounding like a fool. She
squints at me in disbelief: "And where am I supposed to get a month's rent and a
month's deposit for an apartment?" I'd been feeling pretty smug about my $500
efficiency, but of course it was made possible only by the $1,300 I had allotted
myself for start-up costs when I began my low-wage life: $1,000 for the first
month's rent and deposit, $100 for initial groceries and cash in my pocket, $200
stuffed away for emergencies. In poverty, as in certain propositions in physics,
starting conditions are everything.

There are no secret economies that nourish the poor; on the contrary, there are   24
a host of special costs. If you can't put up the two months' rent you need to secure
an apartment, you end up paying through the nose for a room by the week. If you
have only a room, with a hot plate at best, you can't save by cooking up huge lentil
stews that can be frozen for the week ahead. You eat fast food or the hot dogs and
Styrofoam cups of soup that can be microwaved in a convenience store. If you have
no money for health insurance—and the Hearthside's niggardly plan kicks in only
after three months—you go without routine care or prescription drugs and end up
paying the price. Gail, for example, was doing fine, healthwise anyway, until she
ran out of money for estrogen pills. She is supposed to be on the company health
plan by now, but they claim to have lost her application form and to be beginning
the paperwork all over again. So she spends $9 a pop for pills to control the
migraines she wouldn't have, she insists, if her estrogen supplements were covered.
Similarly, Marianne's boyfriend lost his job as a roofer because he missed so much
time after getting a cut on his foot for which he couldn't afford the prescribed
antibiotic.

My own situation, when I sit down to assess it after two weeks of work, would   25
not be much better if this were my actual life. The seductive thing about waitressing is that you don't have to wait for payday to feel a few bills in your pocket, and
my tips usually cover meals and gas, plus something left over to stuff into the
kitchen drawer I use as a bank. But as the tourist business slows in the summer
heat, I sometimes leave work with only $20 in tips (the gross is higher, but servers
share about 15 percent of their tips with the busboys and bartenders). With wages
included, this amounts to about the minimum wage of $5.15 an hour. The sum in
the drawer is piling up but at the present rate of accumulation will be more than
$100 short of my rent when the end of the month comes around. Nor can I see any
expenses to cut. True, I haven't gone the lentil stew route yet, but that's because I

don't have a large cooking pot, potholders, or a ladle to stir with (which would cost a total of about $30 at Kmart, somewhat less at a thrift store), not to mention onions, carrots, and the indispensable bay leaf. I do make my lunch almost every day—usually some slow-burning, high-protein combo like frozen chicken patties with melted cheese on top and canned pinto beans on the side. Dinner is at the Hearthside, which offers its employees a choice of BLT, fish sandwich, or hamburger for only $2. The burger lasts longest especially if it's heaped with gut-puckering jalapeños, but by midnight my stomach is growling again.

So unless I want to start using my car as a residence, I have to find a second or 26 an alternative job. I call all the hotels I'd filled out housekeeping applications at weeks ago—the Hyatt, Holiday Inn, Econo Lodge, HoJo's, Best Western, plus a half dozen locally run guest houses. Nothing. Then I start making the rounds again, wasting whole mornings waiting for some assistant manager to show up, even dipping into places so creepy that the front-desk clerk greets you from behind bullet-proof glass and sells pints of liquor over the counter. But either someone has exposed my real-life housekeeping habits—which are, shall we say, mellow—or I am at the wrong end of some infallible ethnic equation: most, but by no means all, of the working housekeepers I see on my job searches are African Americans, Spanish-speaking, or refugees from the Central European post-Communist world, while servers are almost invariably white and monolingually English-speaking. When I finally get a positive response, I have been identified, once again as server material. Jerry's—again, not the real name—which is part of a well-known national chain and physically attached here to another budget hotel, is ready to use me at once. The prospect is both exciting and terrifying because, with about the same number of tables and counter seats, Jerry's attracts three or four times the volume of customers as the gloomy old Hearthside.

READING WITH AN EYE FOR THE METHODS

1. Most of the time, Ehrenreich is telling the story of her experience as a waitress in Florida. Where and how does she use this NARRATIVE to make an ARGUMENT about the lives of low-wage earners in general? Point out several instances, and explain how the details of her narrative support (or fail to support) her contentions.

2. Ehrenreich directly COMPARES (and contrasts) her work as a server to her work in "the writing business" (10). What are some of the main points of similarity? Of difference? Why is Ehrenreich drawing the comparison?

3. With no experience in the service industry, Ehrenreich has to learn how to wait tables. Who teaches her? Where and how does she ANALYZE THE PROCESS of learning to do those various tasks?

4. What other methods of development does Ehrenreich use in "Serving in Florida"? Point out and explain how they contribute to her argument.

USING THE METHODS

1. Write a paragraph in which you relate how you learned to iron, set a table, make a bed, clean a room, or do some other "menial" but still useful task. Then tell your reader how to do the task.

2. Write a NARRATIVE about a phase of your work experience, whether as a lifeguard, camp counselor, babysitter, construction worker, or in some other temporary job. What did these experiences teach you about yourself and about the workplace in general?

ERIC SCHLOSSER

What We Eat

Eric Schlosser earned a bachelor's degree in American history from Princeton University and later studied the history of the British monarchy at Oxford University. He is an investigative reporter for the Atlantic Monthly *and other magazines. On assignment for* Rolling Stone, *he began to look into a different kind of history—that of consumer culture, particularly fast food, as represented in the American marketplace by McDonald's and other fast food outlets. The result was* Fast Food Nation: What the All-American Meal Is Doing to the World *(2001). Schlosser is also the author of* Reefer Madness: Sex, Drugs, and Cheap Labor in the American Black Market *(2003).*

"What We Eat," a selection from Fast Food Nation, *argues not only that the fast food industry has changed the way Americans eat, but that its methods and values have become the country's chief export. Schlosser supports this argument with a host of examples, stories, and statistics. "In trying to tie together all these different threads," he told an interviewer for Powells.com, "there was a huge risk that it would be a total mess." Actually, this selection, like the rest of Schlosser's book, is tightly organized. The secret of combining many topics and methods at once, he says, is "balance"—something he finds lacking in the American meal and in consumer culture as a whole.*

OVER THE LAST THREE DECADES, fast food has infiltrated every nook and 1
cranny of American society. An industry that began with a handful of modest hot dog and hamburger stands in southern California has spread to every corner of the nation, selling a broad range of foods wherever paying customers may be found. Fast food is now served at restaurants and drive-throughs, at stadiums, airports, zoos, high schools, elementary schools, and universities, on cruise ships, trains, and airplanes, at K-Marts, Wal-Marts, gas stations, and even at hospital cafeterias. In 1970, Americans spent about $6 billion on fast food; in 2001, they spent more than $110 billion. Americans now spend more money on fast food than on higher education, personal computers, computer software, or new cars. They spend more on fast food than on movies, books, magazines, newspapers, videos, and recorded music—combined.

Pull open the glass door, feel the rush of cool air, walk in, get on line, study the 2
backlit color photographs above the counter, place your order, hand over a few dollars, watch teenagers in uniforms pushing various buttons, and moments later take hold of a plastic tray full of food wrapped in colored paper and cardboard. The whole experience of buying fast food has become so routine, so thoroughly unexceptional and mundane, that it is now taken for granted, like brushing your teeth

or stopping for a red light. It has become a social custom as American as a small, rectangular, hand-held, frozen, and reheated apple pie.

. . . Fast food has proven to be a revolutionary force in American life; I am inter-   3
ested in it both as a commodity and as a metaphor. What people eat (or don't eat) has always been determined by a complex interplay of social, economic, and technological forces. The early Roman Republic was fed by its citizen-farmers; the Roman Empire, by its slaves. A nation's diet can be more revealing than its art or literature. On any given day in the United States about one-quarter of the adult population visits a fast food restaurant. During a relatively brief period of time, the fast food industry has helped to transform not only the American diet, but also our landscape, economy, workforce, and popular culture. Fast food and its consequences have become inescapable, regardless of whether you eat it twice a day, try to avoid it, or have never taken a single bite.

The extraordinary growth of the fast food industry has been driven by funda-   4
mental changes in American society. Adjusted for inflation, the hourly wage of the average U.S. worker peaked in 1973 and then steadily declined for the next twenty-five years. During that period, women entered the workforce in record numbers, often motivated less by a feminist perspective than by a need to pay the bills. In 1975, about one-third of American mothers with young children worked outside the home; today almost two-thirds of such mothers are employed. As the sociologists Cameron Lynne Macdonald and Carmen Sirianni have noted, the entry of so many women into the workforce has greatly increased demand for the types of services that housewives traditionally perform: cooking, cleaning, and child care. A generation ago, three-quarters of the money used to buy food in the United States was spent to prepare meals at home. Today about half of the money used to buy food is spent at restaurants—mainly at fast food restaurants.

The McDonald's Corporation has become a powerful symbol of America's ser-   5
vice economy, which is now responsible for 90 percent of the country's new jobs. In 1968, McDonald's operated about one thousand restaurants. Today it has about thirty thousand restaurants worldwide and opens almost two thousand new ones each year. An estimated one out of every eight workers in the United States has at some point been employed by McDonald's. The company annually hires about one million people, more than any other American organization, public or private. McDonald's is the nation's largest purchaser of beef, pork, and potatoes—and the second largest purchaser of chicken. The McDonald's Corporation is the largest owner of retail property in the world. Indeed, the company earns the majority of its profits not from selling food but from collecting rent. McDonald's spends more money on advertising and marketing than any other brand. As a result it has replaced Coca-Cola as the world's most famous brand. McDonald's operates more

playgrounds than any other private entity in the United States. It is responsible for the nation's bestselling line of children's clothing (McKids) and is one of the largest distributors of toys. A survey of American schoolchildren found that 96 percent could identify Ronald McDonald. The only fictional character with a higher degree of recognition was Santa Claus. The impact of McDonald's on the way we live today is hard to overstate. The Golden Arches are now more widely recognized than the Christian cross.

In the early 1970s, the farm activist Jim Hightower warned of "the McDonald-ization of America." He viewed the emerging fast food industry as a threat to independent businesses, as a step toward a food economy dominated by giant corporations, and as a homogenizing influence on American life. In *Eat Your Heart Out* (1975), he argued that "bigger is *not* better." Much of what Hightower feared has come to pass. The centralized purchasing decisions of the large restaurant chains and their demand for standardized products have given a handful of corporations an unprecedented degree of power over the nation's food supply. Moreover, the tremendous success of the fast food industry has encouraged other industries to adopt similar business methods. The basic thinking behind fast food has become the operating system of today's retail economy, wiping out small businesses, obliterating regional differences, and spreading identical stores throughout the country like a self-replicating code. 6

America's main streets and malls now boast the same Pizza Huts and Taco Bells, Gaps and Banana Republics, Starbucks and Jiffy-Lubes, Foot Lockers, Snip N' Clips, Sunglass Huts, and Hobbytown USAs. Almost every facet of American life has now been franchised or chained. From the maternity ward at a Columbia/HCA hospital to an embalming room owned by Service Corporation International—"the world's largest provider of death care services," based in Houston, Texas, which since 1968 has grown to include 3,823 funeral homes, 523 cemeteries, and 198 crematoriums, and which today handles the final remains of one out of every nine Americans—a person can now go from the cradle to the grave without spending a nickel at an independently owned business. 7

The key to a successful franchise, according to many texts on the subject, can be expressed in one word: "uniformity." Franchises and chain stores strive to offer exactly the same product or service at numerous locations. Customers are drawn to familiar brands by an instinct to avoid the unknown. A brand offers a feeling of reassurance when its products are always and everywhere the same. "We have found out . . . that we cannot trust some people who are nonconformists," declared Ray Kroc, one of the founders of McDonald's, angered by some of his franchisees. "We will make conformists out of them in a hurry . . . The organization cannot trust the individual; the individual must trust the organization." 8

One of the ironies of America's fast food industry is that a business so dedicated   9
to conformity was founded by iconoclasts and self-made men, by entrepreneurs
willing to defy conventional opinion. Few of the people who built fast food empires
ever attended college, let alone business school. They worked hard, took risks, and
followed their own paths. In many respects, the fast food industry embodies the
best and the worst of American capitalism at the start of the twenty-first century—
its constant stream of new products and innovations, its widening gulf between
rich and poor. The industrialization of the restaurant kitchen has enabled the fast
food chains to rely upon a low-paid and unskilled workforce. While a handful of
workers manage to rise up the corporate ladder, the vast majority lack full-time
employment, receive no benefits, learn few skills, exercise little control over their
workplace, quit after a few months, and float from job to job. The restaurant industry is now America's largest private employer, and it pays some of the lowest wages.
During the economic boom of the 1990s, when many American workers enjoyed
their first pay raises in a generation, the real value of wages in the restaurant industry continued to fall. The roughly 3.5 million fast food workers are by far the largest
group of minimum wage earners in the United States. The only Americans who
consistently earn a lower hourly wage are migrant farm workers.

A hamburger and french fries became the quintessential American meal in the   10
1950s, thanks to the promotional efforts of the fast food chains. The typical American now consumes approximately three hamburgers and four orders of french fries
every week. But the steady barrage of fast food ads, full of thick juicy burgers and
long golden fries, rarely mentions where these foods come from nowadays or
what ingredients they contain. The birth of the fast food industry coincided with
Eisenhower-era glorifications of technology, with optimistic slogans like "Better
Living through Chemistry" and "Our Friend the Atom." The sort of technological
wizardry that Walt Disney promoted on television and at Disneyland eventually
reached its fulfillment in the kitchens of fast food restaurants. Indeed, the corporate culture of McDonald's seems inextricably linked to that of the Disney empire,
sharing a reverence for sleek machinery, electronics, and automation. The leading
fast food chains still embrace a boundless faith in science—and as a result have
changed not just what Americans eat, but also how their food is made.

The current methods for preparing fast food are less likely to be found in cook-   11
books than in trade journals such as *Food Technologist* and *Food Engineering.* Aside
from the salad greens and tomatoes, most fast food is delivered to the restaurant
already frozen, canned, dehydrated, or freeze-dried. A fast food kitchen is merely
the final stage in a vast and highly complex system of mass production. Foods that
may look familiar have in fact been completely reformulated. What we eat has
changed more in the last forty years than in the previous forty thousand. Like

Cheyenne Mountain,[1] today's fast food conceals remarkable technological advances behind an ordinary-looking façade. Much of the taste and aroma of American fast food, for example, is now manufactured at a series of large chemical plants off the New Jersey Turnpike.

In the fast food restaurants of Colorado Springs, behind the counters, amid the   12
plastic seats, in the changing landscape outside the window, you can see all the virtues and destructiveness of our fast food nation. I chose Colorado Springs as a focal point . . . because the changes that have recently swept through the city are emblematic of those that fast food—and the fast food mentality—have encouraged throughout the United States. Countless other suburban communities, in every part of the country, could have been used to illustrate the same points. The extraordinary growth of Colorado Springs neatly parallels that of the fast food industry: during the last few decades, the city's population has more than doubled. Subdivisions, shopping malls, and chain restaurants are appearing in the foothills of Cheyenne Mountain and the plains rolling to the east. The Rocky Mountain region as a whole has the fastest-growing economy in the United States, mixing high-tech and service industries in a way that may define America's workforce for years to come. And new restaurants are opening there at a faster pace than anywhere else in the nation.

Fast food is now so commonplace that it has acquired an air of inevitability, as   13
though it were somehow unavoidable, a fact of modern life. And yet the dominance of the fast food giants was no more preordained than the march of colonial split-levels, golf courses, and manmade lakes across the deserts of the American West. The political philosophy that now prevails in so much of the West—with its demand for lower taxes, smaller government, an unbridled free market—stands in total contradiction to the region's true economic underpinnings. No other region of the United States has been so dependent on government subsidies for so long, from the nineteenth-century construction of its railroads to the twentieth-century financing of its military bases and dams. One historian has described the federal government's 1950s highway-building binge as a case study in "interstate socialism"—a phrase that aptly describes how the West was really won. The fast food industry took root alongside that interstate highway system, as a new form of restaurant sprang up beside the new off-ramps. Moreover, the extraordinary growth of this industry over the past quarter-century did not occur in a political

---

1. *Cheyenne Mountain:* a bi-national (United States and Canada) military operations center and high-level command post near Colorado Springs, Colorado, containing missile sensors and other high-tech equipment. The center is built inside a mountain and is entered through a 540-meter tunnel; it is designed to withstand direct nuclear attack.

vacuum. It took place during a period when the inflation-adjusted value of the minimum wage declined by about 40 percent, when sophisticated mass marketing techniques were for the first time directed at small children, and when federal agencies created to protect workers and consumers too often behaved like branch offices of the companies that were supposed to be regulated. Ever since the administration of President Richard Nixon, the fast food industry has worked closely with its allies in Congress and the White House to oppose new worker safety, food safety, and minimum wage laws. While publicly espousing support for the free market, the fast food chains have quietly pursued and greatly benefited from a wide variety of government subsidies. Far from being inevitable, America's fast food industry in its present form is the logical outcome of certain political and economic choices.

In the potato fields and processing plants of Idaho, in the ranchlands east of Colorado Springs, in the feedlots and slaughterhouses of the High Plains, you can see the effects of fast food on the nation's rural life, its environment, its workers, and its health. The fast food chains now stand atop a huge food-industrial complex that has gained control of American agriculture. During the 1980s, large multinationals—such as Cargill, ConAgra, and IBP—were allowed to dominate one commodity market after another. Farmers and cattle ranchers are losing their independence, essentially becoming hired hands for the agribusiness giants or being forced off the land. Family farms are now being replaced by gigantic corporate farms with absentee owners. Rural communities are losing their middle class and becoming socially stratified, divided between a small, wealthy elite and large numbers of the working poor. Small towns that seemingly belong in a Norman Rockwell painting are being turned into rural ghettos. The hardy, independent farmers whom Thomas Jefferson considered the bedrock of American democracy are a truly vanishing breed. The United States now has more prison inmates than full-time farmers.

The fast food chains' vast purchasing power and their demand for a uniform product have encouraged fundamental changes in how cattle are raised, slaughtered, and processed into ground beef. These changes have made meatpacking—once a highly skilled, highly paid occupation—into the most dangerous job in the United States, performed by armies of poor, transient immigrants whose injuries often go unrecorded and uncompensated. And the same meat industry practices that endanger these workers have facilitated the introduction of deadly pathogens, such as *E. coli* O157:H7, into America's hamburger meat, a food aggressively marketed to children. Again and again, efforts to prevent the sale of tainted ground beef have been thwarted by meat industry lobbyists and their allies in Congress. The federal government has the legal authority to recall a defective toaster oven or stuffed animal—but still lacks the power to recall tons of contaminated, potentially lethal meat.

I do not mean to suggest that fast food is solely responsible for every social prob- 16
lem now haunting the United States. In some cases (such as the malling and
sprawling of the West) the fast food industry has been a catalyst and a symptom of
larger economic trends. In other cases (such as the rise of franchising and the
spread of obesity) fast food has played a more central role. By tracing the diverse
influences of fast food I hope to shed light not only on the workings of an important industry, but also on a distinctively American way of viewing the world.

Elitists have always looked down at fast food, criticizing how it tastes and 17
regarding it as another tacky manifestation of American popular culture. The aes-
thetics of fast food are of much less concern to me than its impact upon the lives of
ordinary Americans, both as workers and consumers. Most of all, I am concerned
about its impact on the nation's children. Fast food is heavily marketed to children
and prepared by people who are barely older than children. This is an industry that
both feeds and feeds off the young. During the two years spent researching this
book, I ate an enormous amount of fast food. Most of it tasted pretty good. That is
one of the main reasons people buy fast food; it has been carefully designed to taste
good. It's also inexpensive and convenient. But the value meals, two-for-one deals,
and free refills of soda give a distorted sense of how much fast food actually costs.
The real price never appears on the menu.

The sociologist George Ritzer has attacked the fast food industry for celebrating 18
a narrow measure of efficiency over every other human value, calling the triumph
of McDonald's "the irrationality of rationality." Others consider the fast food industry proof of the nation's great economic vitality, a beloved American institution
that appeals overseas to millions who admire our way of life. Indeed, the values,
the culture, and the industrial arrangements of our fast food nation are now being
exported to the rest of the world. Fast food has joined Hollywood movies, blue
jeans, and pop music as one of America's most prominent cultural exports. Unlike
other commodities, however, fast food isn't viewed, read, played, or worn. It enters
the body and becomes part of the consumer. No other industry offers, both literally
and figuratively, so much insight into the nature of mass consumption.

Reading with an Eye for the Methods

1. The fast food industry in America, says Schlosser, has seen "extraordinary
   growth" in recent decades (4). What are some of the main CAUSES of this phenomenon, according to his analysis?

2. Where else in his essay does Schlosser analyze CAUSES AND EFFECTS? What are
   some of them, especially in rural areas?

3. Why does Schlosser choose Colorado Springs as a "focal point" for his essay and the book that it introduces (12)? What does the town EXEMPLIFY and why is it, in his opinion, a good example?

4. What other methods, such as NARRATIVE and ARGUMENT, does Schlosser use in this selection? How and where does he combine them to help explain "the nature of mass consumption" (18)?

USING THE METHODS

1. "Pull open the glass door, feel the rush of cool air, walk in," and DESCRIBE in a paragraph what you see inside a familiar fast food restaurant (2).

2. Write an essay in which you attack or agree with Schlosser's thesis that "fast food has proven to be a revolutionary force in American life" (3). Give numerous examples.

STEVEN JOHNSON

Watching TV Makes You Smarter

Steven Johnson, who studied semiotics and English literature at Brown and Columbia Universities, teaches in the telecommunications program at New York University and writes a monthly column, "Emerging Technology," for Discover *magazine. He is also a contributing editor to* Wired *and the co-founder of FEED and Plastics.com, two award-winning websites. In* Emergence: The Connected Lives of Ants, Brains, Cities, and Software *(2002),* Mind Wide Open *(2004), and* Everything Bad Is Good For You *(2005), Johnson explores the frontiers where science, technology, and popular culture come together.*

"Watching TV Makes You Smarter" appeared in the New York Times *in 2005. It exemplifies the principle set forth in the title of the book from which it is adapted:* Everything Bad Is Good For You. *(The idea for the book came to him, says Johnson, from playing video games.) Johnson does more than just give examples, however. He defines what he calls the "Sleeper Curve." He argues that watching television (and other forms of popular culture) makes us smarter. And he supports his argument by comparing and contrasting the television programs of today with those of yesteryear. One of the basic differences between shows like* ER *and* Dragnet, *Johnson finds, has to do with how they are narrated.*

> SCIENTIST A: Has he asked for anything special?
>
> SCIENTIST B: Yes, this morning for breakfast . . . he requested something called "wheat germ, organic honey and tiger's milk."
>
> SCIENTIST A: Oh, yes. Those were the charmed substances that some years ago were felt to contain life-preserving properties.
>
> SCIENTIST B: You mean there was no deep fat? No steak or cream pies or . . . hot fudge?
>
> SCIENTIST A: Those were thought to be unhealthy.
>
> from WOODY ALLEN's *Sleeper*

ON JANUARY 24, the Fox network showed an episode of its hit drama *24*, the real-time thriller known for its cliffhanger tension and often-gruesome violence. Over the preceding weeks, a number of public controversies had erupted around *24*, mostly focused on its portrait of Muslim terrorists and its penchant for torture scenes. The episode that was shown on the 24th only fanned the flames higher: in one scene, a terrorist enlists a hit man to kill his child for not fully supporting the jihadist cause; in another scene, the secretary of defense authorizes the torture of his son to uncover evidence of a terrorist plot.

615

But the explicit violence and the post-9/11 terrorist anxiety are not the only ele- 2
ments of 24 that would have been unthinkable on prime-time network television
20 years ago. Alongside the notable change in content lies an equally notable
change in form. During its 44 minutes—a real-time hour, minus 16 minutes for
commercials—the episode connects the lives of 21 distinct characters, each with a
clearly defined "story arc," as the Hollywood jargon has it: a defined personality
with motivations and obstacles and specific relationships with other characters.
Nine primary narrative threads wind their way through those 44 minutes, each
drawing extensively upon events and information revealed in earlier episodes.
Draw a map of all those intersecting plots and personalities, and you get structure
that—where formal complexity is concerned—more closely resembles *Middlemarch*[1] than a hit TV drama of years past like *Bonanza*.

For decades, we've worked under the assumption that mass culture follows a 3
path declining steadily toward lowest-comon-denominator standards, presumably
because the "masses" want dumb, simple pleasures and big media companies try to
give the masses what they want. But as that 24 episode suggests, the exact opposite
is happening: the culture is getting more cognitively demanding, not less. To make
sense of an episode of 24, you have to integrate far more information than you
would have a few decades ago watching a comparable show. Beneath the violence
and the ethnic stereotypes, another trend appears: to keep up with entertainment
like 24, you have to pay attention, make inferences, track shifting social relationships. This is what I call the Sleeper Curve: the most debased forms of mass diversion—video games and violent television dramas and juvenile sitcoms—turn out to
be nutritional after all.

I believe that the Sleeper Curve is the single most important new force altering 4
the mental development of young people today, and I believe it is largely a force for
good: enhancing our cognitive faculties, not dumbing them down. And yet you
almost never hear this story in popular accounts of today's media. Instead, you hear
dire tales of addiction, violence, mindless escapism. It's assumed that shows that
promote smoking or gratuitous violence are bad for us, while those that thunder
against teen pregnancy or intolerance have a positive role in society. Judged by that
morality-play standard, the story of popular culture over the past 50 years—if not
500—is a story of decline: the morals of the stories have grown darker and more
ambiguous, and the antiheroes have multiplied.

The usual counterargument here is that what media have lost in moral clarity, 5
they have gained in realism. The real world doesn't come in nicely packaged
public-service announcements, and we're better off with entertainment like *The*

---

1. *Middlemarch*: a complex nineteenth-century British novel by George Eliot (the *nom de plume* of
Mary Anne Evans) that follows several main characters through their interrelated lives.

Sopranos that reflects our fallen state with all its ethical ambiguity. I happen to be sympathetic to that argument, but it's not the one I want to make here. I think there is another way to assess the social virtue of pop culture, one that looks at media as a kind of cognitive workout, not as a series of life lessons. There may indeed be more "negative messages" in the mediasphere today. But that's not the only way to evaluate whether our television shows or video games are having a positive impact. Just as important—if not more important—is the kind of thinking you have to do to make sense of a cultural experience. That is where the Sleeper Curve becomes visible.

Televised Intelligence

Consider the cognitive demands that televised narratives place on their viewers. 6
With many shows that we associate with "quality" entertainment—*The Mary Tyler Moore Show, Murphy Brown, Frasier*[2]—the intelligence arrives fully formed in the words and actions of the characters on-screen. They say witty things to one another and avoid lapsing into tired sitcom clichés, and we smile along in our living rooms, enjoying the company of these smart people. But assuming we're bright enough to understand the sentences they're saying, there's no intellectual labor involved in enjoying the show as a viewer. You no more challenge your mind by watching these intelligent shows than you challenge your body watching *Monday Night Football*. The intellectual work is happening on-screen, not off.

But another kind of televised intelligence is on the rise. Think of the cognitive 7
benefits conventionally ascribed to reading: attention, patience, retention, the parsing of narrative threads. Over the last half-century, programming on TV has increased the demands it places on precisely these mental faculties. This growing complexity involves three primary elements: multiple threading, flashing arrows and social networks.

According to television lore, the age of multiple threads began with the arrival 8
in 1981 of *Hill Street Blues*, the Steven Bochco police drama invariably praised for its "gritty realism." Watch an episode of *Hill Street Blues* side by side with any major drama from the preceding decades—*Starsky and Hutch*, for instance, or *Dragnet*— and the structural transformation will jump out at you. The earlier shows follow one or two lead characters, adhere to a single dominant plot and reach a decisive conclusion at the end of the episode. Draw an outline of the narrative threads in almost every *Dragnet* episode, and it will be a single line: from the initial crime scene, through the investigation, to the eventual cracking of the case. A typical

2. *The Mary Tyler Moore Show, Murphy Brown, Frasier*: thirty-minute sitcoms that aired from 1970 to 1977 (*Moore*), 1988 to 1998 (*Brown*), and 1993 to 2004 (*Frasier*).

Starsky and Hutch episode offers only the slightest variation on this linear formula: the introduction of a comic subplot that usually appears only at the tail ends of the episode, creating a structure that looks like the graph below. The vertical axis represents the number of individual threads, and the horizontal axis is time.

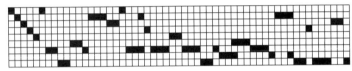

Starsky and Hutch (any episode)

A *Hill Street Blues* episode complicates the picture in a number of profound 9 ways. The narrative weaves together a collection of distinct strands—sometimes as many as 10, though at least half of the threads involve only a few quick scenes scattered through the episode. The number of primary characters—and not just bit parts—swells significantly. And the episode has fuzzy borders: picking up one or two threads from previous episodes at the outset and leaving one or two threads open at the end. Charted graphically, an average episode looks like this:

Hill Street Blues (episode 85)

Critics generally cite *Hill Street Blues* as the beginning of "serious drama" native 10 to the television medium—differentiating the series from the single-episode dramatic programs from the 50's, which were Broadway plays performed in front of a camera. But the *Hill Street* innovations weren't all that original; they'd long played a defining role in popular television, just not during the evening hours. The structure of a *Hill Street* episode—and indeed of all the critically acclaimed dramas that followed, from *thirtysomething* to *Six Feet Under*—is the structure of a soap opera. *Hill Street Blues* might have sparked a new golden age of television drama during its seven-year run, but it did so by using a few crucial tricks that *Guiding Light* and *General Hospital* mastered long before.

Bochco's genius with *Hill Street* was to marry complex narrative structure with 11 complex subject matter. *Dallas* had already shown that the extended, interwoven threads of the soap-opera genre could survive the weeklong interruptions of a prime-time show, but the actual content of *Dallas* was fluff. (The most probing issue it addressed was the question, now folkloric, of who shot J.R.[3]) *All in the Fam-*

---

3. *Who shot J.R.:* a reference to the final moments of the 1980 season-ending episode of *Dallas*, in which the character J.R. Ewing was shot by an unknown assailant. The question was the subject of much speculation throughout the following summer; the shooter was not revealed until the following November.

ily and *Rhoda* showed that you could tackle complex social issues, but they did their tackling in the comfort of the sitcom living room. *Hill Street* had richly drawn characters confronting difficult social issues and a narrative structure to match.

Since *Hill Street* appeared, the multi-threaded drama has become the most widespread fictional genre on prime time: *St. Elsewhere*, *L.A. Law*, *thirtysomething*, *Twin Peaks*, *N.Y.P.D. Blue*, *E.R.*, *The West Wing*, *Alias*, *Lost*. (The only prominent holdouts in drama are shows like *Law and Order* that have essentially updated the venerable *Dragnet* format and thus remained anchored to a single narrative line.) Since the early 80's, however, there has been a noticeable increase in narrative complexity in these dramas. The most ambitious show on TV to date, *The Sopranos*, routinely follows up to a dozen distinct threads over the course of an episode, with more than 20 recurring characters. An episode from late in the first season looks like this: 12

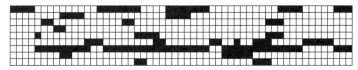

The Sopranos (episode 8)

The total number of active threads equals the multiple plots of *Hill Street*, but here each thread is more substantial. The show doesn't offer a clear distinction between dominant and minor plots; each story line carries its weight in the mix. The episode also displays a chordal mode of storytelling entirely absent from *Hill Street*: a single scene in *The Sopranos* will often connect to three different threads at the same time, layering one plot atop another. And every single thread in this *Sopranos* episode builds on events from previous episodes and continues on through the rest of the season and beyond. 13

Put those charts together, and you have a portrait of the Sleeper Curve rising over the past 30 years of popular television. In a sense, this is as much a map of cognitive changes in the popular mind as it is a map of on-screen developments, as if the media titans decided to condition our brains to follow ever-larger numbers of simultaneous threads. Before *Hill Street*, the conventional wisdom among television execs was that audiences wouldn't be comfortable following more than three plots in a single episode, and indeed, the *Hill Street* pilot, which was shown in January 1981, brought complaints from viewers that the show was too complicated. Fast-forward two decades, and shows like *The Sopranos* engage their audiences with narratives that make *Hill Street* look like *Three's Company*.[4] Audiences happily embrace that complexity because they've been trained by two decades of multi-threaded dramas. 14

4. *Three's Company*: thirty-minute sitcom that ran from 1977 to 1984.

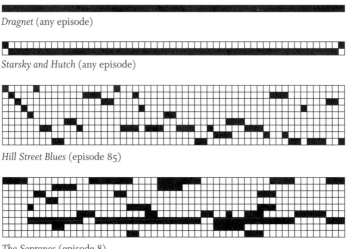

Dragnet (any episode)

Starsky and Hutch (any episode)

Hill Street Blues (episode 85)

The Sopranos (episode 8)

Multi-threading is the most celebrated structural feature of the modern tele- 15
vision drama, and it certainly deserves some of the honor that has been doled out
to it. And yet multi-threading is only part of the story.

The Case for Confusion

Shortly after the arrival of the first-generation slasher movies—*Halloween*, *Friday* 16
the 13th—Paramount released a mock-slasher flick called *Student Bodies*, parodying
the genre just as the *Scream* series would do 15 years later. In one scene, the obligatory nubile teenage baby sitter hears a noise outside a suburban house; she opens
the door to investigate, finds nothing and then goes back inside. As the door shuts
behind her, the camera swoops in on the doorknob, and we see that she has left the
door unlocked. The camera pulls back and then swoops down again for emphasis.
And then a flashing arrow appears on the screen, with text that helpfully explains:
"Unlocked!"

That flashing arrow is parody, of course, but it's merely an exaggerated version 17
of a device popular stories use all the time. When a sci-fi script inserts into some
advanced lab a nonscientist who keeps asking the science geeks to explain what
they're doing with that particle accelerator, that's a flashing arrow that gives the
audience precisely the information it needs in order to make sense of the ensuing
plot. ("Whatever you do, don't spill water on it, or you'll set off a massive explosion!") These hints serve as a kind of narrative hand-holding. Implicitly, they say to
the audience, "We realize you have no idea what a particle accelerator is, but here's

the deal: all you need to know is that it's a big fancy thing that explodes when wet." They focus the mind on relevant details: "Don't worry about whether the baby sitter is going to break up with her boyfriend. Worry about that guy lurking in the bushes." They reduce the amount of analytic work you need to do to make sense of a story. All you have to do is follow the arrows.

By this standard, popular television has never been harder to follow. If narrative threads have experienced a population explosion over the past 20 years, flashing arrows have grown correspondingly scarce. Watching our pinnacle of early 80's TV drama, *Hill Street Blues*, we find there's an informational wholeness to each scene that differs markedly from what you see on shows like *The West Wing* or *The Sopranos* or *Alias* or *E.R.* 18

Hill Street has ambiguities about future events: will a convicted killer be executed? Will Furillo marry Joyce Davenport? Will Renko find it in himself to bust a favorite singer for cocaine possession? But the present tense of each scene explains itself to the viewer with little ambiguity. There's an open question or a mystery driving each of these stories—how will it all turn out?—but there's no mystery about the immediate activity on the screen. A contemporary drama like *The West Wing*, on the other hand, constantly embeds mysteries into the present-tense events: you see characters performing actions or discussing events about which crucial information has been deliberately withheld. Anyone who has watched more than a handful of *The West Wing* episodes closely will know the feeling: scene after scene refers to some clearly crucial but unexplained piece of information, and after the sixth reference, you'll find yourself wishing you could rewind the tape to figure out what they're talking about, assuming you've missed something. And then you realize that you're supposed to be confused. The open question posed by these sequences is not "How will this turn out in the end?" The question is "What's happening right now?" 19

The deliberate lack of hand-holding extends down to the microlevel of dialogue as well. Popular entertainment that addresses technical issues—whether they are the intricacies of passing legislation, or of performing a heart bypass, or of operating a particle accelerator—conventionally switches between two modes of information in dialogue: texture and substance. Texture is all the arcane verbiage provided to convince the viewer that they're watching Actual Doctors at Work; substance is the material planted amid the background texture that the viewer needs to make sense of the plot. 20

Conventionally, narratives demarcate the line between texture and substance by inserting cues that flag or translate the important data. There's an unintentionally comical moment in the 2004 blockbuster *The Day After Tomorrow* in which the beleaguered climatologist (played by Dennis Quaid) announces his theory about the imminent arrival of a new ice age to a gathering of government officials. In his 21 speech, he warns that "we have hit a critical desalinization point!" At this moment, the writer-director Roland Emmerich—a master of brazen arrow-flashing—has an official follow with the obliging remark: "It would explain what's driving this extreme weather." They might as well have had a flashing "Unlocked!" arrow on the screen.

The dialogue on shows like *The West Wing* and *E.R.*, on the other hand, doesn't 22 talk down to its audiences. It rushes by, the words accelerating in sync with the high-speed tracking shots that glide through the corridors and operating rooms. The characters talk faster in these shows, but the truly remarkable thing about the dialogue is not purely a matter of speed; it's the willingness to immerse the audience in information that most viewers won't understand. Here's a typical scene from *E.R.*:

[WEAVER *and* WRIGHT *push a gurney containing a 16-year-old girl. Her parents,* JANNA *and* FRANK MIKAMI, *follow close behind.* CARTER *and* LUCY *fall in.*]

WEAVER: 16-year-old, unconscious, history of biliary atresia.
CARTER: Hepatic coma?
WEAVER: Looks like it.
MR. MIKAMI: She was doing fine until six months ago.
CARTER: What medication is she on?
MRS. MIKAMI: Ampicillin, tobramycin, vitamins A, D and K.
LUCY: Skin's jaundiced.
WEAVER: Same with the sclera. Breath smells sweet.
CARTER: Fetor hepaticus?
WEAVER: Yep.
LUCY: What's that?
WEAVER: Her liver's shut down. Let's dip a urine. [To CARTER] Guys, it's getting a little crowded in here, why don't you deal with the parents? Start lactulose, 30 cc's per NG.
CARTER: We're giving medicine to clean her blood.
WEAVER: Blood in the urine, two-plus.
CARTER: The liver failure is causing her blood not to clot.
MRS. MIKAMI: Oh, God. . . .
CARTER: Is she on the transplant list?
MR. MIKAMI: She's been Status 2a for six months, but they haven't been able to find her a match.
CARTER: Why? What's her blood type?
MR. MIKAMI: AB.

[*This hits* CARTER *like a lightning bolt. Lucy gets it, too. They share a look.*]

There are flashing arrows here, of course—"The liver failure is causing her   23
blood not to clot"—but the ratio of medical jargon to layperson translation is
remarkably high. From a purely narrative point of view, the decisive line arrives at
the very end: "AB." The 16-year-old's blood type connects her to an earlier plot line,
involving a cerebral-hemorrhage victim who—after being dramatically revived in
one of the opening scenes—ends up brain-dead. Far earlier, before the liver-failure
scene above, Carter briefly discusses harvesting the hemorrhage victim's organs for
transplants, and another doctor makes a passing reference to his blood type being
the rare AB (thus making him an unlikely donor). The twist here revolves around a
statistically unlikely event happening at the E.R.—an otherwise perfect liver donor
showing up just in time to donate his liver to a recipient with the same rare blood
type. But the show reveals this twist with remarkable subtlety. To make sense of
that last "AB" line—and the look of disbelief on Carter's and Lucy's faces—you have
to recall a passing remark uttered earlier regarding a character who belongs to a
completely different thread. Shows like *E.R.* may have more blood and guts than
popular TV had a generation ago, but when it comes to storytelling, they possess a
quality that can only be described as subtlety and discretion.

Even Bad TV Is Better

Skeptics might argue that I have stacked the deck here by focusing on relatively   24
highbrow titles like *The Sopranos* or *The West Wing*, when in fact the most significant change in the last five years of narrative entertainment involves reality TV.
Does the contemporary pop cultural landscape look quite as promising if the representative show is *Joe Millionaire*[5] instead of *The West Wing*?

I think it does, but to answer that question properly, you have to avoid the ten-   25
dency to sentimentalize the past. When people talk about the golden age of television in the early 70's—invoking shows like *The Mary Tyler Moore Show* and *All in
the Family*—they forget to mention how awful most television programming was
during much of that decade. If you're going to look at pop-culture trends, you have
to compare apples to apples, or in this case, lemons to lemons. The relevant comparison is not between *Joe Millionaire* and *MASH*; it's between *Joe Millionaire* and
The Newlywed Game, or between *Survivor* and *The Love Boat*.[6]

5. *Joe Millionaire*: a 2003 reality show in which women competed for the heart of a man they
believed to be a millionaire—only to discover at the end of the series that he was a construction
worker.
6. *The Love Boat*: comedy, set aboard a cruise ship, that aired from 1977 to 1986. *MASH*: critically
acclaimed sitcom about military doctors and nurses set during the Korean War; it aired from 1972 to
1983. *The Newlywed Game*: game show that ran from 1966 to 1974 and 1977 to 1980 in which newlywed
couples answered questions about how well they knew each other. *Survivor*: reality show that premiered in 2000, in which contestants in a remote location compete for $1 million.

What you see when you make these head-to-head comparisons is that a rising   26
tide of complexity has been lifting programming at the bottom of the quality spectrum and at the top. *The Sopranos* is several times more demanding of its audiences
than *Hill Street* was, and *Joe Millionaire* has made comparable advances over *Battle
of the Network Stars*.[7] This is the ultimate test of the Sleeper Curve theory: even the
junk has improved.

If early television took its cues from the stage, today's reality programming is   27
reliably structured like a video game: a series of competitive tests, growing more
challenging over time. Many reality shows borrow a subtler device from gaming
culture as well: the rules aren't fully established at the outset. You learn as you play.

On a show like *Survivor* or *The Apprentice*,[8] the participants—and the audi-   28
ence—know the general objective of the series, but each episode involves new
challenges that haven't been ordained in advance. The final round of the first season of *The Apprentice*, for instance, threw a monkey wrench into the strategy that
governed the play up to that point, when Trump announced that the two remaining apprentices would have to assemble and manage a team of subordinates who
had already been fired in earlier episodes of the show. All of a sudden the overarch-
ing objective of the game—do anything to avoid being fired—presented a potential
conflict to the remaining two contenders: the structure of the final round favored
the survivor who had maintained the best relationships with his comrades. Suddenly, it wasn't enough just to have clawed your way to the top; you had to have
made friends while clawing. The original *Joe Millionaire* went so far as to undermine the most fundamental convention of all—that the show's creators don't
openly lie to the contestants about the prizes—by inducing a construction worker
to pose as man of means while 20 women competed for his attention.

Reality programming borrowed another key ingredient from games: the intel-   29
lectual labor of probing the system's rules for weak spots and opportunities. As
each show discloses its conventions, and each participant reveals his or her personality traits and background, the intrigue in watching comes from figuring out how
the participants should best navigate the environment that has been created for
them. The pleasure in these shows comes not from watching other people being
humiliated on national television; it comes from depositing other people in a complex, high-pressure environment where no established strategies exist and watching them find their bearings. That's why the water-cooler conversation about these
shows invariably tracks in on the strategy displayed on the previous night's episode:

7. *Battle of the Network Stars*: specials that aired periodically between 1976 and 1988, in which television stars from each major network competed in physical challenges.

8. *The Apprentice*: reality show that premiered in 2004, in which contestants compete to become
an apprentice to Donald Trump and run one of his companies for one year.

why did Kwame pick Omarosa in that final round? What devious strategy is Richard Hatch concocting now?[9]

When we watch these shows, the part of our brain that monitors the emotional lives of the people around us—the part that tracks subtle shifts in intonation and gesture and facial expression—scrutinizes the action on the screen, looking for clues. We trust certain characters implicitly and vote others off the island in a heartbeat. Traditional narrative shows also trigger emotional connections to the characters, but those connections don't have the same participatory effect, because traditional narratives aren't explicitly about strategy. The phrase "Monday-morning quarterbacking" describes the engaged feeling that spectators have in relation to games as opposed to stories. We absorb stories, but we second-guess games. Reality programming has brought that second-guessing to prime time, only the game in question revolves around social dexterity rather than the physical kind.

The Rewards of Smart Culture

The quickest way to appreciate the Sleeper Curve's cognitive training is to sit down and watch a few hours of hit programming from the late 70's on Nick at Nite[10] or the SOAPnet channel or on DVD. The modern viewer who watches a show like *Dallas* today will be bored by the content—not just because the show is less salacious than today's soap operas (which it is by a small margin) but also because the show contains far less information in each scene, despite the fact that its soap-opera structure made it one of the most complicated narratives on television in its prime. With *Dallas*, the modern viewer doesn't have to think to make sense of what's going on, and not having to think is boring. Many recent hit shows—*24, Survivor, The Sopranos, Alias, Lost, The Simpsons, E.R.*—take the opposite approach, layering each scene with a thick network of affiliations. You have to focus to follow the plot, and in focusing you're exercising the parts of your brain that map social networks, that fill in missing information, that connect multiple narrative threads.

Of course, the entertainment industry isn't increasing the cognitive complexity of its products for charitable reasons. The Sleeper Curve exists because there's money to be made by making culture smarter. The economics of television syndication and DVD sales mean that there's a tremendous financial pressure to make programs that can be watched multiple times, revealing new nuances and shadings on the third viewing. Meanwhile, the Web has created a forum for annotation and commentary that allows more complicated shows to prosper, thanks to the fan

---

9. *Kwame / Omarosa / Richard Hatch*: notable contestants on the reality shows *The Apprentice* and *Survivor*.

10. *Nick at Nite*: evening programming on the children's television channel Nickelodeon; the lineup has featured classic sitcoms from the late 1950s to the early 2000s.

sites where each episode of shows like *Lost* or *Alias* is dissected with an intensity usually reserved for Talmud scholars. Finally, interactive games have trained a new generation of media consumers to probe complex environments and to think on their feet, and that gamer audience has now come to expect the same challenges from their television shows. In the end, the Sleeper Curve tells us something about the human mind. It may be drawn toward the sensational where content is concerned—sex does sell, after all. But the mind also likes to be challenged; there's real pleasure to be found in solving puzzles, detecting patterns or unpacking a complex narrative system.

In pointing out some of the ways that popular culture has improved our minds, I am not arguing that parents should stop paying attention to the way their children amuse themselves. What I am arguing for is a change in the criteria we use to determine what really is cognitive junk food and what is genuinely nourishing. Instead of a show's violent or tawdry content, instead of wardrobe malfunctions or the F-word, the true test should be whether a given show engages or sedates the mind. Is it a single thread strung together with predictable punch lines every 30 seconds? Or does it map a complex social network? Is your on-screen character running around shooting everything in sight, or is she trying to solve problems and manage resources? If your kids want to watch reality TV, encourage them to watch *Survivor* over *Fear Factor*. If they want to watch a mystery show, encourage 24 over *Law and Order*. If they want to play a violent game, encourage Grand Theft Auto over Quake. Indeed, it might be just as helpful to have a rating system that used mental labor and not obscenity and violence as its classification scheme for the world of mass culture. 33

Kids and grown-ups each can learn from their increasingly shared obsessions. Too often we imagine the blurring of kid and grown-up cultures as a series of violations: the 9-year-olds who have to have nipple brooches explained to them thanks to Janet Jackson; the middle-aged guy who can't wait to get home to his Xbox. But this demographic blur has a commendable side that we don't acknowledge enough. The kids are forced to think like grown-ups: analyzing complex social networks, managing resources, tracking subtle narrative intertwinings, recognizing long-term patterns. The grown-ups, in turn, get to learn from the kids: decoding each new technological wave, parsing the interfaces and discovering the intellectual rewards of play. Parents should see this as an opportunity, not a crisis. Smart culture is no longer something you force your kids to ingest, like green vegetables. It's something you share. 34

Reading with an Eye for the Methods

1. Johnson draws an extended COMPARISON between recent TV shows and those of the past. What are some of the main differences as he sees them?

2. How and how well does Johnson use this comparison to support his ARGUMENT that watching television makes us smarter?

3. How does Johnson DEFINE "the Sleeper Curve" (3) and how, according to him, does watching TV EXEMPLIFY this phenomenon?

4. Point out other methods of development in Johnson's essay. How and how well do they support his main point about the intellectual benefits of watching TV?

Using the Methods

1. In a paragraph, give an EXAMPLE of how a television show you have watched uses one of the NARRATIVE conventions that Johnson cites, such as "multi-threading" (15) or "the flashing arrow" (17).

2. Write an essay in which you ARGUE that watching too much television can still be unhealthy, even though individual shows make more demands on the viewer's intellect than the old shows did.

MALCOLM GLADWELL

The Tipping Point: Hush Puppies, Crime, Yawning, and Other Contagions

Malcolm Gladwell (b. 1963) was born in England but grew up in Canada. Gladwell produced his first prize-winning story when he was 16—an interview with God. After graduating from the University of Toronto in 1984, he became a science and business writer and a bureau chief for the Washington Post. *In 1996, Gladwell joined the writing staff of the* New Yorker. *Drawing on research in sociology, psychology, and social psychology, Gladwell's articles and books—including the best-selling* The Tipping Point *(2000) and* Blink *(2005)—deal with the large-scale implications of apparently insignificant events.*

In The Tipping Point, *Gladwell studies the structure of epidemics, taking the field of epidemiology well beyond the realm of disease to show "how little things can make a big difference" in all aspects of life. In the following chapter from* The Tipping Point, *Gladwell illustrates this principle with a number of specific examples, notably a sudden rise in the sales of Hush Puppies ("the classic American brushed-suede shoes with the lightweight crepe sole")[1] and the sudden decrease in the rate of violent crime on the streets of New York.*

FOR HUSH PUPPIES—the classic American brushed-suede shoes with the lightweight crepe sole—the Tipping Point came somewhere between late 1994 and early 1995. The brand had been all but dead until that point. Sales were down to 30,000 pairs a year, mostly to backwoods outlets and small-town family stores. Wolverine, the company that makes Hush Puppies, was thinking of phasing out the shoes that made them famous. But then something strange happened. At a fashion shoot, two Hush Puppies executives—Owen Baxter and Geoffrey Lewis—ran into a stylist from New York who told them that the classic Hush Puppies had suddenly become hip in the clubs and bars of downtown Manhattan. "We were being told," Baxter recalls, "that there were resale shops in the Village, in Soho, where the shoes were being sold. People were going to the Ma and Pa stores, the little stores that still carried

1

---

1. *Hush Puppies*: before they were shoes, hush puppies were (and still are) a treat in the cuisine of the southern United States. They are small, deep-fried balls of seasoned dough, mainly cornmeal, and they are eaten for breakfast and also as a side dish, often with catfish. The etymology of the name is unknown, but one theory is that hush puppies were originally fed to dogs to keep them quiet while people were eating or cooking; thus, they hushed the puppies. Wolverine, the footwear company that makes Hush Puppies, cites that etymology of the name.

them, and buying them up." Baxter and Lewis were baffled at first. It made no sense to them that shoes that were so obviously out of fashion could make a comeback. "We were told that Isaac Mizrahi[2] was wearing the shoes himself," Lewis says. "I think it's fair to say that at the time we had no idea who Isaac Mizrahi was."

By the fall of 1995, things began to happen in a rush. First the designer John Bartlett called. He wanted to use Hush Puppies in his spring collection. Then another Manhattan designer, Anna Sui, called, wanting shoes for her show as well. In Los Angeles, the designer Joel Fitzgerald put a twenty-five-foot inflatable basset hound—the symbol of the Hush Puppies brand—on the roof of his Hollywood store and gutted an adjoining art gallery to turn it into a Hush Puppies boutique. While he was still painting and putting up shelves, the actor Pee-wee Herman walked in and asked for a couple of pairs. "It was total word of mouth," Fitzgerald remembers.

In 1995, the company sold 430,000 pairs of the classic Hush Puppies, and the next year it sold four times that, and the year after that still more, until Hush Puppies were once again a staple of the wardrobe of the young American male. In 1996, Hush Puppies won the prize for best accessory at the Council of Fashion Designers awards dinner at Lincoln Center, and the president of the firm stood up on the stage with Calvin Klein and Donna Karan and accepted an award for an achievement that—as he would be the first to admit—his company had almost nothing to do with. Hush Puppies had suddenly exploded, and it all started with a handful of kids in the East Village and Soho.

How did that happen? Those first few kids, whoever they were, weren't deliberately trying to promote Hush Puppies. They were wearing them precisely because no one else would wear them. Then the fad spread to two fashion designers who used the shoes to peddle something else—haute couture. The shoes were an incidental touch. No one was trying to make Hush Puppies a trend. Yet, somehow, that's exactly what happened. The shoes passed a certain point in popularity and they tipped. How does a thirty-dollar pair of shoes go from a handful of downtown Manhattan hipsters and designers to every mall in America in the space of two years?

I.

There was a time, not very long ago, in the desperately poor New York City neighborhoods of Brownsville and East New York, when the streets would turn into ghost towns at dusk. Ordinary working people wouldn't walk on the sidewalks. Children wouldn't ride their bicycles on the streets. Old folks wouldn't sit on stoops and park benches. The drug trade ran so rampant and gang warfare was so

2. *Isaac Mizrahi*: well-known fashion designer.

ubiquitous in that part of Brooklyn that most people would take to the safety of their apartment at nightfall. Police officers who served in Brownsville in the 1980s and early 1990s say that, in those years, as soon as the sun went down their radios exploded with chatter between beat officers and their dispatchers over every conceivable kind of violent and dangerous crime. In 1992, there were 2,154 murders in New York City and 626,182 serious crimes, with the weight of those crimes falling hardest in places like Brownsville and East New York. But then something strange happened. At some mysterious and critical point, the crime rate began to turn. It tipped. Within five years, murders had dropped 64.3 percent to 770 and total crimes had fallen by almost half to 355,893. In Brownsville and East New York, the sidewalks filled up again, the bicycles came back, and old folks reappeared on the stoops. "There was a time when it wasn't uncommon to hear rapid fire, like you would hear somewhere in the jungle in Vietnam," says Inspector Edward Messadri, who commands the police precinct in Brownsville. "I don't hear the gunfire anymore."

The New York City police will tell you that what happened in New York was   6 that the city's policing strategies dramatically improved. Criminologists point to the decline of the crack trade and the aging of the population. Economists, meanwhile, say that the gradual improvement in the city's economy over the course of the 1990s had the effect of employing those who might otherwise have become criminals. These are the conventional explanations for the rise and fall of social problems, but in the end none is any more satisfying than the statement that kids in the East Village caused the Hush Puppies revival. The changes in the drug trade, the population, and the economy are all long-term trends, happening all over the country. They don't explain why crime plunged in New York City so much more than in other cities around the country, and they don't explain why it all happened in such an extraordinarily short time. As for the improvements made by the police, they are important too. But there is a puzzling gap between the scale of the changes in policing and the size of the effect on places like Brownsville and East New York. After all, crime didn't just slowly ebb in New York as conditions gradually improved. It plummeted. How can a change in a handful of economic and social indices cause murder rates to fall by two-thirds in five years?

2.

. . .

The rise of Hush Puppies and the fall of New York's crime rate are textbook exam-   7 ples of epidemics in action. Although they may sound as if they don't have very much in common, they share a basic, underlying pattern. First of all, they are clear examples of contagious behavior. No one took out an advertisement and told people that the traditional Hush Puppies were cool and they should start wearing them. Those kids simply wore the shoes when they went to clubs or cafes or walked the streets of downtown New York, and in so doing exposed other people to their fashion sense. They infected them with the Hush Puppies "virus."

The crime decline in New York surely happened the same way. It wasn't that 8 some huge percentage of would-be murderers suddenly sat up in 1993 and decided not to commit any more crimes. Nor was it that the police managed magically to intervene in a huge percentage of situations that would otherwise have turned deadly. What happened is that the small number of people in the small number of situations in which the police or the new social forces had some impact started behaving very differently, and that behavior somehow spread to other would-be criminals in similar situations. Somehow a large number of people in New York got "infected" with an anti-crime virus in a short time.

The second distinguishing characteristic of these two examples is that in both 9 cases little changes had big effects. All of the possible reasons for why New York's crime rate dropped are changes that happened at the margin; they were incremental changes. The crack trade leveled off. The population got a little older. The police force got a little better. Yet the effect was dramatic. So too with Hush Puppies. How many kids are we talking about who began wearing the shoes in downtown Manhattan? Twenty? Fifty? One hundred—at the most? Yet their actions seem to have single-handedly started an international fashion trend.

Finally, both changes happened in a hurry. They didn't build steadily and slowly. 10 It is instructive to look at a chart of the crime rate in New York City from, say, the mid-1960s to the late 1990s. It looks like a giant arch. In 1965, there were 200,000 crimes in the city and from that point on the number begins a sharp rise, doubling in two years and continuing almost unbroken until it hits 650,000 crimes a year in the mid-1970s. It stays steady at that level for the next two decades, before plunging downward in 1992 as sharply as it rose thirty years earlier. Crime did not taper off. It didn't gently decelerate. It hit a certain point and jammed on the brakes.

These three characteristics—one, contagiousness; two, the fact that little causes 11 can have big effects; and three, that change happens not gradually but at one dramatic moment—are the same three principles that define how measles moves through a grade-school classroom or the flu attacks every winter. Of the three, the third trait—the idea that epidemics can rise or fall in one dramatic moment—is the most important, because it is the principle that makes sense of the first two and that permits the greatest insight into why modern change happens the way it does. The name given to that one dramatic moment in an epidemic when everything can change all at once is the Tipping Point.

3.

A world that follows the rules of epidemics is a very different place from the world 12 we think we live in now. Think, for a moment, about the concept of contagiousness. If I say that word to you, you think of colds and the flu or perhaps something very dangerous like HIV or Ebola. We have, in our minds, a very specific, biological notion of what contagiousness means. But if there can be epidemics of crime or epidemics of fashion, there must be all kinds of things just as contagious as viruses. Have you ever thought about yawning, for instance? Yawning is a surprisingly powerful act. Just because you read the word "yawning" in the previous two sentences—and the two additional "yawns" in this sentence—a good number of you will probably yawn within the next few minutes. Even as I'm writing this, I've yawned twice. If you're reading this in a public place, and you've just yawned, chances are that a good proportion of everyone who saw you yawn is now yawning too, and a good proportion of the people watching the people who watched you yawn are now yawning as well, and on and on, in an ever-widening, yawning circle.

Yawning is incredibly contagious. I made some of you reading this yawn simply by writing the word "yawn." The people who yawned when they saw you yawn, meanwhile, were infected by the sight of you yawning—which is a second kind of contagion. They might even have yawned if they only heard you yawn, because yawning is also aurally contagious: if you play an audiotape of a yawn to blind people, they'll yawn too. And finally, if you yawned as you read this, did the thought cross your mind—however unconsciously and fleetingly—that you might be tired? I suspect that for some of you it did, which means that yawns can also be emotionally contagious. Simply by writing the word, I can plant a feeling in your mind. Can the flu virus do that? Contagiousness, in other words, is an unexpected property of all kinds of things, and we have to remember that, if we are to recognize and diagnose epidemic change. 13

The second of the principles of epidemics—that little changes can somehow have big effects—is also a fairly radical notion. We are, as humans, heavily socialized to make a kind of rough approximation between cause and effect. If we want to communicate a strong emotion, if we want to convince someone that, say, we love them, we realize that we need to speak passionately and forthrightly. If we want to break bad news to someone, we lower our voices and choose our words carefully. We are trained to think that what goes into any transaction or relationship or system must be directly related, in intensity and dimension, to what comes out. Consider, for example, the following puzzle. I give you a large piece of paper, and I ask you to fold it over once, and then take that folded paper and fold it over again, and then again, and again, until you have refolded the original paper 50 times. How tall do you think the final stack is going to be? In answer to that question, most people will fold the sheet in their mind's eye, and guess that the pile would be as thick as a phone book or, if they're really courageous, they'll say that it would be as tall as a refrigerator. But the real answer is that the height of the stack would approximate the distance to the sun. And if you folded it over one 14 more time, the stack would be as high as the distance to the sun and back. This is an example of what in mathematics is called a geometric progression. Epidemics are another example of geometric progression: when a virus spreads through a population, it doubles and doubles again, until it has (figuratively) grown from a single sheet of paper all the way to the sun in fifty steps. As human beings we have a hard time with this kind of progression, because the end result—the effect— seems far out of proportion to the cause. To appreciate the power of epidemics, we have to abandon this expectation about proportionality. We need to prepare our- selves for the possibility that sometimes big changes follow from small events, and that sometimes these changes can happen very quickly.

This possibility of sudden change is at the center of the idea of the Tipping Point 15 and might well be the hardest of all to accept. The expression first came into popu- lar use in the 1970s to describe the flight to the suburbs of whites living in the older cities of the American Northeast. When the number of incoming African Americans in a particular neighborhood reached a certain point—20 percent, say—sociologists observed that the community would "tip": most of the remaining whites would leave almost immediately. The Tipping Point is the moment of criti- cal mass, the threshold, the boiling point. There was a Tipping Point for violent crime in New York in the early 1990s, and a Tipping Point for the reemergence of Hush Puppies, just as there is a Tipping Point for the introduction of any new tech- nology. Sharp introduced the first low-priced fax machine in 1984, and sold about 80,000 of those machines in the United States in that first year. For the next three years, businesses slowly and steadily bought more and more faxes, until, in 1987, enough people had faxes that it made sense for everyone to get a fax. Nineteen eighty-seven was the fax machine Tipping Point. A million machines were sold that year, and by 1989 two million new machines had gone into operation. Cellular phones have followed the same trajectory. Through the 1990s, they got smaller and cheaper, and service got better until 1998, when the technology hit a Tipping Point and suddenly everyone had a cell phone. . . .

All epidemics have Tipping Points. Jonathan Crane, a sociologist at the Univer- 16 sity of Illinois, has looked at the effect the number of role models in a commu- nity—the professionals, managers, teachers whom the Census Bureau has defined as "high status"—has on the lives of teenagers in the same neighborhood. He found little difference in pregnancy rates or school drop-out rates in neighborhoods of between 40 and 5 percent of high-status workers. But when the number of profes- sionals dropped below 5 percent, the problems exploded. For black schoolchildren, for example, as the percentage of high-status workers falls just 2.2 percentage points—from 5.6 percent to 3.4 percent—drop-out rates more than double. At the same Tipping Point, the rates of child-bearing for teenaged girls—which barely move at all up to that point—nearly double. We assume, intuitively, that neighbor-

hoods and social problems decline in some kind of steady progression. But sometimes they may not decline steadily at all; at the Tipping Point, schools can lose
control of their students, and family life can disintegrate all at once.

I remember once as a child seeing our family's puppy encounter snow for the   17
first time. He was shocked and delighted and overwhelmed, wagging his tail nervously, sniffing about in this strange, fluffy substance, whimpering with the mystery of it all. It wasn't much colder on the morning of his first snowfall than it had
been the evening before. It might have been 34 degrees the previous evening, and
now it was 31 degrees. Almost nothing had changed, in other words, yet—and this
was the amazing thing—everything had changed. Rain had become something
entirely different. Snow! We are all, at heart, gradualists, our expectations set by
the steady passage of time. But the world of the Tipping Point is a place where the
unexpected becomes expected, where radical change is more than possibility. It
is—contrary to all our expectations—a certainty.

Two simple questions . . . lie at the heart of what we would all like to accom-   18
plish as educators, parents, marketers, business people, and policymakers. Why is
it that some ideas or behaviors or products start epidemics and others don't? And
what can we do to deliberately start and control positive epidemics of our own?

Reading with an Eye for the Methods

1. Besides giving specific EXAMPLES of epidemics, Gladwell is ANALYZING CAUSES
   for why epidemics occur. What are some of the causes?

2. How does Gladwell DEFINE a "Tipping Point," and how does this definition contribute to his analysis of how and why epidemics take place?

3. Where does Gladwell use other methods of development, such as NARRATION,
   DESCRIPTION, or PROCESS ANALYSIS? Point out several instances, and explain
   how they support his analysis.

Using the Methods

1. In a paragraph, explain how, according to Gladwell, the sales of Hush Puppies
   EXEMPLIFY an epidemic in action.

2. Write an essay in which you use (and give full credit to) Gladwell's tipping-point
   theory to ANALYZE THE CAUSES of one of the following: an emerging trend in
   fashion, the ascension of a top-ten tune, the spread of a rumor, the sale of a
   product or idea by word-of-mouth advertising, or the spread of a disease.

BILLY COLLINS

Fishing on the Susquehanna in July

Billy Collins (b. 1941) grew up in New York, the son of an electrician and a nurse. He studied at Holy Cross College and the University of California, Riverside, where he earned a Ph.D. in romantic poetry. The poet laureate of the United States from 2001 to 2003, Collins teaches English at Lehman College of New York University.

"Fishing on the Susquehanna in July" is from Collins's poetry collection Picnic, Lightning *(1998). The poem is a description of "American scenes"—particularly of a man fishing on a river in Maryland—as depicted in paintings that Collins once viewed in a Philadelphia art gallery. As Collins looks at the fisherman, however, he goes beyond merely describing the tranquil scene to demonstrate how art, including the art of writing, "manufactures" experience.*

I have never been fishing on the Susquehanna[1]   1
or on any river for that matter
to be perfectly honest.

Not in July or any month
have I had the pleasure—if it is a pleasure—   5
of fishing on the Susquehanna.

I am more likely to be found
in a quiet room like this one—
a painting of a woman on the wall,

a bowl of tangerines on the table—   10
trying to manufacture the sensation
of fishing on the Susquehanna.

There is little doubt
that others have been fishing
on the Susquehanna,   15

---

1. *Susquehanna*: the longest river in the northeastern part of the United States; it passes through the states of New York and Pennsylvania and empties into the northernmost tip of the Chesapeake Bay, in the state of Maryland.

rowing upstream in a wooden boat,
sliding the oars under the water
then raising them to drip in the light.

But the nearest I have ever come to
fishing on the Susquehanna   20
was one afternoon in a museum in Philadelphia,

when I balanced a little egg of time
in front of a painting
in which that river curled around a bend

under a blue cloud-ruffled sky,   25
dense trees along the banks,
and a fellow with a red bandana

sitting in a small, green
flat-bottom boat
holding the thin whip of a pole.   30

That is something I am unlikely
ever to do, I remember
saying to myself and the person next to me.

Then I blinked and moved on
to other American scenes   35
of haystacks, water whitening over rocks,

even one of a brown hare
who seemed so wired with alertness
I imagined him springing right out of the frame.

READING WITH AN EYE FOR THE METHODS

1. In stanzas 7–13 (lines 19–39), Collins is DESCRIBING what he saw "one afternoon in a museum in Philadelphia" (21). What place is he describing in stanzas three and four (lines 7–12)? Why is Collins more likely to be found in places like these than in a boat on a lake or river?

2. Of all the five senses—sight, sound, touch, smell, and taste—which one is most important in Collins's description? What DOMINANT IMPRESSION does he create by exercising it?

3. Among other methods of development, Collins draws heavily on NARRATION. What are some of the narrative elements of his poem, and what story do they help him to tell?

USING THE METHODS

1. Write a paragraph DESCRIBING the objects or scene depicted in a painting or photograph that has captured your imagination.

2. In an essay, DESCRIBE that painting or photograph *and* how it makes you think and feel as you observe and examine it.

3. In an essay, ANALYZE THE PROCESS of "trying to manufacture" the sensation of fishing (or any other experience) as that process is depicted in Collins's poem.

Using Sources
in Your Writing

Research is formalized curiosity. It is poking and prying with a purpose.
—ZORA NEALE HURSTON

In much of the writing you do, you will need to draw on the work of other writers. This appendix will show you how to do research and use what you find in your own writing, and how to document your sources accurately.

Finding Sources

To analyze the 2007 controversy about the student loan industry, you examine news stories and blogs published at the time. To write an essay interpreting "My Last Duchess," you study the poem and read several critical interpretations in literary journals. In both of these cases, you go beyond your own knowledge to consult additional sources of information.

The following section gives you some tips for finding a range of sources—print and online, general and specialized, published and firsthand. Keep in mind that as you do research, finding and evaluating sources are two activities that usually take place simultaneously. So this section and the next one go hand in hand.

Kinds of Sources

PRIMARY AND SECONDARY SOURCES

Your research will likely lead you to both primary and secondary sources. Primary sources include historical documents, literary works, eyewitness accounts, field reports, diaries, letters, and lab studies. Secondary sources include scholarly books and articles, reviews, biographies, textbooks, and other works that interpret or discuss primary sources. Novels and poems are primary sources; articles interpreting them are secondary sources. The Declaration of Independence is a primary historical document; a historian's description of the events surrounding the Declaration's writing is secondary.

PRINT AND ONLINE SOURCES

Some sources are available only in print; some are available only online. But many print sources are also available on the Web. When it comes to finding sources, it's likely that you'll search for most sources online, through the library's website. In general, there are four kinds of sources you'll want to consult: reference works, books, periodicals, and material on the Web.

- *Reference works.* The reference section of your school's library is the place to find encyclopedias, dictionaries, atlases, almanacs, bibliographies, and other reference works in print. Many of these sources are also online. Remember, though, that reference works are only a starting point, a place where you can get an overview of your topic or basic facts about it. Some reference works are *general*, such as *The New Encyclopaedia Britannica* or the *Statistical Abstract of the United States*. Others are *specialized*, providing in-depth information on a single field or topic.

- *Books.* The library catalog is your primary source for finding books. Most library catalogs are computerized and can be accessed through the library's website. You can search by author, title, subject, or keyword. When you click on a specific source, you'll find bibliographic data about author, title, and publication; the call number (which identifies the book's location on the library's shelves); related subject headings (which may lead to other useful materials in the library)—and more.

- *Periodicals.* To find journal and magazine articles, you will need to search periodical indexes and databases, many of which are online. Indexes (such as the *New York Times Index*) provide listings of articles organized by topics; databases (such as LexisNexis) provide the full texts. Although some databases are available for free, many are available only by subscription and so must be accessed through a library.

- *The Web.* The Web provides access to countless sites containing information posted by governments, educational institutions, organizations, businesses, and individuals. Websites are different from other sources in several ways: (1) they often provide entire texts, not just citations of texts, (2) their content varies greatly in its reliability, and (3) they are not stable: what you see on a site today may be different (or gone) tomorrow. Anyone who wants to can post texts on the Web, so you need to evaluate carefully what you find there.

Searching Electronically

Whether you're searching for books, articles in periodicals, or material available on the Web, chances are you'll conduct much of your search electronically. In each case, you can search for authors, titles, or subjects.

The key to searching efficiently is to come up with keywords that focus on the information you need. Most search engines have "advanced search" options that will help you focus your research. Keep in mind that specific commands vary among search engines and within databases. Here are some common ones to try:

- Type quotation marks around words to search for an exact phrase—"Thomas Jefferson."
- Type AND to find sources that include more than one keyword: Jefferson AND Adams.
- Type OR if you're looking for sources that include one of several terms: Jefferson OR Adams OR Madison.
- Type NOT to find sources *without* a certain word: Jefferson NOT Adams.
- Type an asterisk—or some other symbol—to search for words in different forms—*teach** will yield sources containing *teacher* and *teaching*, for example. Check the search engine's search tips to find out what symbol to use.
- Some search engines allow you to ask questions in conversational language: What did Thomas Jefferson write about slavery?
- If you don't get results with one set of keywords, substitute synonyms (if *folk medicine* doesn't generate much information, try *home remedy*).

Evaluating Sources

Searching the Wilson Education Index for sources on the student loan industry, you find more than five hundred sites. How do you decide which sources to read? This section helps you determine whether a source is reliable and useful for your purpose.

First, think about your purpose. Are you trying to persuade readers to believe or do something? To inform them about something? If the former, try to find sources representing various stances; if the latter, you may need sources that are more factual or informative. Reconsider your audience. What kinds of sources will they find persuasive? Following are some questions that can help you select reliable and use-ful sources:

- *Is it relevant?* How does the source relate to your purpose? What will it add to your work? Look at the title and at any introductory material—a preface, abstract, or introduction—to see what it covers.

- *What are the author's credentials?* What are the author's qualifications to write on the subject? Is he or she associated with a particular position on the issue? You might do a Web search to see what else you can learn about the author.

- *What is the stance?* Does the source cover various points of view or advocate one particular point of view? Does its title suggest a certain slant?

- *Who is the publisher?* If it's a book, what kind of company published it; if an arti-cle, what kind of periodical did it appear in? University presses and scholarly journals review books or articles by experts before they are published, but that is typically not the case for other kinds of publications.

- *If it's a website, who is the sponsor?* Is the site maintained by an organization? An interest group? A government agency? An individual? What is the sponsor's pur-pose—to sell a product, for example, or to convey objective information?

- *What is the level?* Texts written for a general audience might be easier to under-stand but not authoritative enough. Texts written for scholars will be more authoritative but may be hard to comprehend.

- *When was it published?* See when books and articles were published and when websites were last updated. (If the site lists no date, see if links to other sites still work.) Recent does not necessarily mean better—some topics require cur-rent information whereas others call for older sources.

Quoting, Paraphrasing, and Summarizing

In an essay about the writings of E. B. White, you quote a memorable line from "Once More to the Lake." For an essay on the Iraq War, you summarize some key debates about that war. Like all writers, you work with the ideas and words of oth-ers. This section will help you with the specifics of quoting, paraphrasing, and sum-marizing source materials.

Taking Notes

When you find material you think will be useful, take careful notes. Write down enough information so that when you refer to it later, you will be reminded of the main points, and keep a precise record of where the information comes from.

- *Use index cards, a computer file, or a notebook,* labeling each entry with the information that will allow you to keep track of where it comes from—author, title, the pages or the URL, and for online sources, the date of access.

- *Take notes in your own words, and use your own sentence patterns.* If you make a note that is a detailed paraphrase, label it as such so that you'll know to provide appropriate documentation if you use it.

- *If you find wording that you'd like to quote,* be sure to enclose the exact words in quotation marks to distinguish your source's words from your own.

- *Label each note with a subject heading.*

Deciding Whether to Quote, Paraphrase, or Summarize

When it comes time to draft, you'll need to decide how to use the sources you've found—in other words, whether to quote, paraphrase, or summarize. You might follow this rule of thumb: quote texts when the wording is worth repeating or makes a point so well that no rewording will do it justice, when you want to cite the exact words of a known authority on your topic, when his or her opinions challenge or disagree with those of others, or when the source is one you want to emphasize. Paraphrase sources that are not worth quoting but contain details you need to include. Summarize longer passages whose main points are important but whose details are not. In all of these instances, you need to identify the source and use proper documentation (see p. 646).

Quoting

When you use someone else's exact words, you need to reproduce the source exactly, though you can modify it to omit unnecessary details (with ellipses).

> Journalist David Brooks makes this assertion: "The dream of diversity is like the dream of equality. Both are based on ideals we celebrate even as we undermine them daily" (90).

> In her analysis of life and death, Mary Roach notes that "a gurney with a cadaver commands no urgency. It is wheeled by a single person, . . . like a shopping cart" (167).

Paraphrasing

When you paraphrase, you restate information from a source *in your own words,* using *your own sentence structures.* Paraphrase when the source material is important but the original wording is not. Because it includes all the main points of the source, a paraphrase is usually about the same length as the original.

Here is a paragraph from Diane Ackerman's essay "Why Leaves Turn Color in the Fall." It is followed by two example paraphrases. The first demonstrates some of the challenges of paraphrasing:

ORIGINAL SOURCE

Where do the colors come from? Sunlight rules most living things with its golden edicts. When the days begin to shorten, soon after the summer solstice on June 21, a tree reconsiders its leaves. All summer it feeds them so they can process sunlight, but in the dog days of summer the tree begins pulling nutrients back into its trunk and roots, pares down, and gradually chokes off its leaves. A corky layer of cells forms at the leaves' slender petioles, then scars over. Undernourished, the leaves stop producing the pigment chlorophyll, and photosynthesis ceases. Animals can migrate, hibernate, or store food to prepare for winter. But where can a tree go? It survives by dropping its leaves, and by the end of autumn only a few fragile threads of fluid-carrying xylem hold leaves to their stems.

UNACCEPTABLE PARAPHRASE

Ackerman tells us where the colors of leaves come from. The amount of sunlight is the trigger, as is true for most living things. At the end of June, as daylight lessens, a tree begins to treat its leaves differently. It feeds them all summer so they can turn sunlight into food, but in August a tree begins to redirect its food into its trunk and roots, gradually choking the leaves. A corky group of cells develops at the petioles, and a scar forms. By autumn, the leaves don't have enough food, so they stop producing chlorophyll, and photosynthesis also stops. Although animals are able to migrate, hibernate, or stow food for the winter, a tree cannot go anywhere. It survives only by dropping its leaves, and by the time winter comes only a few leaves remain on their stems.

This paraphrase borrows too much of the language of the original or changes it only slightly. It also follows the original sentence structure too closely. This acceptable paraphrase avoids both of these pitfalls:

ACCEPTABLE PARAPHRASE

Ackerman explains why leaves change color. Diminishing sunlight is the main instigator. A tree nourishes its leaves—and encourages photosynthesis—for most of the summer. By August, however, as daylight continues to lessen, a tree starts to reroute its food to the roots and trunk, a process that saves the tree but eventually kills the leaves. In autumn, because the leaves are almost starving, they can neither manufacture chlorophyll to stay green nor carry out photosynthesis. By this time, the base of the petiole, or leaf's stem, has hardened, in preparation for the final drop. Unlike animals, who have many ways to get ready for winter—hiding food ahead of time, moving to a warm climate, sleeping through winter—a tree is immobile. It can make it through the winter only by losing its leaves (257).

Summarizing

A summary states the main ideas found in a source concisely and in your own words. Unlike a paraphrase, a summary does not present all the details so it is generally as brief as possible. Summaries may boil down an entire book or essay into a single sentence, or they may take a paragraph or more to present the main ideas. Here, for example, is a summary of the Ackerman paragraph:

> As Ackerman explains, in late summer and fall trees put most of their food into their roots and trunk, which causes leaves to change color and die but enables trees to live through the winter (257).

Incorporating Source Materials into Your Text

You need to introduce quotations, paraphrases, and summaries clearly, letting readers know who the author is—and, if need be, something about his or her credentials. Consider this sentence:

> Professor and textbook author Elaine Tyler May claims that many high school history books are too bland to interest young readers (531).

The beginning ("Professor and textbook author Elaine Tyler May claims") functions as a signal phrase, telling readers who is making the assertion and why she has the authority to speak on the topic. The verb you use in a signal phrase can be neutral (*says* or *thinks*) or it can suggest something about the stance—the source's or your own. The preceding example about the textbook author uses the verb *claims*, suggesting that what she says is arguable (or that the writer believes it is). How would it change your understanding if the signal verb were *observes* or *suggests*?

Acknowledging Sources and Avoiding Plagiarism

Whenever you do research-based writing, you are entering a conversation—"putting in your oar," as the rhetorician Kenneth Burke once wrote. As a writer, you need to acknowledge any words and ideas that come from others—to give credit where credit is due, to recognize the various authorities and many perspectives you have considered, to show readers where they can find your sources, and to situate your own arguments in the ongoing conversation. Using other people's words and ideas without acknowledgment is plagiarism, a serious academic and ethical offense. This section will give you some tips on acknowledging the materials you use and avoiding plagiarism.

Acknowledging Sources

Your reader needs to know where your source's words or ideas begin and end. Therefore, you should introduce a source by naming the author in a signal phrase, and follow it with a brief parenthetical in-text citation or by naming the author in a parenthetical citation (see p. 647).

SOURCES THAT NEED ACKNOWLEDGMENT

- Direct quotations, paraphrases, and summaries
- Arguable statements and any information that is not commonly known
- The opinions and assertions of others
- Visuals that you did not create yourself (charts, photographs, and so on)
- Collaborative help you received from others.

SOURCES THAT DON'T NEED ACKNOWLEDGMENT

- Information that most readers are likely to know or that can be found in many sources, such as the name of the current president of the United States.
- Well-known quotations, such as John F. Kennedy's "Ask not what your country can do for you; ask what you can do for your country."
- Material that you created or gathered yourself, as long as the data are yours as well. A graph that you devised from someone else's research would require acknowledgment.

Avoiding Plagiarism

When you use the words, ideas, or visual images of others, you need to acknowledge who and where the material came from; if you don't credit those sources, you are guilty of plagiarism. Plagiarism is often committed unintentionally—as when a writer paraphrases someone else's ideas in language that is close to the original. It is essential, therefore, to know what constitutes plagiarism: (1) using another writer's words or ideas without in-text citation and documentation, (2) using another writer's exact words without quotation marks, and (3) paraphrasing or summarizing someone else's ideas using language or sentence structures that are too close to theirs.

To avoid plagiarizing, take careful notes as you do your research, clearly labeling as quotations any words you quote directly and being careful to use your own words and sentence structures in paraphrases and summaries. Be sure you know what source material you must document, and give credit to your sources. Be especially careful with material found online—copying written or visual material right into a document you are writing is all too easy to do. You must acknowledge information you find on the Web just as you do all other source materials.

And you must recognize that plagiarism has consequences. Scholars' work will be discredited if it too closely resembles another's. Journalists found to have plagiarized lose their jobs, and students routinely fail courses or are dismissed from their school when they are caught cheating—all too often by submitting as their own essays that they have purchased from online "research" sites. If you're having trouble completing an assignment, seek assistance. Talk with your instructor, or if your school has a writing center, go there for advice on all aspects of your writing, including acknowledging sources and avoiding plagiarism.

Documentation

When you write up the results of a research project, you need to cite the sources you use and tell readers where the ideas came from. The information you give about sources is called documentation.

The documentation style of the Modern Language Association (MLA) is a two-part system, consisting of (1) brief in-text parenthetical documentation for quotations, paraphrases, or summaries and (2) more-detailed documentation in a list of sources at the end of the text. MLA requires that the end-of-text documentation provides the following basic information about each source you cite: author, editor, or organization providing the information; title of work; place of publication; publisher; date of publication; medium of publication; and, for online sources, date when you accessed the source.

MLA is by no means the only documentation style. Many other publishers and organizations have their own style, among them the American Psychological Association (APA), the University of Chicago Press, and the Council of Science Editors. We focus on MLA here because it's one of the styles that college students are often required to use.

Following is an example of how the two parts—the brief parenthetical documentation in your text and the more detailed information at the end—correspond. As the example shows, when you cite a work in your text, you can name the author either in a signal phrase or in parentheses. If you name the author in a signal phrase, give the page number(s) in parentheses; when the author's name is not given in a signal phrase, include it in parentheses. Citing a source appropriately in your text enables readers to locate that source in your works-cited list.

IN-TEXT DOCUMENTATION

As Lester Faigley puts it, "The world has become a bazaar from which to shop for an individual 'lifestyle' " (12).

As one observer suggests, "The world has become a bazaar from which to shop for an individual 'lifestyle' " (Faigley 12).

WORKS-CITED DOCUMENTATION

Faigley, Lester. *Fragments of Rationality: Postmodernity and the Subject of Composition.* Pittsburgh: U of Pittsburgh P, 1992. Print.

MLA In-Text Documentation

In your text, you have three options for citing a source: quoting, paraphrasing, and summarizing. As you cite each source, you will need to decide whether or not to name the author in a signal phrase—"as Toni Morrison writes"—or in parentheses—"(Morrison 24)."

1. AUTHOR NAMED IN A SIGNAL PHRASE

If you mention the author in a signal phrase, put only the page number(s) in parentheses. Do not write *page* or *p.* When citing a direct quotation, note that the parenthetical reference comes after the closing quotation marks but before the period at the end of the sentence.

McCullough describes John Adams as having "the hands of a man accustomed to pruning his own trees, cutting his own hay, and splitting his own firewood" (18).

2. AUTHOR NAMED IN PARENTHESES

If you do not mention the author in a signal phrase, put his or her last name in parentheses along with the page number(s).

One biographer describes John Adams as someone who was not a stranger to manual labor (McCullough 18).

For either style of reference, try to put the parenthetical citation at the end of the sentence or as close as possible to the material you've cited without awkwardly interrupting the sentence.

3. AFTER A BLOCK QUOTATION

When quoting more than three lines of poetry, more than four lines of prose, or dialogue from a drama, set off the quotation from the rest of your text, indenting it one inch (or ten spaces) from the left margin. Do not use quotation marks. Place any parenthetical documentation after the final punctuation.

> In *Eastward to Tartary*, Kaplan captures ancient and contemporary Antioch for us:
>
>> At the height of its glory in the Roman-Byzantine age, when it had an amphitheater, public baths, aqueducts, and sewage pipes, half a million people lived in Antioch. Today the population is only 125,000. With sour relations between Turkey and Syria, and unstable politics throughout the Middle East, Antioch is now a backwater—seedy and tumbledown, with relatively few tourists. I found it altogether charming. (123)

4. TWO OR MORE AUTHORS

For a work by two or three authors, name all the authors.

> Some educators strive to introduce Julio Cortázar, Marjorie Agosín, and other Latin American writers to an audience of English-speaking adolescents (Carlson and Ventura 5).

For a work with four or more authors, you can mention all their names *or* just the name of the first author followed by *et al.*, which means "and others."

> One popular survey of American literature breaks the contents into sixteen thematic groupings (Anderson, Brinnin, Leggett, Arpin, and Toth 19–24).

> One popular survey of American literature breaks the contents into sixteen thematic groupings (Anderson et al. 19–24).

5. ORGANIZATION OR GOVERNMENT AS AUTHOR

If the author is an organization, cite the organization. It's acceptable to shorten long names.

> The U.S. government can be direct when it wants to be. For example, it sternly warns, "If you are overpaid, we will recover any payments not due you" (Social Security Administration 12).

6. AUTHOR UNKNOWN

Use the work's title or a shortened version of the title.

A powerful editorial in last week's paper asserts that healthy liver donor Mike Hurewitz died because of "frightening" faulty postoperative care ("Every Patient's Nightmare").

7. LITERARY WORKS

When referring to literary works that are available in many different editions, you need to cite additional information so that readers of any edition can locate the text you are citing.

Novels: Give the page and chapter number.

> In *Pride and Prejudice*, Mrs. Bennett shows no warmth toward Jane and Elizabeth when they return from Netherfield (105; ch. 12).

Verse plays: Instead of page numbers, give the act, scene, and line numbers; separate them with periods.

> Macbeth develops the vision theme when he addresses the Ghost with "Thou hast no speculation in those eyes / Which thou dost glare with" (3.3.96–97).

Poems: Instead of page numbers, give the line numbers (separated by periods). Use the word *line(s)* in the first reference.

> The mere in *Beowulf* is described as "not a pleasant place!" (line 1372). Later, it is called "the awful place" (1378).

8. TWO OR MORE WORKS CITED TOGETHER

If you cite the works in the same parentheses, separate the references with a semicolon.

> Critics have looked at both *Pride and Prejudice* and *Frankenstein* from a cultural perspective (Tanner 7; Smith viii).

9. SOURCE QUOTED IN ANOTHER SOURCE

When you are quoting text that you found quoted in another source, use the abbreviation *qtd. in* in the parenthetical reference.

> Charlotte Brontë wrote to G. H. Lewes: "Why do you like Miss Austen so very much? I am puzzled on that point" (qtd. in Tanner 7).

10. ELECTRONIC SOURCES WITHOUT PAGE NUMBERS

For works without page numbers, give paragraph, section, or screen numbers, using the abbreviation *par.* or *sec.* or the word *screen*. If you include the author's name in the parenthetical reference, add a comma. If a work has no dividing numbers at all, follow the model for an entire work (below).

> Russell's dismissals from Trinity College at Cambridge and from City College in New York City are seen as examples of the controversy that marked the philosopher's life (Irvine, par. 2).

11. AN ENTIRE WORK

If you refer to an entire work rather than a part of it, there's no need to include page numbers.

> At least one observer considers Turkey and Central Asia explosive (Kaplan).

MLA List of Works Cited

A works-cited list provides full bibliographic information for every source cited in your text. Following is some general advice to help you prepare such a list:

GENERAL FORMAT

- Start the list on a new page, and center the title (Works Cited) one inch from the top of the page.
- Double-space the whole list.
- Put the entries in alphabetical order by the author's last name. If a work has no identifiable author, alphabetize it by the first major word of the title.
- Type the first line of each entry flush with the left-hand margin. Indent subsequent lines one-half inch or five spaces.

INDIVIDUAL ENTRIES

- *Authors*: List the authors by last name first, and include any middle name or initial after the first name. List additional authors, if any, first name before last. When citing the work of an editor, compiler, director, narrator, or translator, follow the name with the appropriate abbreviation (*ed., comp., narr., trans.*).
- *Titles*: Capitalize the first and last words of titles and subtitles and all principal words, including short verbs such as *is* and *are*. Do not capitalize *a, an, the, to,* or any preposition or conjunction unless they begin a title or subtitle. For periodical titles, omit any initial *A, An,* or *The*. The titles of books and periodicals

should be italicized, but put quotation marks around titles of articles and short works.

- *Dates*: In entries for periodicals or electronic sources, abbreviate the names of months except for May, June, or July: Jan., Feb., Mar., Apr., Aug., Sept., Oct., Nov., Dec.

- *Medium*: For books and periodicals, use *Print*. For online sources, use *Web*. For other media, use *Film, Radio, Email, MP3 file, JPEG file*, and so on.

Books

For most books, you'll need to list the author; the title and any subtitle; and the place of publication, publisher, date, and the medium—*Print*. Note that MLA style requires you to use a shortened form of the publisher's name (Norton for W. W. Norton & Company, Princeton UP for Princeton University Press).

1. ONE AUTHOR

Miller, Susan. *Assuming the Positions: Cultural Pedagogy and the Politics of Commonplace Writing*. Pittsburgh: U of Pittsburgh P, 1998. Print.

2. TWO OR MORE WORKS BY THE SAME AUTHOR(S)

Give the author's name in the first entry, and then use three hyphens in the author slot for each of the subsequent works, listing them alphabetically by the first important word of each title.

Kaplan, Robert D. *The Coming Anarchy: Shattering the Dreams of the Post Cold War*. New York: Random, 2000. Print.

- - - . *Eastward to Tartary: Travels in the Balkans, the Middle East, and the Caucasus*. New York: Random, 2000. Print.

3. TWO OR THREE AUTHORS

Follow the order of names on the book's title page.

Malless, Stanley, and Jeffrey McQuain. *Coined by God: Words and Phrases That First Appear in the English Translations of the Bible*. New York: Norton, 2003. Print.

Sebranek, Patrick, Verne Meyer, and Dave Kemper. *Writers INC: A Guide to Writing, Thinking, and Learning*. Burlington: Write Source, 1990. Print.

4. FOUR OR MORE AUTHORS

You may give each author's name or the name of the first author only, followed by *et al.* (and others).

> Anderson, Robert, et al. *Elements of Literature: Literature of the United States.*
>   Austin: Holt, 1993. Print.

5. ORGANIZATION OR GOVERNMENT AS AUTHOR

> Diagram Group. *The Macmillan Visual Desk Reference.* New York: Macmillan,
>   1993. Print.

6. ANTHOLOGY

Use this model only when you are citing the whole anthology or the contributions of the editor(s).

> Kitchen, Judith, and Mary Paumier Jones, eds. *In Short: A Collection of Brief*
>   *Creative Nonfiction.* New York: Norton, 1996. Print.

7. WORK(S) IN AN ANTHOLOGY

Give the inclusive page numbers of the selection you are citing.

> Achebe, Chinua. "Uncle Ben's Choice." *The Seagull Reader: Literature.* Ed.
>   Joseph Kelly. New York: Norton, 2005. 23–27. Print.

To document two or more selections from one anthology, list each selection by author and title, followed by a cross-reference to the anthology. In addition, include in your works-cited list an entry for the anthology itself (see above entry).

> Hiestand, Emily. "Afternoon Tea." Kitchen and Jones 65–67.

> Ozick, Cynthia. "The Shock of Teapots." Kitchen and Jones 68–71.

8. AUTHOR AND EDITOR

Start with the author if you've cited the text itself.

> Austen, Jane. *Emma.* Ed. Stephen M. Parrish. New York: Norton, 2000.
>   Print.

Start with the editor if you've cited his or her work.

> Parrish, Stephen M., ed. *Emma.* By Jane Austen. New York: Norton, 2000.
>   Print.

9. TRANSLATION

> Dostoevsky, Fyodor. *Crime and Punishment*. Trans. Richard Pevear and
> Larissa Volokhonsky. New York: Vintage, 1993. Print.

10. FOREWORD, INTRODUCTION, PREFACE, OR AFTERWORD

> Tanner, Tony. Introduction. *Pride and Prejudice*. By Jane Austen. London:
> Penguin, 1972. 7–46. Print.

11. MULTIVOLUME WORK

If you cite all the volumes, give the number of volumes after the title.

> Sandburg, Carl. *Abraham Lincoln: The War Years*. 4 vols. New York:
> Harcourt, 1939. Print.

If you cite only one volume, give the volume number after the title.

> Sandburg, Carl. *Abraham Lincoln: The War Years*. Vol. 2. New York:
> Harcourt, 1939. Print.

12. EDITION OTHER THAN THE FIRST

> Gibaldi, Joseph. *MLA Handbook for Writers of Research Papers*. 6th ed. New
> York: MLA, 2003. Print.

13. ARTICLE IN A REFERENCE BOOK

If a reference book is well known, list only the edition, if available, and the year of
publication.

> "Iraq." *The New Encyclopaedia Brittanica*. 15th ed. 2007. Print.

If a reference book is less familiar, give complete publication information.

> Benton-Cohen, Katherine. "Women in the Reform and Progressive Era." *A
> History of Women in the United States*. Ed. Doris Weatherford. 4 vols.
> Danbury, CT: Grolier, 2004. Print.

Periodicals

For most articles, you'll need to list the author, the article title and any subtitle, the
periodical title, any volume and issue number, the date, inclusive page numbers,
and the medium—*Print*. A few details to note:

- *Periodical titles*: Omit any initial *A, An,* or *The*.

- *Dates*: Abbreviate the names of months except for May, June, or July.

- *Pages*: If an article does not fall on consecutive pages, give the first page with a plus sign (55+).

14. ARTICLE IN A JOURNAL

> Bartley, William. "Imagining the Future in *The Awakening*." *College English* 62.6 (2000): 719–46. Print.

15. ARTICLE IN A JOURNAL NUMBERED BY ISSUE

For journals that do not have volume numbers, give the issue number after the title, followed by the year of publication and inclusive page numbers.

> Flynn, Kevin. "The Railway in Canadian Poetry." *Canadian Literature* 174 (2002): 70–95. Print.

16. ARTICLE IN A MONTHLY MAGAZINE

> Fellman, Bruce. "Leading the Libraries." *Yale Alumni Magazine* Feb. 2002: 26–31. Print.

17. ARTICLE IN A WEEKLY MAGAZINE

> Cloud, John. "Should SATs Matter?" *Time* 12 Mar. 2001: 62+. Print.

18. ARTICLE IN A DAILY NEWSPAPER

> Springer, Shira. "Celtics Reserves Are Whizzes vs. Wizards." *Boston Globe* 14 Mar. 2005: D4+. Print.

If you are documenting a particular edition of a newspaper, specify the edition (late ed., natl. ed., and so on) in between the date and the section and page reference. The following citation shows that the article begins on page 1 of section G of the late edition.

> Margulius, David L. "Smarter Call Centers: At Your Service?" *New York Times* 14 Mar. 2002, late ed.: G1+. Print.

19. UNSIGNED ARTICLE

> "Coal Mine Inspections Fall Short." *Atlanta Journal-Constitution* 18 Nov. 2007: A7. Print.

20. EDITORIAL OR LETTER TO THE EDITOR

"Gas, Cigarettes Are Safe to Tax." Editorial. *Lakeville Journal* 17 Feb. 2005: A10. Print.

Festa, Roger. "Social Security: Another Phony Crisis." Letter. *Lakeville Journal* 17 Feb. 2005: A10. Print.

21. REVIEW

Lahr, John. "Night for Day." Rev. of *The Crucible*, by Arthur Miller. *New Yorker* 18 Mar. 2002: 149–51. Print.

Electronic Sources

When you cite electronic sources, your goal, as with print sources, is to give readers all the information they need to find the particular source you used. If possible, your citation should include at least the following: (1) author's name; (2) title; (3) name of online site; (4) publisher or sponsoring institution; (5) date of first electronic publication and/or most recent revision; (6) the medium, e.g., *Web*; (7) date you accessed the source. Here is an example of a citation that includes all this information:

Johnson, Charles W. "How Our Laws Are Made." *Thomas: Legislative Information on the Internet.* Lib. of Congress, 31 Jan. 2000. Web. 5 Apr. 2005.

A few details to note:

- *Basic information*: Some citations for electronic sources are based on the style you would follow for a print version, so you may need to consult the previous sections on books and periodicals. Note that the titles of websites and databases are italicized.

- *Dates*: Although MLA asks for the date when materials were first posted or most recently updated, you won't always be able to find that information; if it is unavailable, use *n.d.* The date you *must* include is the date on which you accessed the electronic source.

- *Publisher*: If the name of the publisher or sponsoring institution is unavailable, use *N.p.*

- *URL*: This is only required if your reader will probably be unable to find the site without it. In such cases, give the address of the website at the end of the citation, enclosed in angle brackets. When a URL will not fit on one line, break it only after a slash (and do not add a hyphen).

22. ENTIRE WEBSITE

Zalta, Edward N., ed. *Stanford Encyclopedia of Philosophy*. Metaphysics
Research Lab, Center for the Study of Language and Information,
Stanford U, 2007. Web. 2 Jan. 2008.

23. PERSONAL WEBSITE

Chomsky, Noam. Home page. N.p., 2006. Web. 12 Dec. 2007.

24. WORK WITHIN A WEBSITE

"Medications: Using Them Safely." *KidsHealth*. Nemours Foundation, 2005.
Web. 26 Nov. 2007.

25. ONLINE BOOK OR PART OF A BOOK

To cite part of an online book, list the short work before the book title.

Anderson, Sherwood. "The Philosopher." *Winesburg, Ohio*. New York: B. W.
Huebsch, 1919. *Bartleby.com: Great Books Online*. 1999. Web. 2 Dec. 2007.

26. ARTICLE IN AN ONLINE JOURNAL

Cite the volume, issue, and year as you would for a print journal. If a journal does
not number pages or if it numbers each article separately, use *n. pag.* in place of
page numbers.

Moore, Greggory. "The Process of Life in *2001: A Space Odyssey*." *Images:
A Journal of Film and Popular Culture* 9 (2000): n. pag. Web. 12 May
2009.

27. ARTICLE IN AN ONLINE MAGAZINE

Landsburg, Steven E. "Putting All Your Potatoes in One Basket: The
Economic Lessons of the Great Famine." *Slate.com*. Slate, 13 Mar. 2001.
Web. 8 Dec. 2007.

28. ARTICLE FROM AN ONLINE DATABASE OR SUBSCRIPTION SERVICE

Include the author, title, periodical title, and any information about print publication. End with the name of the database (in the following example, *Academic
Search Premier*), the medium, and the date of access.

Bowman, James. "Moody Blues." *American Spectator* June 1999: 64–65. *Academic Search Premier.* Web. 15 Mar. 2005.

Cite a work from a personal online subscription service such as America Online as you would a work on an online database.

Broder, John M., and Felicity Barringer. "EPA Blocks States on Emission Rules." *New York Times.* 20 Dec. 2007. *America Online.* Web. 27 Dec. 2007.

29. ARTICLE IN AN ONLINE NEWSPAPER

Mitchell, Dan. "Being Skeptical of Green." *New York Times.* New York Times, 24 Nov. 2007. Web. 26 Nov. 2007.

30. ONLINE EDITORIAL

"Outsourcing Your Life." Editorial. *Chicagotribune.com.* Chicago Tribune, 24 Nov. 2004. Web. 3 Jan. 2008.

31. EMAIL

Smith, William. "Teaching Grammar—Some Thoughts." Message to the author. 15 Feb. 2008. Email.

32. POSTING TO AN ELECTRONIC FORUM

Mintz, Stephen H. "Manumission During the Revolution." H-Net List on Slavery. Michigan State U, 14 Sept. 2006. Web. 18 Apr. 2009.

33. CD-ROM OR DVD-ROM

Cite like a book, but indicate any pertinent information about the edition or version.

Othello. Princeton: Films for the Humanities and Sciences, 1998. CD-ROM.

Other Kinds of Sources

This section shows how to prepare works-cited entries for categories other than books, periodicals, and writing found on the Web and CD-ROMs. Many of these categories cover works that can be found both on and off the Web. Author (or performer) names, titles, and dates should be styled as in print versions.

34. ART (PRINT AND ONLINE)

Van Gogh, Vincent. *The Potato Eaters*. 1885. Oil on canvas. Van Gogh
 Museum, Amsterdam.

Warhol, Andy. *Self-Portrait*. 1979. Polaroid Polacolor print. J. Paul Getty
 Museum, Los Angeles. *The Getty*. Web. 5 Jan. 2008.

35. CARTOON OR COMIC STRIP (PRINT AND ONLINE)

Chast, Roz. "The Three Wise Men of Thanksgiving." Cartoon. *New Yorker*
 1 Dec. 2003: 174. Print.

Adams, Scott. "Dilbert." Comic strip. *Dilbert.com*. United Features Syndicate,
 9 Nov. 2007. Web. 26 Nov. 2007.

36. FILM, VIDEO, OR DVD

Casablanca. Dir. Michael Curtiz. Perf. Humphrey Bogart, Ingrid Bergman,
 and Claude Rains. Warner, 1942. Film.

Easter Parade. Dir. Charles Walters. Perf. Judy Garland and Fred Astaire.
 MGM, 1948. DVD.

37. BROADCAST, PUBLISHED, AND PERSONAL INTERVIEW

Gates, Henry Louis, Jr. Interview. *Fresh Air*. NPR. WNYC, New York. 9 Apr.
 2002. Radio.

Brzezinski, Zbigniew. "Against the Neocons." *American Prospect* Mar. 2005:
 26–27. Print.

Berra, Yogi. Personal interview. 17 June 2001.

38. PUBLISHED LETTER

White, E. B. Letter to Carol Angell. 28 May 1970. *Letters of E. B. White*. Ed.
 Dorothy Lobarno Guth. New York: Harper, 1976. 600. Print.

39. MAP (PRINT AND ONLINE)

Toscana. Map. Milan: Touring Club Italiano, 1987. Print.

"Portland, Oregon." Map. *Google Maps*. Google, 25 Apr. 2009. Web. 25 Apr.
 2009.

40. MUSICAL SCORE

> Beethoven, Ludwig van. *String Quartet No. 13 in B Flat, Op. 130.* 1825. New York: Dover, 1970. Print.

41. SOUND RECORDING (WITH ONLINE VERSION)

Whether you list the composer, conductor, or performer first depends on where you want to place the emphasis.

> Beethoven, Ludwig van. *Missa Solemnis.* Perf. Westminster Choir and New York Philharmonic. Cond. Leonard Bernstein. Sony, 1992. CD.

> The Beatles. "Can't Buy Me Love." *A Hard Day's Night.* United Artists, 1964. MP3 file.

> Davis, Miles. "So What." *Birth of the Cool.* Columbia, 1959. *Miles Davis.* Web. 14 Feb. 2009.

42. TELEVISION OR RADIO PROGRAM (WITH ONLINE VERSION)

> "Stirred." *The West Wing.* Writ. Aaron Sorkin, Dir. Jeremy Kagan. Perf. Martin Sheen. NBC. WPTV, West Palm Beach, 3 Apr. 2002. Television.

> "Bush's War." *Frontline.* Writ. and Dir. Michael Kirk. *PBS.org.* PBS, 24 Mar. 2008. Web. 10 Apr. 2009.

Sample Student Research Paper

Dylan Borchers wrote the following research paper for a first-year writing class. He used MLA style for his essay, but documentation styles vary from discipline to discipline, so ask your instructor if you're not sure which style you should use.

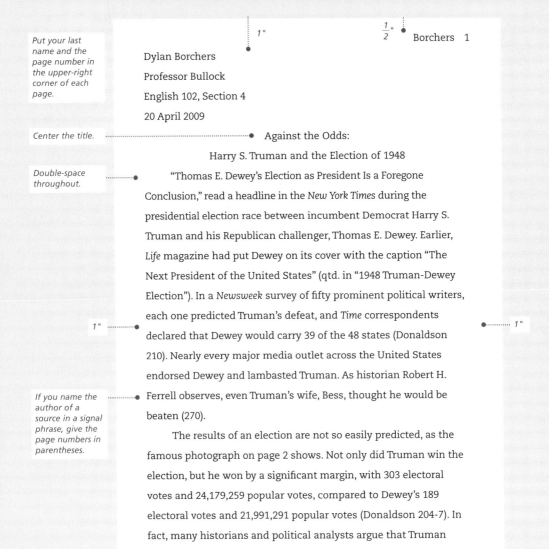

Dylan Borchers

Professor Bullock

English 102, Section 4

20 April 2009

Against the Odds:

Harry S. Truman and the Election of 1948

"Thomas E. Dewey's Election as President Is a Foregone
Conclusion," read a headline in the *New York Times* during the
presidential election race between incumbent Democrat Harry S.
Truman and his Republican challenger, Thomas E. Dewey. Earlier,
Life magazine had put Dewey on its cover with the caption "The
Next President of the United States" (qtd. in "1948 Truman-Dewey
Election"). In a *Newsweek* survey of fifty prominent political writers,
each one predicted Truman's defeat, and *Time* correspondents
declared that Dewey would carry 39 of the 48 states (Donaldson
210). Nearly every major media outlet across the United States
endorsed Dewey and lambasted Truman. As historian Robert H.
Ferrell observes, even Truman's wife, Bess, thought he would be
beaten (270).

The results of an election are not so easily predicted, as the
famous photograph on page 2 shows. Not only did Truman win the
election, but he won by a significant margin, with 303 electoral
votes and 24,179,259 popular votes, compared to Dewey's 189
electoral votes and 21,991,291 popular votes (Donaldson 204-7). In
fact, many historians and political analysts argue that Truman

Put your last name and the page number in the upper-right corner of each page.

Center the title.

Double-space throughout.

1"

1"

If you name the author of a source in a signal phrase, give the page numbers in parentheses.

1"

Fig. 1. President Harry S. Truman holds up an Election Day edition of the *Chicago Daily Tribune*, which mistakenly announced "Dewey Defeats Truman." St. Louis, 4 Nov. 1948 (Rollins).

Put illustrations close to the text they relate to. Label with figure number, caption, and parenthetical source citation.

would have won by an even greater margin had third-party Progressive candidate Henry A. Wallace not split the Democratic vote in New York State and Dixiecrat Strom Thurmond not won four states in the South (McCullough 711). Although Truman's defeat was heavily predicted, those predictions themselves, Dewey's passiveness as a campaigner, and Truman's zeal turned the tide for a Truman victory.

    In the months preceding the election, public opinion polls predicted that Dewey would win by a large margin. Pollster Elmo Roper stopped polling in September, believing there was no reason to continue, given a seemingly inevitable Dewey landslide. Although the margin narrowed as the election drew near, the other pollsters

Indent paragraphs 5 spaces or $\frac{1}{2}$ inch .

Give the author and page in parentheses when there's no signal phrase.

predicted a Dewey win by at least 5 percent (Donaldson 209). Many historians believe that these predictions aided the president in the long run. First, surveys showing Dewey in the lead may have prompted some of Dewey's supporters to feel overconfident about their candidate's chances and therefore to stay home from the polls on Election Day. Second, these same surveys may have energized Democrats to mount late get-out-the-vote efforts ("1948 Truman-Dewey Election"). Other analysts believe that the overwhelming predictions of a Truman loss also kept at home some Democrats who approved of Truman's policies but saw a Truman loss as inevitable. According to political analyst Samuel Lubell, those Democrats may have saved Dewey from an even greater defeat (Hamby, *Man of the People* 465). Whatever the impact on the voters, the polling numbers had a decided effect on Dewey.

Historians and political analysts alike cite Dewey's overly cautious campaign as one of the main reasons Truman was able to achieve victory. Dewey firmly believed in public opinion polls. With all indications pointing to an easy victory, Dewey and his staff believed that all he had to do was bide his time and make no foolish mistakes. Dewey himself said, "When you're leading, don't talk"

If you quote text that's quoted in another source, cite that source in a parenthetical reference.

(qtd. in McCullough 672). Each of Dewey's speeches was well-crafted and well-rehearsed. As the leader in the race, he kept his remarks faultlessly positive, with the result that he failed to deliver a solid message or even mention Truman or any of Truman's policies. Eventually, Dewey began to be perceived as aloof and stuffy. One observer compared him to the plastic groom on top of a wedding cake (Hamby, "Harry S. Truman"), and others noted his stiff, cold demeanor (McCullough 671-74).

If you cite 2 or more works closely together, give a parenthetical citation for each one.

As his campaign continued, observers noted that Dewey seemed uncomfortable in crowds, unable to connect with ordinary people. And he made a number of blunders. One took place at a train stop when the candidate, commenting on the number of children in the crowd, said he was glad they had been let out of school for his arrival. Unfortunately for Dewey, it was a Saturday ("1948: The Great Truman Surprise"). Such gaffes gave voters the feeling that Dewey was out of touch with the public.

Again and again through the autumn of 1948, Dewey's campaign speeches failed to address the issues, with the candidate declaring that he did not want to "get down in the gutter" (qtd. in McCullough 701). When told by fellow Republicans that he was losing ground, Dewey insisted that his campaign not alter its course. Even *Time* magazine, though it endorsed and praised him, conceded that his speeches were dull (McCullough 696). According to historian Zachary Karabell, they were "notable only for taking place, not for any specific message" (244). Dewey's numbers in the polls slipped in the weeks before the election, but he still held a comfortable lead over Truman. It would take Truman's famous whistle-stop campaign to make the difference.

Few candidates in U.S. history have campaigned for the presidency with more passion and faith than Harry Truman. In the autumn of 1948, he wrote to his sister, "It will be the greatest campaign any President ever made. Win, lose, or draw, people will know where I stand" (91). For thirty-three days, Truman traveled the nation, giving hundreds of speeches from the back of the *Ferdinand Magellan* railroad car. In the same letter, he described the pace: "We made about 140 stops and I spoke over 147 times, shook hands with at least 30,000 and am in good condition to start out again tomorrow for Wilmington, Philadelphia, Jersey City, Newark, Albany and Buffalo" (91). McCullough writes of Truman's campaign:

> No President in history had ever gone so far in quest of support from the people, or with less cause for the effort, to judge by informed opinion. . . . As a test of his skills and judgment as a professional politician, not to say his stamina and disposition at age sixty-four, it would be like no other experience in his long, often difficult career, as he himself understood perfectly. More than any other event in his public life, or in his presidency thus far, it would reveal the kind of man he was. (655)

He spoke in large cities and small towns, defending his policies and attacking Republicans. As a former farmer and relatively late bloomer, Truman was able to connect with the public. He developed an energetic style, usually speaking from notes rather than from a prepared speech, and often mingled with the crowds that met his train. These crowds grew larger as the campaign

Set off quotations of 4 or more lines by indenting 1 inch (or 10 spaces).

Put parenthetical references after final punctuation in a block quotation.

progressed. In Chicago, over half a million people lined the streets as he passed, and in St. Paul the crowd numbered over 25,000. When Dewey entered St. Paul two days later, he was greeted by only 7,000 supporters ("1948 Truman-Dewey Election"). Reporters brushed off the large crowds as mere curiosity seekers wanting to see a president (McCullough 682). Yet Truman persisted, even if he often seemed to be the only one who thought he could win. By going directly to the American people and connecting with them, Truman built the momentum needed to surpass Dewey and win the election.

If you cite a work with no known author, use the title in your parenthetical reference.

The legacy and lessons of Truman's whistle-stop campaign continue to be studied by political analysts, and politicians today often mimic his campaign methods by scheduling multiple visits to key states, as Truman did. He visited California, Illinois, and Ohio 48 times, compared with 6 visits to those states by Dewey. Political scientist Thomas M. Holbrook concludes that his strategic campaigning in those states and others gave Truman the electoral votes he needed to win (61, 65).

The 1948 election also had an effect on pollsters, who, as Elmo Roper admitted, "couldn't have been more wrong" (qtd. in Karabell 255). *Life* magazine's editors concluded that pollsters as well as reporters and commentators were too convinced of a Dewey victory to analyze the polls seriously, especially the opinions of undecided voters (Karabell 256). Pollsters assumed that undecided voters would vote in the same proportion as decided voters -- and that turned out to be a false assumption (Karabell 258). In fact, the lopsidedness of the polls might have led voters who supported Truman to call themselves undecided out of an unwillingness to associate themselves with the losing side, further skewing the polls' results (McDonald, Glynn, Kim, and Ostman 152). Such errors led pollsters to change their methods significantly after the 1948 election.

In a work by 4 or more authors, either cite them all or name the first one followed by et al.

After the election, many political analysts, journalists, and historians concluded that the Truman upset was in fact a victory for the American people, who, the *New Republic* noted, "couldn't be ticketed by the polls, knew its own mind and had picked the rather unlikely but courageous figure of Truman to carry its banner" (qtd. in McCullough 715). How "unlikely" is unclear, however; Truman biographer Alonzo Hamby notes that "polls of scholars consistently rank Truman among the top eight presidents in American history" (*Man of the People* 641). But despite Truman's high standing, and despite the fact that the whistle-stop campaign is now part of our political landscape, politicians have increasingly imitated the style of the Dewey campaign, with its "packaged candidate who ran so as not to lose, who steered clear of controversy, and who made a good show of appearing presidential" (Karabell 266). The election of 1948 shows that voters are not necessarily swayed by polls, but it may have presaged the packaging of candidates by public relations experts, to the detriment of public debate on the issues in future presidential elections.

1"

Works Cited

Donaldson, Gary A. *Truman Defeats Dewey*. Lexington: UP of

Kentucky, 1999. Print.

Ferrell, Robert H. *Harry S. Truman: A Life*. Columbia: U of Missouri P,

1994. Print.

Hamby, Alonzo L., ed. "Harry S. Truman (1945-1953)."

AmericanPresident.org. Miller Center of Public Affairs, U of

Virginia, 11 Dec. 2003. Web. 12 Jan. 2009.

---. *Man of the People: A Life of Harry S. Truman*. New York: Oxford UP,

1995. Print.

Holbrook, Thomas M. "Did the Whistle-Stop Campaign Matter?" *PS:

Political Science and Politics* 35.1 (2002): 59-66. Print.

Karabell, Zachary. *The Last Campaign: How Harry Truman Won the 1948

Election*. New York: Knopf, 2000. Print.

McCullough, David. *Truman*. New York: Simon & Schuster, 1992. Print.

McDonald, Daniel G., Carroll J. Glynn, Sei-Hill Kim, and Ronald E.

Ostman. "The Spiral of Silence in the 1948 Presidential

Election." *Communication Research* 28.2 (2001): 139-55. Print.

"1948 Truman-Dewey Election." *Electronic Government Project: Eagleton

Digital Archive of American Politics*. Eagleton Inst. of Politics,

Rutgers, State U of New Jersey, 2004. Web. 11 Jan. 2009.

"1948: The Great Truman Surprise." *Media and Politics Online

Projects: Media Coverage of Presidential Campaigns*. Dept. of

Center the heading.

Double-space throughout.

Alphabetize the list by authors' last names or by title for works with no author.

Begin each entry at the left margin; indent subsequent lines $\frac{1}{2}$-inch or 5 spaces.

If you cite more than one work by a single author, list them alphabetically by title, and use 3 hyphens instead of repeating the author's name after the first entry.

Political Science and International Affairs, Kennesaw State U,

29 Oct. 2003. Web. 11 Jan. 2009.

Rollins, Byron. Untitled photograph. "The First 150 Years: 1948." AP

History. Associated Press, n.d. Web. 10 Jan. 2009.

Truman, Harry S. "Campaigning, Letter, October 5, 1948." *Harry S.

Truman*. Ed. Robert H. Ferrell. Washington: CQ P, 2003. 91. Print.

Check to be sure that every source you use is on the list of works cited.

Credits

Text

ZOE SHEWER: "Ready, Willing, and Able." Reprinted by permission of the author.

BRYAN SYKES: From THE SEVEN DAUGHTERS OF EVE by Bryan Sykes. Copyright © 2001 by Bryan Sykes. Used by permission of W.W. Norton & Company, Inc.

AMY TAN: "Mother Tongue" first appeared in *The Threepenny Review*. Copyright © 1990 by Amy Tan. Reprinted by permission of the author and the Sandra Dijkstra Literary Agency.

DEBORAH TANNEN: "But What Do You Mean?" by Deborah Tannen, *Redbook*, Oct. 1994, copyright © by Deborah Tannen. Reprinted by permission of the author.

HAL R. VARIAN: "Analyzing the Marriage Gap" published as "Economic Scene: Ask Not What You Can Do For Marriage Can Do For Your Bottom Line" from *The New York Times*, July 29, 2004. Copyright © 2004 The New York Times. All rights reserved. Used by permission and protected by the Copyright Laws of the United States. The printing, copying, redistribution, or retransmission of the Material without express written permission is prohibited.

ROBERT VOAS: "There's No Benefit to Lowering the Drinking Age" is reprinted by permission of the author from The Christian Science Monitor, Jan. 12, 2006.

BRYAN WALSH: "Skip the Steak" by Bryan Walsh. Copyright © 2008 Time Inc. All rights reserved. Reprinted from *Time* magazine with permission.

MICHELLE WATSON: "Shades of Character" by Michelle Watson is used by permission of the author, Michelle Watson DeBord.

E. B. WHITE: "Once More to the Lake" from ONE MAN'S MEAT, text copyright © 1941 by E. B. White, copyright renewed. Reprinted by permission of Tilbury House, Publishers, Gardiner, Maine.

MONICA WUNDERLICH: "My Technologically Challenged Life" first appeared in DELTA WINDS 2004. Reprinted by permission of the author.

Every effort has been made to contact the copyright holder of each of the selections. Rights holders of any selections not credited should contact Permissions Department, W. W. Norton & Company, Inc., 500 Fifth Avenue, New York, NY 10110, in order for a correction to be made in the next reprinting of our work.

Illustrations

p. 6: Anna Quindlen, *How Reading Changed My Life*. Copyright 1998. Reprinted with permission of Ballantine Books, Random House. **p. 37**: Doug Steley B / Alamy. **p. 65**: Gordon Marshal. **p. 72**: From *The 9/11 Commission Report*. New York: Norton. **p. 123**: From *Sneakers: The Complete Collector's Guide*, written and designed by Unorthodox Styles, Thames & Hudson Inc., New York. Text and layout © 2005 Thames & Hudson Ltd., London. Photographs © 2005 Unorthodox Styles. Reprinted by kind permission of Thames & Hudson. **p. 177**: Courtesy of Ebay.com. **p. 179**: Naum Kazhdan / *The New York Times*. **p. 223**: Christopher Hirsheimer. **p. 226**: *The Worst-Case Scenario Survival Handbook: College* by Joshua Piven et al., illustrated by Brenda Brown. Copyright © 2004 by Quirk Productions, Inc. Used with permission of Chronicle Books LLC, San Francisco. Visit ChronicleBooks.com. **p. 251**: Courtesy of Victor Pollaci. **000**: [7.1?] Used by permission of Bill Morrison. **p. 319**: AP Images. **p. 377**: Cartoon Bank. **p. 435**: Courtesy of Aeroports de Paris. **p. 445**: Rube Goldberg, Inc. **p. 507**: Courtesy of The Life Is Good Company. **p. 593**: Mary Roach, *Stiff*. New York: Norton. Photo by Mark Atkins / Panoptika.net; **pp. 618–20**: From Steven Johnson, *Everything Bad Is Good for You.* (Riverhead 2005) Drawings by Christoph Niemann. **p. 661**: Bettman / Corbis.

Glossary / Index

This glossary / index defines key terms and concepts and directs you to pages in the book where you can find specific information on these and other topics. Please note that words set in SMALL CAPITAL LETTERS are themselves defined in the glossary / index.

CAUSES Conditions or events necessary to produce an effect. The *immediate* cause of an effect is the one closest to it in time and most directly responsible for producing the effect. *Remote* causes are further in time from an effect and less direct in producing it. The *main* cause of an effect is the most important cause; it is not only necessary to produce the effect but sufficient to do so. *Contributing* causes are less important but still necessary to the effect; they are not, however, sufficient to produce it on their own.

CHRONOLOGICAL ORDER The sequence of events in time.

CLAIM In TOULMIN ARGUMENT, the claim is the main point of an argument and is supported both by the GROUNDS and by the WARRANT.

CLASSIFICATION, 306–61, 316, 586 Writing that explains what category or categories a person or thing belongs to. Strictly speaking, classification assigns individuals to categories (*Red is an Irish setter*) and division separates a category into subcategories (*The dogs at the pound included pit bulls, greyhounds, and Boston terriers*).

F

FALLACY, 497, 499 An error in logical reasoning. Common logical fallacies include reasoning *post hoc, ergo prompter hoc; non sequiturs;* begging the question; arguing *ad hominem;* and false analogies.

FIGURE OF SPEECH Words and phrases used in an unusual or nonliteral way. *See also specific figures of speech*

FIRST PERSON The grammatical and narrative point of view of the person speaking in a text, expressed by the personal pronouns *I* or *we.*

FLASHBACK, 57 A scene dropped into a narrative to show what happened in the past, before the events of the main plot.

FLASH-FORWARD, 57 A scene dropped into a narrative to show what happens in the future, after the events of the main plot.

FREEWRITING, 18, 19 A means of GENERATING IDEAS by writing, without stopping, whatever thoughts come to mind over a set period of time.

G

GENERATING IDEAS, 17–23 Part of the writing process that deals with the discovery of ideas, topics, points to consider, examples, and other raw materials for a text. *See also specific ways of generating ideas;* IDEAS

GROUNDS In TOULMIN ARGUMENT, the facts and other data on which a writer bases a CLAIM.

H

HYPERBOLE Exaggeration: The *mountain reached to the sky.*

HYPOTHESIS A tentative explanation; a theory to be tested. One hypothesis for explaining the extinction of the dinosaurs, for example, is that they were killed by a cataclysmic event, such as a meteor striking the earth.

I

INDUCTION A form of logical reasoning that proceeds from specific examples to general conclusions. *See also* DEDUCTION

IRONY A statement that implies something other than what the words literally mean. *Situational irony*, as opposed to *verbal iron*, occurs when events turn out differently than expected. It would be ironic, for example, if you barely graduated from high school and then ended up at the head of your class in college.

JOURNALING, 22–23, 369 Keeping a regular notebook or journal as source of inspiration and means of GENERATING IDEAS for a text.

LISTING, 20, 169, 212, 366–67 GENERATING IDEAS for a text by making lists of specific words, phrases, topics, examples, and other details as they occur to you, either while working by yourself or with others.

LOOPING, 18–20 A directed form of FREEWRITING in which you GENERATE IDEAS for a text by narrowing your focus—and summarizing what you have just written—each time you freewrite.

METAPHOR, 118   A direct comparison that identifies one thing with another, without the use of a stated connecting word: *Throughout the battle, Sergeant Phillips was a rock.*

METONYMY   The use of one word or name in place of another commonly associated with it: *The White House* [for the president] *awarded the sergeant a medal.*

N

NARRATION, 49–107, 584, 592   An account of actions and events that happen to someone or something. Because narration is essentially storytelling, it is often used in fiction; however, it is also an important element in almost all writing and speaking. The opening of Lincoln's Gettysburg Address, for example, is in the narrative mode: "Fourscore and seven years ago our fathers bought forth on this continent a new nation."

NARRATOR   The speaker in a narrative, the person (or thing) telling the story.

ONOMATOPOEIA The use of words that sound like what they refer to: *buzz, purr, bark, tick-tock.*

OXYMORON A FIGURE OF SPEECH that brings together opposite or contradictory terms for rhetorical or humorous effect, as in *eloquent silence, mournful optimist,* or (some would say) *military intelligence.*

P

PARADOX A statement that appears to contradict itself but that, on closer examination, makes sense. For example: *They have ears but hear not.*

PARALLELISM, 175 Using the same grammatical form for words and / or sentences of equal importance. This example isn't parallel: *The program included someone lecturing, a PowerPoint presentation, and a film.* This one is: *This program included a lecture, a PowerPoint presentation, and a film.*

PARAPHRASE, 642–44 Stating someone's else's ideas or writing in your own words. The source of a paraphrase must be fully acknowledged and DOCUMENTED.

PARODY A comic imitation of a type or particular example of writing, music, film, or other art form; a spoof. For example, "Weird Al" Yankovic's "Girls Just Want to Have Lunch" is a parody of Cyndi Lauper's hit song "Girls Just Want to Have Fun."

PERSONIFICATION, 118 FIGURE OF SPEECH that attributes human characteristics to inanimate objects or ideas: *Death lurked around the corner.*

PERSUASION The art of moving an audience to action or belief.

PLAGIARISM Using someone else's ideas or words without giving them credit. To avoid plagiarism, always DOCUMENT your sources.

PLOT   The sequence of events in a story arranged in such a way that they have a beginning,
a middle, and ending.

POINT-BY-POINT COMPARISON   A way of organizing a comparison in which the traits of two or
more subjects are compared one by one. A point-
by-point comparison of London and New York
might first address nightlife in each city, then
museums, then theater, then history. *See also*
SUBJECT-BY-SUBJECT COMPARISON

POINT OF VIEW   The vantage from which a story
is told or an account given. *See also* FIRST PER-
SON; THIRD PERSON

PRINCIPLE OF CLASSIFICATION   The basis on
which the various categories of a classification
system are determined. Bicycles, for example,
are often classified by function (mountain bikes,
racing bikes, touring bikes); but they can also be
classified by some other principle, such as the
position of the rider (upright or recumbent) or
the gearing system (internal hub, shaft-driven
derailleur, single gear, retro-direct).

PROCESS / PROCESS ANALYSIS, 209–56, 585–86
A series of actions or events leading to a particular end result. A *process analysis* explains, step by
step, how to do something such as mow the
lawn—or how something, such as lawnmower,
works or is made.

PUN   A play on words, usually involving different words that sound alike or different meanings of the same word: *The undertaker was a grave man.*

PURPOSE, 13–15   The general intent of a piece of writing—whether to explain, inform, entertain, record, persuade, express one's self, or serve some other goal.

Q

QUALIFIER   A verbal or grammatical element that limits or modifies the meaning of another word, phrase, or statement. In the sentence *I have been true to you after my fashion,* "after my fashion" restricts the meaning of the statement.

QUOTATION, 642   Someone else's exact words. All quotations should be fully attributed to their original sources.

R

REMOTE CAUSE, 436. *See also* CAUSES